BAREFOOT GEN

A CARTOON STORY OF HIROSHIMA

KEIJI NAKAZAWA

Translated by Project Gen

LAST GASP OF SAN FRANCISCO

Barefoot Gen: A Cartoon Story of Hiroshima
Volume One

By Keiji Nakazawa

Published by Last Gasp of San Francisco
777 Florida Street, San Francisco, California, 94110
www.lastgasp.com

First serialized under the title *Hadashi no Gen* in Japan, 1972-3.

13th printing, 2020
ISBN 978-0-86719-602-3

© Keiji Nakazawa, 2004.
Introduction © Art Spiegelman, 1990.
English language translation rights arranged with Misayo Nakazawa
c/o Project Gen through Japan UNI Agency, Inc., Tokyo.

Translation by Project Gen
Volume 1 Translators: Kazuko Futakuchi, Kiyoko Nishita, George Stenson,
Alan Gleason, Libby Hopkins, Hiromi Matsuoka.

Project Gen Volunteers: Namie Asazuma, Kazuko Futakuchi, Michael
Gordon, Kyoko Honda, Yukari Kimura, Nobutoshi Kohara, Nante Kotta,
Michiko Tanaka, Kazuko Yamada.

Edited by Alan Gleason and Colin Turner
Production: Colin Turner
Cover design: Evan Hayden

Printed in China by Prolong Press Ltd.

Barefoot Gen: Comics
After the Bomb

An Introduction by Art Spiegelman

Gen haunts me. The first time I read it was in the late 1970s, shortly after I'd begun working on *Maus*, my own extended comic-book chronicle of the twentieth century's other central cataclysm. I had the flu at the time and read it while high on fever. *Gen* burned its way into my heated brain with all the intensity of a fever-dream. I've found myself remembering images and events from the *Gen* books with a clarity that made them seem like memories from my own life, rather than Nakazawa's. I will never forget the people dragging their own melted skin as they walk through the ruins of Hiroshima, the panic-stricken horse on fire galloping through the city, the maggots crawling out of the sores of a young girl's ruined face. *Gen* deals with the trauma of the atom bomb without flinching. There are no irradiated Godzillas or super-mutants, only tragic realities. I've just reread the books recently and I'm glad to discover that the vividness of *Barefoot Gen* emanates from the work itself and not simply from my fever. Or, more accurately, it emanates from something intrinsic to the comics medium itself and from the events Nakazawa lived through and depicted.

Comics are a highly charged medium, delivering densely con-centrated information in relatively few words and simplified code-images. It seems to me that this is a model of how the brain for-mulates thoughts and remembers. We think in cartoons. Comics have often demonstrated how well suited they are to telling action adventure stories or jokes, but the small scale of the images and the directness of a medium that has something in common with handwriting allow comics a kind of intimacy that also make them surprisingly well suited to autobiography.

It's odd that, until the development of underground comics in the late 1960s, overtly autobiographical comics have not com-prised an important "genre." Rarer still are works that overtly grapple with the intersection between personal history and world history. Perhaps it was necessary to have a concept of comics as suitable adult fare for the medium to move toward autobiography. Or so I thought until I became more aware of Keiji Nakazawa's career. In 1972 Nakazawa, then 33, wrote and drew a directly autobiographical account of surviving the atomic blast at Hiroshima for a Japanese children's comic weekly. It was called, with chilling directness, "I Saw It." A year later he began his *Gen* series, a slightly fictionalized narrative also based on having seen "It," an adventure story of a boy caught in hell, a "Disasters of War" with speech balloons.

In Japan there is no stigma attached to reading comics; they're consumed in truly astonishing numbers (some comics weeklies have been known to sell over 3 million copies of a single issue) by all classes and ages. There are comics devoted to economic theory, mah jongg, and male homosexual love stories designed for pre-pubescent girls, as well as more familiar tales of samurai, robots and mutants. However, I should confess to a very limited knowledge of Japanese comics. They form a vast unexplored universe only tangentially connected to my own. Sometimes that seems true of everything about Japan, and *Gen* may be an ideal starting point for the twain to meet.

The modern comic book is a specifically Western form (making it all the more appropriate as a medium for reporting on the horrors brought to the East by the atom bomb), but Japanese comics have stylistic quirks and idioms that are quite different from ours, and these must be learned and accepted as part of the process of reading *Gen*. The stories are often quite long (the entire *Gen* saga reportedly runs to close on 2,000 pages), usually with rather few words on a page, allowing an entire 200-page book to be read during a short commuter ride. Overt symbolism is characteristic of Japanese comics; for Nakazawa it takes the form of a relentlessly reappearing sun that glares implacably through the pages. It is the marker of time passing, the giver of life, the flag of Japan, and a metronome that gives rhythm to Gen's story.

The degree of casual violence in Japanese comics is typically far greater than in our homegrown products. Gen's pacifist father freely wallops his kids with a frequency and force that we might easily perceive as criminal child abuse rather than the sign of affection that is intended. The sequence of Gen brawling with the chairman's son and literally biting his fingers off is (forgive me, I can't resist) especially hard to swallow. Yet these casual small-scale brutalities pale to naturalistic proportions when compared to the enormity of dropping a nuclear weapon on a civilian population.

The physiognomy of the characters often leans to the cloyingly cute, with special emphasis on Disney-like oversized Caucasian eyes and generally neotenic faces. Nakazawa is hardly the worst offender, though his cartoon style derives from that tradition. His draftsmanship is somewhat graceless, even homely, and without much nuance, but it gets the job done. It is clear and efficient, and it performs the essential magic trick of all good narrative art: the characters come to living, breathing life. The drawing's greatest virtue is its straightforward, blunt sincerity. Its conviction and honesty allow you to believe in the unbelievable and impossible things that did, indeed, happen in Hiroshima. It is the inexorable art of the witness.

Although the strangeness of the unfamiliar idioms and conventions of Japanese comics language may set up a hurdle for the Western reader first confronted with this book, it also offers one of its central pleasures. Nakazawa is an exceptionally skillful storyteller who knows how to keep his reader's attention in order to tell the Grim Things That Must Be Told. He effortlessly communicates a wealth of information about day-to-day life in wartime Japan and the anatomy of survival without slowing down the trajectory of his narrative. There is a paradox inherent in talking about such pleasures in the context of a work that illuminates the reality of mass death, yet the exposure to another culture's frame of reference, the sympathetic identification one develops with the protagonists and the very nature of narrative itself are all intrinsically pleasurable. Arguably, by locating the causes of the bombings exclusively in the evils of Japanese militaristic nationalism rather than in the *Realpolitik* of Western racism and cold-war power-jockeying, Nakazawa may make the work a little *too* pleasurable for American and British readers.

Ultimately, *Gen* is a very optimistic work. Nakazawa believes that his story can have a cautionary effect, that mankind can be improved to the point of acting in its own genuine self-interest. Indeed, Gen is a plucky little hero, embodying such virtues as loyalty, bravery, and industriousness. Nakazawa's faith in the possibility for Goodness may mark the work in some cynical eyes as true Literature for Children, but the underlying fact is that the artist is reporting on his own survival — not simply on the *events* that he lived through, but on the philosophical/psychological basis for that survival. His work is humanistic and humane, demonstrating and stressing the necessity for empathy among humans if we're to survive into another century.

A Note from the Author

Keiji Nakazawa

The atomic bomb exploded 600 meters above my hometown of Hiroshima on August 6, 1945 at 8:15 a.m. I was a little over a kilometer away from the epicenter, standing at the back gate of Kanzaki Primary School, when I was hit by a terrible blast of wind and searing heat. I was six years old. I owe my life to the school's concrete wall. If I hadn't been standing in its shadow, I would have been burned to death instantly by the 5,000-degree heat flash. Instead, I found myself in a living hell, the details of which remain etched in my brain as if it happened yesterday.

My mother, Kimiyo, was eight months pregnant. She was on the second floor balcony of our house, had just finished hanging up the wash to dry, and was turning to go back inside when the bomb exploded. The blast blew the entire balcony, with my mother on it, into the alley behind our house. Miraculously, my mother survived without a scratch.

The blast blew our house flat. The second floor collapsed onto the first, trapping my father, my sister Eiko, and my brother Susumu under it. My brother had been sitting in the front doorway, playing with a toy ship. His head was caught under the rafter over the doorway. He frantically kicked his legs and cried out for my mother. My father, trapped inside the house, begged my mother to do something. My sister had been crushed by a rafter and killed instantly.

My mother frantically tried to lift the rafters off them, but she wasn't strong enough to do it by herself. She begged passersby to stop and help, but nobody would. In that atomic hell, people could only think of their own survival; they had no time for anyone else. My mother tried everything she could, but to no avail. Finally, in despair, she sat down in the doorway, clutching my crying brother and helplessly pushing at the rafter that was crushing him.

The fires that followed the blast soon reached our house. It was quickly enveloped in flame. My brother yelled that he was burning; my father kept begging my mother to get some help. My mother, half-mad with grief and desperation, sobbed that she would stay and die with them. But our next-door neighbor found my mother just in time and dragged her away.

For the rest of her days, my mother never forgot the sound of the voices of her husband and son, crying out for her to save them. The shock sent my mother into labor, and she gave birth to a daughter by the side of the road that day. She named the baby Tomoko. But Tomoko died only four months later -- perhaps from malnutrition, perhaps from radiation sickness, we didn't know.

After escaping the flames near the school, I found my mother there by the roadside with her newborn baby. Together we sat and watched the scenes of hell unfolding around us.

My father had been a painter of lacquer work and traditional-style Japanese painting. He was also a member of an anti-war theater group that performed plays like Gorky's "The Lower Depths." Eventually the thought police arrested the entire troupe and put them in the Hiroshima Prefectural Prison. My father was held there for a year and a half. Even when I was a young child, my father constantly told me that Japan had been stupid and reckless to start the war.

Thanks, no doubt, to my father's influence, I enjoyed drawing from an early age. After the war I began reading Osamu Tezuka's comic magazine *Shin-Takarajima* (*New Treasure Island*); that had a huge impact on me. I began slavishly copying Tezuka's draw-ings and turned into a manga maniac. Hiroshima was an empty, burnt-out wasteland and we went hungry every day, but when I drew comics, I was happy and forgot everything else. I vowed early on to become a professional cartoonist when I grew up.

In 1961 I pursued my dream by moving to Tokyo. A year later I published my first cartoon serial in the manga monthly *Shonen Gaho* (*Boys' Pictorial*). From then on I was a full-time cartoonist.

In 1966, after seven years of illness, my mother died in the A-Bomb Victims Hospital in Hiroshima. When I went to the crema-torium to collect her ashes, I was shocked. There were no bones left in my mother's ashes, as there normally are after a cremation. Radioactive cesium from the bomb had eaten away at her bones to the point that they disintegrated. The bomb had even deprived me of my mother's bones. I was overcome with rage. I vowed that I would never forgive the Japanese militarists who started the war, nor the Americans who had so casually dropped the bomb on us.

I began drawing comics about the A-bomb as a way to avenge my mother. I vented my anger through a "Black" series of six manga published in an adult manga magazine, starting with *Kuroi Ame ni Utarete* (*Struck by Black Rain*). Then I moved to *Shukan Shonen Jump* (*Weekly Boys' Jump*), where I began a series of works about the war and the A-bomb starting with *Aru Hi Totsuzen ni* (*One Day, Suddenly*). When the monthly edition of *Jump* launched a series of autobiographical works by its cartoonists, I was asked to lead off with my own story. My 45-page manga auto-biography was titled *Ore wa Mita* (*I Saw It*). My editor at *Jump*, Tadasu Nagano, commenting that I must have more to say that wouldn't fit in 45 pages, urged me to draw a longer series based on my personal experiences. I gratefully began the series right away. That was in 1972.

I named my new story *Hadashi no Gen* (*Barefoot Gen*). The young protagonist's name, Gen, has several meanings in Japanese. It can mean the "root" or "origin" of something, but also "elemental" in the sense of an atomic element, as well as a "source" of vitality and happiness. I envisioned Gen as barefoot, standing firmly atop the burnt-out rubble of Hiroshima, raising his voice against war and nuclear weapons. Gen is my alter ego, and his family is just like my own. The episodes in *Barefoot Gen* are all based on what really happened to me or to other people in Hiroshima.

Human beings are foolish. Thanks to bigotry, religious fanaticism, and the greed of those who traffic in war, the Earth is never at peace, and the specter of nuclear war is never far away. I hope that Gen's story conveys to its readers the preciousness of peace and the courage we need to live strongly, yet peacefully. In *Barefoot Gen*, wheat appears as a symbol of that strength and courage. Wheat pushes its shoots up through the winter frost, only to be trampled again and again. But the trampled wheat sends strong roots into the earth and grows straight and tall. And one day, that wheat bears fruit.

BAREFOOT GEN

A CARTOON STORY OF HIROSHIMA

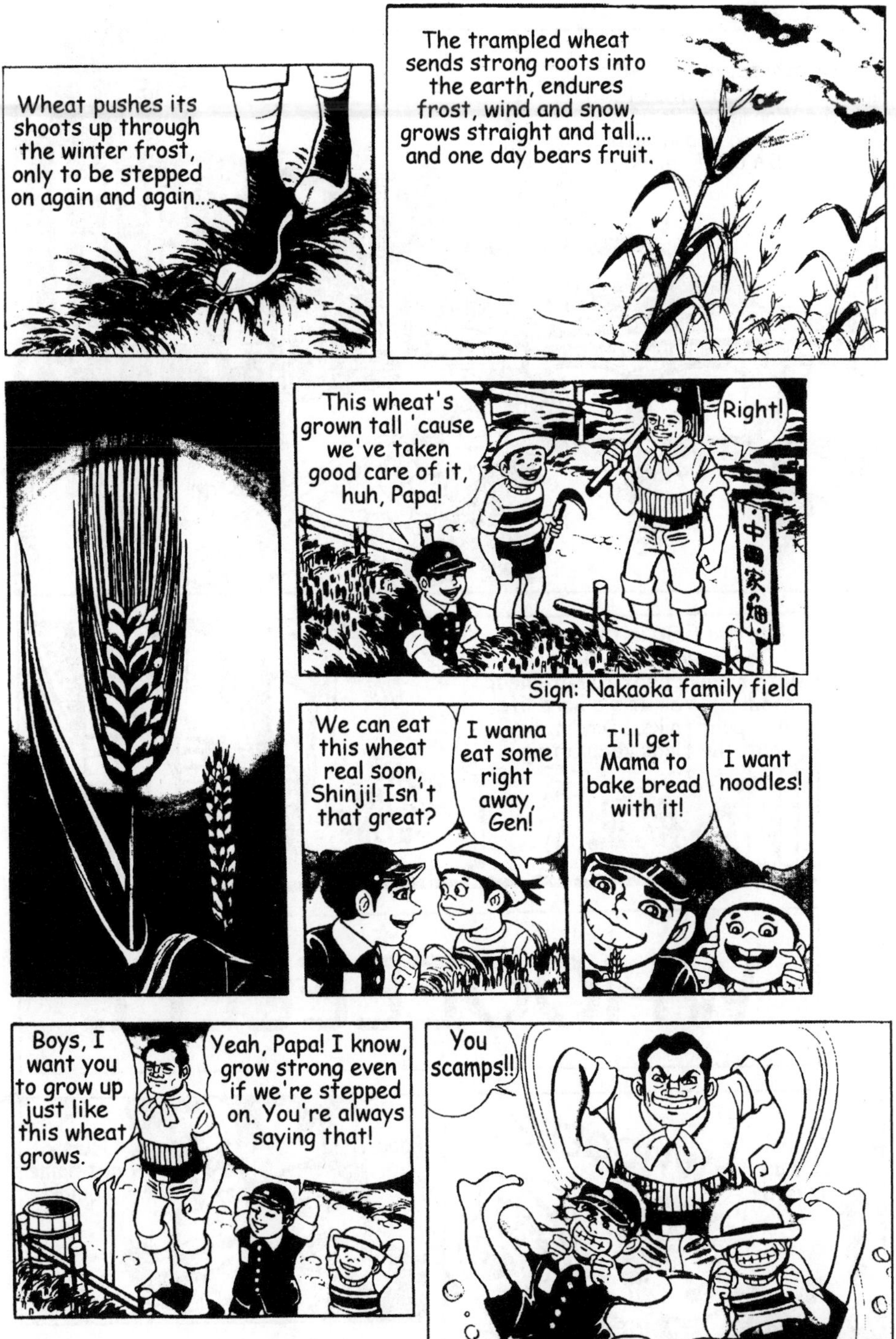
Wheat pushes its shoots up through the winter frost, only to be stepped on again and again...
The trampled wheat sends strong roots into the earth, endures frost, wind and snow, grows straight and tall... and one day bears fruit.
This wheat's grown tall 'cause we've taken good care of it, huh, Papa!
Right!
中岡家の畑
Sign: Nakaoka family field
We can eat this wheat real soon, Shinji! Isn't that great?
I wanna eat some right away, Gen!
I'll get Mama to bake bread with it!
I want noodles!
Boys, I want you to grow up just like this wheat grows.
Yeah, Papa! I know, grow strong even if we're stepped on. You're always saying that!
You scamps!!

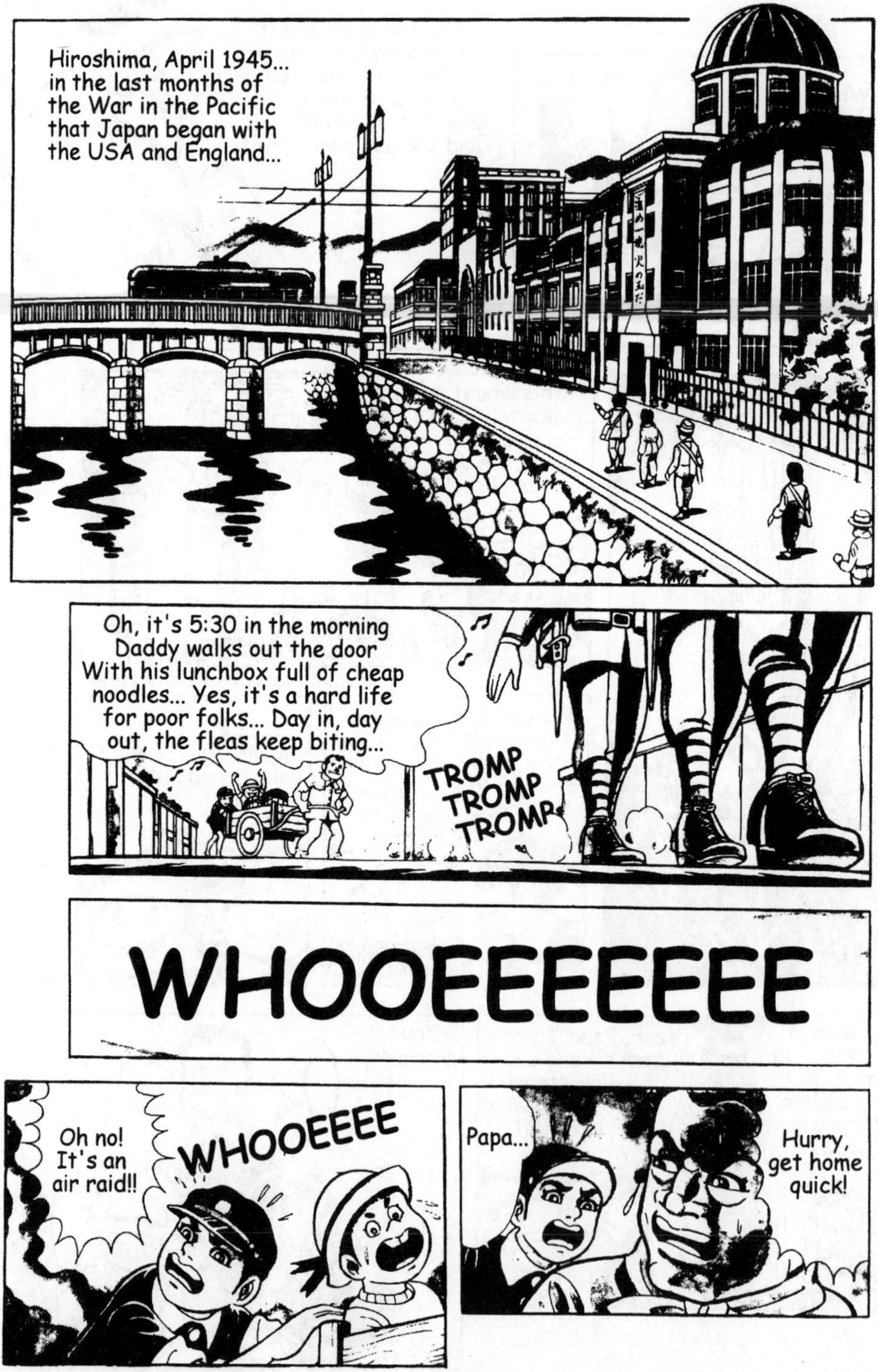
Hiroshima, April 1945... in the last months of the War in the Pacific that Japan began with the USA and England...
進め一億火の玉だ
Oh, it's 5:30 in the morning Daddy walks out the door With his lunchbox full of cheap noodles... Yes, it's a hard life for poor folks... Day in, day out, the fleas keep biting...
TROMP TROMP TROMP
WHOOEEEEEEEE
Oh no! It's an air raid!!
WHOOEEEE
Papa...
Hurry, get home quick!

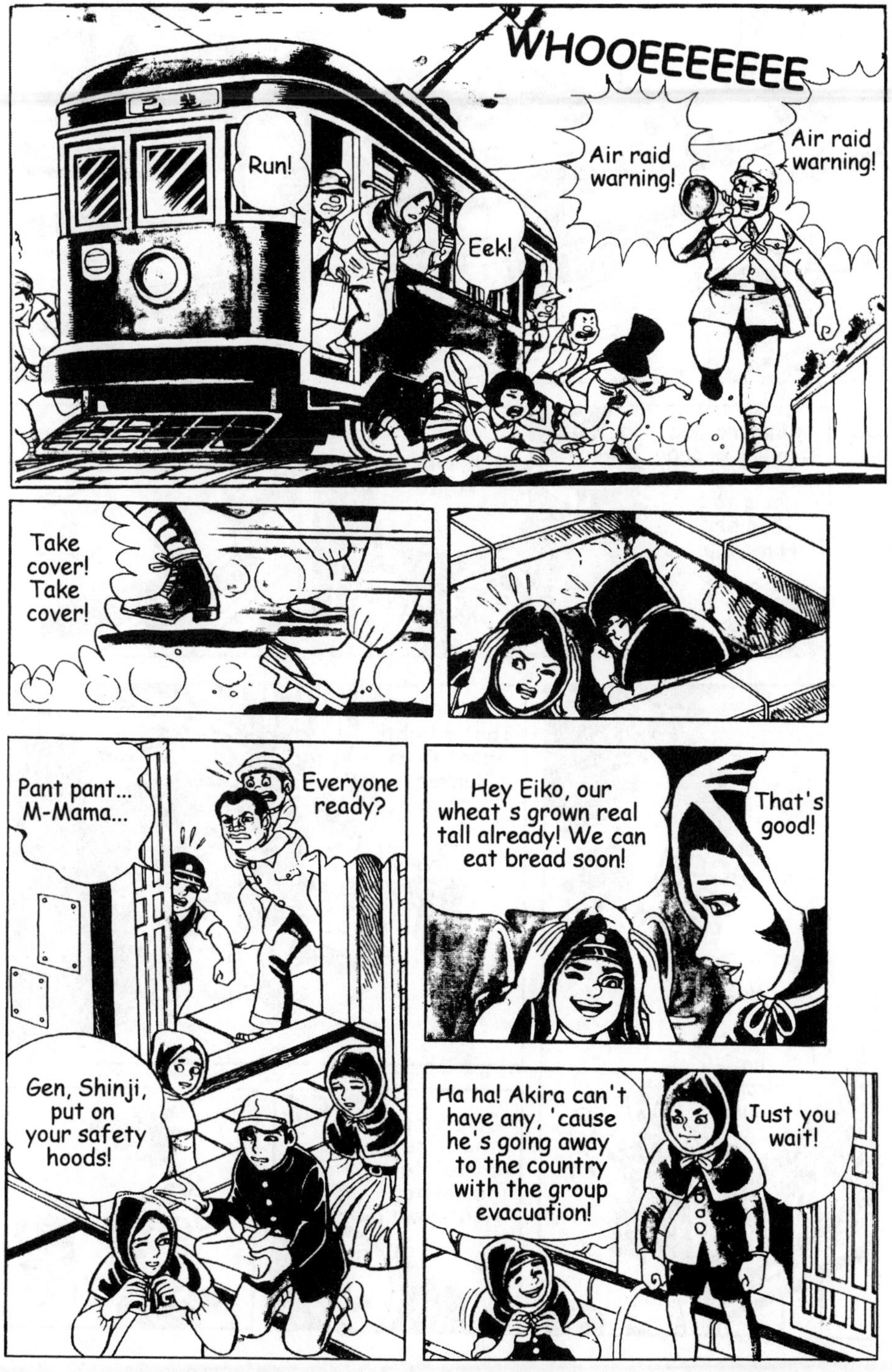
WHOOEEEEEEE
Run!
Eek!
Air raid warning!
Air raid warning!
Take cover! Take cover!
Pant pant... M-Mama...
Everyone ready?
Gen, Shinji, put on your safety hoods!
Hey Eiko, our wheat's grown real tall already! We can eat bread soon!
That's good!
Ha ha! Akira can't have any, 'cause he's going away to the country with the group evacuation!
Just you wait!

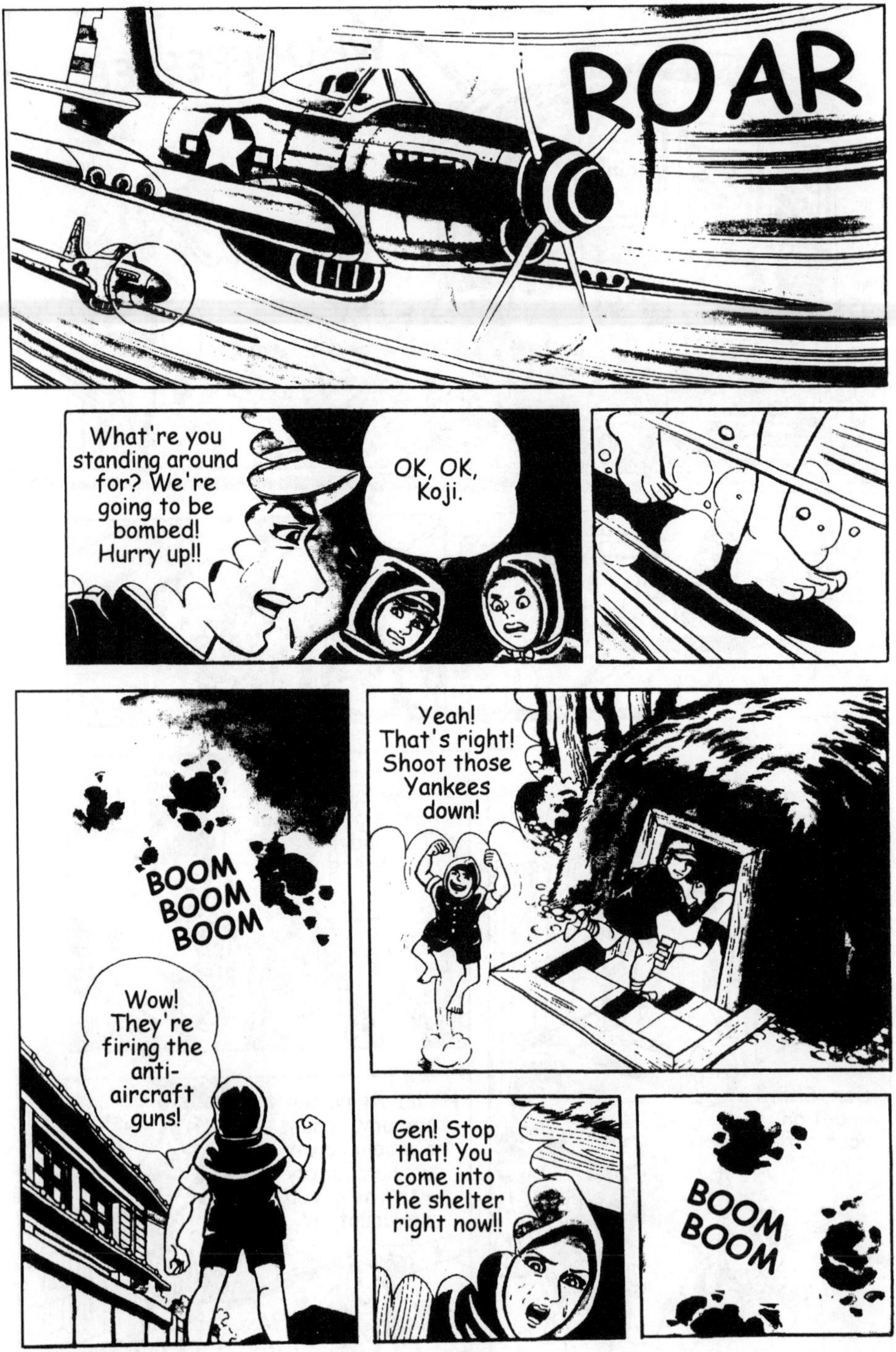
ROAR
What're you standing around for? We're going to be bombed! Hurry up!!
OK, OK, Koji.
BOOM BOOM BOOM
Wow! They're firing the anti-aircraft guns!
Yeah! That's right! Shoot those Yankees down!
Gen! Stop that! You come into the shelter right now!!
BOOM BOOM

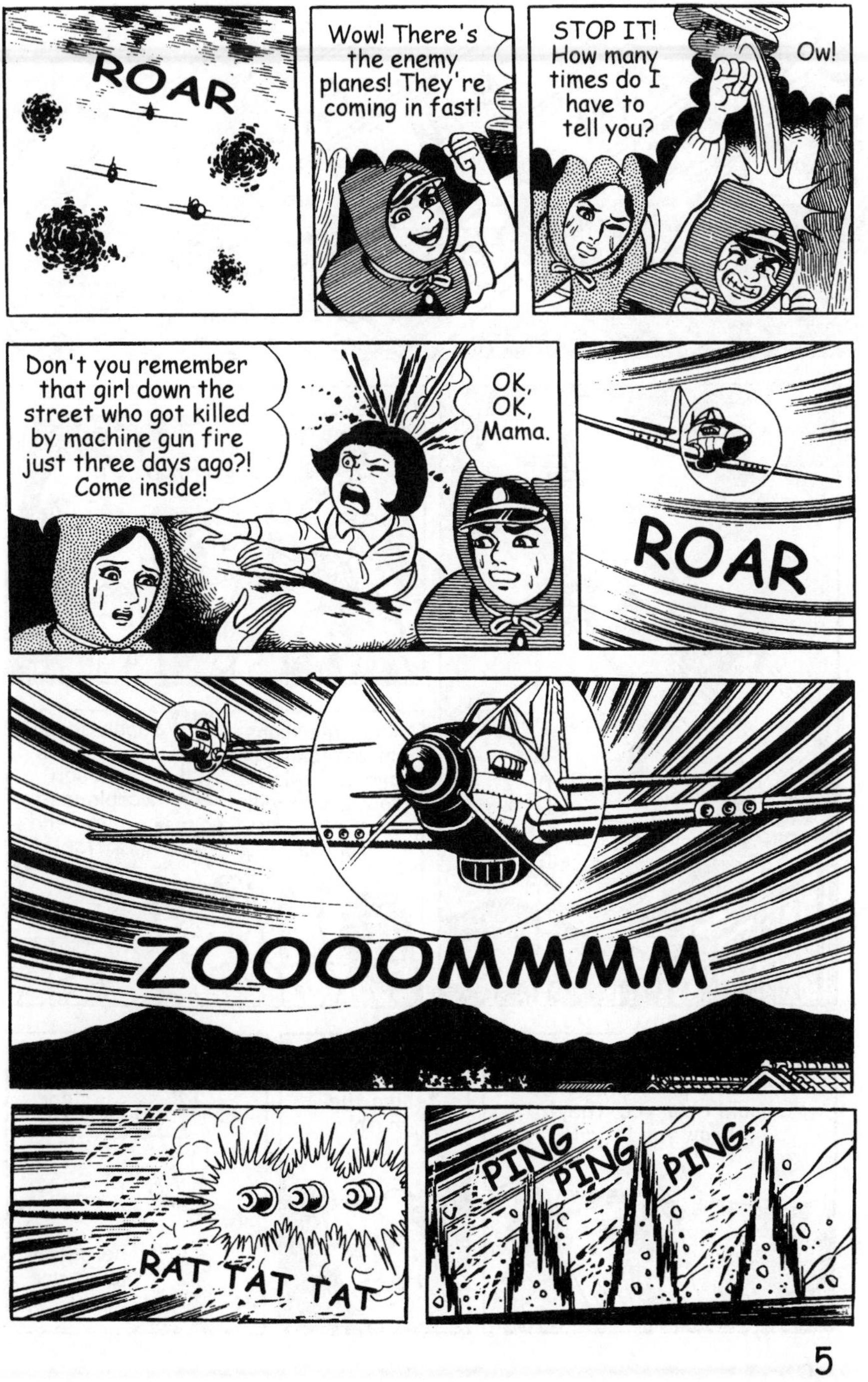
ROAR
Wow! There's the enemy planes! They're coming in fast!
STOP IT! How many times do I have to tell you?
Ow!
Don't you remember that girl down the street who got killed by machine gun fire just three days ago?! Come inside!
OK, OK, Mama.
ROAR
ZOOOOMMMMM
RAT TAT TAT
PING PING PING

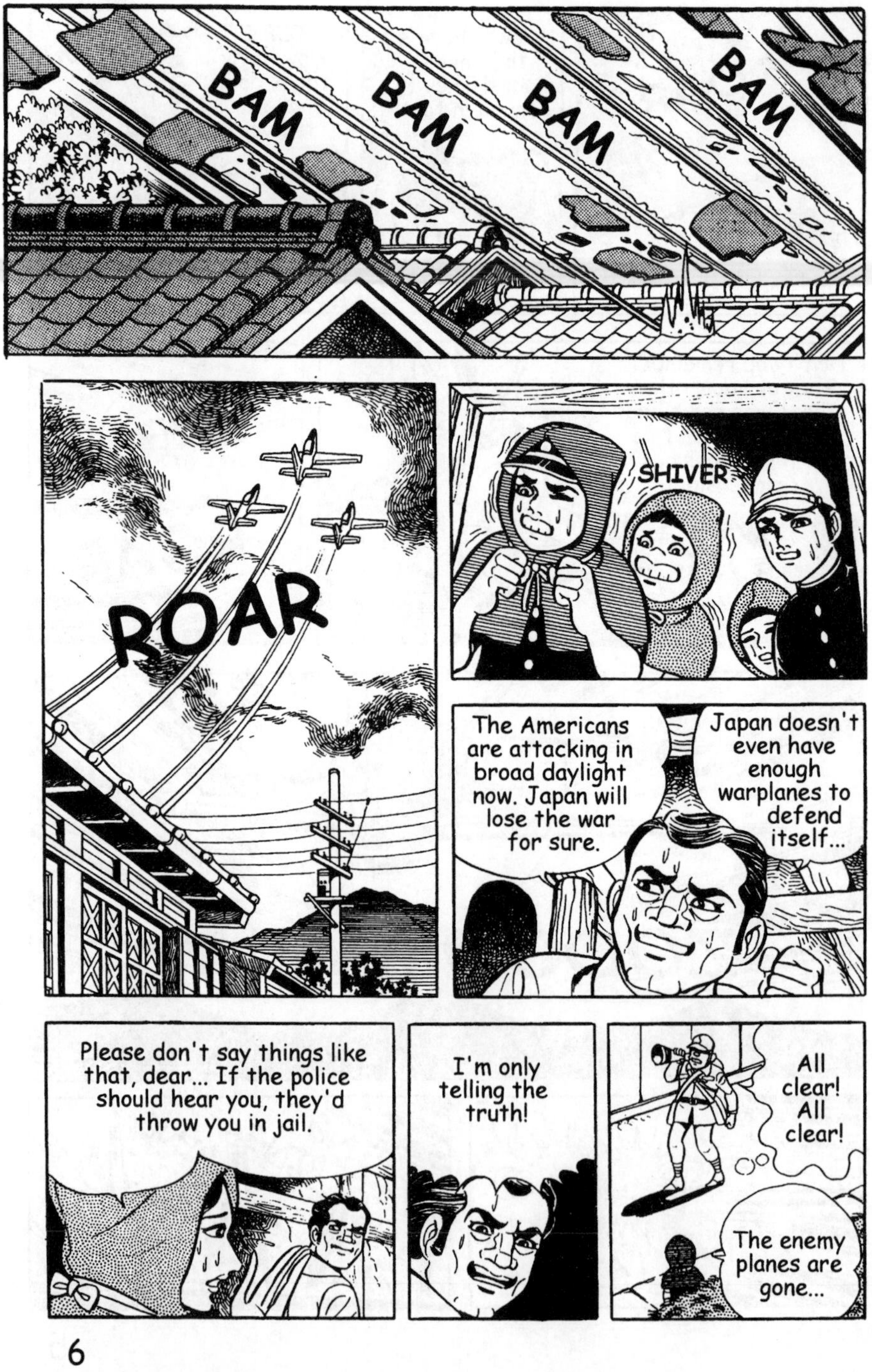
BAM
BAM
BAM
BAM
ROAR
SHIVER
The Americans are attacking in broad daylight now. Japan will lose the war for sure.
Japan doesn't even have enough warplanes to defend itself...
Please don't say things like that, dear... If the police should hear you, they'd throw you in jail.
I'm only telling the truth!
All clear! All clear!
The enemy planes are gone...

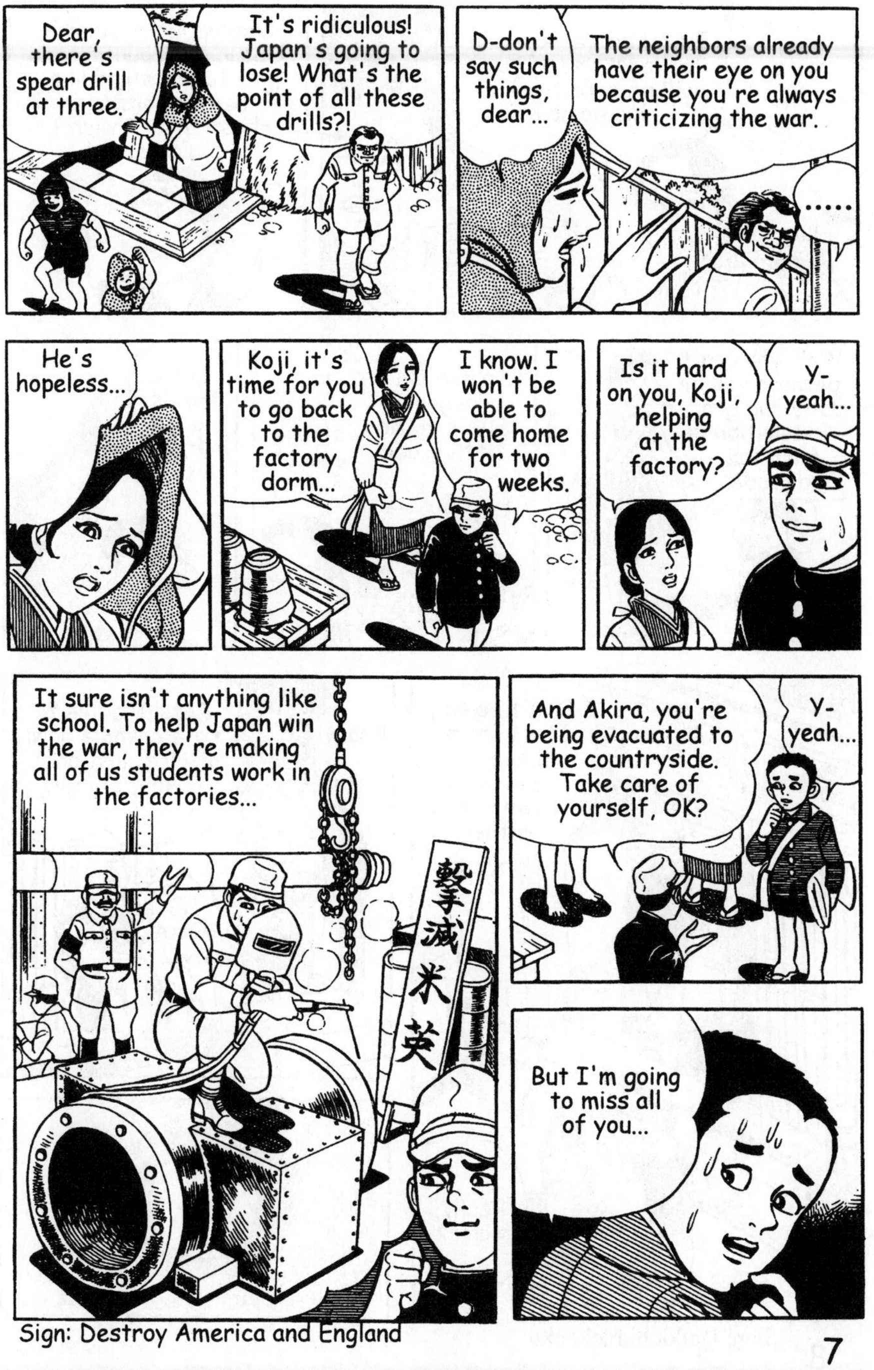
Dear, there's spear drill at three.
It's ridiculous! Japan's going to lose! What's the point of all these drills?!
D-don't say such things, dear...
The neighbors already have their eye on you because you're always criticizing the war.
.....
He's hopeless...
Koji, it's time for you to go back to the factory dorm...
I know. I won't be able to come home for two weeks.
Is it hard on you, Koji, helping at the factory?
Y-yeah...
It sure isn't anything like school. To help Japan win the war, they're making all of us students work in the factories...
撃滅米英
And Akira, you're being evacuated to the countryside. Take care of yourself, OK?
Y-yeah...
But I'm going to miss all of you...
Sign: Destroy America and England

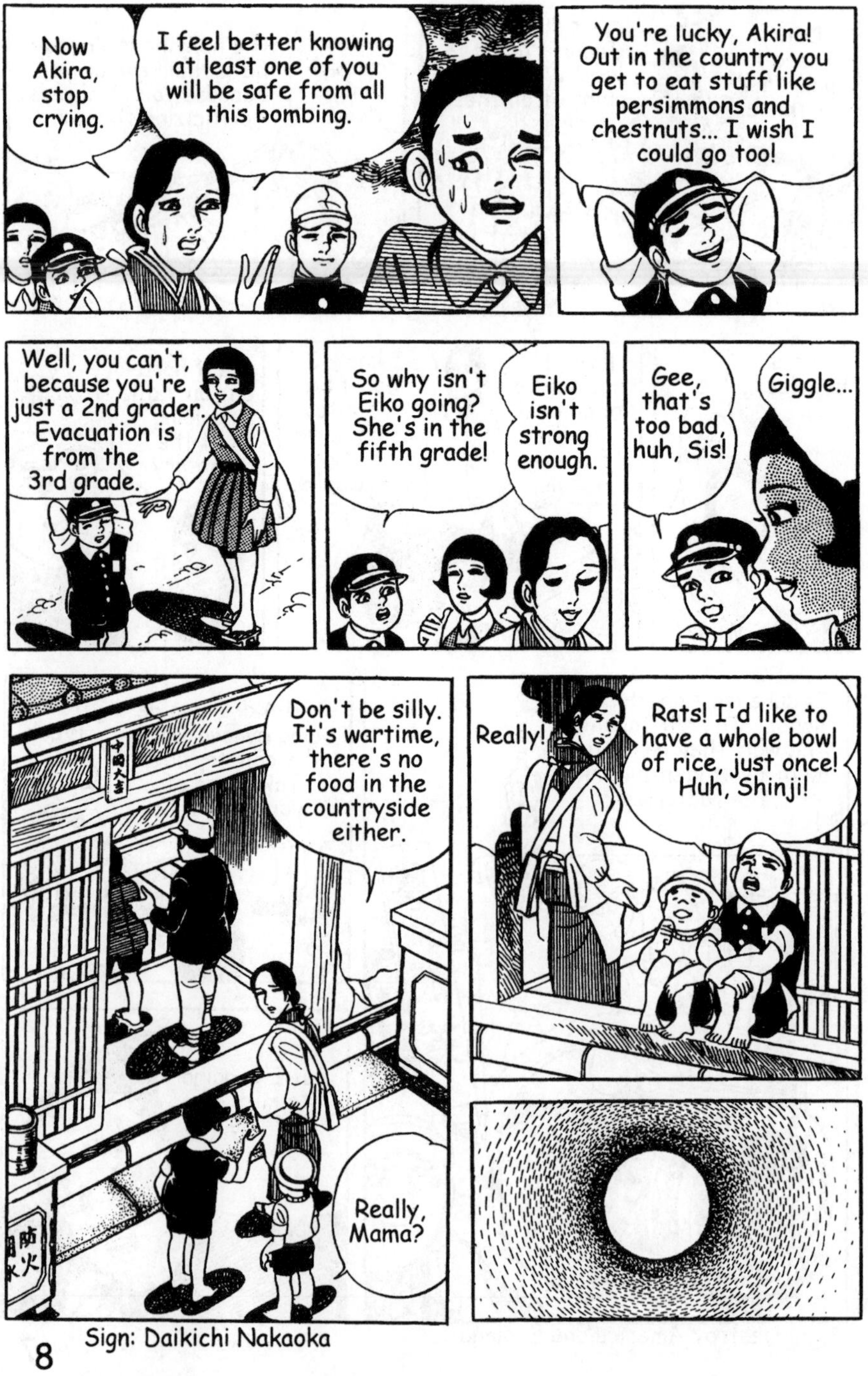
Now Akira, stop crying.
I feel better knowing at least one of you will be safe from all this bombing.
You're lucky, Akira! Out in the country you get to eat stuff like persimmons and chestnuts... I wish I could go too!
Well, you can't, because you're just a 2nd grader. Evacuation is from the 3rd grade.
So why isn't Eiko going? She's in the fifth grade!
Eiko isn't strong enough.
Gee, that's too bad, huh, Sis!
Giggle...
Don't be silly. It's wartime, there's no food in the countryside either.
Really, Mama?
Really!
Rats! I'd like to have a whole bowl of rice, just once! Huh, Shinji!

Sign: Daikichi Nakaoka

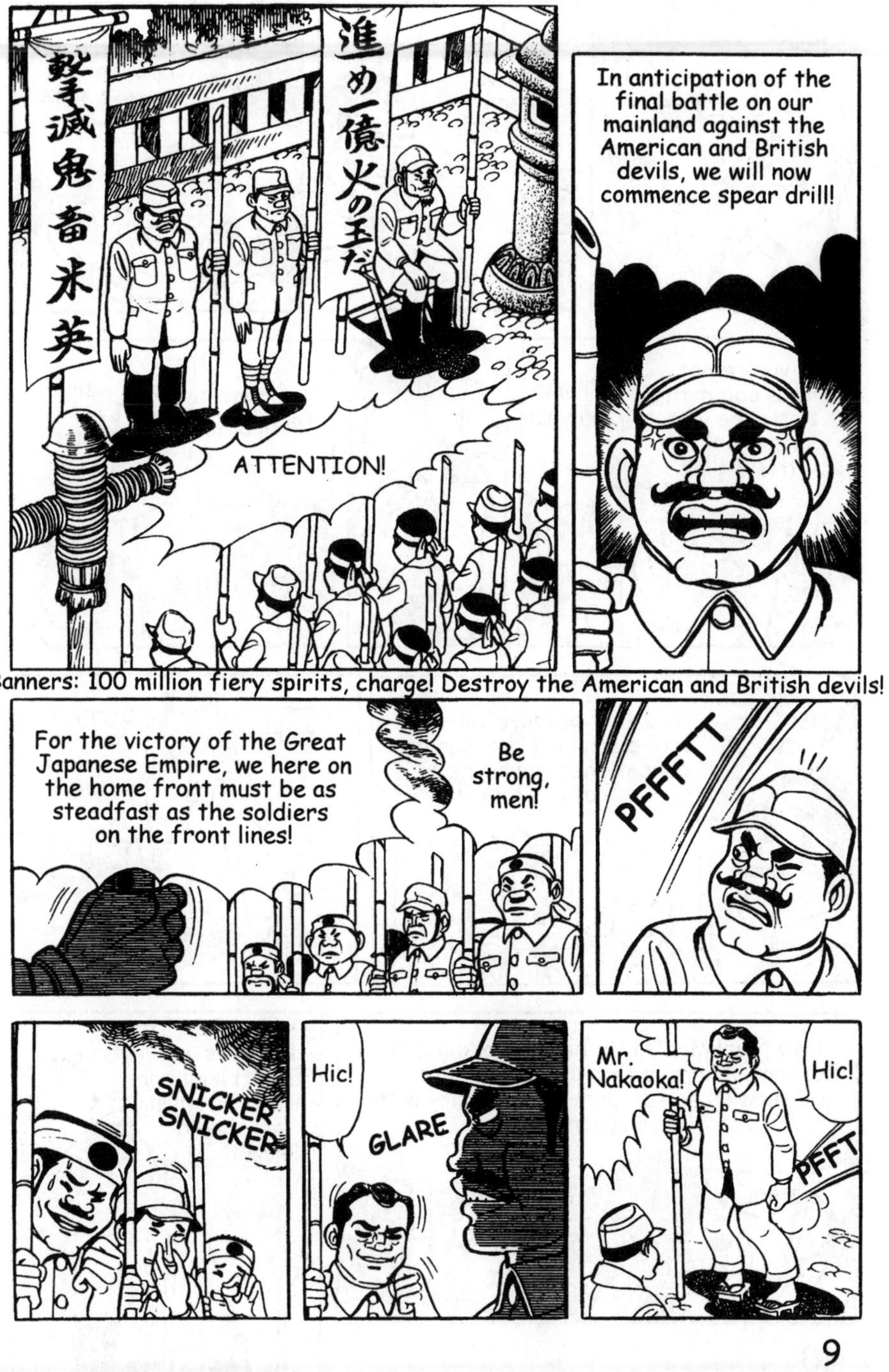
撃滅鬼畜米英
進め一億火の玉だ
ATTENTION!
In anticipation of the final battle on our mainland against the American and British devils, we will now commence spear drill!
Banners: 100 million fiery spirits, charge! Destroy the American and British devils!
For the victory of the Great Japanese Empire, we here on the home front must be as steadfast as the soldiers on the front lines!
Be strong, men!
PFFFTT
SNICKER SNICKER
Hic!
GLARE
Mr. Nakaoka!
Hic!
PFFT

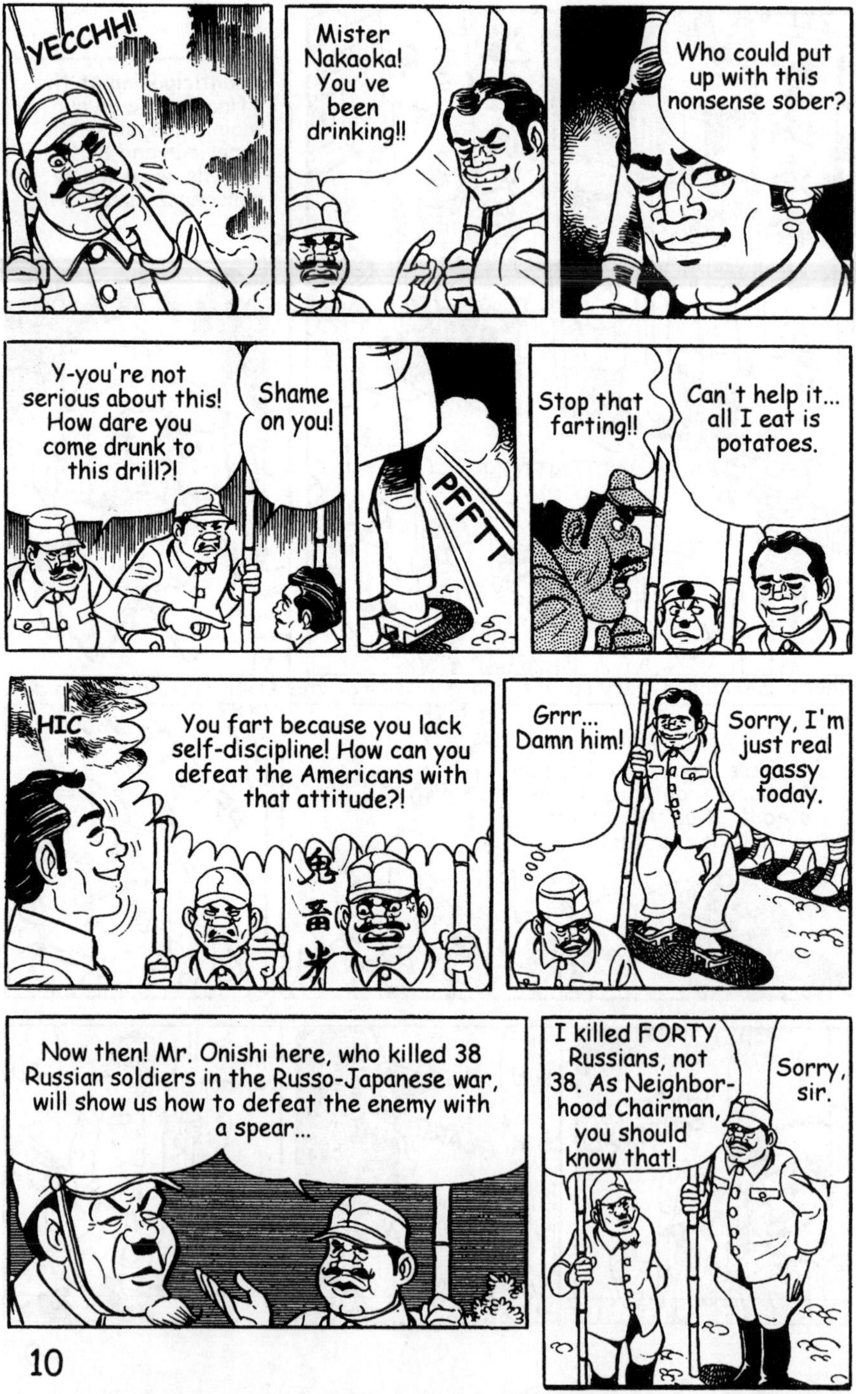
YECCHH!
Mister Nakaoka! You've been drinking!!
Who could put up with this nonsense sober?
Y-you're not serious about this! How dare you come drunk to this drill?!
Shame on you!
PFFTT
Stop that farting!!
Can't help it... all I eat is potatoes.
HIC
You fart because you lack self-discipline! How can you defeat the Americans with that attitude?!
鬼畜米
Grrr... Damn him!
Sorry, I'm just real gassy today.
Now then! Mr. Onishi here, who killed 38 Russian soldiers in the Russo-Japanese war, will show us how to defeat the enemy with a spear...
I killed FORTY Russians, not 38. As Neighbor-hood Chairman, you should know that!
Sorry, sir.

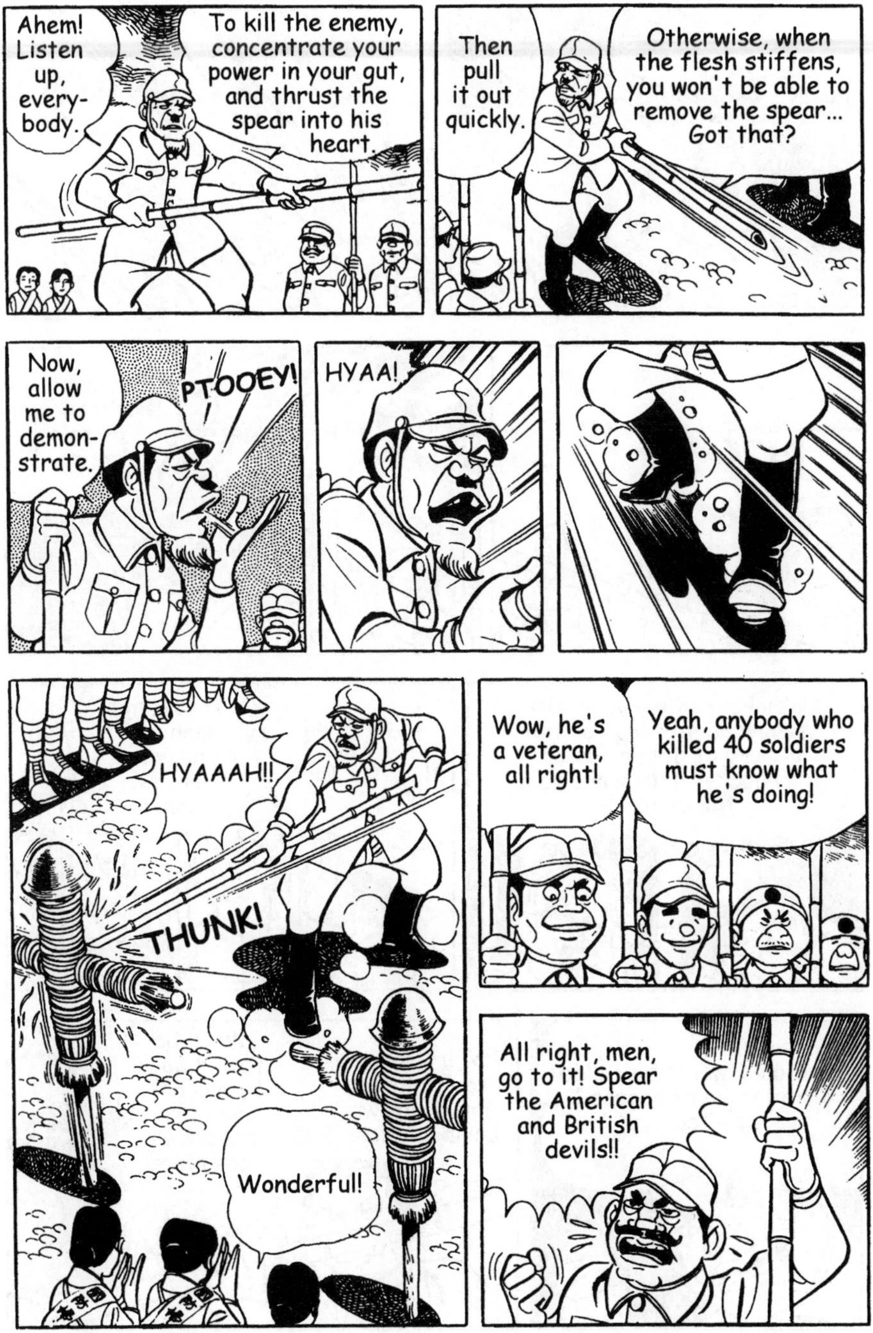
Ahem! Listen up, everybody.
To kill the enemy, concentrate your power in your gut, and thrust the spear into his heart.
Then pull it out quickly.
Otherwise, when the flesh stiffens, you won't be able to remove the spear... Got that?
Now, allow me to demonstrate.
PTOOEY!
HYAA!
HYAAAH!!
THUNK!
Wonderful!
Wow, he's a veteran, all right!
Yeah, anybody who killed 40 soldiers must know what he's doing!
All right, men, go to it! Spear the American and British devils!!

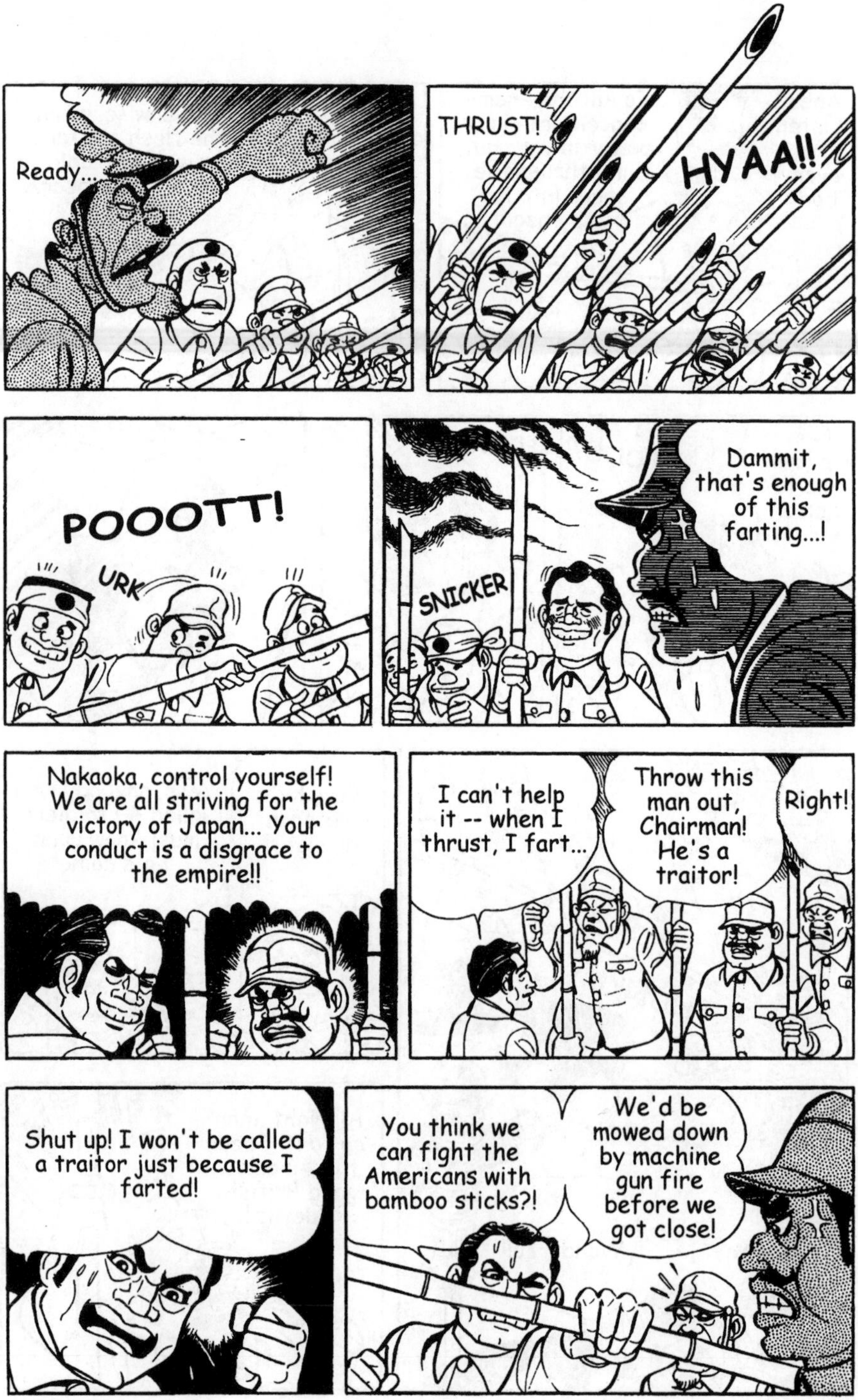
Ready...
THRUST!
HYAA!!
POOOTT!
URK
SNICKER
Dammit, that's enough of this farting...!
Nakaoka, control yourself! We are all striving for the victory of Japan... Your conduct is a disgrace to the empire!!
I can't help it -- when I thrust, I fart...
Throw this man out, Chairman! He's a traitor!
Right!
Shut up! I won't be called a traitor just because I farted!
You think we can fight the Americans with bamboo sticks?!
We'd be mowed down by machine gun fire before we got close!

America has more resources than Japan does. A small country like Japan can only survive by foreign trade. We should keep peace with the rest of the world.

Japan has no business fighting a war!

W-what?!

The military was misled by the rich. They started the war to grab resources by force, and drew us all in...

You're all sick with war fever! This war is wrong!

Y-you won't get away with this, traitor!

Go to hell. I'm tired of war!

I'm through with all this!

CRACK!

You'll see how stupid this war is soon enough. Try thinking for yourselves for a change!

Y-you TRAITOR!!

13

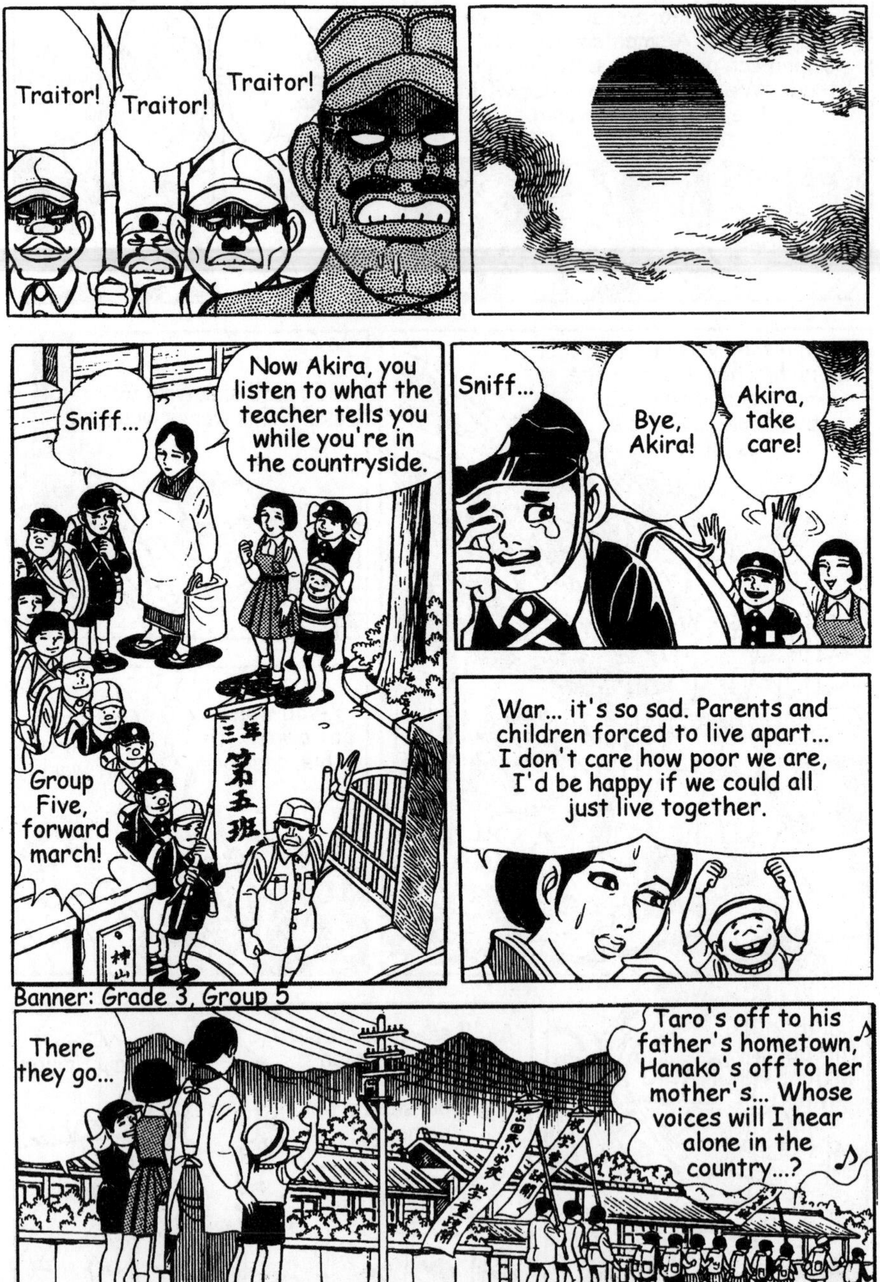
Traitor!
Traitor!
Traitor!
Sniff...
Now Akira, you listen to what the teacher tells you while you're in the countryside.
三年 第五班
Group Five, forward march!
Sniff...
Bye, Akira!
Akira, take care!
War... it's so sad. Parents and children forced to live apart... I don't care how poor we are, I'd be happy if we could all just live together.
Banner: Grade 3, Group 5
There they go...
Taro's off to his father's hometown, Hanako's off to her mother's... Whose voices will I hear alone in the country...?
Banners: Kamiyama Primary School Group Evacuation

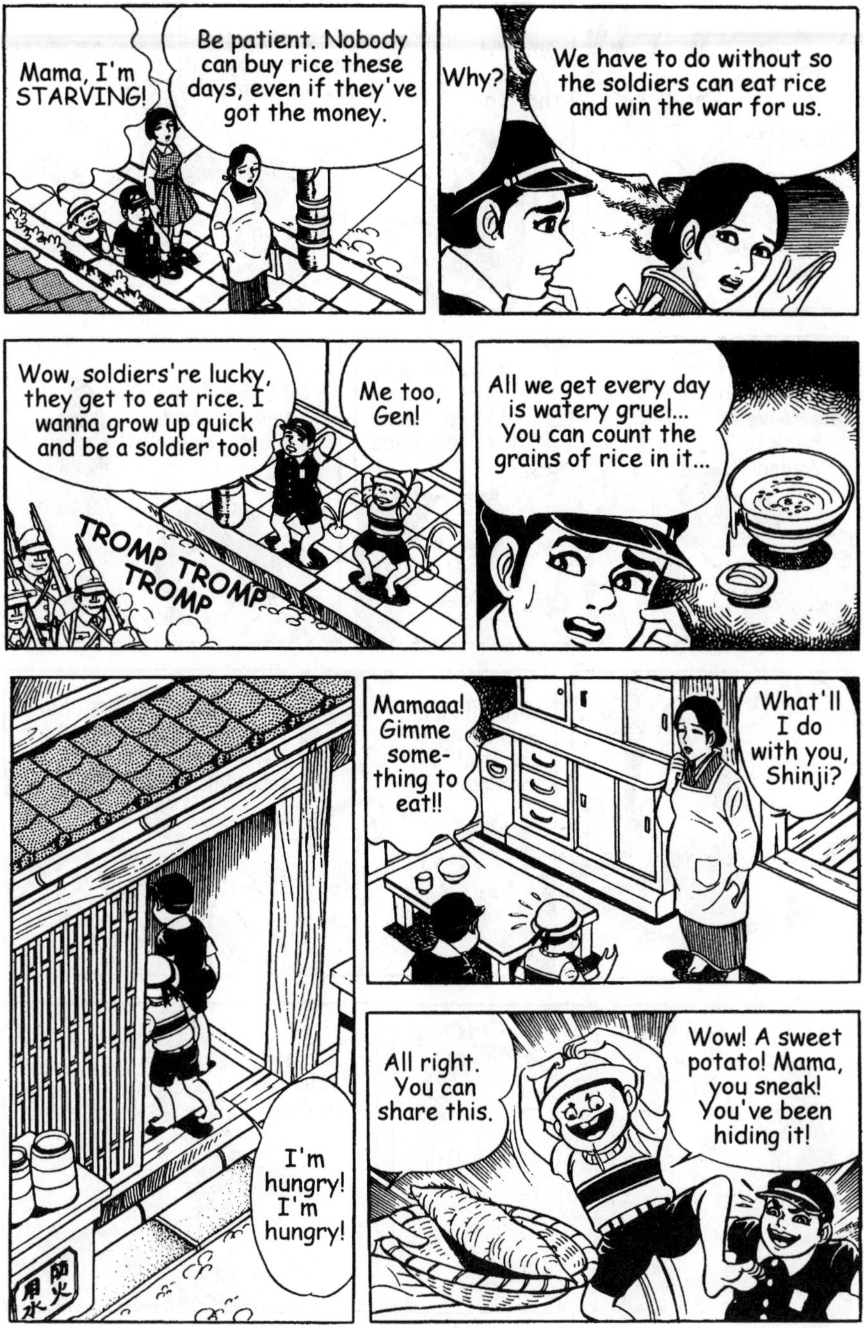
Mama, I'm STARVING!
Be patient. Nobody can buy rice these days, even if they've got the money.
Why?
We have to do without so the soldiers can eat rice and win the war for us.
Wow, soldiers're lucky, they get to eat rice. I wanna grow up quick and be a soldier too!
Me too, Gen!
TROMP TROMP TROMP
All we get every day is watery gruel... You can count the grains of rice in it...
I'm hungry! I'm hungry!
防火用水
Mamaaa! Gimme some-thing to eat!!
What'll I do with you, Shinji?
All right. You can share this.
Wow! A sweet potato! Mama, you sneak! You've been hiding it!

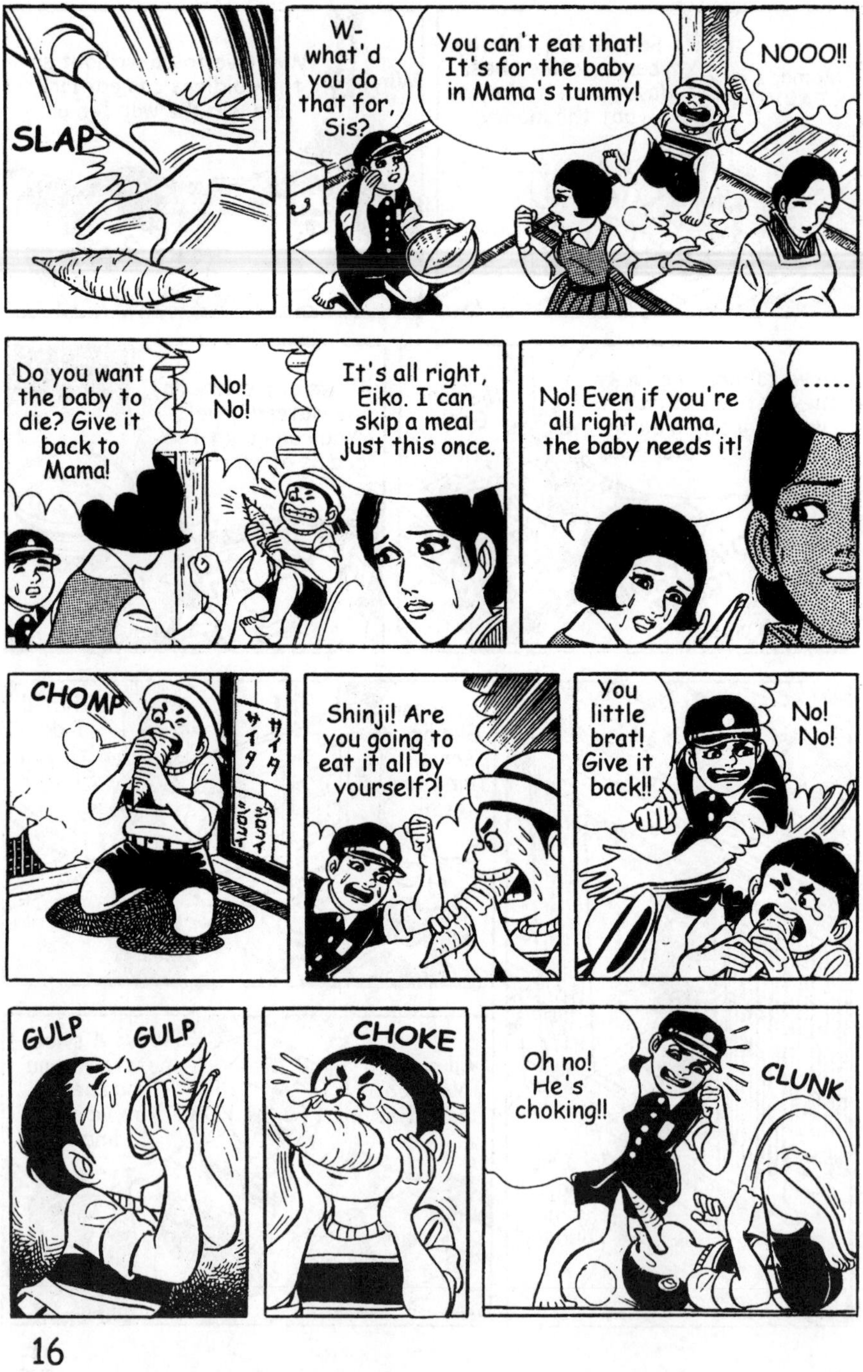
SLAP
W- what'd you do that for, Sis?
You can't eat that! It's for the baby in Mama's tummy!
NOOO!!
Do you want the baby to die? Give it back to Mama!
No! No!
It's all right, Eiko. I can skip a meal just this once.
No! Even if you're all right, Mama, the baby needs it!
.....
CHOMP
サイタ
サイタ
Shinji! Are you going to eat it all by yourself?!
You little brat! Give it back!!
No! No!
GULP
GULP
CHOKE
Oh no! He's choking!!
CLUNK

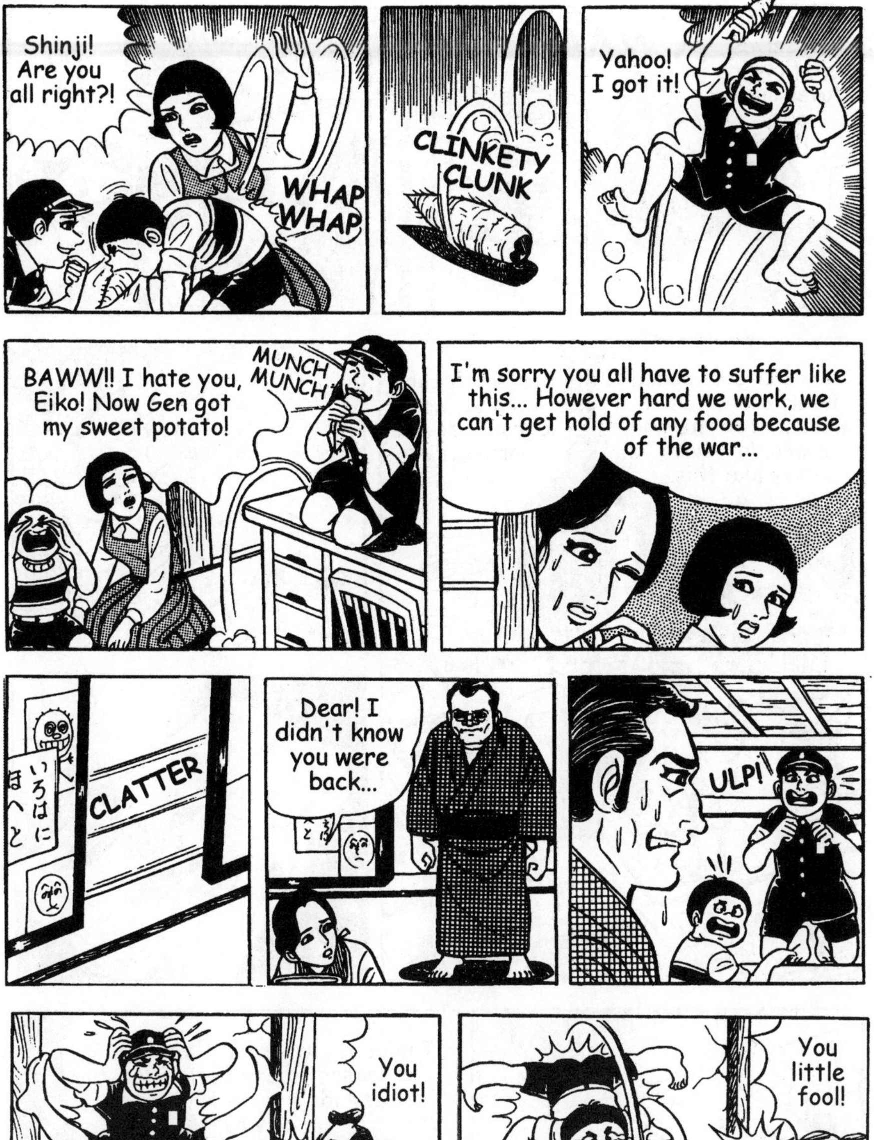
Shinji! Are you all right?!
WHAP WHAP
CLINKETY CLUNK
Yahoo! I got it!
BAWW!! I hate you, Eiko! Now Gen got my sweet potato!
MUNCH MUNCH
I'm sorry you all have to suffer like this... However hard we work, we can't get hold of any food because of the war...
いろはにほへと
CLATTER
Dear! I didn't know you were back...
ULP!
You idiot!
You little fool!

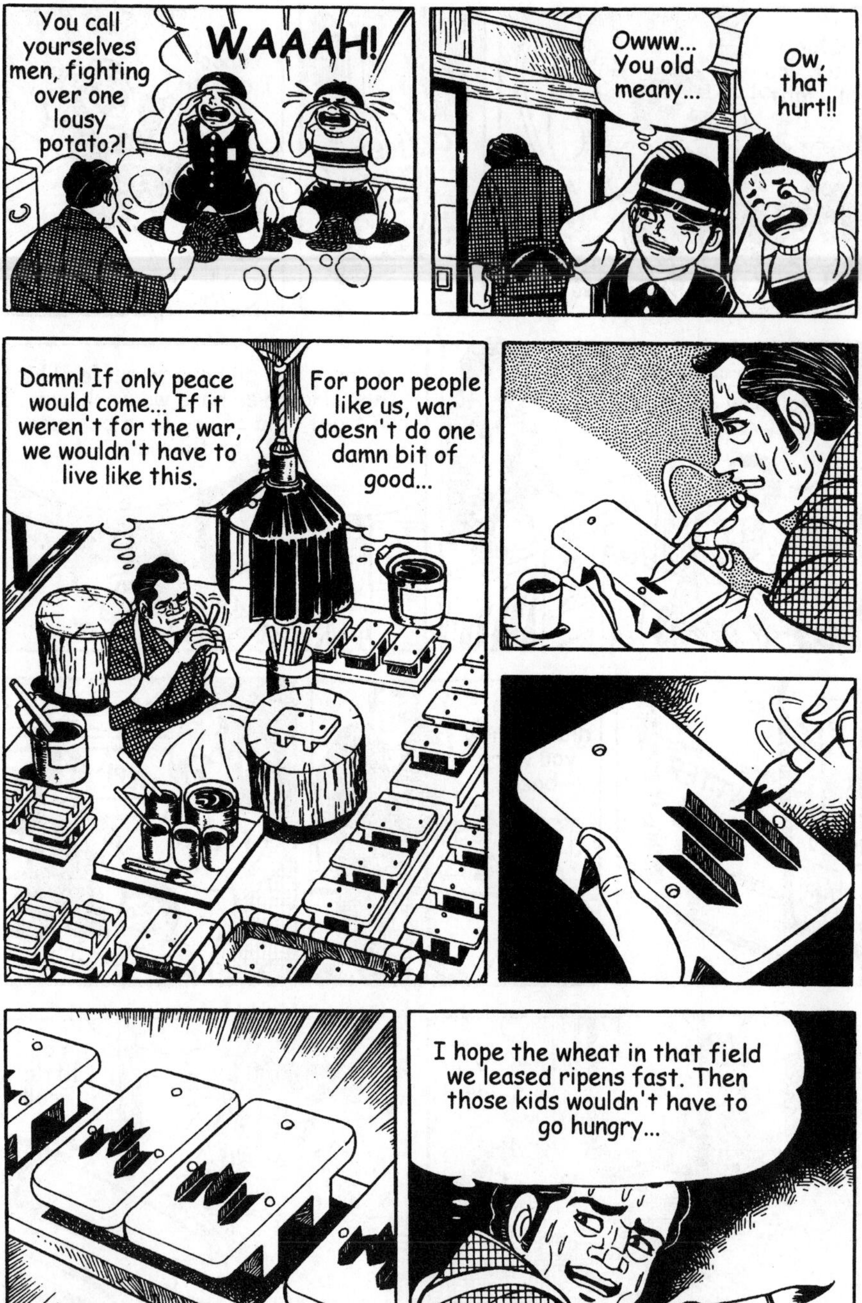
You call yourselves men, fighting over one lousy potato?!
WAAAH!
Owww... You old meany...
Ow, that hurt!!
Damn! If only peace would come... If it weren't for the war, we wouldn't have to live like this.
For poor people like us, war doesn't do one damn bit of good...
I hope the wheat in that field we leased ripens fast. Then those kids wouldn't have to go hungry...

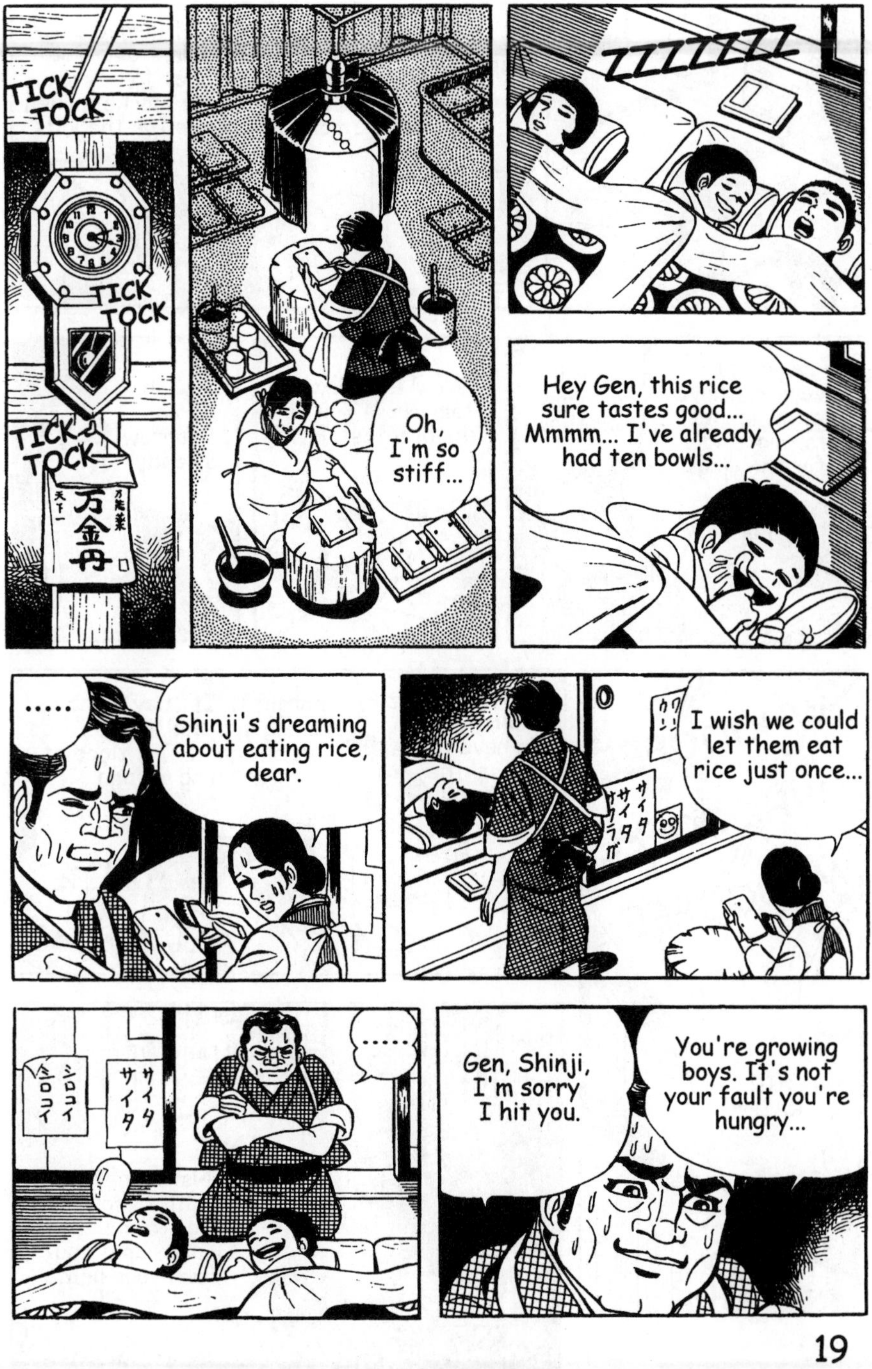
TICK TOCK
TICK TOCK
TICK TOCK
万金丹
Oh, I'm so stiff...
ZZZZZZZ
Hey Gen, this rice sure tastes good... Mmmm... I've already had ten bowls...
.....
Shinji's dreaming about eating rice, dear.
I wish we could let them eat rice just once...
サイタ サイタ サクラガ
.....
Gen, Shinji, I'm sorry I hit you.
You're growing boys. It's not your fault you're hungry...

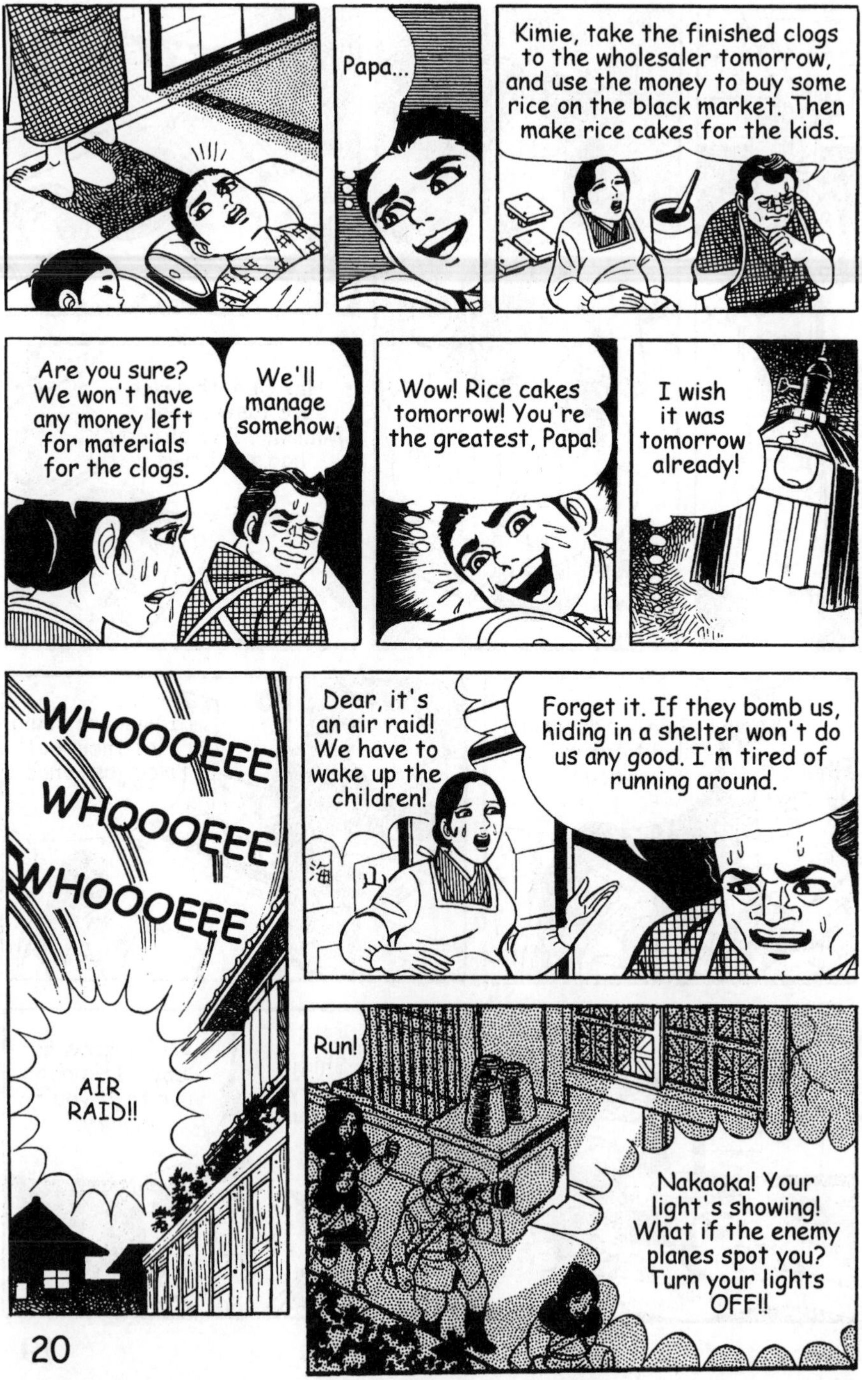

Papa...
Kimie, take the finished clogs to the wholesaler tomorrow, and use the money to buy some rice on the black market. Then make rice cakes for the kids.
Are you sure? We won't have any money left for materials for the clogs.
We'll manage somehow.
Wow! Rice cakes tomorrow! You're the greatest, Papa!
I wish it was tomorrow already!
WHOOOEEE
WHOOOEEE
WHOOOEEE
AIR RAID!!
Dear, it's an air raid! We have to wake up the children!
Forget it. If they bomb us, hiding in a shelter won't do us any good. I'm tired of running around.
Run!
Nakaoka! Your light's showing! What if the enemy planes spot you? Turn your lights OFF!!

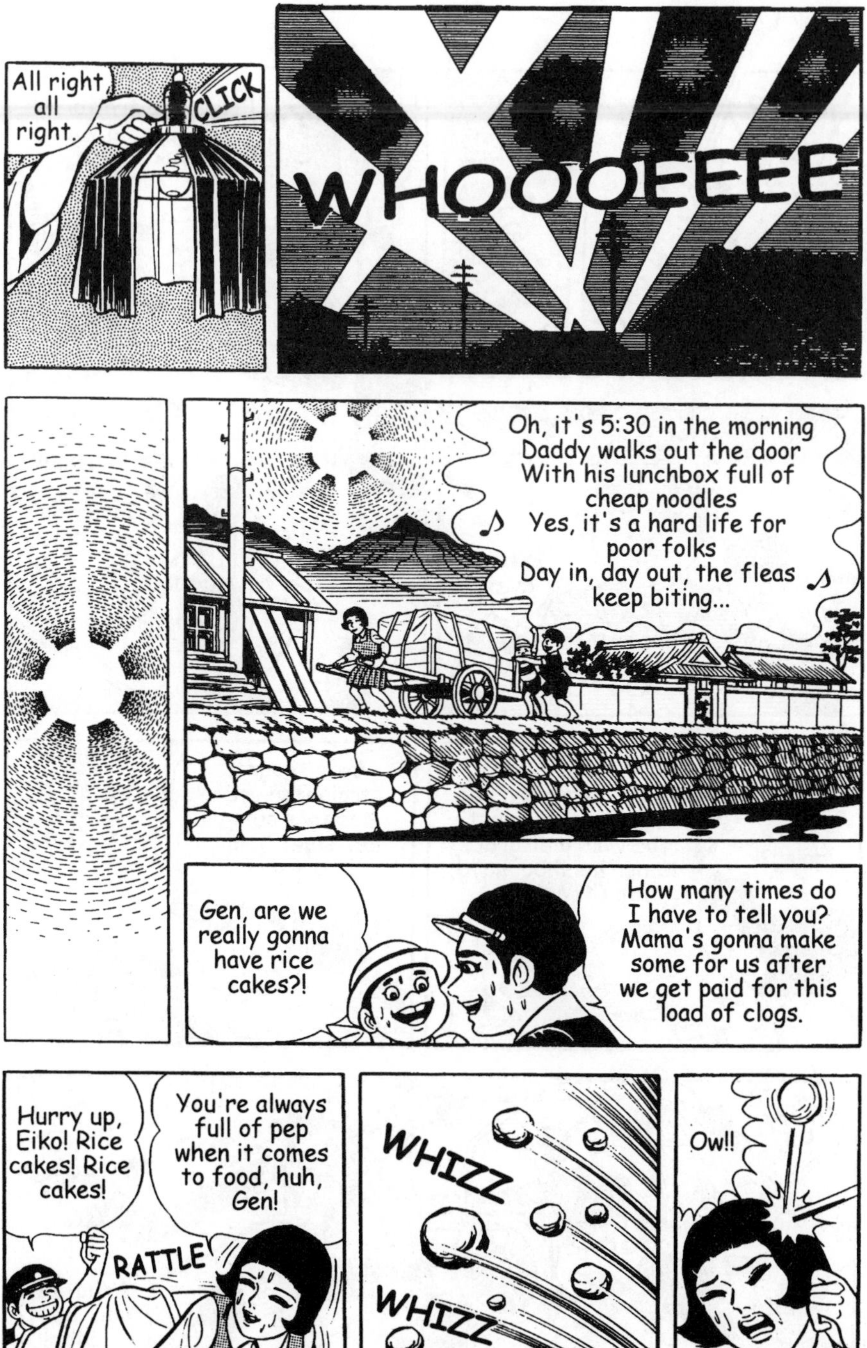
All right, all right.
CLICK
WHOOOEEEE
Oh, it's 5:30 in the morning
Daddy walks out the door
With his lunchbox full of cheap noodles
Yes, it's a hard life for poor folks
Day in, day out, the fleas keep biting...
Gen, are we really gonna have rice cakes?!
How many times do I have to tell you? Mama's gonna make some for us after we get paid for this load of clogs.
Hurry up, Eiko! Rice cakes! Rice cakes!
You're always full of pep when it comes to food, huh, Gen!
RATTLE
WHIZZ
WHIZZ
Ow!!

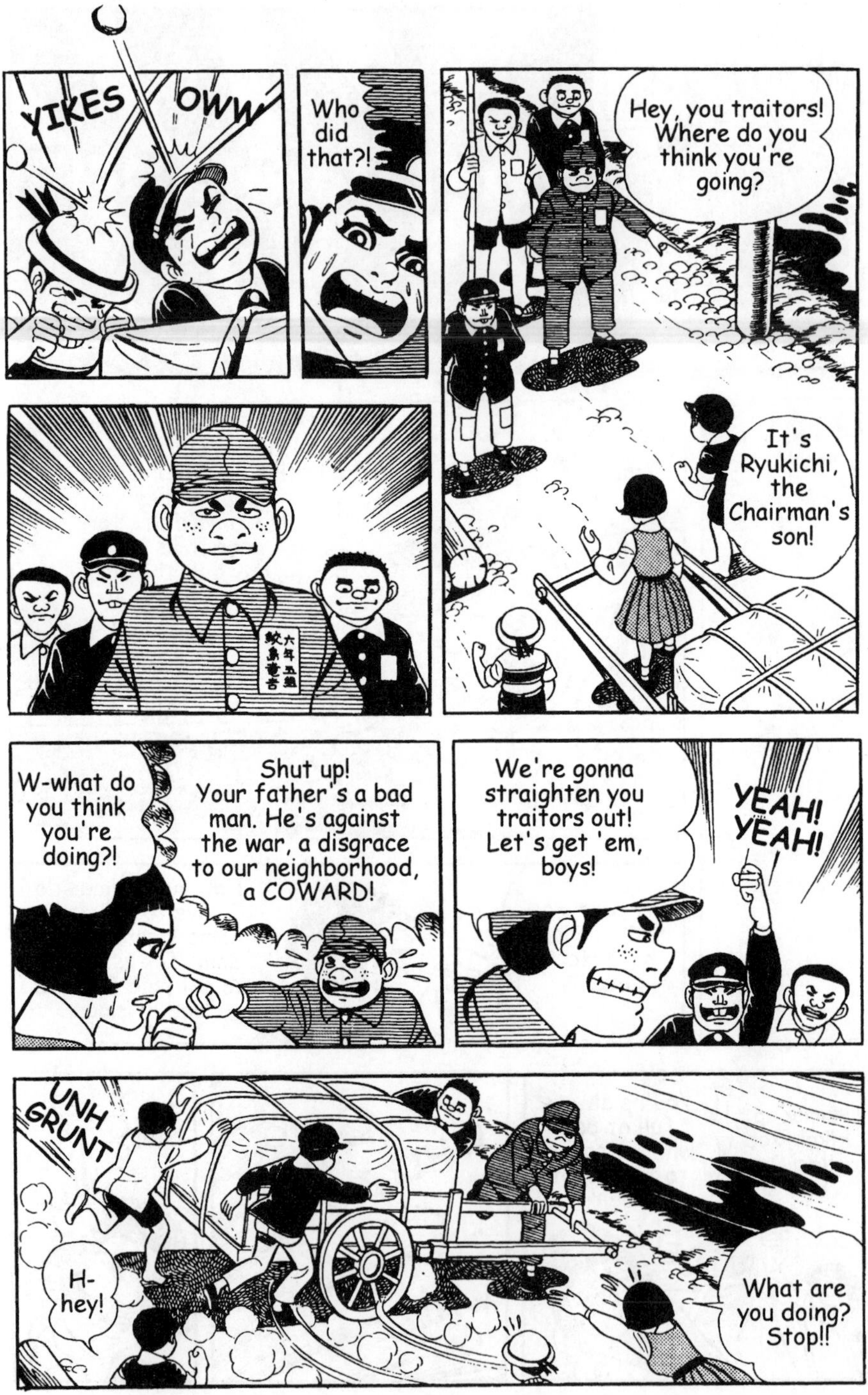
YIKES
OWW
Who did that?!
Hey, you traitors! Where do you think you're going?
It's Ryukichi, the Chairman's son!
W-what do you think you're doing?!
Shut up! Your father's a bad man. He's against the war, a disgrace to our neighborhood, a COWARD!
We're gonna straighten you traitors out! Let's get 'em, boys!
YEAH! YEAH!
UNH GRUNT
H-hey!
What are you doing? Stop!!

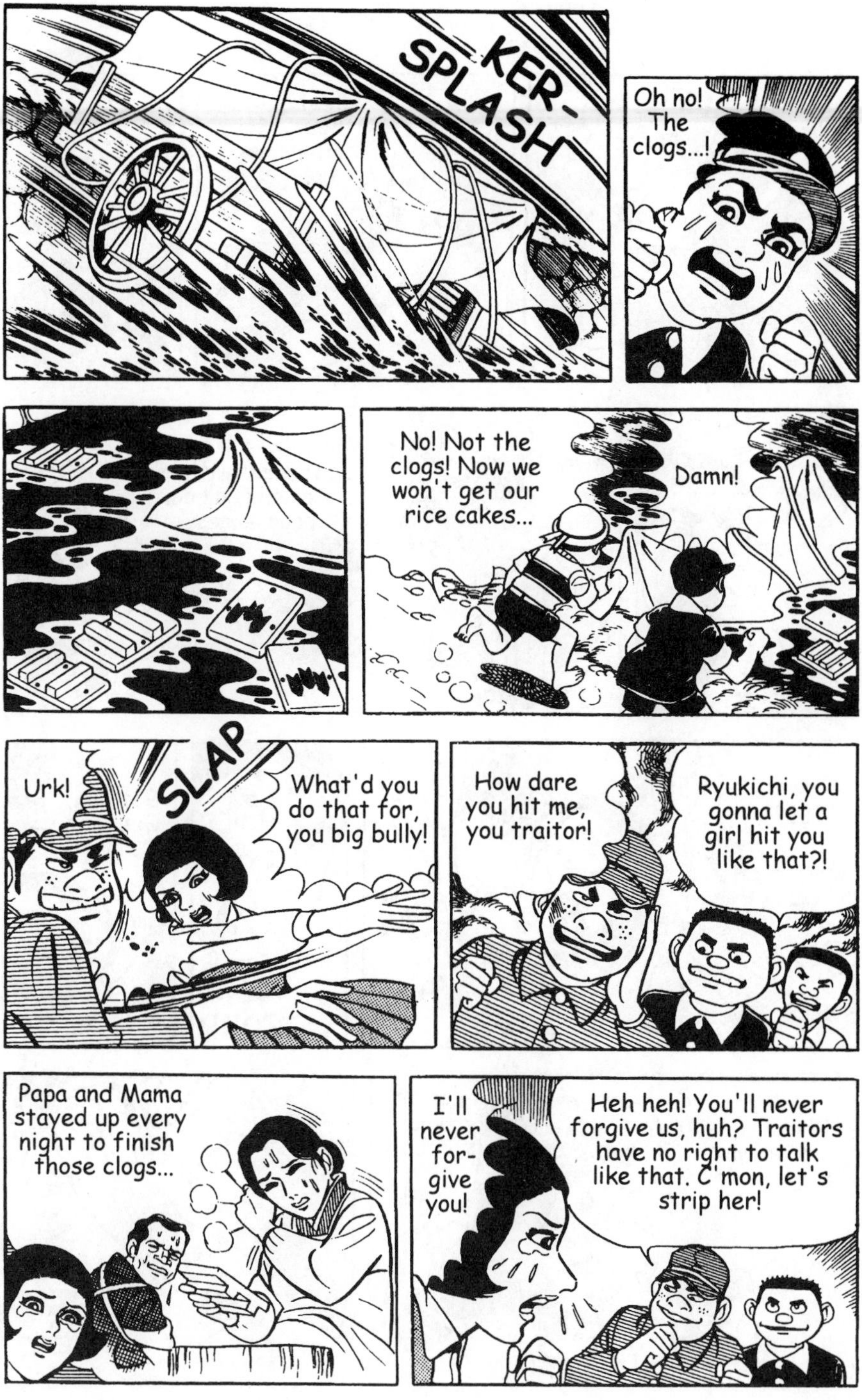
KER-SPLASH
Oh no! The clogs...!
No! Not the clogs! Now we won't get our rice cakes...
Damn!
Urk!
SLAP
What'd you do that for, you big bully!
How dare you hit me, you traitor!
Ryukichi, you gonna let a girl hit you like that?!
Papa and Mama stayed up every night to finish those clogs...
I'll never for-give you!
Heh heh! You'll never forgive us, huh? Traitors have no right to talk like that. C'mon, let's strip her!

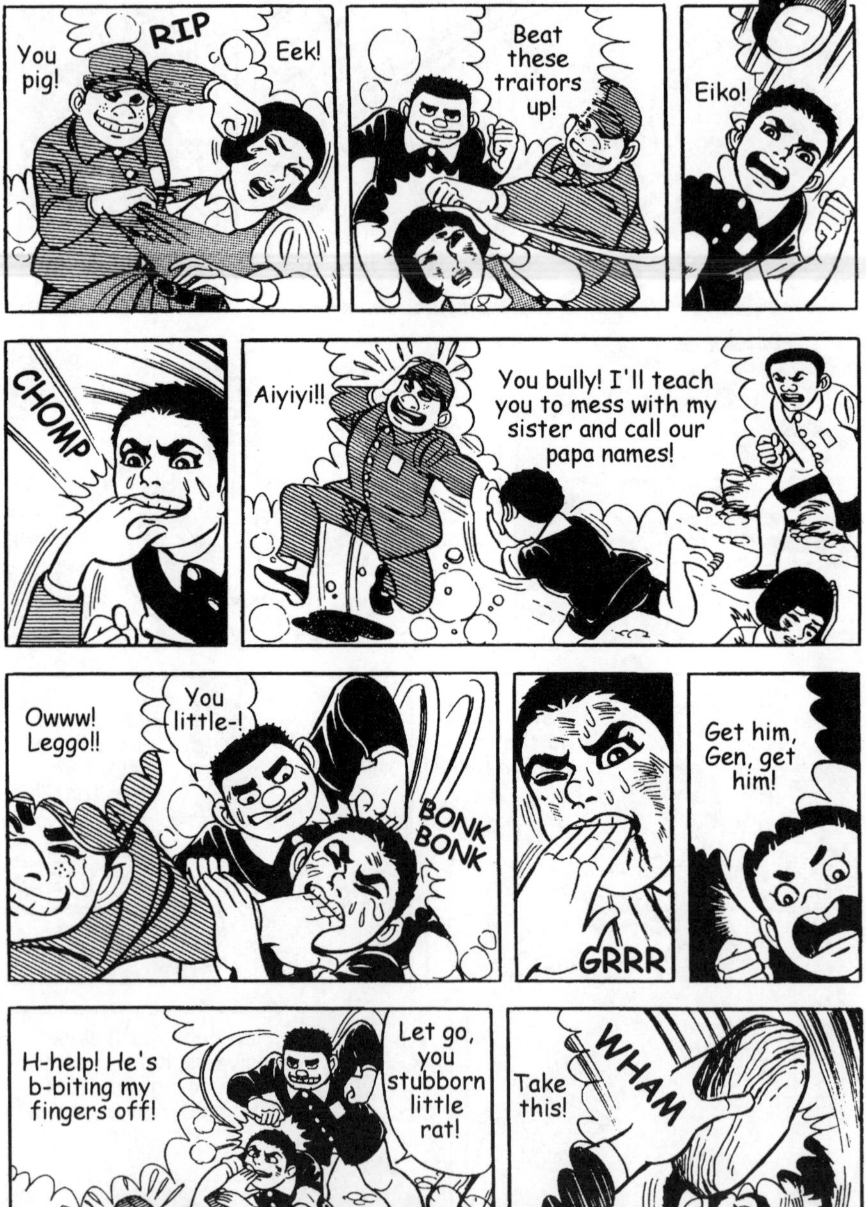
You pig!
RIP
Eek!
Beat these traitors up!
Eiko!
CHOMP
Aiyiyi!!
You bully! I'll teach you to mess with my sister and call our papa names!
Owww! Leggo!!
You little-!
BONK BONK
GRRR
Get him, Gen, get him!
H-help! He's b-biting my fingers off!
Let go, you stubborn little rat!
Take this!
WHAM

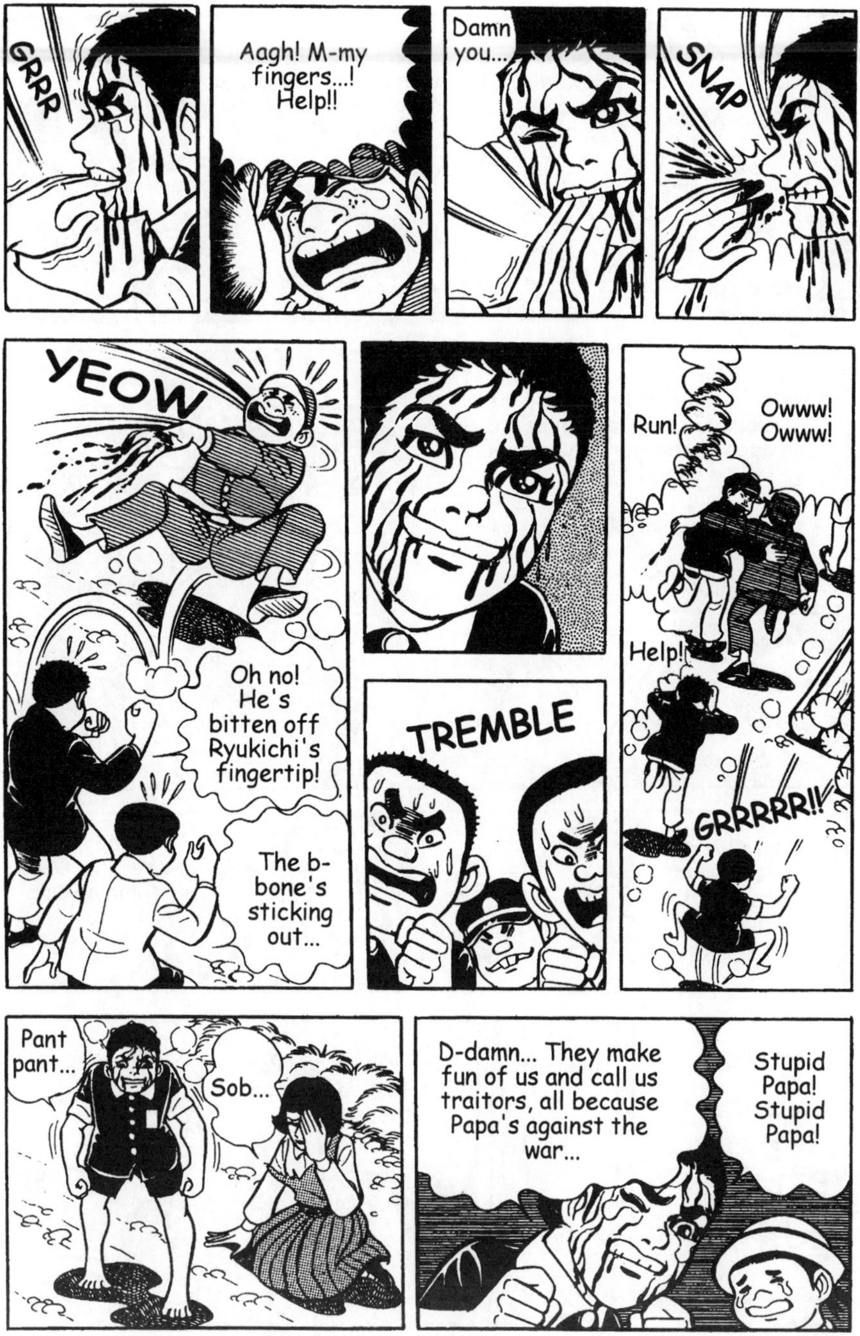
GRRR
Aagh! M-my fingers...! Help!!
Damn you...
SNAP
YEOW
Oh no! He's bitten off Ryukichi's fingertip!
The b-bone's sticking out...
TREMBLE
Run!
Owww! Owww!
Help!
GRRRRR!!
Pant pant...
Sob...
D-damn... They make fun of us and call us traitors, all because Papa's against the war...
Stupid Papa! Stupid Papa!

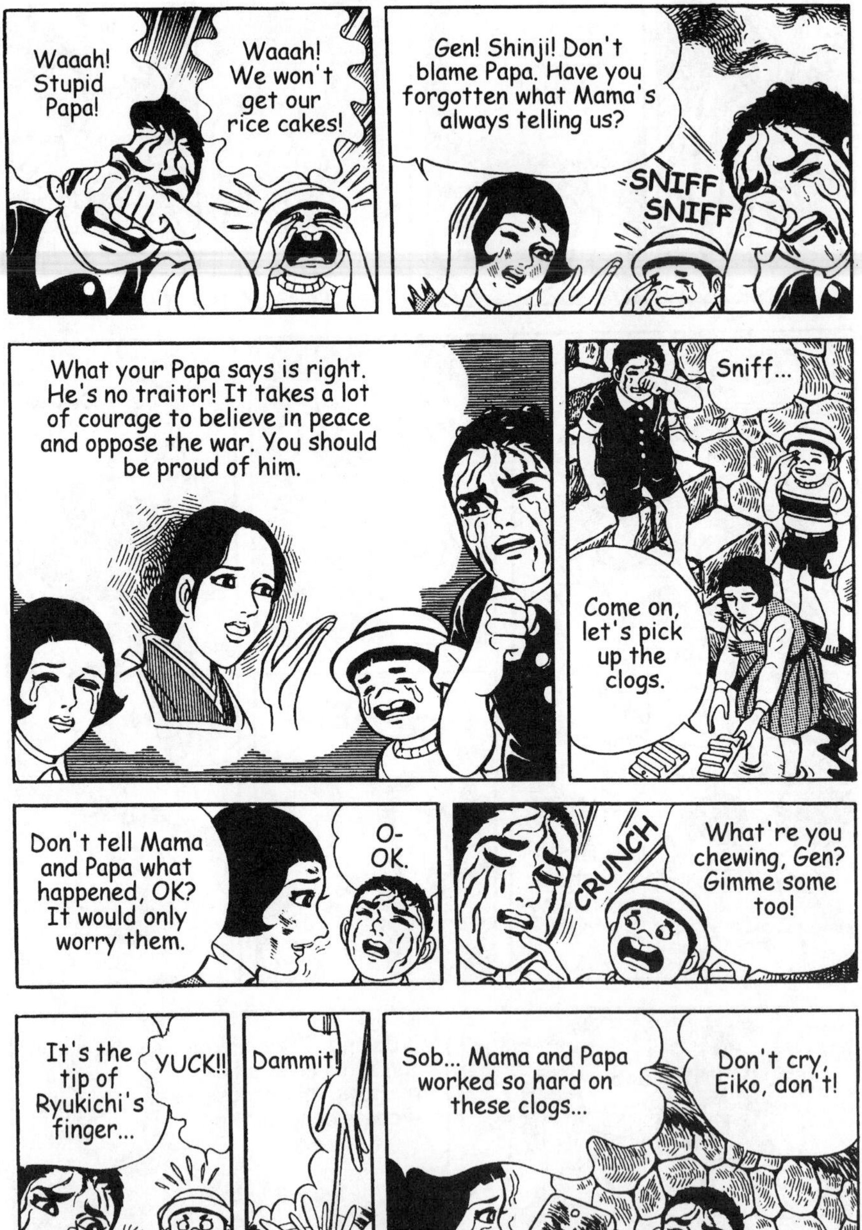
Waaah! Stupid Papa!
Waaah! We won't get our rice cakes!
Gen! Shinji! Don't blame Papa. Have you forgotten what Mama's always telling us?
SNIFF SNIFF
What your Papa says is right. He's no traitor! It takes a lot of courage to believe in peace and oppose the war. You should be proud of him.
Sniff...
Come on, let's pick up the clogs.
Don't tell Mama and Papa what happened, OK? It would only worry them.
O- OK.
CRUNCH
What're you chewing, Gen? Gimme some too!
It's the tip of Ryukichi's finger...
YUCK!!
Dammit!
Sob... Mama and Papa worked so hard on these clogs...
Don't cry, Eiko, don't!

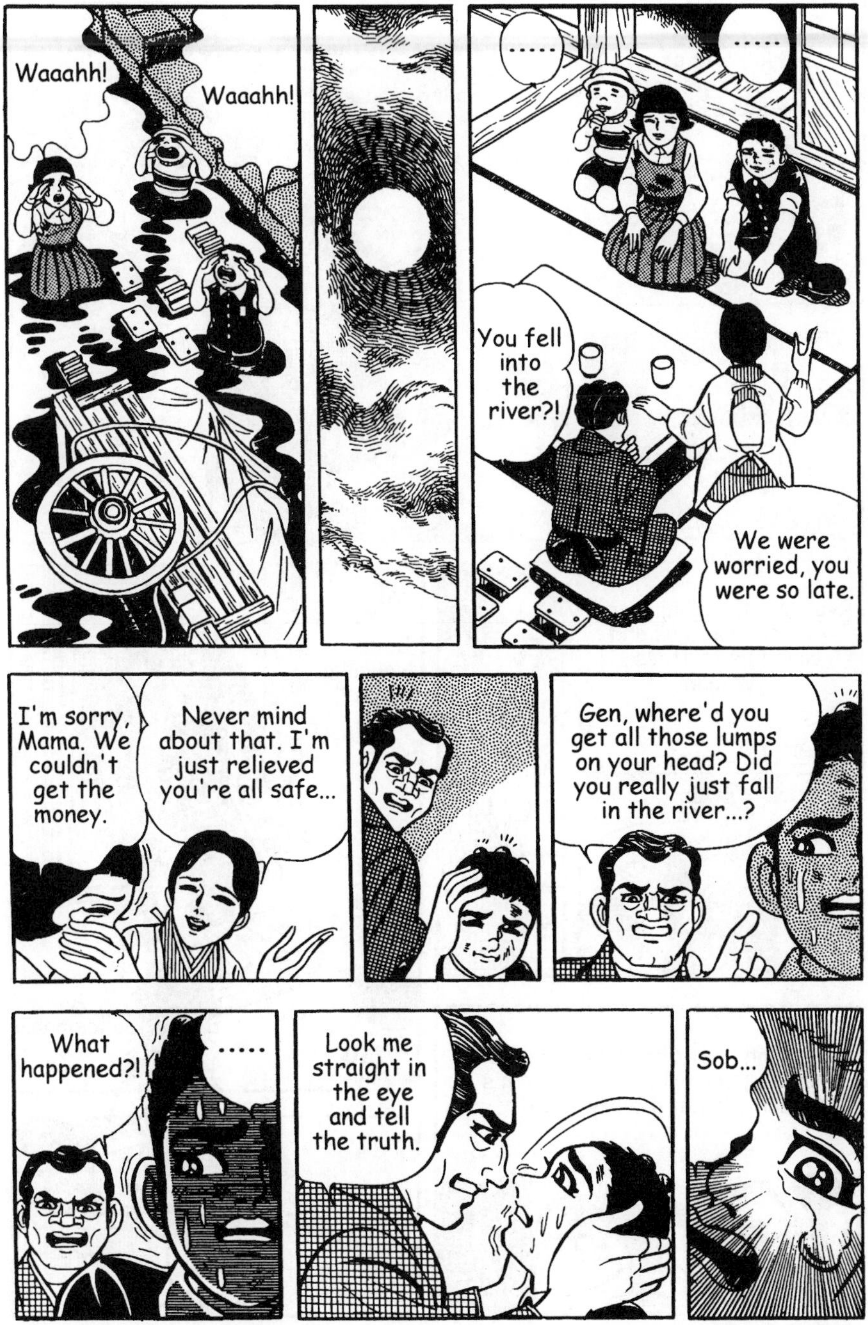
Waaahh!
Waaahh!
.....
.....
You fell into the river?!
We were worried, you were so late.
I'm sorry, Mama. We couldn't get the money.
Never mind about that. I'm just relieved you're all safe...
Gen, where'd you get all those lumps on your head? Did you really just fall in the river...?
What happened?!
.....
Look me straight in the eye and tell the truth.
Sob...

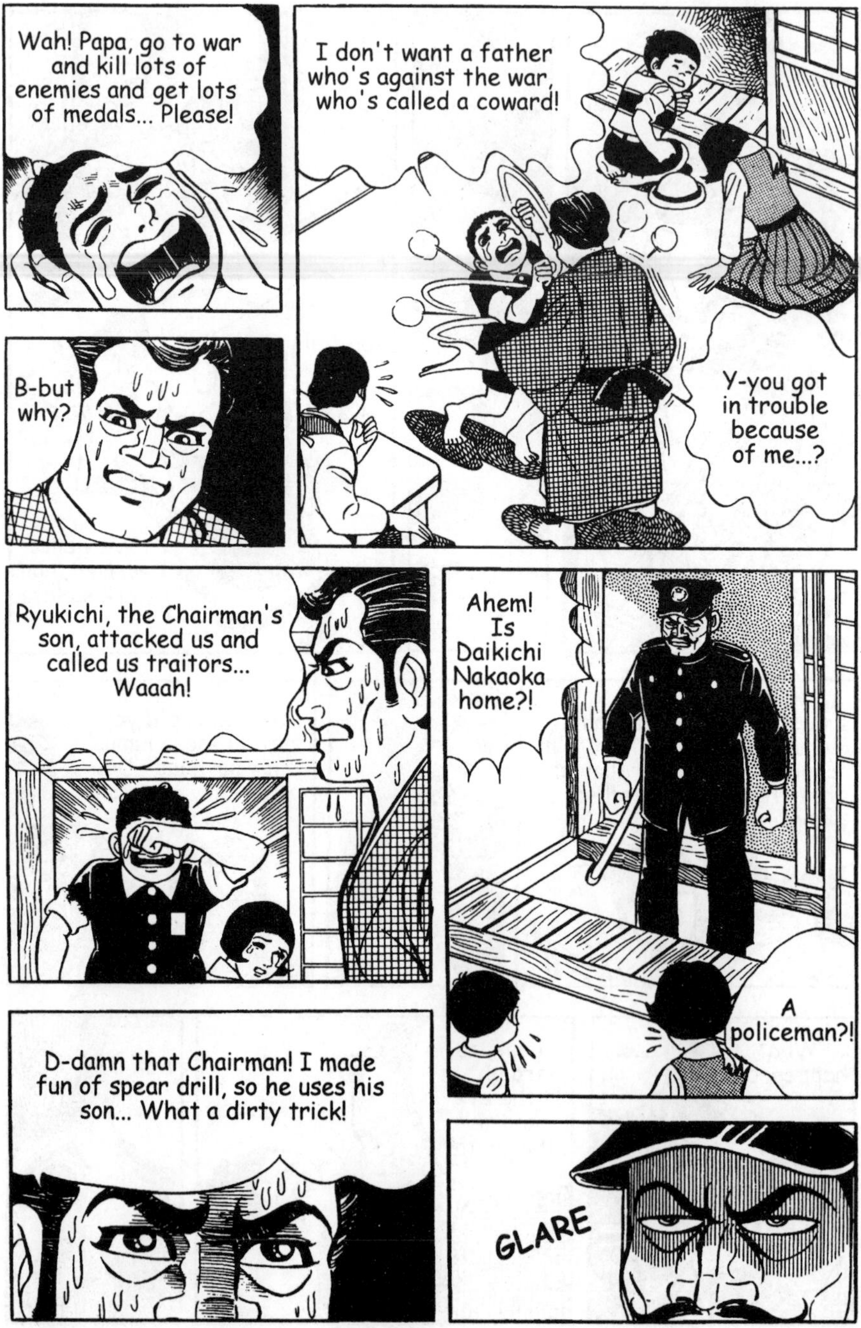

Wah! Papa, go to war and kill lots of enemies and get lots of medals... Please!
I don't want a father who's against the war, who's called a coward!
Y-you got in trouble because of me...?
B-but why?
Ryukichi, the Chairman's son, attacked us and called us traitors... Waaah!
Ahem! Is Daikichi Nakaoka home?!
A policeman?!
D-damn that Chairman! I made fun of spear drill, so he uses his son... What a dirty trick!
GLARE

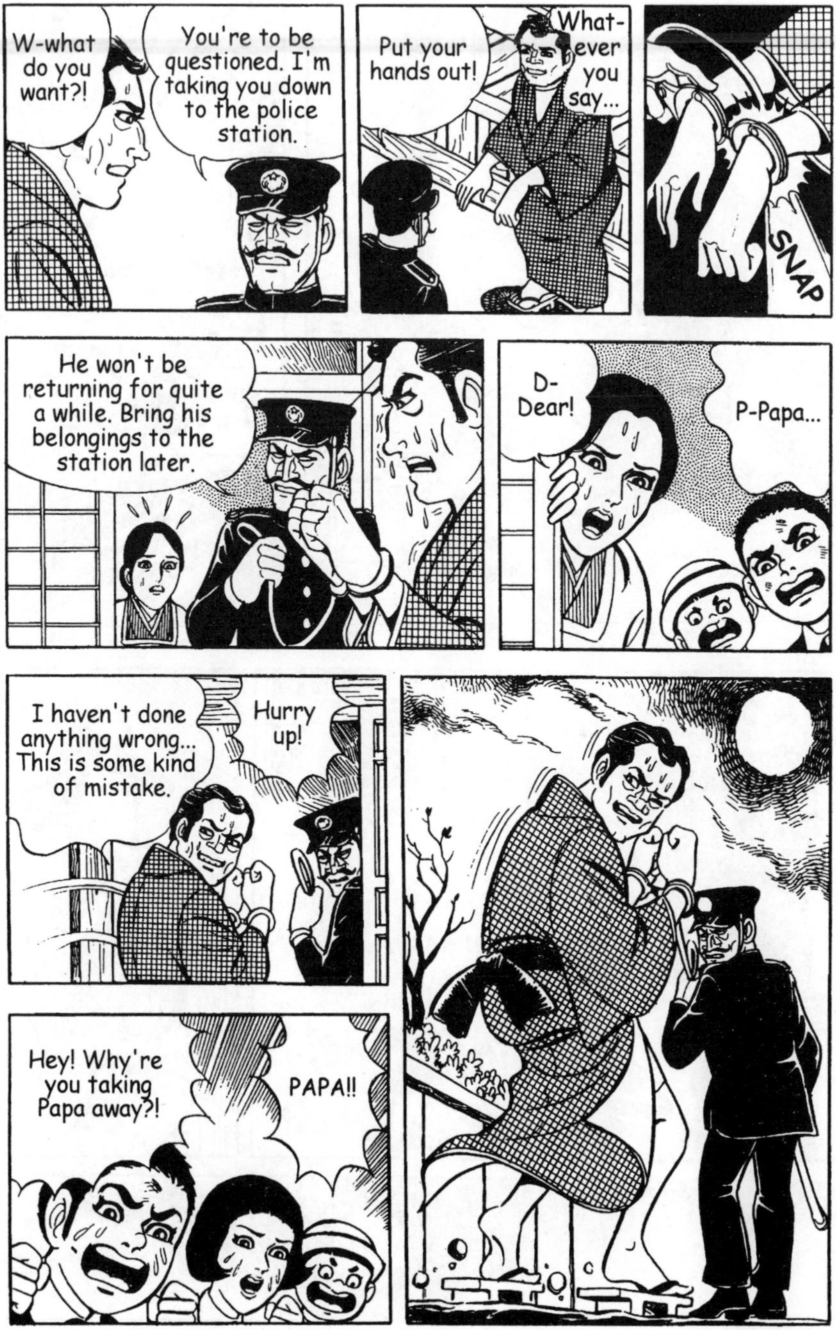
W-what do you want?!
You're to be questioned. I'm taking you down to the police station.
Put your hands out!
Whatever you say...
SNAP
He won't be returning for quite a while. Bring his belongings to the station later.
D-Dear!
P-Papa...
I haven't done anything wrong... This is some kind of mistake.
Hurry up!
Hey! Why're you taking Papa away?!
PAPA!!

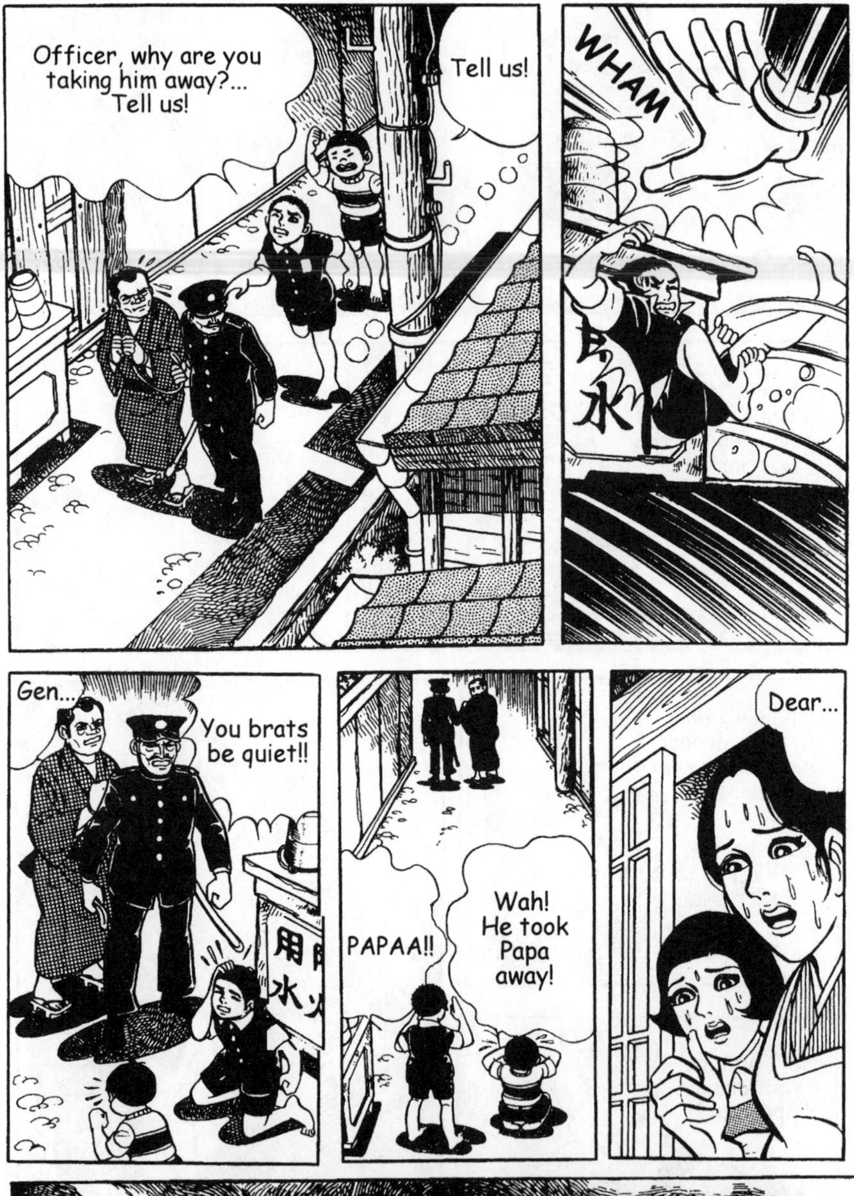
Officer, why are you taking him away?... Tell us!
Tell us!
WHAM
Gen...
You brats be quiet!!
PAPAA!!
Wah! He took Papa away!
Dear...

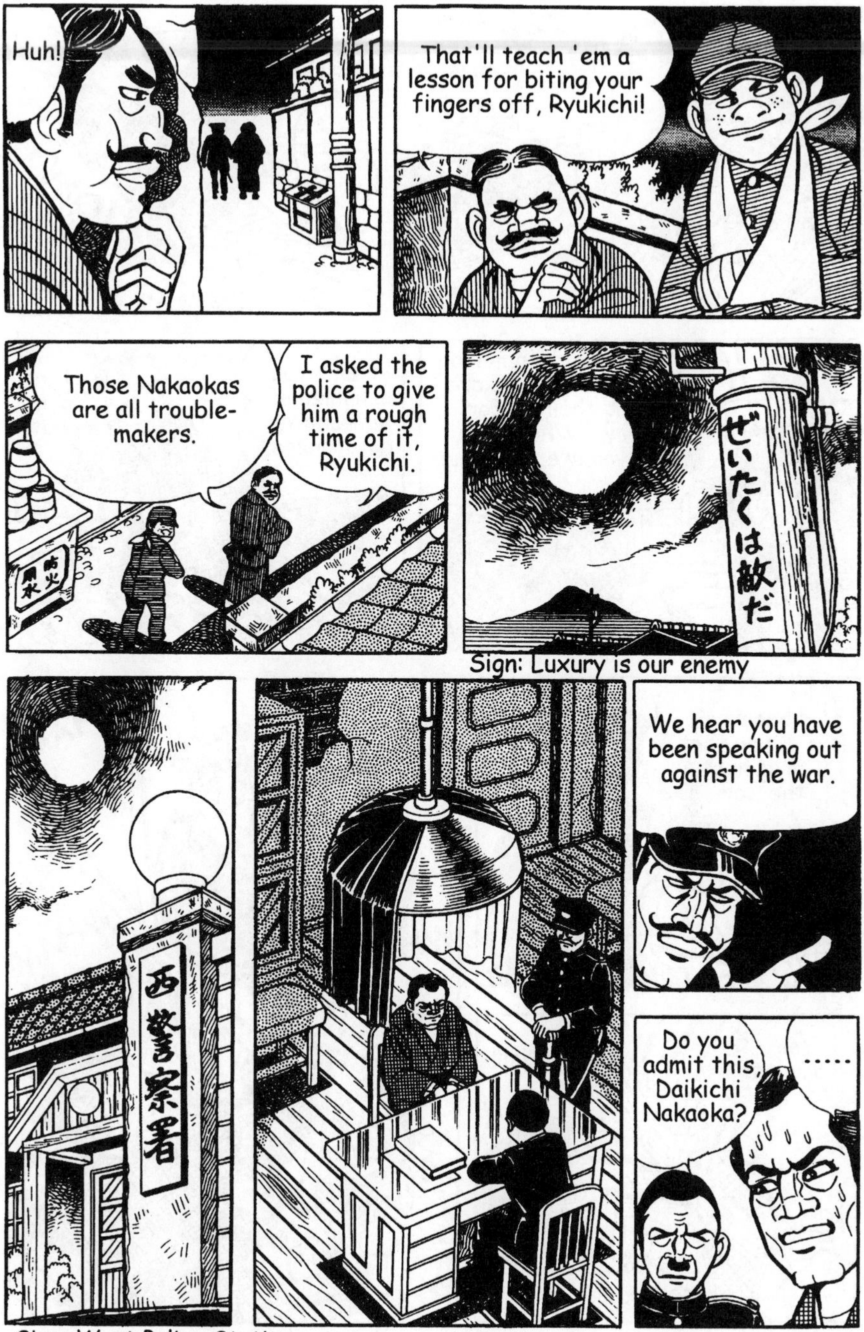
Huh!
That'll teach 'em a lesson for biting your fingers off, Ryukichi!
Those Nakaokas are all trouble-makers.
I asked the police to give him a rough time of it, Ryukichi.
ぜいたくは敵だ
西警察署
We hear you have been speaking out against the war.
Do you admit this, Daikichi Nakaoka?
.....

Sign: Luxury is our enemy

Sign: West Police Station

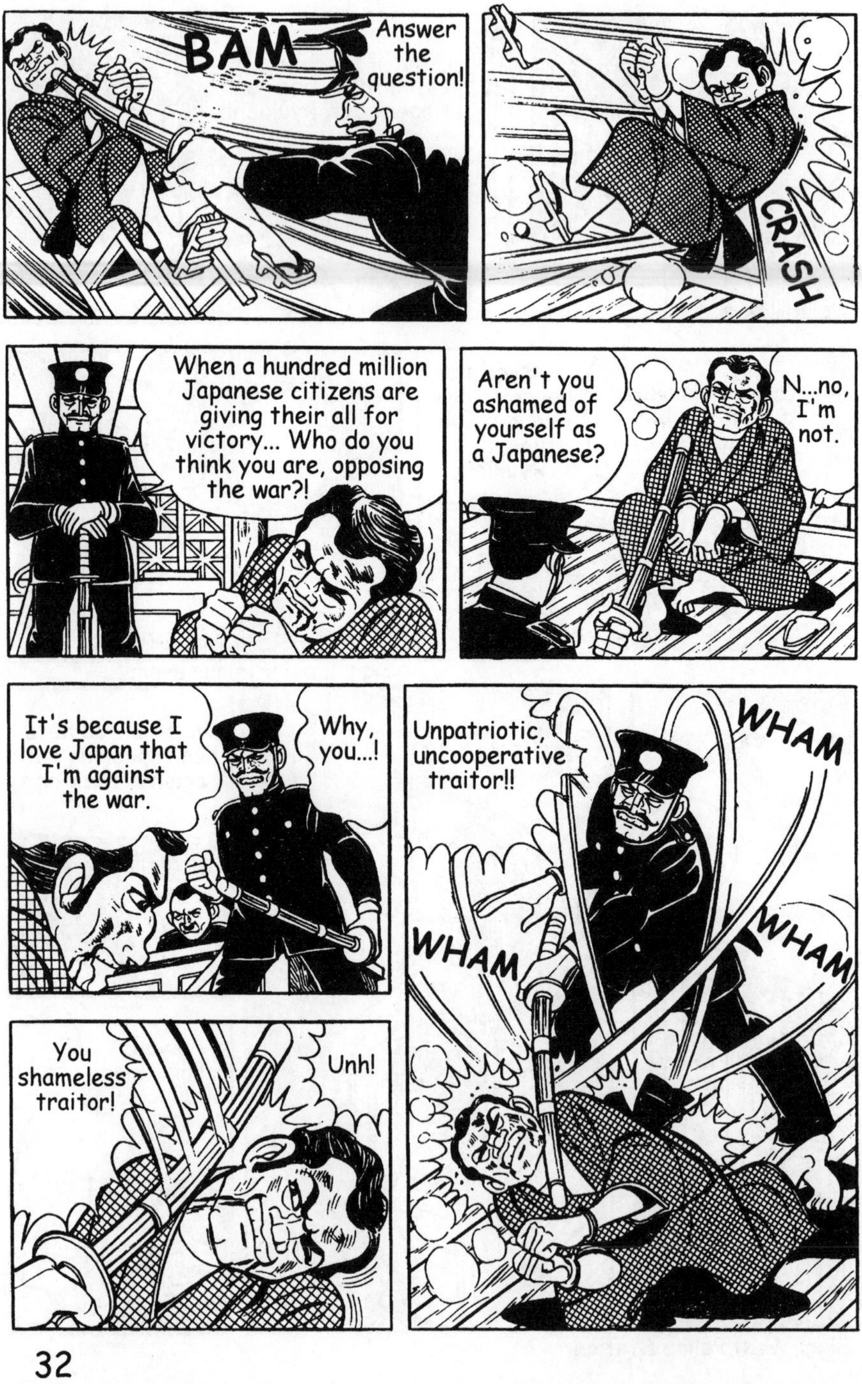
BAM
Answer the question!
CRASH
When a hundred million Japanese citizens are giving their all for victory... Who do you think you are, opposing the war?!
Aren't you ashamed of yourself as a Japanese?
N...no, I'm not.
It's because I love Japan that I'm against the war.
Why, you...!
Unpatriotic, uncooperative traitor!!
WHAM
WHAM
WHAM
You shameless traitor!
Unh!

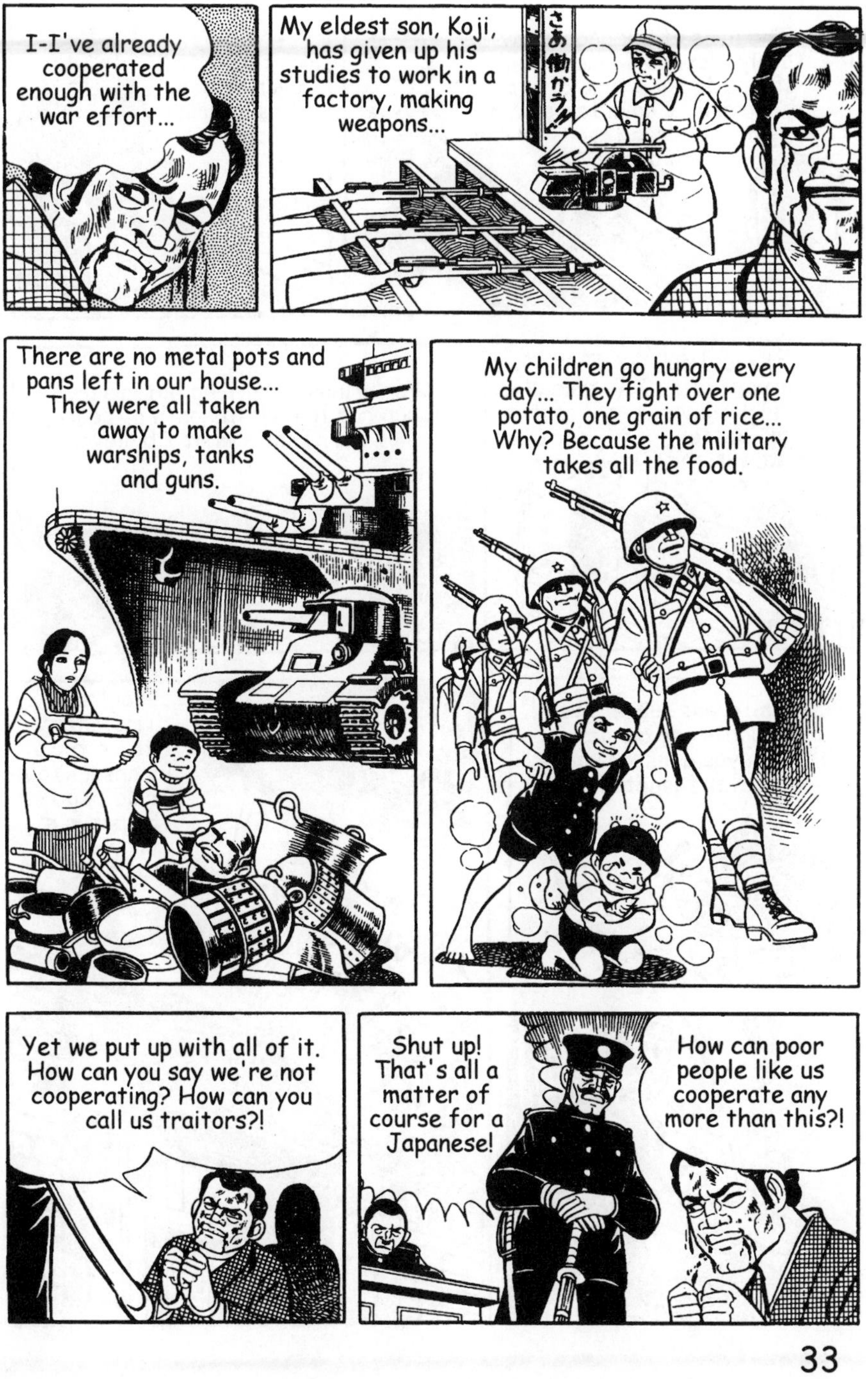
I-I've already cooperated enough with the war effort...
My eldest son, Koji, has given up his studies to work in a factory, making weapons...
There are no metal pots and pans left in our house... They were all taken away to make warships, tanks and guns.
My children go hungry every day... They fight over one potato, one grain of rice... Why? Because the military takes all the food.
Yet we put up with all of it. How can you say we're not cooperating? How can you call us traitors?!
Shut up! That's all a matter of course for a Japanese!
How can poor people like us cooperate any more than this?!

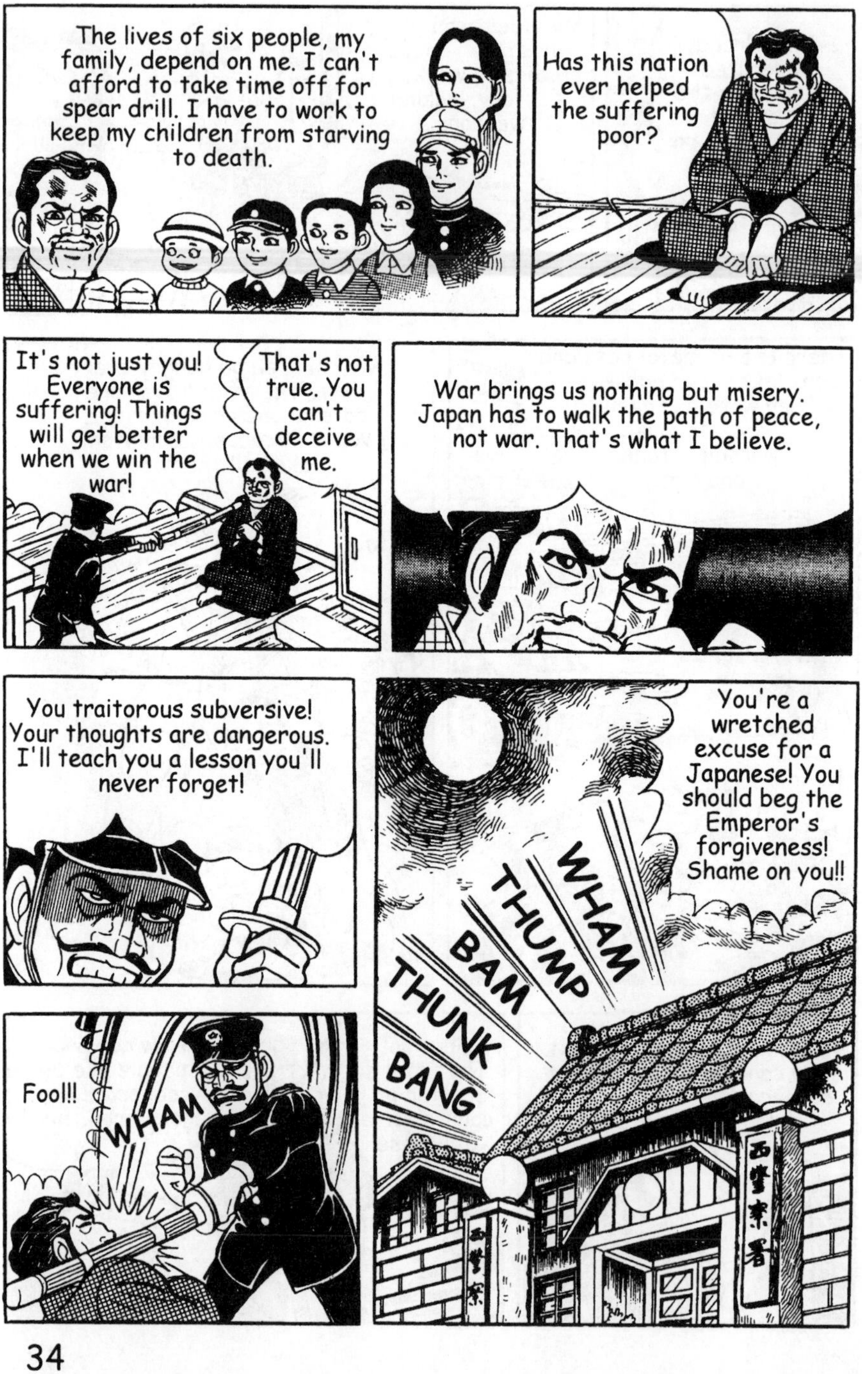
The lives of six people, my family, depend on me. I can't afford to take time off for spear drill. I have to work to keep my children from starving to death.
Has this nation ever helped the suffering poor?
It's not just you! Everyone is suffering! Things will get better when we win the war!
That's not true. You can't deceive me.
War brings us nothing but misery. Japan has to walk the path of peace, not war. That's what I believe.
You traitorous subversive! Your thoughts are dangerous. I'll teach you a lesson you'll never forget!
Fool!!
WHAM
You're a wretched excuse for a Japanese! You should beg the Emperor's forgiveness! Shame on you!!
WHAM
THUMP
BAM
THUNK
BANG

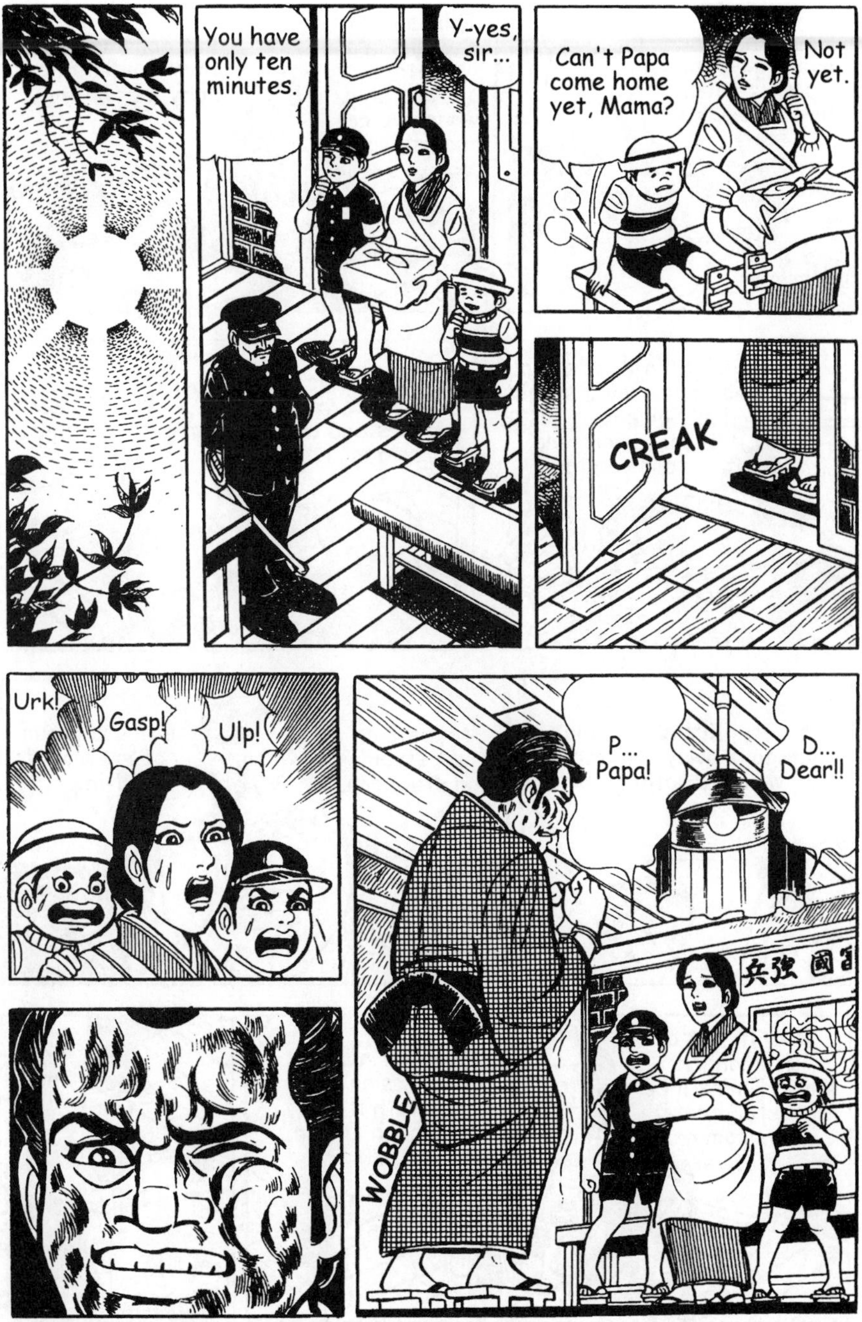
You have only ten minutes.
Y-yes, sir...
Can't Papa come home yet, Mama?
Not yet.
CREAK
Urk!
Gasp!
Ulp!
P... Papa!
D... Dear!!
WOBBLE

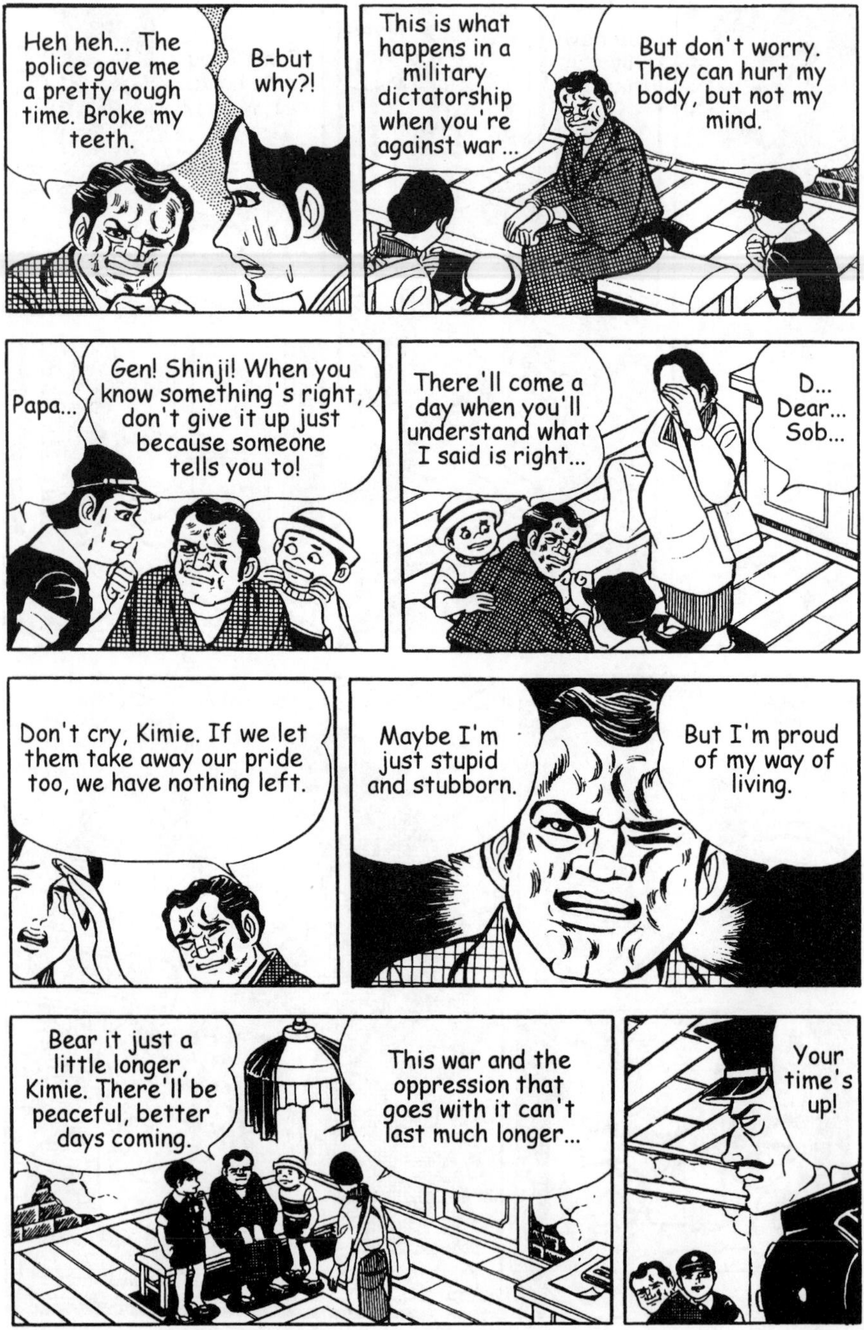
Heh heh... The police gave me a pretty rough time. Broke my teeth.
B-but why?!
This is what happens in a military dictatorship when you're against war...
But don't worry. They can hurt my body, but not my mind.
Papa...
Gen! Shinji! When you know something's right, don't give it up just because someone tells you to!
There'll come a day when you'll understand what I said is right...
D... Dear... Sob...
Don't cry, Kimie. If we let them take away our pride too, we have nothing left.
Maybe I'm just stupid and stubborn.
But I'm proud of my way of living.
Bear it just a little longer, Kimie. There'll be peaceful, better days coming.
This war and the oppression that goes with it can't last much longer...
Your time's up!

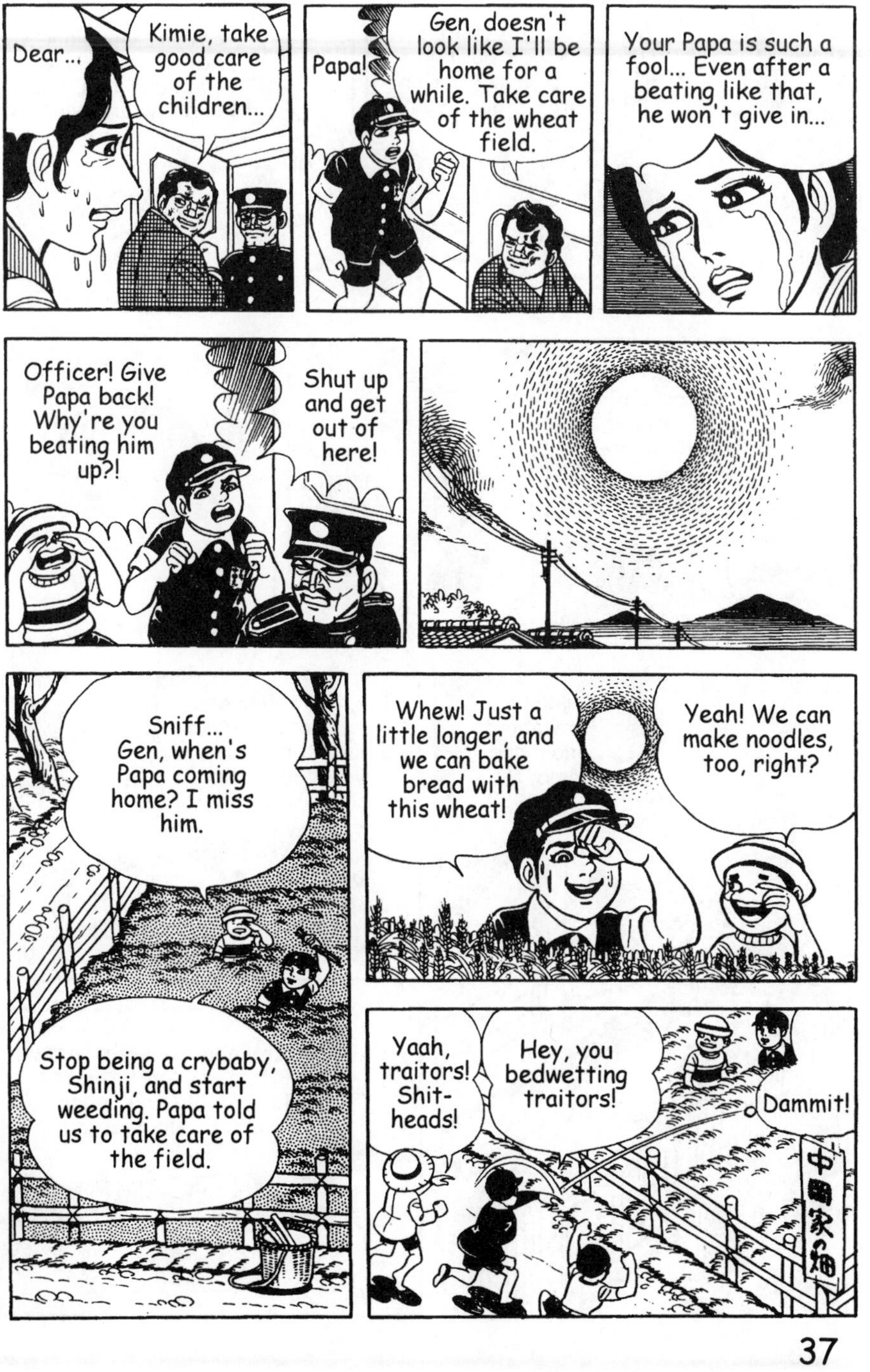
Dear...
Kimie, take good care of the children...
Papa!
Gen, doesn't look like I'll be home for a while. Take care of the wheat field.
Your Papa is such a fool... Even after a beating like that, he won't give in...
Officer! Give Papa back! Why're you beating him up?!
Shut up and get out of here!
Sniff... Gen, when's Papa coming home? I miss him.
Stop being a crybaby, Shinji, and start weeding. Papa told us to take care of the field.
Whew! Just a little longer, and we can bake bread with this wheat!
Yeah! We can make noodles, too, right?
Yaah, traitors! Shit-heads!
Hey, you bedwetting traitors!
Dammit!
中岡家の畑

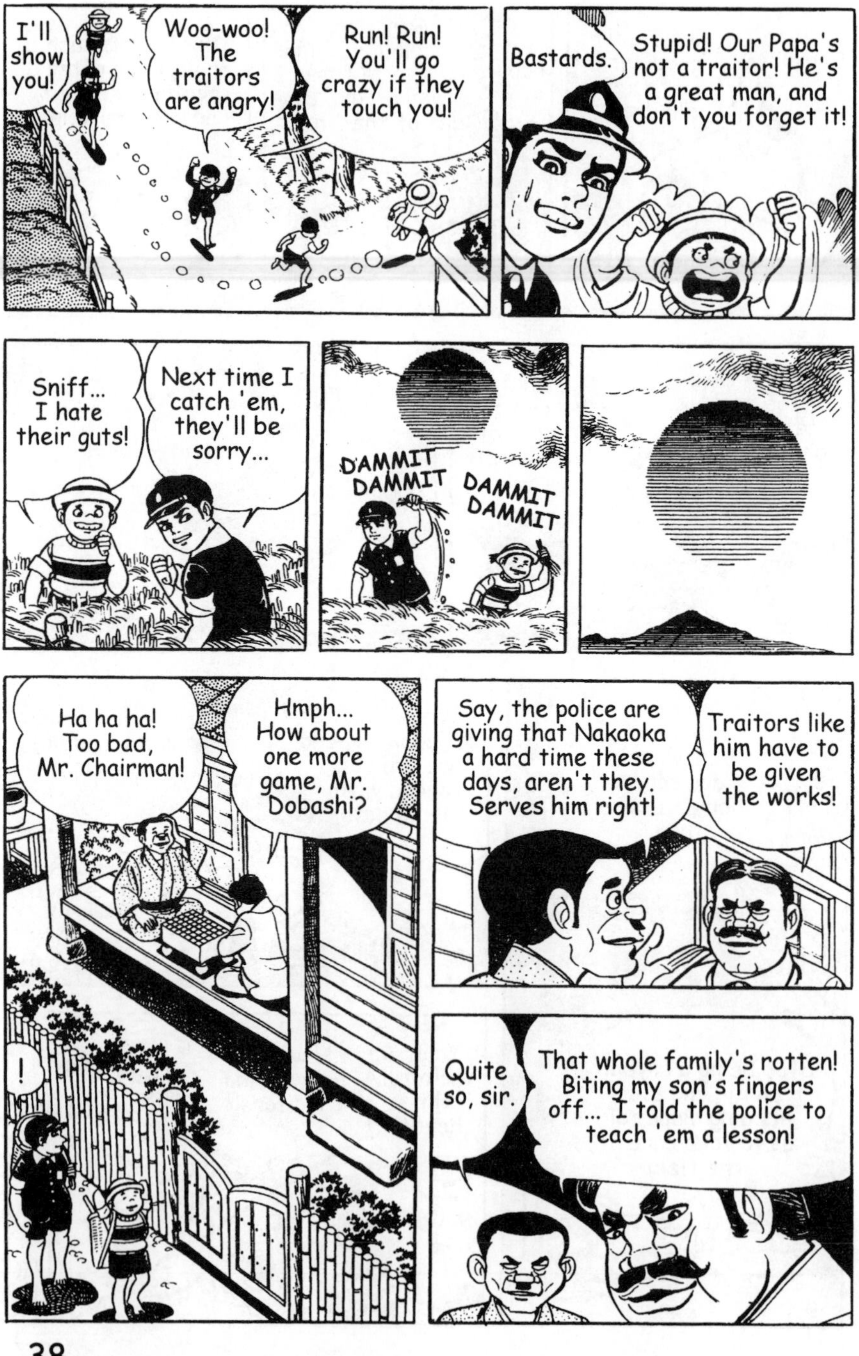

I'll show you!
Woo-woo! The traitors are angry!
Run! Run! You'll go crazy if they touch you!
Bastards.
Stupid! Our Papa's not a traitor! He's a great man, and don't you forget it!
Sniff... I hate their guts!
Next time I catch 'em, they'll be sorry...
DAMMIT DAMMIT
DAMMIT DAMMIT
Ha ha ha! Too bad, Mr. Chairman!
Hmph... How about one more game, Mr. Dobashi?
!
Say, the police are giving that Nakaoka a hard time these days, aren't they. Serves him right!
Traitors like him have to be given the works!
Quite so, sir.
That whole family's rotten! Biting my son's fingers off... I told the police to teach 'em a lesson!

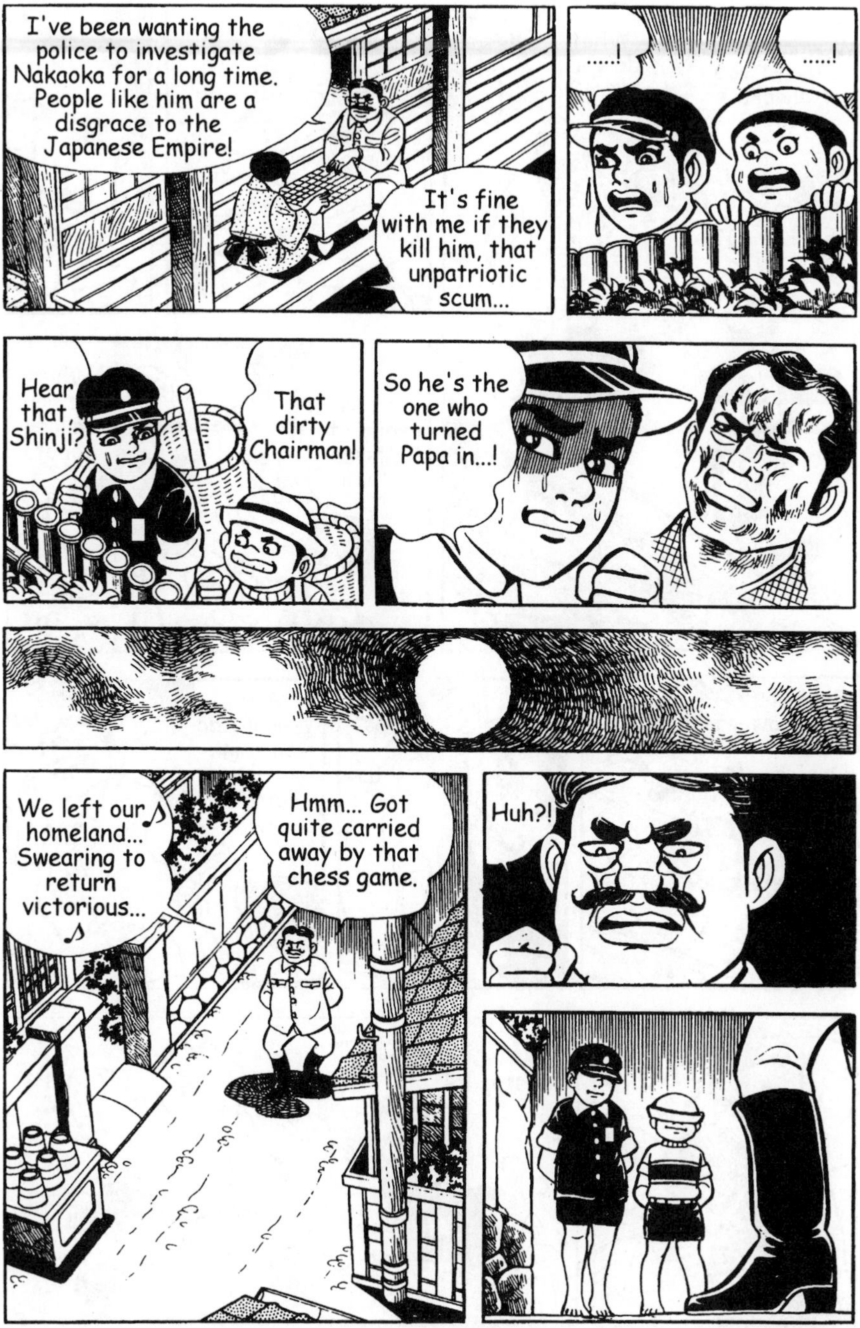
I've been wanting the police to investigate Nakaoka for a long time. People like him are a disgrace to the Japanese Empire!
It's fine with me if they kill him, that unpatriotic scum...
.....!
.....!
Hear that, Shinji?
That dirty Chairman!
So he's the one who turned Papa in...!
We left our homeland... Swearing to return victorious...
Hmm... Got quite carried away by that chess game.
Huh?!

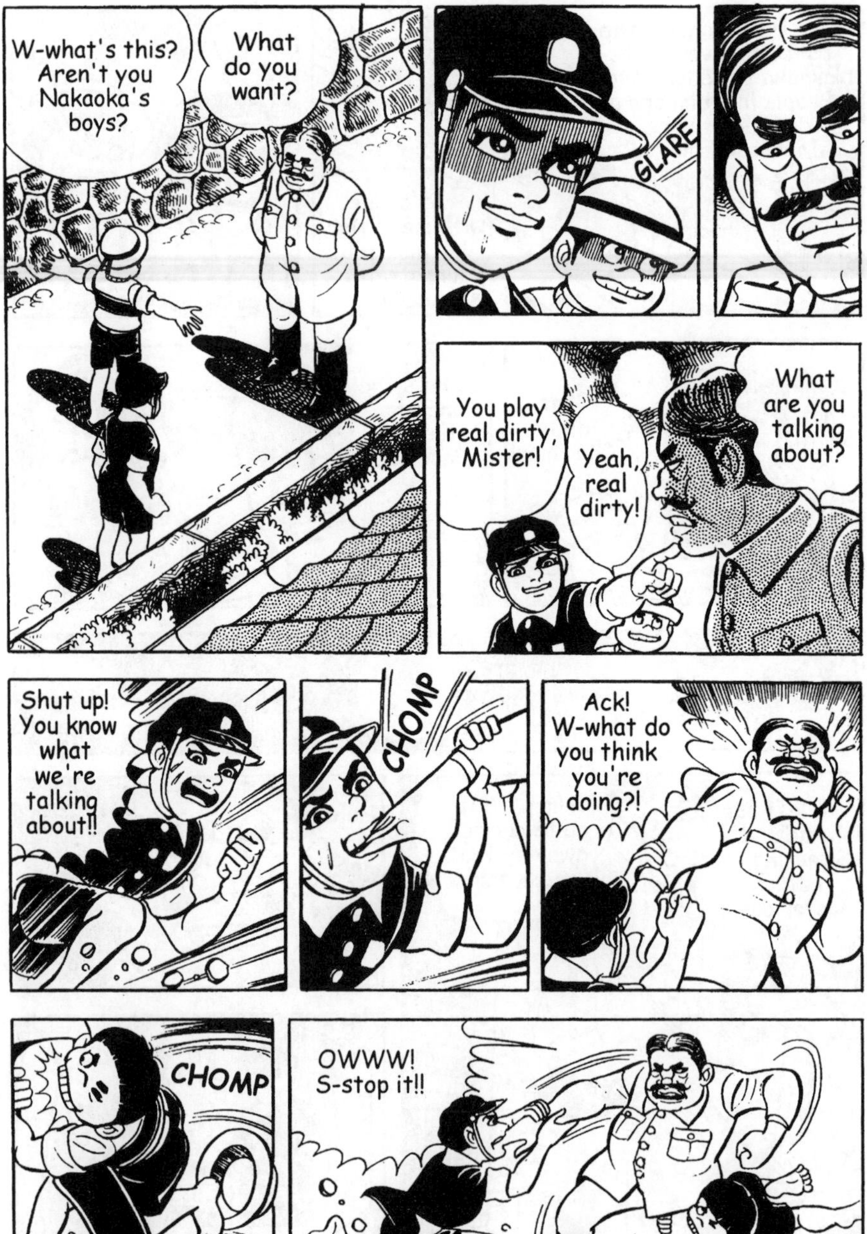
W-what's this? Aren't you Nakaoka's boys?
What do you want?
GLARE
You play real dirty, Mister!
Yeah, real dirty!
What are you talking about?
Shut up! You know what we're talking about!!
CHOMP
Ack! W-what do you think you're doing?!
CHOMP
OWWW! S-stop it!!

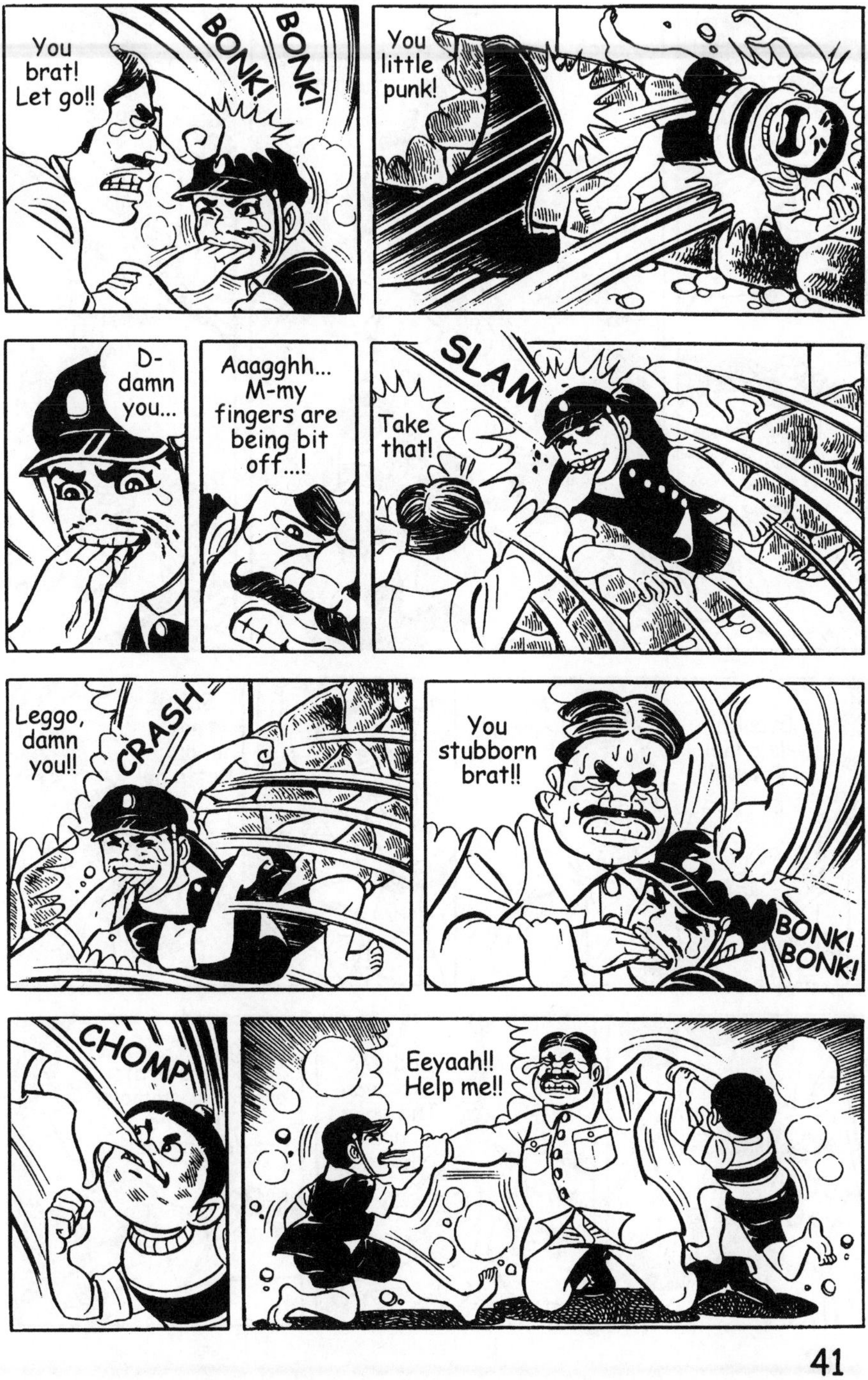
You brat! Let go!!
BONK! BONK!
You little punk!
D-damn you...
Aaagghh... M-my fingers are being bit off...!
SLAM
Take that!
Leggo, damn you!!
CRASH
You stubborn brat!!
BONK! BONK!
CHOMP
Eeyaah!! Help me!!

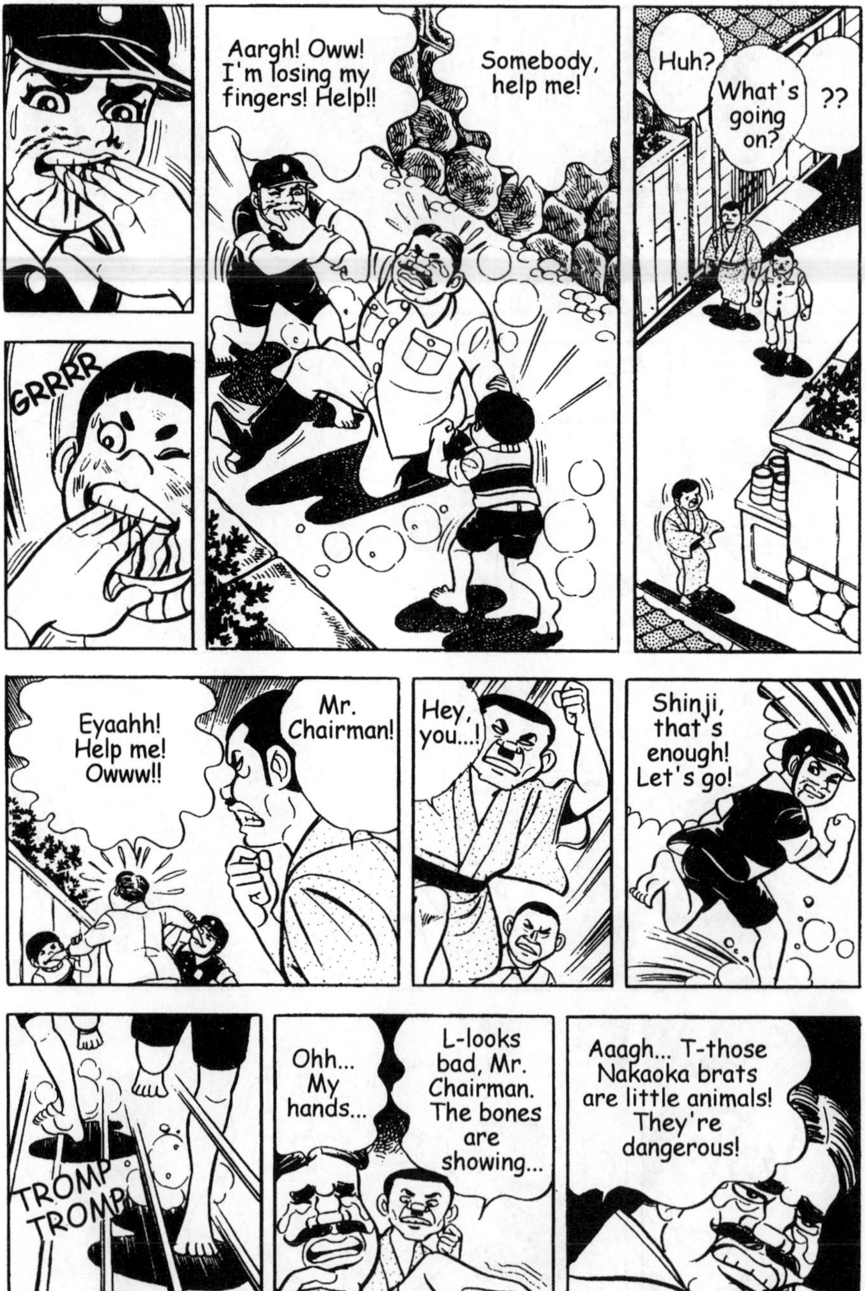
GRRRR
Aargh! Oww! I'm losing my fingers! Help!!
Somebody, help me!
Huh?
What's going on?
??
Eyaahh! Help me! Owww!!
Mr. Chairman!
Hey, you...!
Shinji, that's enough! Let's go!
TROMP TROMP
Ohh... My hands...
L-looks bad, Mr. Chairman. The bones are showing...
Aaagh... T-those Nakaoka brats are little animals! They're dangerous!

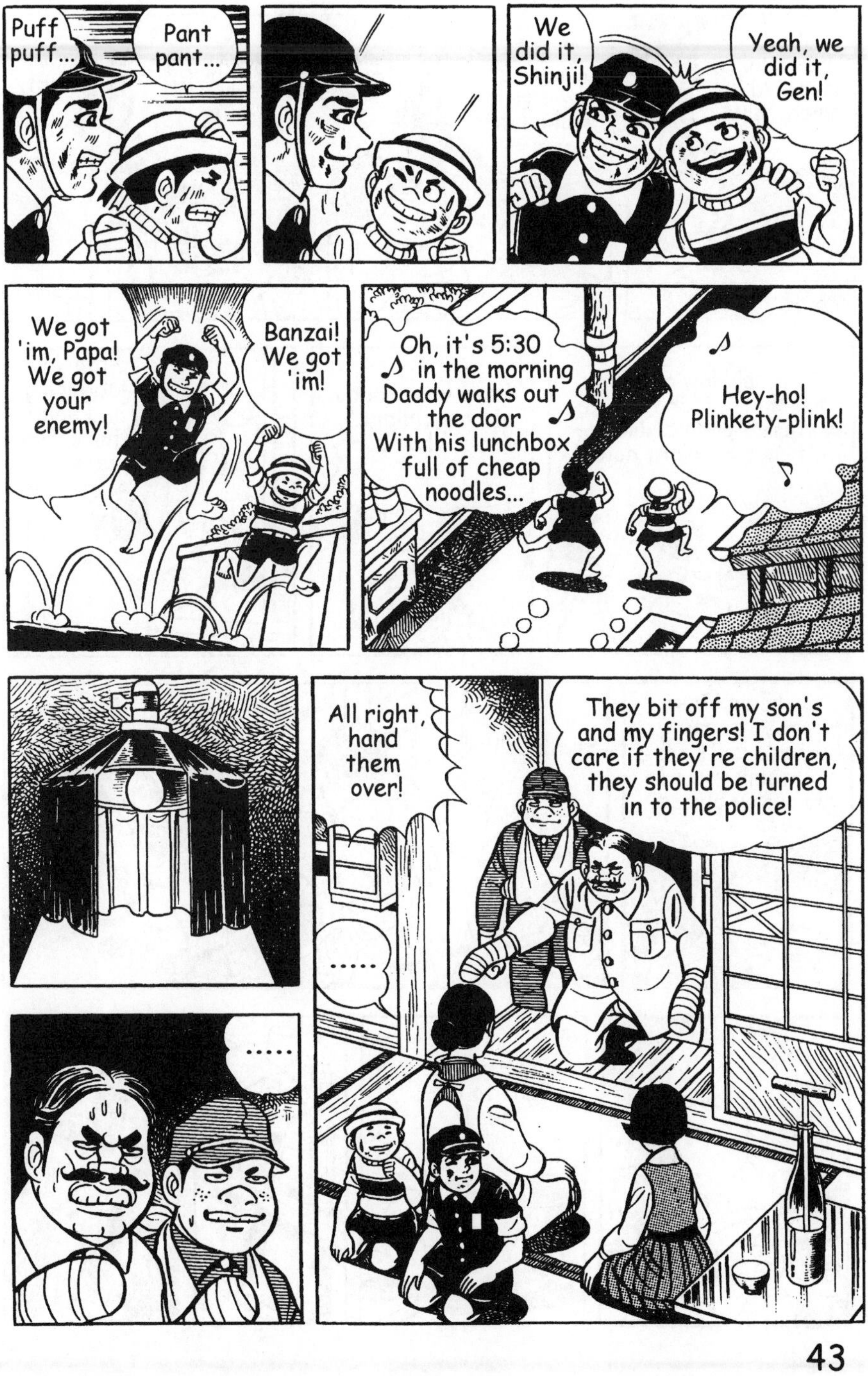

Puff puff...
Pant pant...
We did it, Shinji!
Yeah, we did it, Gen!
We got 'im, Papa! We got your enemy!
Banzai! We got 'im!
Oh, it's 5:30 in the morning Daddy walks out the door With his lunchbox full of cheap noodles...
Hey-ho! Plinkety-plink!
All right, hand them over!
They bit off my son's and my fingers! I don't care if they're children, they should be turned in to the police!
.....
.....

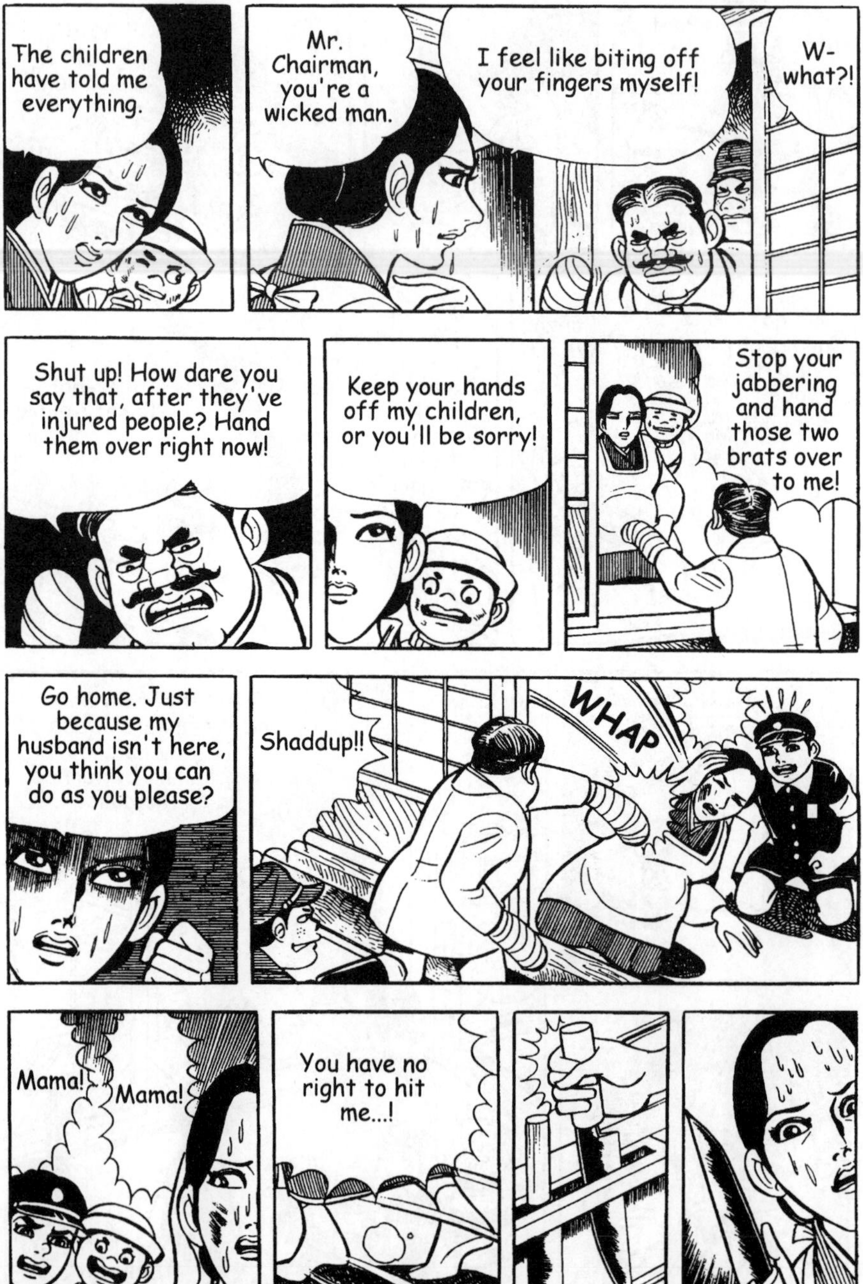

The children have told me everything.
Mr. Chairman, you're a wicked man.
I feel like biting off your fingers myself!
W-what?!
Shut up! How dare you say that, after they've injured people? Hand them over right now!
Keep your hands off my children, or you'll be sorry!
Stop your jabbering and hand those two brats over to me!
Go home. Just because my husband isn't here, you think you can do as you please?
Shaddup!!
WHAP
Mama!
Mama!
You have no right to hit me...!

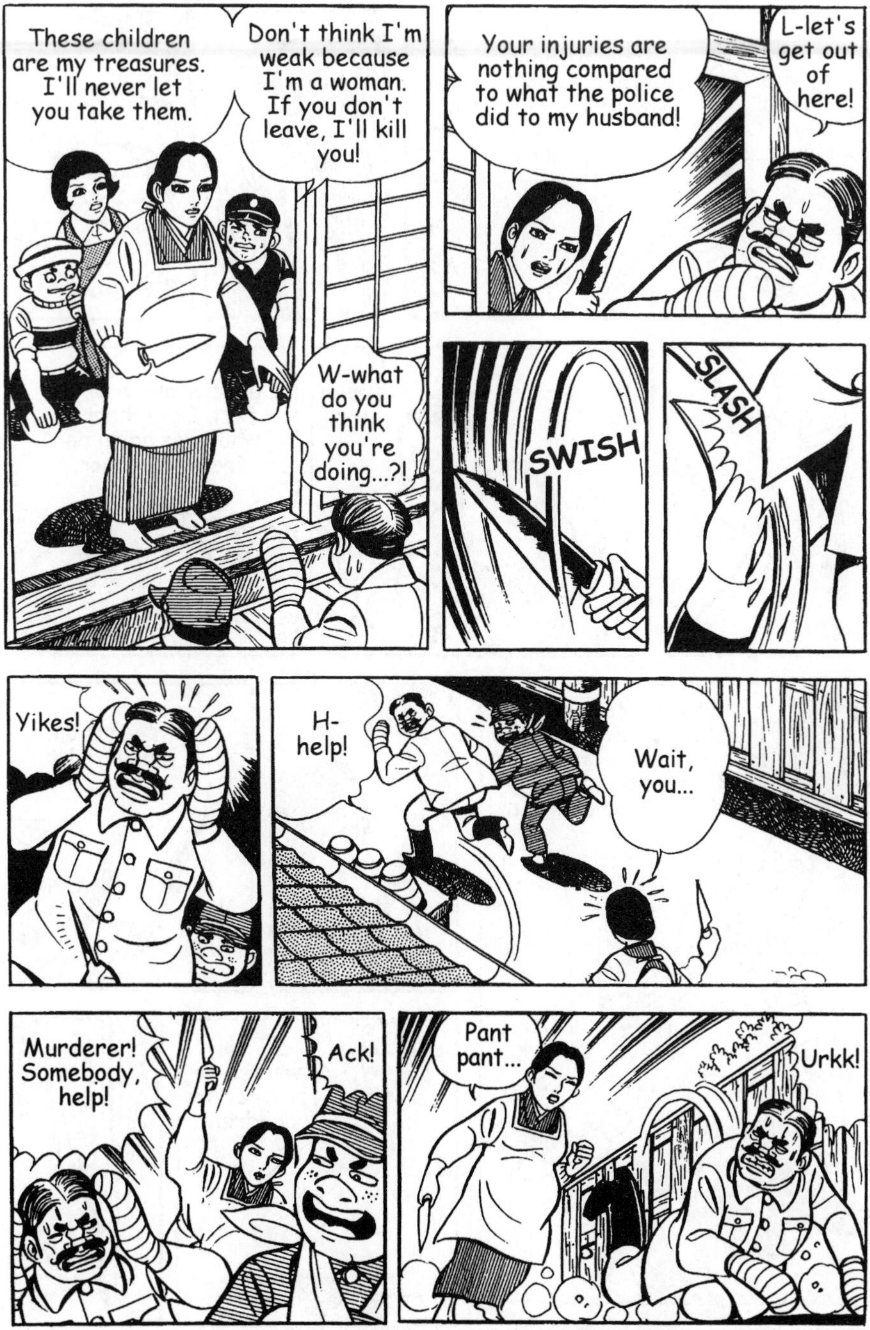
These children are my treasures. I'll never let you take them.
Don't think I'm weak because I'm a woman. If you don't leave, I'll kill you!
W-what do you think you're doing...?!
Your injuries are nothing compared to what the police did to my husband!
L-let's get out of here!
SWISH
SLASH
Yikes!
H-help!
Wait, you...
Murderer! Somebody, help!
Ack!
Pant pant...
Urkk!

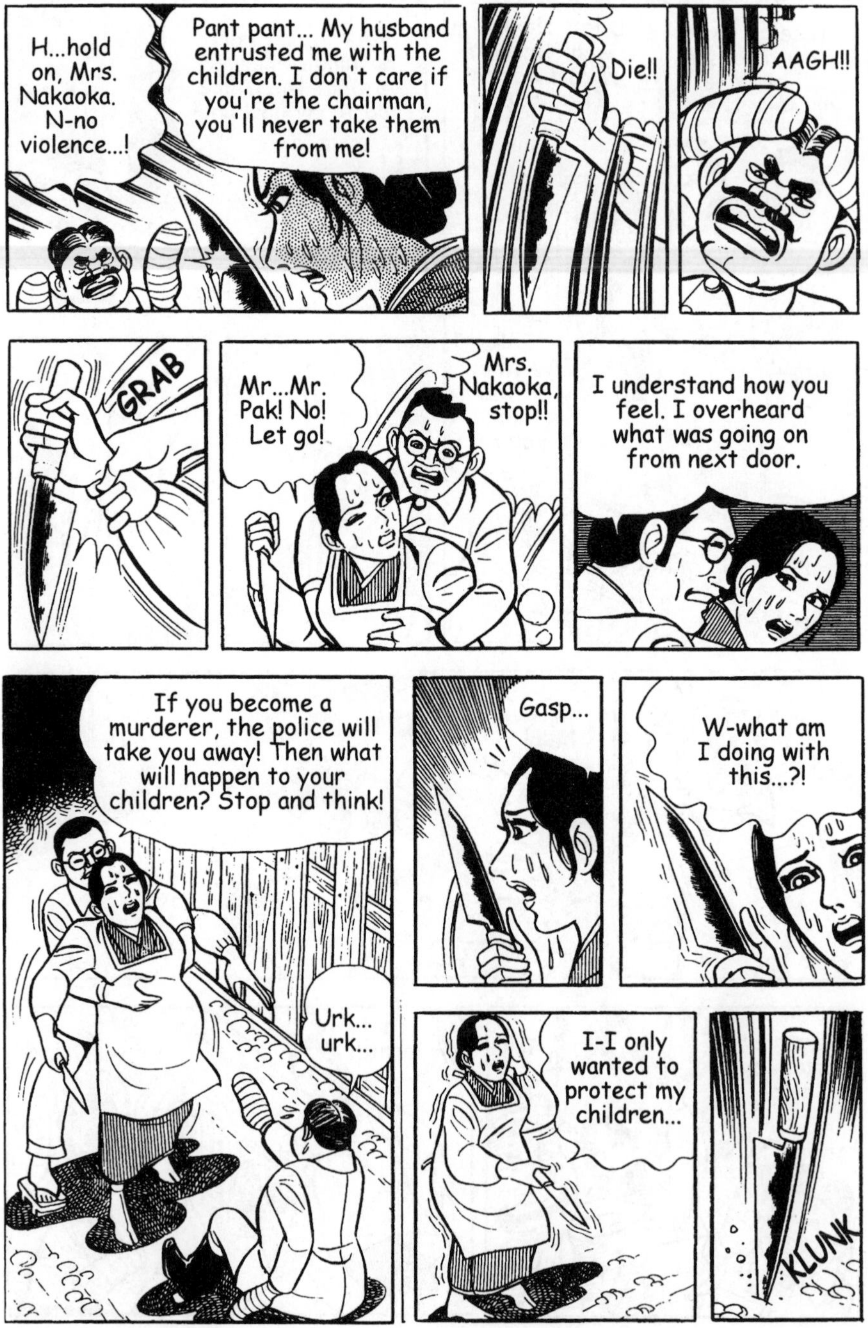
H...hold on, Mrs. Nakaoka. N-no violence...!
Pant pant... My husband entrusted me with the children. I don't care if you're the chairman, you'll never take them from me!
Die!!
AAGH!!
GRAB
Mr...Mr. Pak! No! Let go!
Mrs. Nakaoka, stop!!
I understand how you feel. I overheard what was going on from next door.
If you become a murderer, the police will take you away! Then what will happen to your children? Stop and think!
Urk... urk...
Gasp...
W-what am I doing with this...?!
I-I only wanted to protect my children...
KLUNK

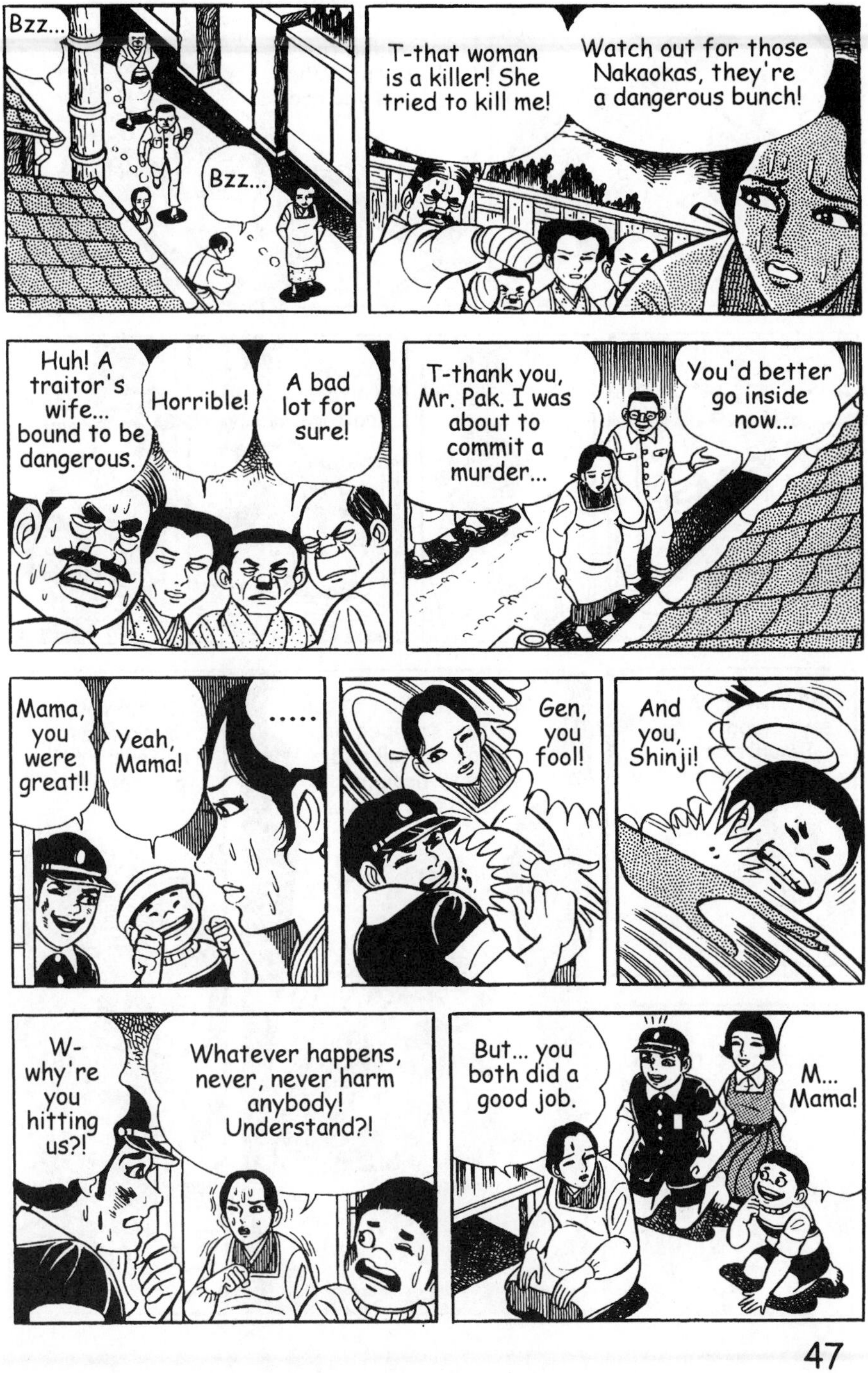

Bzz...
Bzz...
T-that woman is a killer! She tried to kill me!
Watch out for those Nakaokas, they're a dangerous bunch!
Huh! A traitor's wife... bound to be dangerous.
Horrible!
A bad lot for sure!
T-thank you, Mr. Pak. I was about to commit a murder...
You'd better go inside now...
Mama, you were great!!
Yeah, Mama!
.....
Gen, you fool!
And you, Shinji!
W-why're you hitting us?!
Whatever happens, never, never harm anybody! Understand?!
But... you both did a good job.
M... Mama!

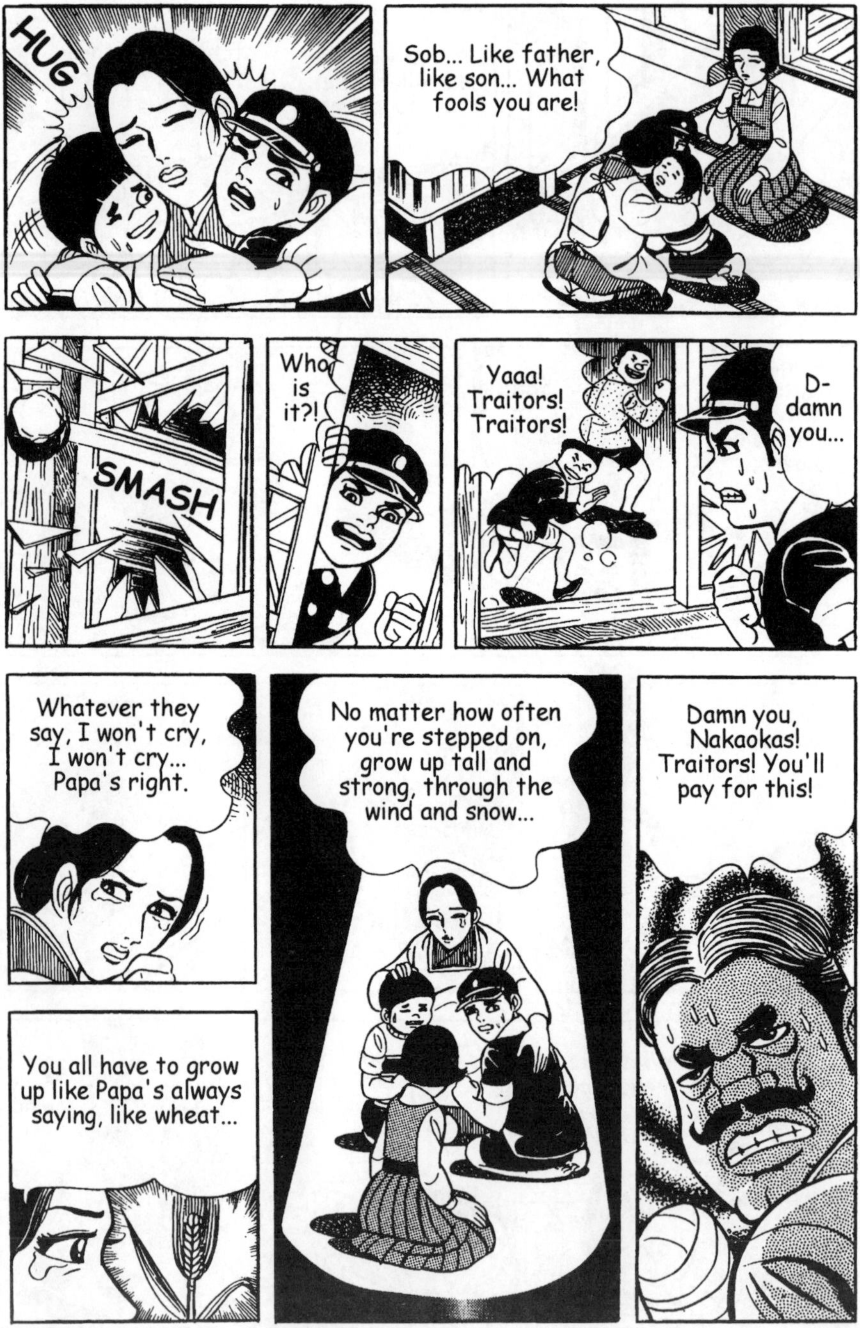
HUG
Sob... Like father, like son... What fools you are!
SMASH
Who is it?!
Yaaa! Traitors! Traitors!
D-damn you...
Whatever they say, I won't cry, I won't cry... Papa's right.
You all have to grow up like Papa's always saying, like wheat...
No matter how often you're stepped on, grow up tall and strong, through the wind and snow...
Damn you, Nakaokas! Traitors! You'll pay for this!

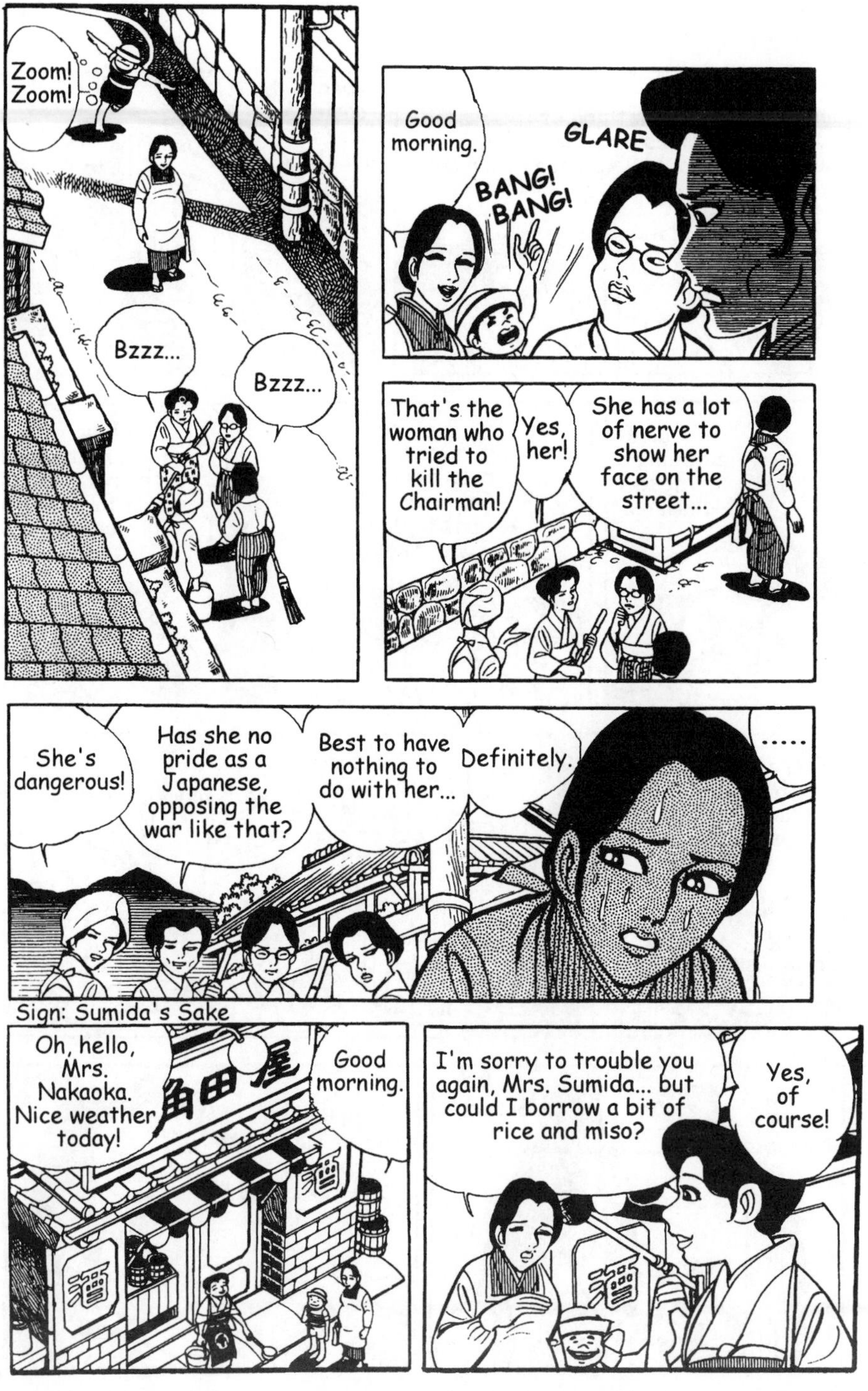
Zoom! Zoom!
Bzzz...
Bzzz...
Good morning.
BANG! BANG!
GLARE
That's the woman who tried to kill the Chairman!
Yes, her!
She has a lot of nerve to show her face on the street...
She's dangerous!
Has she no pride as a Japanese, opposing the war like that?
Best to have nothing to do with her...
Definitely.
.....
Sign: Sumida's Sake
Oh, hello, Mrs. Nakaoka. Nice weather today!
Good morning.
I'm sorry to trouble you again, Mrs. Sumida... but could I borrow a bit of rice and miso?
Yes, of course!

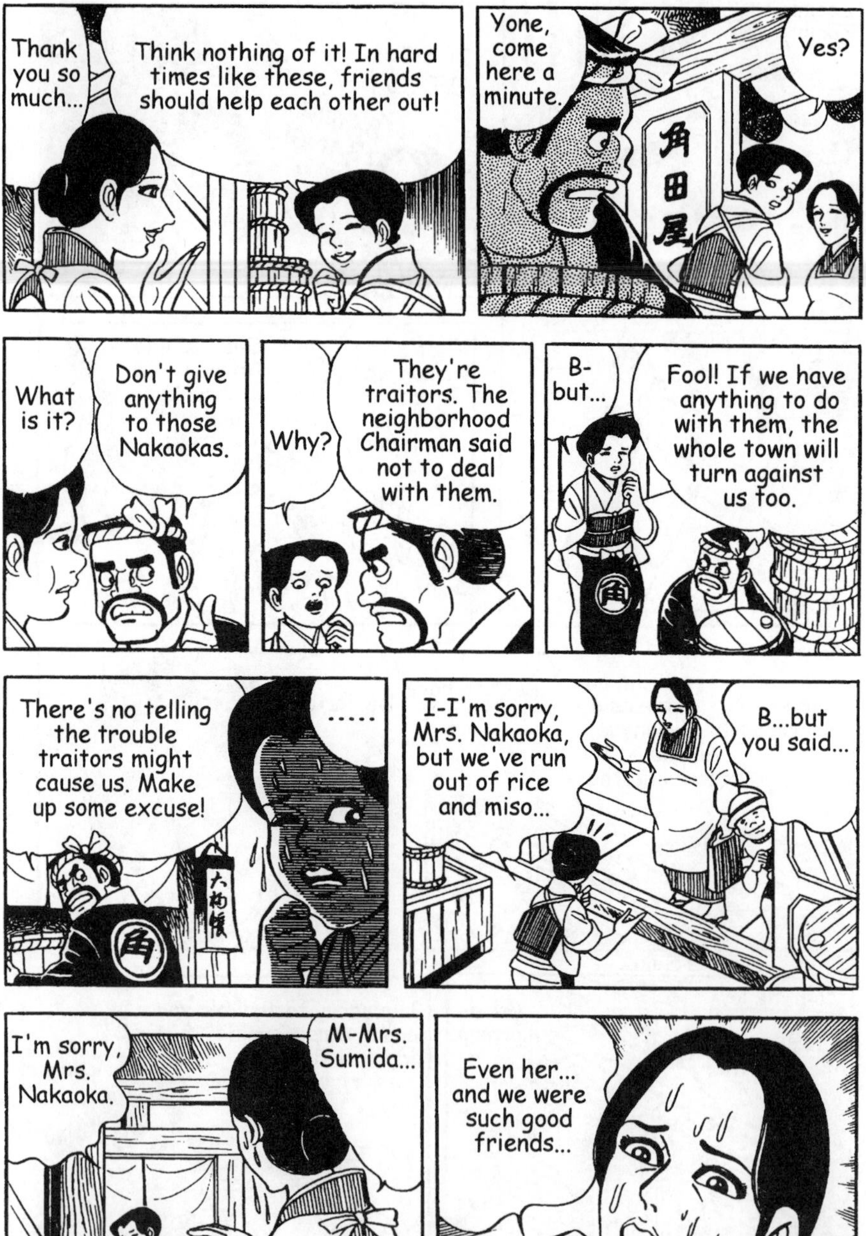
Thank you so much...
Think nothing of it! In hard times like these, friends should help each other out!
Yone, come here a minute.
角田屋
Yes?
What is it?
Don't give anything to those Nakaokas.
Why?
They're traitors. The neighborhood Chairman said not to deal with them.
B-but...
Fool! If we have anything to do with them, the whole town will turn against us too.
There's no telling the trouble traitors might cause us. Make up some excuse!
.....
I-I'm sorry, Mrs. Nakaoka, but we've run out of rice and miso...
B...but you said...
I'm sorry, Mrs. Nakaoka.
M-Mrs. Sumida...
Even her... and we were such good friends...

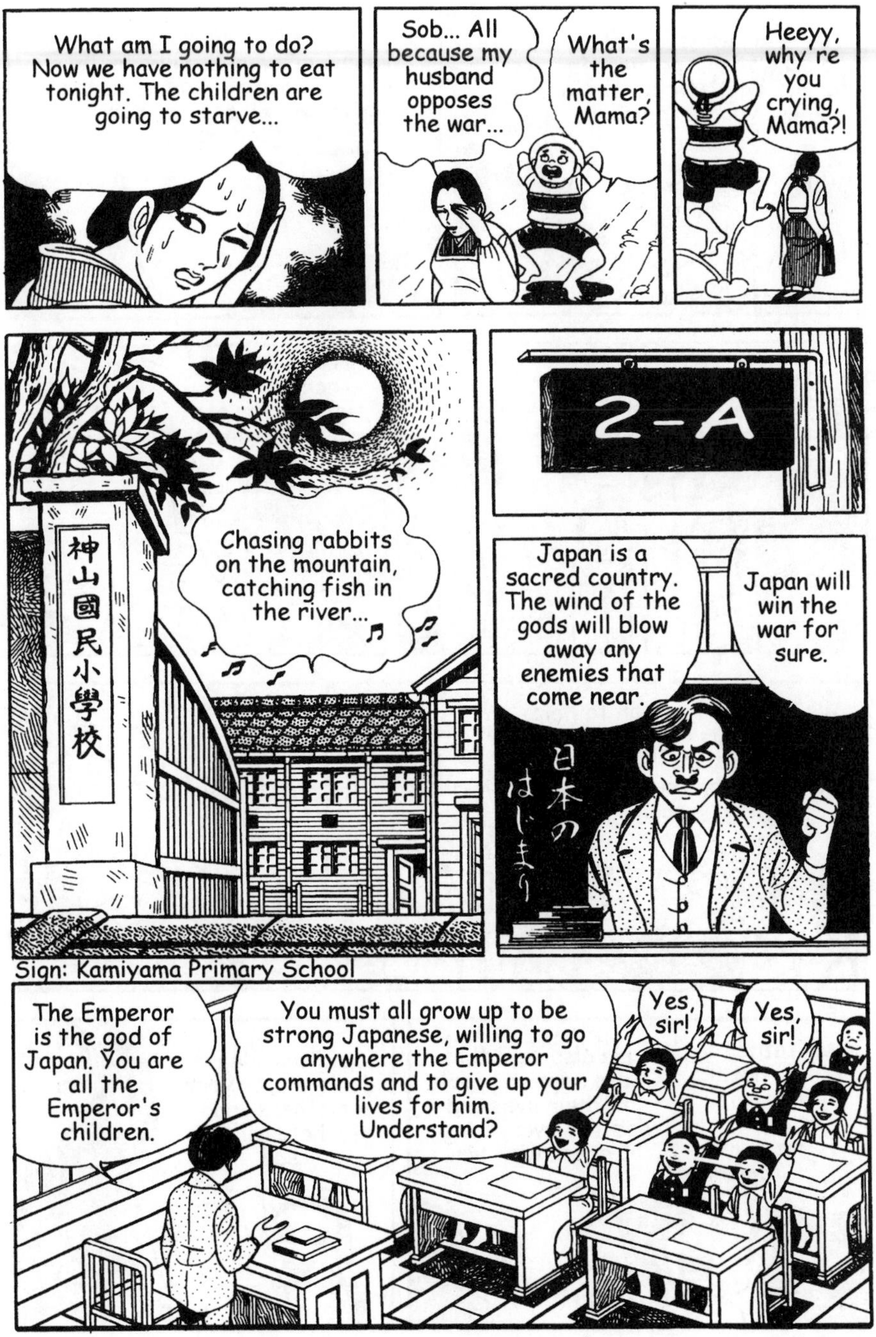
What am I going to do? Now we have nothing to eat tonight. The children are going to starve...
Sob... All because my husband opposes the war...
What's the matter, Mama?
Heeyy, why're you crying, Mama?!
神山國民小學校
Chasing rabbits on the mountain, catching fish in the river...
Sign: Kamiyama Primary School
2-A
Japan is a sacred country. The wind of the gods will blow away any enemies that come near.
Japan will win the war for sure.
日本のはじまり
The Emperor is the god of Japan. You are all the Emperor's children.
You must all grow up to be strong Japanese, willing to go anywhere the Emperor commands and to give up your lives for him. Understand?
Yes, sir!
Yes, sir!

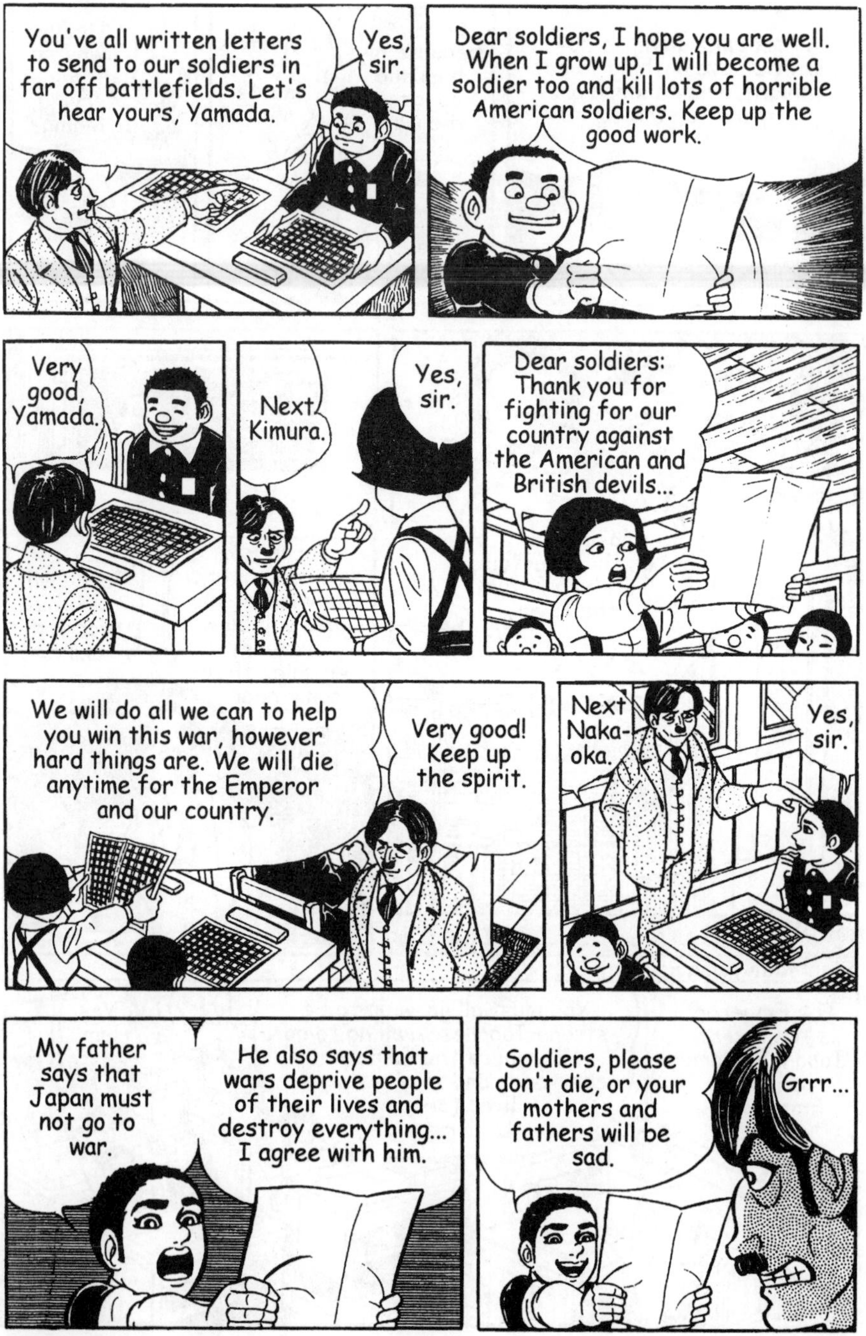
You've all written letters to send to our soldiers in far off battlefields. Let's hear yours, Yamada.
Yes, sir.
Dear soldiers, I hope you are well. When I grow up, I will become a soldier too and kill lots of horrible American soldiers. Keep up the good work.
Very good, Yamada.
Next Kimura.
Yes, sir.
Dear soldiers: Thank you for fighting for our country against the American and British devils...
We will do all we can to help you win this war, however hard things are. We will die anytime for the Emperor and our country.
Very good! Keep up the spirit.
Next Naka-oka.
Yes, sir.
My father says that Japan must not go to war.
He also says that wars deprive people of their lives and destroy everything... I agree with him.
Soldiers, please don't die, or your mothers and fathers will be sad.
Grrr...

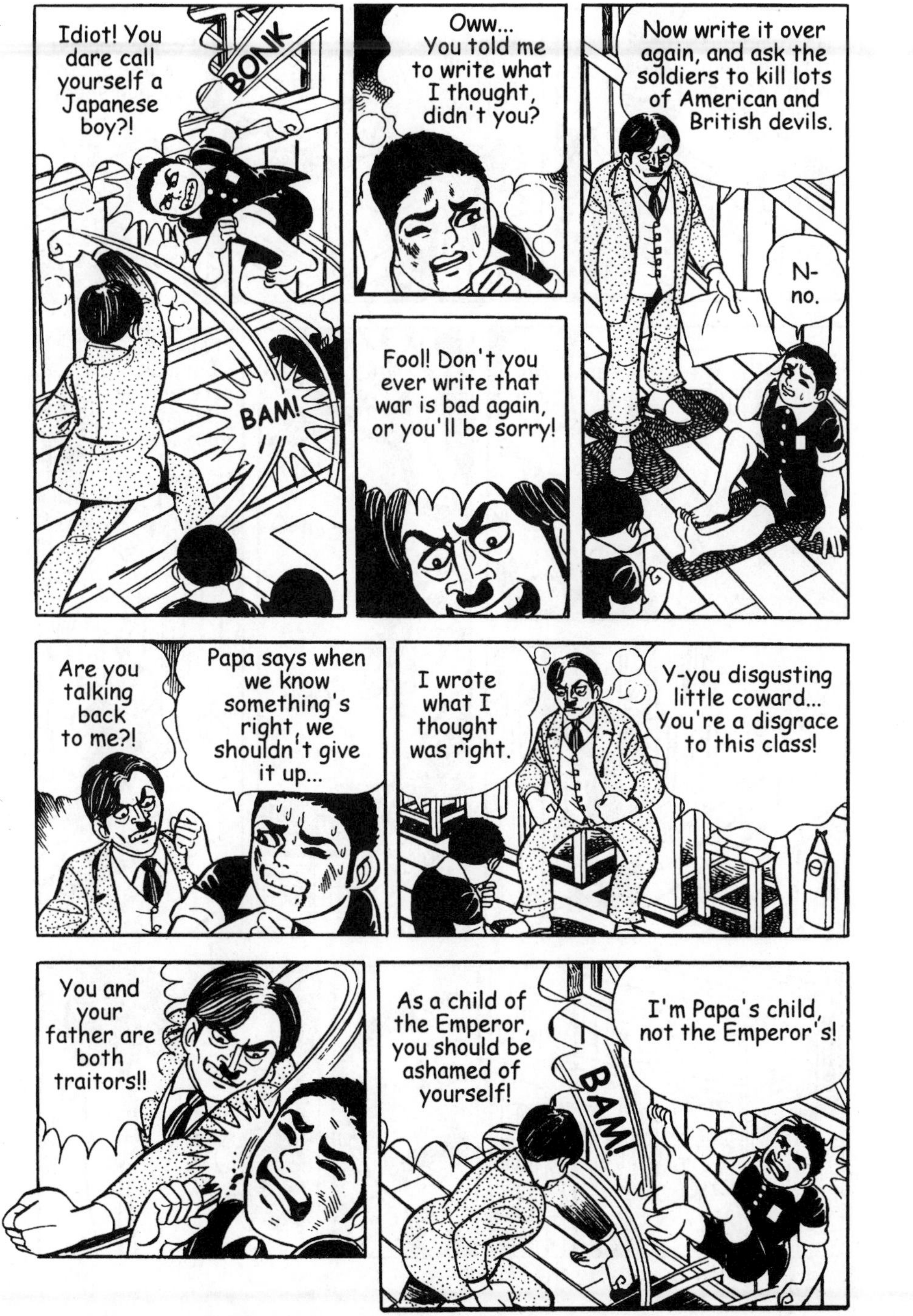
Idiot! You dare call yourself a Japanese boy?!
BONK
BAM!
Oww... You told me to write what I thought, didn't you?
Fool! Don't you ever write that war is bad again, or you'll be sorry!
Now write it over again, and ask the soldiers to kill lots of American and British devils.
N-no.
Are you talking back to me?!
Papa says when we know something's right, we shouldn't give it up...
I wrote what I thought was right.
Y-you disgusting little coward... You're a disgrace to this class!
You and your father are both traitors!!
As a child of the Emperor, you should be ashamed of yourself!
I'm Papa's child, not the Emperor's!
BAM!

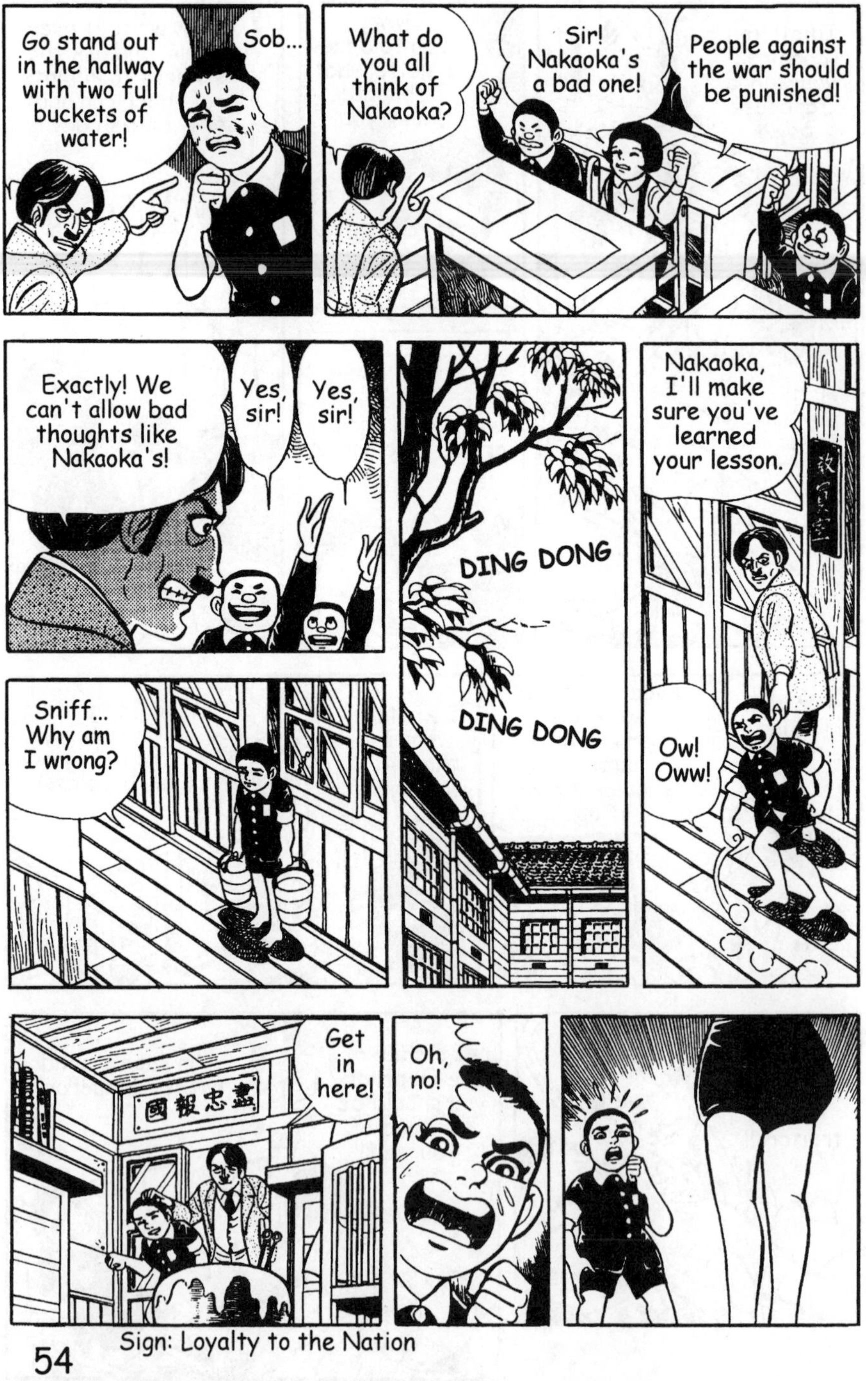
Go stand out in the hallway with two full buckets of water!
Sob...
What do you all think of Nakaoka?
Sir! Nakaoka's a bad one!
People against the war should be punished!
Exactly! We can't allow bad thoughts like Nakaoka's!
Yes, sir!
Yes, sir!
Sniff... Why am I wrong?
DING DONG
DING DONG
Nakaoka, I'll make sure you've learned your lesson.
Ow! Oww!
盡忠報國
Get in here!
Oh, no!

Sign: Loyalty to the Nation

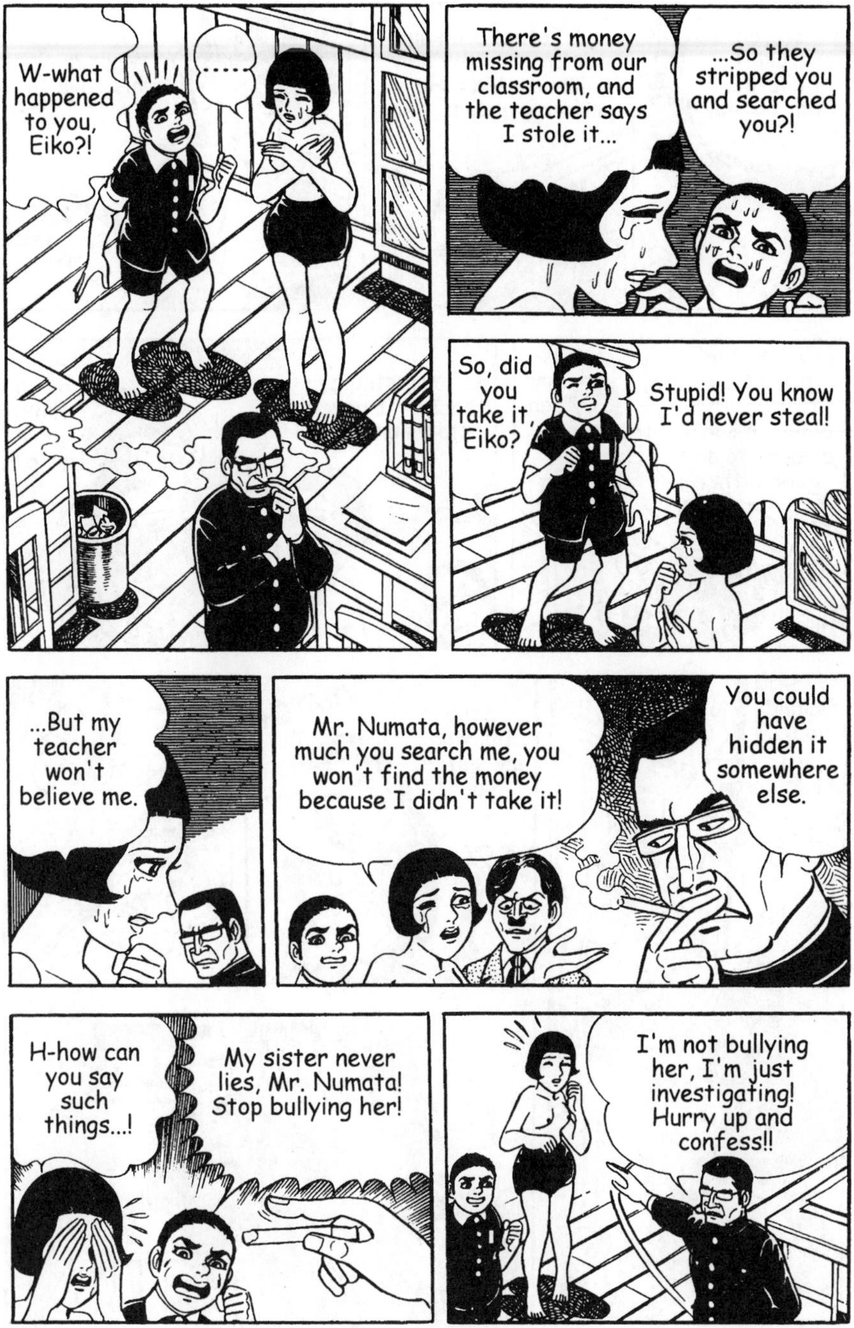
W-what happened to you, Eiko?!
.....
There's money missing from our classroom, and the teacher says I stole it...
...So they stripped you and searched you?!
So, did you take it, Eiko?
Stupid! You know I'd never steal!
...But my teacher won't believe me.
Mr. Numata, however much you search me, you won't find the money because I didn't take it!
You could have hidden it somewhere else.
H-how can you say such things...!
My sister never lies, Mr. Numata! Stop bullying her!
I'm not bullying her, I'm just investigating! Hurry up and confess!!

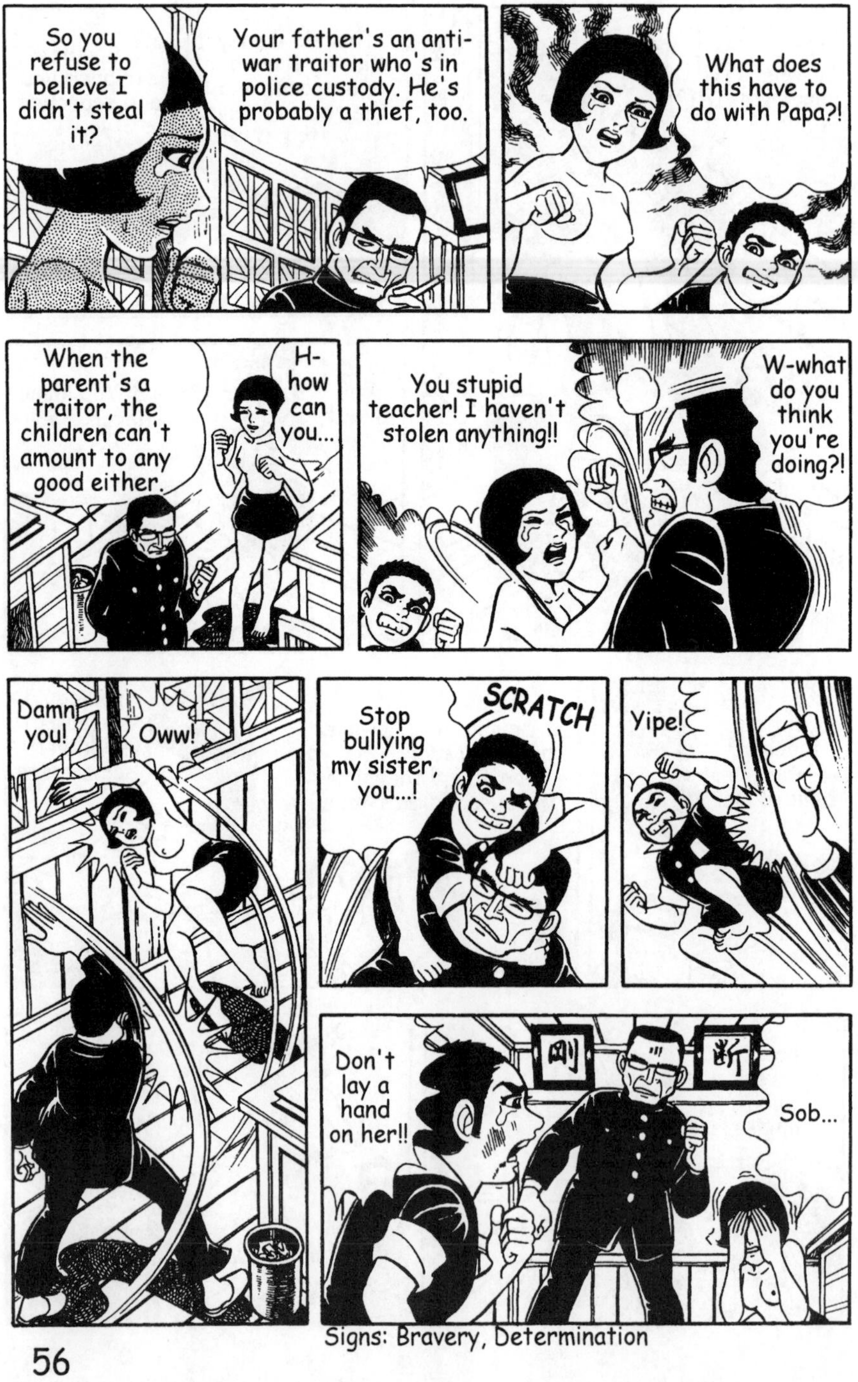
So you refuse to believe I didn't steal it?
Your father's an anti-war traitor who's in police custody. He's probably a thief, too.
What does this have to do with Papa?!
When the parent's a traitor, the children can't amount to any good either.
H-how can you...
You stupid teacher! I haven't stolen anything!!
W-what do you think you're doing?!
Damn you!
Oww!
Stop bullying my sister, you...!
SCRATCH
Yipe!
Don't lay a hand on her!!
Sob...
Signs: Bravery, Determination

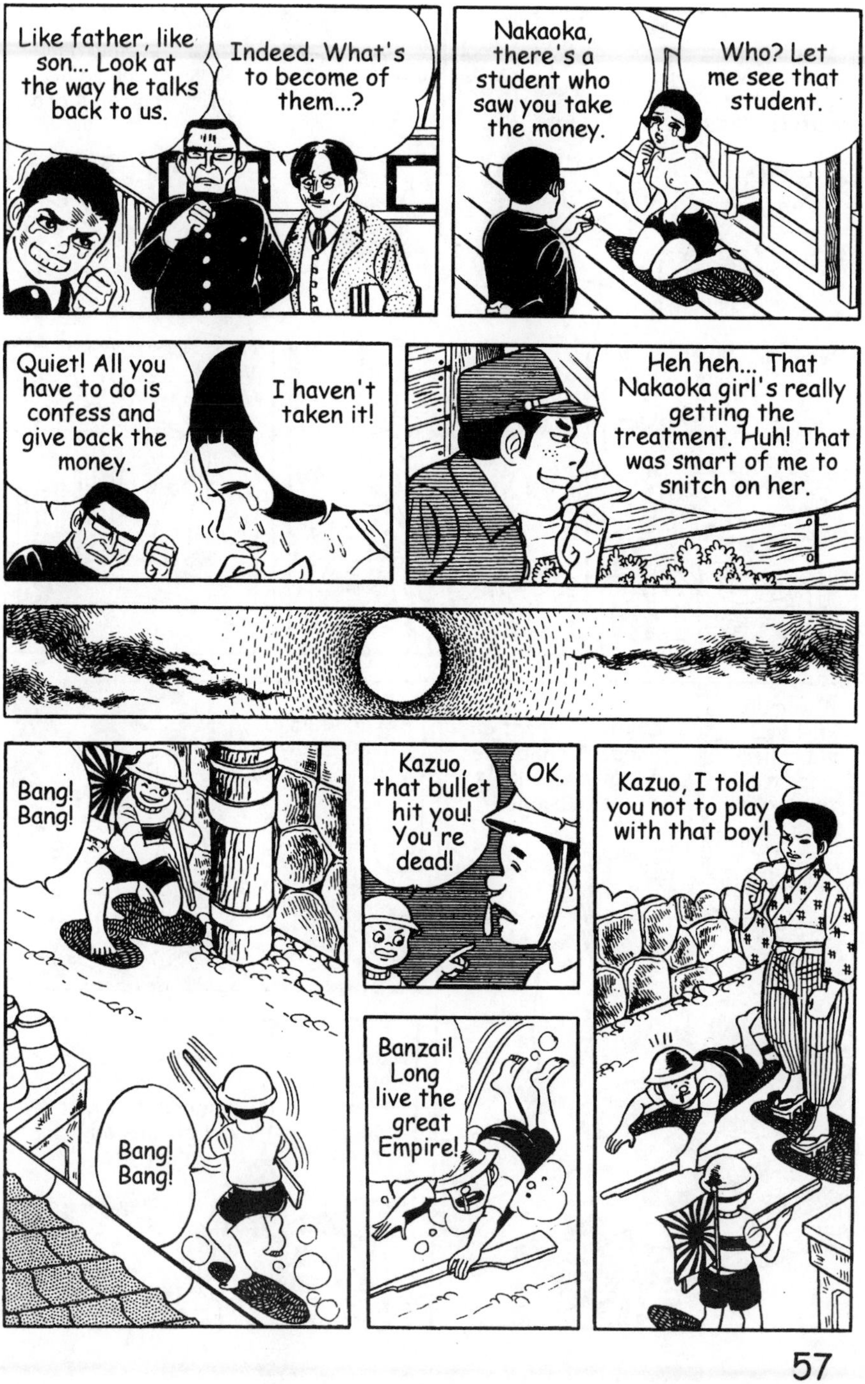

Like father, like son... Look at the way he talks back to us.
Indeed. What's to become of them...?
Nakaoka, there's a student who saw you take the money.
Who? Let me see that student.
Quiet! All you have to do is confess and give back the money.
I haven't taken it!
Heh heh... That Nakaoka girl's really getting the treatment. Huh! That was smart of me to snitch on her.
Bang! Bang!
Bang! Bang!
Kazuo, that bullet hit you! You're dead!
OK.
Banzai! Long live the great Empire!
Kazuo, I told you not to play with that boy!

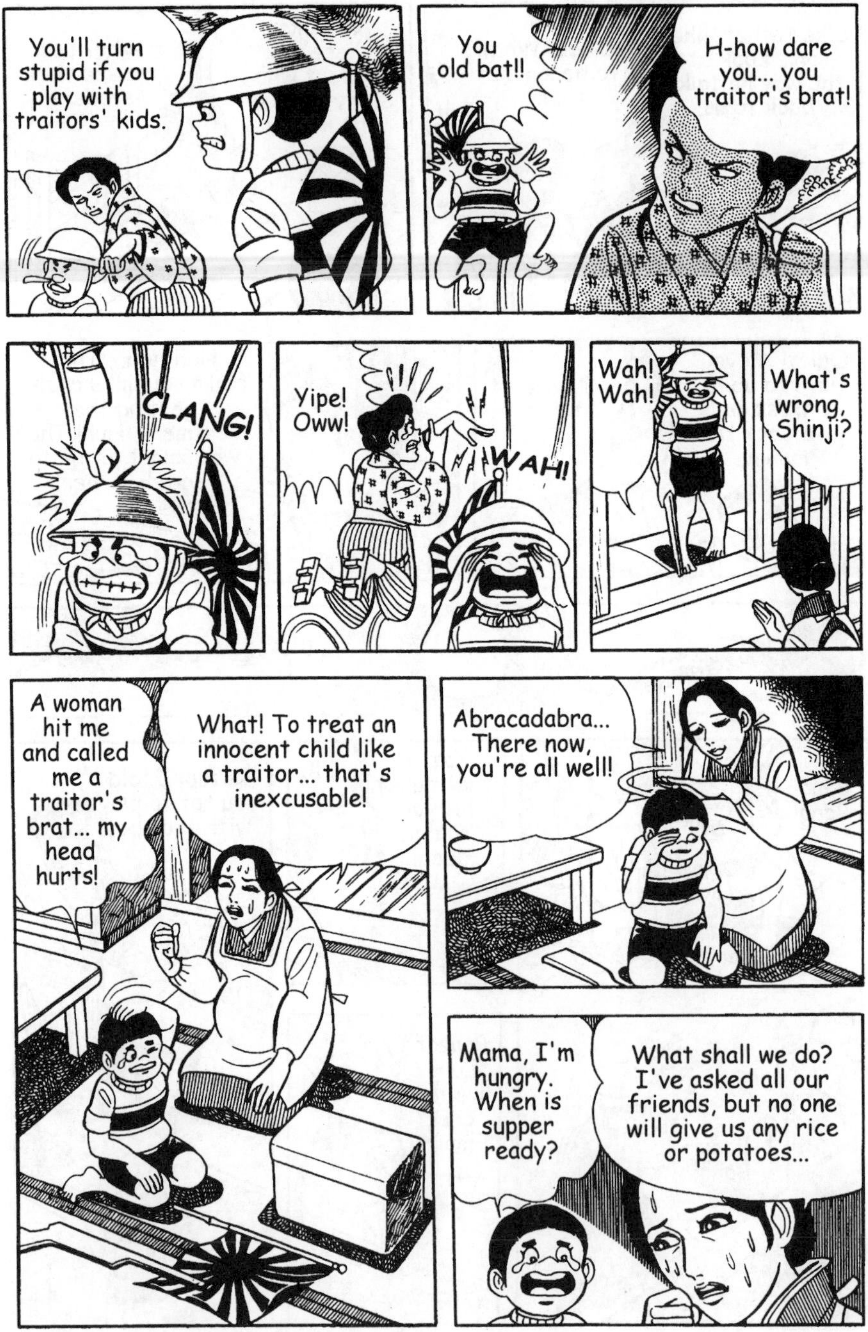
You'll turn stupid if you play with traitors' kids.
You old bat!!
H-how dare you... you traitor's brat!
CLANG!
Yipe! Oww!
WAH!
Wah! Wah!
What's wrong, Shinji?
A woman hit me and called me a traitor's brat... my head hurts!
What! To treat an innocent child like a traitor... that's inexcusable!
Abracadabra... There now, you're all well!
Mama, I'm hungry. When is supper ready?
What shall we do? I've asked all our friends, but no one will give us any rice or potatoes...

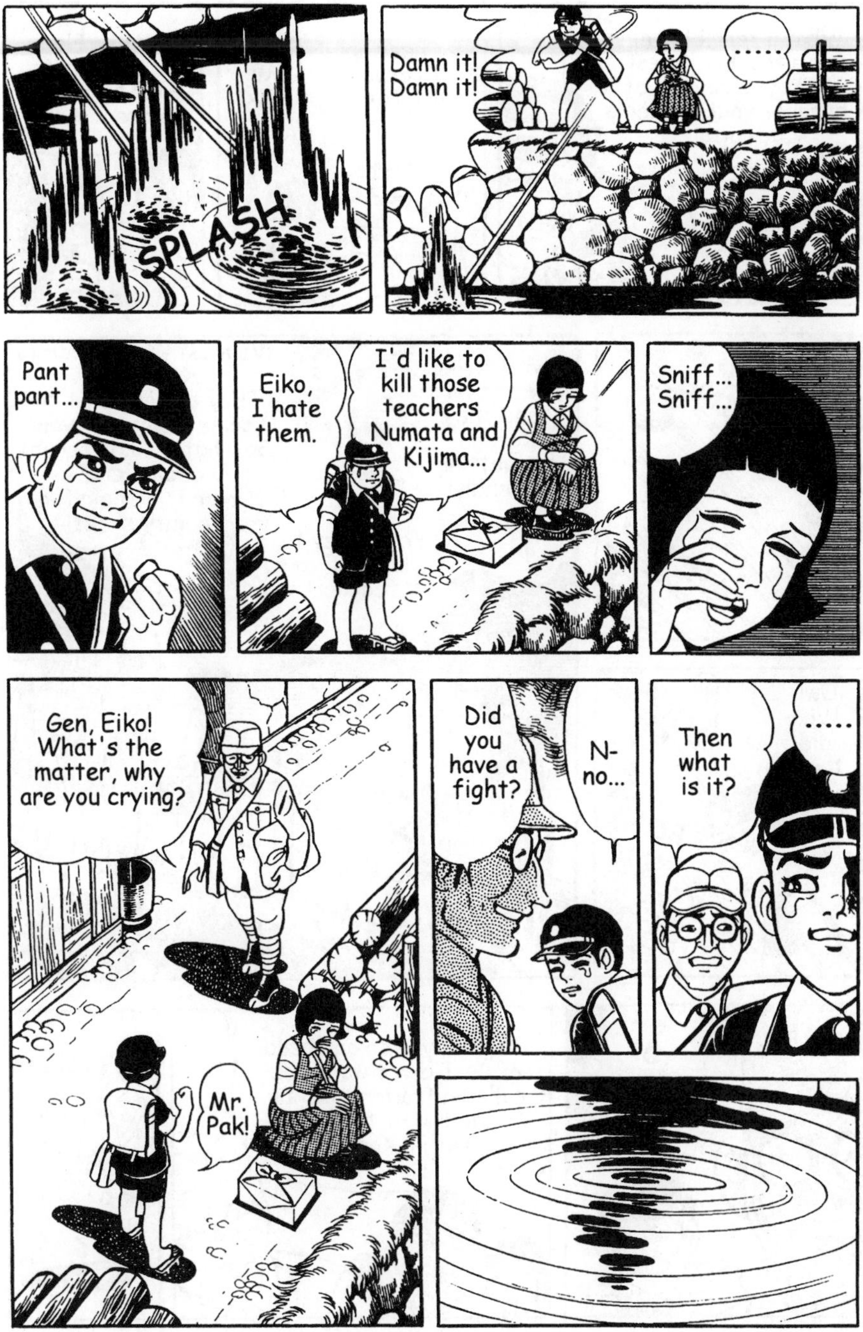
SPLASH
Damn it! Damn it!
......
Pant pant...
Eiko, I hate them.
I'd like to kill those teachers Numata and Kijima...
Sniff... Sniff...
Gen, Eiko! What's the matter, why are you crying?
Mr. Pak!
Did you have a fight?
N-no...
Then what is it?
......

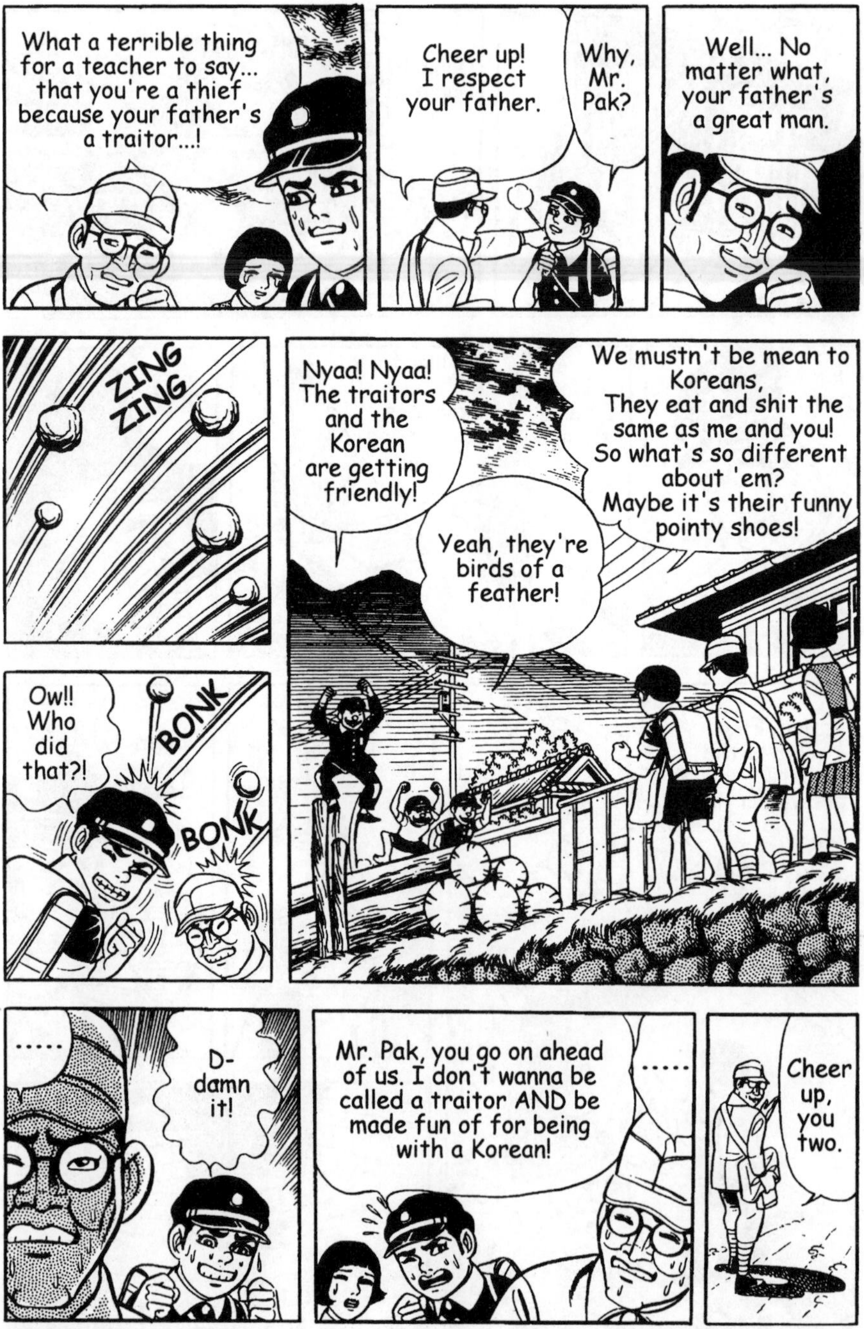

What a terrible thing for a teacher to say... that you're a thief because your father's a traitor...!
Cheer up! I respect your father.
Why, Mr. Pak?
Well... No matter what, your father's a great man.
ZING
ZING
Ow!! Who did that?!
BONK
BONK
Nyaa! Nyaa! The traitors and the Korean are getting friendly!
We mustn't be mean to Koreans, They eat and shit the same as me and you! So what's so different about 'em? Maybe it's their funny pointy shoes!
Yeah, they're birds of a feather!
.....
D-damn it!
Mr. Pak, you go on ahead of us. I don't wanna be called a traitor AND be made fun of for being with a Korean!
.....
Cheer up, you two.

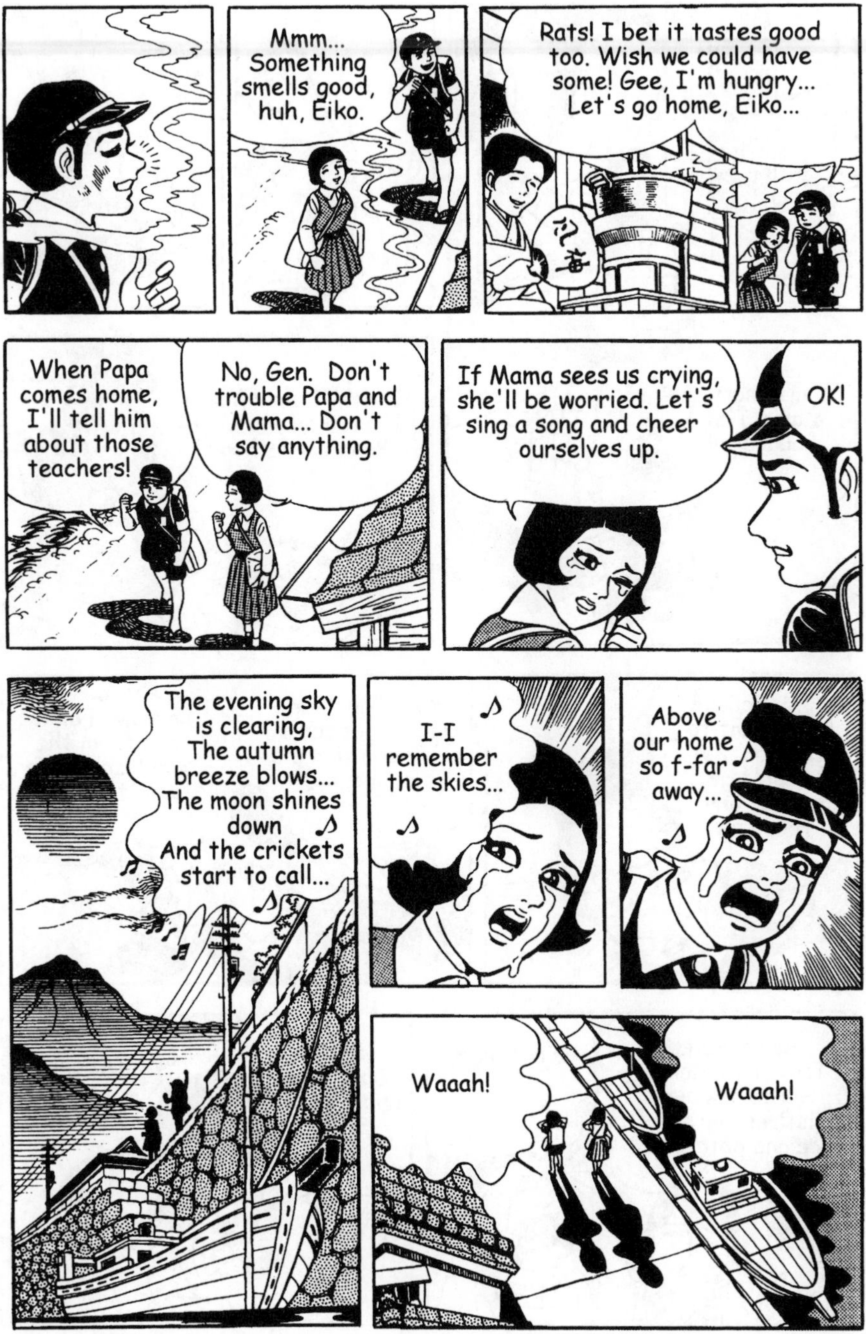
Mmm... Something smells good, huh, Eiko.
Rats! I bet it tastes good too. Wish we could have some! Gee, I'm hungry... Let's go home, Eiko...
When Papa comes home, I'll tell him about those teachers!
No, Gen. Don't trouble Papa and Mama... Don't say anything.
If Mama sees us crying, she'll be worried. Let's sing a song and cheer ourselves up.
OK!
The evening sky is clearing, The autumn breeze blows... The moon shines down And the crickets start to call...
I-I remember the skies...
Above our home so f-far away...
Waaah!
Waaah!

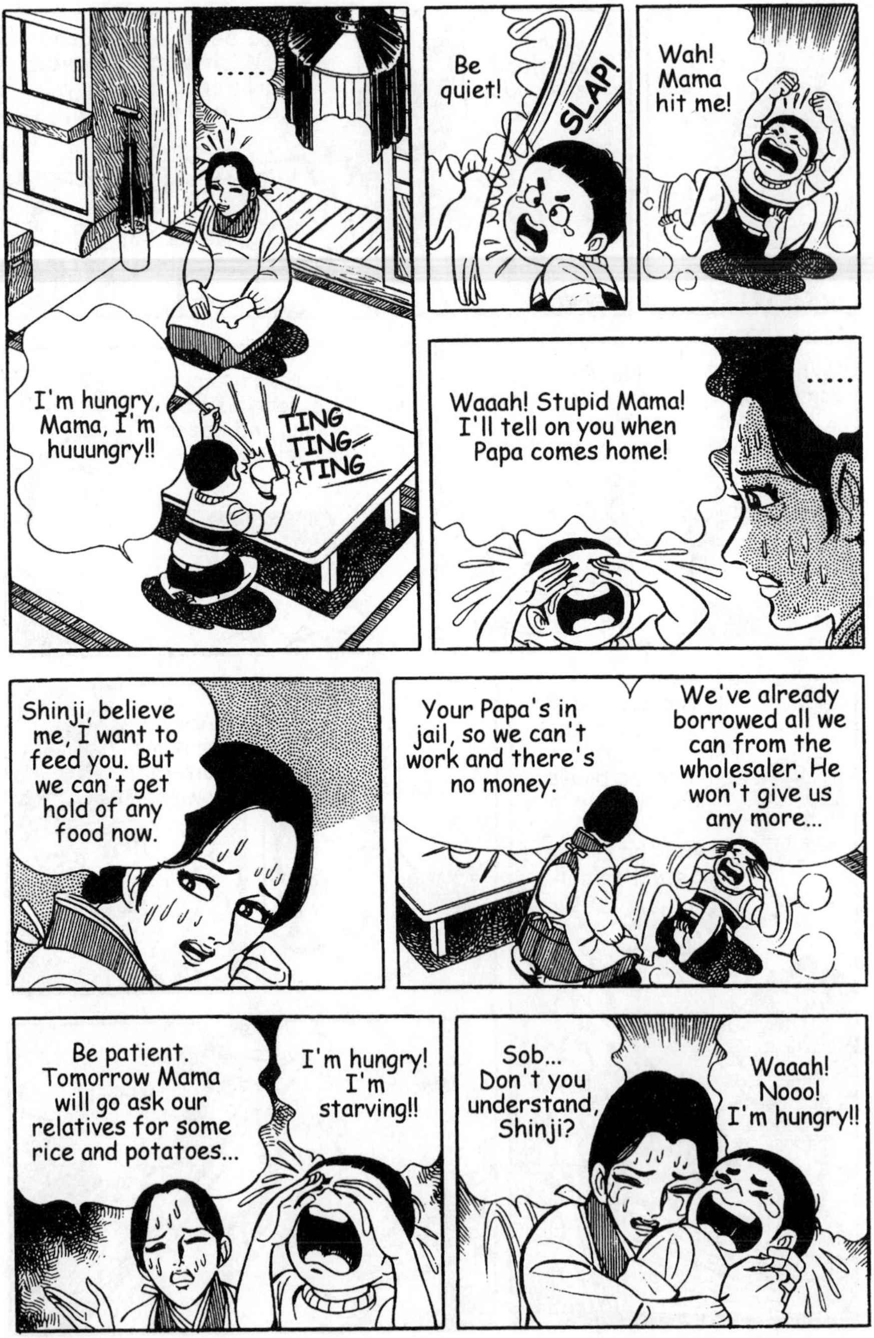
......
I'm hungry, Mama, I'm huuungry!!
TING TING TING
Be quiet!
SLAP!
Wah! Mama hit me!
Waaah! Stupid Mama! I'll tell on you when Papa comes home!
......
Shinji, believe me, I want to feed you. But we can't get hold of any food now.
Your Papa's in jail, so we can't work and there's no money.
We've already borrowed all we can from the wholesaler. He won't give us any more...
Be patient. Tomorrow Mama will go ask our relatives for some rice and potatoes...
I'm hungry! I'm starving!!
Sob... Don't you understand, Shinji?
Waaah! Nooo! I'm hungry!!

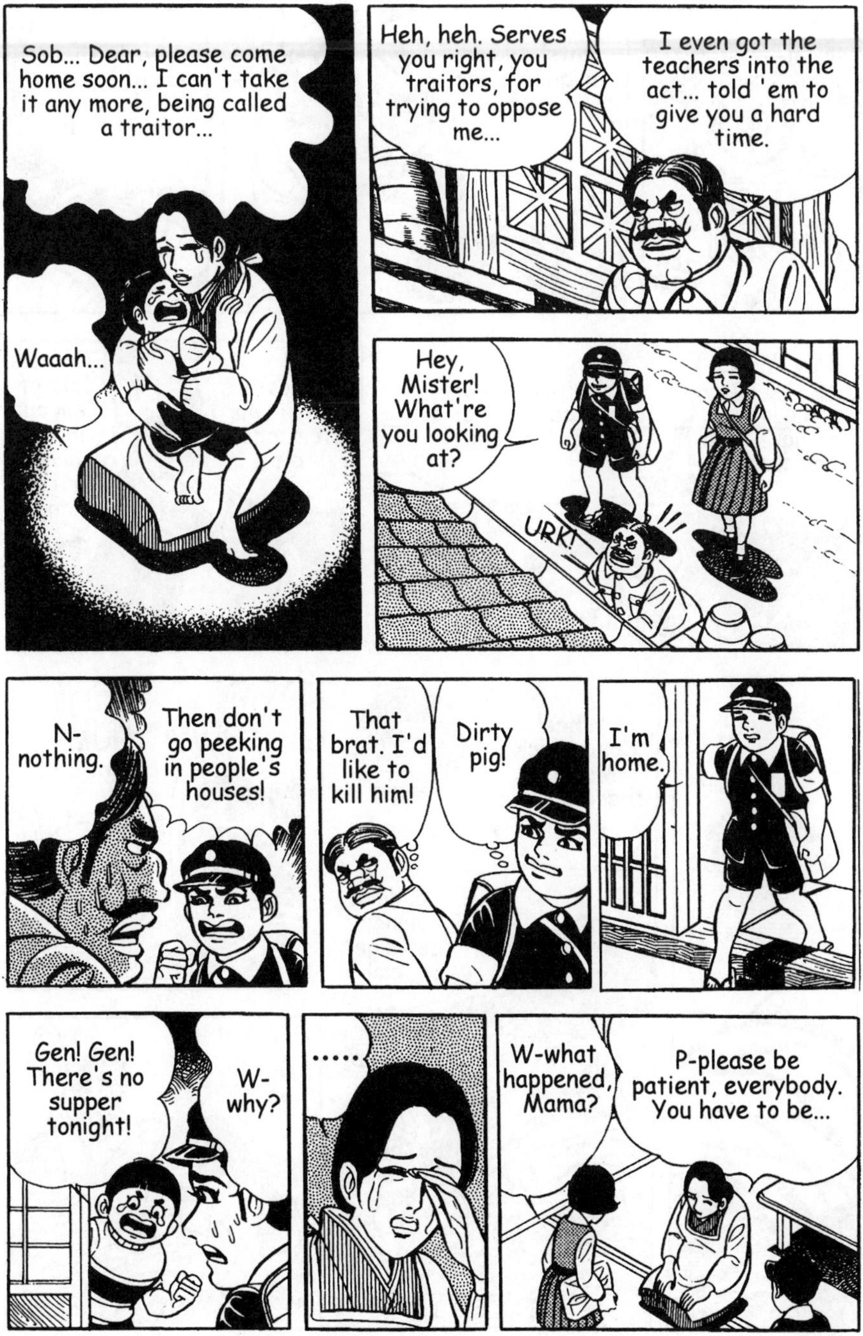

Sob... Dear, please come home soon... I can't take it any more, being called a traitor...
Waaah...
Heh, heh. Serves you right, you traitors, for trying to oppose me...
I even got the teachers into the act... told 'em to give you a hard time.
Hey, Mister! What're you looking at?
URK!
N-nothing.
Then don't go peeking in people's houses!
That brat. I'd like to kill him!
Dirty pig!
I'm home.
Gen! Gen! There's no supper tonight!
W-why?
.....
W-what happened, Mama?
P-please be patient, everybody. You have to be...

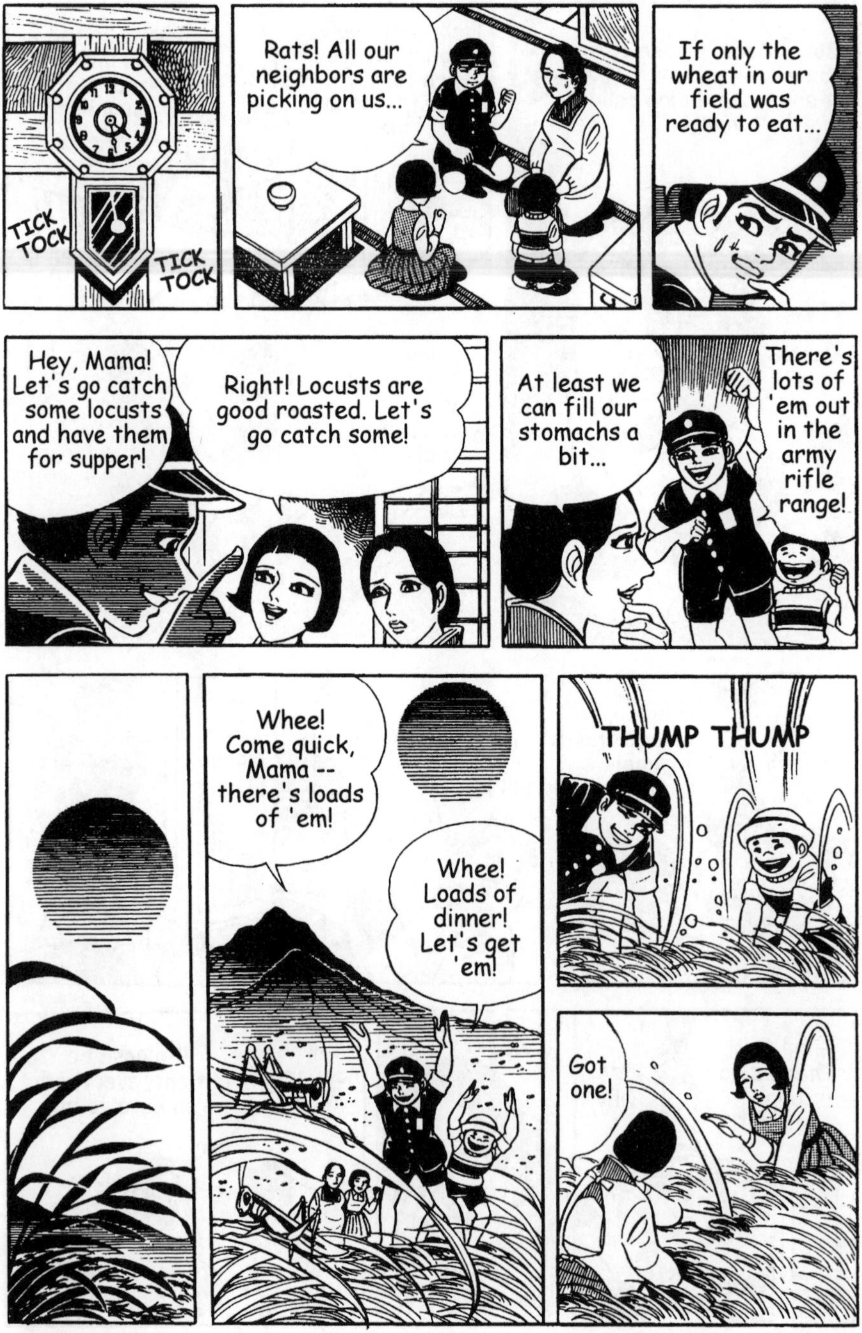
TICK TOCK
TICK TOCK
Rats! All our neighbors are picking on us...
If only the wheat in our field was ready to eat...
Hey, Mama! Let's go catch some locusts and have them for supper!
Right! Locusts are good roasted. Let's go catch some!
At least we can fill our stomachs a bit...
There's lots of 'em out in the army rifle range!
Whee! Come quick, Mama -- there's loads of 'em!
Whee! Loads of dinner! Let's get 'em!
THUMP THUMP
Got one!

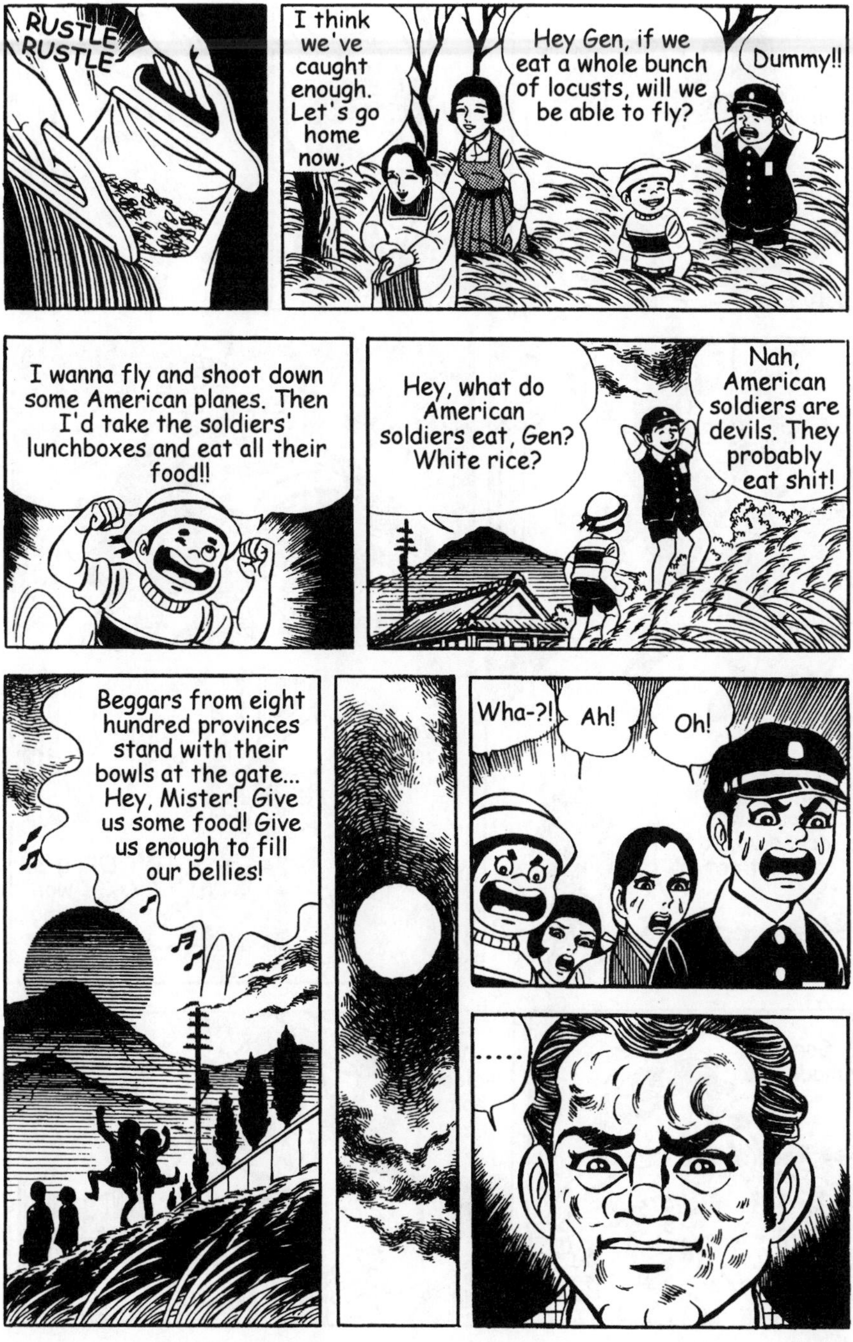
RUSTLE RUSTLE
I think we've caught enough. Let's go home now.
Hey Gen, if we eat a whole bunch of locusts, will we be able to fly?
Dummy!!
I wanna fly and shoot down some American planes. Then I'd take the soldiers' lunchboxes and eat all their food!!
Hey, what do American soldiers eat, Gen? White rice?
Nah, American soldiers are devils. They probably eat shit!
Beggars from eight hundred provinces stand with their bowls at the gate... Hey, Mister! Give us some food! Give us enough to fill our bellies!
Wha-?!
Ah!
Oh!
.....

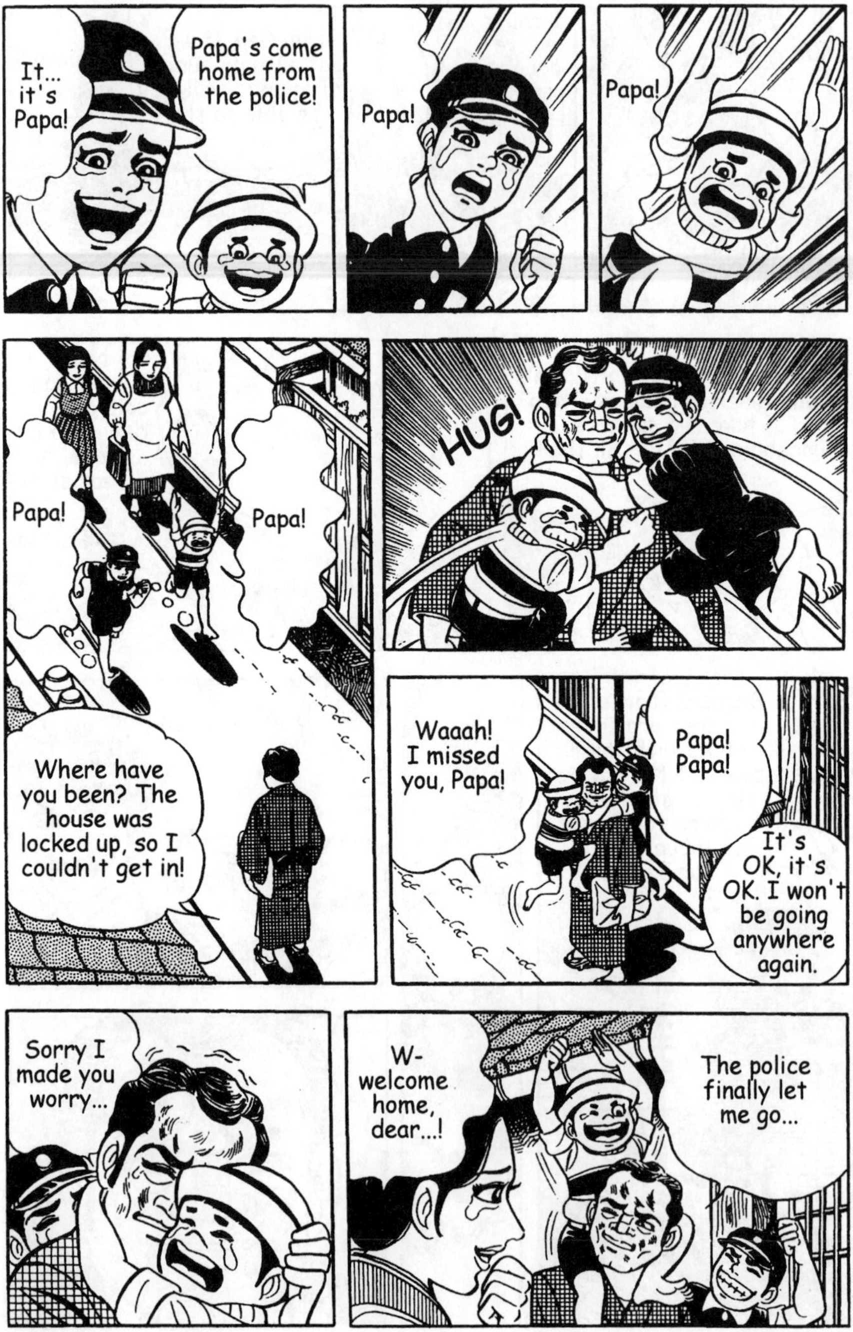

It... it's Papa!
Papa's come home from the police!
Papa!
Papa!
Papa!
Papa!
HUG!
Where have you been? The house was locked up, so I couldn't get in!
Waaah! I missed you, Papa!
Papa! Papa!
It's OK, it's OK. I won't be going anywhere again.
Sorry I made you worry...
W- welcome home, dear...!
The police finally let me go...

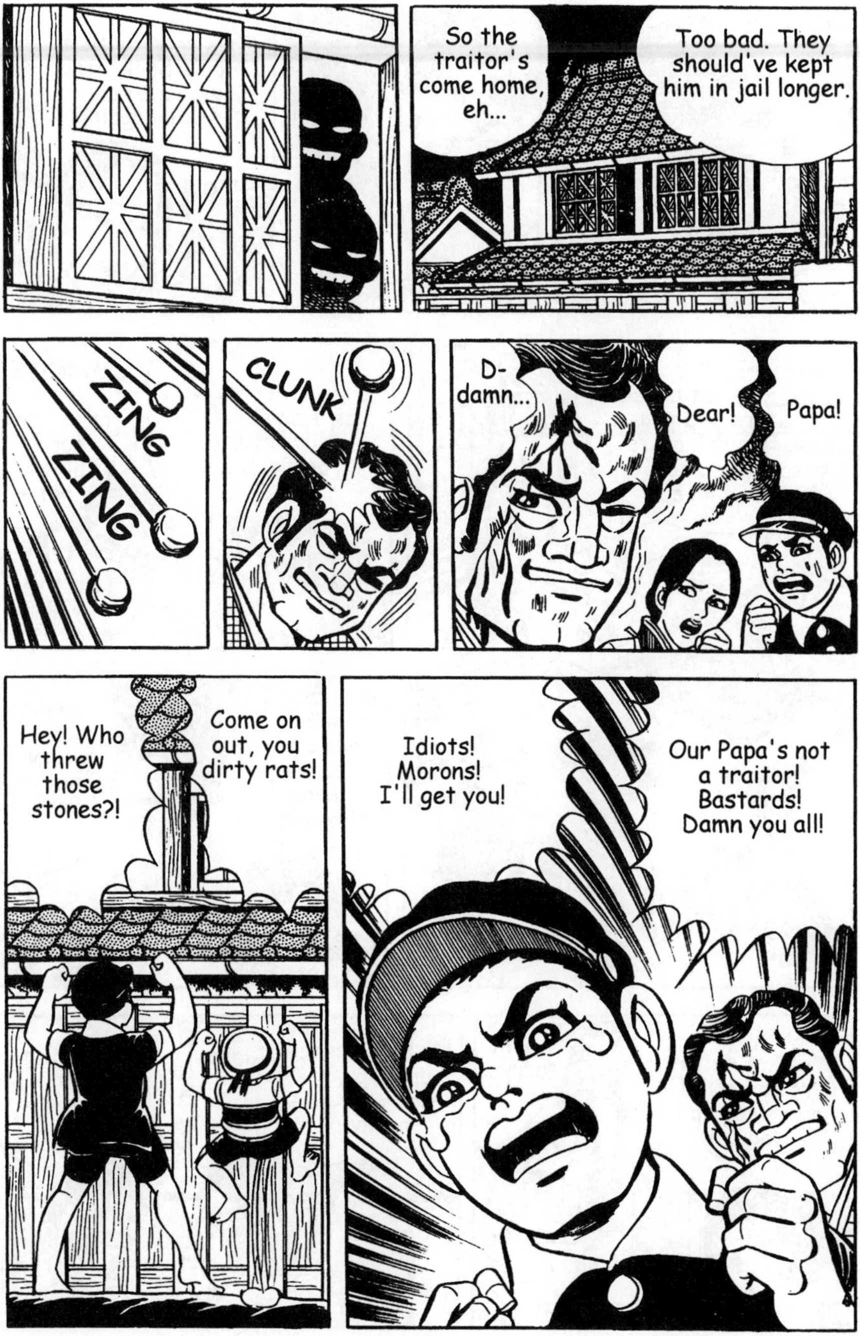
So the traitor's come home, eh...
Too bad. They should've kept him in jail longer.
ZING
ZING
CLUNK
D- damn...
Dear!
Papa!
Hey! Who threw those stones?!
Come on out, you dirty rats!
Idiots! Morons! I'll get you!
Our Papa's not a traitor! Bastards! Damn you all!

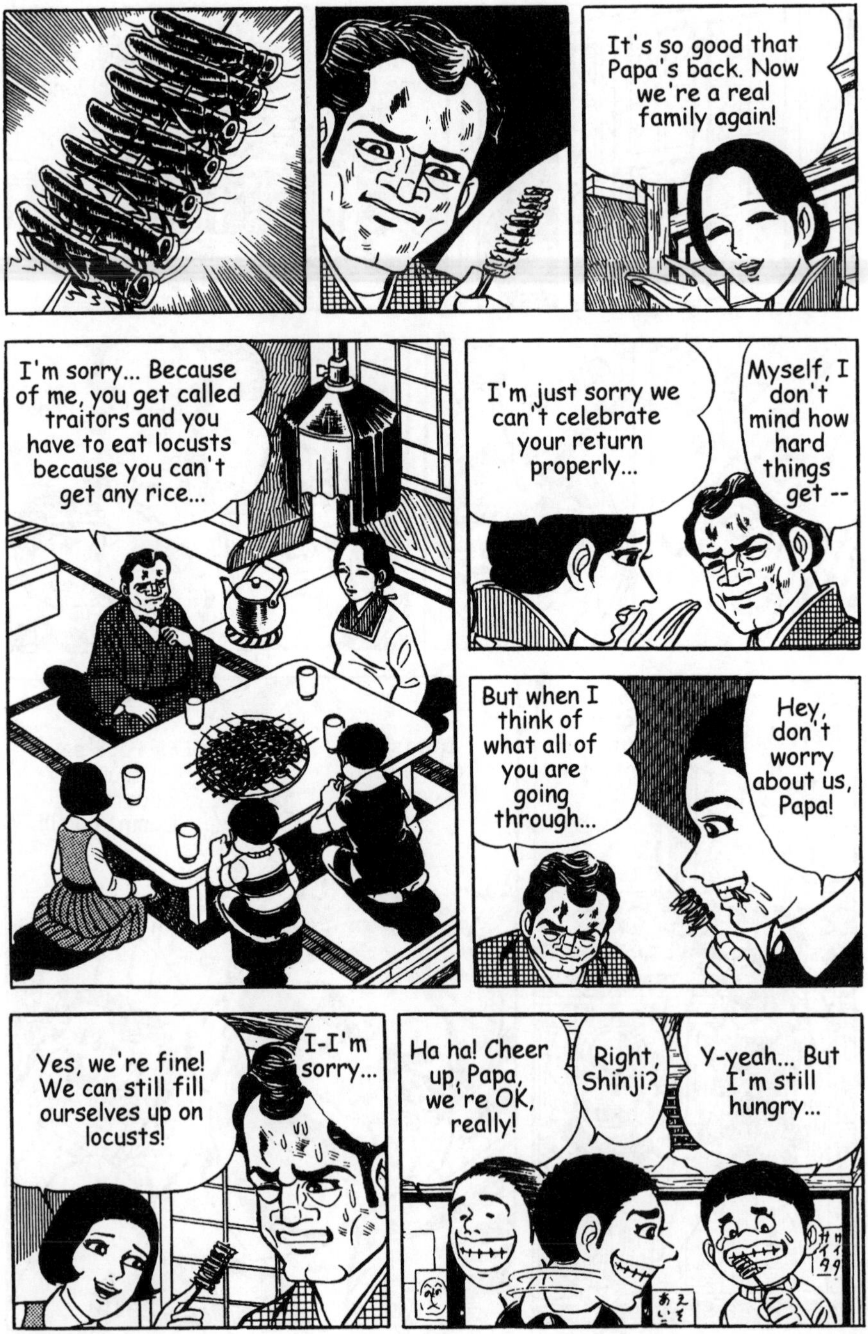
It's so good that Papa's back. Now we're a real family again!
I'm sorry... Because of me, you get called traitors and you have to eat locusts because you can't get any rice...
I'm just sorry we can't celebrate your return properly...
Myself, I don't mind how hard things get --
But when I think of what all of you are going through...
Hey, don't worry about us, Papa!
Yes, we're fine! We can still fill ourselves up on locusts!
I-I'm sorry...
Ha ha! Cheer up, Papa, we're OK, really!
Right, Shinji?
Y-yeah... But I'm still hungry...

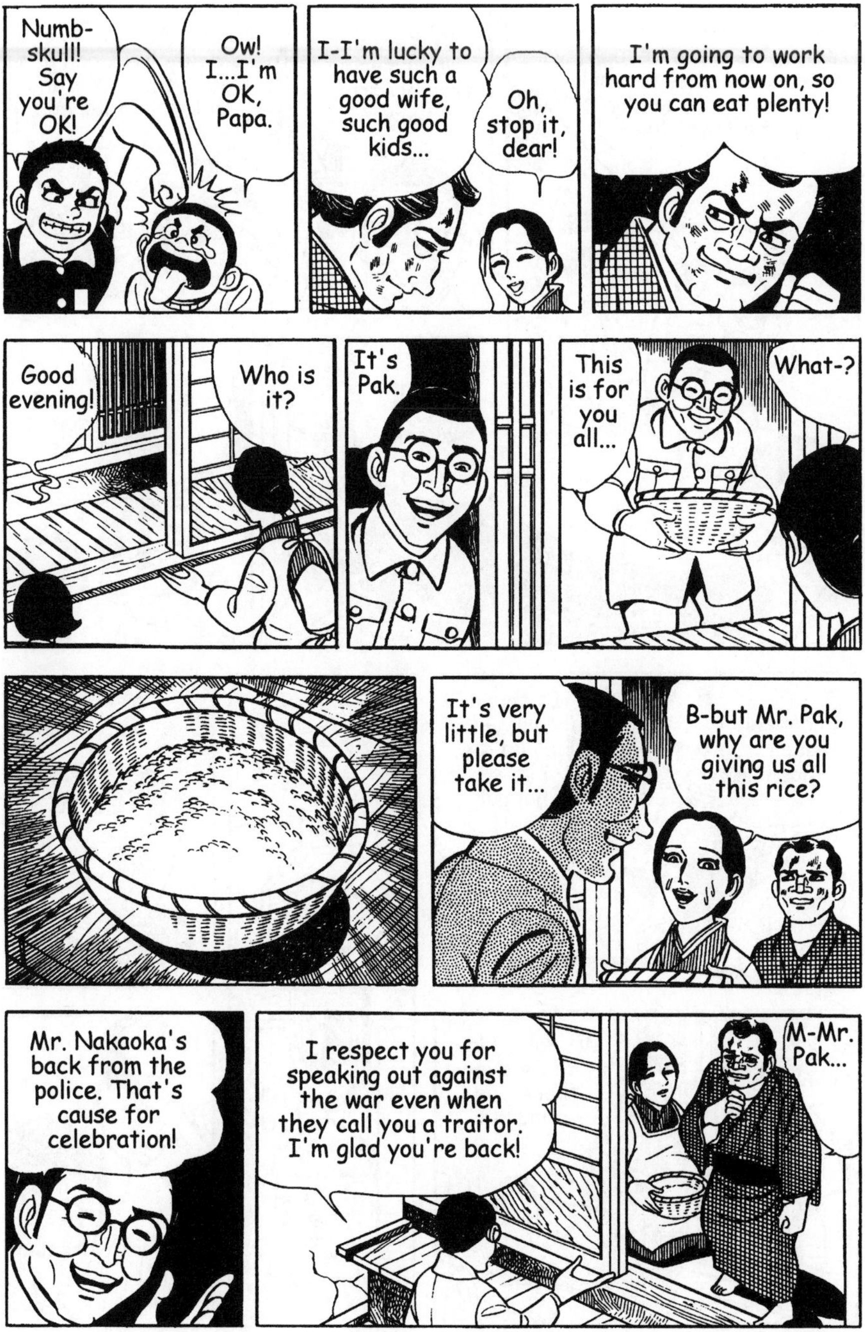
Numb-skull! Say you're OK!
Ow! I...I'm OK, Papa.
I-I'm lucky to have such a good wife, such good kids...
Oh, stop it, dear!
I'm going to work hard from now on, so you can eat plenty!
Good evening!
Who is it?
It's Pak.
This is for you all...
What-?
It's very little, but please take it...
B-but Mr. Pak, why are you giving us all this rice?
Mr. Nakaoka's back from the police. That's cause for celebration!
I respect you for speaking out against the war even when they call you a traitor. I'm glad you're back!
M-Mr. Pak...

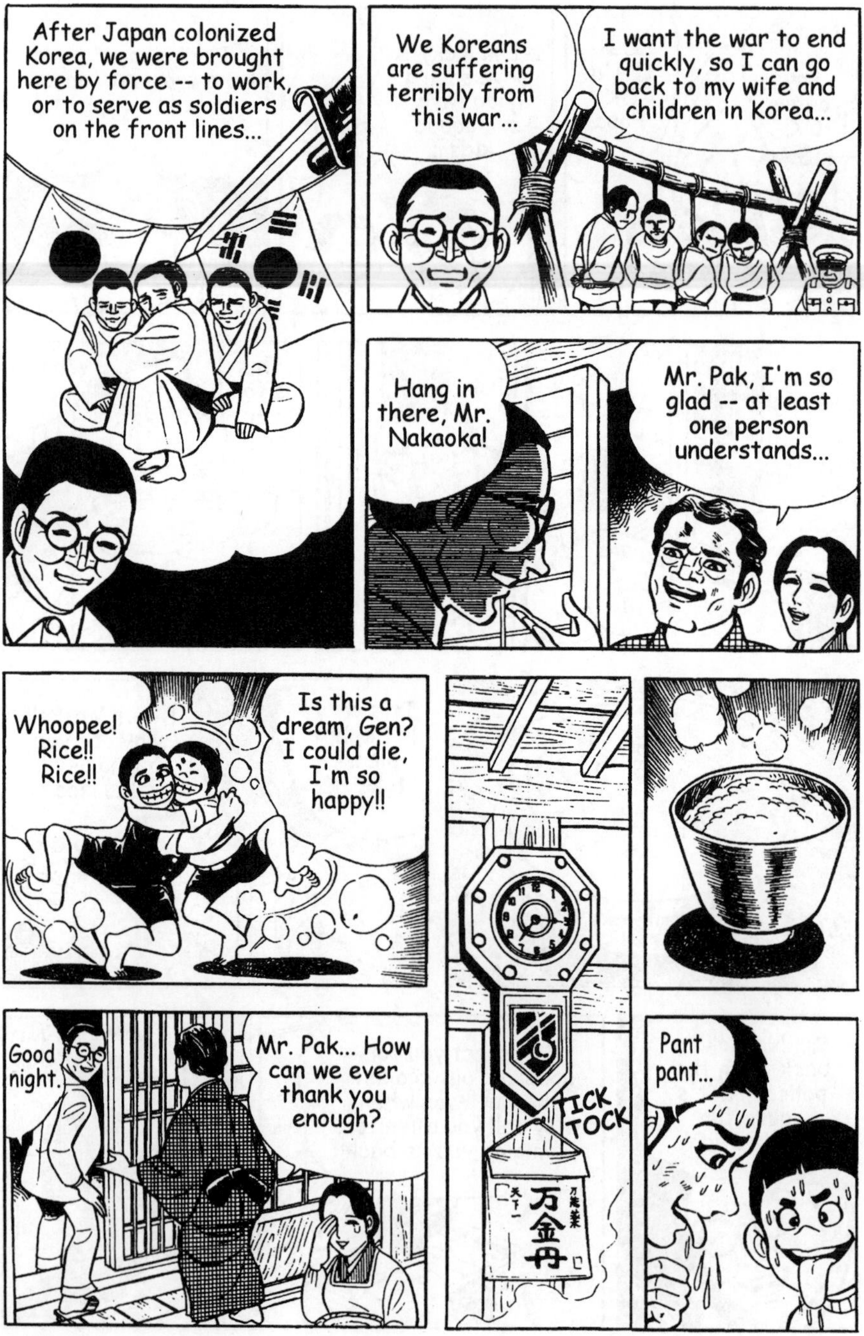
After Japan colonized Korea, we were brought here by force -- to work, or to serve as soldiers on the front lines...
We Koreans are suffering terribly from this war...
I want the war to end quickly, so I can go back to my wife and children in Korea...
Hang in there, Mr. Nakaoka!
Mr. Pak, I'm so glad -- at least one person understands...
Whoopee! Rice!! Rice!!
Is this a dream, Gen? I could die, I'm so happy!!
Good night.
Mr. Pak... How can we ever thank you enough?
TICK TOCK
天下一
万金丹
万能薬
Pant pant...

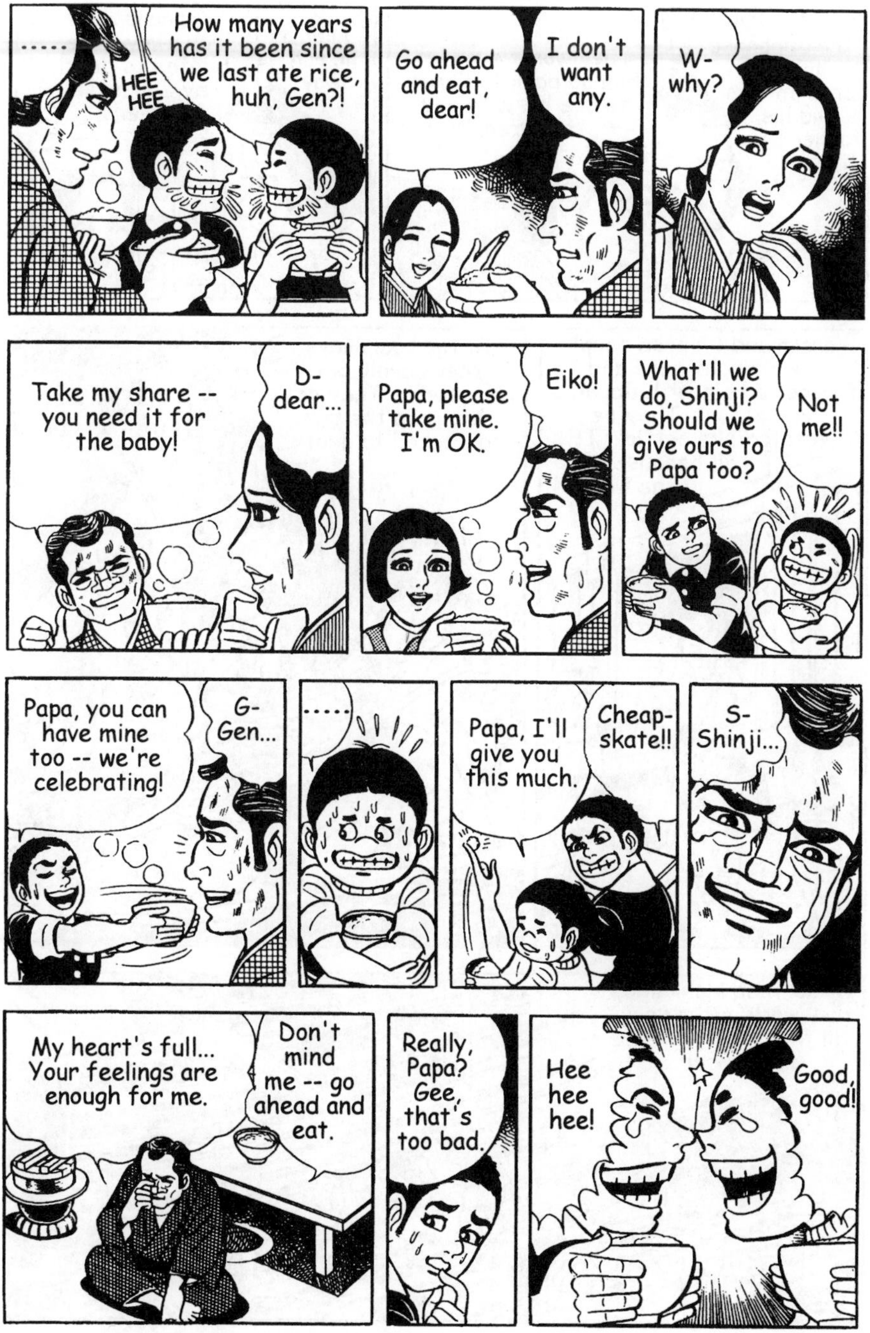

.....
How many years has it been since we last ate rice, huh, Gen?!
HEE HEE
Go ahead and eat, dear!
I don't want any.
W- why?
Take my share -- you need it for the baby!
D- dear...
Papa, please take mine. I'm OK.
Eiko!
What'll we do, Shinji? Should we give ours to Papa too?
Not me!!
Papa, you can have mine too -- we're celebrating!
G- Gen...
.....
Papa, I'll give you this much.
Cheap- skate!!
S- Shinji...
My heart's full... Your feelings are enough for me.
Don't mind me -- go ahead and eat.
Really, Papa? Gee, that's too bad.
Hee hee hee!
Good, good!

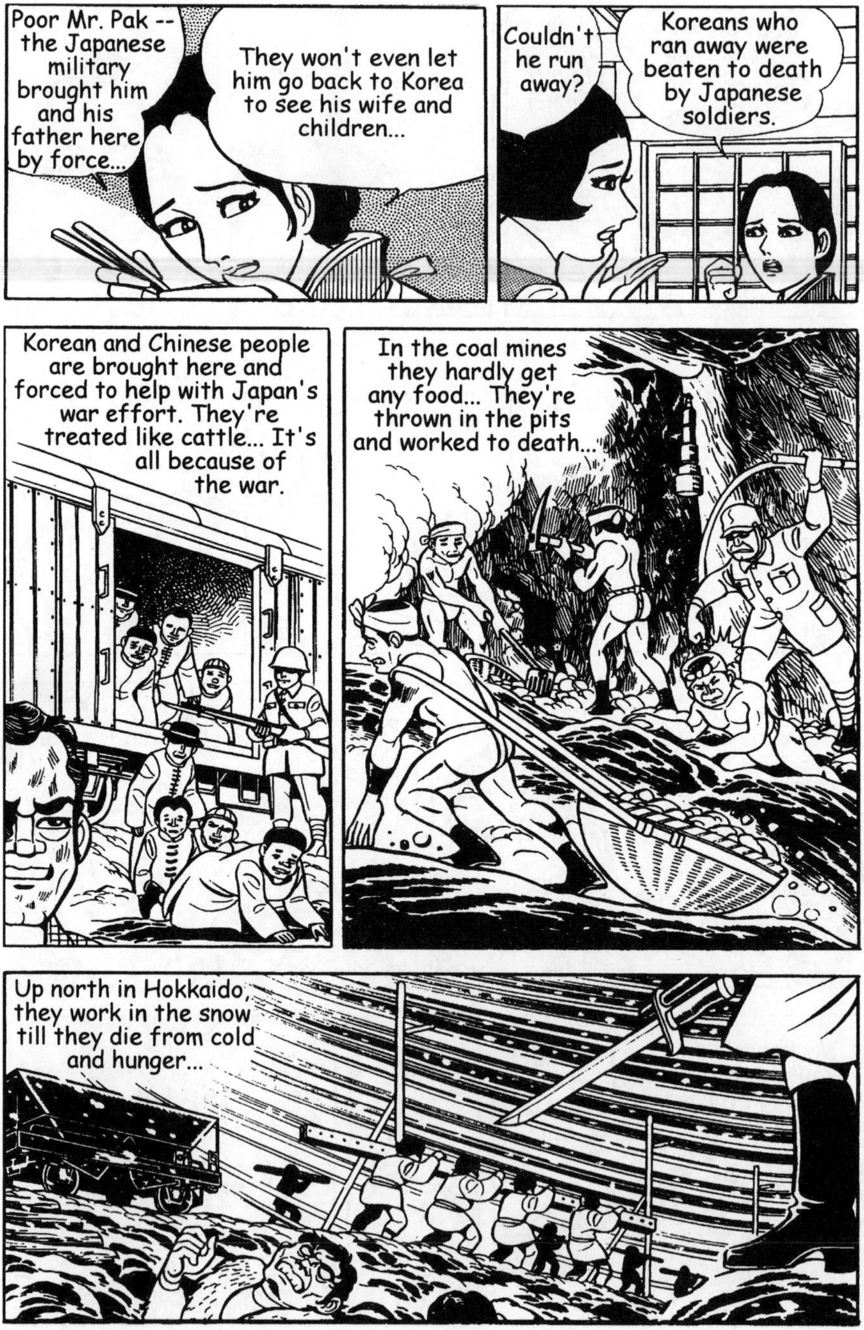
Poor Mr. Pak -- the Japanese military brought him and his father here by force...
They won't even let him go back to Korea to see his wife and children...
Couldn't he run away?
Koreans who ran away were beaten to death by Japanese soldiers.
Korean and Chinese people are brought here and forced to help with Japan's war effort. They're treated like cattle... It's all because of the war.
In the coal mines they hardly get any food... They're thrown in the pits and worked to death...
Up north in Hokkaido, they work in the snow till they die from cold and hunger...

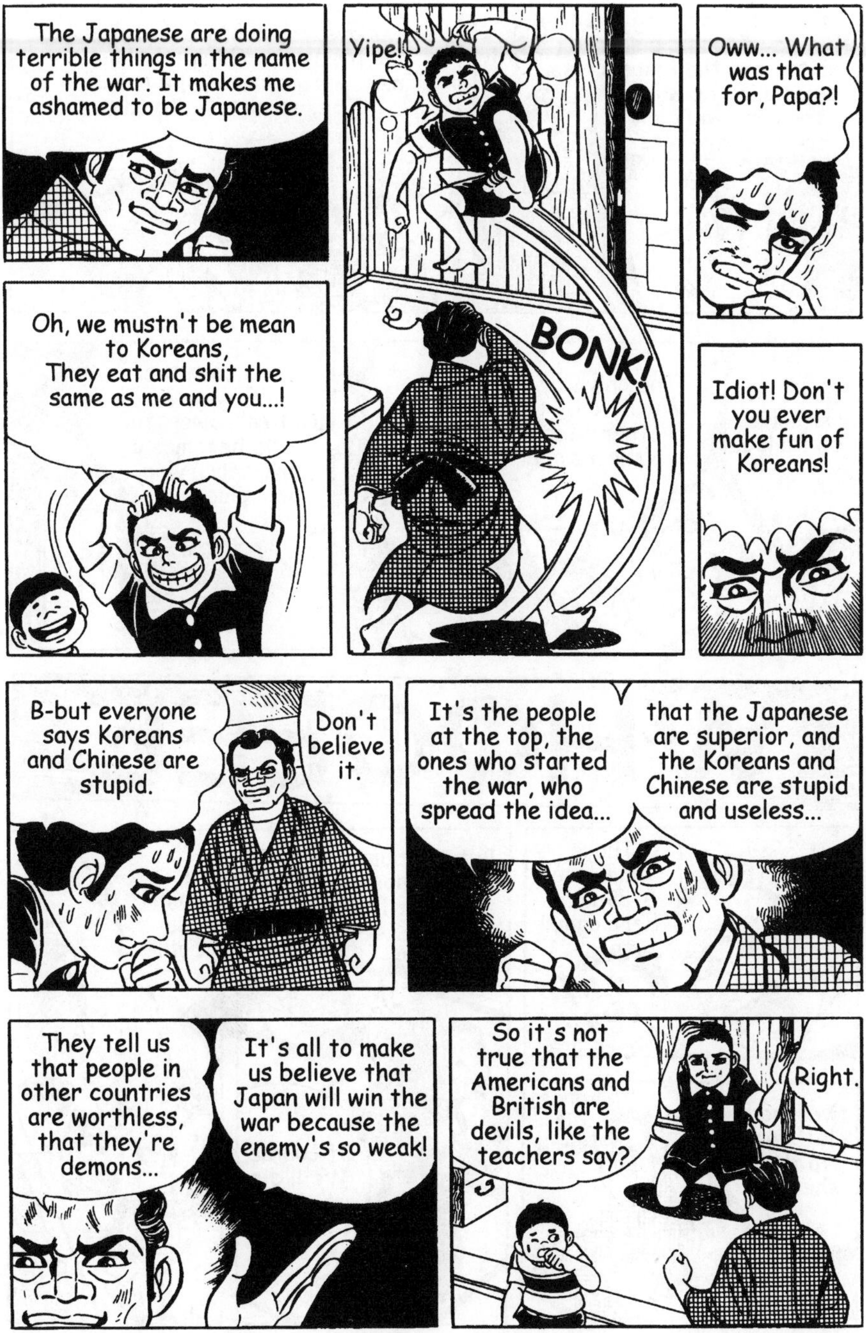
The Japanese are doing terrible things in the name of the war. It makes me ashamed to be Japanese.
Oh, we mustn't be mean to Koreans, They eat and shit the same as me and you...!
Yipe!
BONK!
Oww... What was that for, Papa?!
Idiot! Don't you ever make fun of Koreans!
B-but everyone says Koreans and Chinese are stupid.
Don't believe it.
It's the people at the top, the ones who started the war, who spread the idea...
that the Japanese are superior, and the Koreans and Chinese are stupid and useless...
They tell us that people in other countries are worthless, that they're demons...
It's all to make us believe that Japan will win the war because the enemy's so weak!
So it's not true that the Americans and British are devils, like the teachers say?
Right.

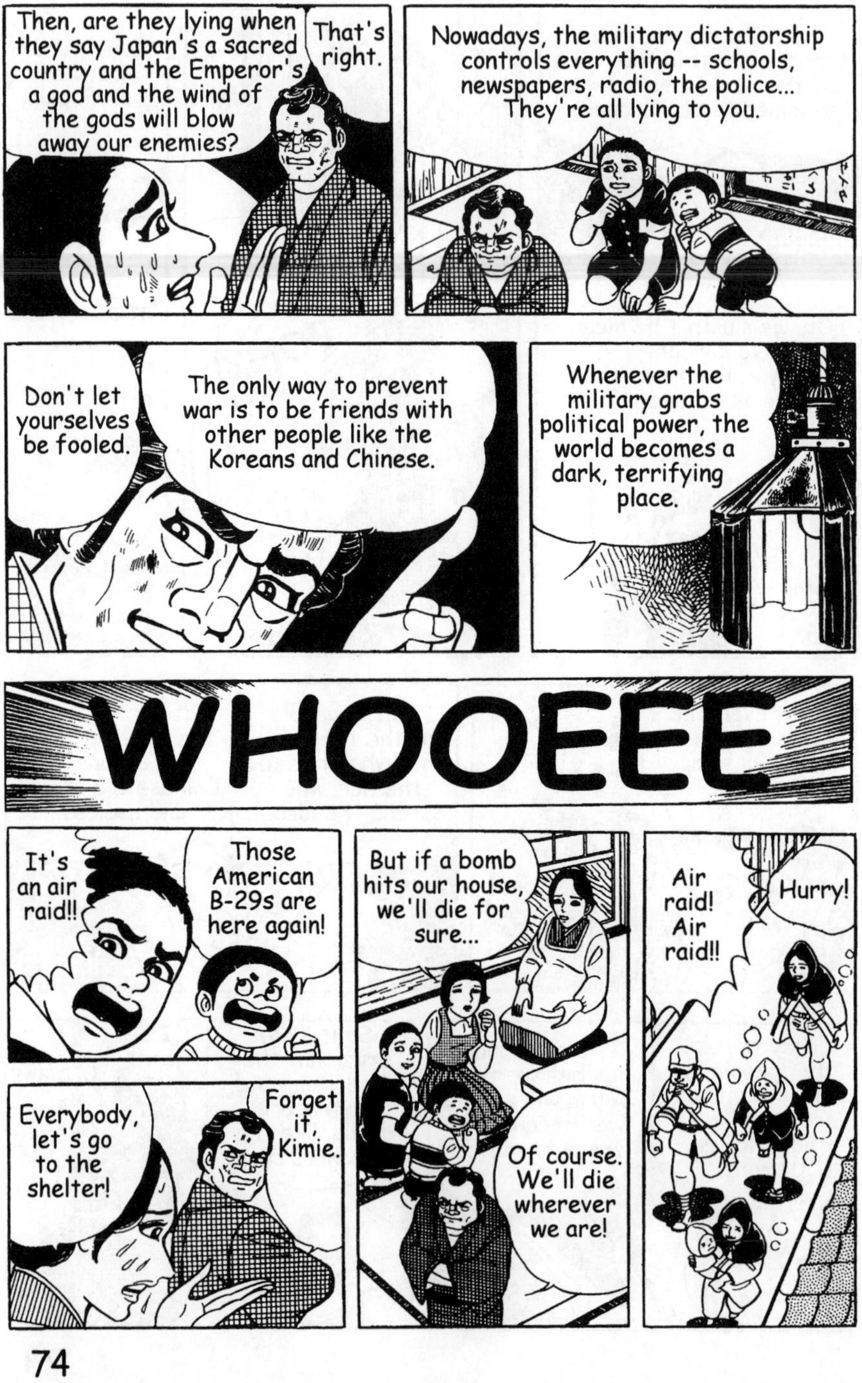

Then, are they lying when they say Japan's a sacred country and the Emperor's a god and the wind of the gods will blow away our enemies?
That's right.
Nowadays, the military dictatorship controls everything -- schools, newspapers, radio, the police... They're all lying to you.
Don't let yourselves be fooled.
The only way to prevent war is to be friends with other people like the Koreans and Chinese.
Whenever the military grabs political power, the world becomes a dark, terrifying place.
WHOOEEE
It's an air raid!!
Those American B-29s are here again!
Everybody, let's go to the shelter!
Forget it, Kimie.
But if a bomb hits our house, we'll die for sure...
Of course. We'll die wherever we are!
Air raid! Air raid!!
Hurry!

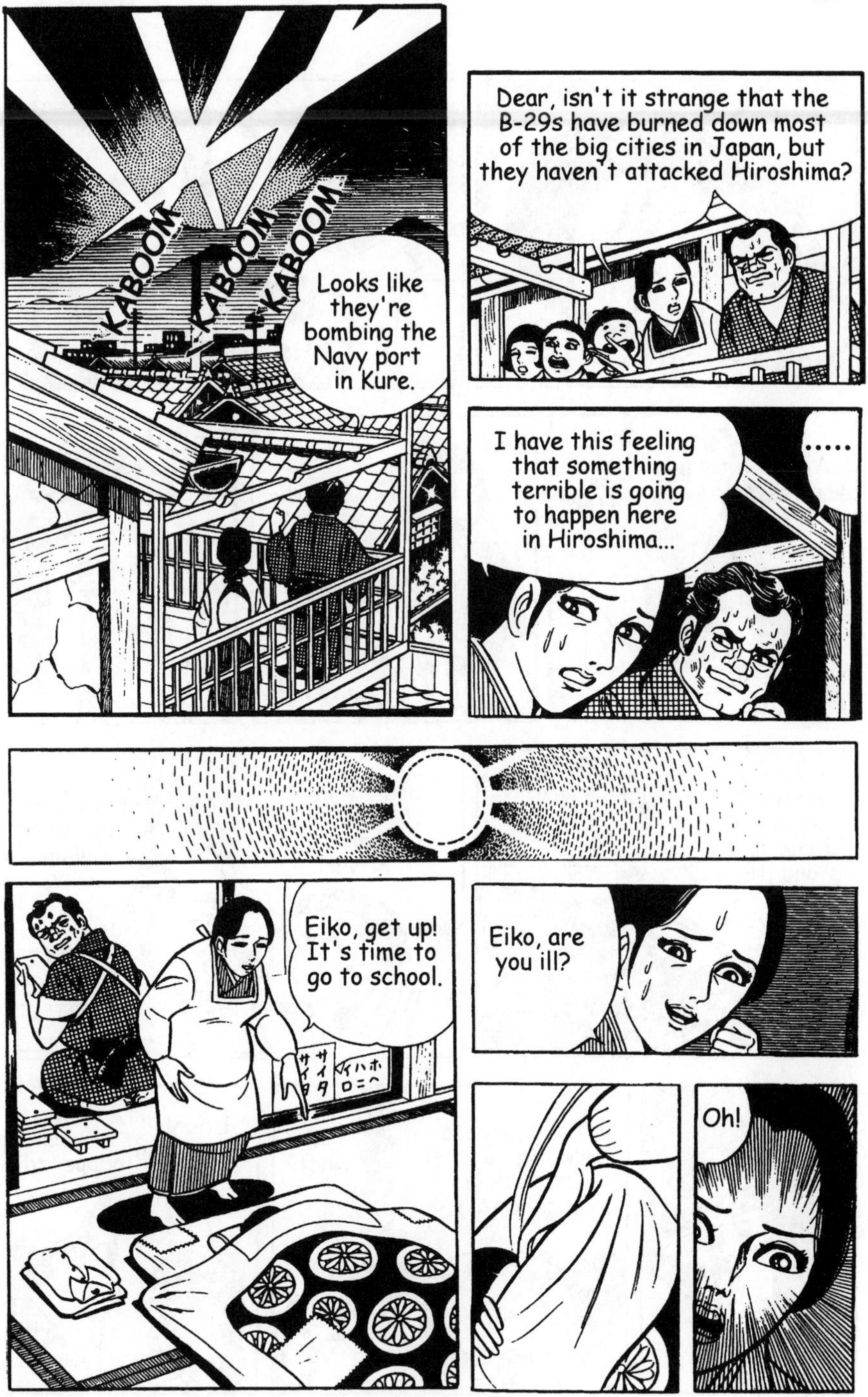
KABOOM
KABOOM
KABOOM
Looks like they're bombing the Navy port in Kure.
Dear, isn't it strange that the B-29s have burned down most of the big cities in Japan, but they haven't attacked Hiroshima?
I have this feeling that something terrible is going to happen here in Hiroshima...
.....
Eiko, get up! It's time to go to school.
サイタ サイタ
イロハニホヘ
Eiko, are you ill?
Oh!

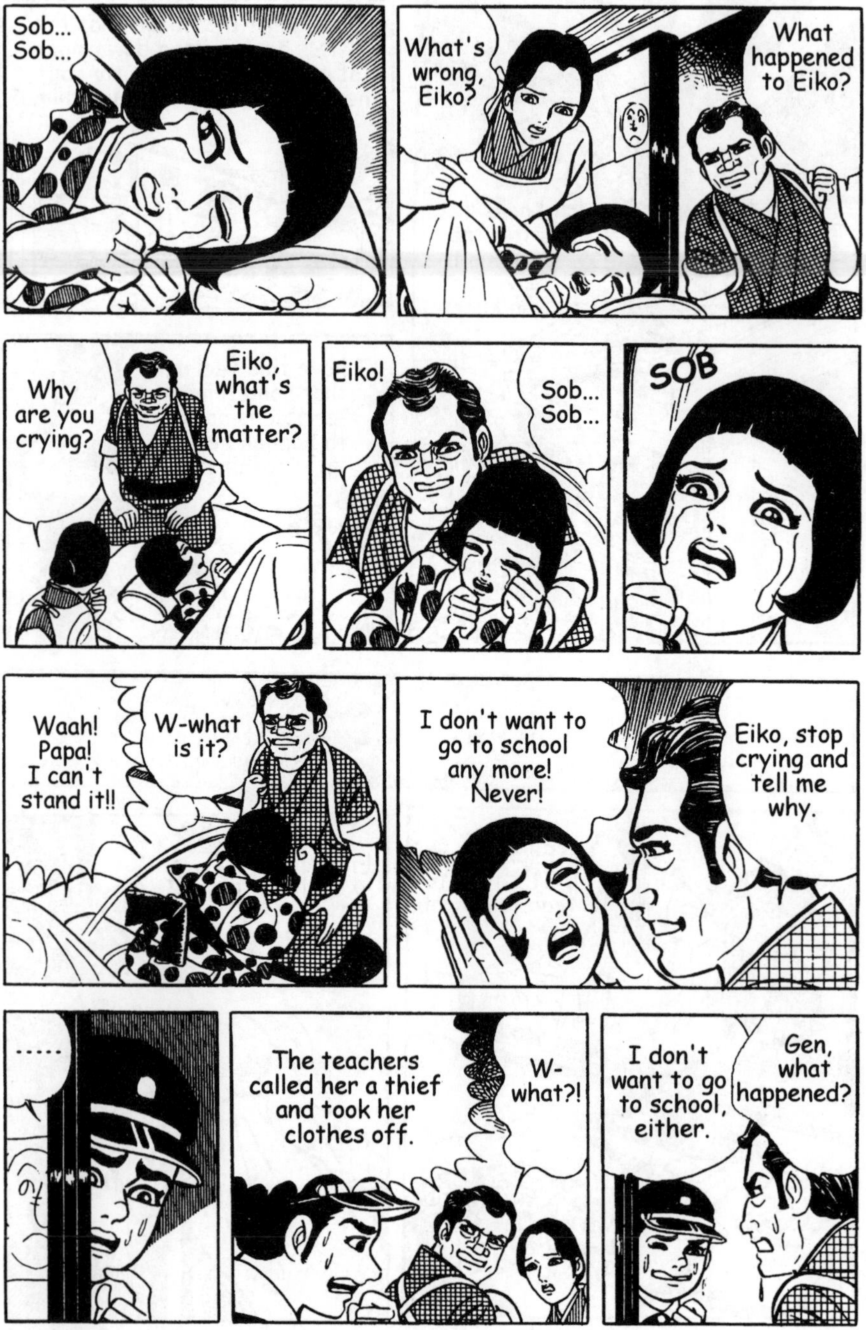
Sob... Sob...
What's wrong, Eiko?
What happened to Eiko?
Why are you crying?
Eiko, what's the matter?
Eiko!
Sob... Sob...
SOB
Waah! Papa! I can't stand it!!
W-what is it?
I don't want to go to school any more! Never!
Eiko, stop crying and tell me why.

The teachers called her a thief and took her clothes off.
W- what?!
I don't want to go to school, either.
Gen, what happened?

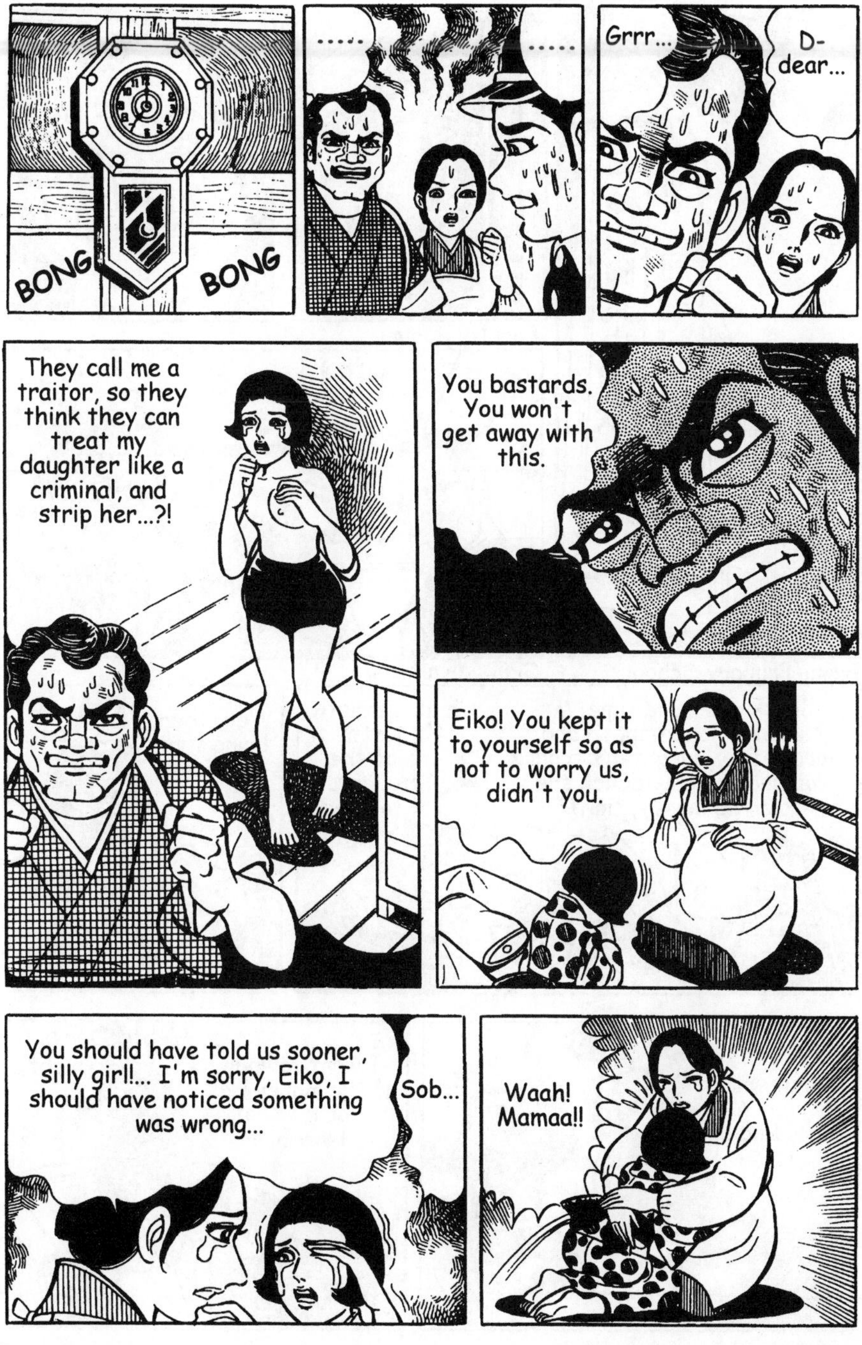
BONG
BONG
.....
.....
Grrr...
D-dear...
They call me a traitor, so they think they can treat my daughter like a criminal, and strip her...?!
You bastards. You won't get away with this.
Eiko! You kept it to yourself so as not to worry us, didn't you.
You should have told us sooner, silly girl!!... I'm sorry, Eiko, I should have noticed something was wrong...
Sob...
Waah! Mamaa!!

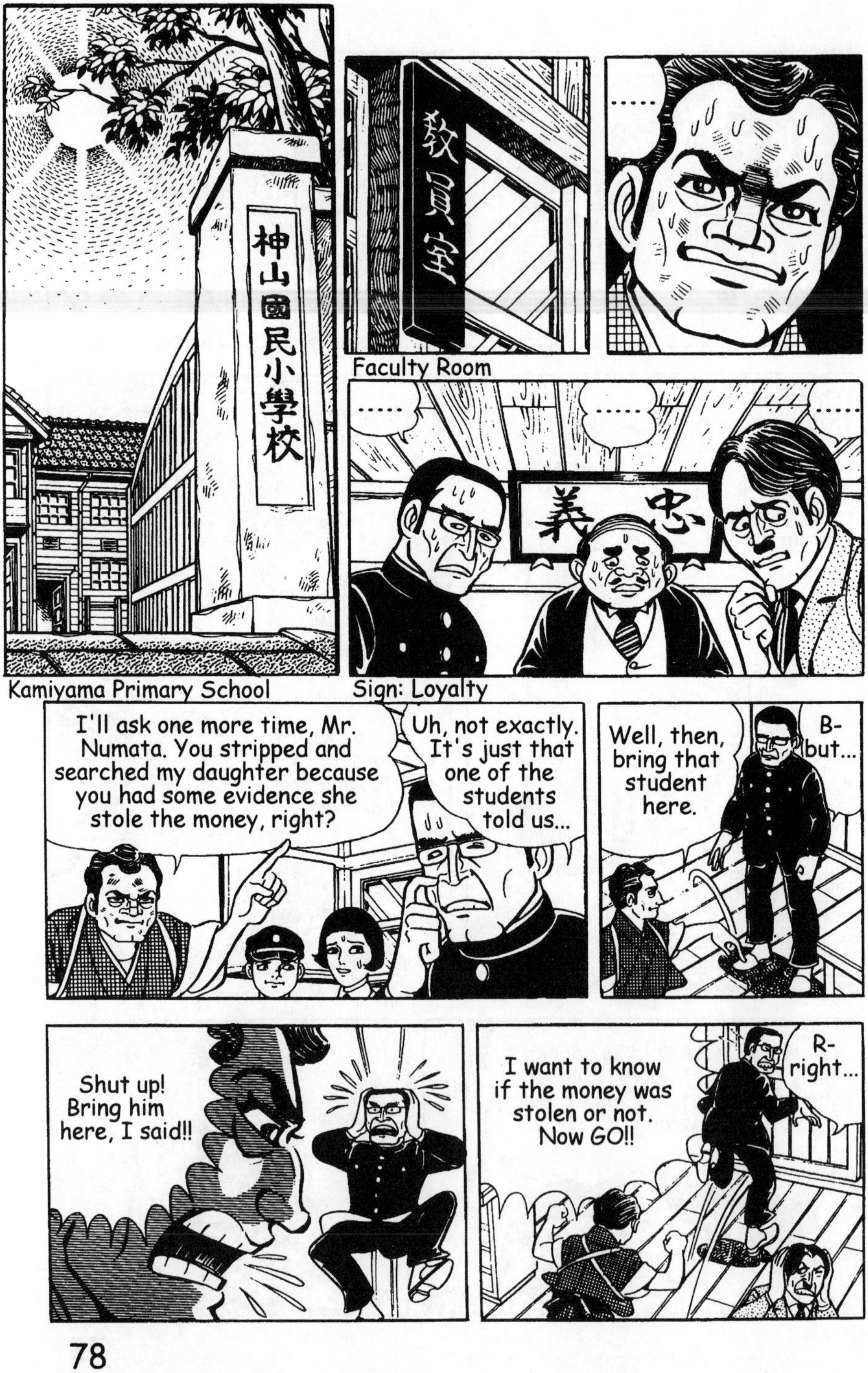

神山國民小學校
Kamiyama Primary School
教員室
Faculty Room
......
......
......
......
忠義
Sign: Loyalty
I'll ask one more time, Mr. Numata. You stripped and searched my daughter because you had some evidence she stole the money, right?
Uh, not exactly. It's just that one of the students told us...
Well, then, bring that student here.
B-but...
Shut up! Bring him here, I said!!
I want to know if the money was stolen or not. Now GO!!
R-right...

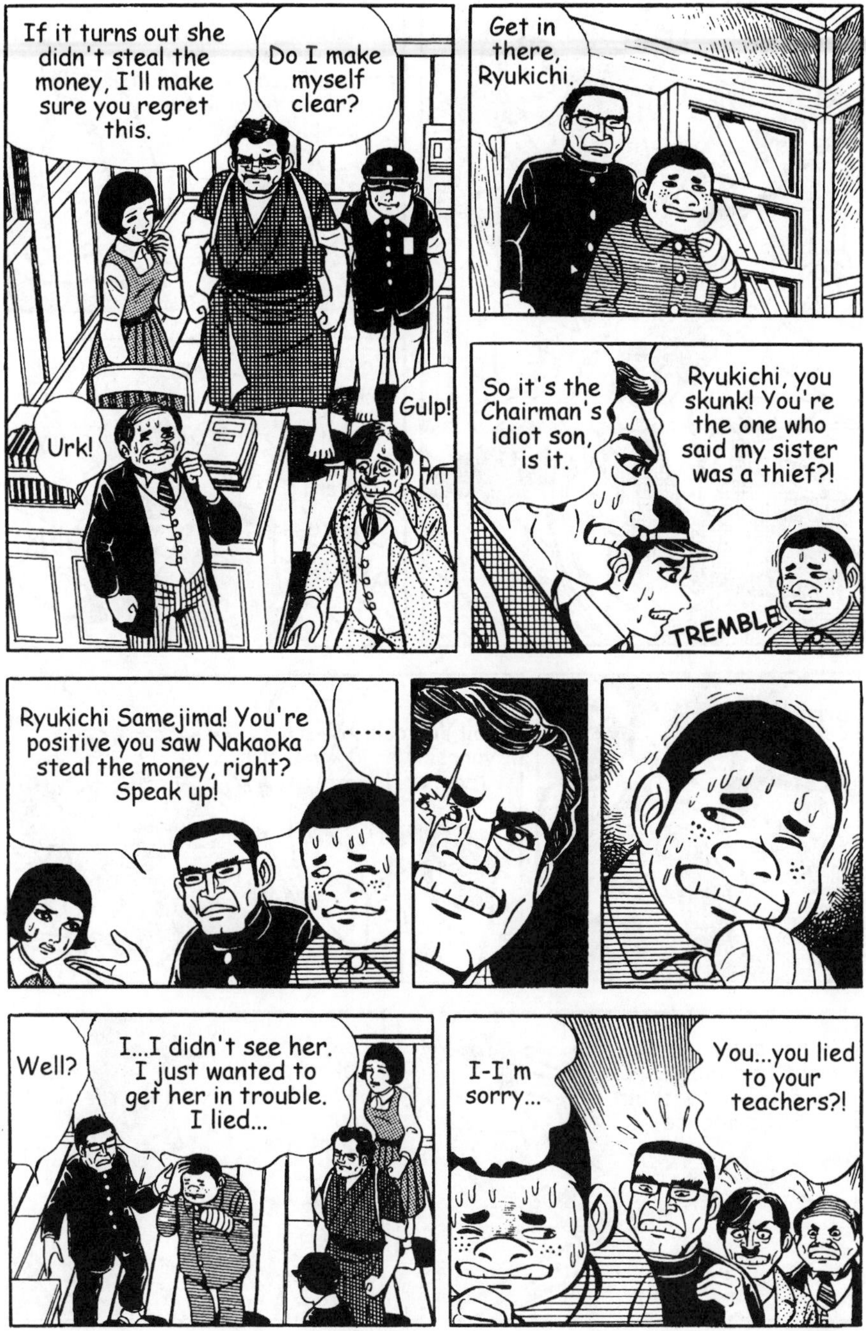

If it turns out she didn't steal the money, I'll make sure you regret this.
Do I make myself clear?
Urk!
Gulp!
Get in there, Ryukichi.
So it's the Chairman's idiot son, is it.
Ryukichi, you skunk! You're the one who said my sister was a thief?!
TREMBLE
Ryukichi Samejima! You're positive you saw Nakaoka steal the money, right? Speak up!
.....
Well?
I...I didn't see her. I just wanted to get her in trouble. I lied...
I-I'm sorry...
You...you lied to your teachers?!

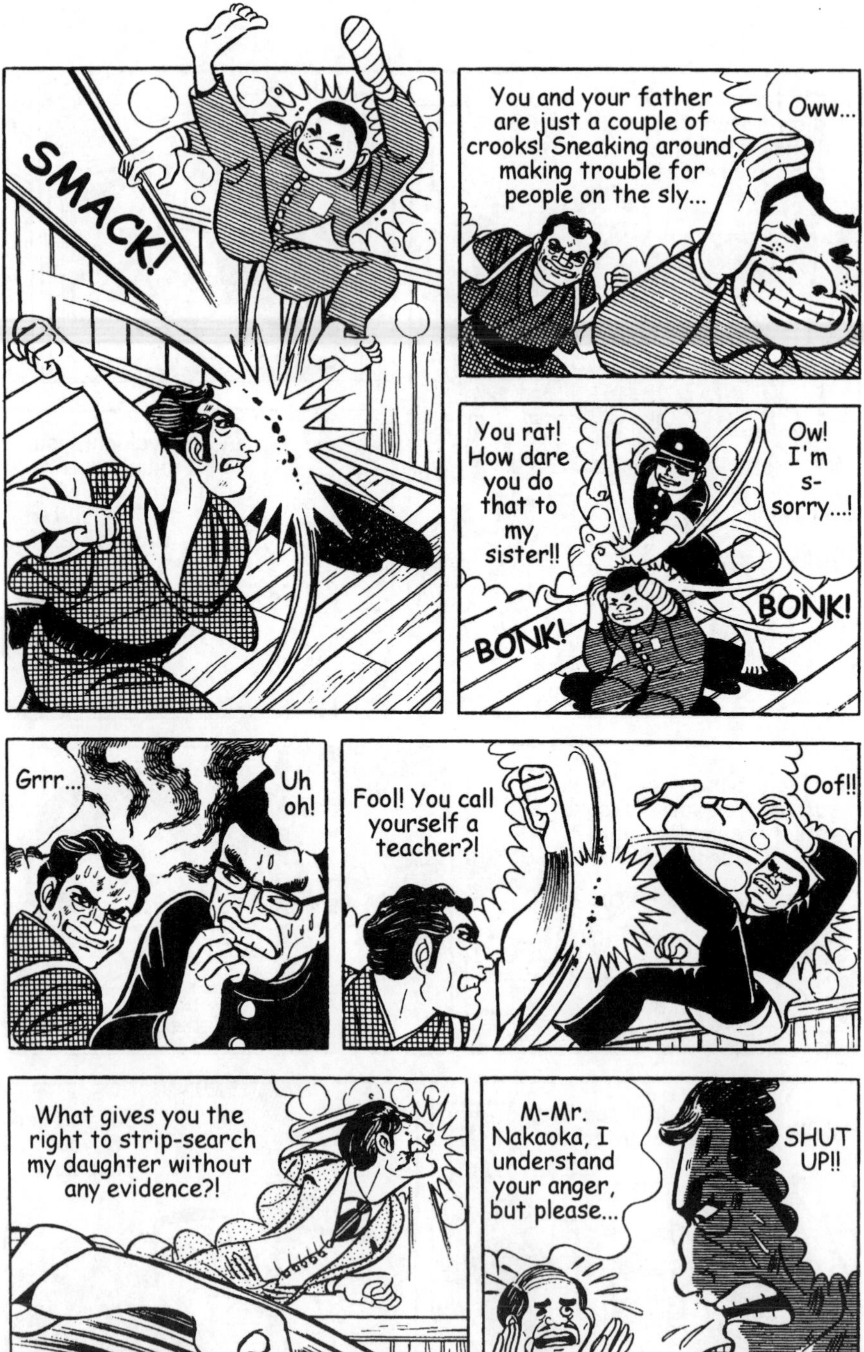
SMACK!
You and your father are just a couple of crooks! Sneaking around, making trouble for people on the sly...
Oww...
You rat! How dare you do that to my sister!!
Ow! I'm s-sorry...!
BONK!
BONK!
Grrr...
Uh oh!
Fool! You call yourself a teacher?!
Oof!!
What gives you the right to strip-search my daughter without any evidence?!
M-Mr. Nakaoka, I understand your anger, but please...
SHUT UP!!

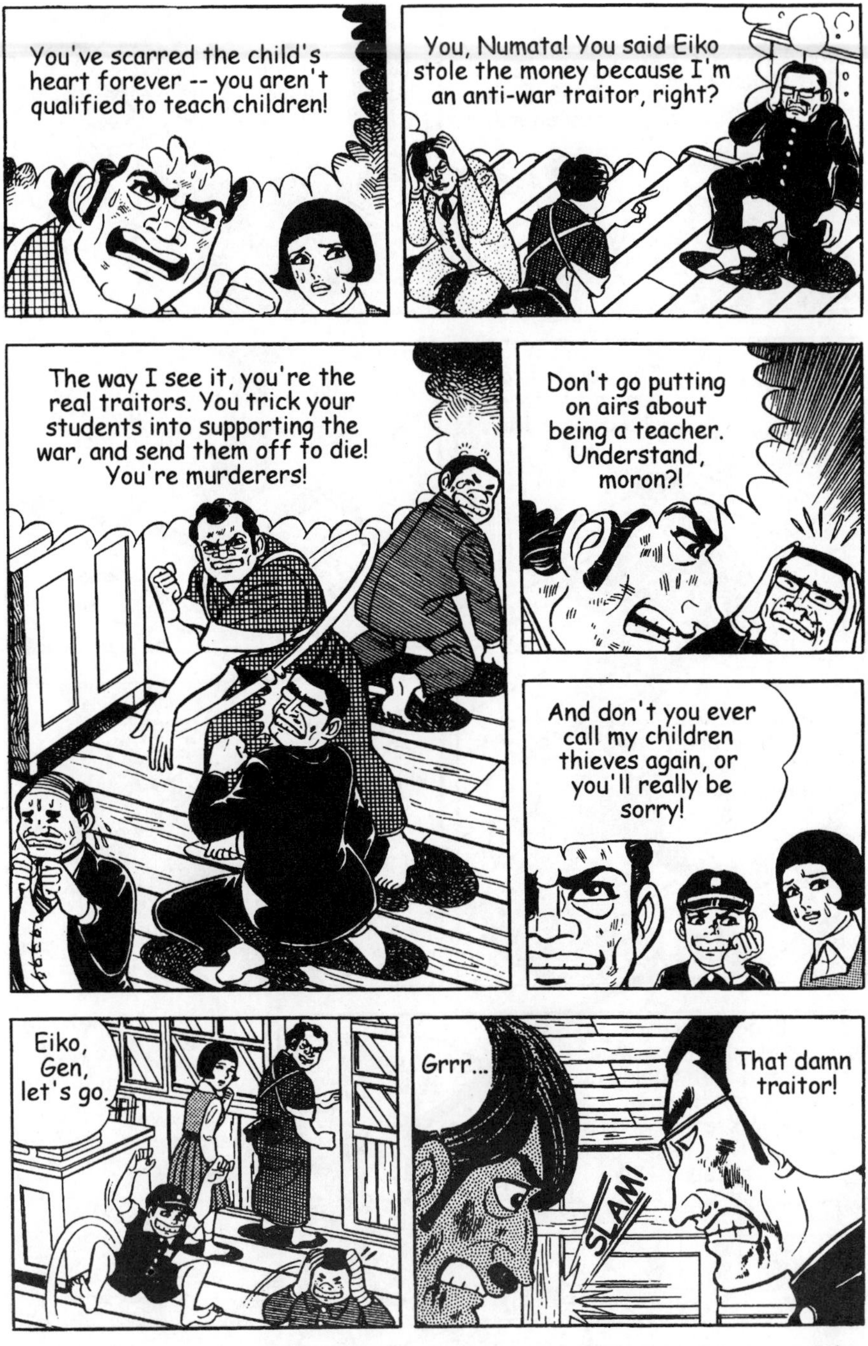
You've scarred the child's heart forever -- you aren't qualified to teach children!
You, Numata! You said Eiko stole the money because I'm an anti-war traitor, right?
The way I see it, you're the real traitors. You trick your students into supporting the war, and send them off to die! You're murderers!
Don't go putting on airs about being a teacher. Understand, moron?!
And don't you ever call my children thieves again, or you'll really be sorry!
Eiko, Gen, let's go.
Grrr...
SLAM!
That damn traitor!

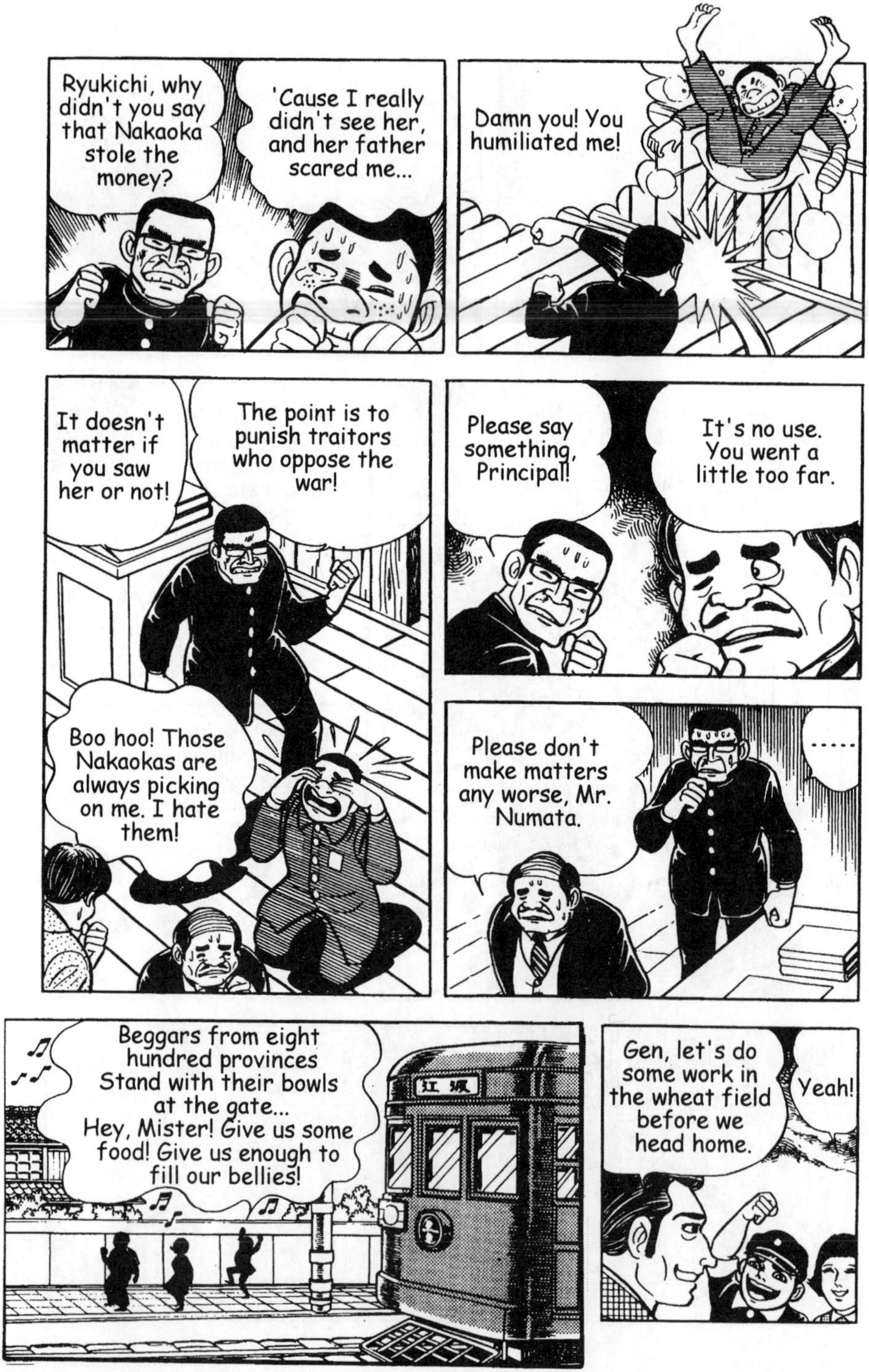
Ryukichi, why didn't you say that Nakaoka stole the money?
'Cause I really didn't see her, and her father scared me...
Damn you! You humiliated me!
It doesn't matter if you saw her or not!
The point is to punish traitors who oppose the war!
Boo hoo! Those Nakaokas are always picking on me. I hate them!
Please say something, Principal!
It's no use. You went a little too far.
Please don't make matters any worse, Mr. Numata.

Beggars from eight hundred provinces Stand with their bowls at the gate... Hey, Mister! Give us some food! Give us enough to fill our bellies!
Gen, let's do some work in the wheat field before we head home.
Yeah!

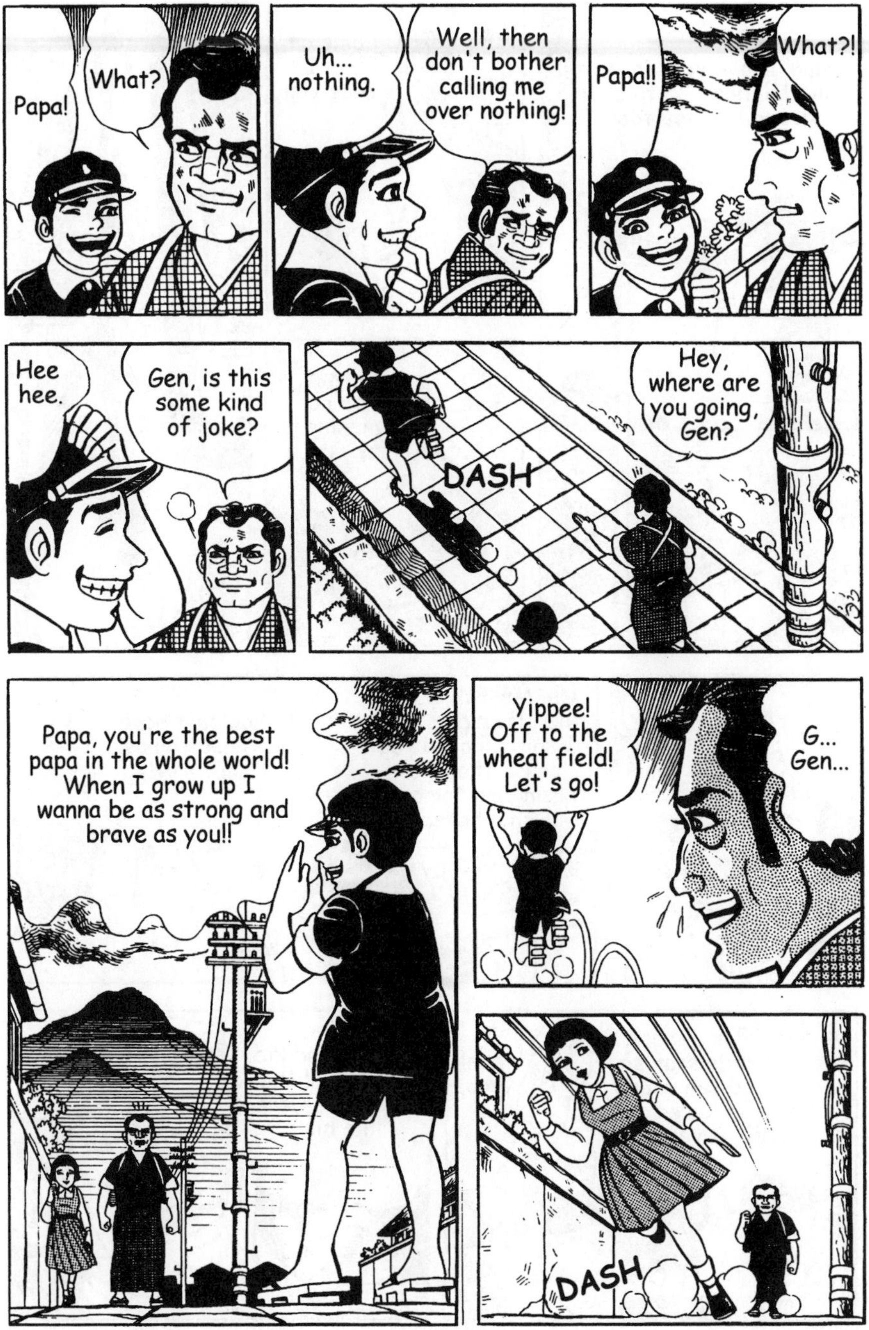

Papa!
What?
Uh... nothing.
Well, then don't bother calling me over nothing!
Papa!!
What?!
Hee hee.
Gen, is this some kind of joke?
DASH
Hey, where are you going, Gen?
Papa, you're the best papa in the whole world! When I grow up I wanna be as strong and brave as you!!
Yippee! Off to the wheat field! Let's go!
G... Gen...
DASH

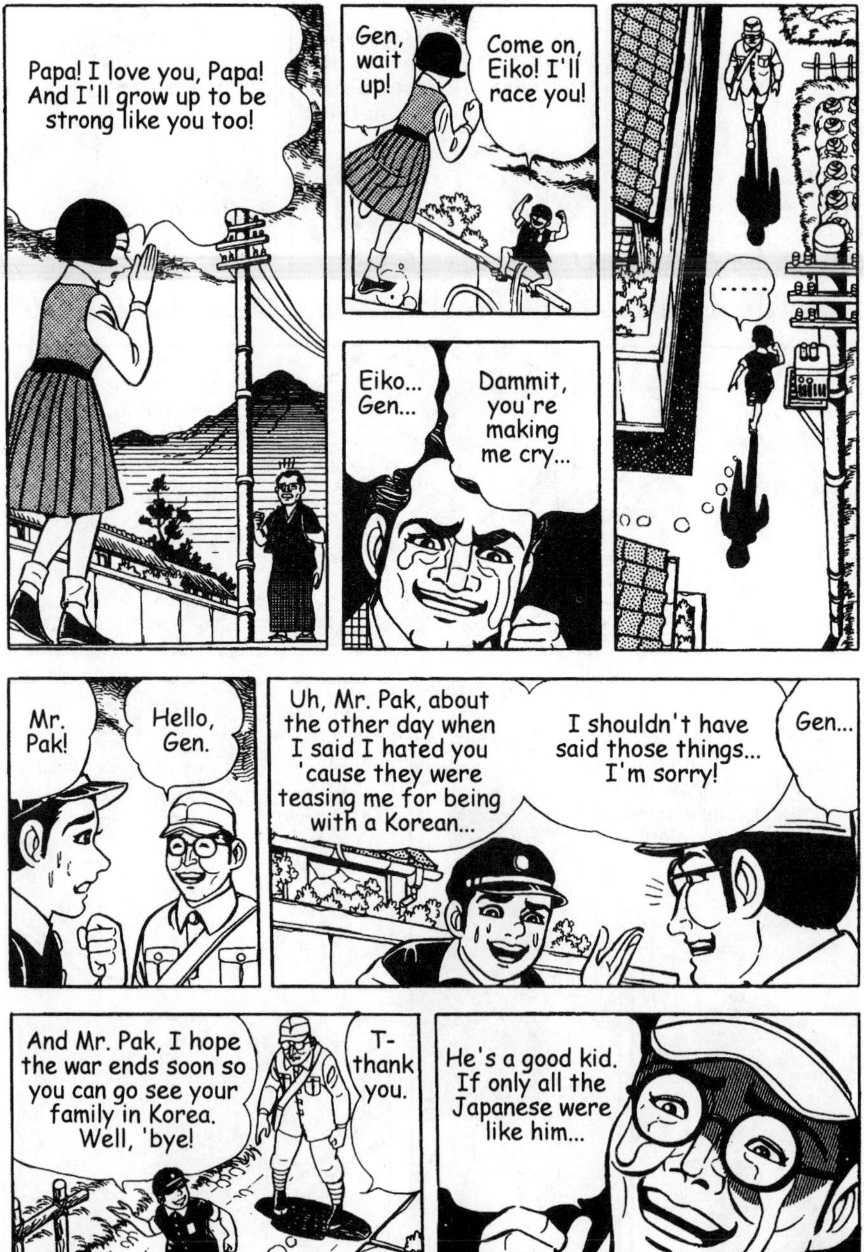
Papa! I love you, Papa! And I'll grow up to be strong like you too!
Gen, wait up!
Come on, Eiko! I'll race you!
Eiko... Gen...
Dammit, you're making me cry...
......
Mr. Pak!
Hello, Gen.
Uh, Mr. Pak, about the other day when I said I hated you 'cause they were teasing me for being with a Korean...
I shouldn't have said those things... I'm sorry!
Gen...
And Mr. Pak, I hope the war ends soon so you can go see your family in Korea. Well, 'bye!
T-thank you.
He's a good kid. If only all the Japanese were like him...

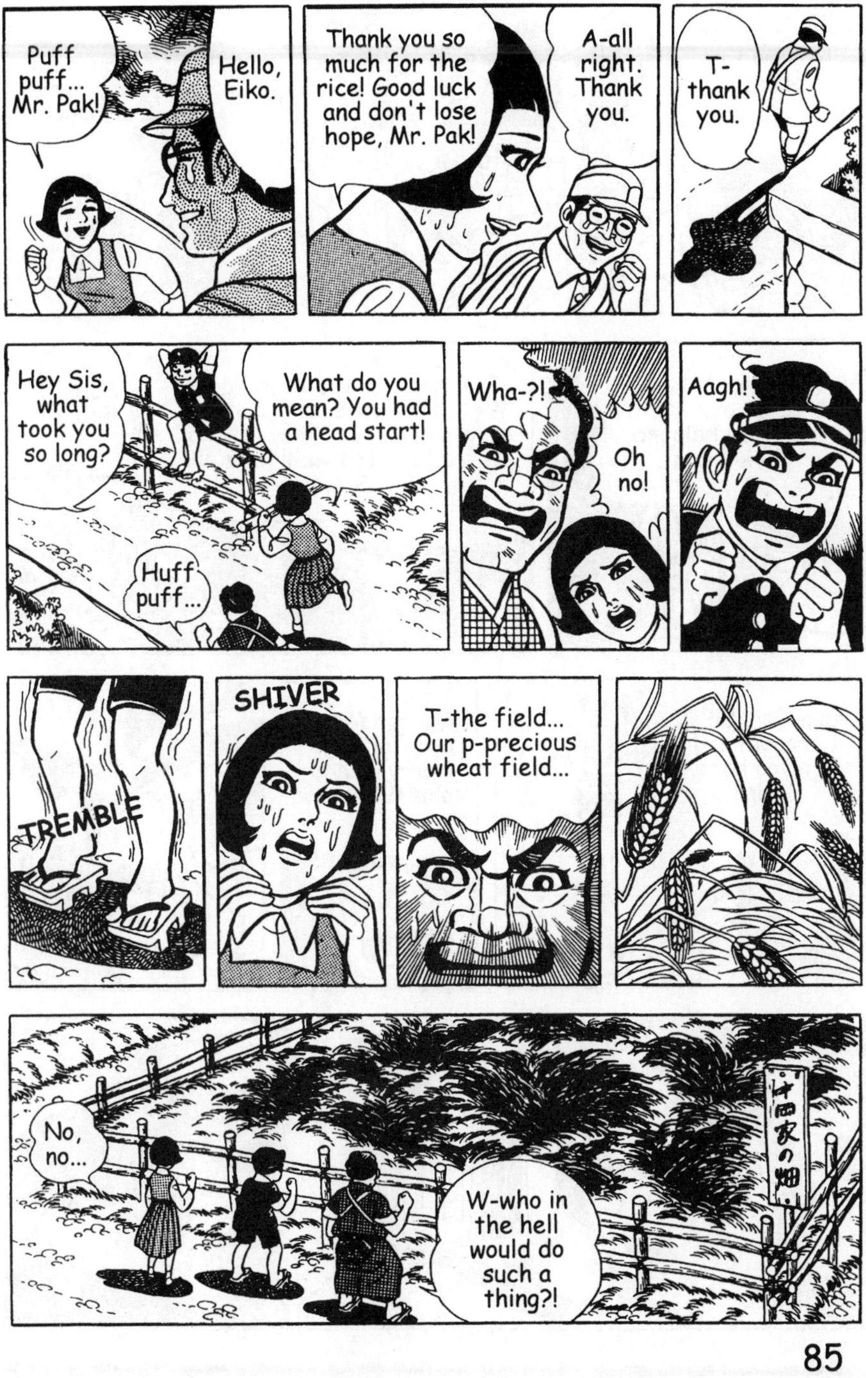
Puff puff... Mr. Pak!
Hello, Eiko.
Thank you so much for the rice! Good luck and don't lose hope, Mr. Pak!
A-all right. Thank you.
T- thank you.
Hey Sis, what took you so long?
What do you mean? You had a head start!
Huff puff...
Wha-?!
Oh no!
Aagh!
TREMBLE
SHIVER
T-the field... Our p-precious wheat field...
No, no...
中岡家の畑
W-who in the hell would do such a thing?!

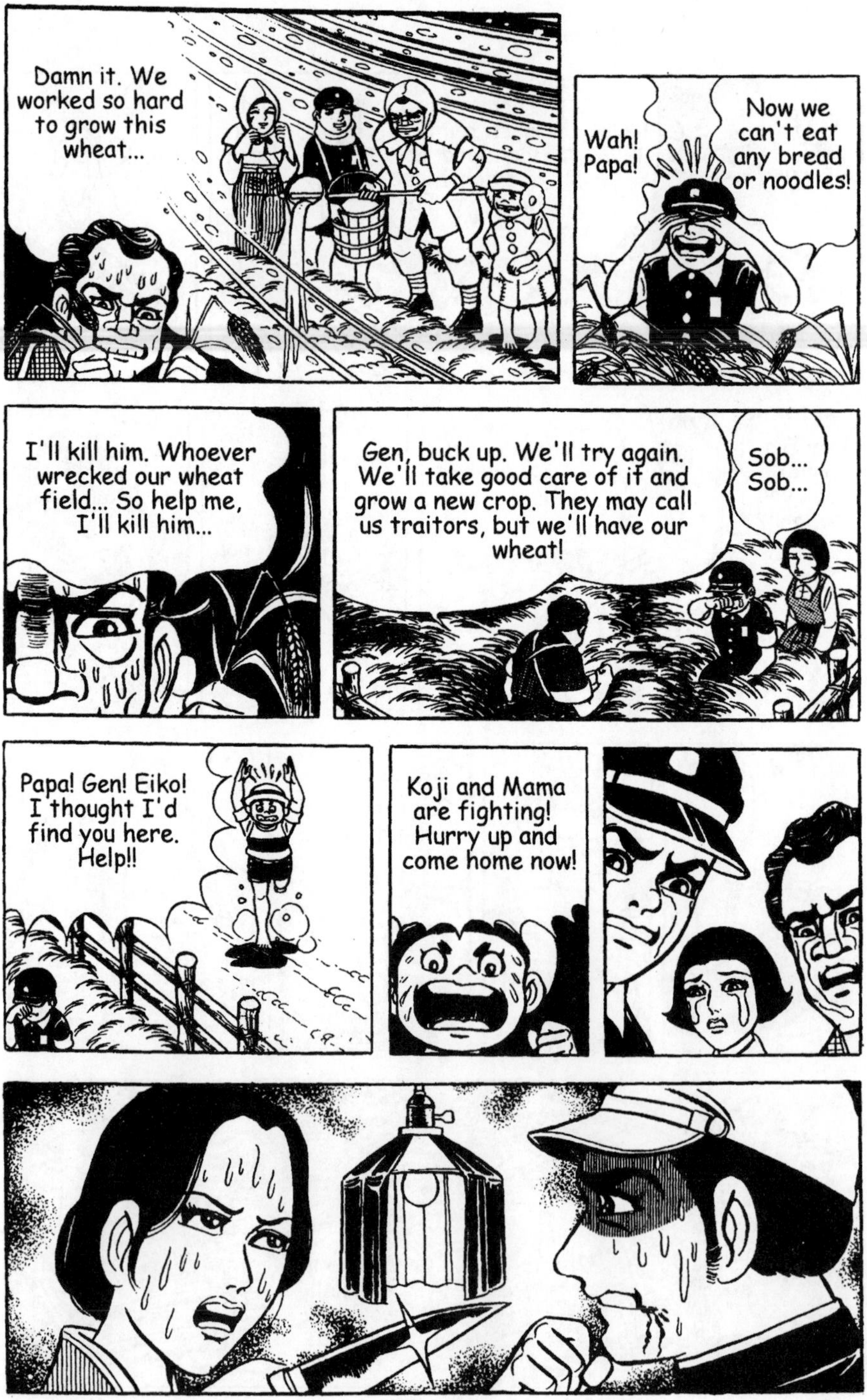

Damn it. We worked so hard to grow this wheat...
Wah! Papa!
Now we can't eat any bread or noodles!
I'll kill him. Whoever wrecked our wheat field... So help me, I'll kill him...
Gen, buck up. We'll try again. We'll take good care of it and grow a new crop. They may call us traitors, but we'll have our wheat!
Sob... Sob...
Papa! Gen! Eiko! I thought I'd find you here. Help!!
Koji and Mama are fighting! Hurry up and come home now!

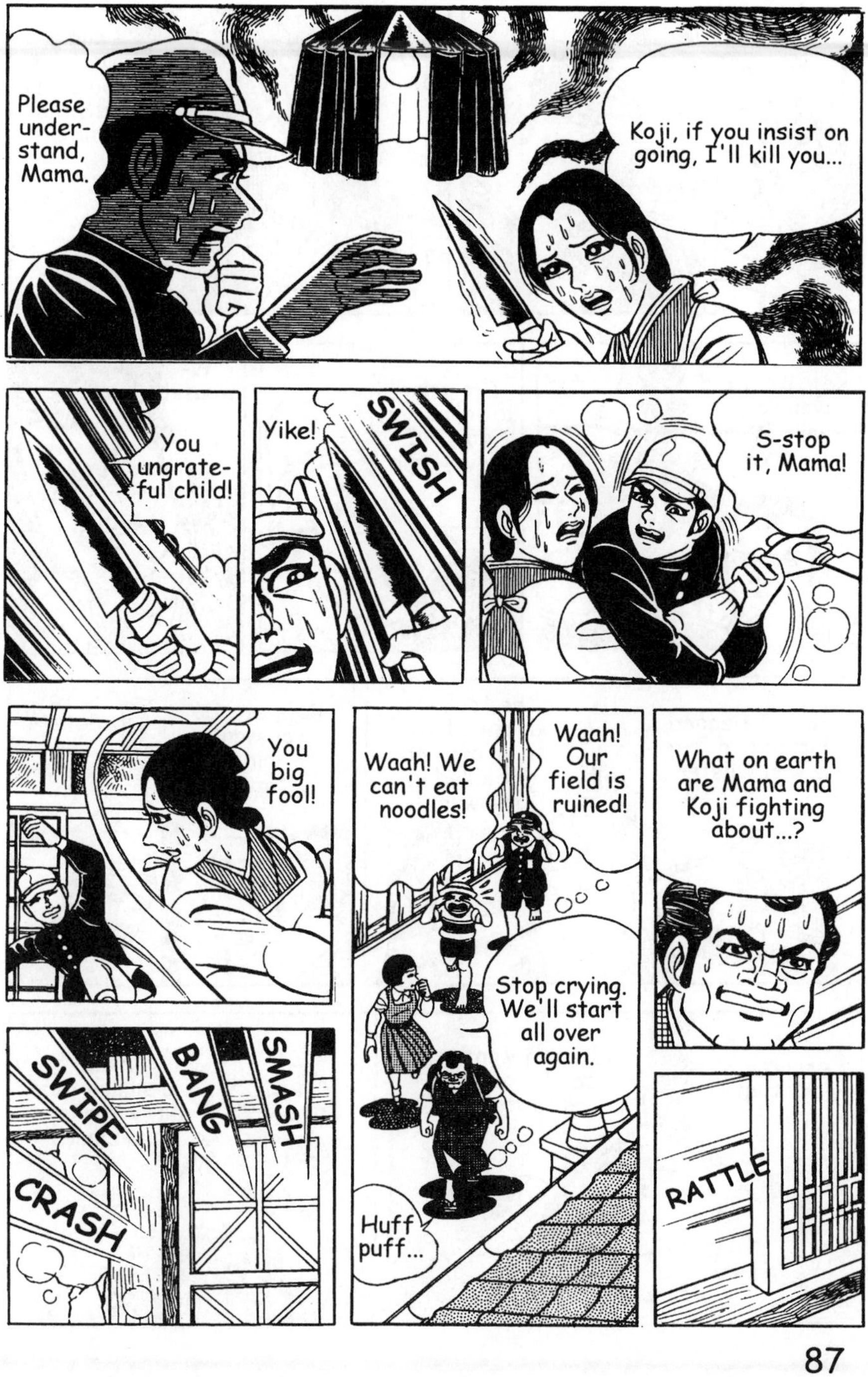
Please understand, Mama.
Koji, if you insist on going, I'll kill you...
You ungrateful child!
Yike!
SWISH
S-stop it, Mama!
You big fool!
Waah! We can't eat noodles!
Waah! Our field is ruined!
Stop crying. We'll start all over again.
Huff puff...
What on earth are Mama and Koji fighting about...?
SWIPE
BANG
SMASH
CRASH
RATTLE

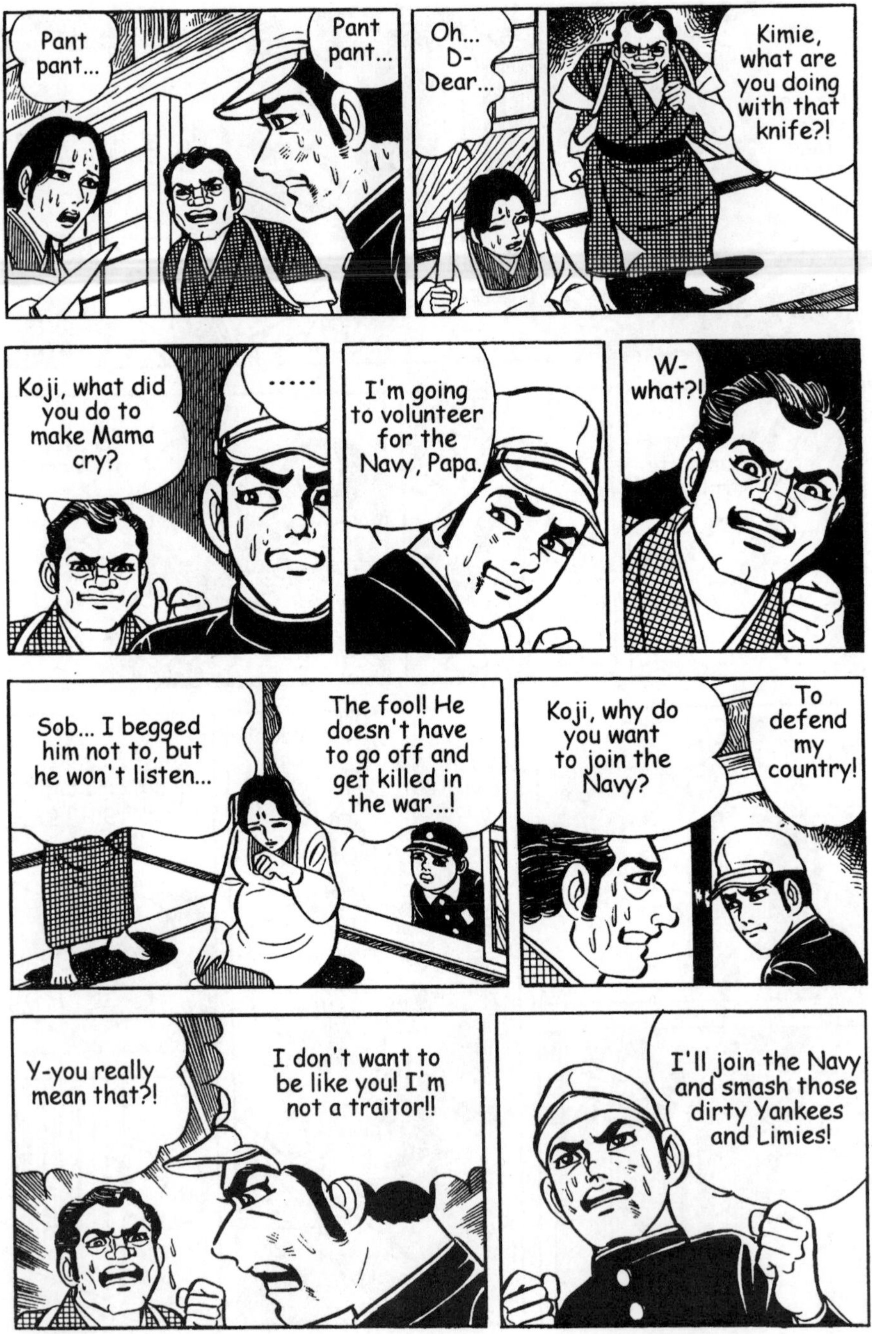
Pant pant...
Pant pant...
Oh... D-Dear...
Kimie, what are you doing with that knife?!
Koji, what did you do to make Mama cry?
.....
I'm going to volunteer for the Navy, Papa.
W-what?!
Sob... I begged him not to, but he won't listen...
The fool! He doesn't have to go off and get killed in the war...!
Koji, why do you want to join the Navy?
To defend my country!
Y-you really mean that?!
I don't want to be like you! I'm not a traitor!!
I'll join the Navy and smash those dirty Yankees and Limies!

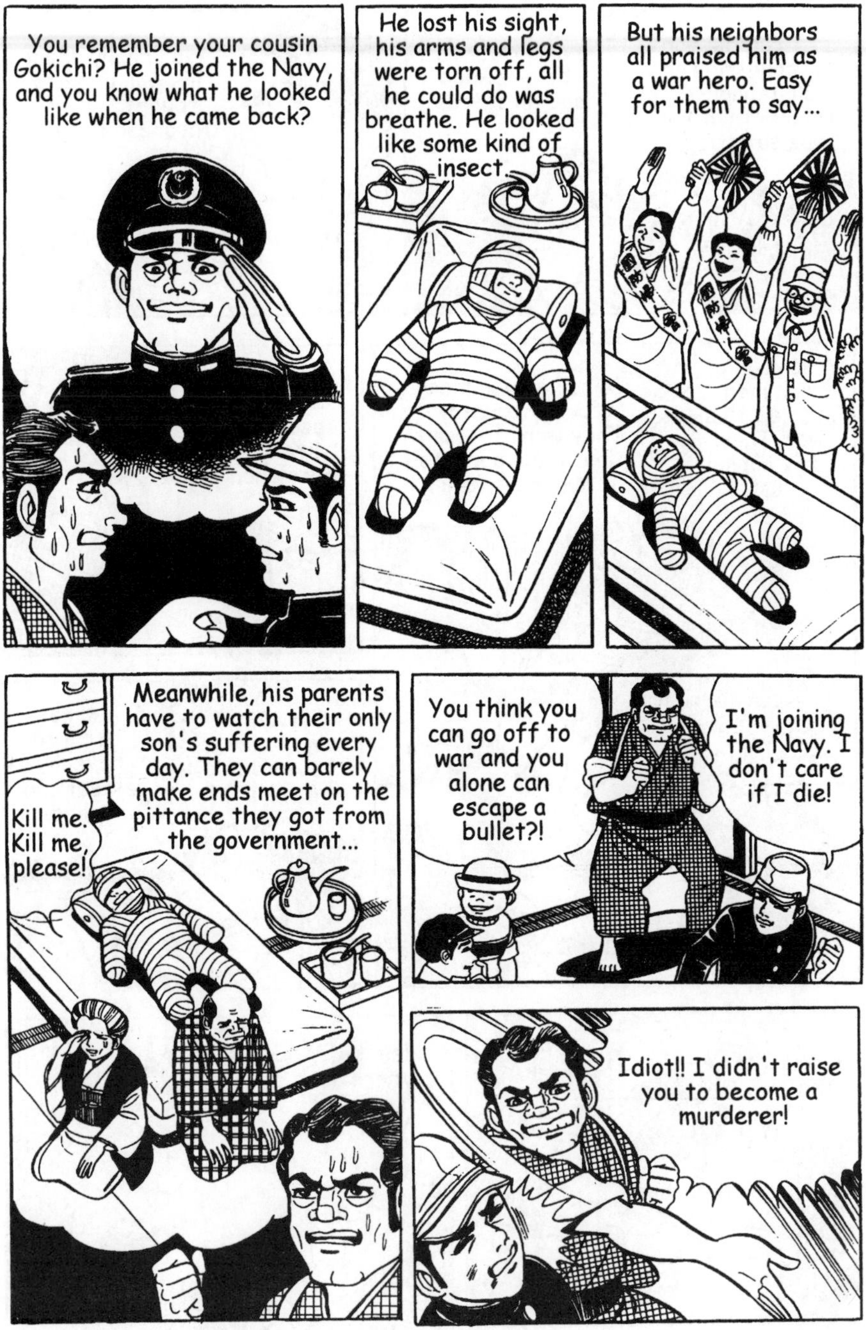
You remember your cousin Gokichi? He joined the Navy, and you know what he looked like when he came back?
He lost his sight, his arms and legs were torn off, all he could do was breathe. He looked like some kind of insect.
But his neighbors all praised him as a war hero. Easy for them to say...
Meanwhile, his parents have to watch their only son's suffering every day. They can barely make ends meet on the pittance they got from the government...
Kill me. Kill me, please!
You think you can go off to war and you alone can escape a bullet?!
I'm joining the Navy. I don't care if I die!
Idiot!! I didn't raise you to become a murderer!

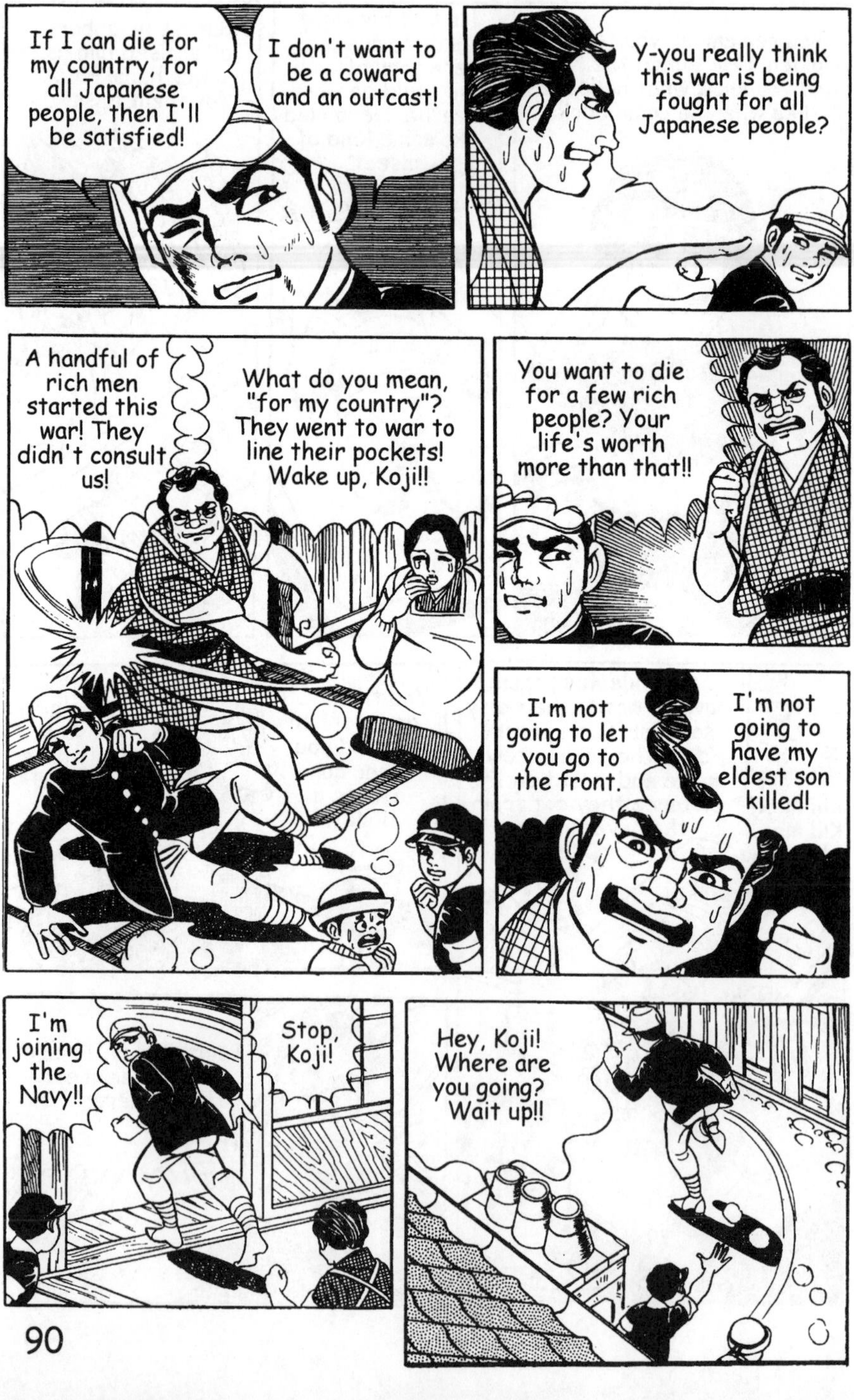
If I can die for my country, for all Japanese people, then I'll be satisfied!
I don't want to be a coward and an outcast!
Y-you really think this war is being fought for all Japanese people?
A handful of rich men started this war! They didn't consult us!
What do you mean, "for my country"? They went to war to line their pockets! Wake up, Koji!!
You want to die for a few rich people? Your life's worth more than that!!
I'm not going to let you go to the front.
I'm not going to have my eldest son killed!
I'm joining the Navy!!
Stop, Koji!
Hey, Koji! Where are you going? Wait up!!

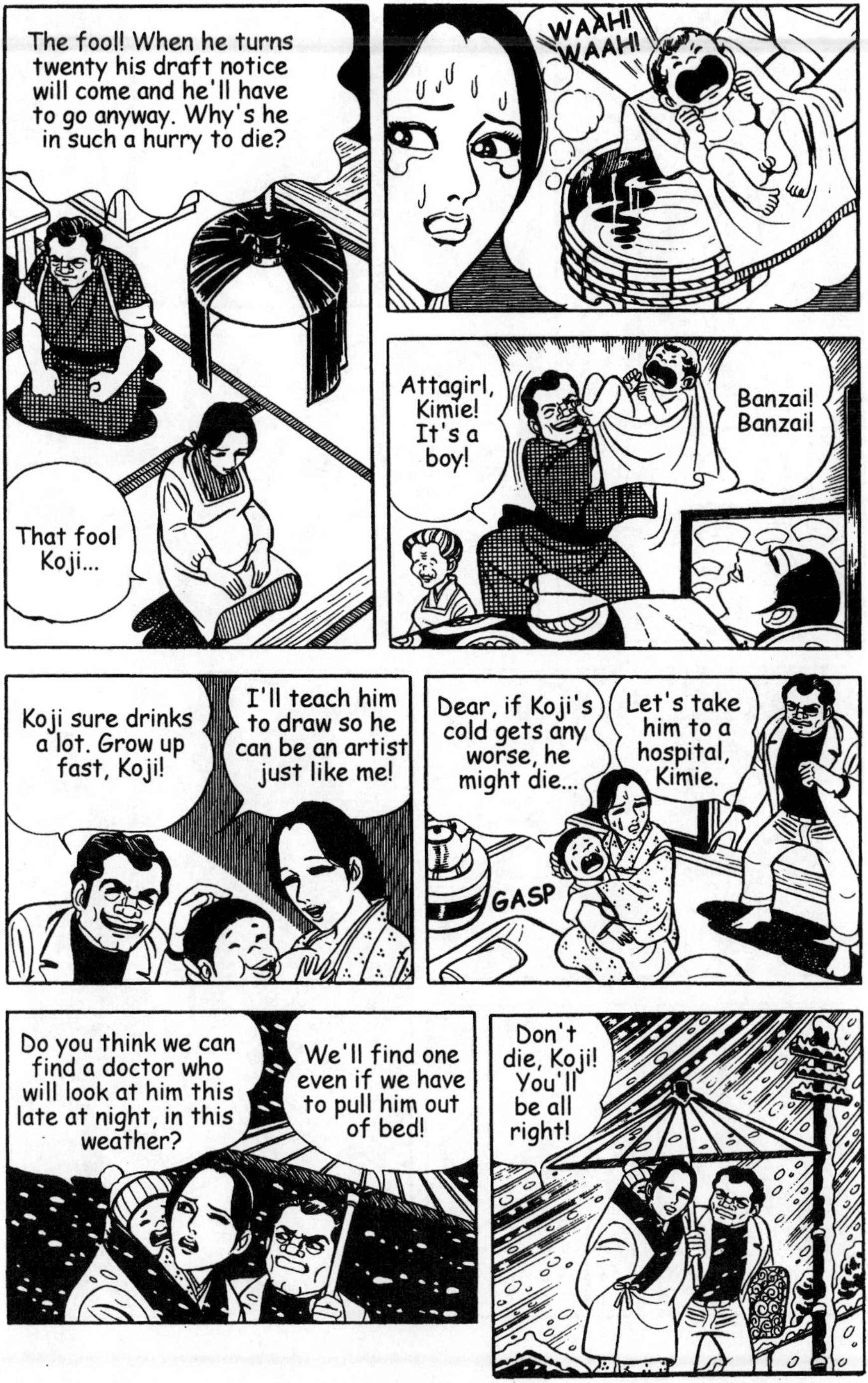
The fool! When he turns twenty his draft notice will come and he'll have to go anyway. Why's he in such a hurry to die?
That fool Koji...
WAAH! WAAH!
Attagirl, Kimie! It's a boy!
Banzai! Banzai!
Koji sure drinks a lot. Grow up fast, Koji!
I'll teach him to draw so he can be an artist just like me!
Dear, if Koji's cold gets any worse, he might die...
Let's take him to a hospital, Kimie.
GASP
Do you think we can find a doctor who will look at him this late at night, in this weather?
We'll find one even if we have to pull him out of bed!
Don't die, Koji! You'll be all right!

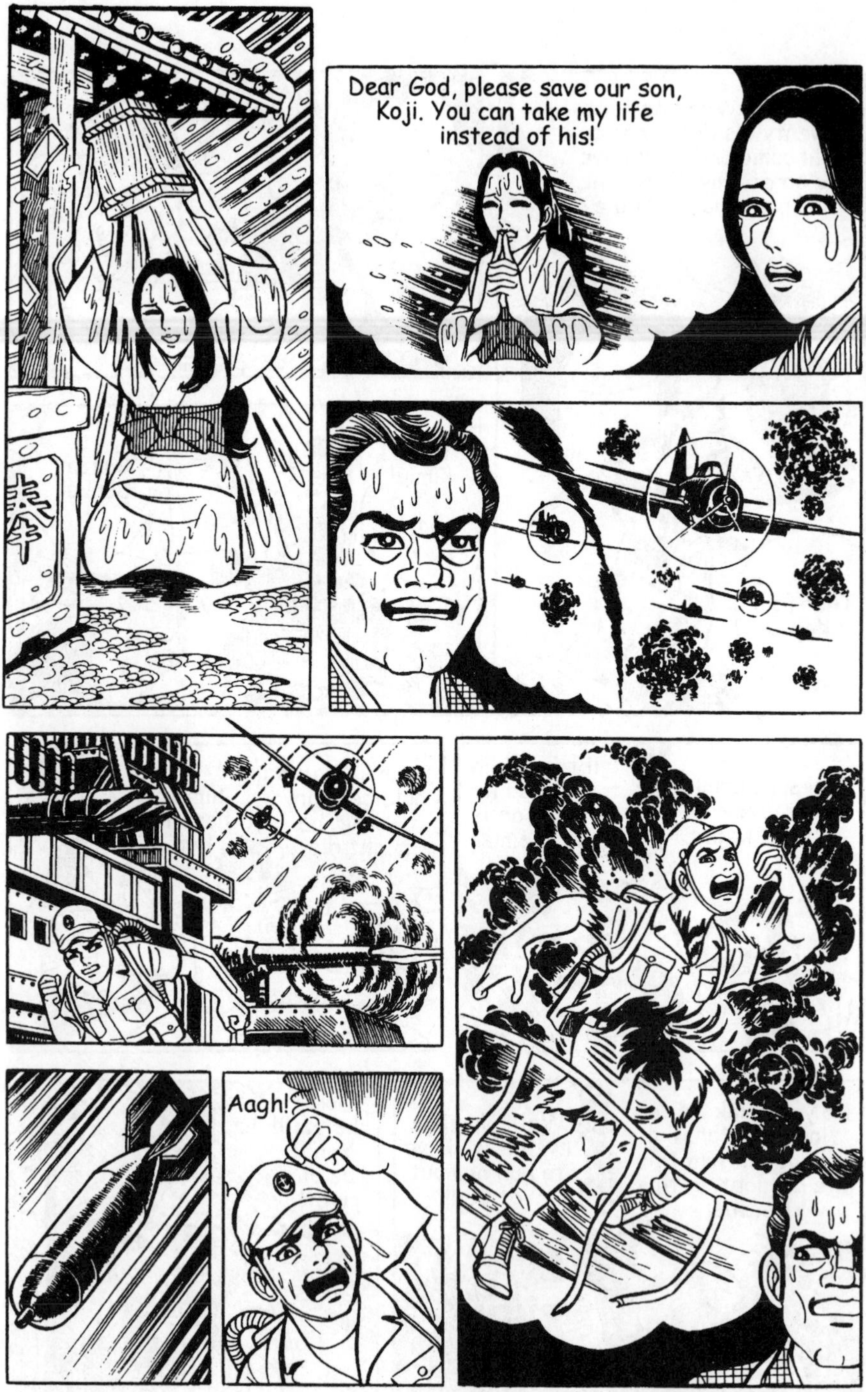
奉
Dear God, please save our son, Koji. You can take my life instead of his!
Aagh!

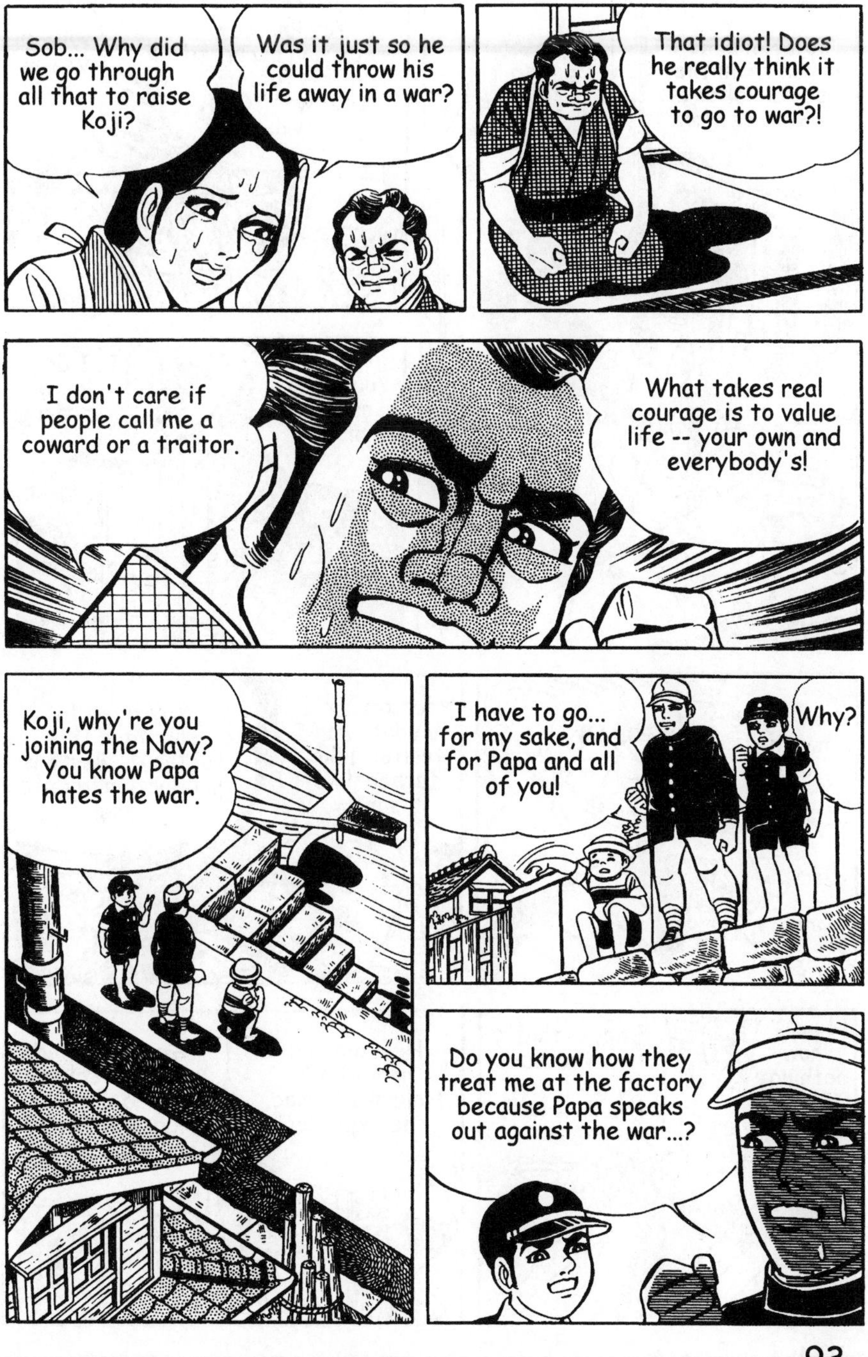

Sob... Why did we go through all that to raise Koji?
Was it just so he could throw his life away in a war?
That idiot! Does he really think it takes courage to go to war?!
I don't care if people call me a coward or a traitor.
What takes real courage is to value life -- your own and everybody's!
Koji, why're you joining the Navy? You know Papa hates the war.
I have to go... for my sake, and for Papa and all of you!
Why?
Do you know how they treat me at the factory because Papa speaks out against the war...?

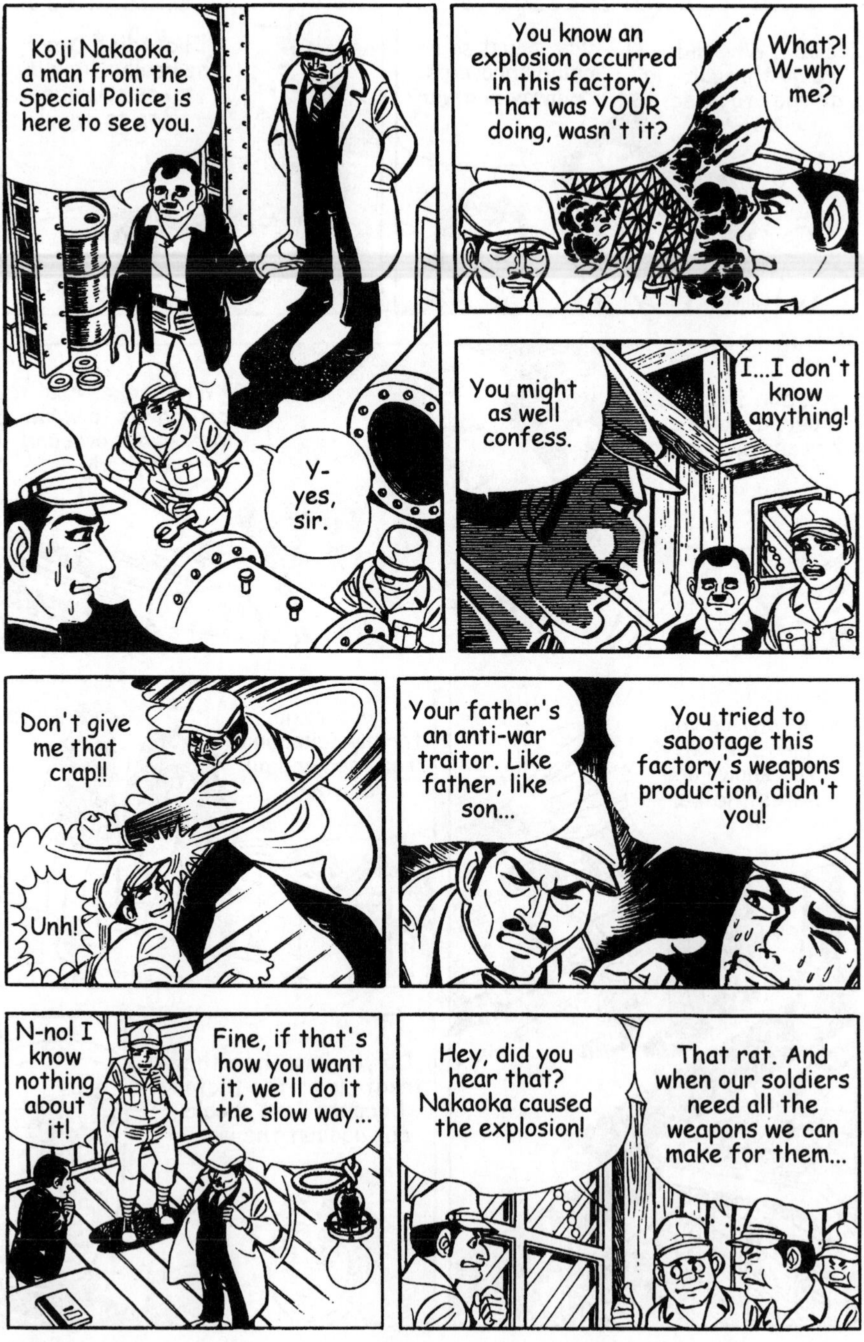
Koji Nakaoka, a man from the Special Police is here to see you.
Y-yes, sir.
You know an explosion occurred in this factory. That was YOUR doing, wasn't it?
What?! W-why me?
You might as well confess.
I...I don't know anything!
Don't give me that crap!!
Unh!
Your father's an anti-war traitor. Like father, like son...
You tried to sabotage this factory's weapons production, didn't you!
N-no! I know nothing about it!
Fine, if that's how you want it, we'll do it the slow way...
Hey, did you hear that? Nakaoka caused the explosion!
That rat. And when our soldiers need all the weapons we can make for them...

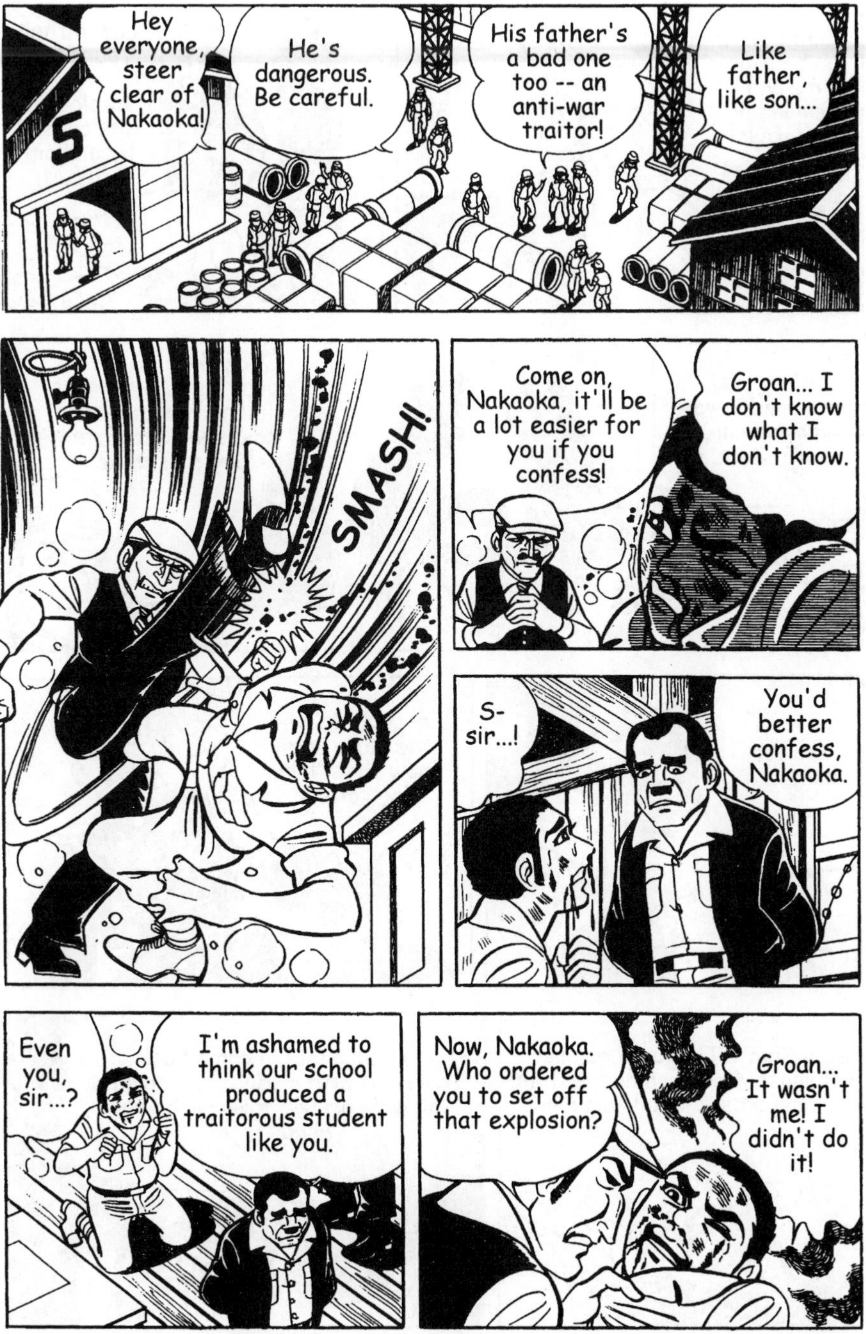
Hey everyone, steer clear of Nakaoka!
He's dangerous. Be careful.
His father's a bad one too -- an anti-war traitor!
Like father, like son...
SMASH!
Come on, Nakaoka, it'll be a lot easier for you if you confess!
Groan... I don't know what I don't know.
S- sir...!
You'd better confess, Nakaoka.
Even you, sir...?
I'm ashamed to think our school produced a traitorous student like you.
Now, Nakaoka. Who ordered you to set off that explosion?
Groan... It wasn't me! I didn't do it!

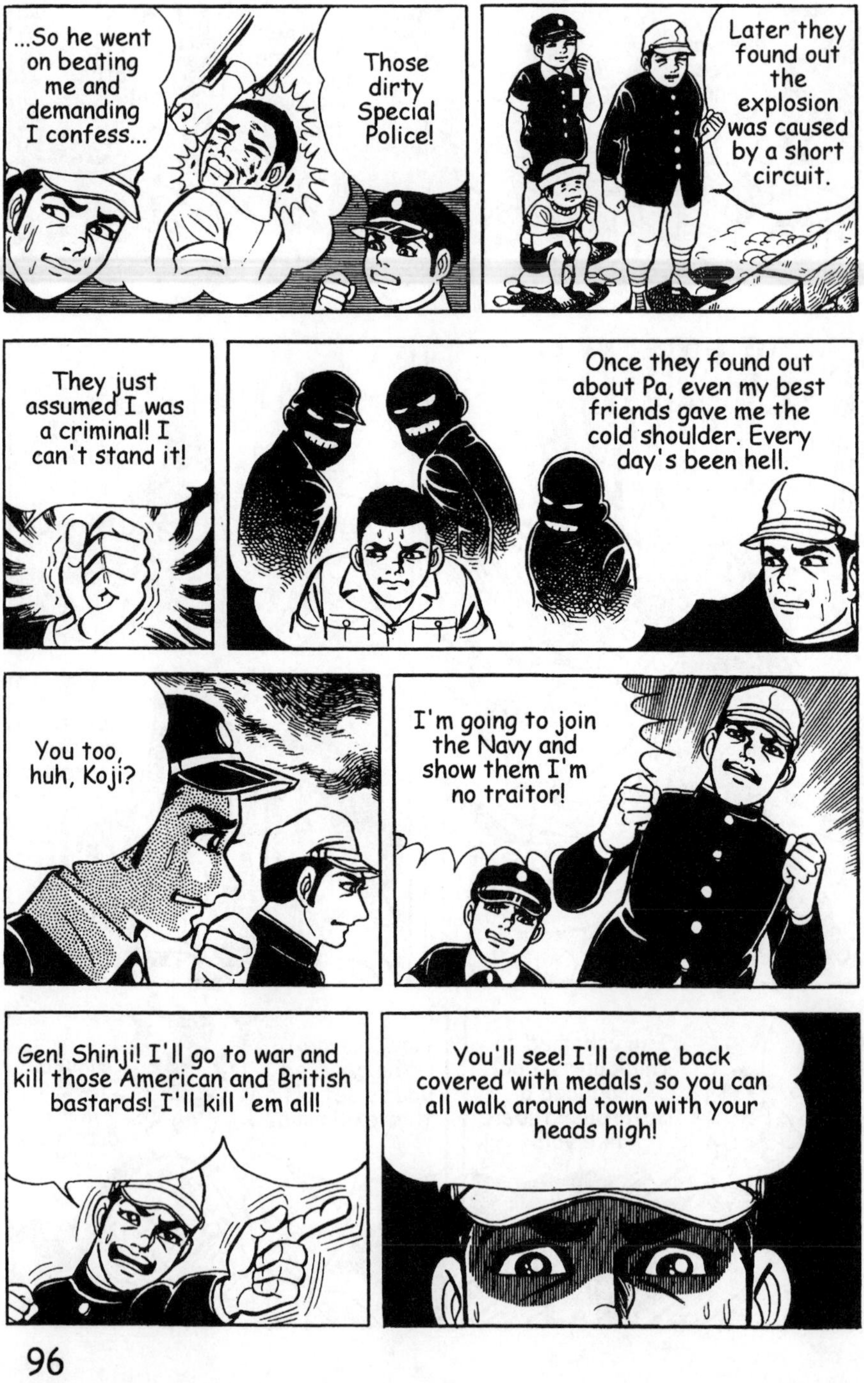
...So he went on beating me and demanding I confess...
Those dirty Special Police!
Later they found out the explosion was caused by a short circuit.
They just assumed I was a criminal! I can't stand it!
Once they found out about Pa, even my best friends gave me the cold shoulder. Every day's been hell.
You too, huh, Koji?
I'm going to join the Navy and show them I'm no traitor!
Gen! Shinji! I'll go to war and kill those American and British bastards! I'll kill 'em all!
You'll see! I'll come back covered with medals, so you can all walk around town with your heads high!

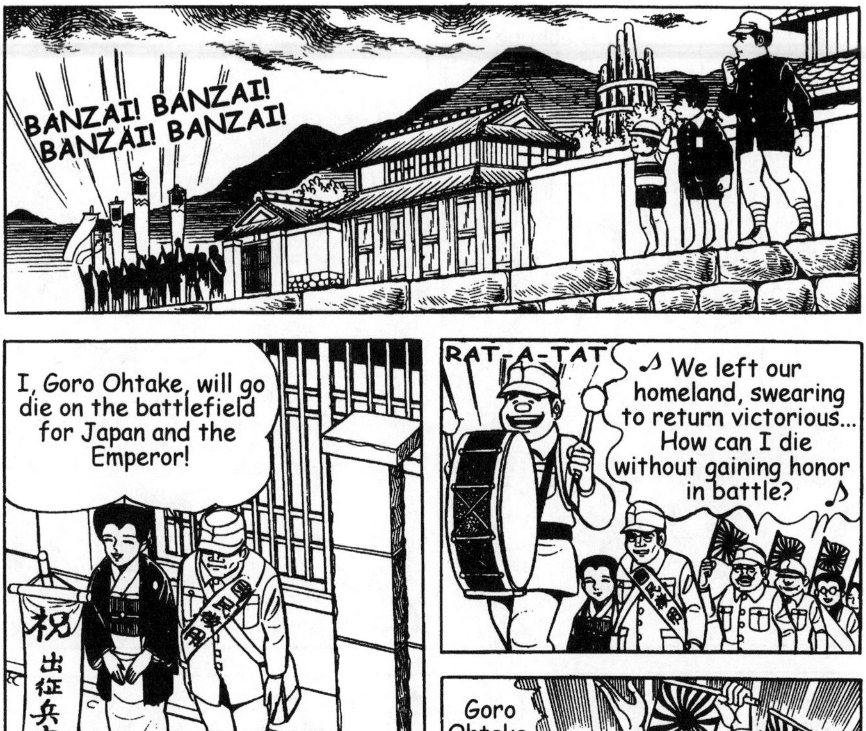
BANZAI! BANZAI!
BANZAI! BANZAI!
I, Goro Ohtake, will go die on the battlefield for Japan and the Emperor!
祝 出征兵士 大竹吾郎君
祝 大竹吾郎
Do your best!
RAT-A-TAT
♪ We left our homeland, swearing to return victorious... How can I die without gaining honor in battle? ♪
Goro Ohtake, Banzai!

Banners: Congratulations Goro Ohtake

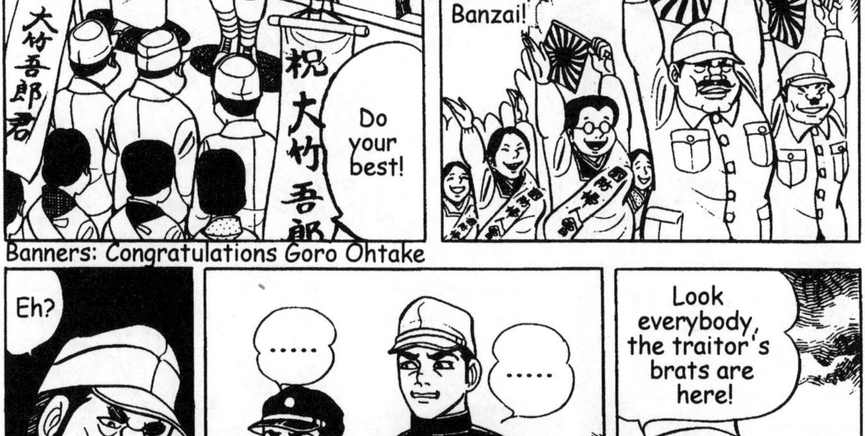
Eh?
.....
.....
Look everybody, the traitor's brats are here!

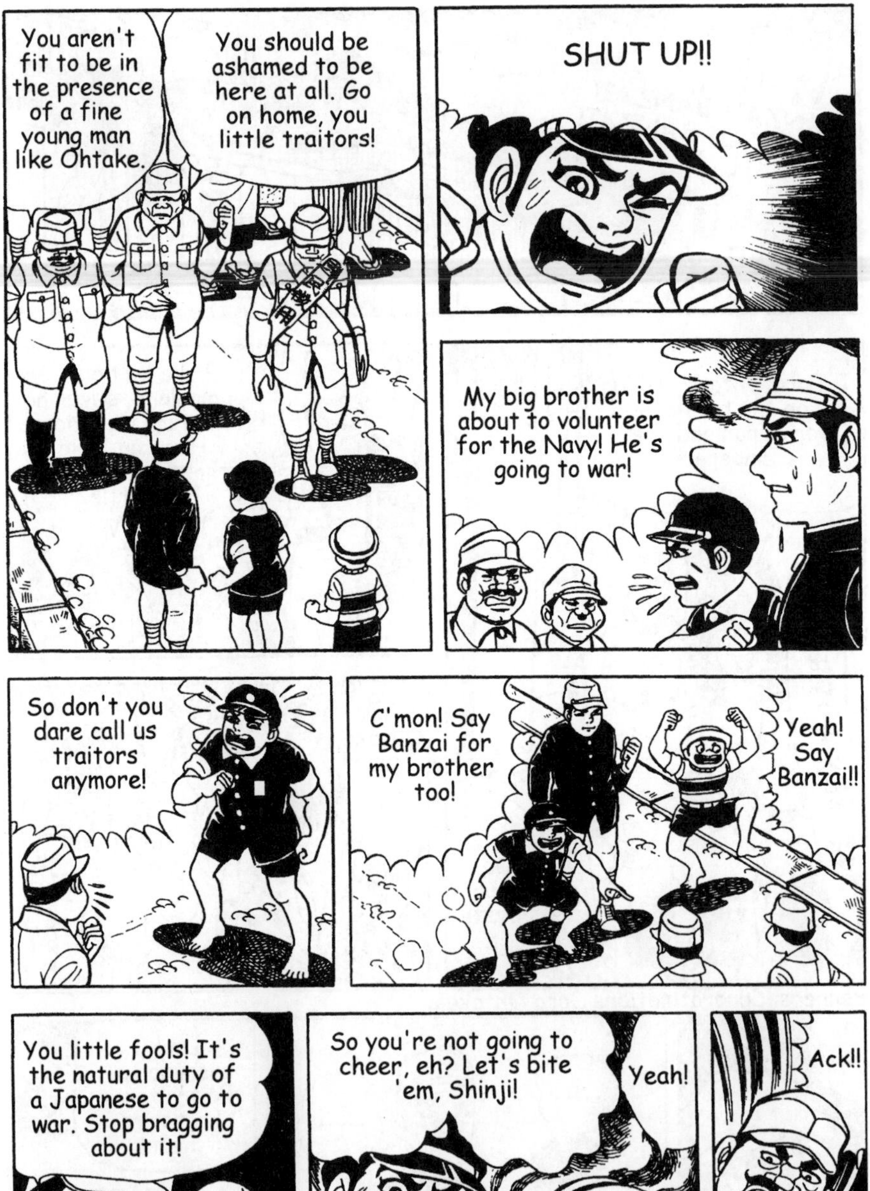
You aren't fit to be in the presence of a fine young man like Ohtake.
You should be ashamed to be here at all. Go on home, you little traitors!
SHUT UP!!
My big brother is about to volunteer for the Navy! He's going to war!
So don't you dare call us traitors anymore!
C'mon! Say Banzai for my brother too!
Yeah! Say Banzai!!
You little fools! It's the natural duty of a Japanese to go to war. Stop bragging about it!
So you're not going to cheer, eh? Let's bite 'em, Shinji!
Yeah!
Ack!!

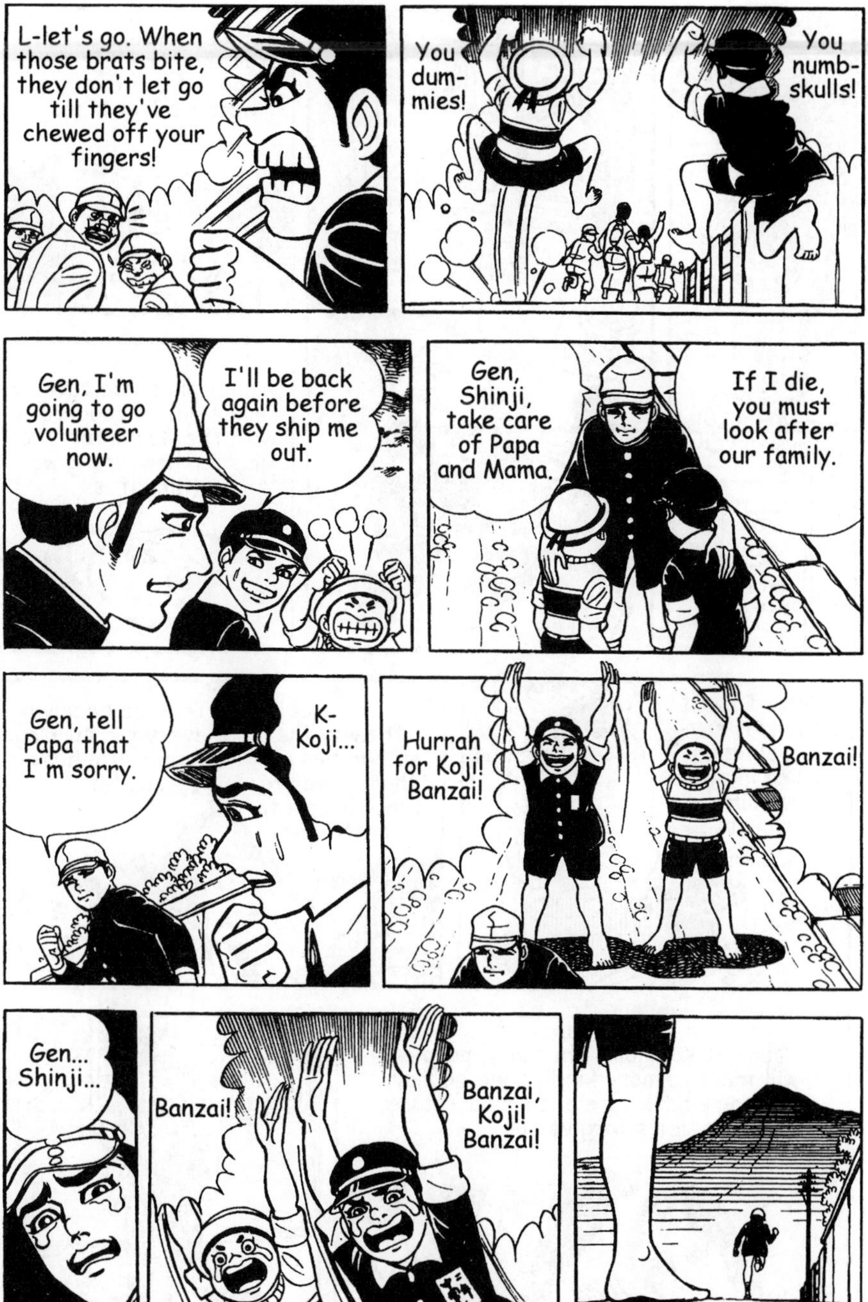
L-let's go. When those brats bite, they don't let go till they've chewed off your fingers!
You dum-mies!
You numb-skulls!
Gen, I'm going to go volunteer now.
I'll be back again before they ship me out.
Gen, Shinji, take care of Papa and Mama.
If I die, you must look after our family.
Gen, tell Papa that I'm sorry.
K-Koji...
Hurrah for Koji! Banzai!
Banzai!
Gen... Shinji...
Banzai!
Banzai, Koji! Banzai!

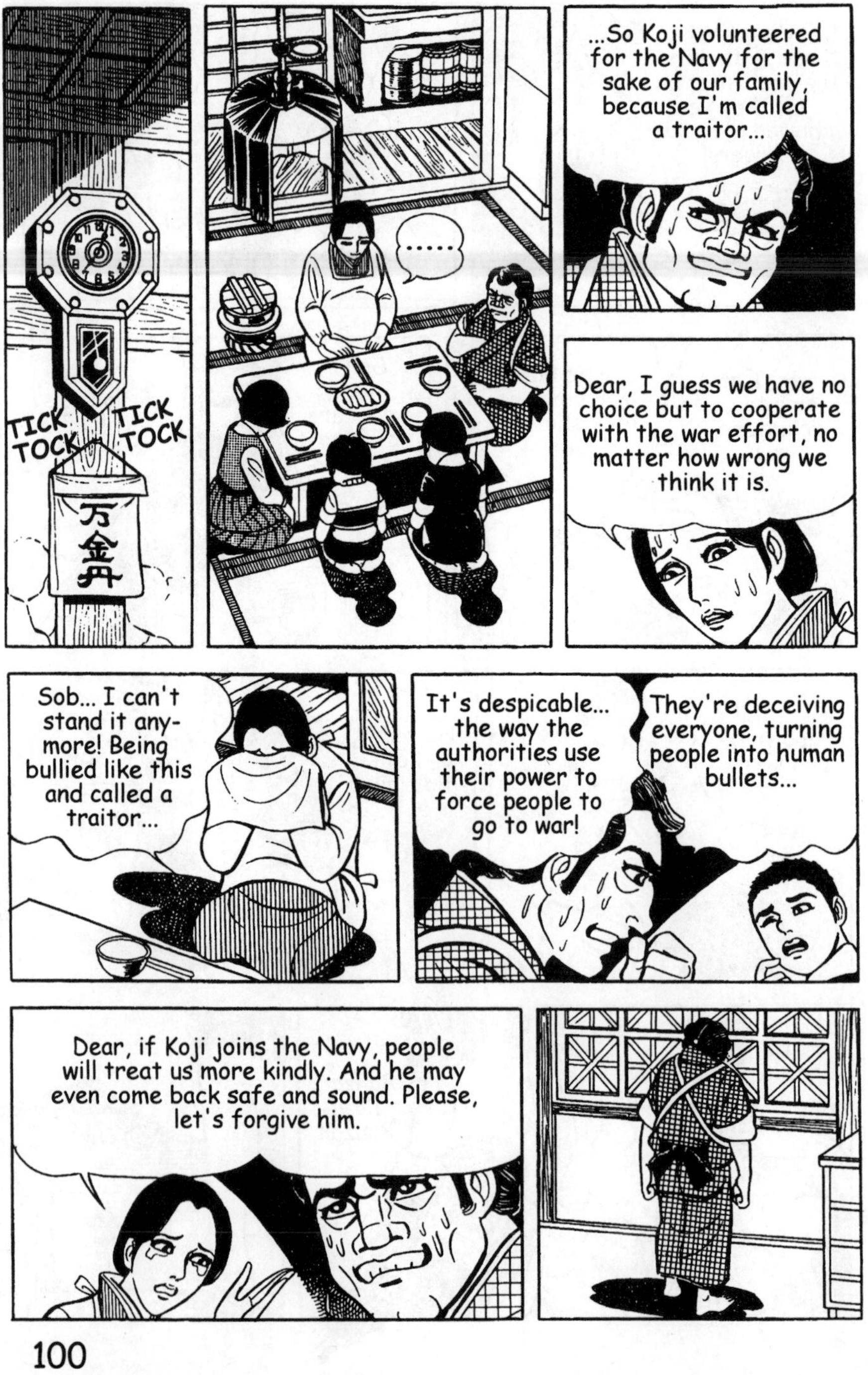
TICK TOCK
TICK TOCK
万金丹
......
...So Koji volunteered for the Navy for the sake of our family, because I'm called a traitor...
Dear, I guess we have no choice but to cooperate with the war effort, no matter how wrong we think it is.
Sob... I can't stand it any-more! Being bullied like this and called a traitor...
It's despicable... the way the authorities use their power to force people to go to war!
They're deceiving everyone, turning people into human bullets...
Dear, if Koji joins the Navy, people will treat us more kindly. And he may even come back safe and sound. Please, let's forgive him.

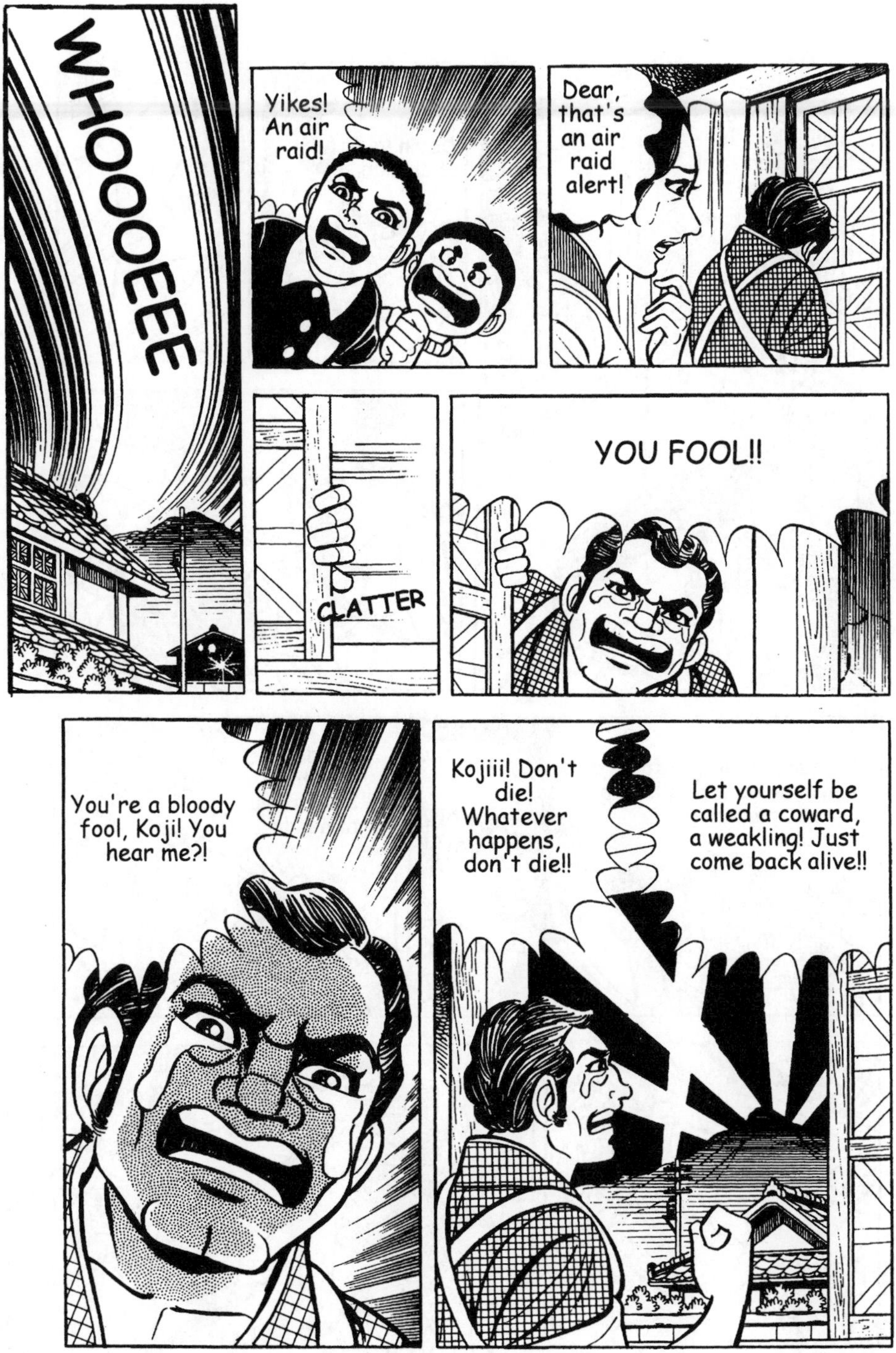
WHOOOEEE
Yikes! An air raid!
Dear, that's an air raid alert!
CLATTER
YOU FOOL!!
You're a bloody fool, Koji! You hear me?!
Kojiii! Don't die! Whatever happens, don't die!!
Let yourself be called a coward, a weakling! Just come back alive!!

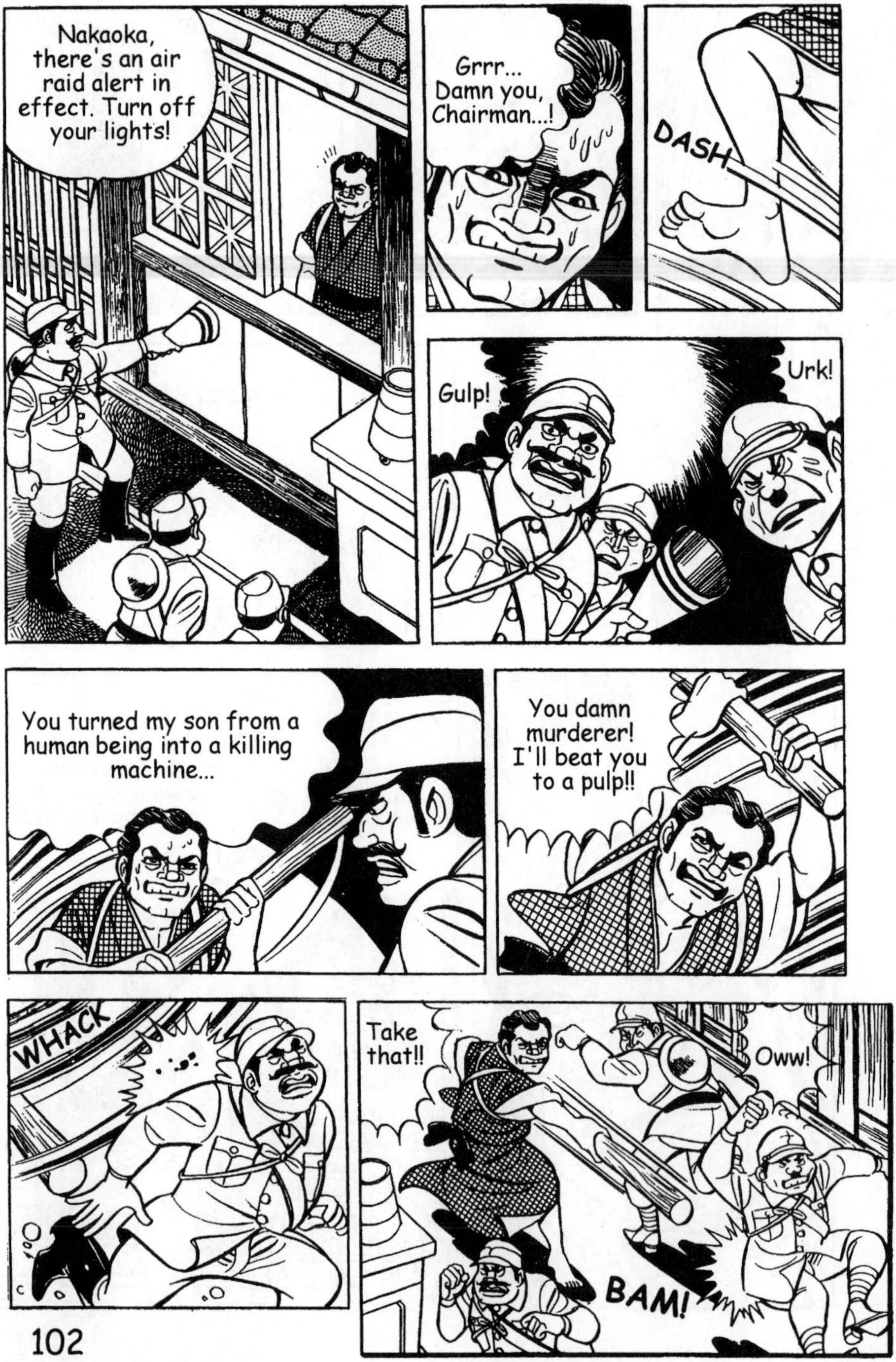

Nakaoka, there's an air raid alert in effect. Turn off your lights!
Grrr... Damn you, Chairman...!
DASH
Gulp!
Urk!
You turned my son from a human being into a killing machine...
You damn murderer! I'll beat you to a pulp!!
WHACK
Take that!!
Oww!
BAM!

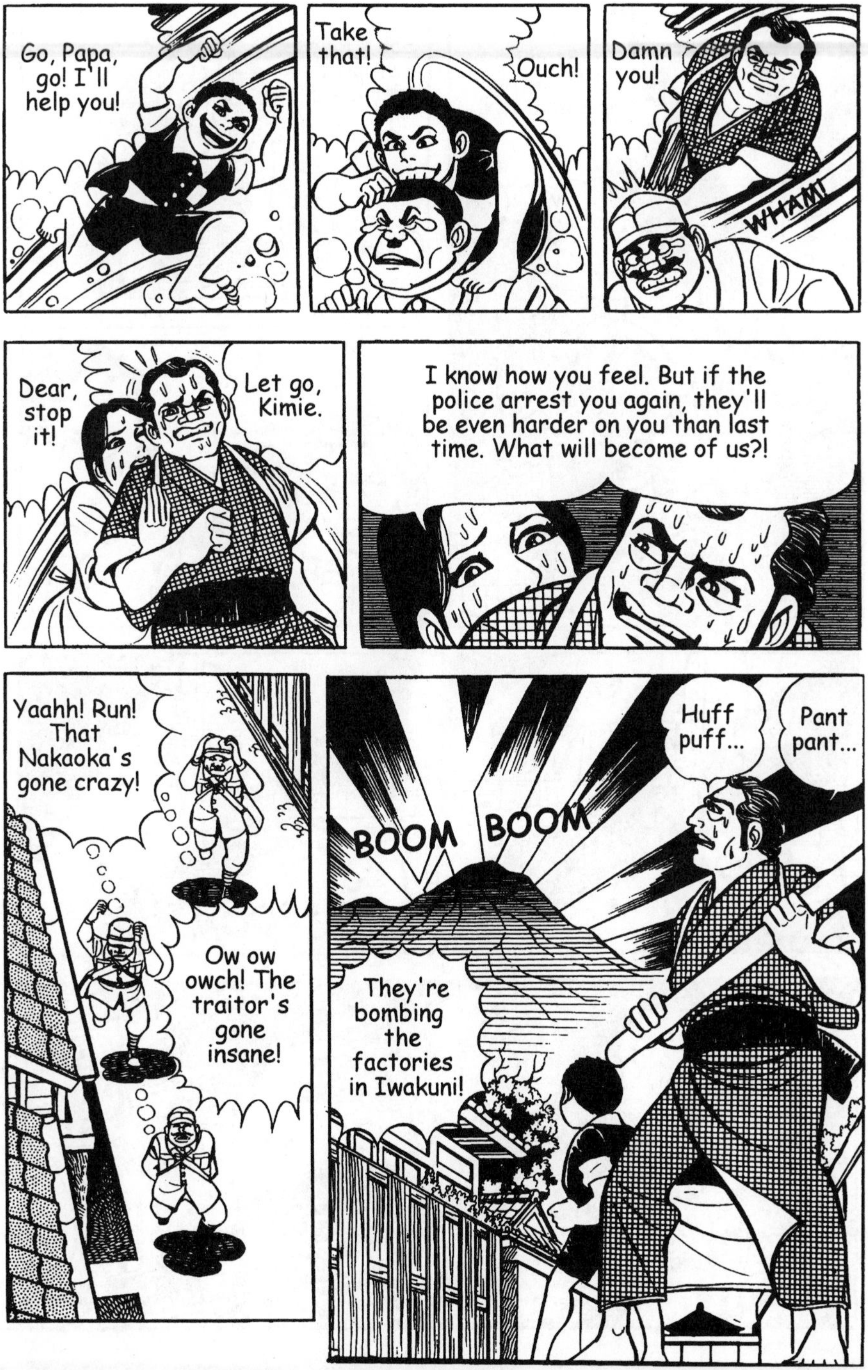
Go, Papa, go! I'll help you!
Take that!
Ouch!
Damn you!
WHAM!
Dear, stop it!
Let go, Kimie.
I know how you feel. But if the police arrest you again, they'll be even harder on you than last time. What will become of us?!
Yaahh! Run! That Nakaoka's gone crazy!
Ow ow owch! The traitor's gone insane!
BOOM
BOOM
Huff puff...
Pant pant...
They're bombing the factories in Iwakuni!

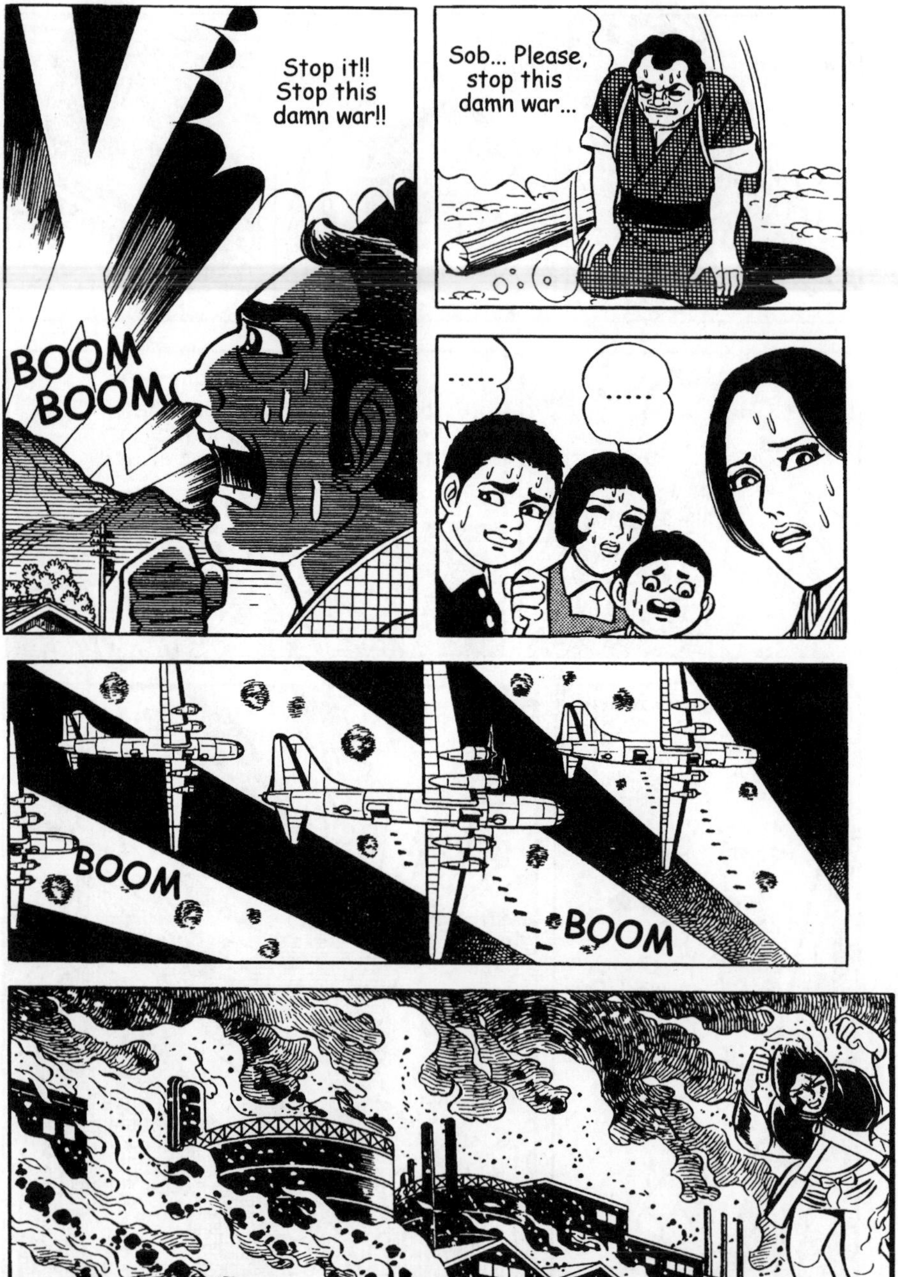
Stop it!! Stop this damn war!!
BOOM
BOOM
Sob... Please, stop this damn war...
......
......
BOOM
BOOM

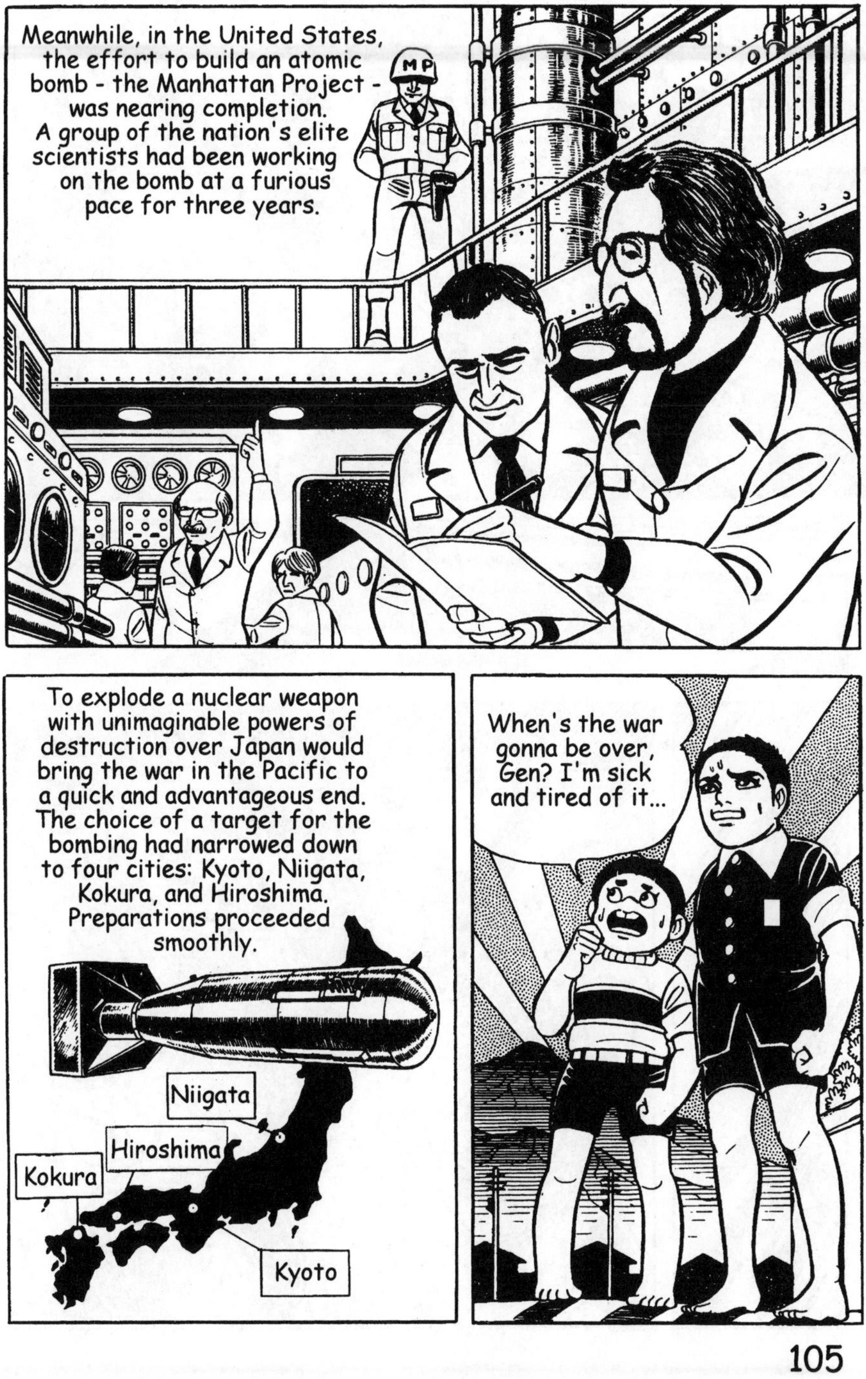

Meanwhile, in the United States, the effort to build an atomic bomb - the Manhattan Project - was nearing completion. A group of the nation's elite scientists had been working on the bomb at a furious pace for three years.
MP
To explode a nuclear weapon with unimaginable powers of destruction over Japan would bring the war in the Pacific to a quick and advantageous end. The choice of a target for the bombing had narrowed down to four cities: Kyoto, Niigata, Kokura, and Hiroshima. Preparations proceeded smoothly.
Niigata
Hiroshima
Kokura
Kyoto
When's the war gonna be over, Gen? I'm sick and tired of it...

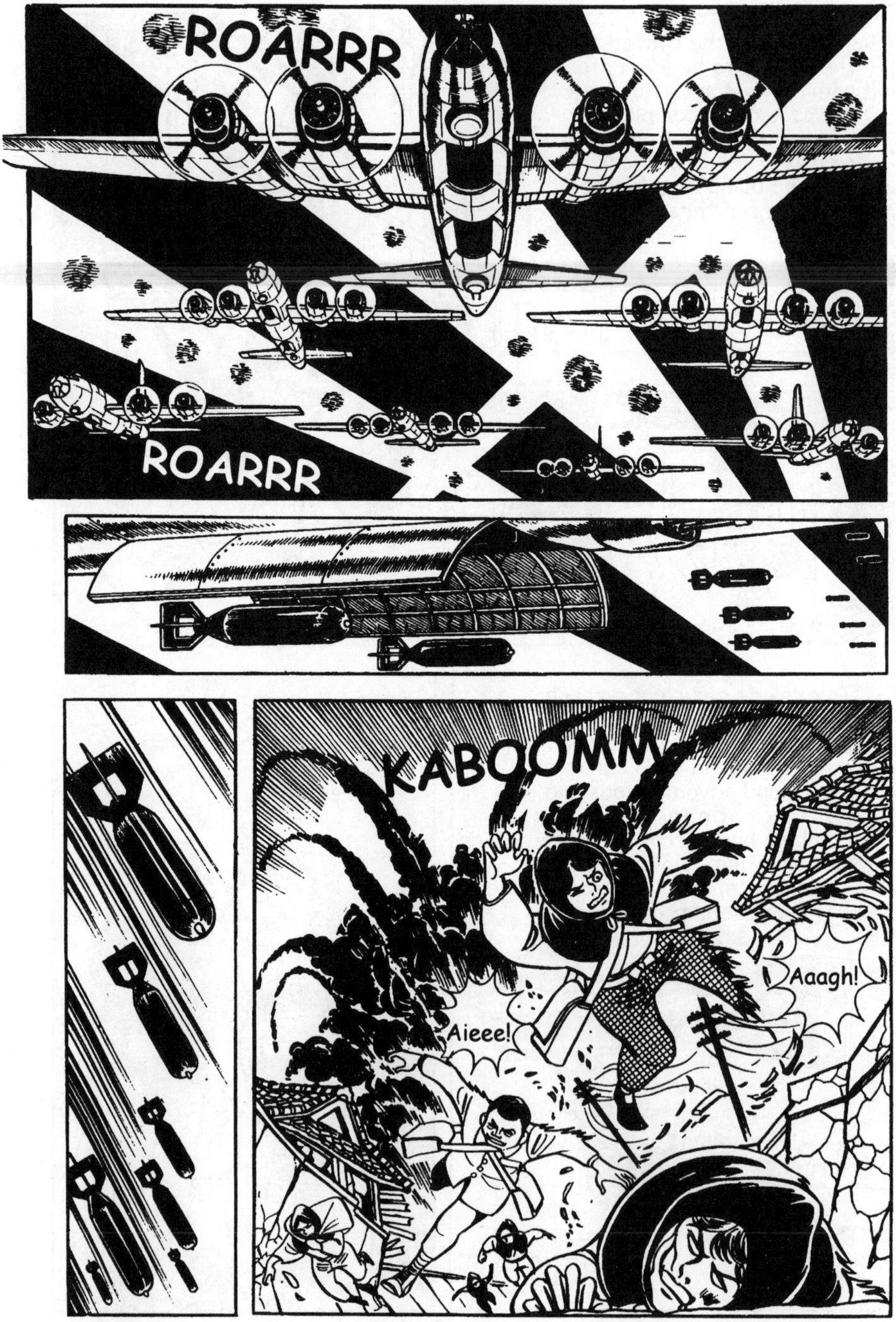
ROARRR
ROARRR
KABOOMM
Aaagh!
Aieee!

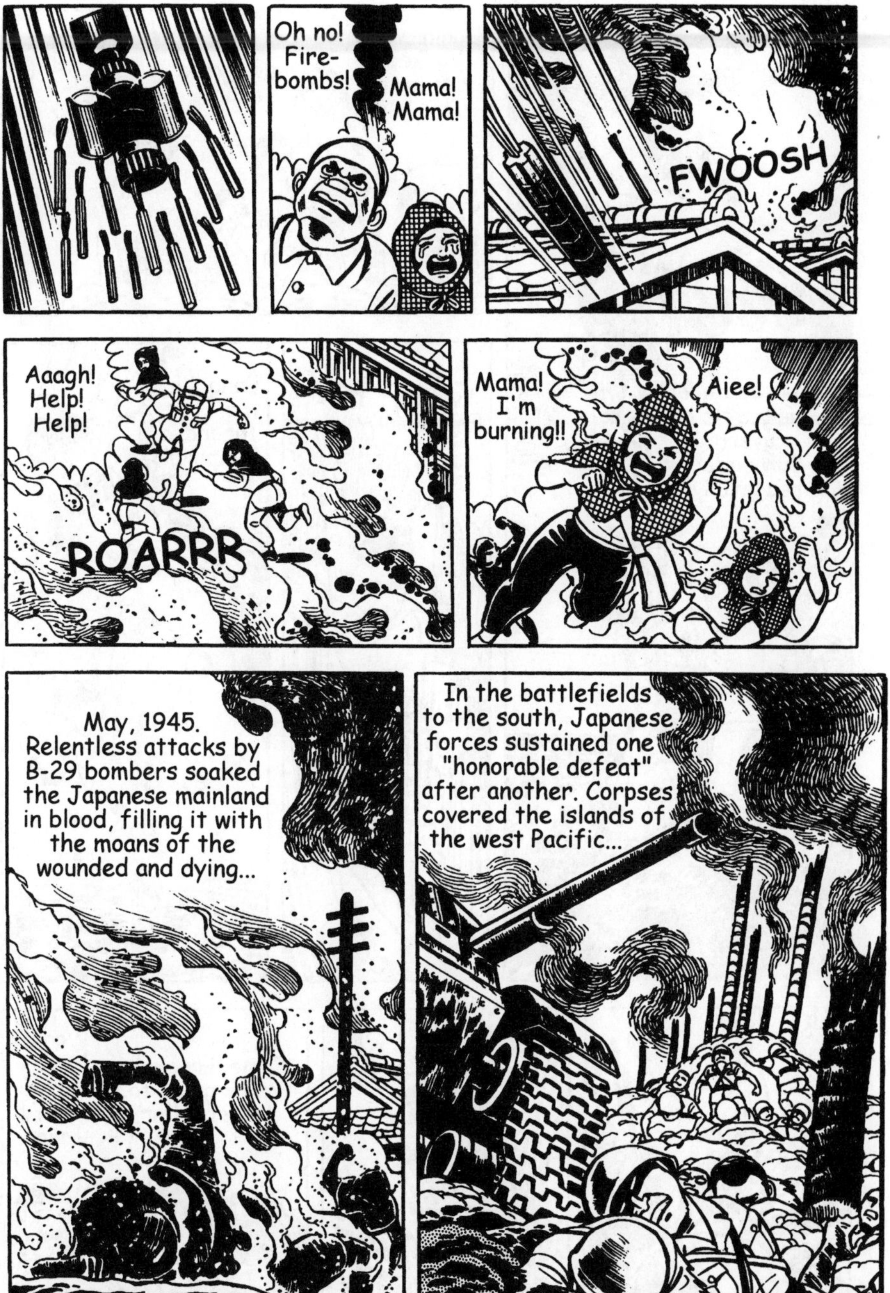
Oh no! Fire-bombs!
Mama! Mama!
FWOOSH
Aaagh! Help! Help!
ROARRR
Mama! I'm burning!!
Aiee!
May, 1945. Relentless attacks by B-29 bombers soaked the Japanese mainland in blood, filling it with the moans of the wounded and dying...
In the battlefields to the south, Japanese forces sustained one "honorable defeat" after another. Corpses covered the islands of the west Pacific...

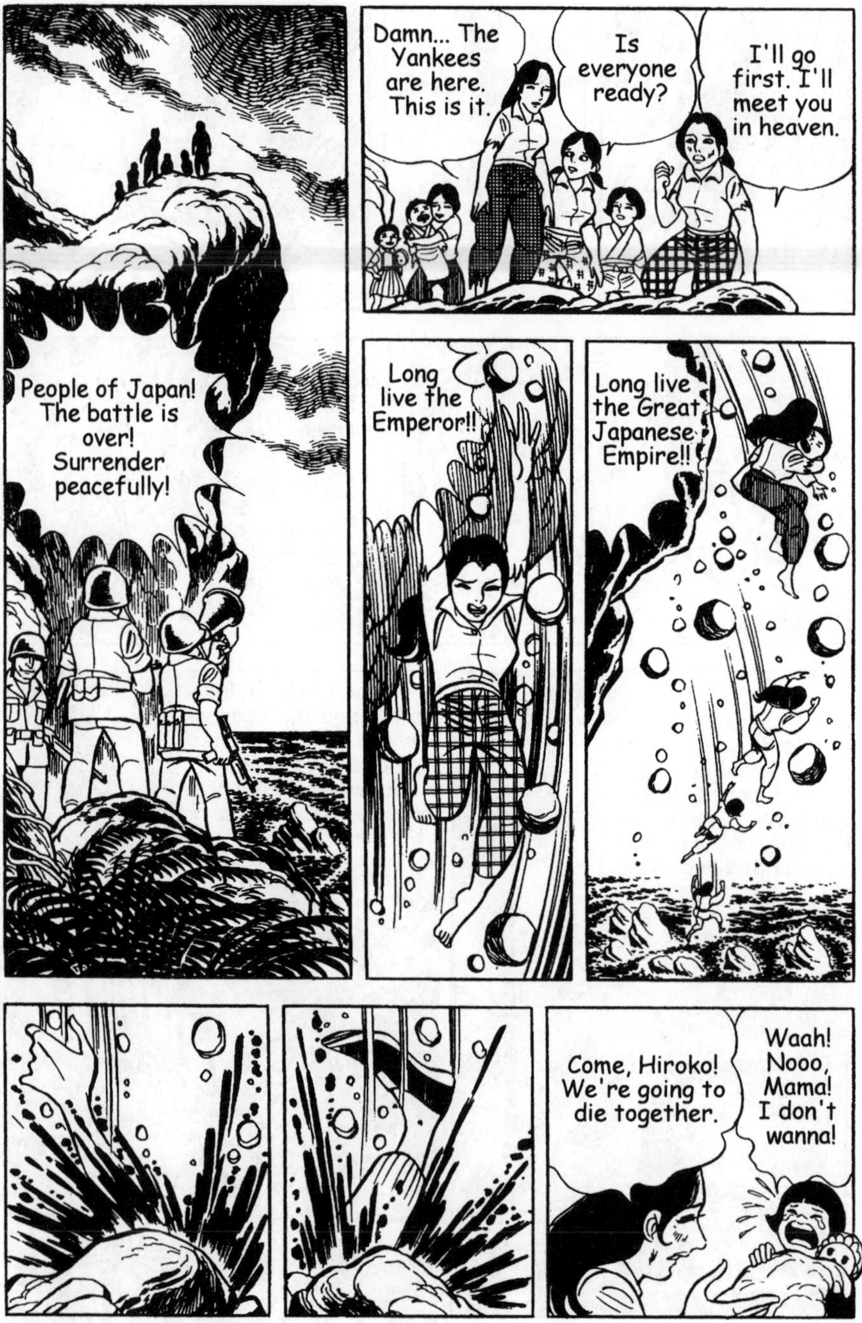
People of Japan! The battle is over! Surrender peacefully!
Damn... The Yankees are here. This is it.
Is everyone ready?
I'll go first. I'll meet you in heaven.
Long live the Emperor!!
Long live the Great Japanese Empire!!
Come, Hiroko! We're going to die together.
Waah! Nooo, Mama! I don't wanna!

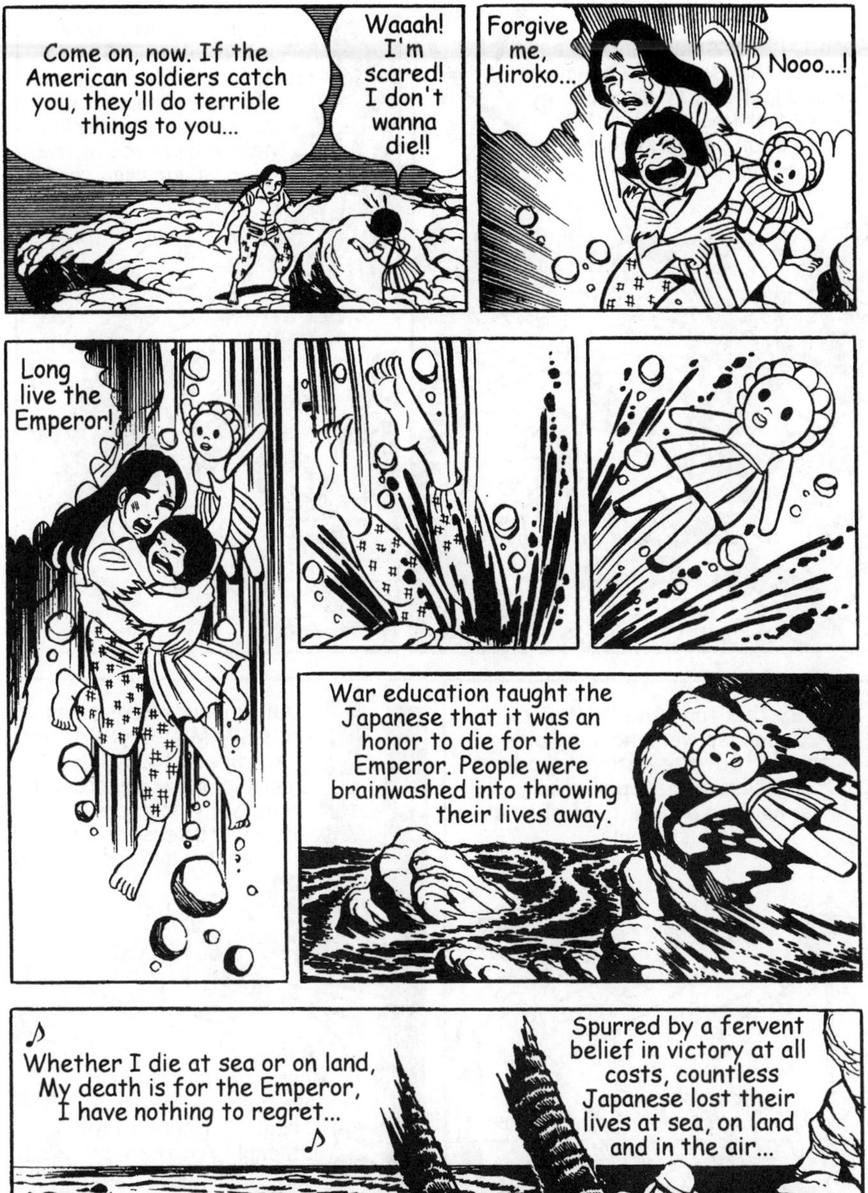

Come on, now. If the American soldiers catch you, they'll do terrible things to you...
Waaah! I'm scared! I don't wanna die!!
Forgive me, Hiroko...
Nooo...!
Long live the Emperor!
War education taught the Japanese that it was an honor to die for the Emperor. People were brainwashed into throwing their lives away.
♪ Whether I die at sea or on land,
My death is for the Emperor,
I have nothing to regret... ♪
Spurred by a fervent belief in victory at all costs, countless Japanese lost their lives at sea, on land and in the air...

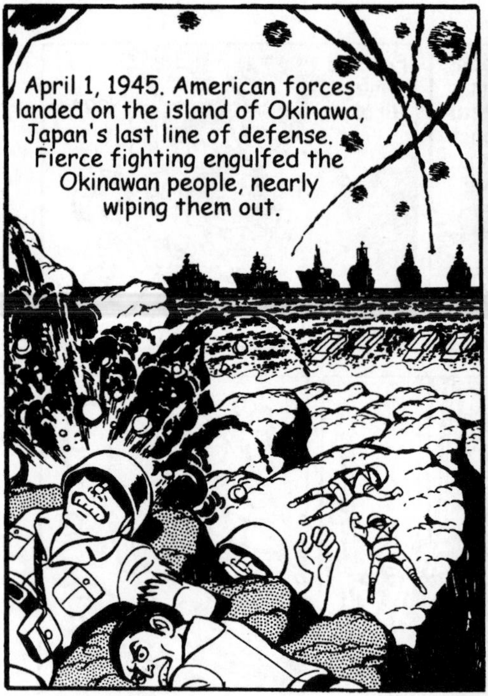
April 1, 1945. American forces landed on the island of Okinawa, Japan's last line of defense. Fierce fighting engulfed the Okinawan people, nearly wiping them out.

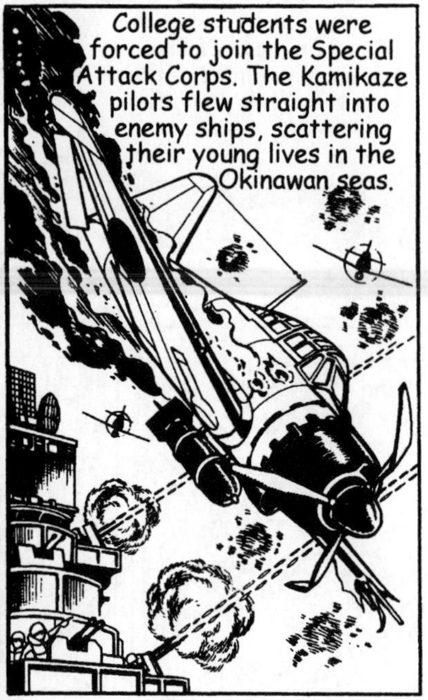
College students were forced to join the Special Attack Corps. The Kamikaze pilots flew straight into enemy ships, scattering their young lives in the Okinawan seas.

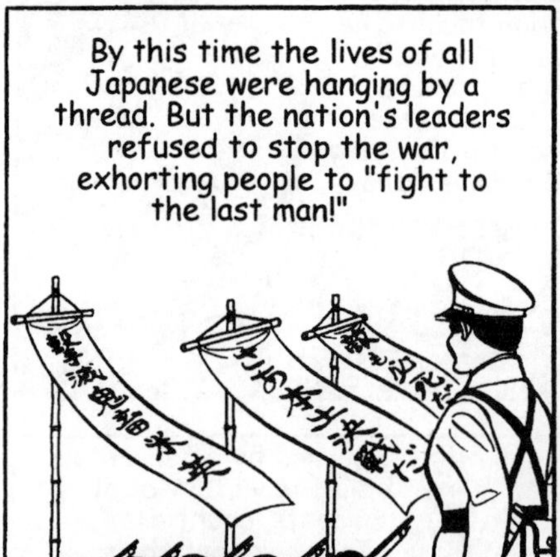
By this time the lives of all Japanese were hanging by a thread. But the nation's leaders refused to stop the war, exhorting people to "fight to the last man!"

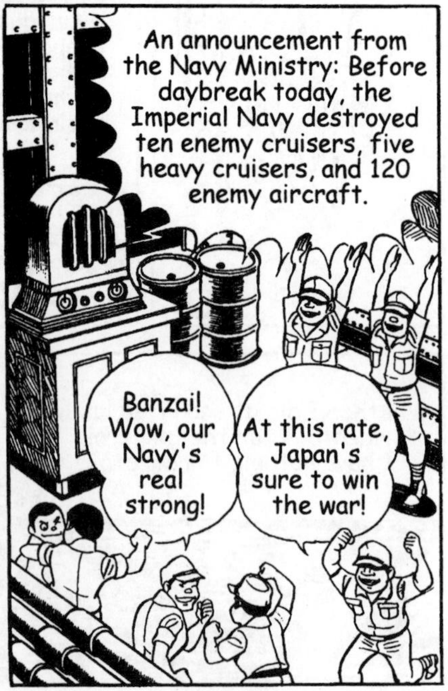
An announcement from the Navy Ministry: Before daybreak today, the Imperial Navy destroyed ten enemy cruisers, five heavy cruisers, and 120 enemy aircraft.
Banzai! Wow, our Navy's real strong!
At this rate, Japan's sure to win the war!

Banners: The enemy is desperate! Prepare to defend the mainland! Wipe out the Americans and British!

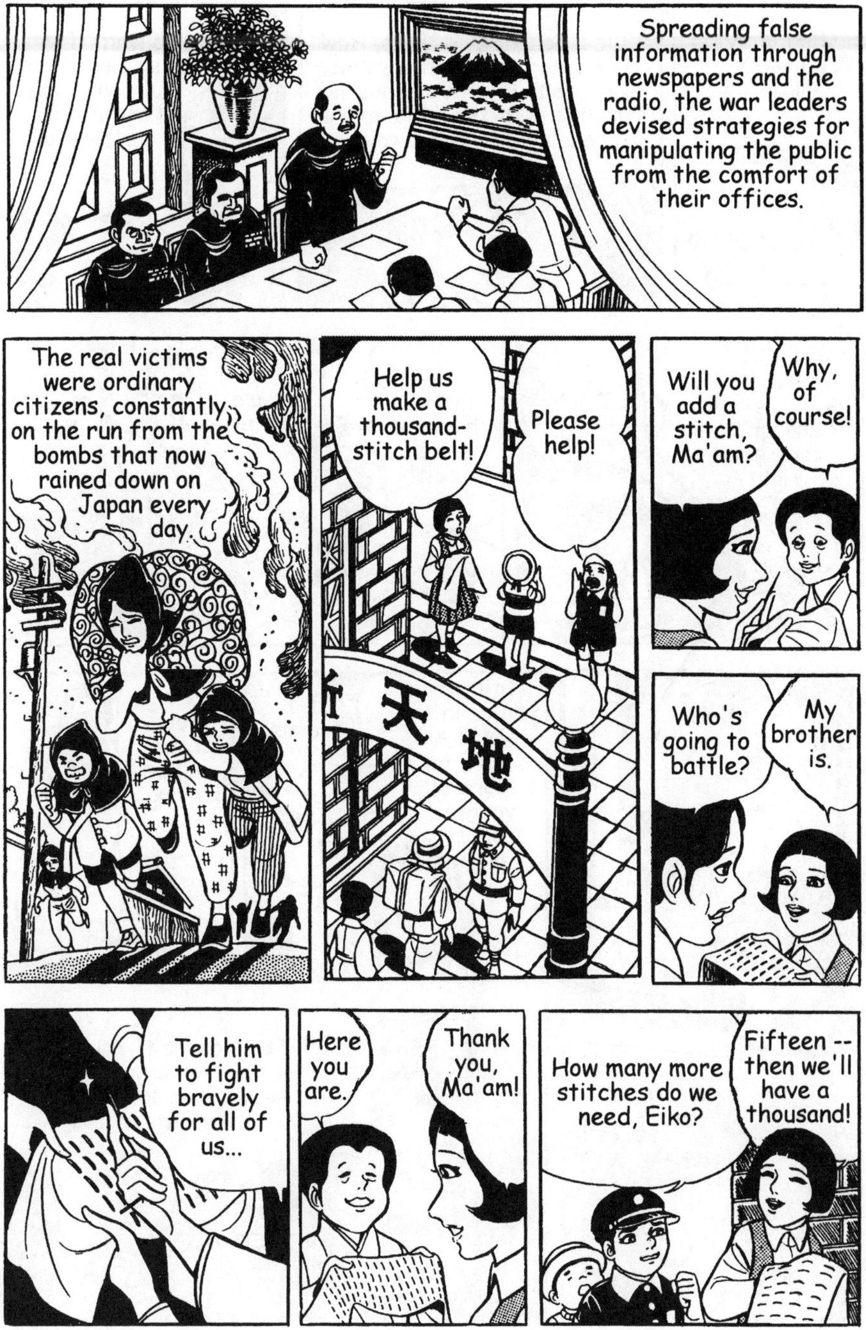
Spreading false information through newspapers and the radio, the war leaders devised strategies for manipulating the public from the comfort of their offices.
The real victims were ordinary citizens, constantly on the run from the bombs that now rained down on Japan every day.
Help us make a thousand-stitch belt!
Please help!
天地
Will you add a stitch, Ma'am?
Why, of course!
Who's going to battle?
My brother is.
Tell him to fight bravely for all of us...
Here you are.
Thank you, Ma'am!
How many more stitches do we need, Eiko?
Fifteen -- then we'll have a thousand!

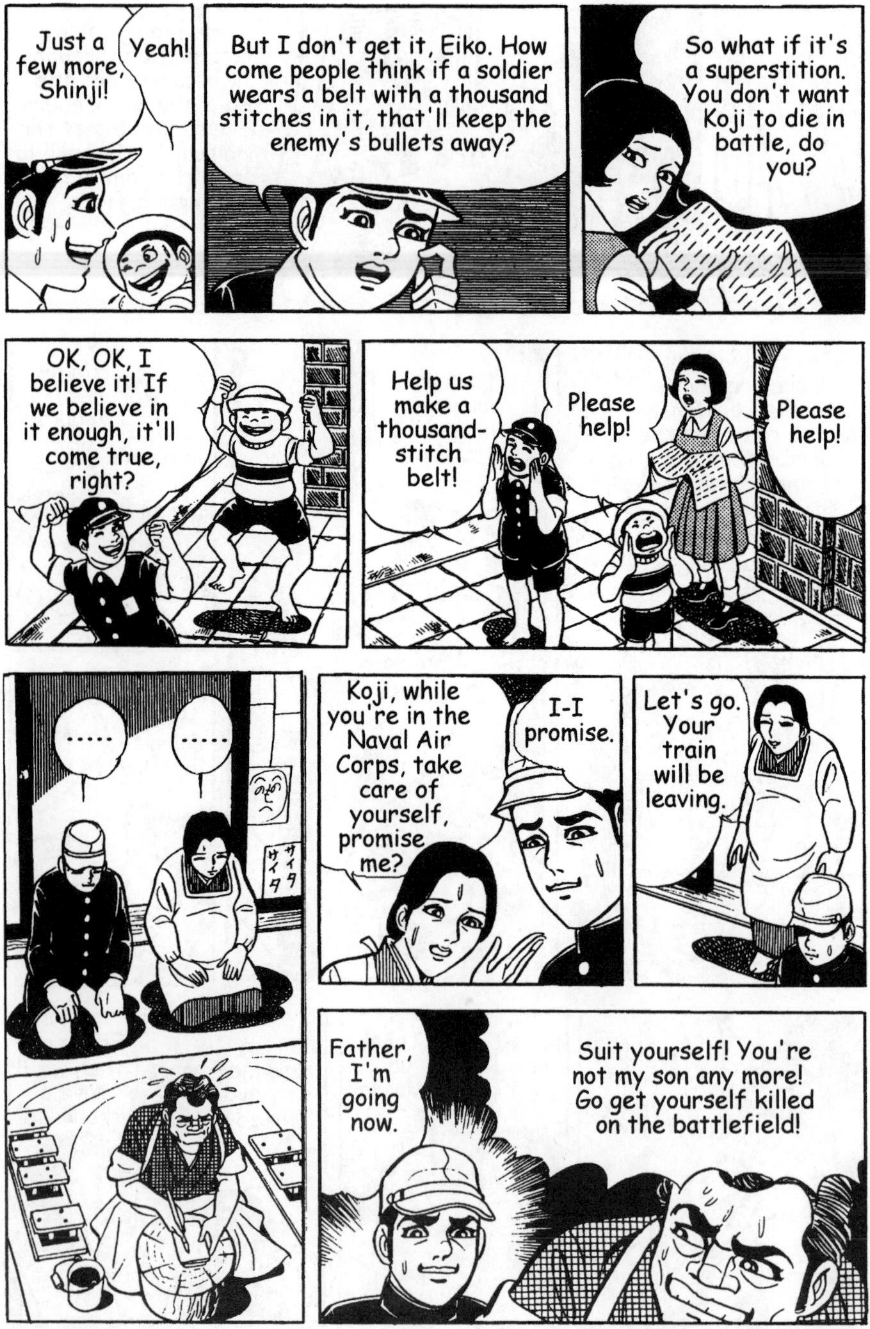
Just a few more, Shinji!
Yeah!
But I don't get it, Eiko. How come people think if a soldier wears a belt with a thousand stitches in it, that'll keep the enemy's bullets away?
So what if it's a superstition. You don't want Koji to die in battle, do you?
OK, OK, I believe it! If we believe in it enough, it'll come true, right?
Help us make a thousand-stitch belt!
Please help!
Please help!

サイタ サイタ
Koji, while you're in the Naval Air Corps, take care of yourself, promise me?
I-I promise.
Let's go. Your train will be leaving.
Father, I'm going now.
Suit yourself! You're not my son any more! Go get yourself killed on the battlefield!

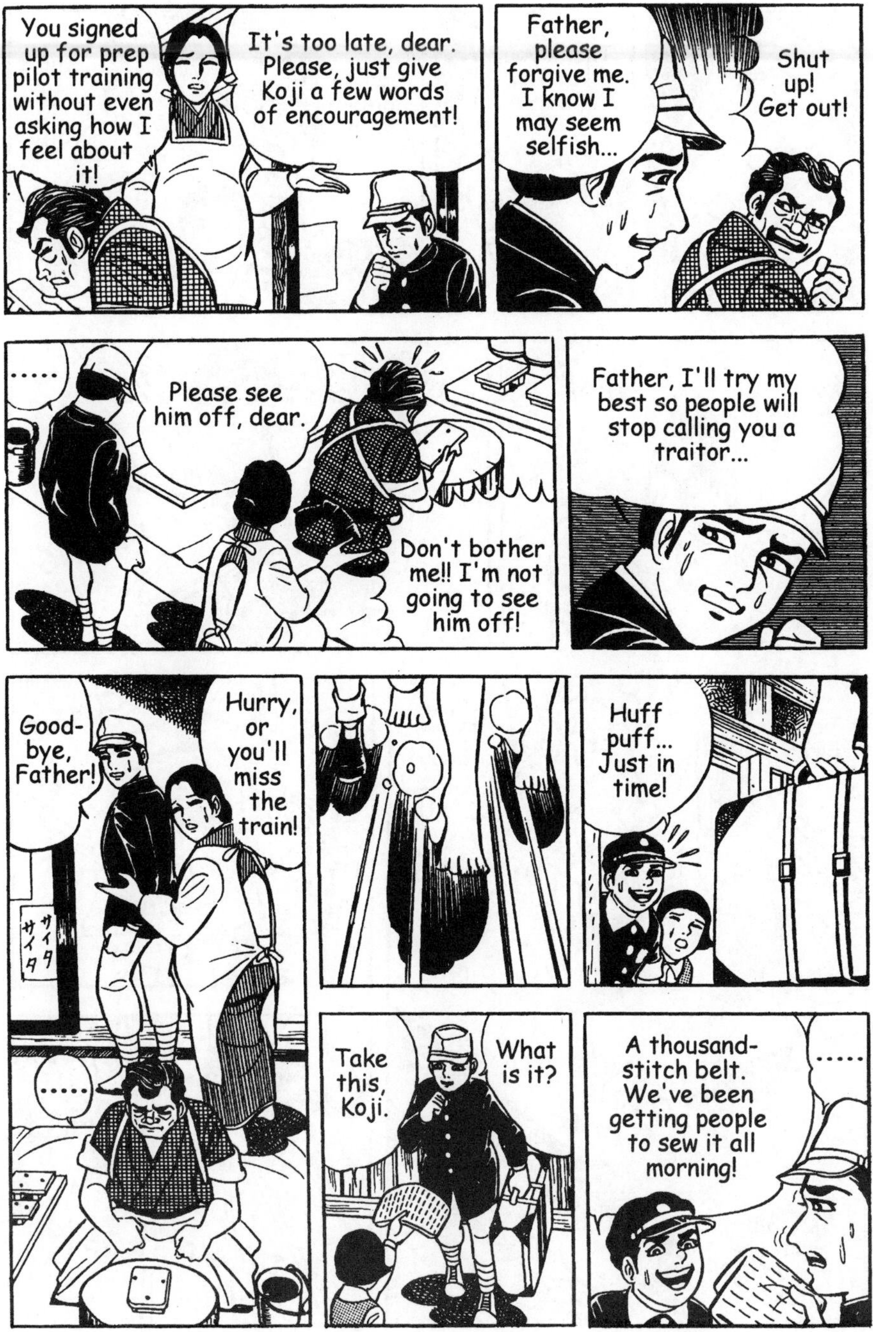
You signed up for prep pilot training without even asking how I feel about it!
It's too late, dear. Please, just give Koji a few words of encouragement!
Father, please forgive me. I know I may seem selfish...
Shut up! Get out!
.....
Please see him off, dear.
Don't bother me!! I'm not going to see him off!
Father, I'll try my best so people will stop calling you a traitor...
Good-bye, Father!
Hurry, or you'll miss the train!
サイタ サイタ
.....
Huff puff... Just in time!
Take this, Koji.
What is it?
A thousand-stitch belt. We've been getting people to sew it all morning!
.....

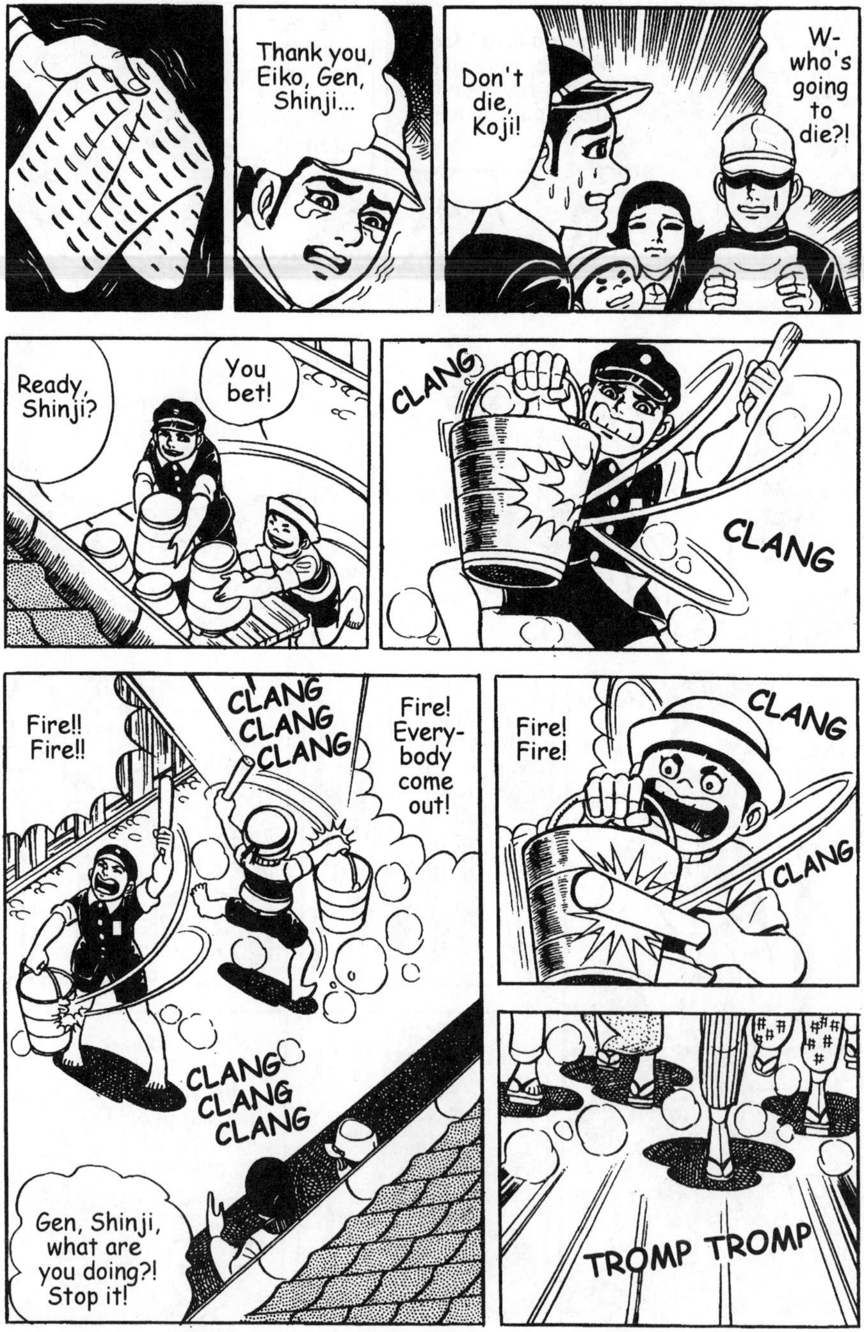
Thank you, Eiko, Gen, Shinji...
Don't die, Koji!
W-who's going to die?!
Ready, Shinji?
You bet!
CLANG
CLANG
Fire!! Fire!!
CLANG CLANG CLANG
Fire! Everybody come out!
CLANG CLANG CLANG
Gen, Shinji, what are you doing?! Stop it!
Fire! Fire!
CLANG
CLANG
TROMP TROMP

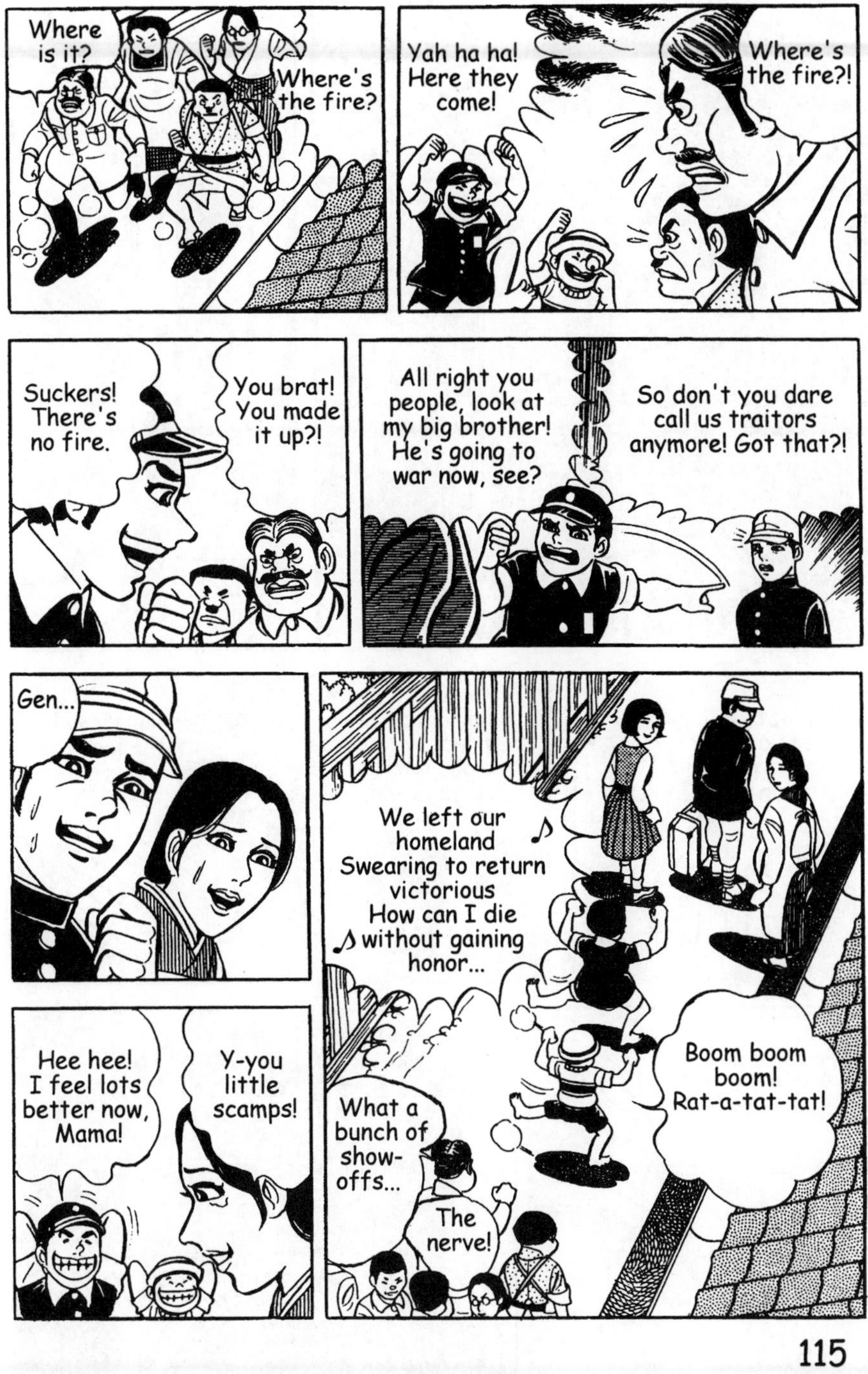

Where is it?
Where's the fire?
Yah ha ha! Here they come!
Where's the fire?!
Suckers! There's no fire.
You brat! You made it up?!
All right you people, look at my big brother! He's going to war now, see?
So don't you dare call us traitors anymore! Got that?!
Gen...
Hee hee! I feel lots better now, Mama!
Y-you little scamps!
We left our homeland ♪ Swearing to return victorious How can I die ♪ without gaining honor...
Boom boom boom! Rat-a-tat-tat!
What a bunch of show-offs...
The nerve!

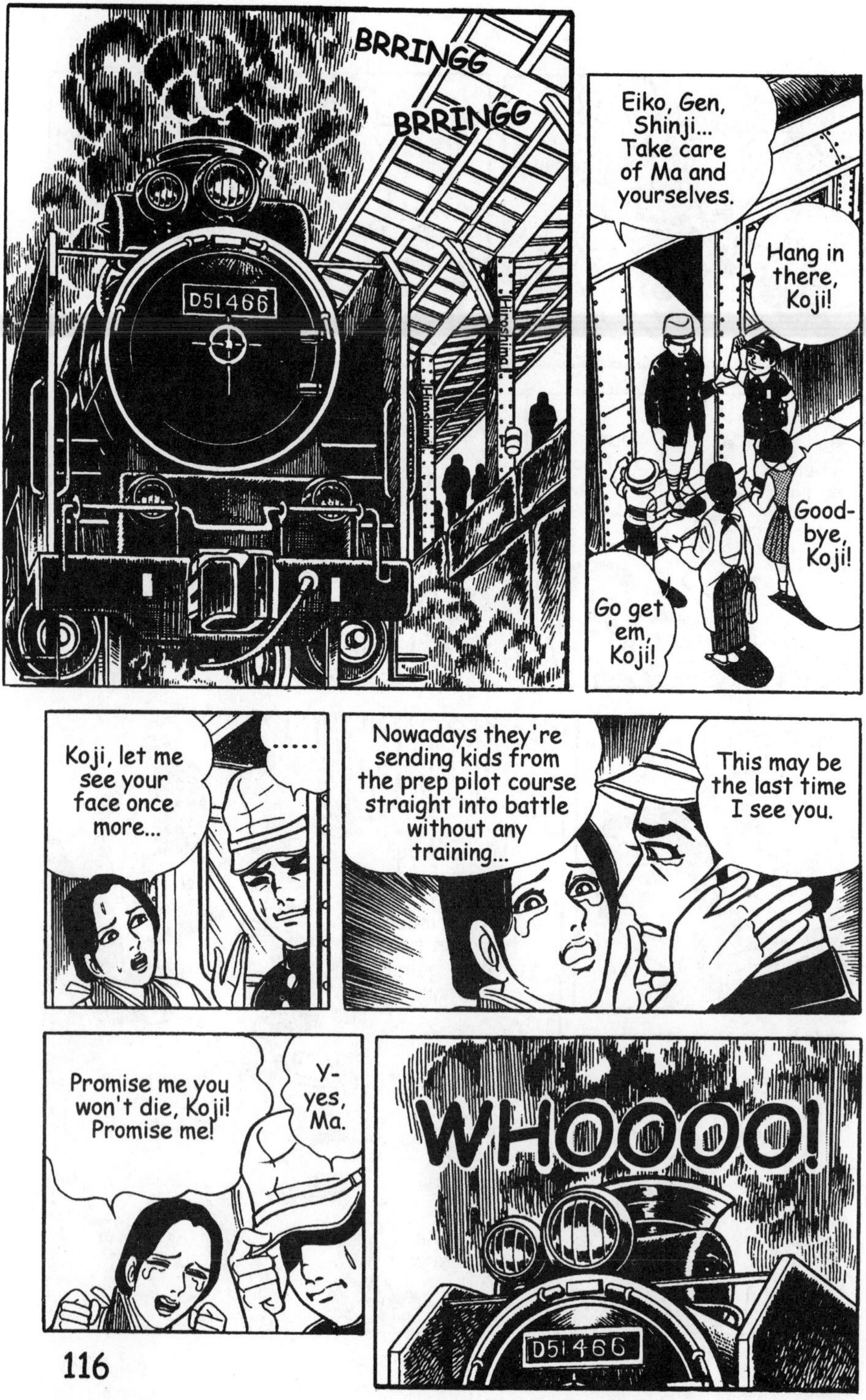
BRRINGG
BRRINGG
D51466
Eiko, Gen, Shinji... Take care of Ma and yourselves.
Hang in there, Koji!
Good-bye, Koji!
Go get 'em, Koji!
Koji, let me see your face once more...
.....
Nowadays they're sending kids from the prep pilot course straight into battle without any training...
This may be the last time I see you.
Promise me you won't die, Koji! Promise me!
Y-yes, Ma.
WHOOOO!
D51466

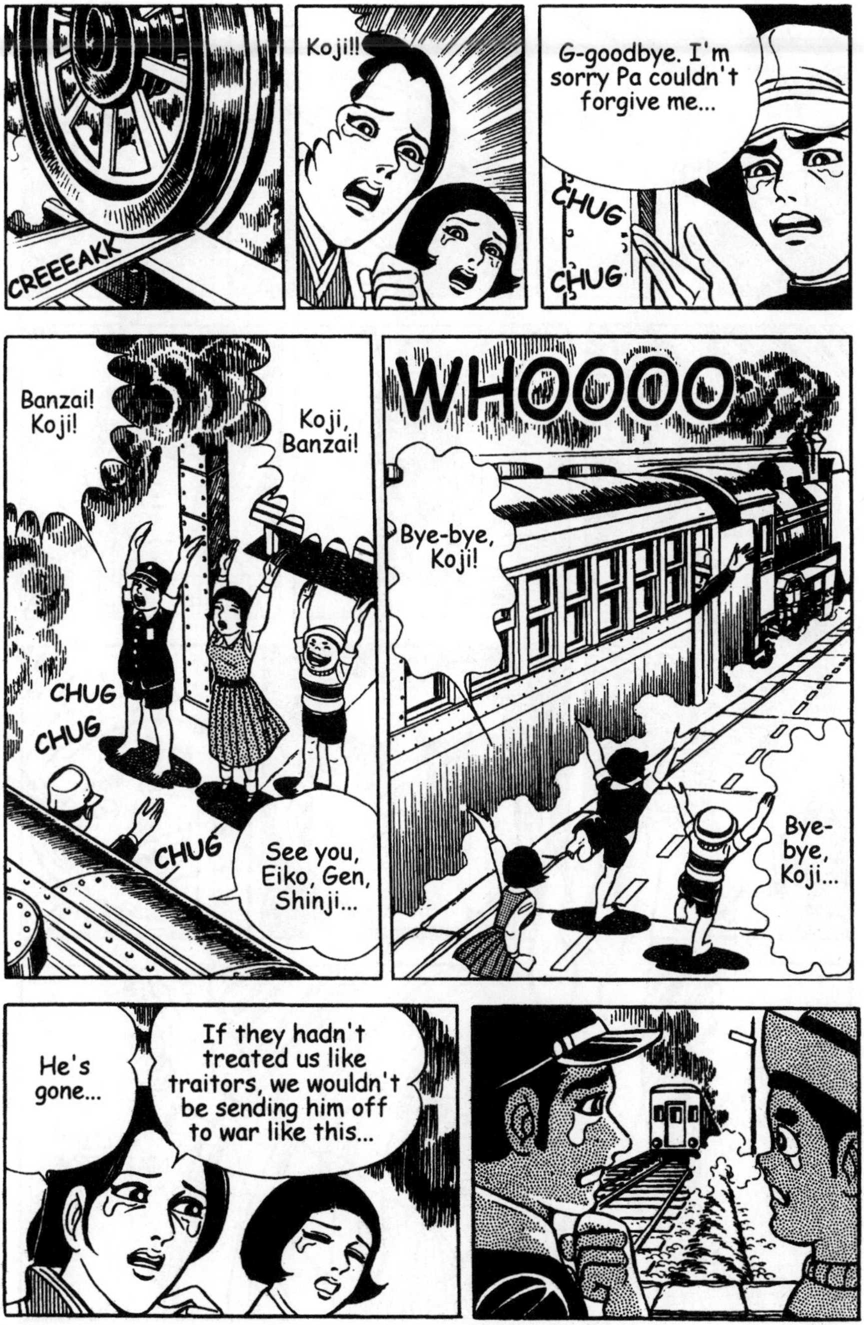

CREEEAKK
Koji!!
G-goodbye. I'm sorry Pa couldn't forgive me...
CHUG
CHUG
Banzai! Koji!
Koji, Banzai!
CHUG
CHUG
CHUG
See you, Eiko, Gen, Shinji...
WHOOOO
Bye-bye, Koji!
Bye-bye, Koji...
He's gone...
If they hadn't treated us like traitors, we wouldn't be sending him off to war like this...

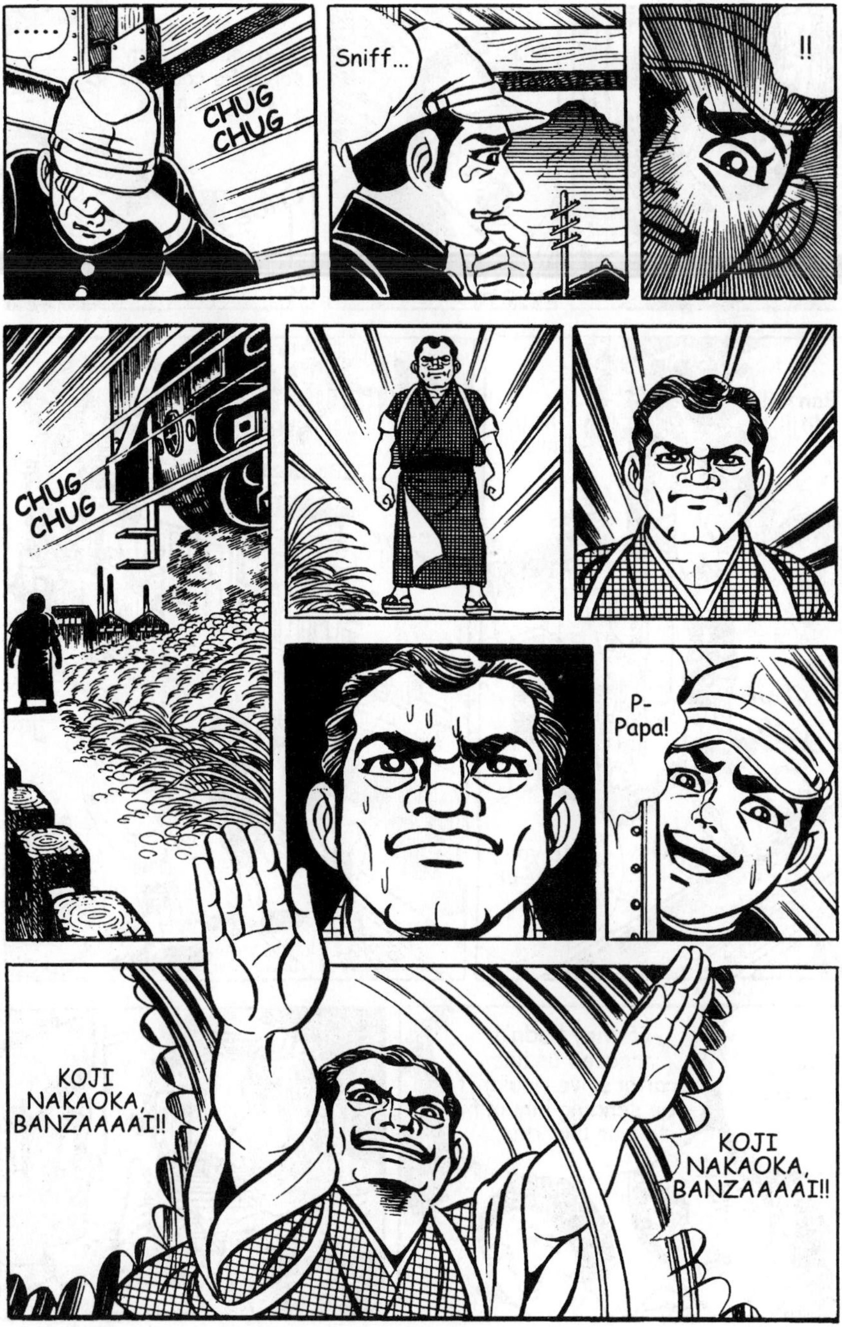
......
CHUG CHUG
Sniff...
!!
CHUG CHUG
P- Papa!
KOJI NAKAOKA, BANZAAAAI!!
KOJI NAKAOKA, BANZAAAAI!!

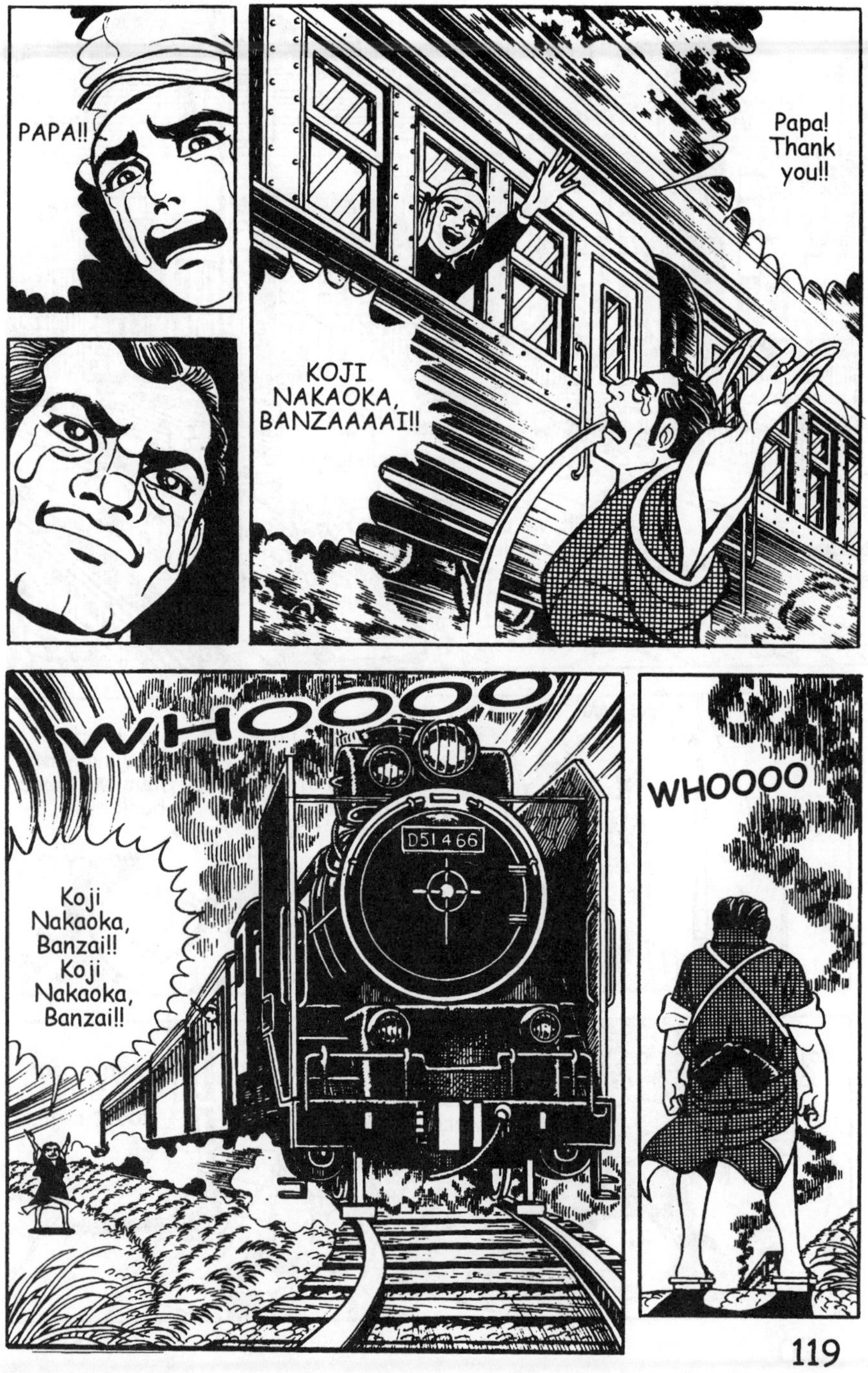
PAPA!!
Papa! Thank you!!
KOJI NAKAOKA, BANZAAAAI!!
WHOOOOO
Koji Nakaoka, Banzai!! Koji Nakaoka, Banzai!!
WHOOOO

Industrial Promotion Hall (now known as the A-Bomb Dome)
I'm hungry! I'm huuungry!!
Oh, we are loyal soldiers, we are the hand of heaven, striking at injustice...
TRAMP
TRAMP
Mama! Those soldiers are going off to the front, too, aren't they.
I wonder how many of them will come back alive...?
Koji, too...
Well, come on. Let's go home and get to work.
長田
I can't bear to think about Koji...

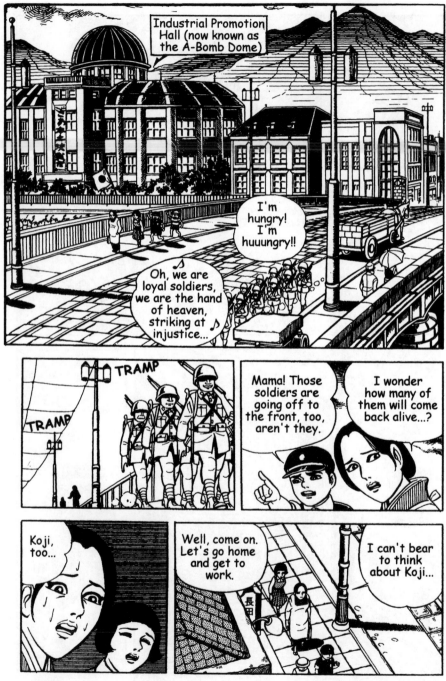

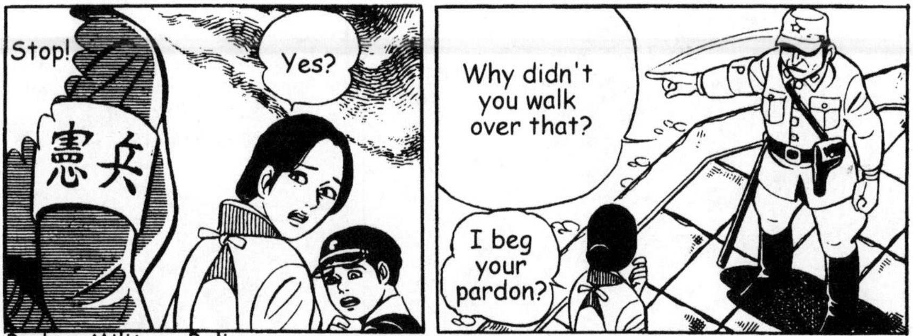
Stop!
Yes?
憲兵
Why didn't you walk over that?
I beg your pardon?

Badge: Military Police

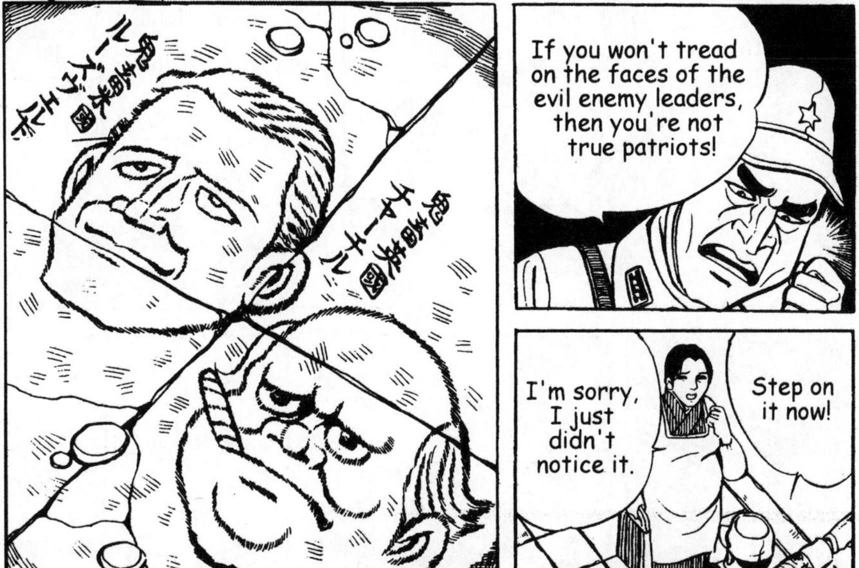
鬼畜米国 ルーズヴェルト
鬼畜英国 チャーチル
If you won't tread on the faces of the evil enemy leaders, then you're not true patriots!
I'm sorry, I just didn't notice it.
Step on it now!

Signs: American Devil Roosevelt, British Devil Churchill

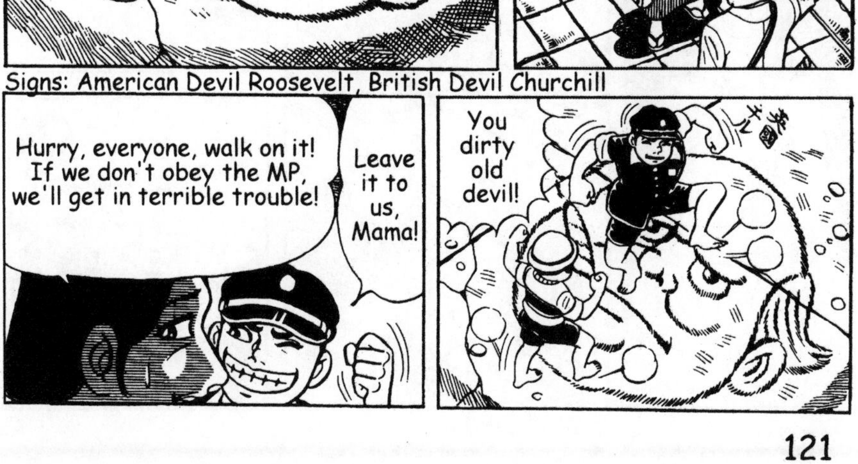
Hurry, everyone, walk on it! If we don't obey the MP, we'll get in terrible trouble!
Leave it to us, Mama!
You dirty old devil!

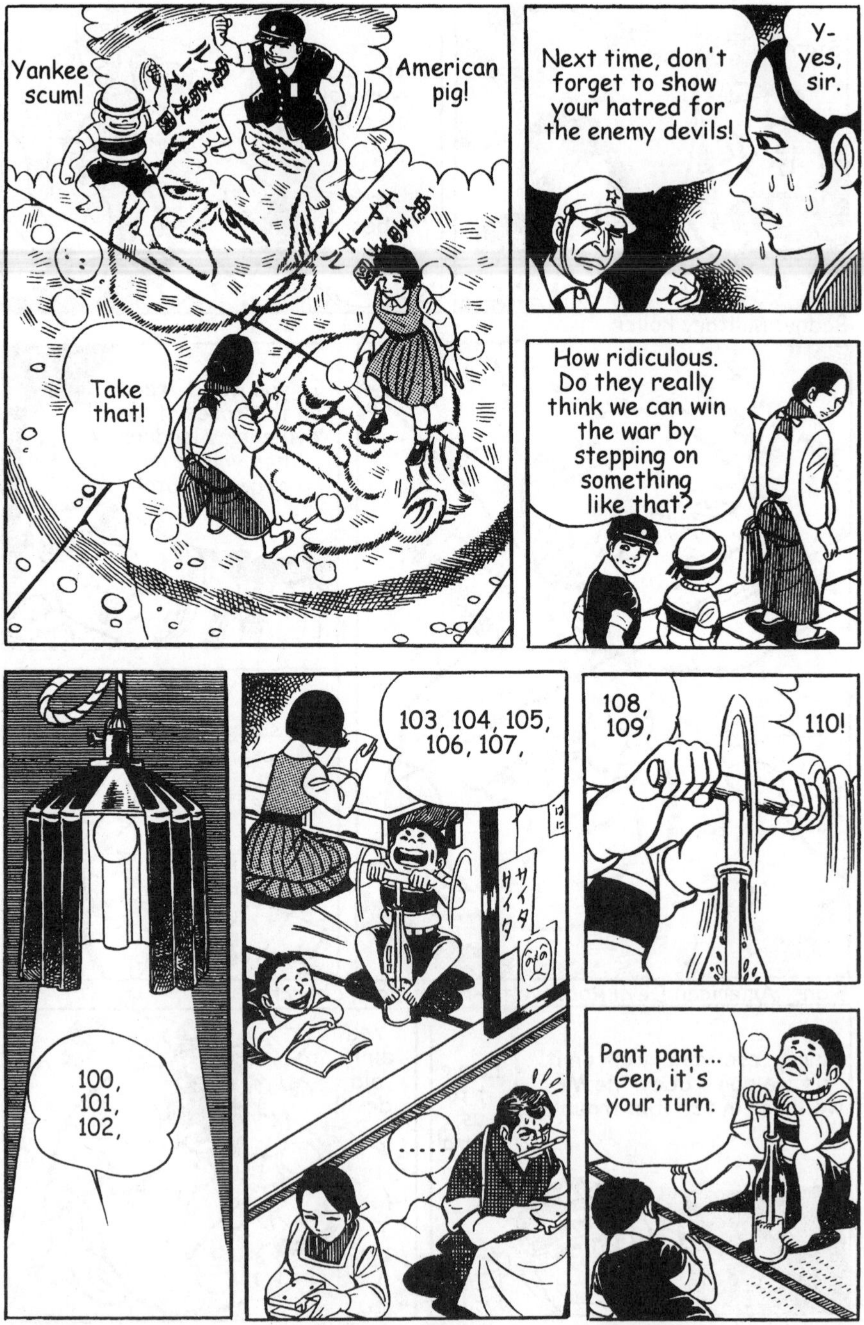

Yankee scum!
American pig!
Take that!
Next time, don't forget to show your hatred for the enemy devils!
Y-yes, sir.
How ridiculous. Do they really think we can win the war by stepping on something like that?
100, 101, 102,
103, 104, 105, 106, 107,
サイタ サイタ
......
108, 109,
110!
Pant pant... Gen, it's your turn.

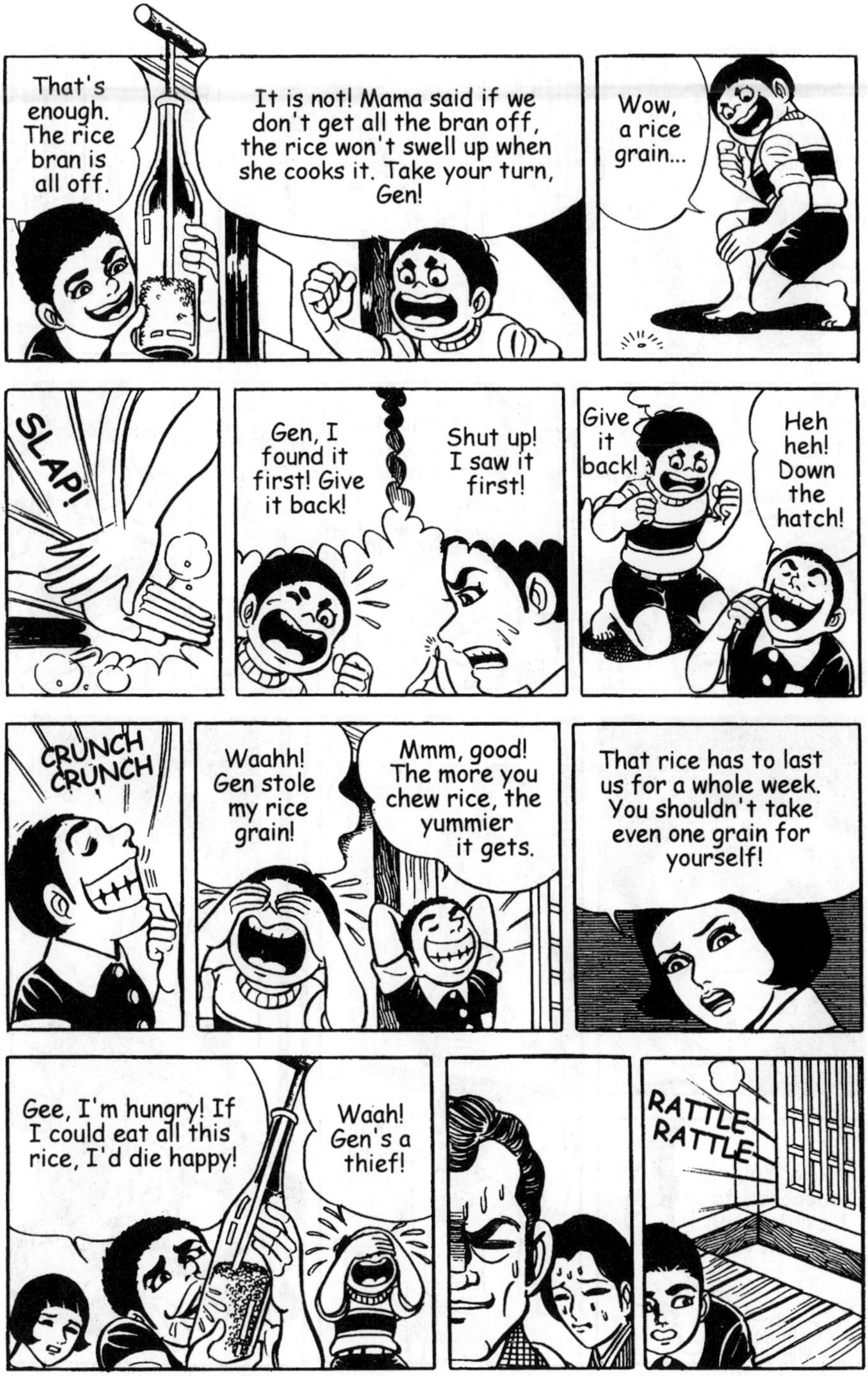
That's enough. The rice bran is all off.
It is not! Mama said if we don't get all the bran off, the rice won't swell up when she cooks it. Take your turn, Gen!
Wow, a rice grain...
SLAP!
Gen, I found it first! Give it back!
Shut up! I saw it first!
Give it back!
Heh heh! Down the hatch!
CRUNCH CRUNCH
Waahh! Gen stole my rice grain!
Mmm, good! The more you chew rice, the yummier it gets.
That rice has to last us for a whole week. You shouldn't take even one grain for yourself!
Gee, I'm hungry! If I could eat all this rice, I'd die happy!
Waah! Gen's a thief!
RATTLE RATTLE

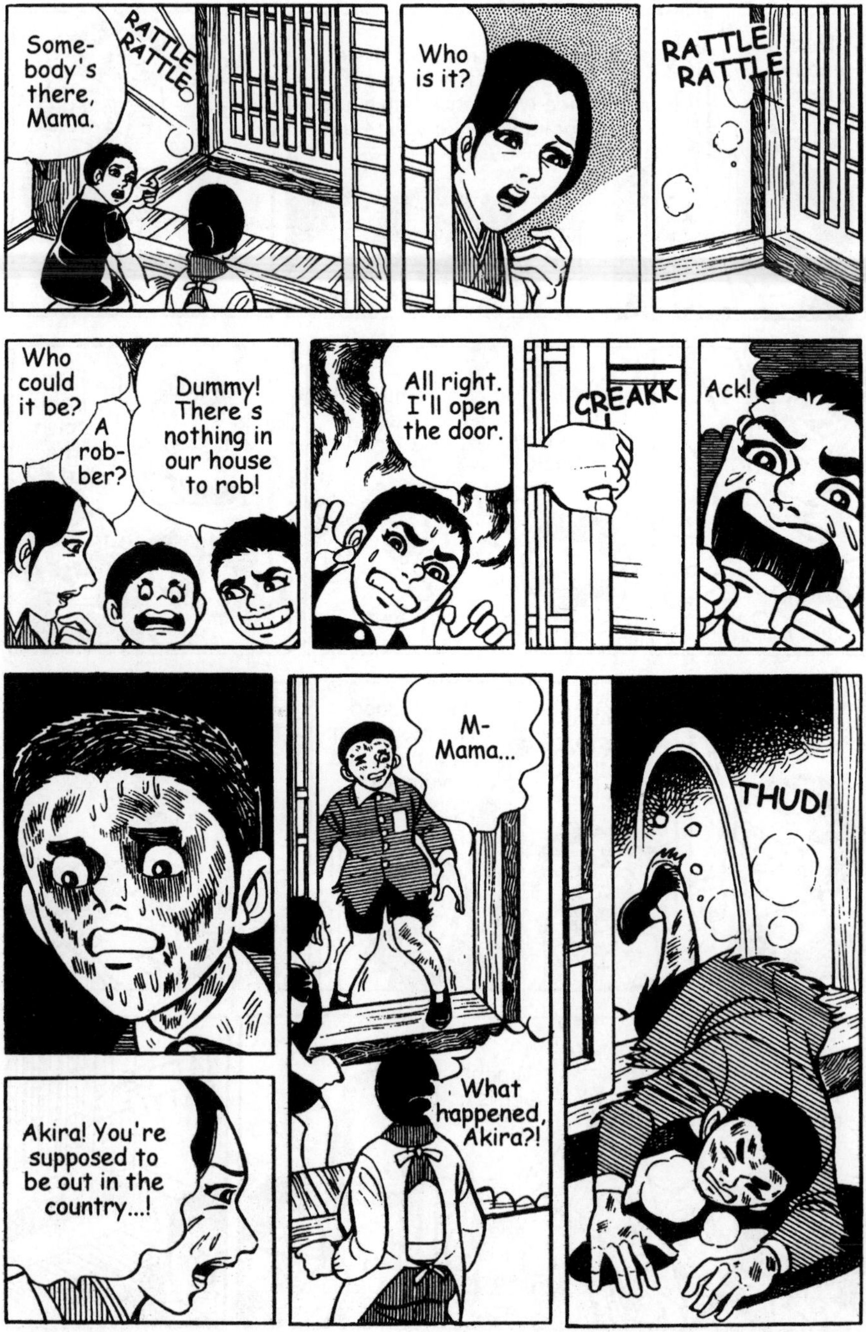
Somebody's there, Mama.
RATTLE RATTLE
Who is it?
RATTLE RATTLE
Who could it be?
A robber?
Dummy! There's nothing in our house to rob!
All right. I'll open the door.
CREAKK
Ack!
Akira! You're supposed to be out in the country...!
M- Mama...
What happened, Akira?!
THUD!

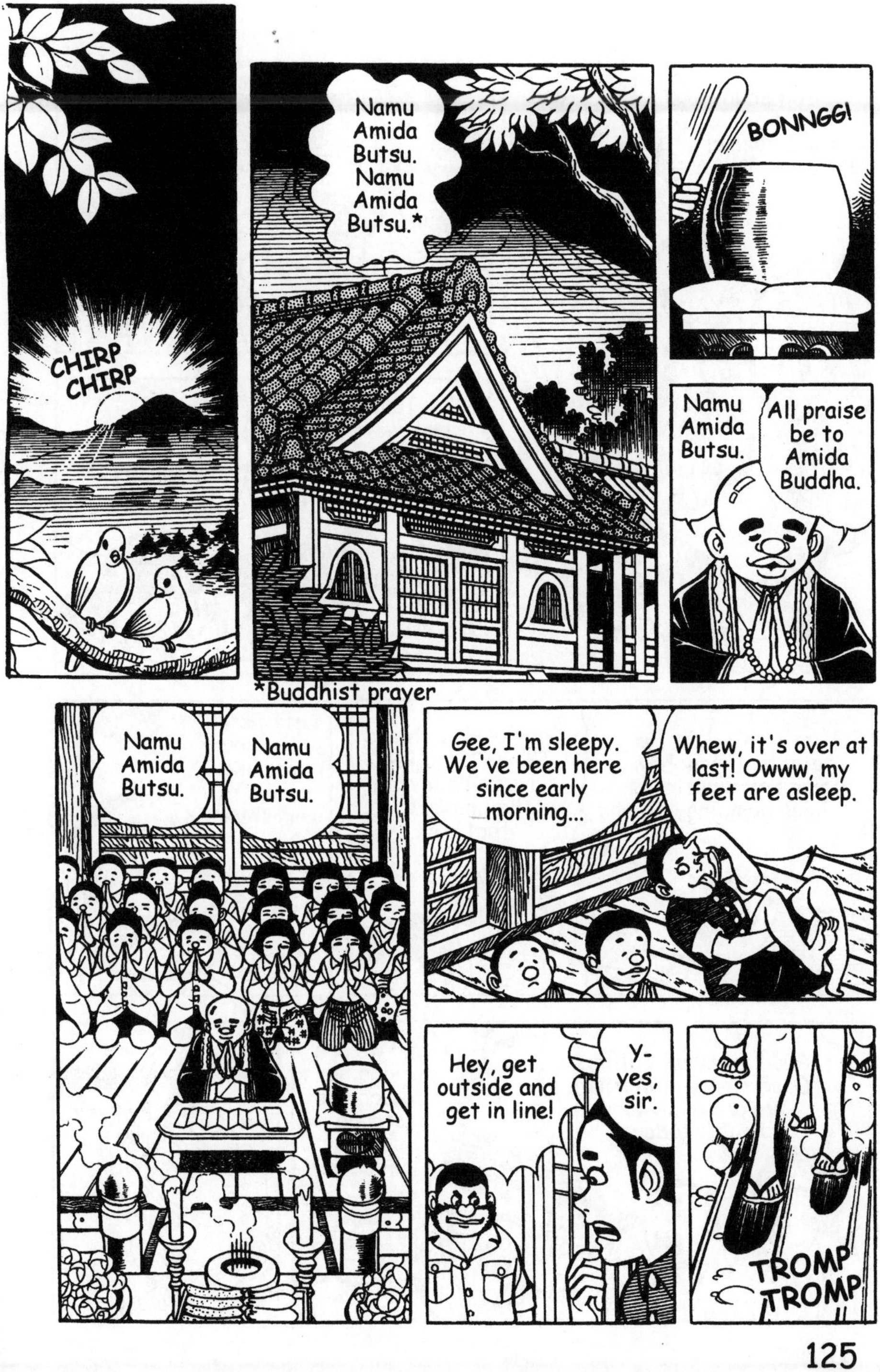
CHIRP CHIRP
Namu Amida Butsu. Namu Amida Butsu.*
BONNGG!
Namu Amida Butsu.
All praise be to Amida Buddha.
*Buddhist prayer
Namu Amida Butsu.
Namu Amida Butsu.
Gee, I'm sleepy. We've been here since early morning...
Whew, it's over at last! Owww, my feet are asleep.
Hey, get outside and get in line!
Y-yes, sir.
TROMP TROMP

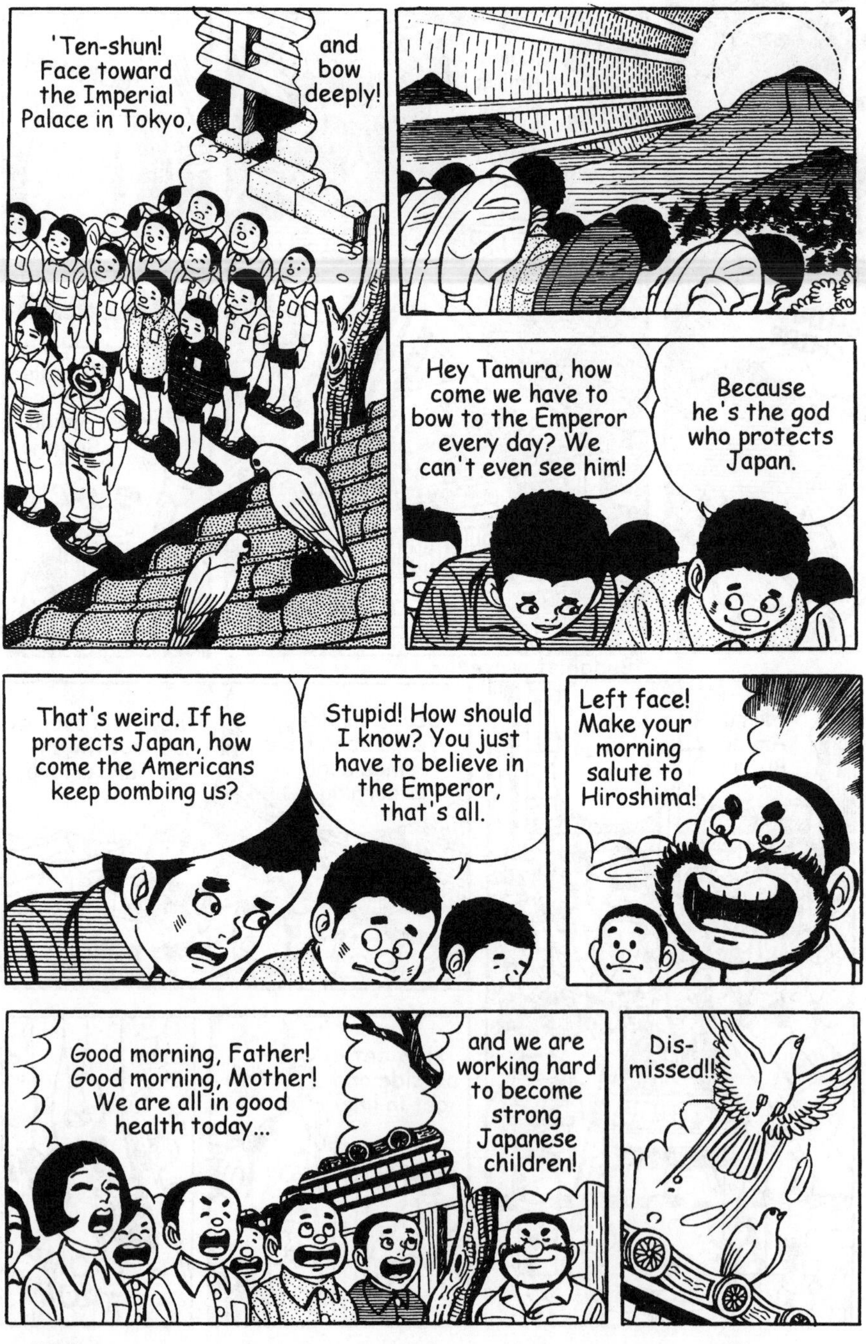
'Ten-shun! Face toward the Imperial Palace in Tokyo,
and bow deeply!
Hey Tamura, how come we have to bow to the Emperor every day? We can't even see him!
Because he's the god who protects Japan.
That's weird. If he protects Japan, how come the Americans keep bombing us?
Stupid! How should I know? You just have to believe in the Emperor, that's all.
Left face! Make your morning salute to Hiroshima!
Good morning, Father! Good morning, Mother! We are all in good health today...
and we are working hard to become strong Japanese children!
Dis- missed!!

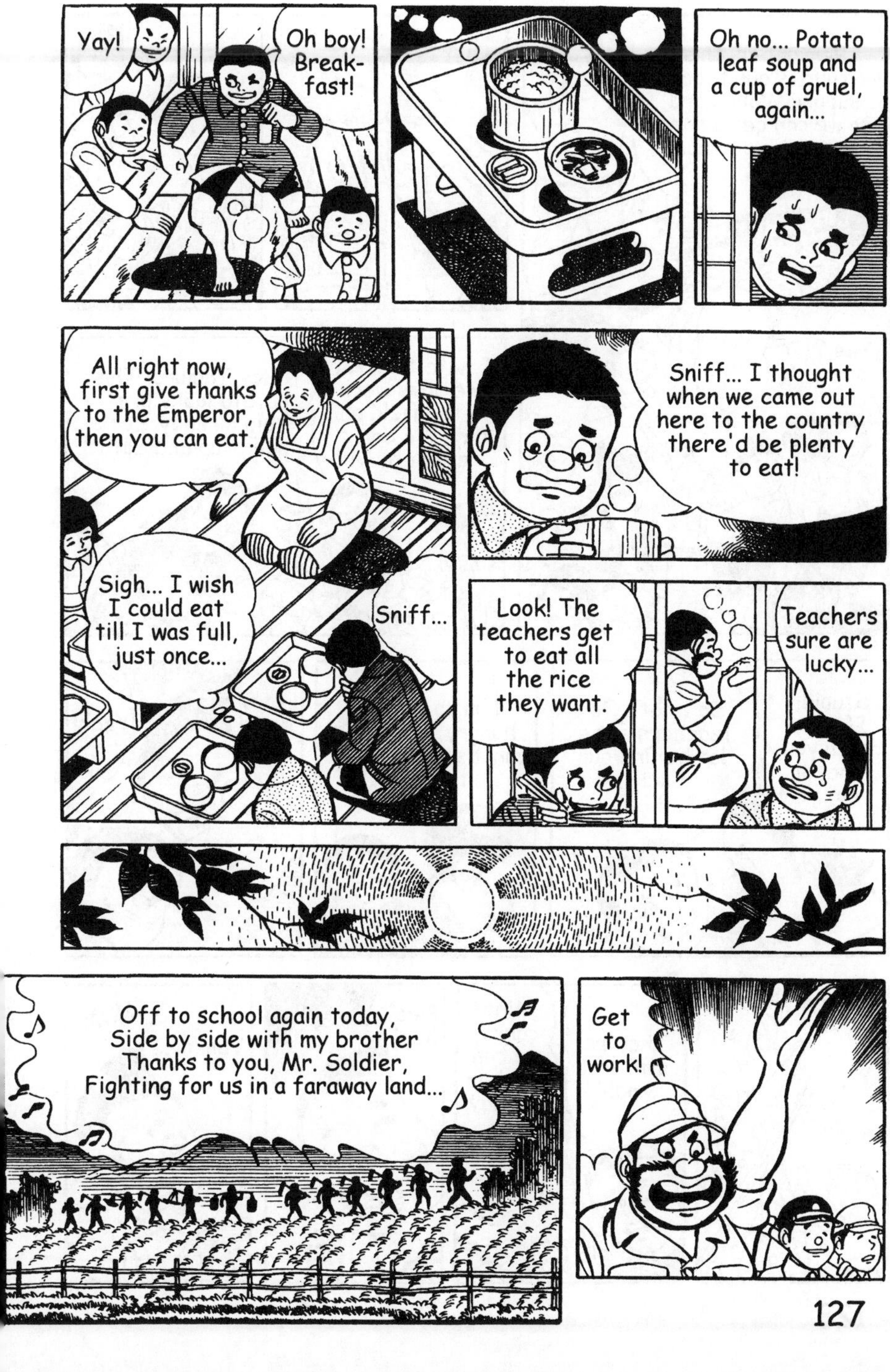
Yay!
Oh boy! Breakfast!
Oh no... Potato leaf soup and a cup of gruel, again...
All right now, first give thanks to the Emperor, then you can eat.
Sigh... I wish I could eat till I was full, just once...
Sniff...
Sniff... I thought when we came out here to the country there'd be plenty to eat!
Look! The teachers get to eat all the rice they want.
Teachers sure are lucky...
Off to school again today,
Side by side with my brother
Thanks to you, Mr. Soldier,
Fighting for us in a faraway land...
Get to work!

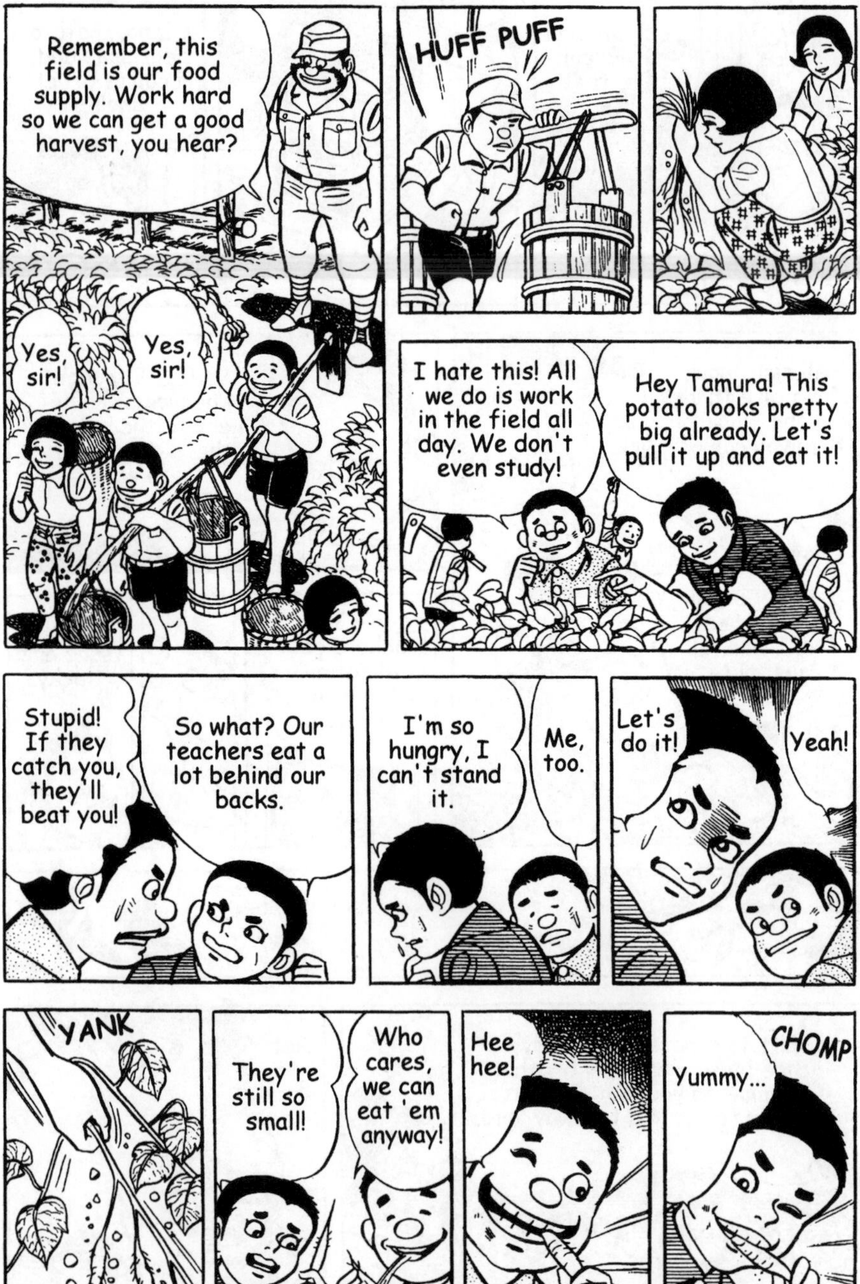
Remember, this field is our food supply. Work hard so we can get a good harvest, you hear?
Yes, sir!
Yes, sir!
HUFF PUFF
I hate this! All we do is work in the field all day. We don't even study!
Hey Tamura! This potato looks pretty big already. Let's pull it up and eat it!
Stupid! If they catch you, they'll beat you!
So what? Our teachers eat a lot behind our backs.
I'm so hungry, I can't stand it.
Me, too.
Let's do it!
Yeah!
YANK
They're still so small!
Who cares, we can eat 'em anyway!
Hee hee!
CHOMP
Yummy...

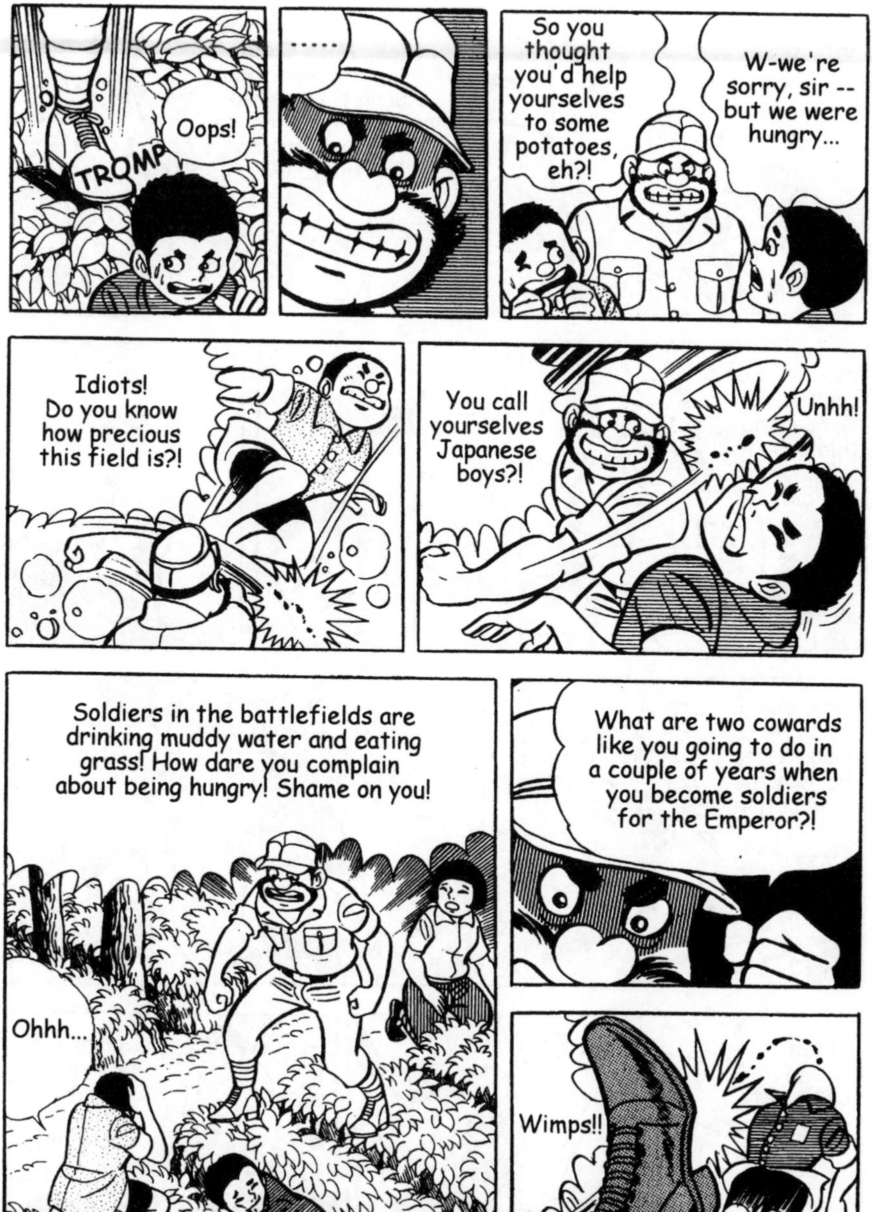
Oops!
TROMP
......
So you thought you'd help yourselves to some potatoes, eh?!
W-we're sorry, sir -- but we were hungry...
Idiots! Do you know how precious this field is?!
You call yourselves Japanese boys?!
Unhh!
Soldiers in the battlefields are drinking muddy water and eating grass! How dare you complain about being hungry! Shame on you!
Ohhh...
What are two cowards like you going to do in a couple of years when you become soldiers for the Emperor?!
Wimps!!

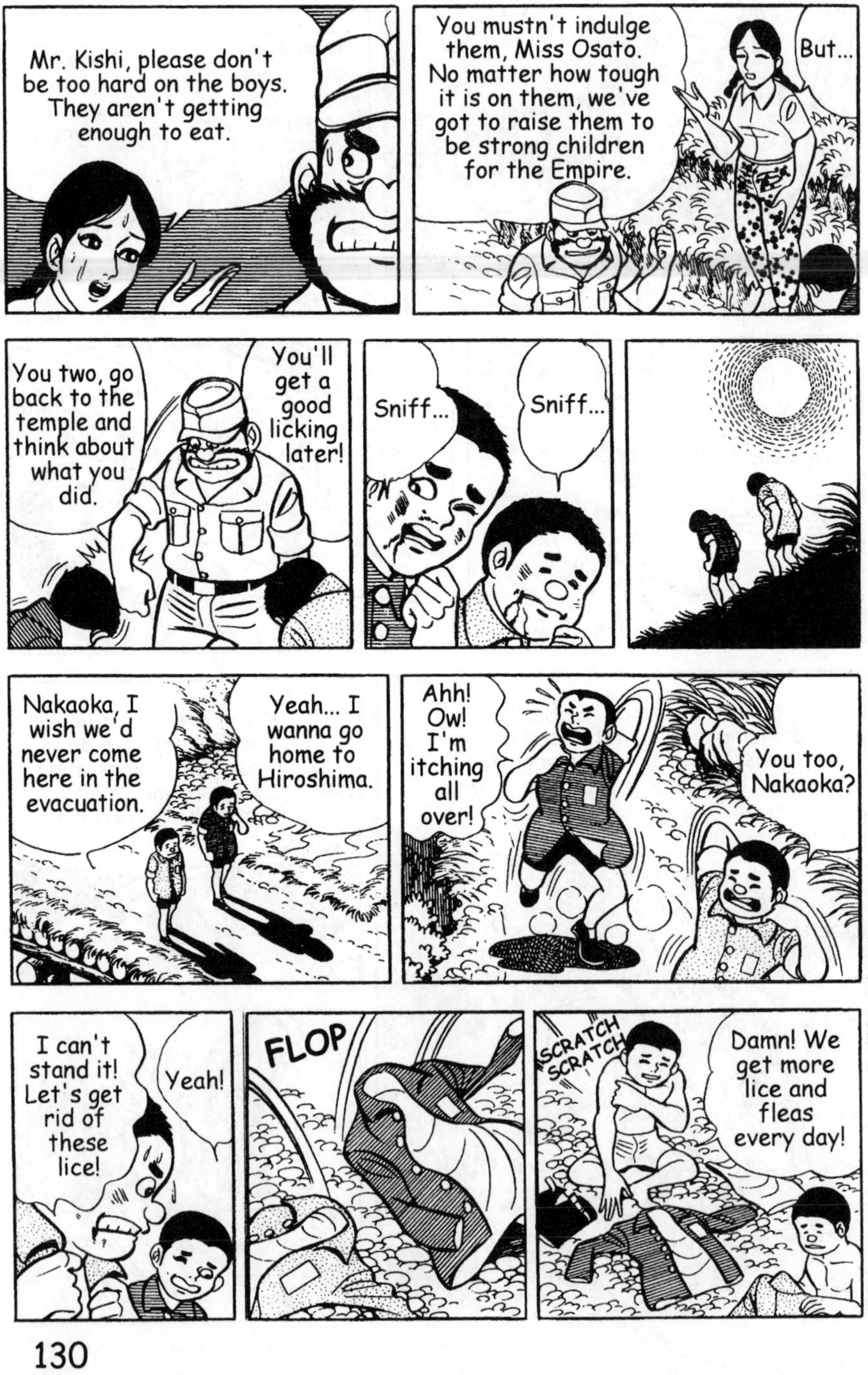
Mr. Kishi, please don't be too hard on the boys. They aren't getting enough to eat.
You mustn't indulge them, Miss Osato. No matter how tough it is on them, we've got to raise them to be strong children for the Empire.
But...
You two, go back to the temple and think about what you did.
You'll get a good licking later!
Sniff...
Sniff...
Nakaoka, I wish we'd never come here in the evacuation.
Yeah... I wanna go home to Hiroshima.
Ahh! Ow! I'm itching all over!
You too, Nakaoka?
I can't stand it! Let's get rid of these lice!
Yeah!
FLOP
SCRATCH SCRATCH
Damn! We get more lice and fleas every day!

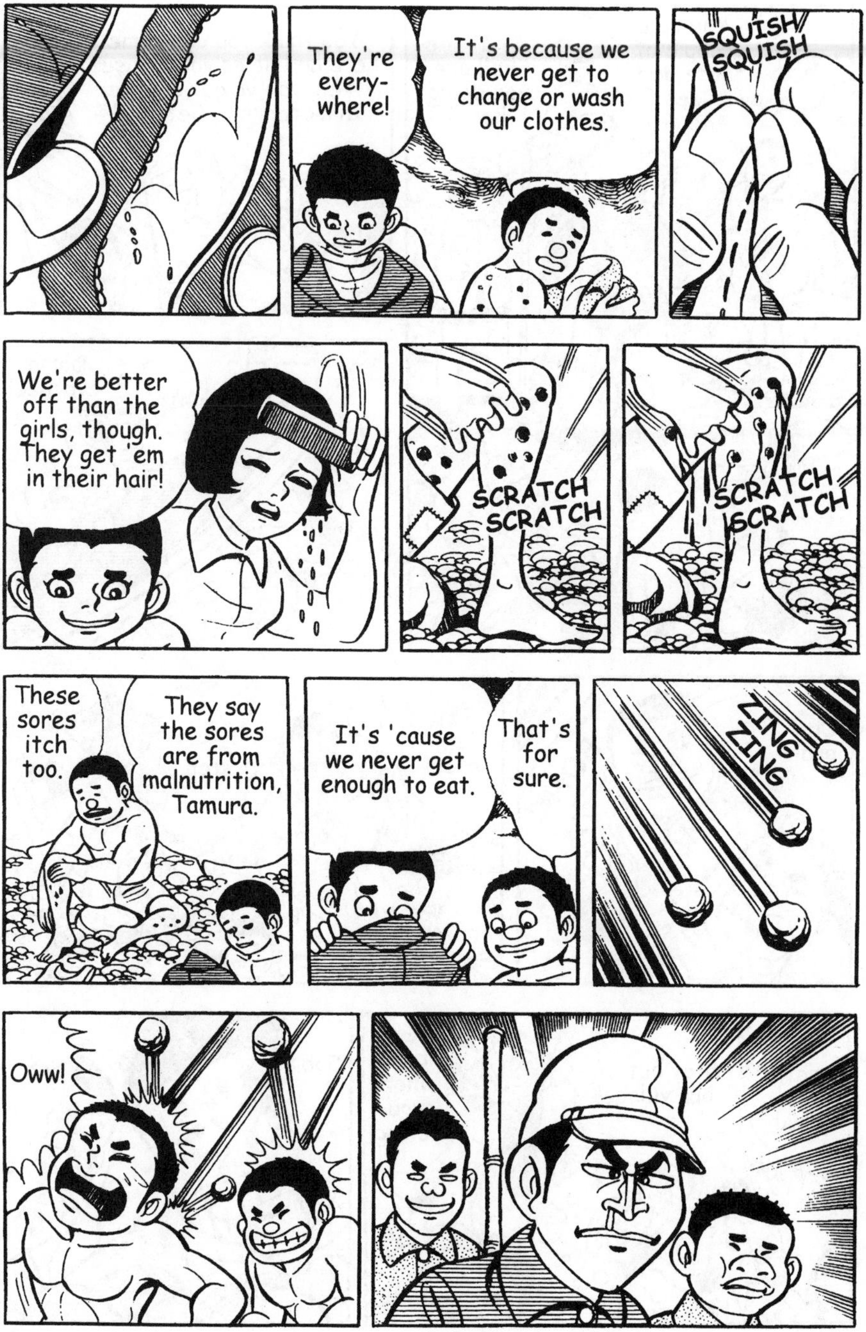
They're every-where!
It's because we never get to change or wash our clothes.
SQUISH SQUISH
We're better off than the girls, though. They get 'em in their hair!
SCRATCH SCRATCH
SCRATCH SCRATCH
These sores itch too.
They say the sores are from malnutrition, Tamura.
It's 'cause we never get enough to eat.
That's for sure.
ZING ZING
Oww!

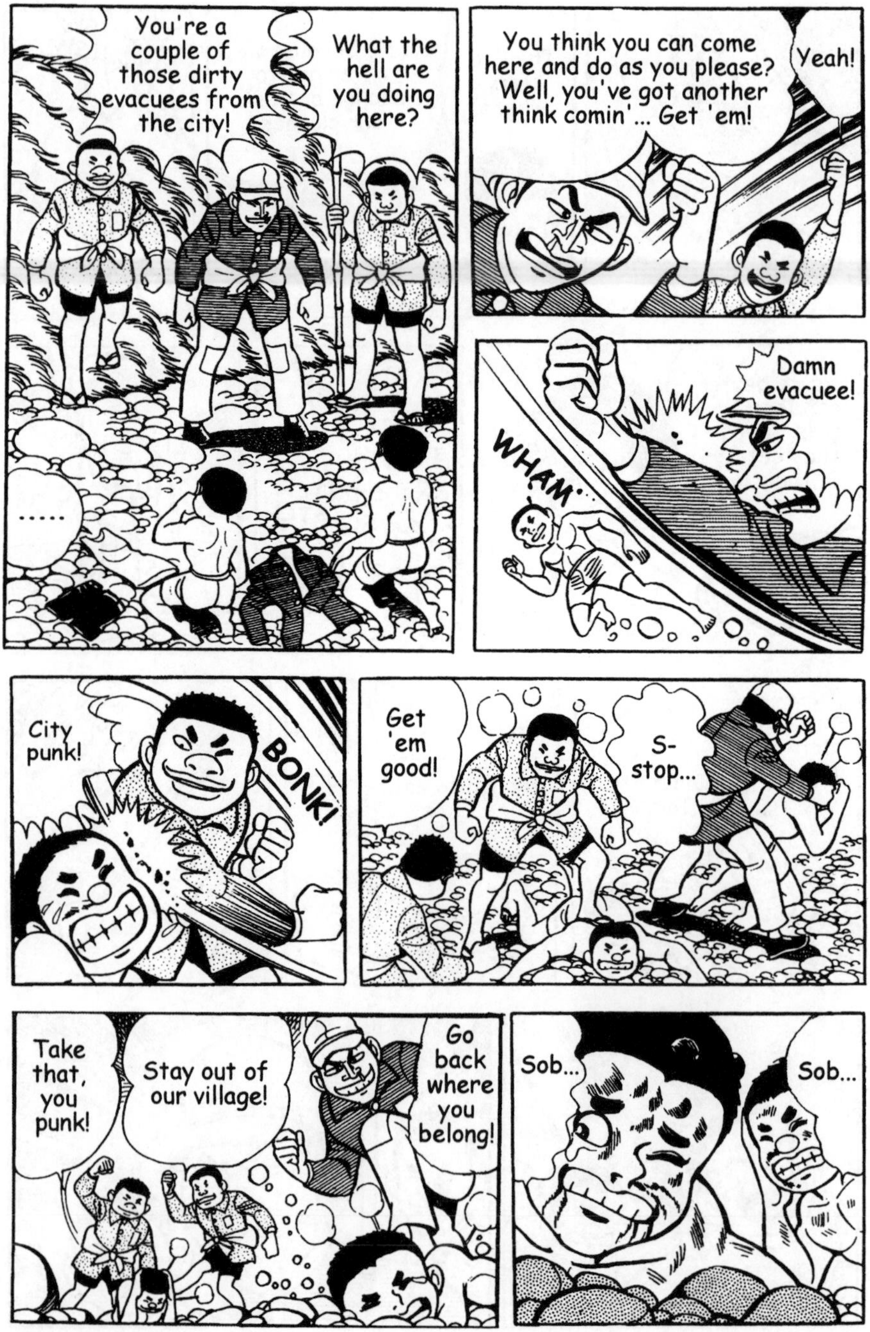
You're a couple of those dirty evacuees from the city!
What the hell are you doing here?
......
You think you can come here and do as you please? Well, you've got another think comin'... Get 'em!
Yeah!
Damn evacuee!
WHAM
City punk!
BONK!
Get 'em good!
S- stop...
Take that, you punk!
Stay out of our village!
Go back where you belong!
Sob...
Sob...

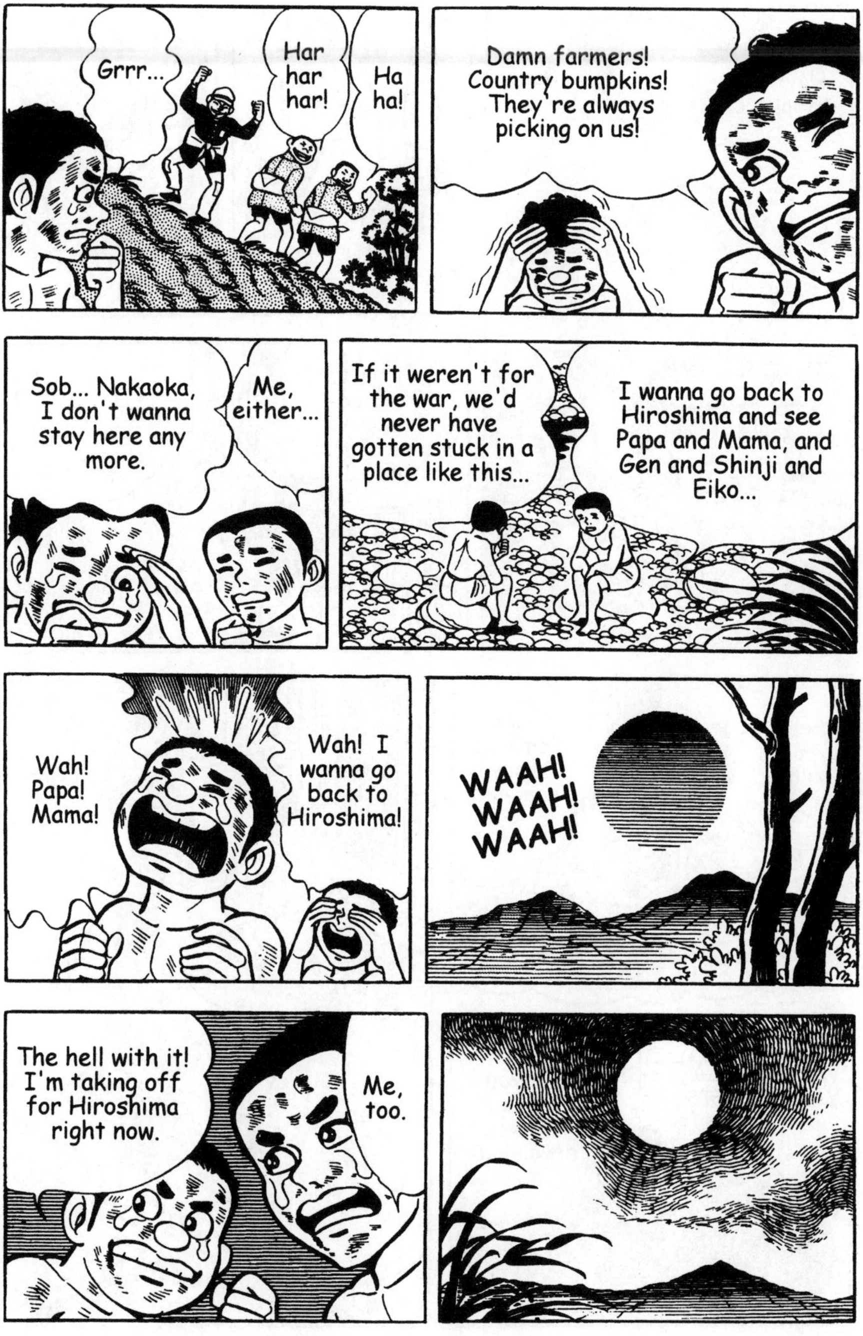
Grrr...
Har har har!
Ha ha!
Damn farmers! Country bumpkins! They're always picking on us!
Sob... Nakaoka, I don't wanna stay here any more.
Me, either...
If it weren't for the war, we'd never have gotten stuck in a place like this...
I wanna go back to Hiroshima and see Papa and Mama, and Gen and Shinji and Eiko...
Wah! Papa! Mama!
Wah! I wanna go back to Hiroshima!
WAAH! WAAH! WAAH!
The hell with it! I'm taking off for Hiroshima right now.
Me, too.

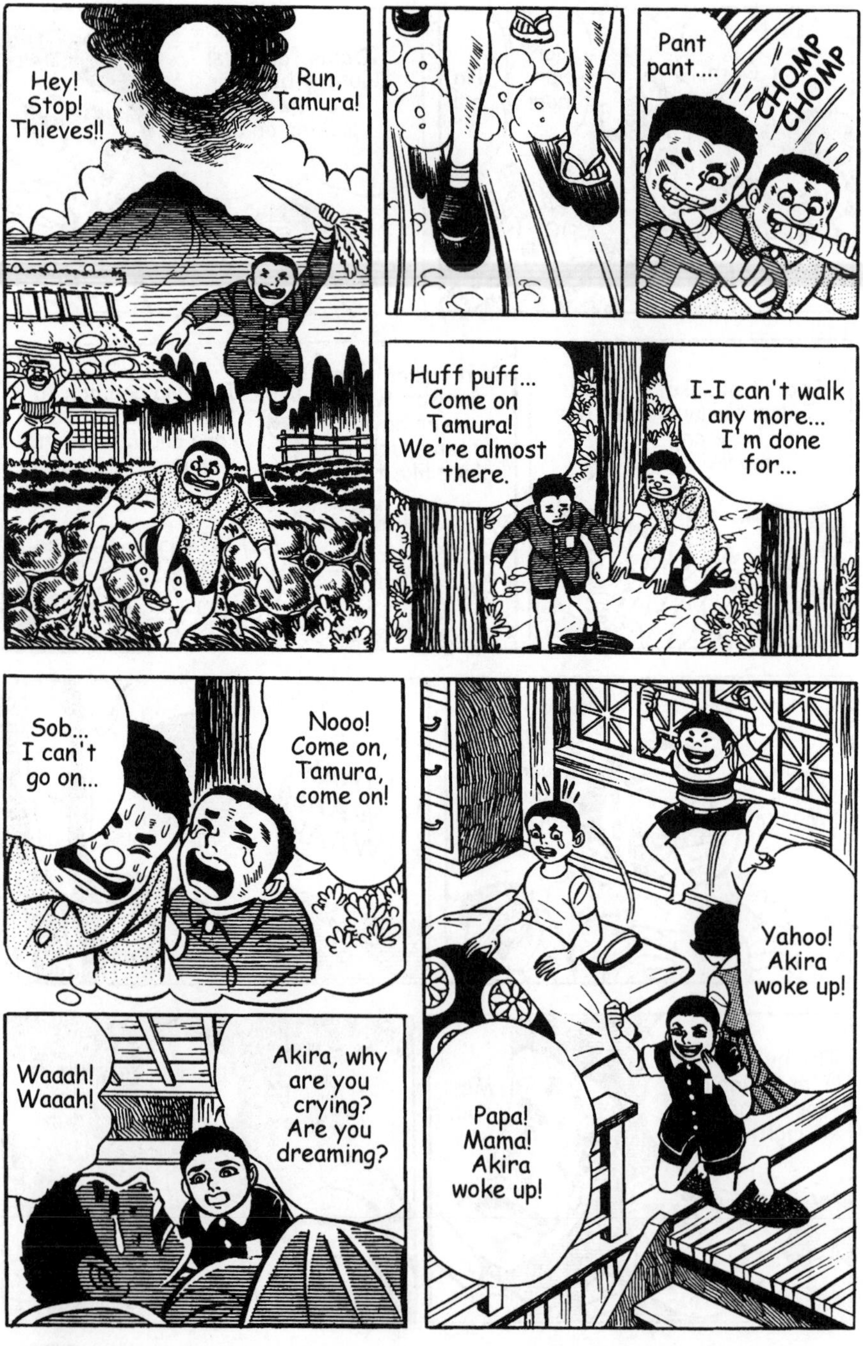
Hey! Stop! Thieves!!
Run, Tamura!
Pant pant....
CHOMP CHOMP
Huff puff... Come on Tamura! We're almost there.
I-I can't walk any more... I'm done for...
Sob... I can't go on...
Nooo! Come on, Tamura, come on!
Waaah! Waaah!
Akira, why are you crying? Are you dreaming?
Yahoo! Akira woke up!
Papa! Mama! Akira woke up!

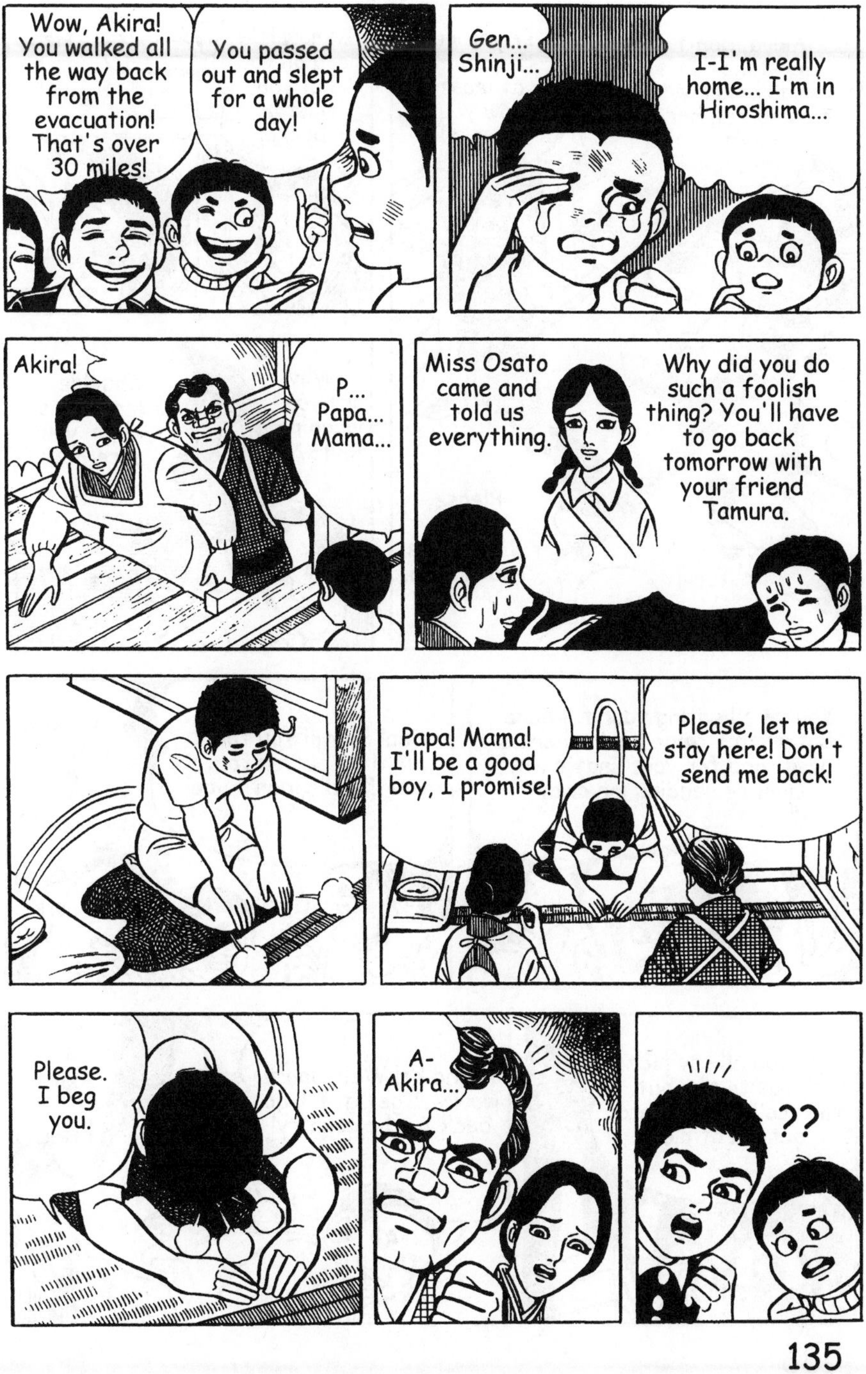
Wow, Akira! You walked all the way back from the evacuation! That's over 30 miles!
You passed out and slept for a whole day!
Gen... Shinji...
I-I'm really home... I'm in Hiroshima...
Akira!
P... Papa... Mama...
Miss Osato came and told us everything.
Why did you do such a foolish thing? You'll have to go back tomorrow with your friend Tamura.
Papa! Mama! I'll be a good boy, I promise!
Please, let me stay here! Don't send me back!
Please. I beg you.
A- Akira...
??

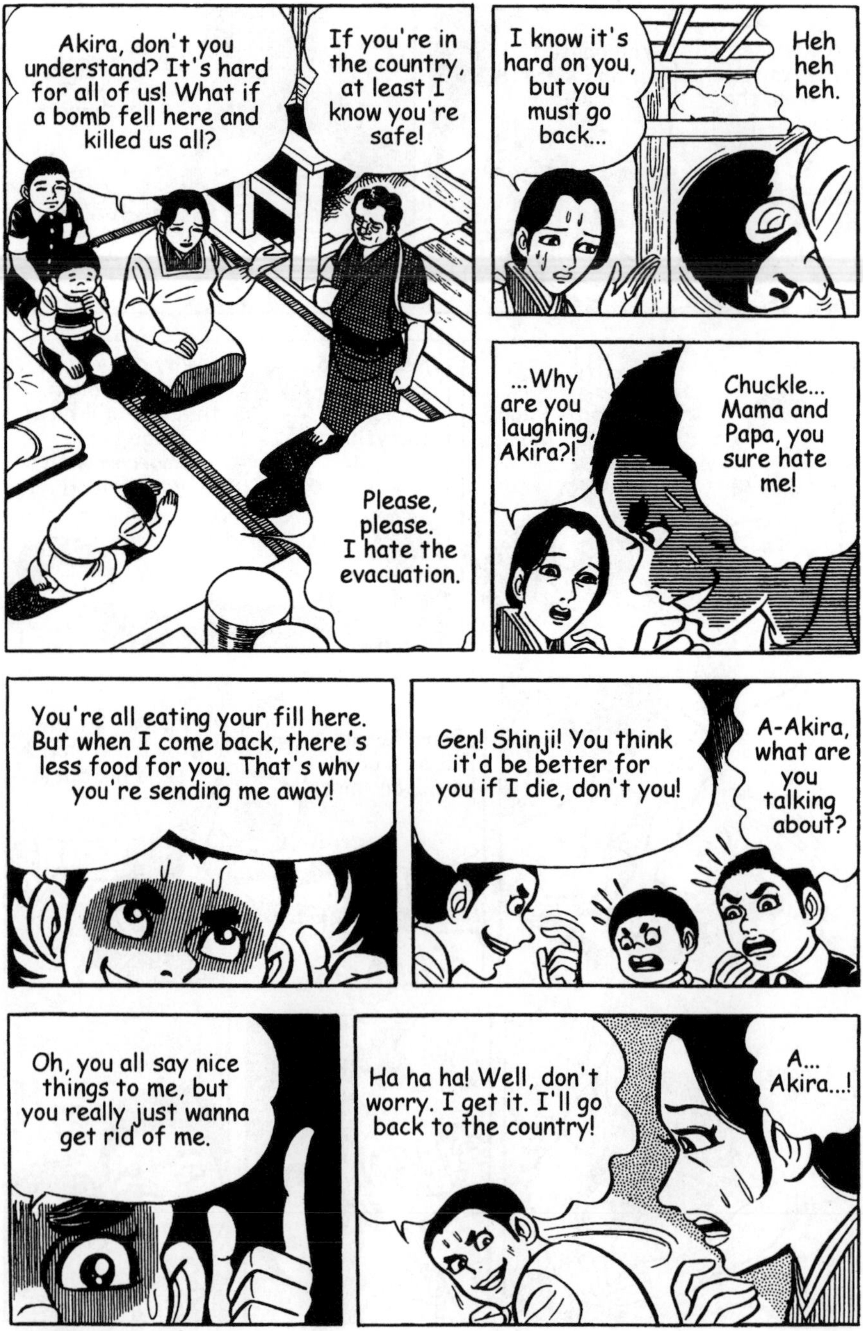
Akira, don't you understand? It's hard for all of us! What if a bomb fell here and killed us all?
If you're in the country, at least I know you're safe!
Please, please. I hate the evacuation.
I know it's hard on you, but you must go back...
Heh heh heh.
...Why are you laughing, Akira?!
Chuckle... Mama and Papa, you sure hate me!
You're all eating your fill here. But when I come back, there's less food for you. That's why you're sending me away!
Gen! Shinji! You think it'd be better for you if I die, don't you!
A-Akira, what are you talking about?
Oh, you all say nice things to me, but you really just wanna get rid of me.
Ha ha ha! Well, don't worry. I get it. I'll go back to the country!
A... Akira...!

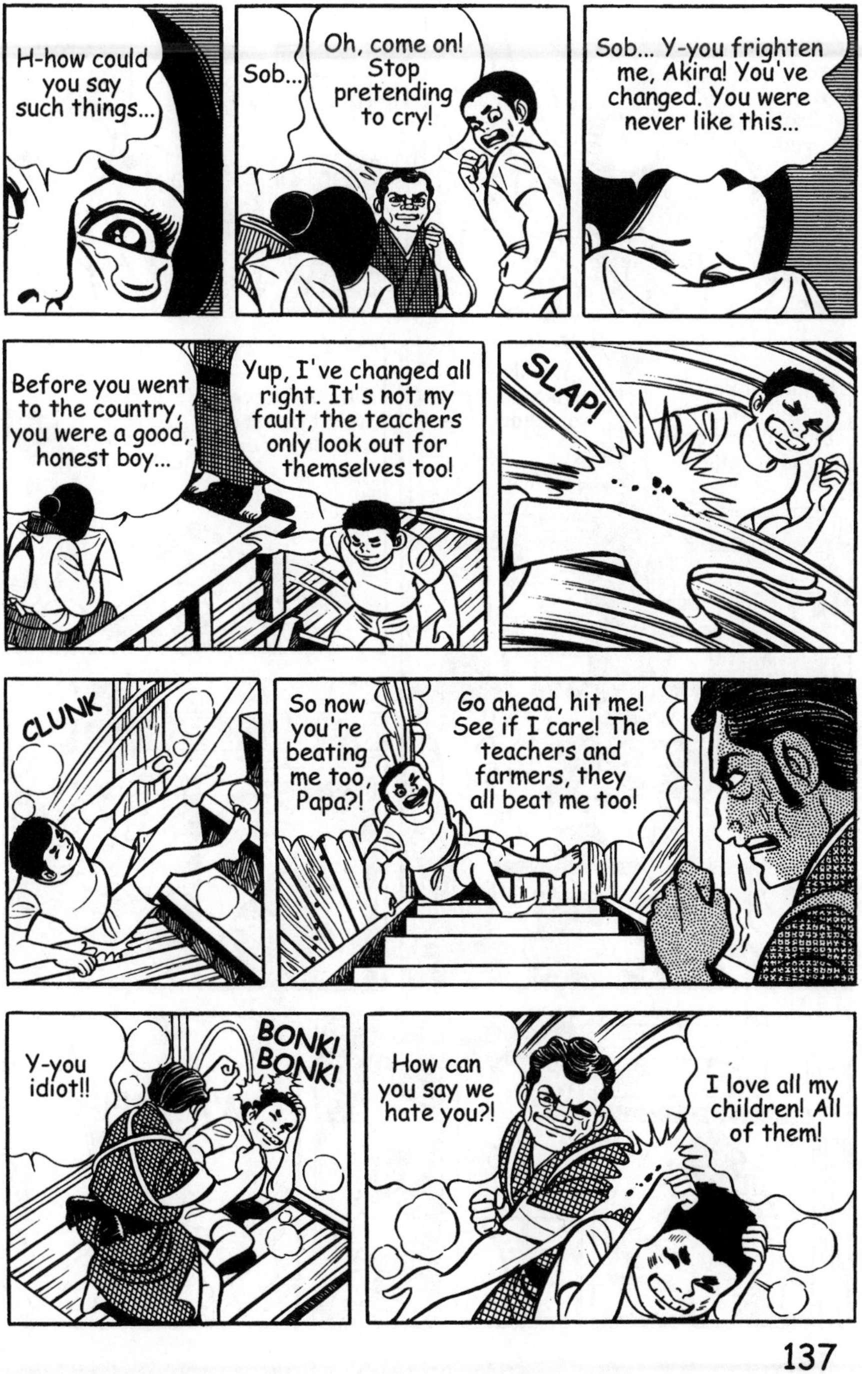
H-how could you say such things...
Sob...
Oh, come on! Stop pretending to cry!
Sob... Y-you frighten me, Akira! You've changed. You were never like this...
Before you went to the country, you were a good, honest boy...
Yup, I've changed all right. It's not my fault, the teachers only look out for themselves too!
SLAP!
CLUNK
So now you're beating me too, Papa?!
Go ahead, hit me! See if I care! The teachers and farmers, they all beat me too!
Y-you idiot!!
BONK! BONK!
How can you say we hate you?!
I love all my children! All of them!

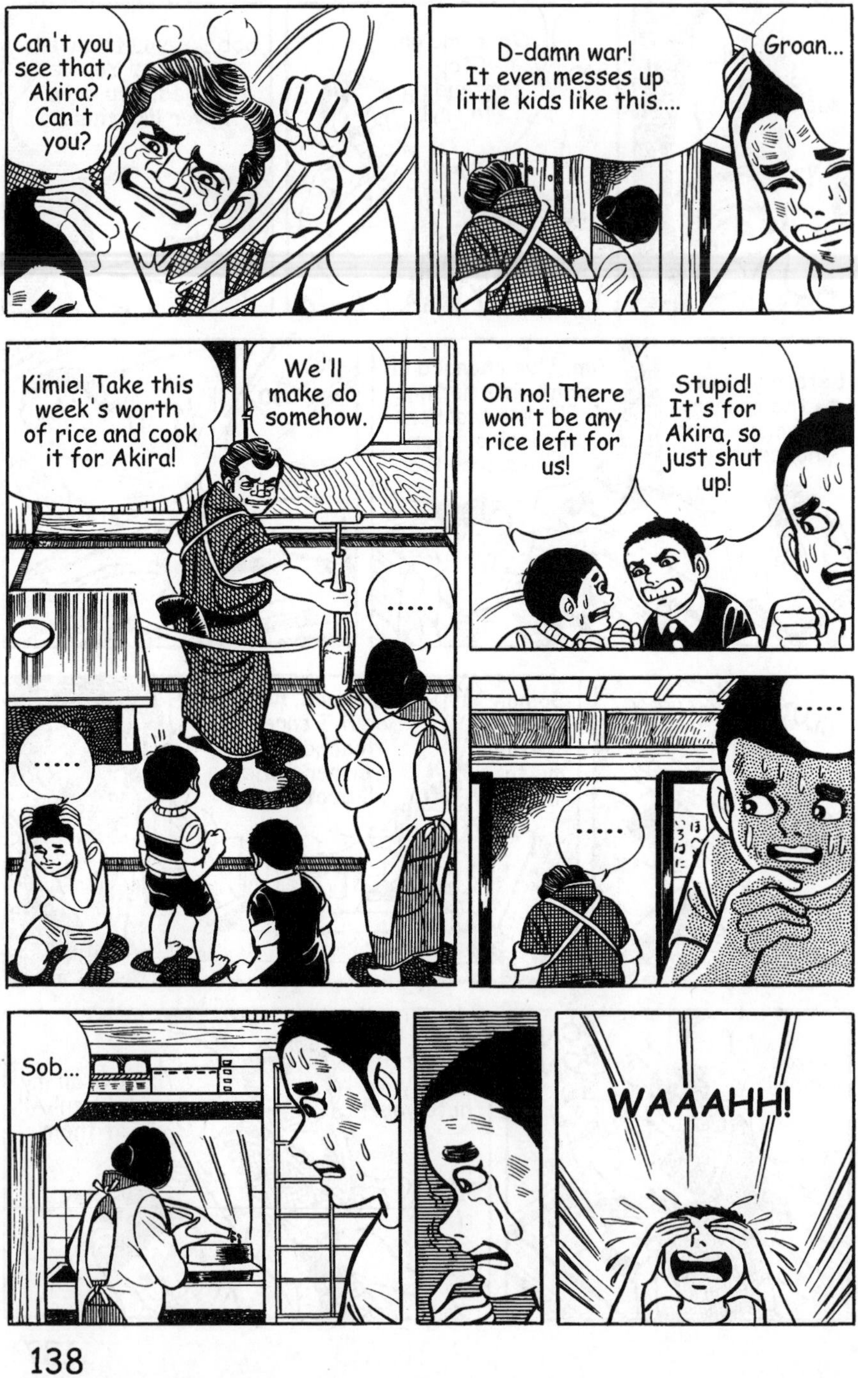
Can't you see that, Akira? Can't you?
D-damn war! It even messes up little kids like this....
Groan...
Kimie! Take this week's worth of rice and cook it for Akira!
We'll make do somehow.
.....
.....
Oh no! There won't be any rice left for us!
Stupid! It's for Akira, so just shut up!
.....
.....
Sob...
WAAAHH!

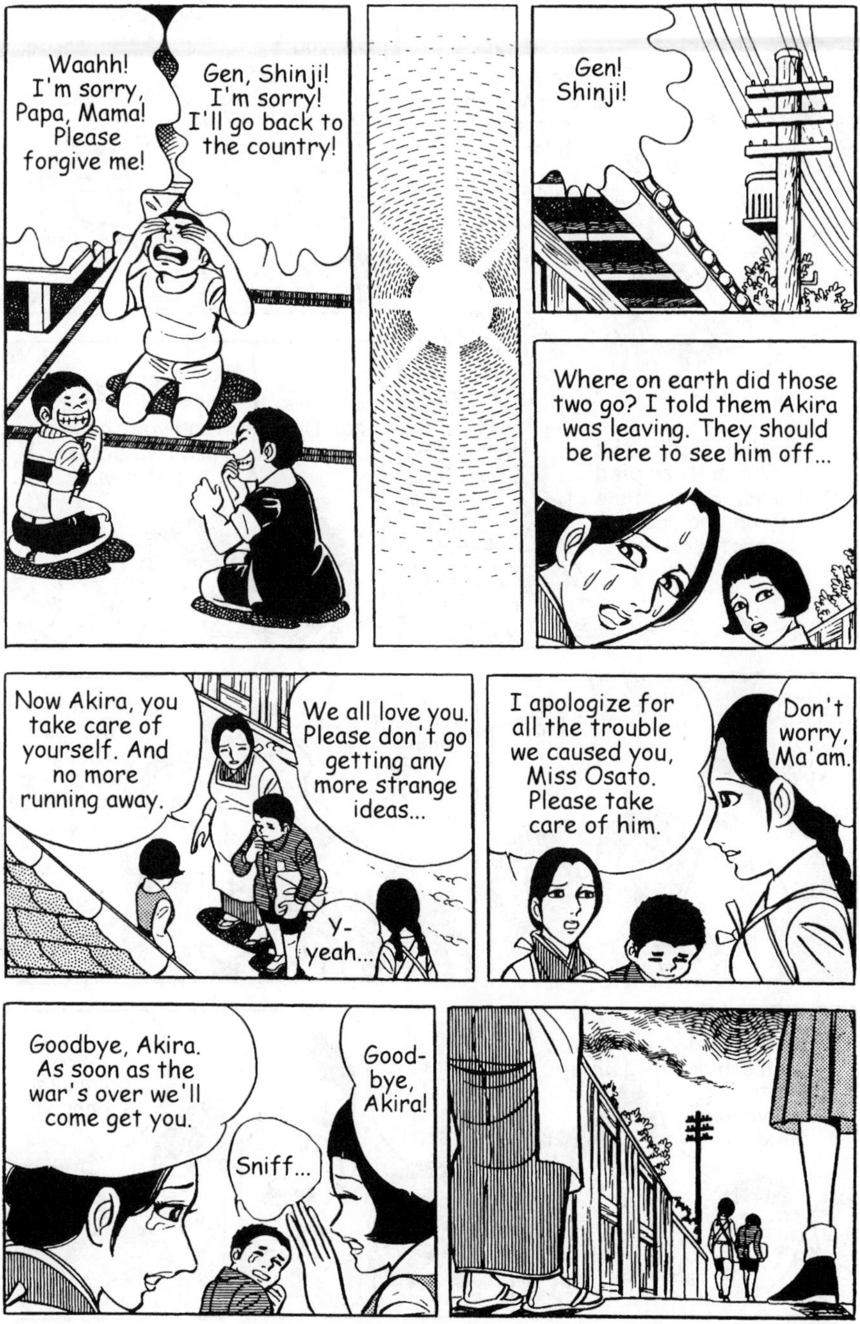
Waahh! I'm sorry, Papa, Mama! Please forgive me!
Gen, Shinji! I'm sorry! I'll go back to the country!
Gen! Shinji!
Where on earth did those two go? I told them Akira was leaving. They should be here to see him off...
Now Akira, you take care of yourself. And no more running away.
We all love you. Please don't go getting any more strange ideas...
Y-yeah...
I apologize for all the trouble we caused you, Miss Osato. Please take care of him.
Don't worry, Ma'am.
Goodbye, Akira. As soon as the war's over we'll come get you.
Good-bye, Akira!
Sniff...

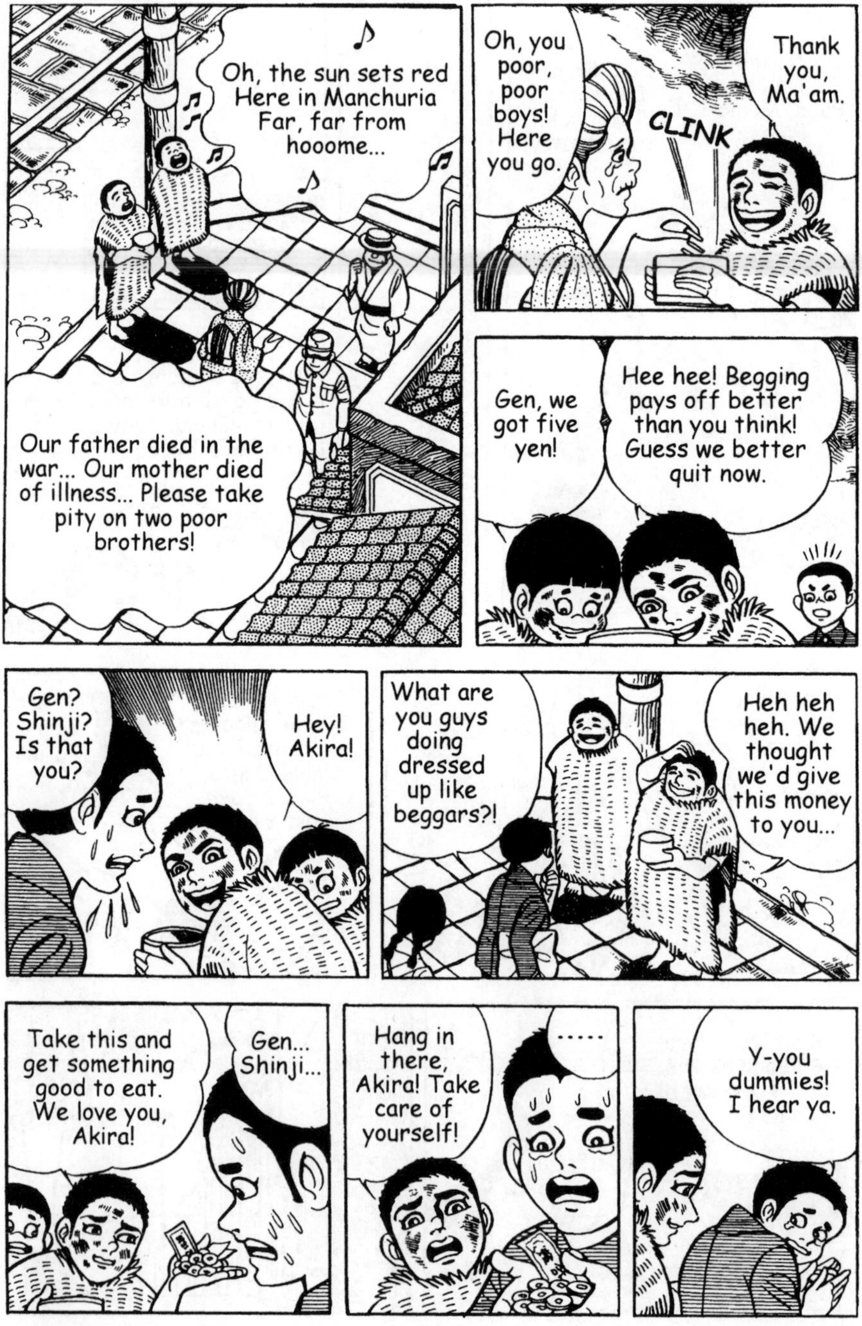
♪ Oh, the sun sets red Here in Manchuria Far, far from hoooome... ♪
Our father died in the war... Our mother died of illness... Please take pity on two poor brothers!
Oh, you poor, poor boys! Here you go.
CLINK
Thank you, Ma'am.
Gen, we got five yen!
Hee hee! Begging pays off better than you think! Guess we better quit now.
Gen? Shinji? Is that you?
Hey! Akira!
What are you guys doing dressed up like beggars?!
Heh heh heh. We thought we'd give this money to you...
Take this and get something good to eat. We love you, Akira!
Gen... Shinji...
Hang in there, Akira! Take care of yourself!
.....
Y-you dummies! I hear ya.

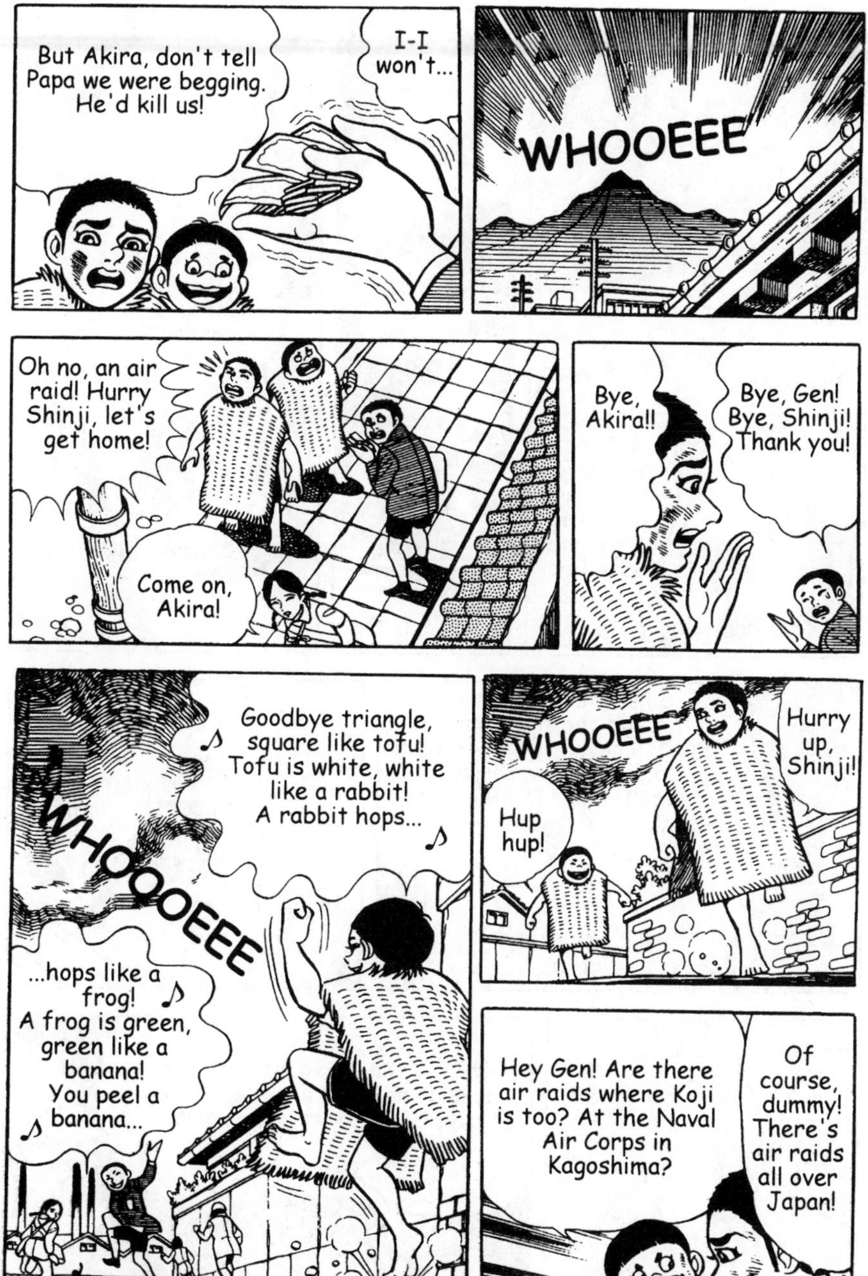
But Akira, don't tell Papa we were begging. He'd kill us!
I-I won't...
WHOOEEE
Oh no, an air raid! Hurry Shinji, let's get home!
Come on, Akira!
Bye, Akira!!
Bye, Gen! Bye, Shinji! Thank you!
WHOOOEEE
Goodbye triangle, square like tofu! Tofu is white, white like a rabbit! A rabbit hops...
...hops like a frog! A frog is green, green like a banana! You peel a banana...
WHOOEEE
Hurry up, Shinji!
Hup hup!
Hey Gen! Are there air raids where Koji is too? At the Naval Air Corps in Kagoshima?
Of course, dummy! There's air raids all over Japan!

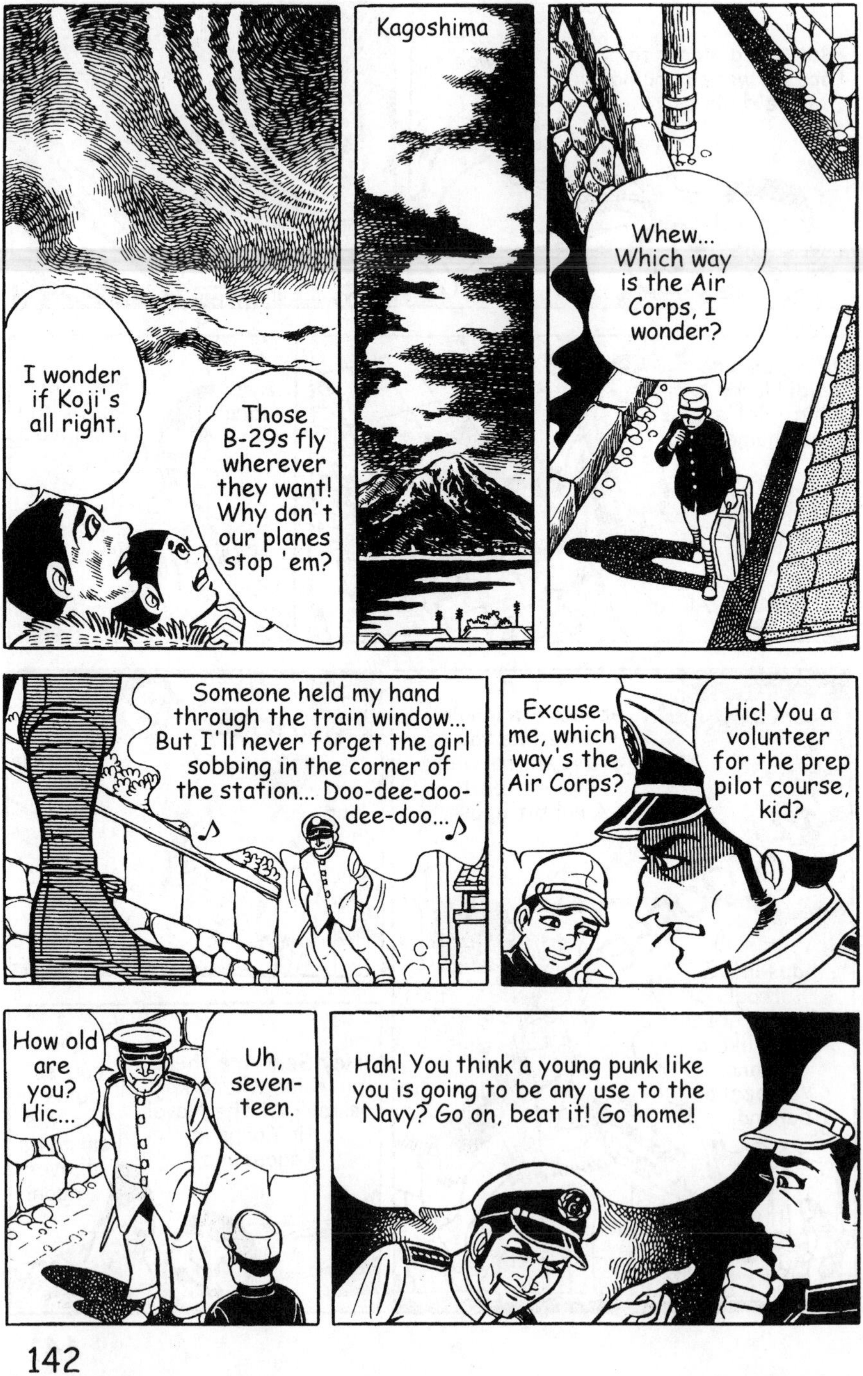
I wonder if Koji's all right.
Those B-29s fly wherever they want! Why don't our planes stop 'em?
Kagoshima
Whew... Which way is the Air Corps, I wonder?
Someone held my hand through the train window... But I'll never forget the girl sobbing in the corner of the station... Doo-dee-doo-dee-doo...♪
Excuse me, which way's the Air Corps?
Hic! You a volunteer for the prep pilot course, kid?
How old are you? Hic...
Uh, seventeen.
Hah! You think a young punk like you is going to be any use to the Navy? Go on, beat it! Go home!

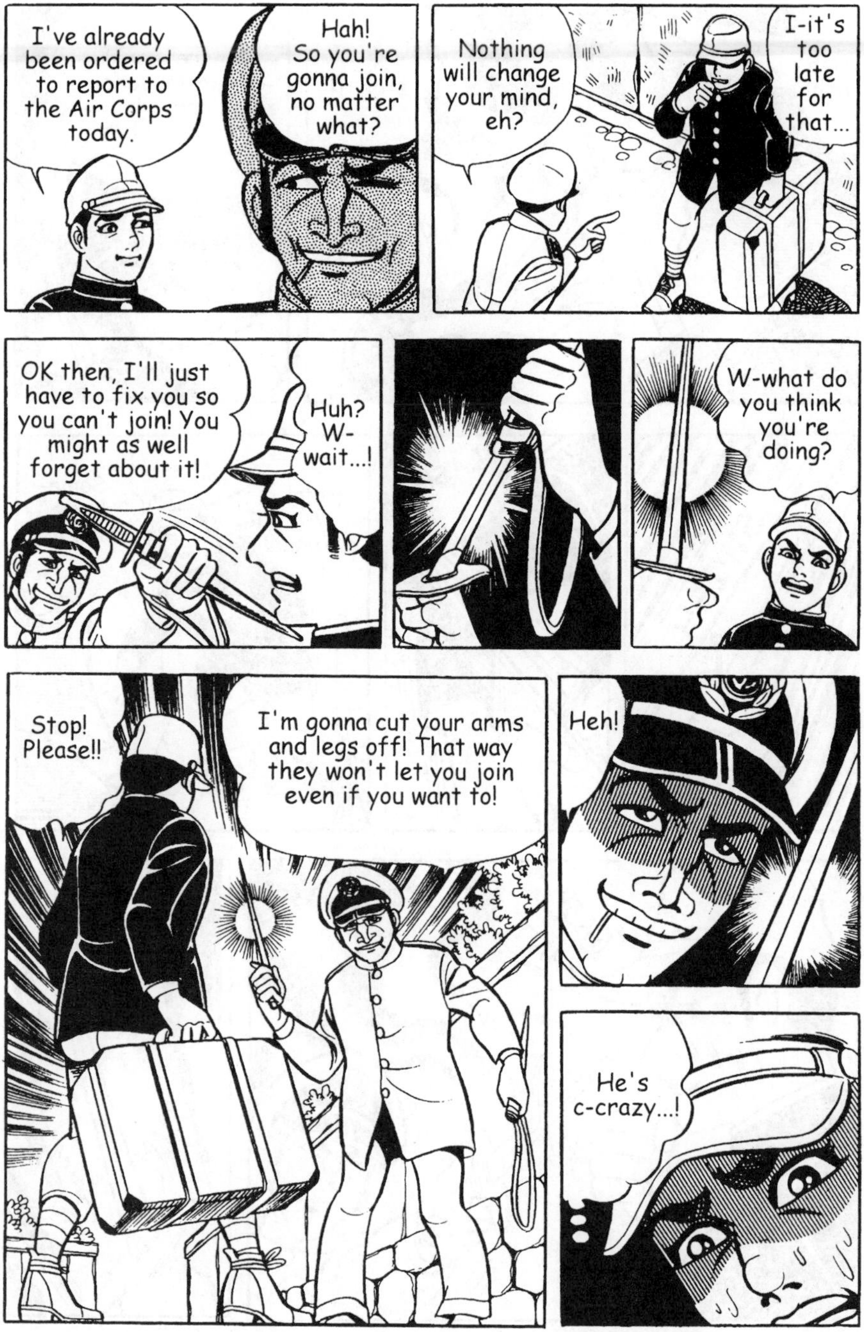
I've already been ordered to report to the Air Corps today.
Hah! So you're gonna join, no matter what?
Nothing will change your mind, eh?
I-it's too late for that...
OK then, I'll just have to fix you so you can't join! You might as well forget about it!
Huh? W- wait...!
W-what do you think you're doing?
Stop! Please!!
I'm gonna cut your arms and legs off! That way they won't let you join even if you want to!
Heh!
He's c-crazy...!

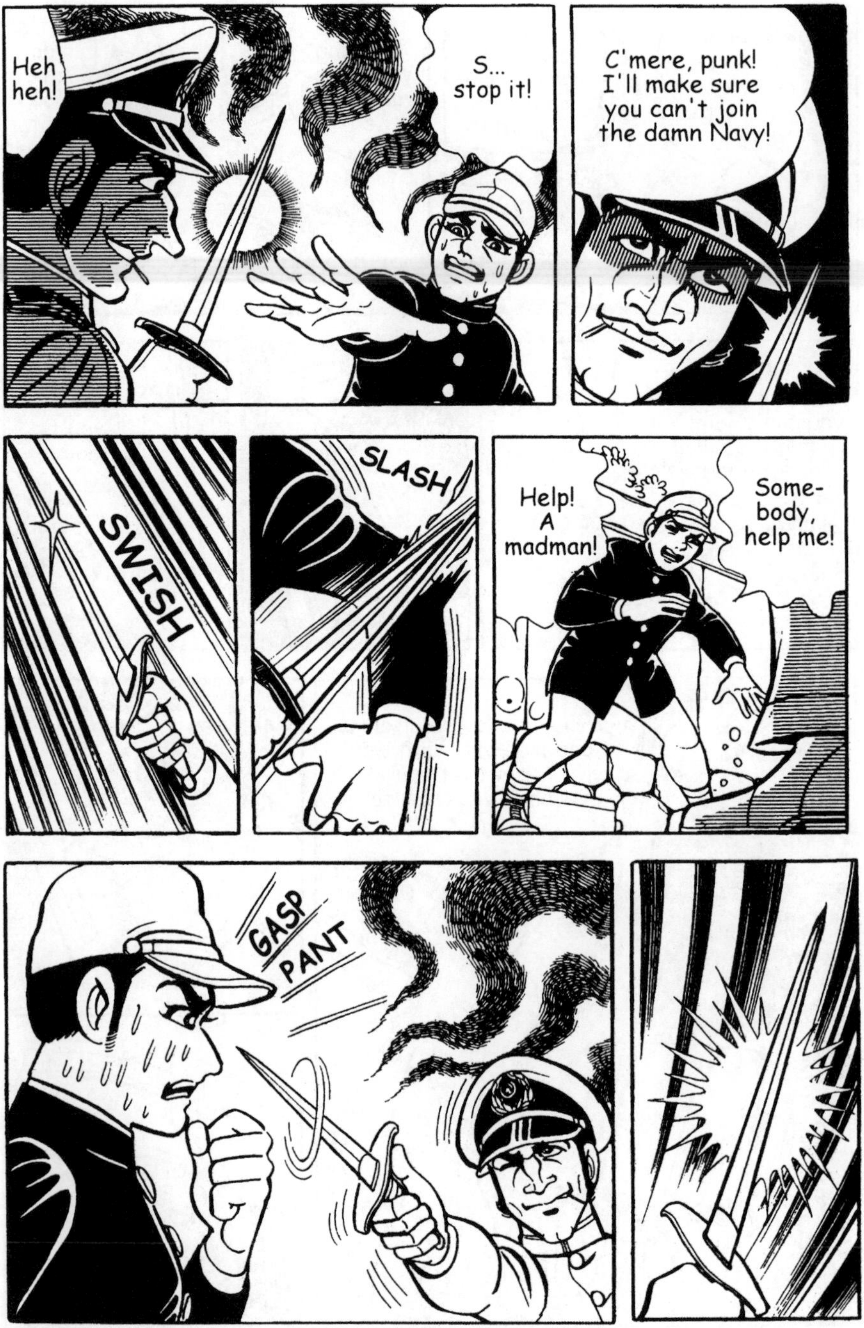
Heh heh!
S... stop it!
C'mere, punk! I'll make sure you can't join the damn Navy!
SWISH
SLASH
Help! A madman!
Some-body, help me!
GASP
PANT

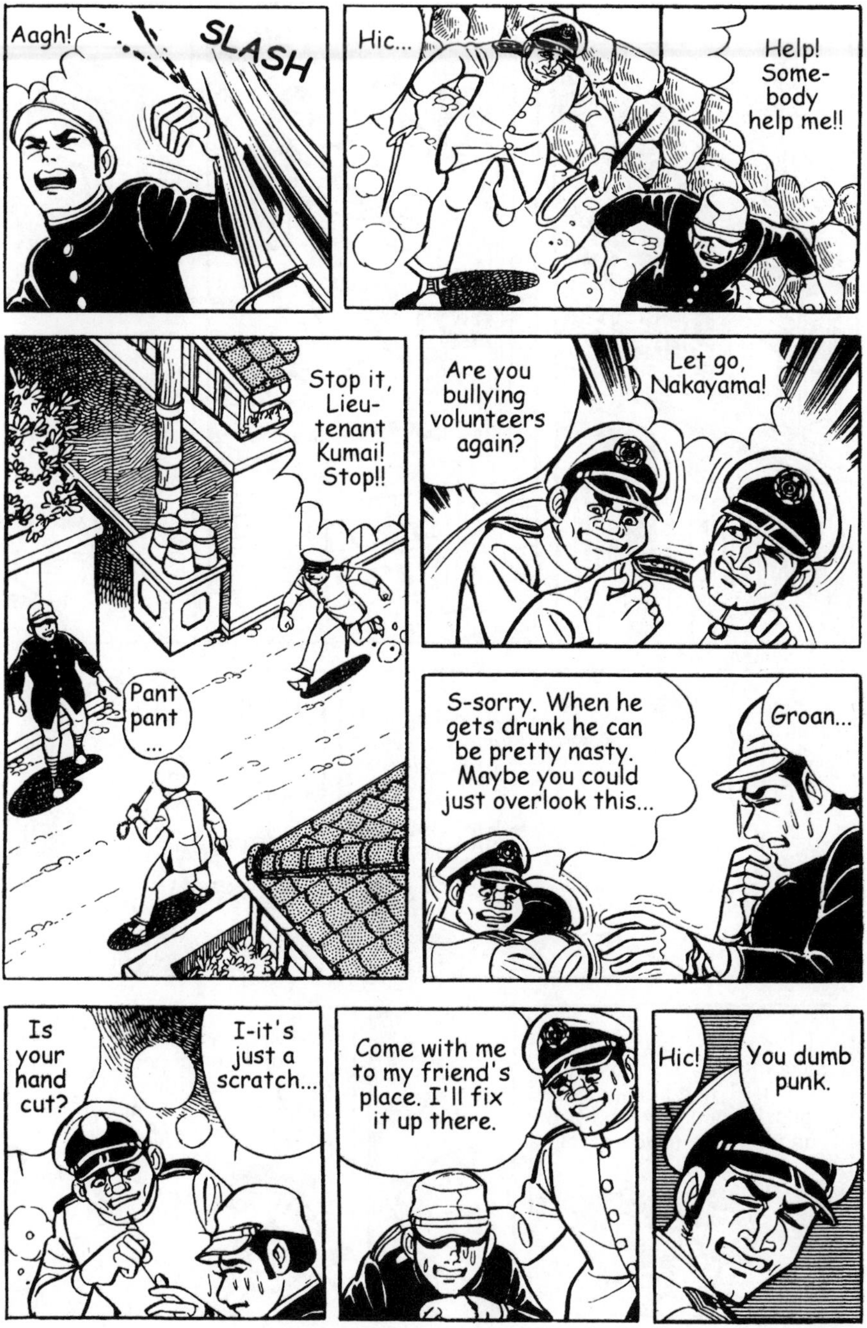
Aagh!
SLASH
Hic...
Help! Some-body help me!!
Stop it, Lieu-tenant Kumai! Stop!!
Pant pant ...
Are you bullying volunteers again?
Let go, Nakayama!
S-sorry. When he gets drunk he can be pretty nasty. Maybe you could just overlook this...
Groan...
Is your hand cut?
I-it's just a scratch...
Come with me to my friend's place. I'll fix it up there.
Hic!
You dumb punk.

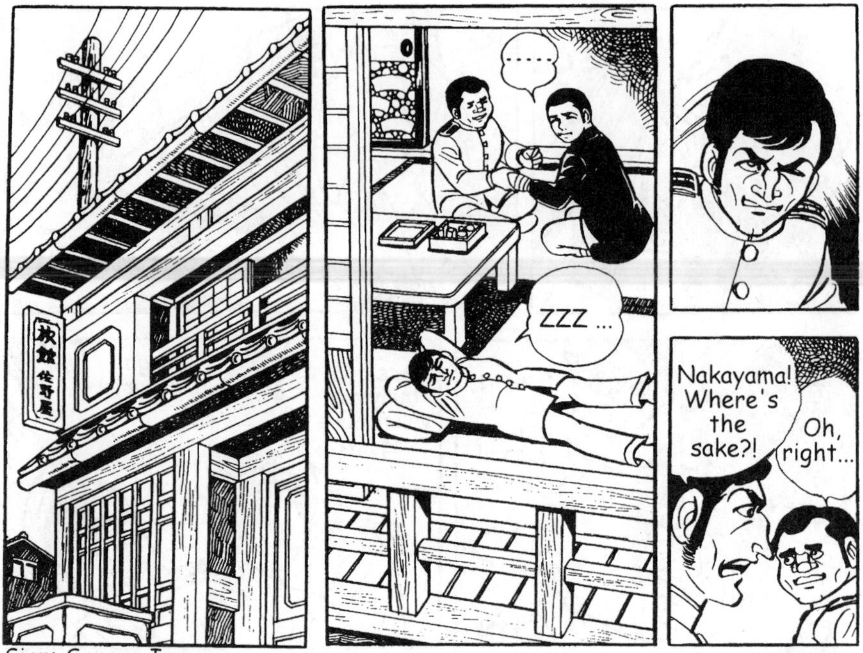

旅館 佐野屋
......
ZZZ ...
Nakayama! Where's the sake?!
Oh, right...

Sign: Sanoya Inn

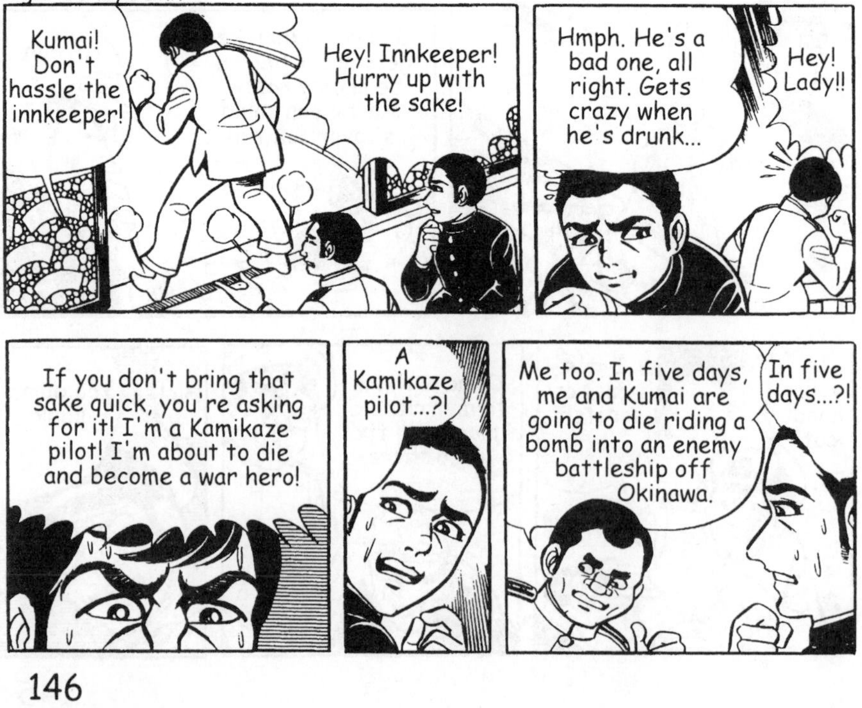

Kumai! Don't hassle the innkeeper!
Hey! Innkeeper! Hurry up with the sake!
Hmph. He's a bad one, all right. Gets crazy when he's drunk...
Hey! Lady!!
If you don't bring that sake quick, you're asking for it! I'm a Kamikaze pilot! I'm about to die and become a war hero!
A Kamikaze pilot...?!
Me too. In five days, me and Kumai are going to die riding a bomb into an enemy battleship off Okinawa.
In five days...?!

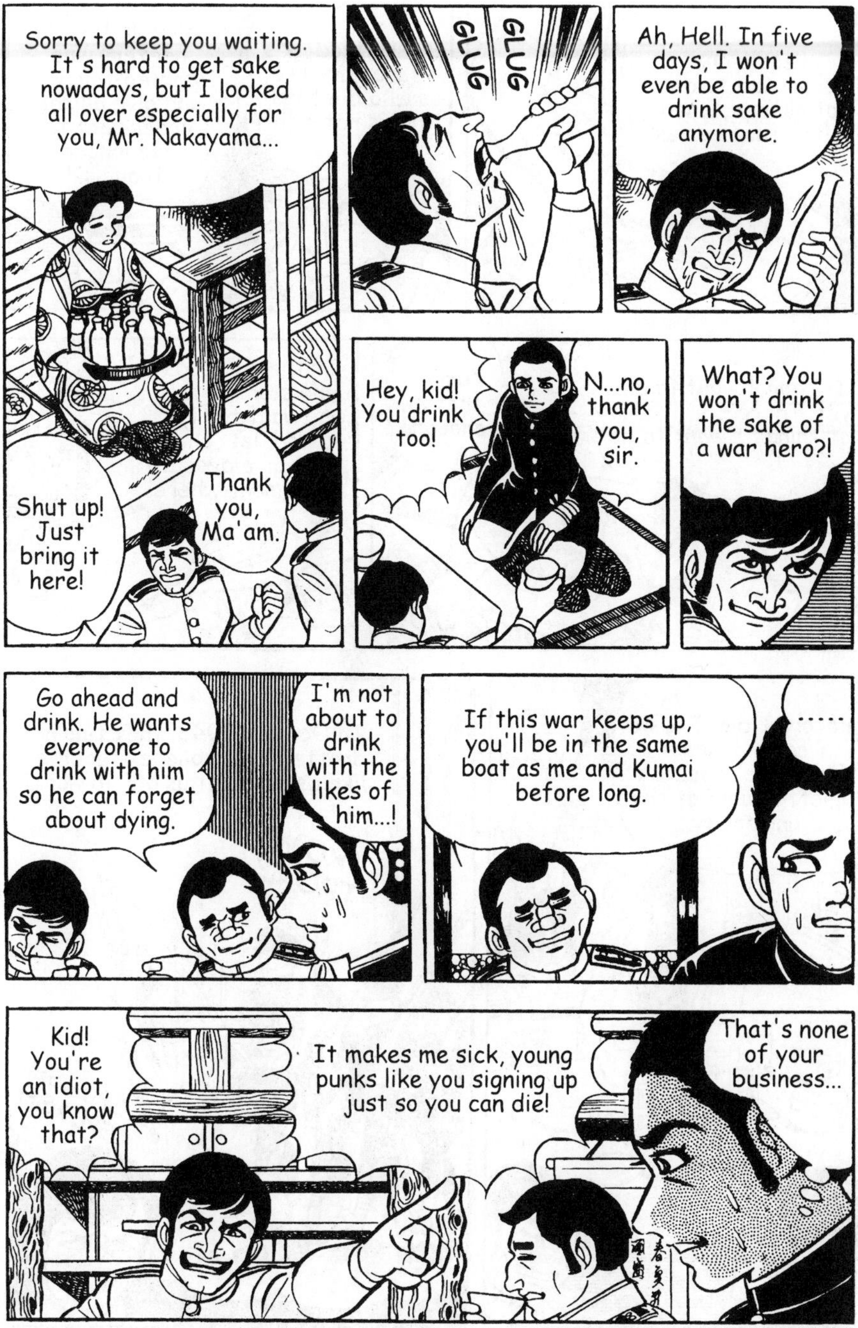
Sorry to keep you waiting. It's hard to get sake nowadays, but I looked all over especially for you, Mr. Nakayama...
Shut up! Just bring it here!
Thank you, Ma'am.
GLUG GLUG
Ah, Hell. In five days, I won't even be able to drink sake anymore.
Hey, kid! You drink too!
N...no, thank you, sir.
What? You won't drink the sake of a war hero?!
Go ahead and drink. He wants everyone to drink with him so he can forget about dying.
I'm not about to drink with the likes of him...!
If this war keeps up, you'll be in the same boat as me and Kumai before long.
.....
Kid! You're an idiot, you know that?
It makes me sick, young punks like you signing up just so you can die!
That's none of your business...

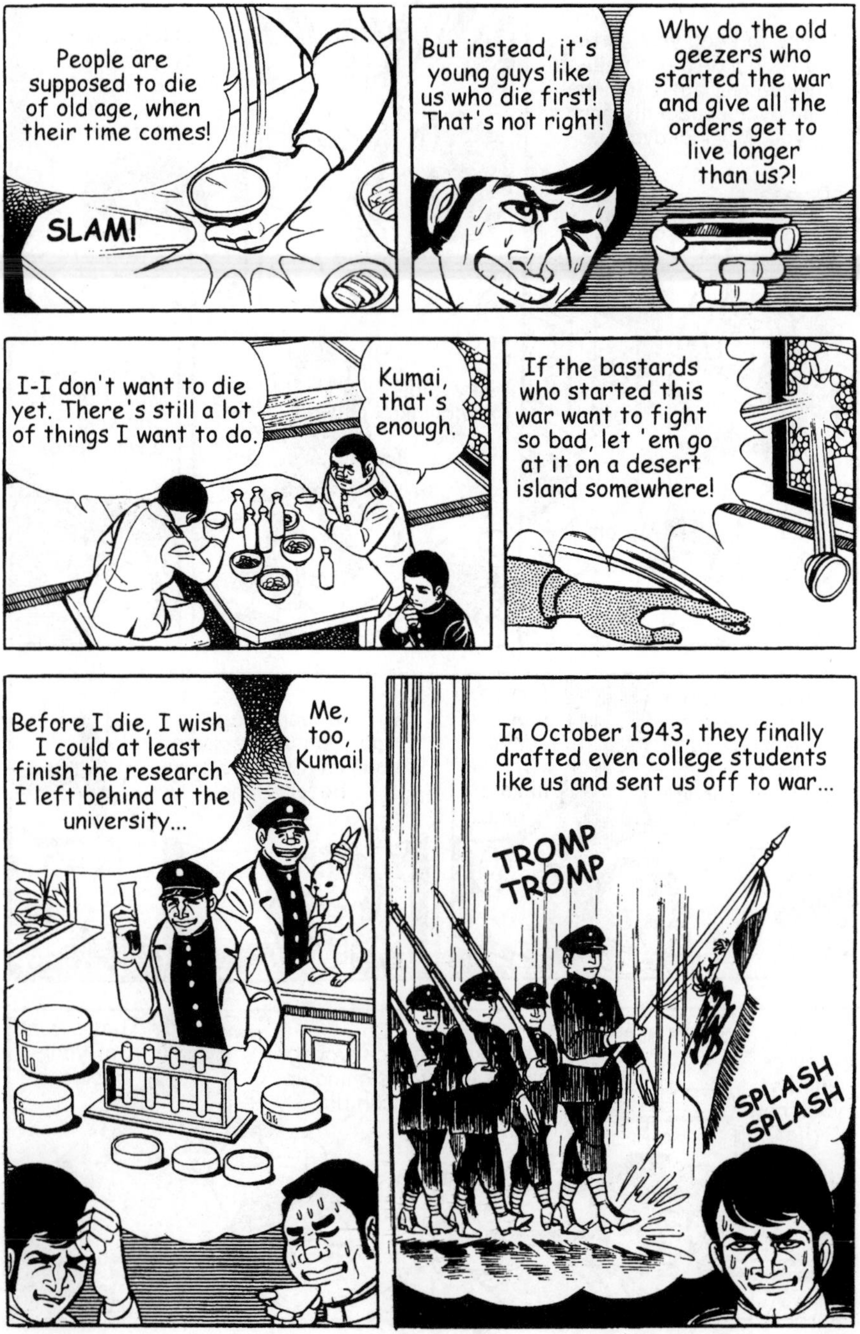

People are supposed to die of old age, when their time comes!
SLAM!
But instead, it's young guys like us who die first! That's not right!
Why do the old geezers who started the war and give all the orders get to live longer than us?!
I-I don't want to die yet. There's still a lot of things I want to do.
Kumai, that's enough.
If the bastards who started this war want to fight so bad, let 'em go at it on a desert island somewhere!
Before I die, I wish I could at least finish the research I left behind at the university...
Me, too, Kumai!
In October 1943, they finally drafted even college students like us and sent us off to war...
TROMP TROMP
SPLASH SPLASH

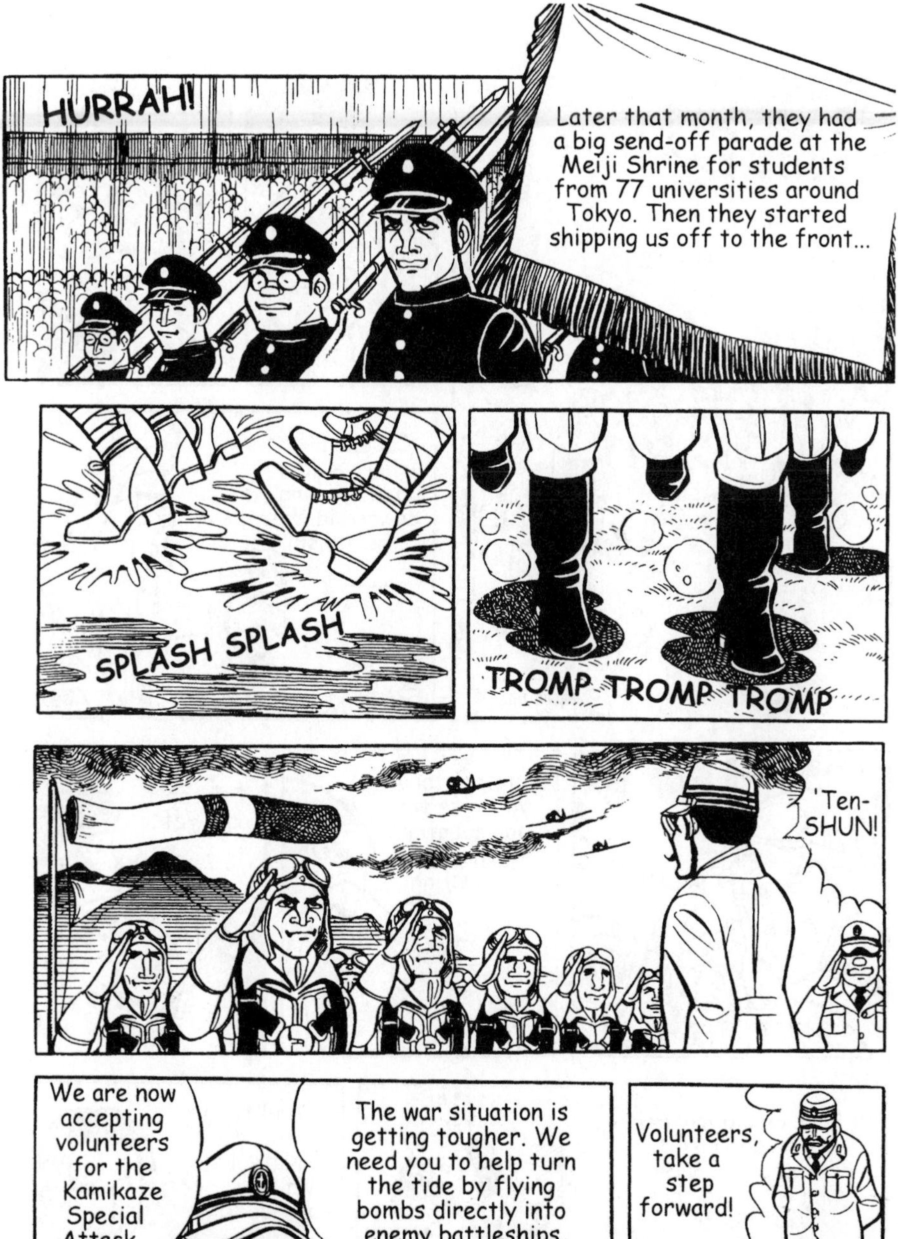
HURRAH!
Later that month, they had a big send-off parade at the Meiji Shrine for students from 77 universities around Tokyo. Then they started shipping us off to the front...
SPLASH SPLASH
TROMP TROMP TROMP
'Ten-SHUN!
We are now accepting volunteers for the Kamikaze Special Attack Corps.
The war situation is getting tougher. We need you to help turn the tide by flying bombs directly into enemy battleships.
Volunteers, take a step forward!

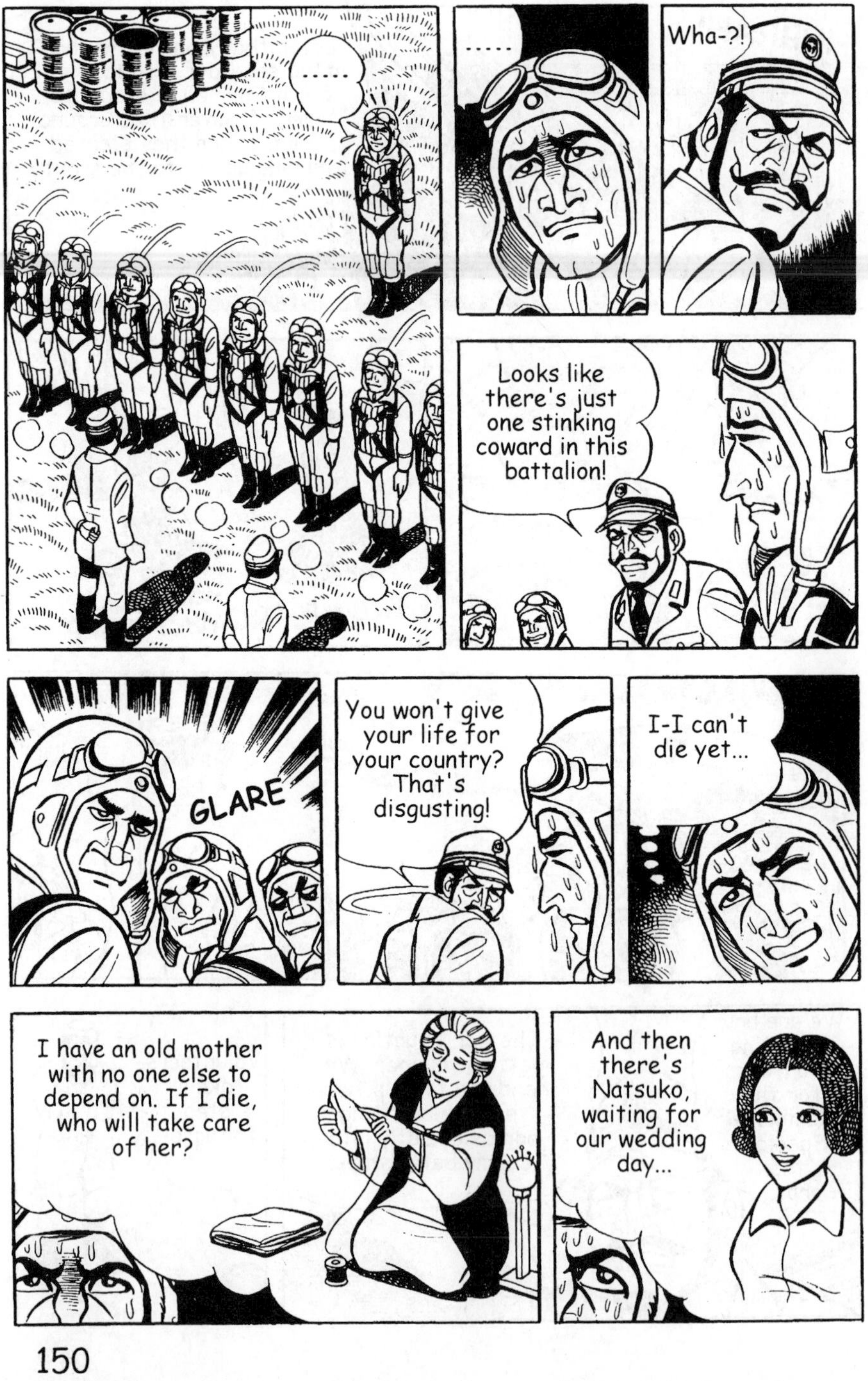
......
......
Wha-?!
Looks like there's just one stinking coward in this battalion!
GLARE
You won't give your life for your country? That's disgusting!
I-I can't die yet...
I have an old mother with no one else to depend on. If I die, who will take care of her?
And then there's Natsuko, waiting for our wedding day...

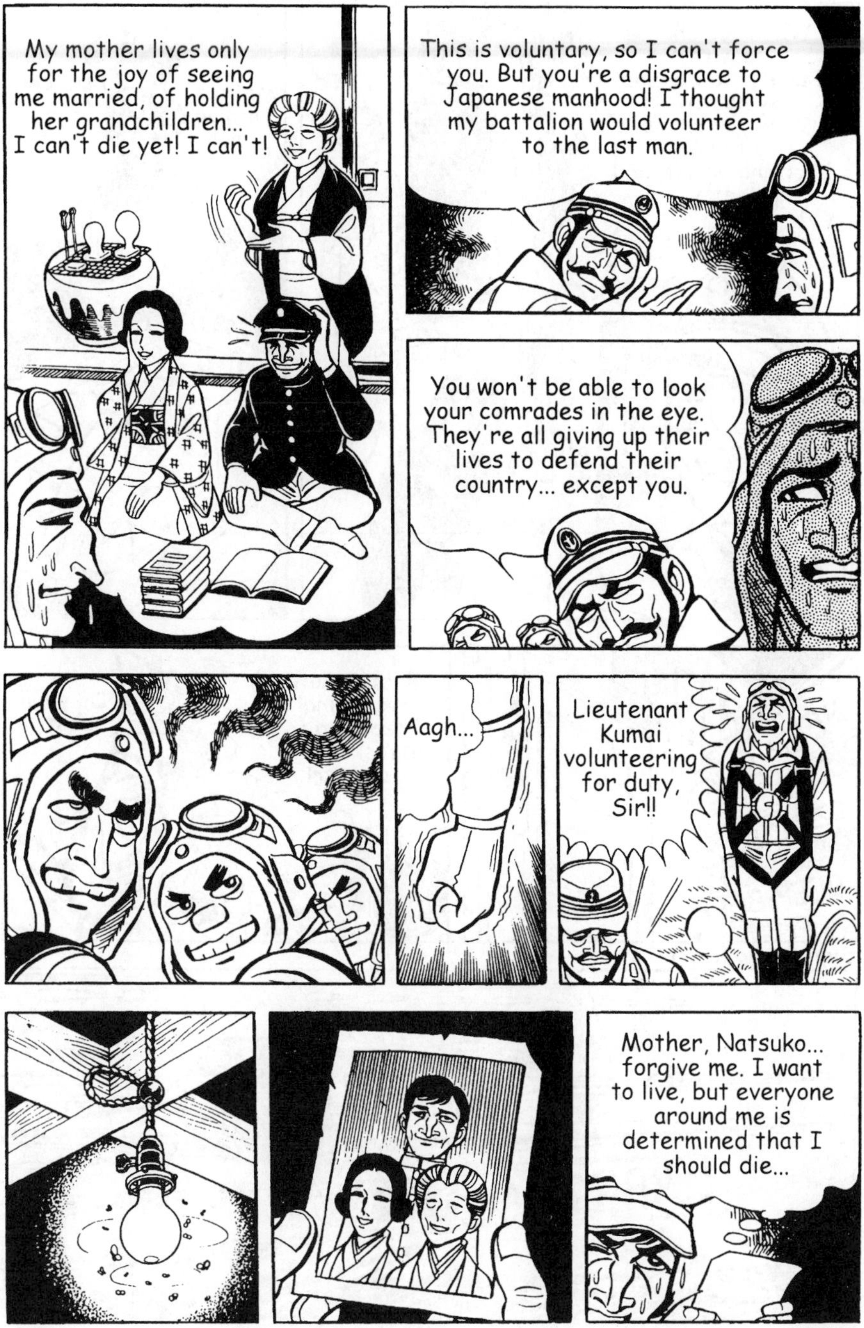
My mother lives only for the joy of seeing me married, of holding her grandchildren... I can't die yet! I can't!
This is voluntary, so I can't force you. But you're a disgrace to Japanese manhood! I thought my battalion would volunteer to the last man.
You won't be able to look your comrades in the eye. They're all giving up their lives to defend their country... except you.
Aagh...
Lieutenant Kumai volunteering for duty, Sir!!
Mother, Natsuko... forgive me. I want to live, but everyone around me is determined that I should die...

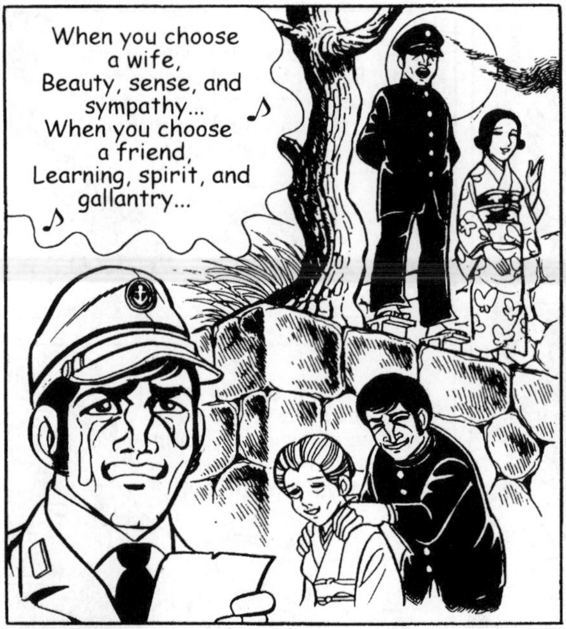
When you choose a wife,
Beauty, sense, and sympathy...
When you choose a friend,
Learning, spirit, and gallantry...

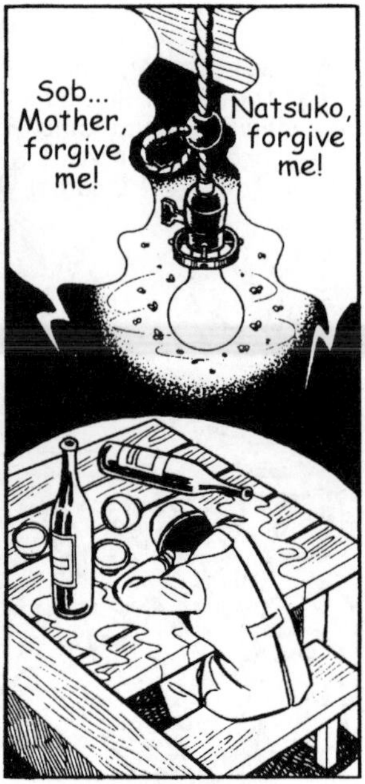
Sob... Mother, forgive me!
Natsuko, forgive me!

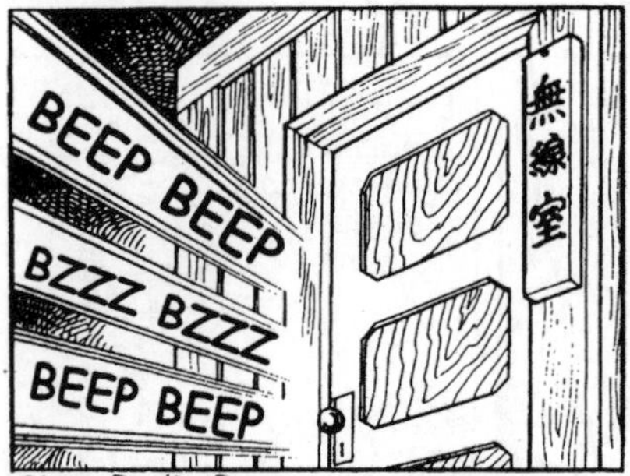
BEEP BEEP
BZZZ BZZZ
BEEP BEEP
無線室

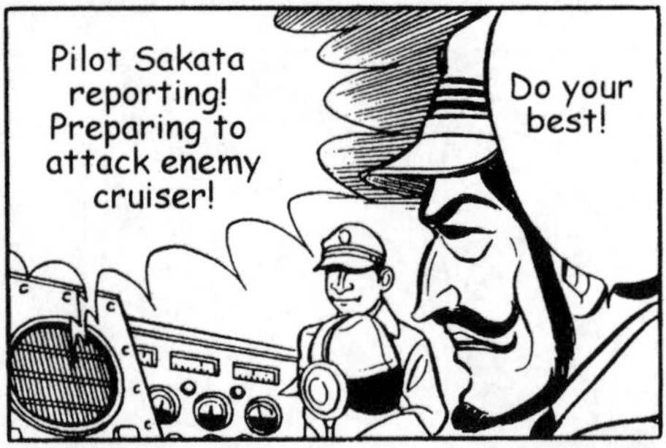
Pilot Sakata reporting! Preparing to attack enemy cruiser!
Do your best!

Sign: Radio Room

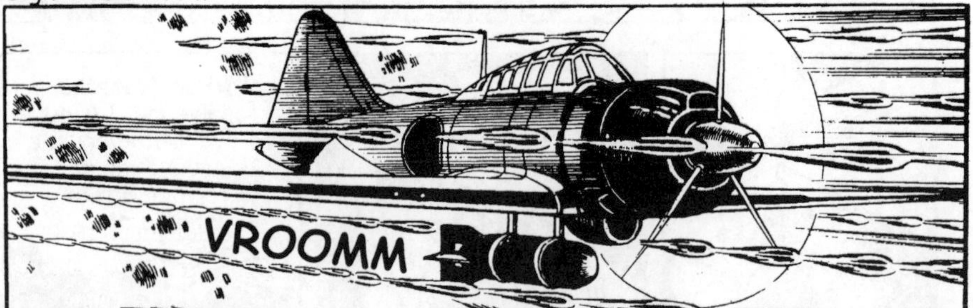
VROOMM

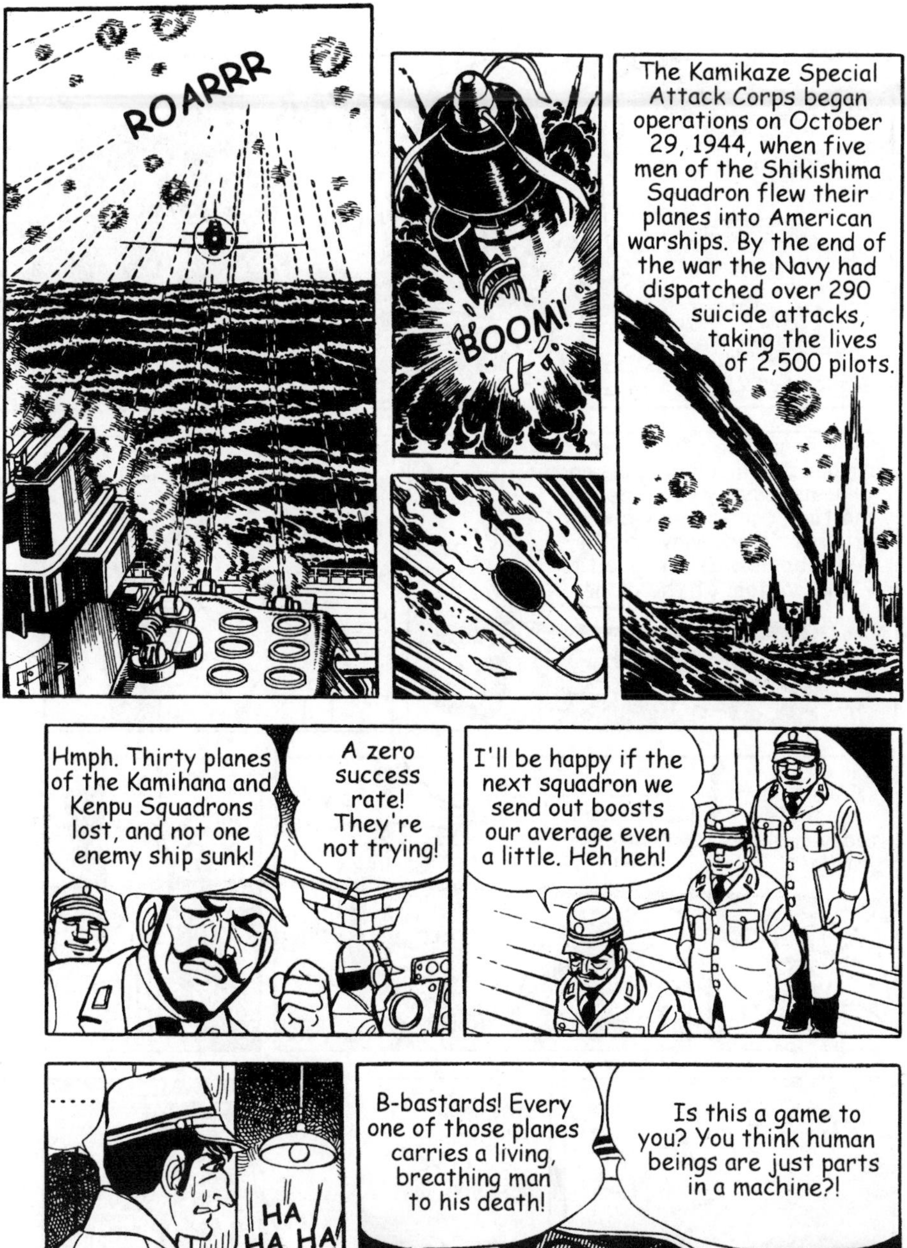
ROARRR
BOOM!
The Kamikaze Special Attack Corps began operations on October 29, 1944, when five men of the Shikishima Squadron flew their planes into American warships. By the end of the war the Navy had dispatched over 290 suicide attacks, taking the lives of 2,500 pilots.
Hmph. Thirty planes of the Kamihana and Kenpu Squadrons lost, and not one enemy ship sunk!
A zero success rate! They're not trying!
I'll be happy if the next squadron we send out boosts our average even a little. Heh heh!
......
HA HA HA
B-bastards! Every one of those planes carries a living, breathing man to his death!
Is this a game to you? You think human beings are just parts in a machine?!

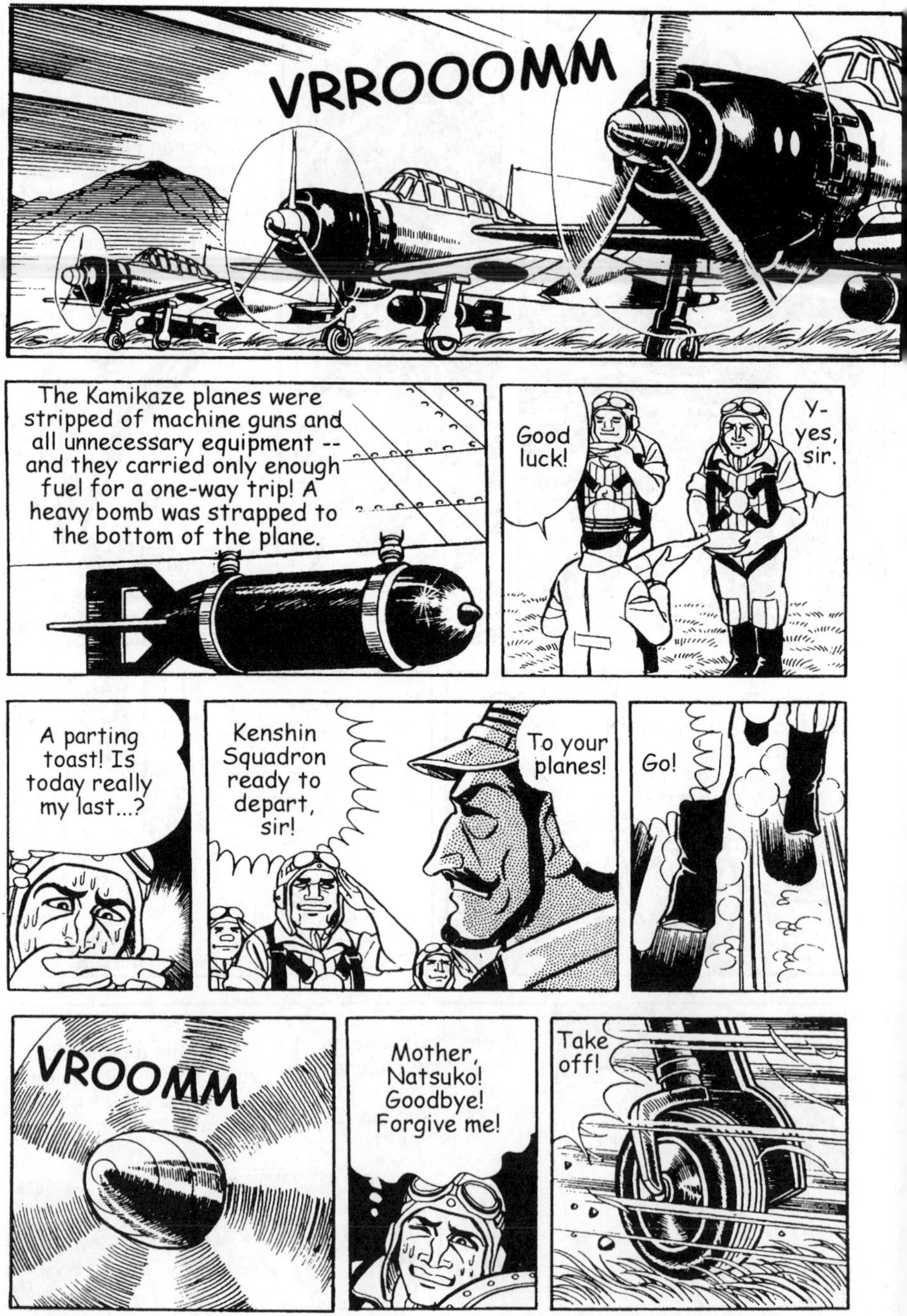
VRROOOMM
The Kamikaze planes were stripped of machine guns and all unnecessary equipment -- and they carried only enough fuel for a one-way trip! A heavy bomb was strapped to the bottom of the plane.
Good luck!
Y-yes, sir.
A parting toast! Is today really my last...?
Kenshin Squadron ready to depart, sir!
To your planes!
Go!
VROOMM
Mother, Natsuko! Goodbye! Forgive me!
Take off!

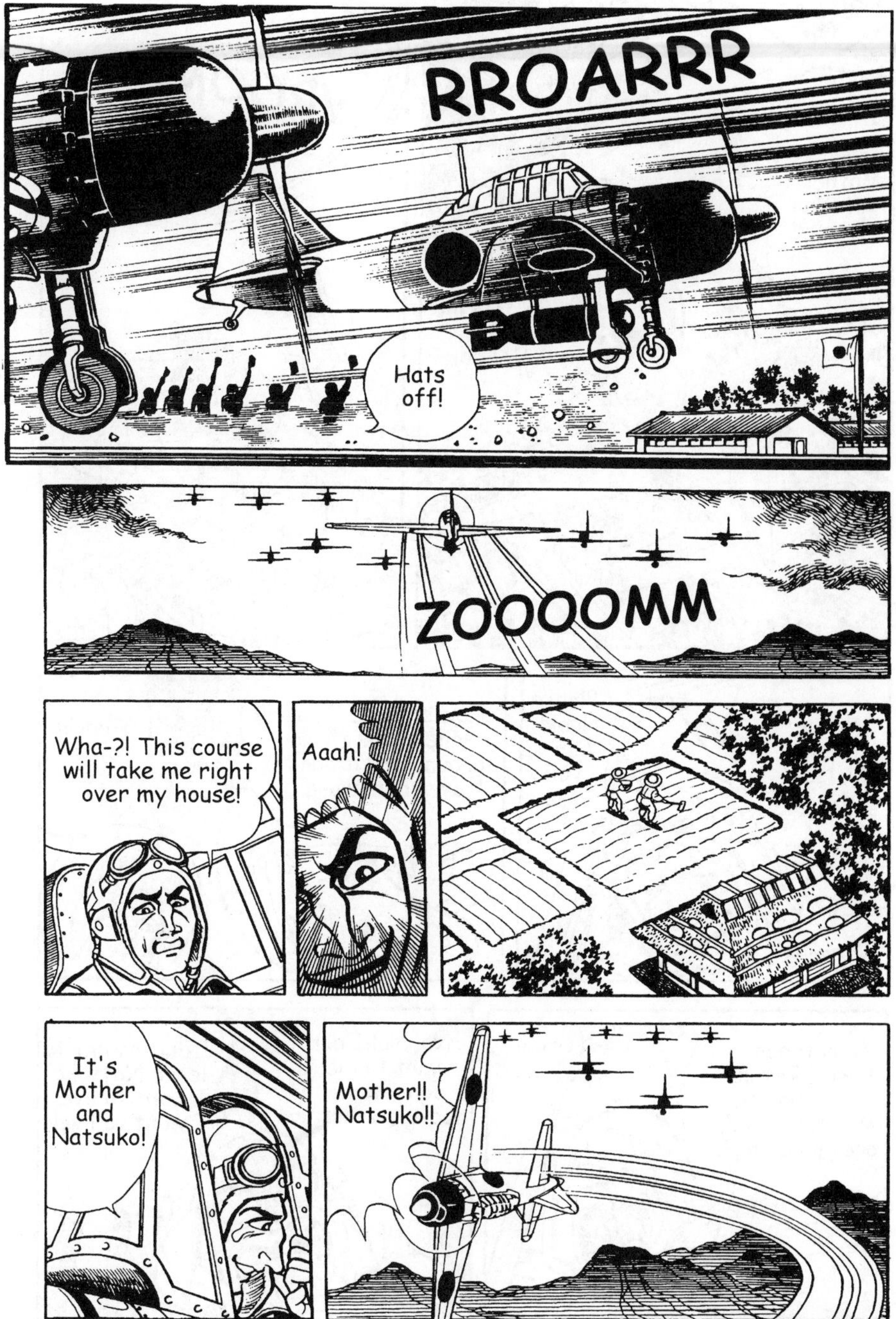
RROARRR
Hats off!
ZOOOOMM
Wha-?! This course will take me right over my house!
Aaah!
It's Mother and Natsuko!
Mother!! Natsuko!!

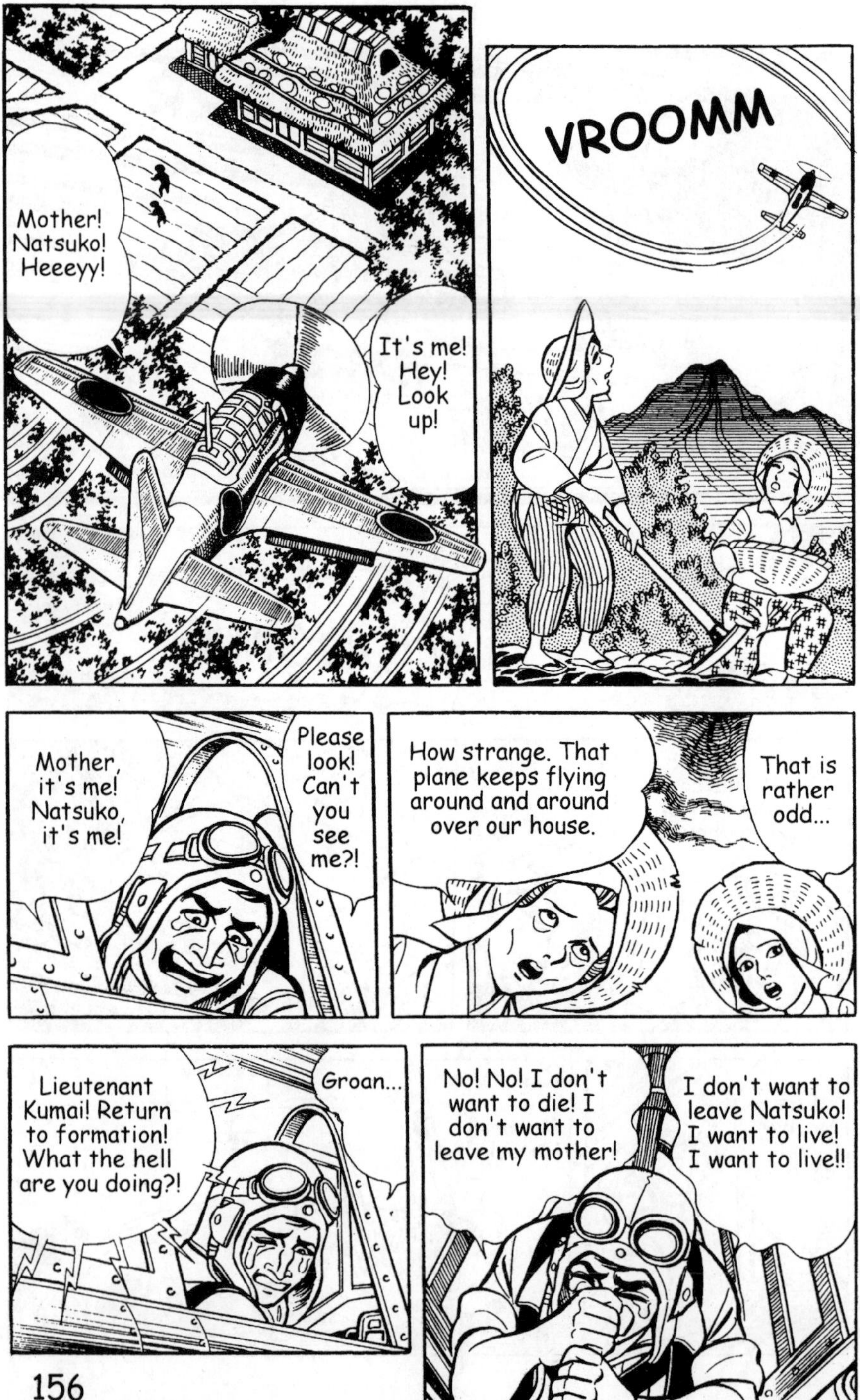
Mother! Natsuko! Heeeyy!
It's me! Hey! Look up!
VROOMM
Mother, it's me! Natsuko, it's me!
Please look! Can't you see me?!
How strange. That plane keeps flying around and around over our house.
That is rather odd...
Lieutenant Kumai! Return to formation! What the hell are you doing?!
Groan...
No! No! I don't want to die! I don't want to leave my mother!
I don't want to leave Natsuko! I want to live! I want to live!!

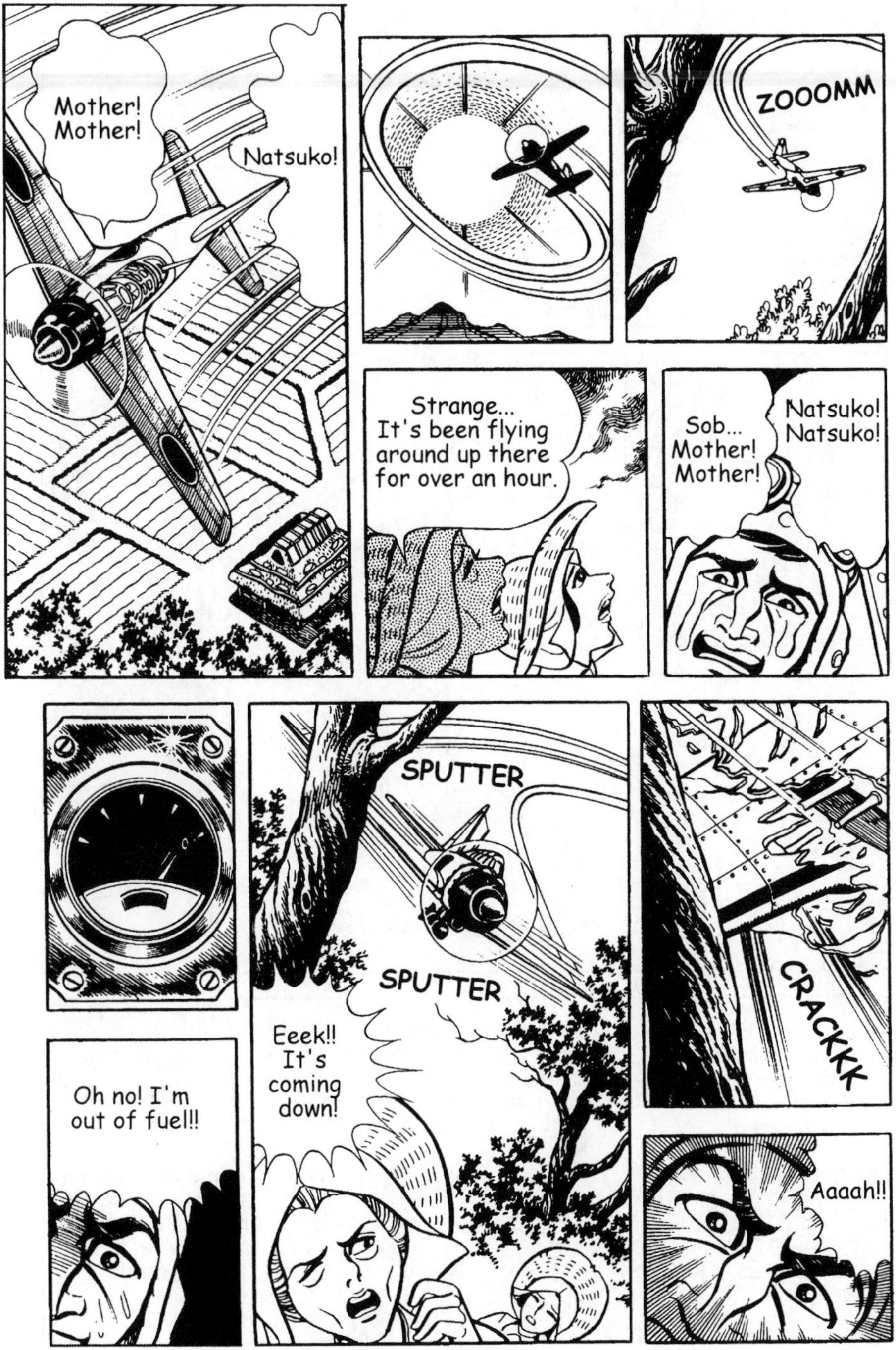

Mother! Mother!
Natsuko!
ZOOOMM
Strange... It's been flying around up there for over an hour.
Sob... Mother! Mother!
Natsuko! Natsuko!
Oh no! I'm out of fuel!!
SPUTTER
SPUTTER
Eeek!! It's coming down!
CRACKKK
Aaaah!!

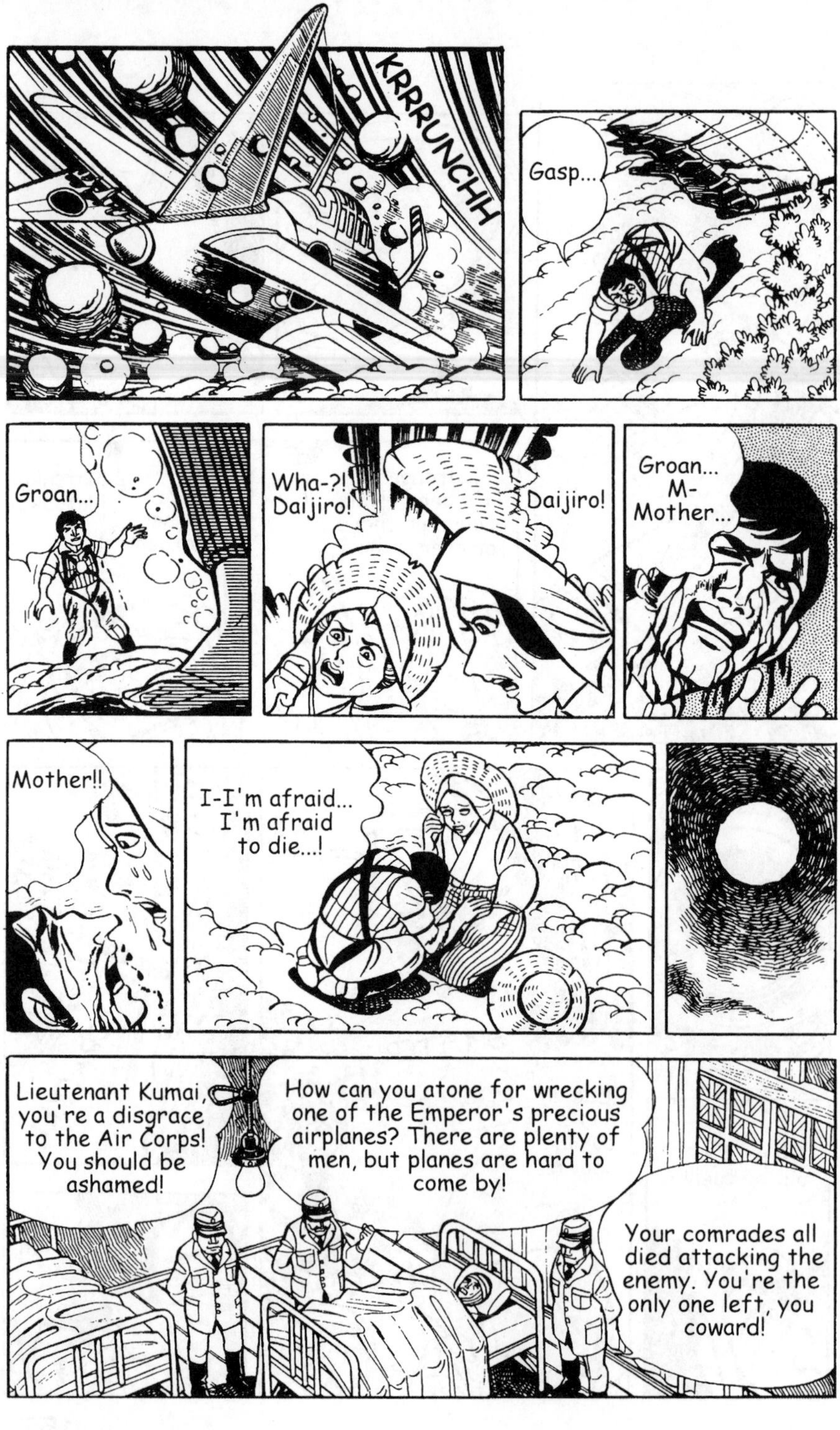
KRRRUNCHH
Gasp...
Groan...
Wha-?! Daijiro!
Daijiro!
Groan... M-Mother...
Mother!!
I-I'm afraid... I'm afraid to die...!
Lieutenant Kumai, you're a disgrace to the Air Corps! You should be ashamed!
How can you atone for wrecking one of the Emperor's precious airplanes? There are plenty of men, but planes are hard to come by!
Your comrades all died attacking the enemy. You're the only one left, you coward!

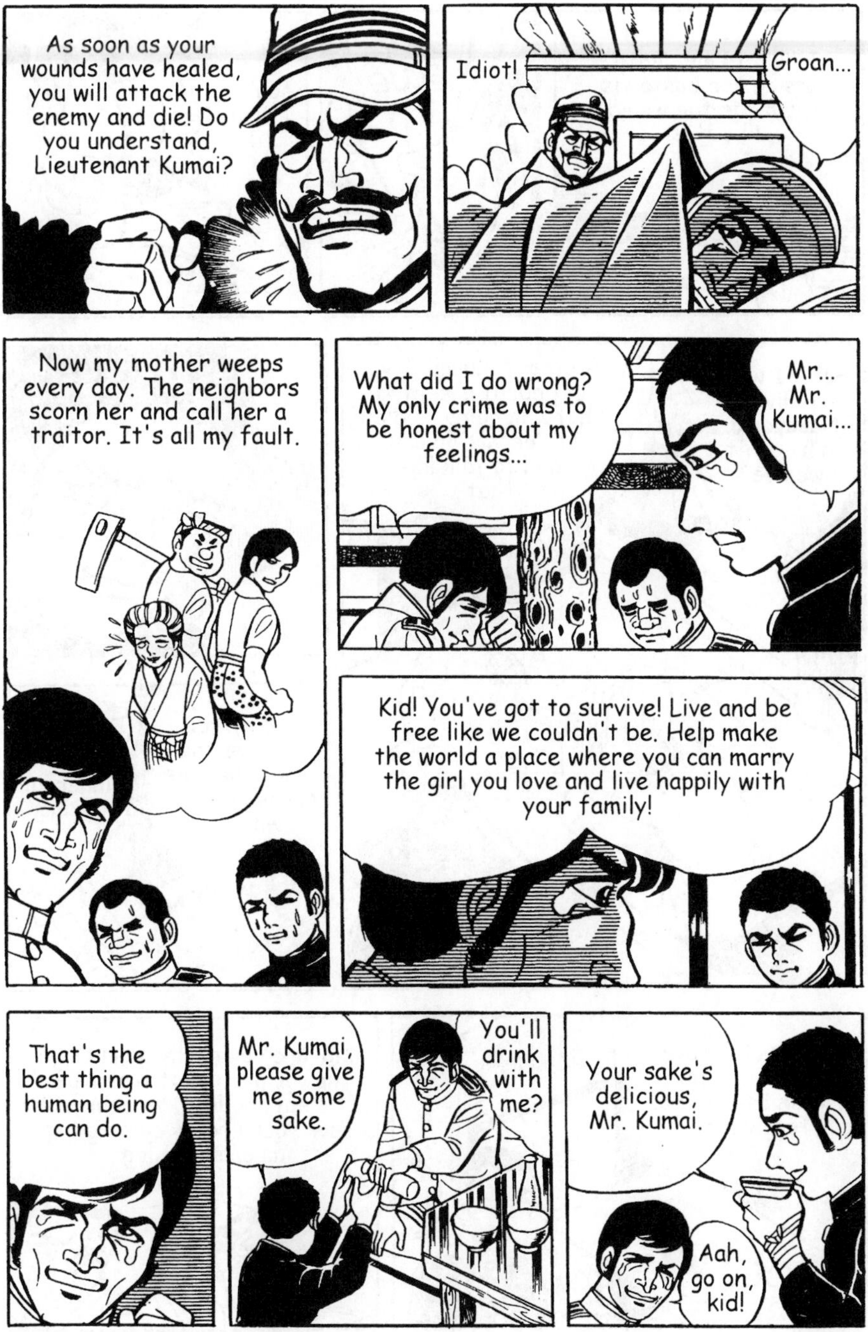
As soon as your wounds have healed, you will attack the enemy and die! Do you understand, Lieutenant Kumai?
Idiot!
Groan...
Now my mother weeps every day. The neighbors scorn her and call her a traitor. It's all my fault.
What did I do wrong? My only crime was to be honest about my feelings...
Mr... Mr. Kumai...
Kid! You've got to survive! Live and be free like we couldn't be. Help make the world a place where you can marry the girl you love and live happily with your family!
That's the best thing a human being can do.
Mr. Kumai, please give me some sake.
You'll drink with me?
Your sake's delicious, Mr. Kumai.
Aah, go on, kid!

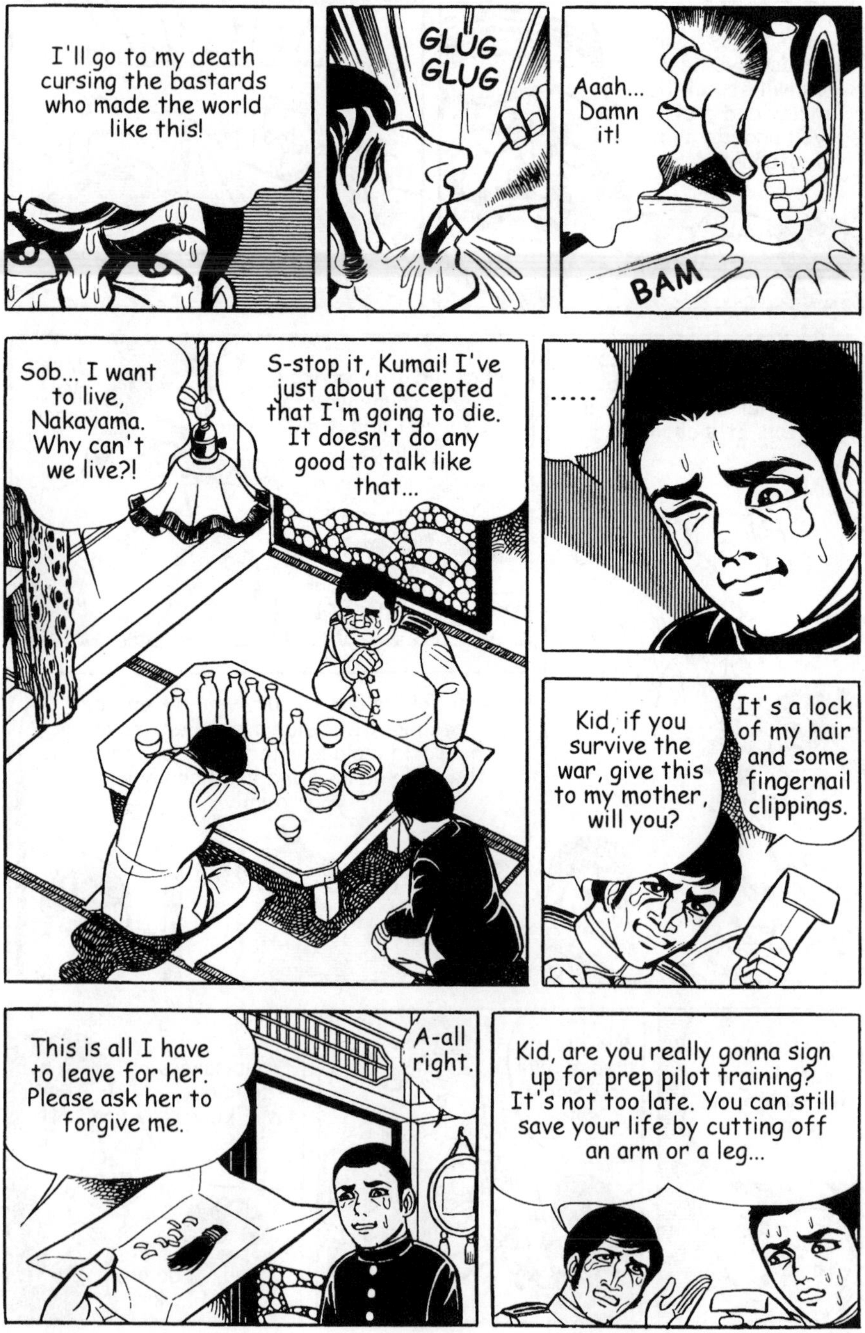

I'll go to my death cursing the bastards who made the world like this!
GLUG GLUG
Aaah... Damn it!
BAM
Sob... I want to live, Nakayama. Why can't we live?!
S-stop it, Kumai! I've just about accepted that I'm going to die. It doesn't do any good to talk like that...
.....
Kid, if you survive the war, give this to my mother, will you?
It's a lock of my hair and some fingernail clippings.
This is all I have to leave for her. Please ask her to forgive me.
A-all right.
Kid, are you really gonna sign up for prep pilot training? It's not too late. You can still save your life by cutting off an arm or a leg...

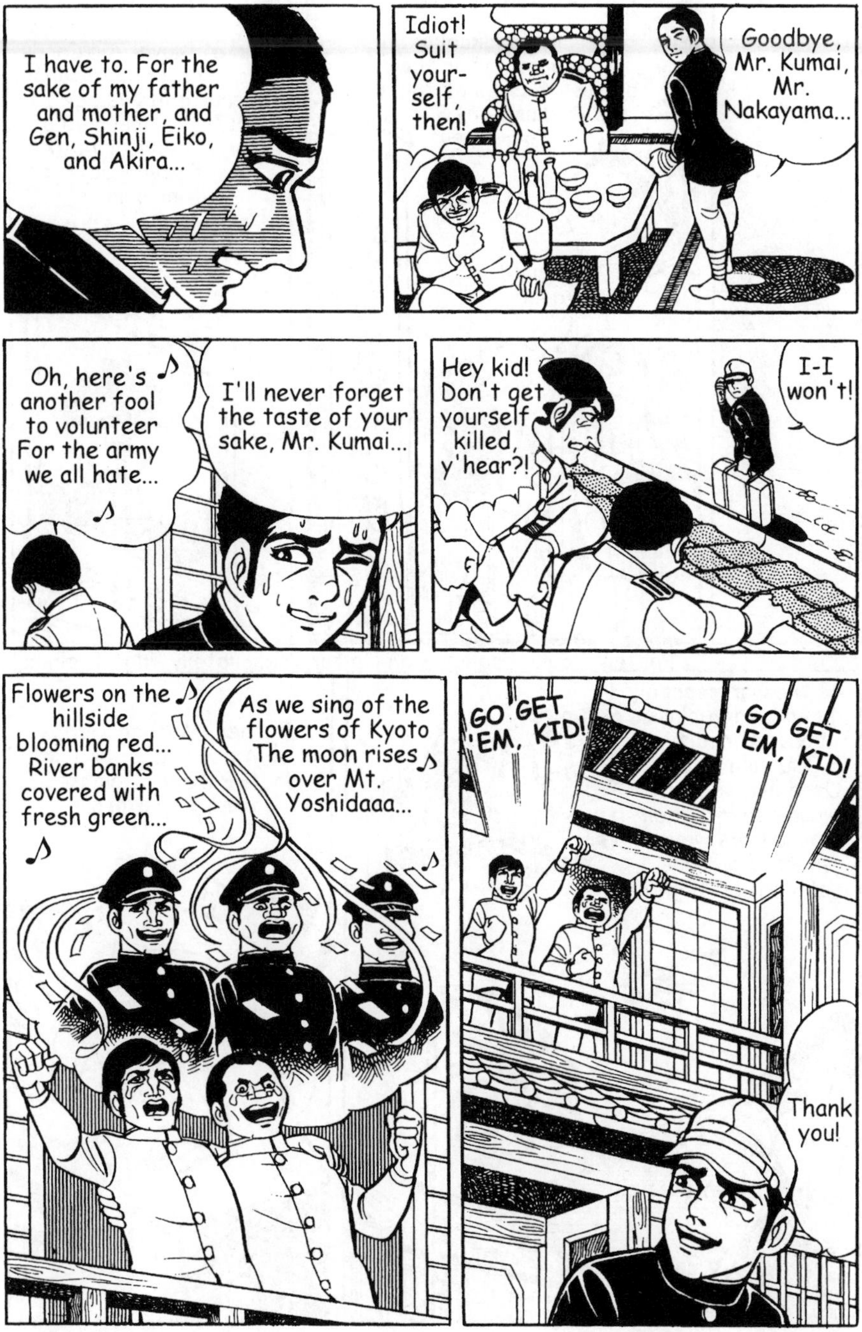
I have to. For the sake of my father and mother, and Gen, Shinji, Eiko, and Akira...
Idiot! Suit your-self, then!
Goodbye, Mr. Kumai, Mr. Nakayama...
Oh, here's another fool to volunteer For the army we all hate...
I'll never forget the taste of your sake, Mr. Kumai...
Hey kid! Don't get yourself killed, y'hear?!
I-I won't!
Flowers on the hillside blooming red... River banks covered with fresh green...
As we sing of the flowers of Kyoto The moon rises over Mt. Yoshidaaa...
GO GET 'EM, KID!
GO GET 'EM, KID!
Thank you!

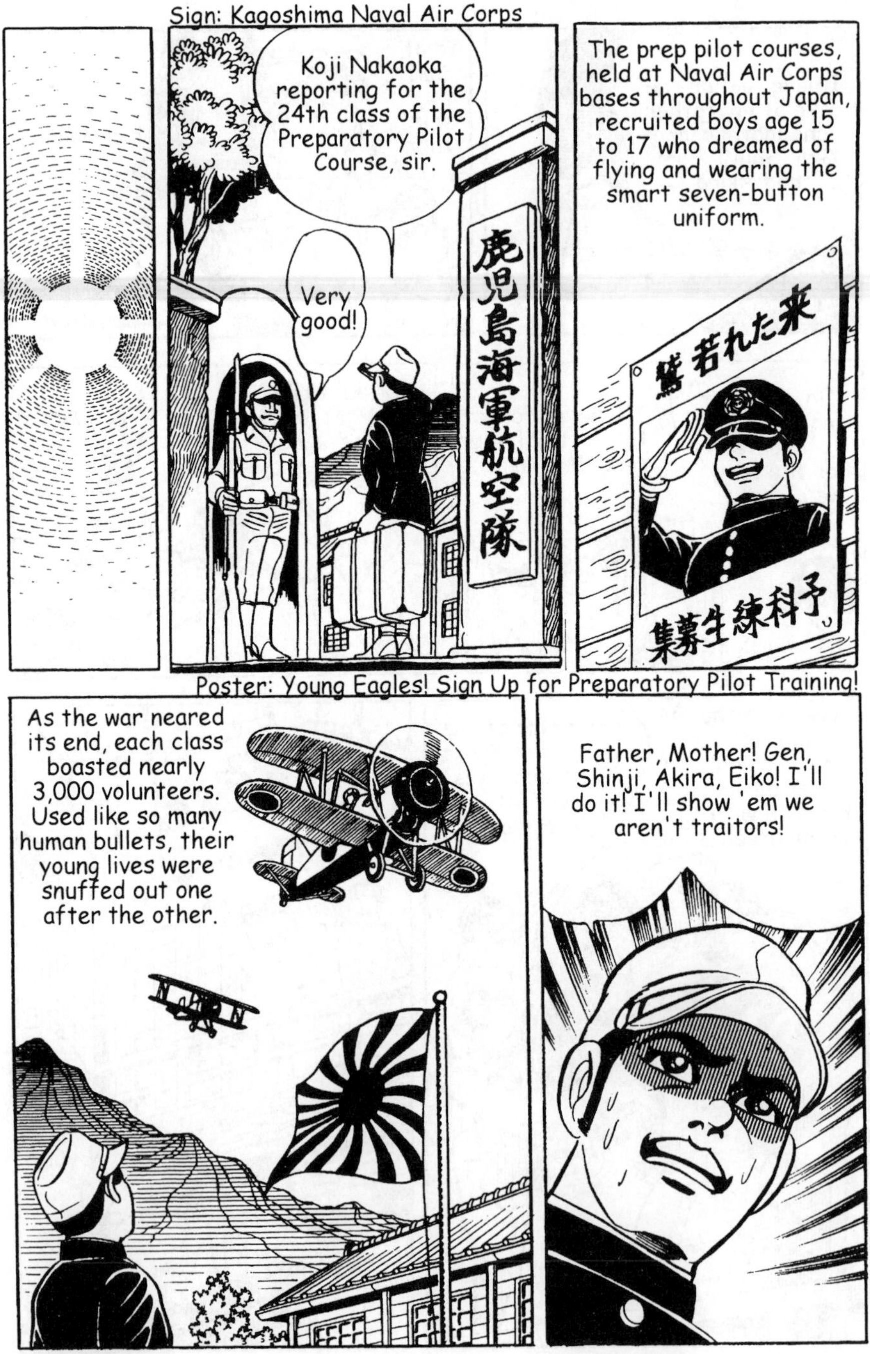
Sign: Kagoshima Naval Air Corps
Koji Nakaoka reporting for the 24th class of the Preparatory Pilot Course, sir.
Very good!
鹿児島海軍航空隊
The prep pilot courses, held at Naval Air Corps bases throughout Japan, recruited boys age 15 to 17 who dreamed of flying and wearing the smart seven-button uniform.
来たれ若鷲
予科練生募集
Poster: Young Eagles! Sign Up for Preparatory Pilot Training!
As the war neared its end, each class boasted nearly 3,000 volunteers. Used like so many human bullets, their young lives were snuffed out one after the other.
Father, Mother! Gen, Shinji, Akira, Eiko! I'll do it! I'll show 'em we aren't traitors!

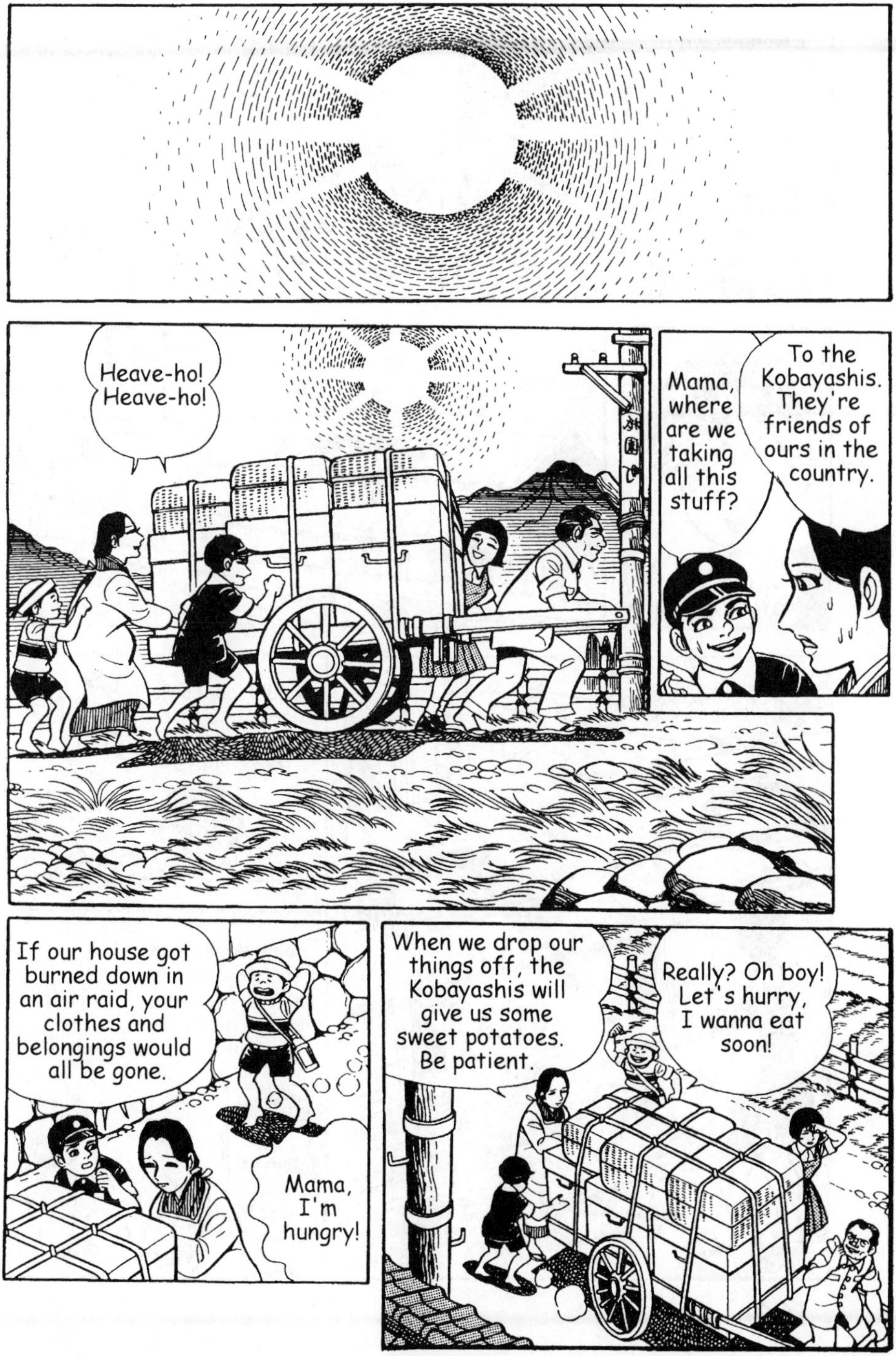
Heave-ho! Heave-ho!
Mama, where are we taking all this stuff?
To the Kobayashis. They're friends of ours in the country.
If our house got burned down in an air raid, your clothes and belongings would all be gone.
Mama, I'm hungry!
When we drop our things off, the Kobayashis will give us some sweet potatoes. Be patient.
Really? Oh boy! Let's hurry, I wanna eat soon!

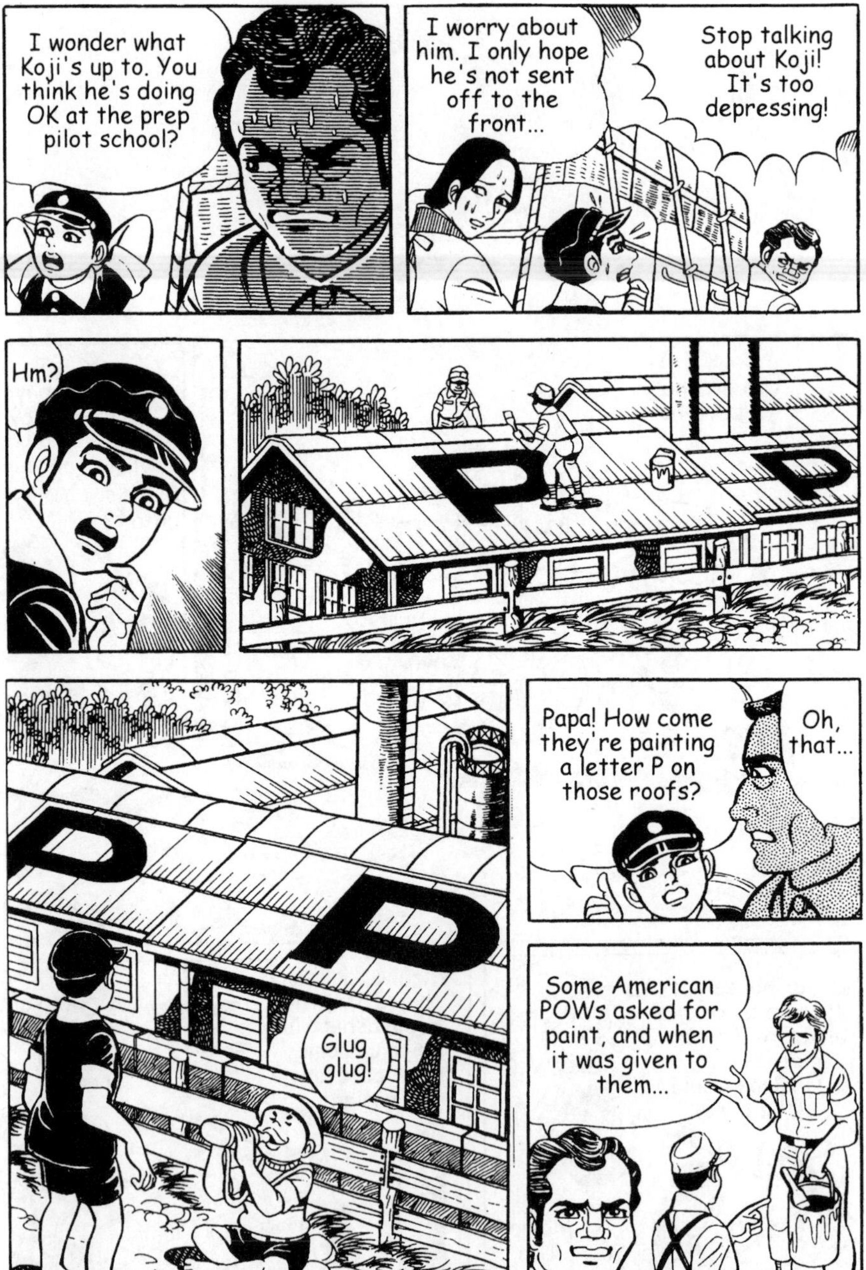
I wonder what Koji's up to. You think he's doing OK at the prep pilot school?
I worry about him. I only hope he's not sent off to the front...
Stop talking about Koji! It's too depressing!
Hm?
Papa! How come they're painting a letter P on those roofs?
Oh, that...
Glug glug!
Some American POWs asked for paint, and when it was given to them...

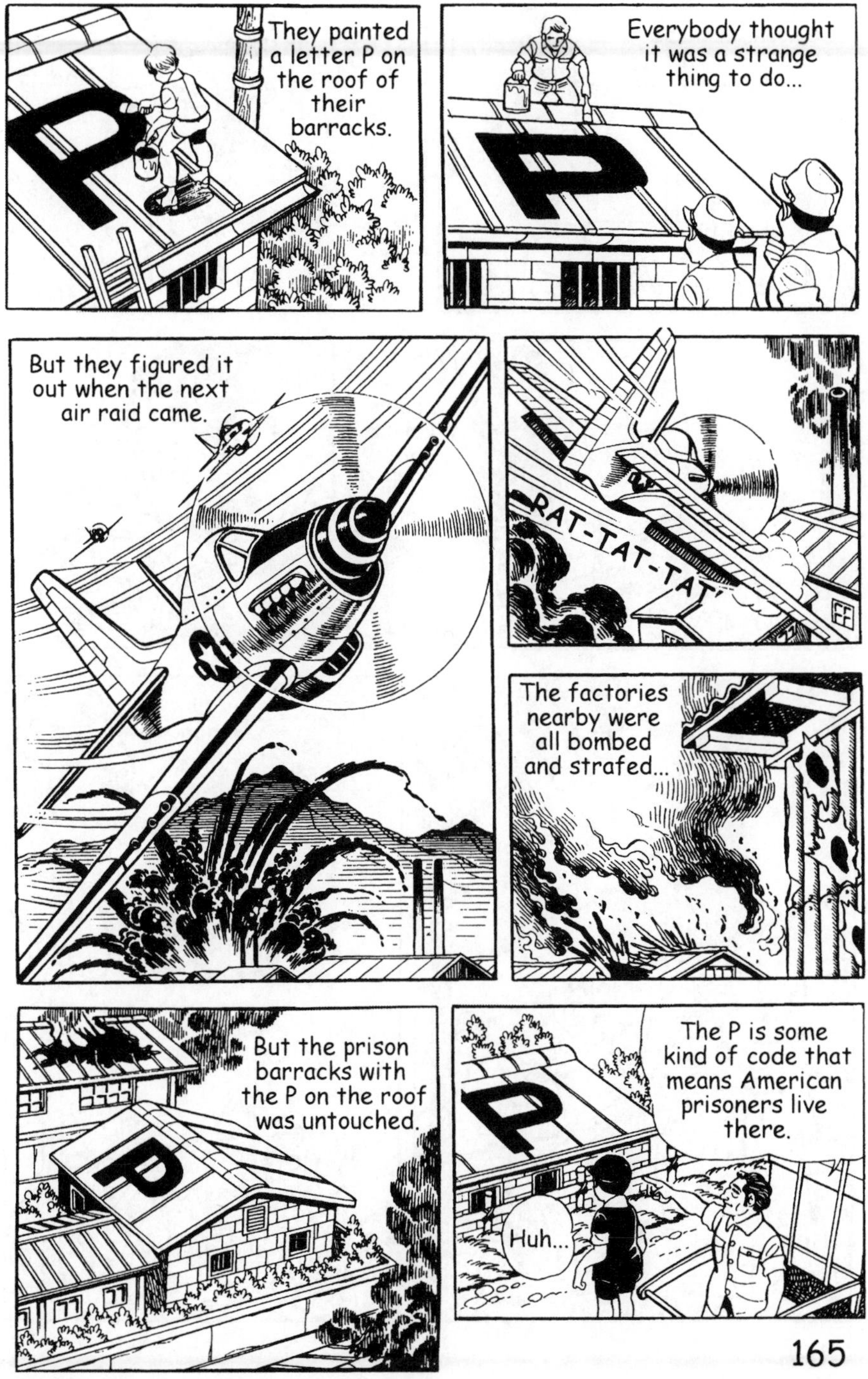
They painted a letter P on the roof of their barracks.
Everybody thought it was a strange thing to do...
But they figured it out when the next air raid came.
RAT-TAT-TAT
The factories nearby were all bombed and strafed...
But the prison barracks with the P on the roof was untouched.
The P is some kind of code that means American prisoners live there.
Huh...

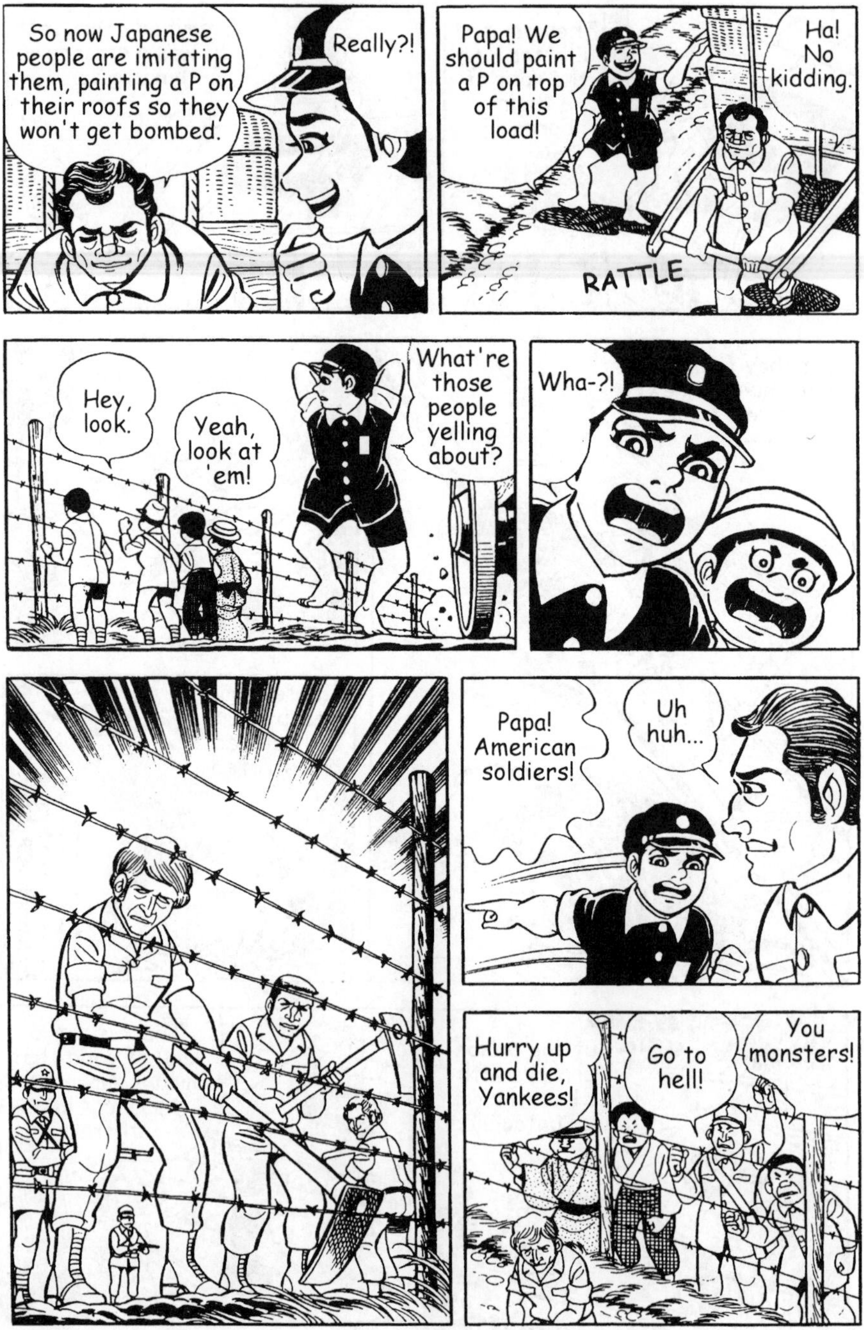
So now Japanese people are imitating them, painting a P on their roofs so they won't get bombed.
Really?!
Papa! We should paint a P on top of this load!
Ha! No kidding.
RATTLE
Hey, look.
Yeah, look at 'em!
What're those people yelling about?
Wha-?!
Papa! American soldiers!
Uh huh...
Hurry up and die, Yankees!
Go to hell!
You monsters!

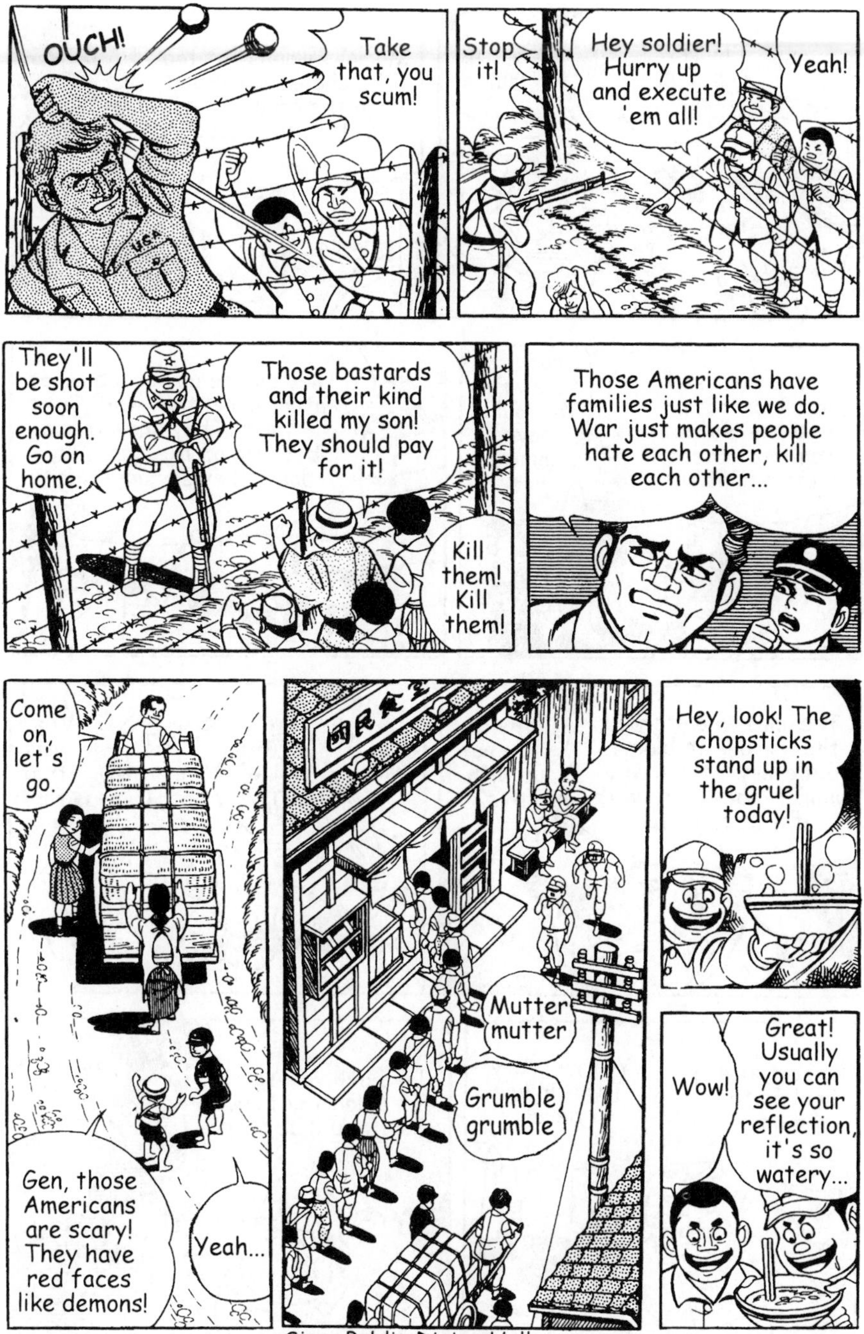
OUCH!
Take that, you scum!
Stop it!
Hey soldier! Hurry up and execute 'em all!
Yeah!
They'll be shot soon enough. Go on home.
Those bastards and their kind killed my son! They should pay for it!
Kill them! Kill them!
Those Americans have families just like we do. War just makes people hate each other, kill each other...
Come on, let's go.
Gen, those Americans are scary! They have red faces like demons!
Yeah...
Mutter mutter
Grumble grumble
Hey, look! The chopsticks stand up in the gruel today!
Wow!
Great! Usually you can see your reflection, it's so watery...
Sign: Public Dining Hall

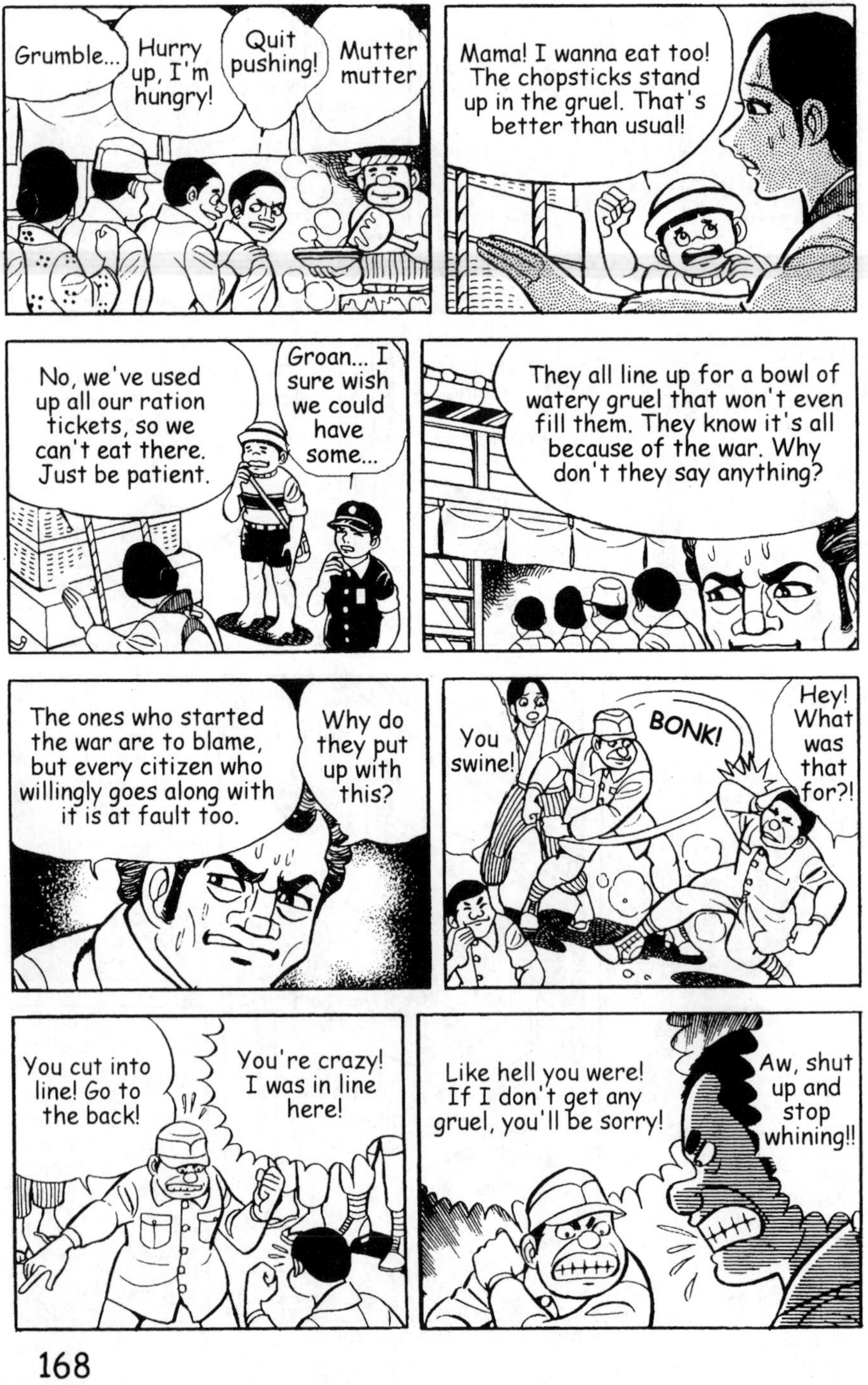
Grumble...
Hurry up, I'm hungry!
Quit pushing!
Mutter mutter
Mama! I wanna eat too! The chopsticks stand up in the gruel. That's better than usual!
No, we've used up all our ration tickets, so we can't eat there. Just be patient.
Groan... I sure wish we could have some...
They all line up for a bowl of watery gruel that won't even fill them. They know it's all because of the war. Why don't they say anything?
The ones who started the war are to blame, but every citizen who willingly goes along with it is at fault too.
Why do they put up with this?
You swine!
BONK!
Hey! What was that for?!
You cut into line! Go to the back!
You're crazy! I was in line here!
Like hell you were! If I don't get any gruel, you'll be sorry!
Aw, shut up and stop whining!!

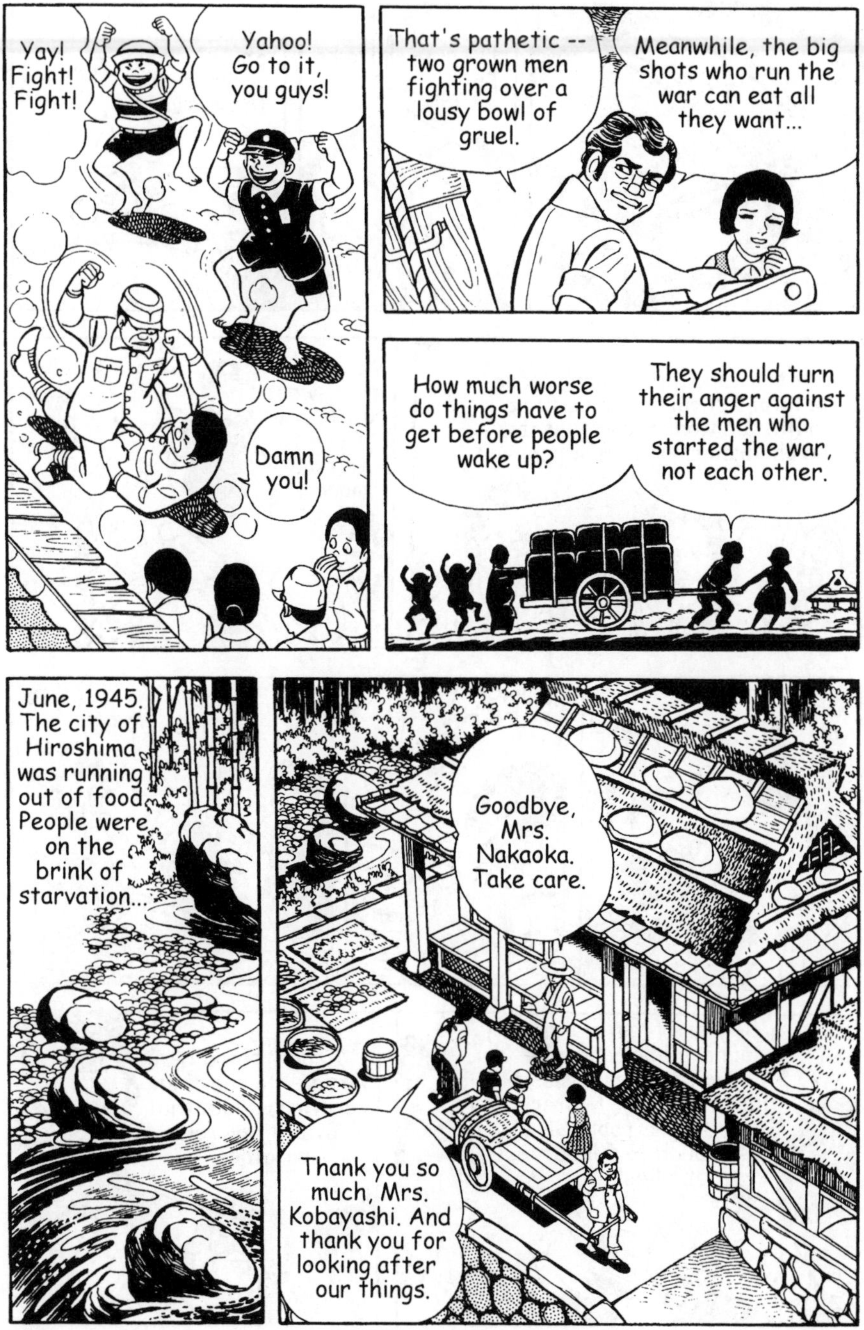
Yay! Fight! Fight!
Yahoo! Go to it, you guys!
Damn you!
That's pathetic -- two grown men fighting over a lousy bowl of gruel.
Meanwhile, the big shots who run the war can eat all they want...
How much worse do things have to get before people wake up?
They should turn their anger against the men who started the war, not each other.
June, 1945. The city of Hiroshima was running out of food People were on the brink of starvation...
Goodbye, Mrs. Nakaoka. Take care.
Thank you so much, Mrs. Kobayashi. And thank you for looking after our things.

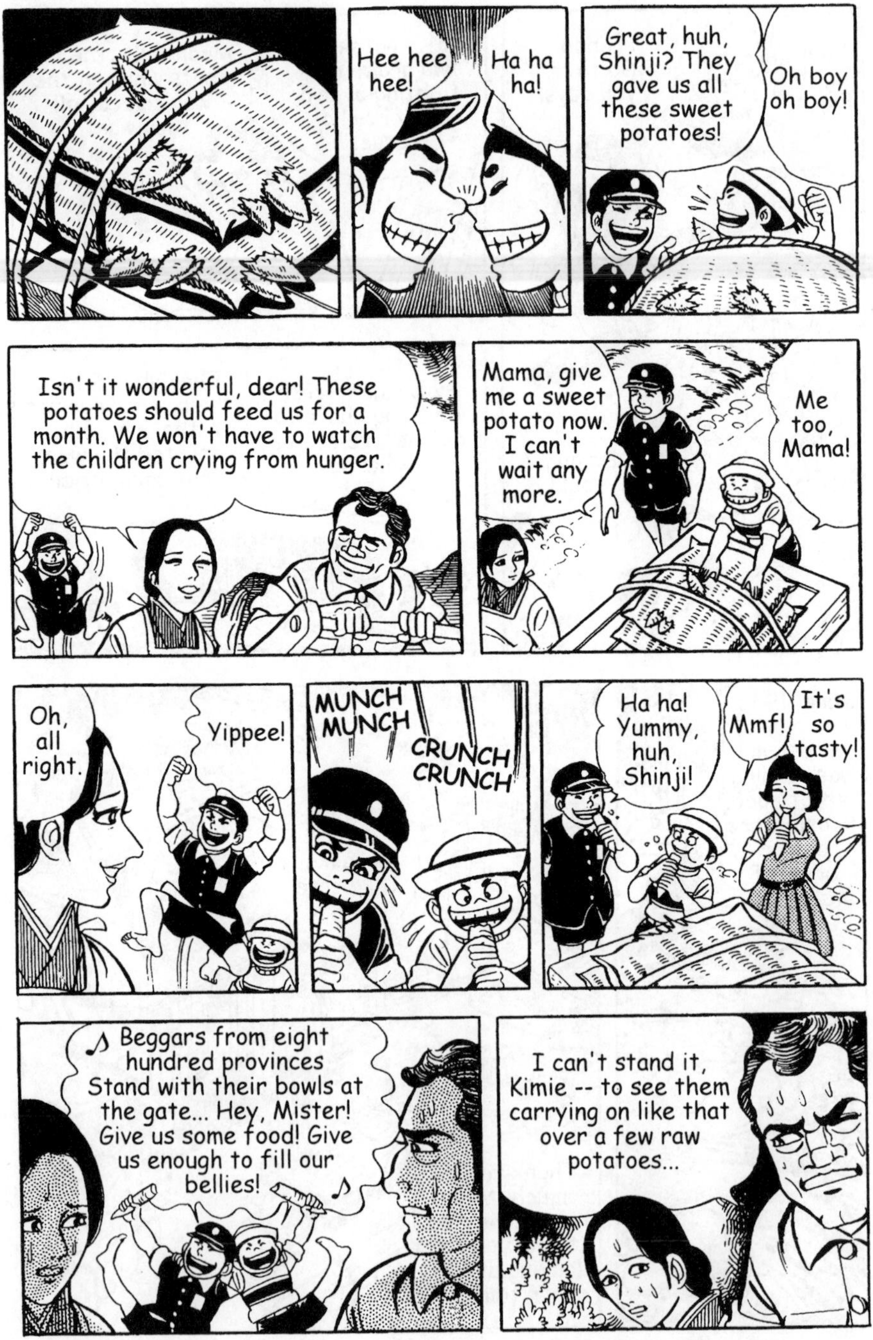
Hee hee hee!
Ha ha ha!
Great, huh, Shinji? They gave us all these sweet potatoes!
Oh boy oh boy!
Isn't it wonderful, dear! These potatoes should feed us for a month. We won't have to watch the children crying from hunger.
Mama, give me a sweet potato now. I can't wait any more.
Me too, Mama!
Oh, all right.
Yippee!
MUNCH MUNCH
CRUNCH CRUNCH
Ha ha! Yummy, huh, Shinji!
Mmf!
It's so tasty!
♪ Beggars from eight hundred provinces Stand with their bowls at the gate... Hey, Mister! Give us some food! Give us enough to fill our bellies! ♪
I can't stand it, Kimie -- to see them carrying on like that over a few raw potatoes...

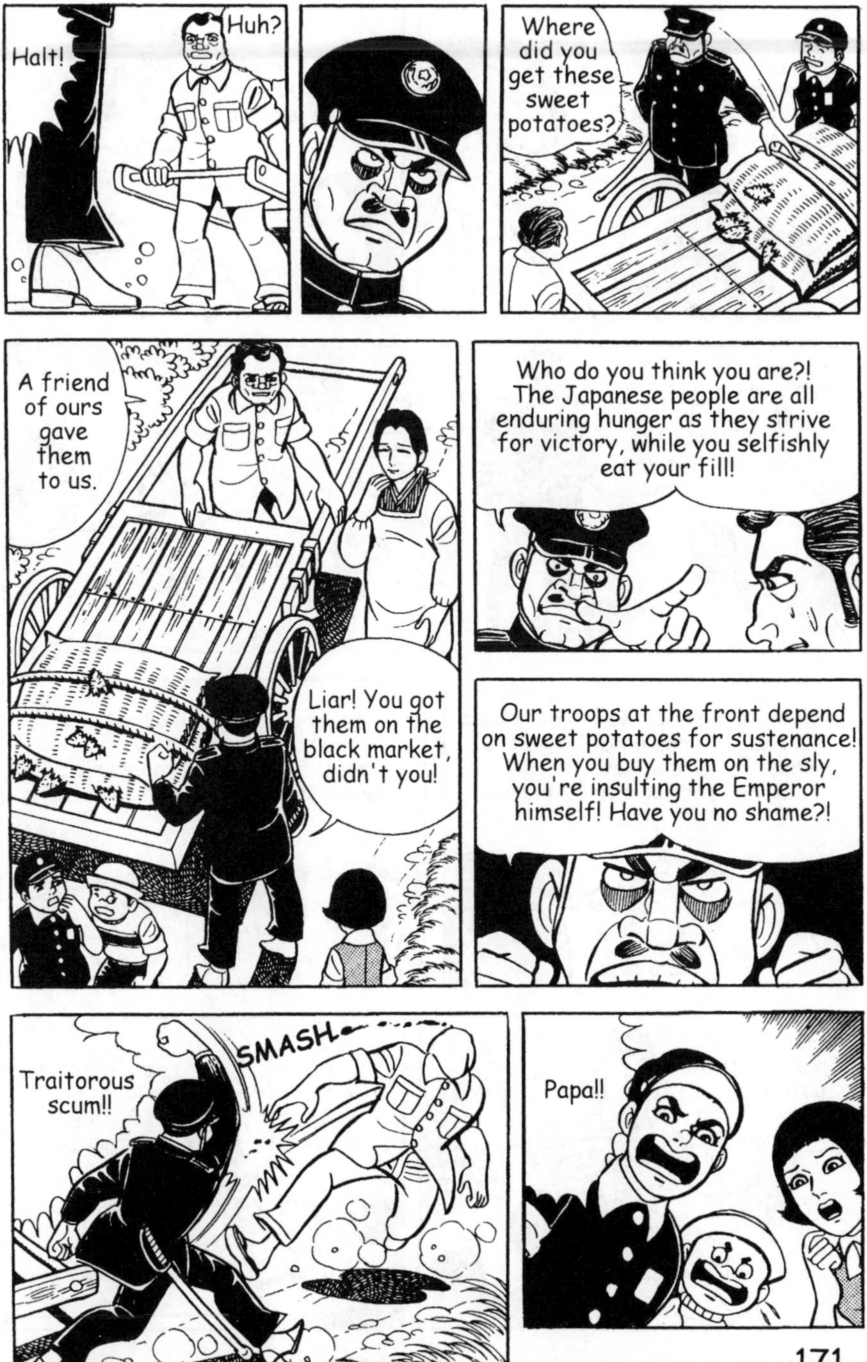
Halt!
Huh?
Where did you get these sweet potatoes?
A friend of ours gave them to us.
Liar! You got them on the black market, didn't you!
Who do you think you are?! The Japanese people are all enduring hunger as they strive for victory, while you selfishly eat your fill!
Our troops at the front depend on sweet potatoes for sustenance! When you buy them on the sly, you're insulting the Emperor himself! Have you no shame?!
Traitorous scum!!
SMASH
Papa!!

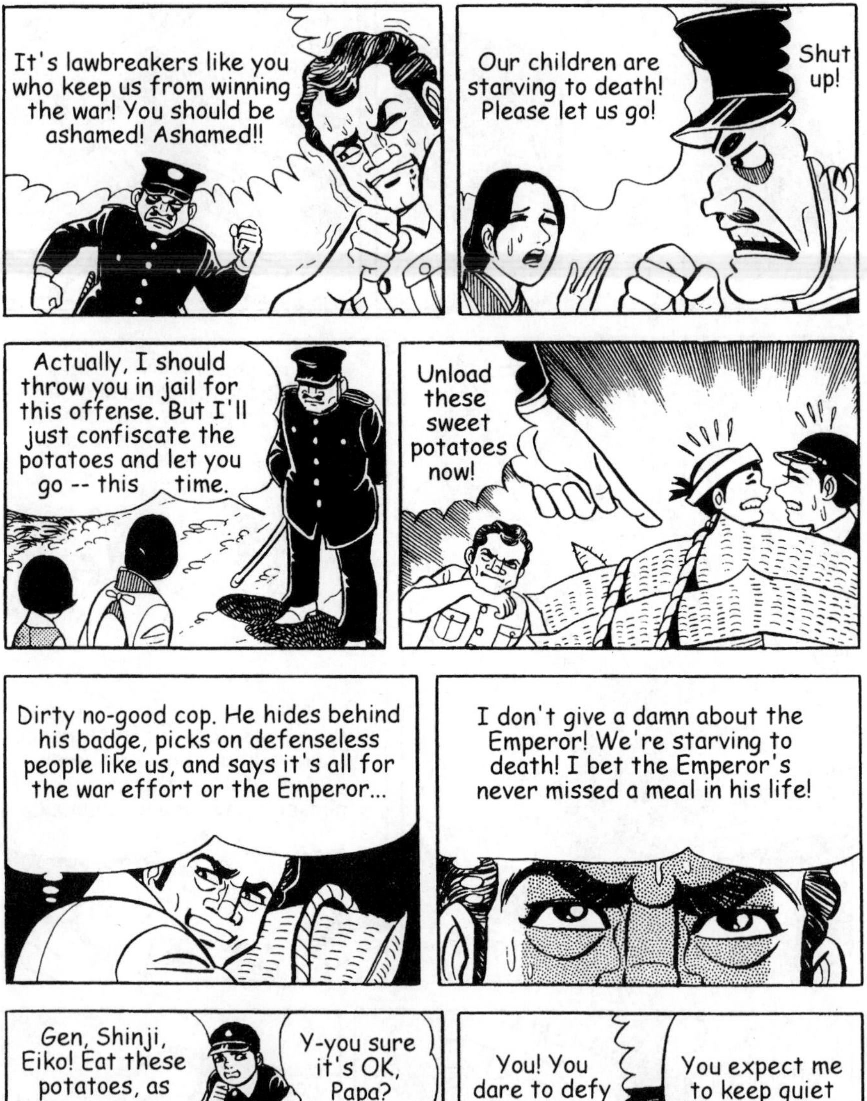
It's lawbreakers like you who keep us from winning the war! You should be ashamed! Ashamed!!
Our children are starving to death! Please let us go!
Shut up!
Actually, I should throw you in jail for this offense. But I'll just confiscate the potatoes and let you go -- this time.
Unload these sweet potatoes now!
Dirty no-good cop. He hides behind his badge, picks on defenseless people like us, and says it's all for the war effort or the Emperor...
I don't give a damn about the Emperor! We're starving to death! I bet the Emperor's never missed a meal in his life!
Gen, Shinji, Eiko! Eat these potatoes, as many as you can!
Y-you sure it's OK, Papa?
You! You dare to defy a police officer?!
You expect me to keep quiet and let my kids starve?

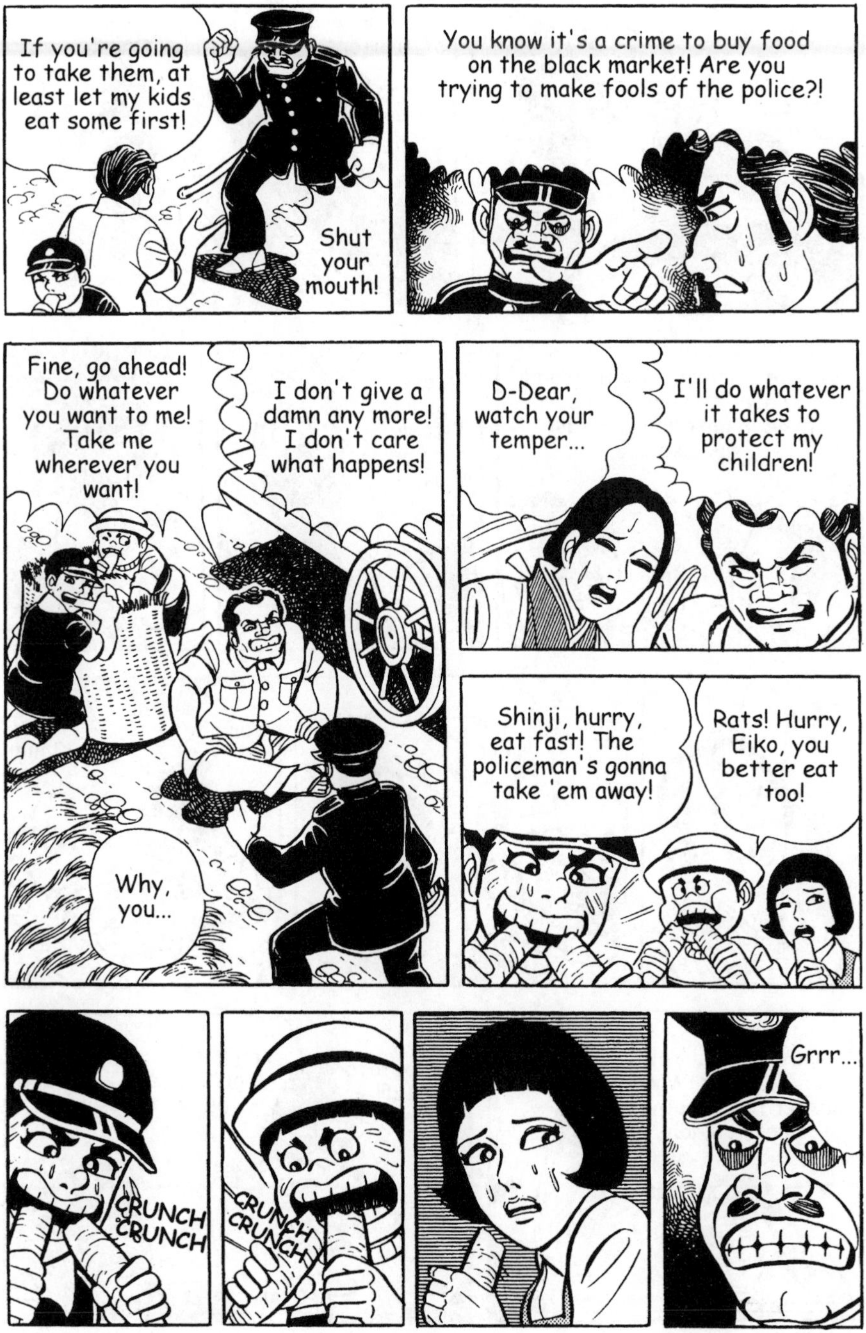
If you're going to take them, at least let my kids eat some first!
Shut your mouth!
You know it's a crime to buy food on the black market! Are you trying to make fools of the police?!
Fine, go ahead! Do whatever you want to me! Take me wherever you want!
I don't give a damn any more! I don't care what happens!
Why, you...
D-Dear, watch your temper...
I'll do whatever it takes to protect my children!
Shinji, hurry, eat fast! The policeman's gonna take 'em away!
Rats! Hurry, Eiko, you better eat too!
CRUNCH CRUNCH
CRUNCH CRUNCH
Grrr...

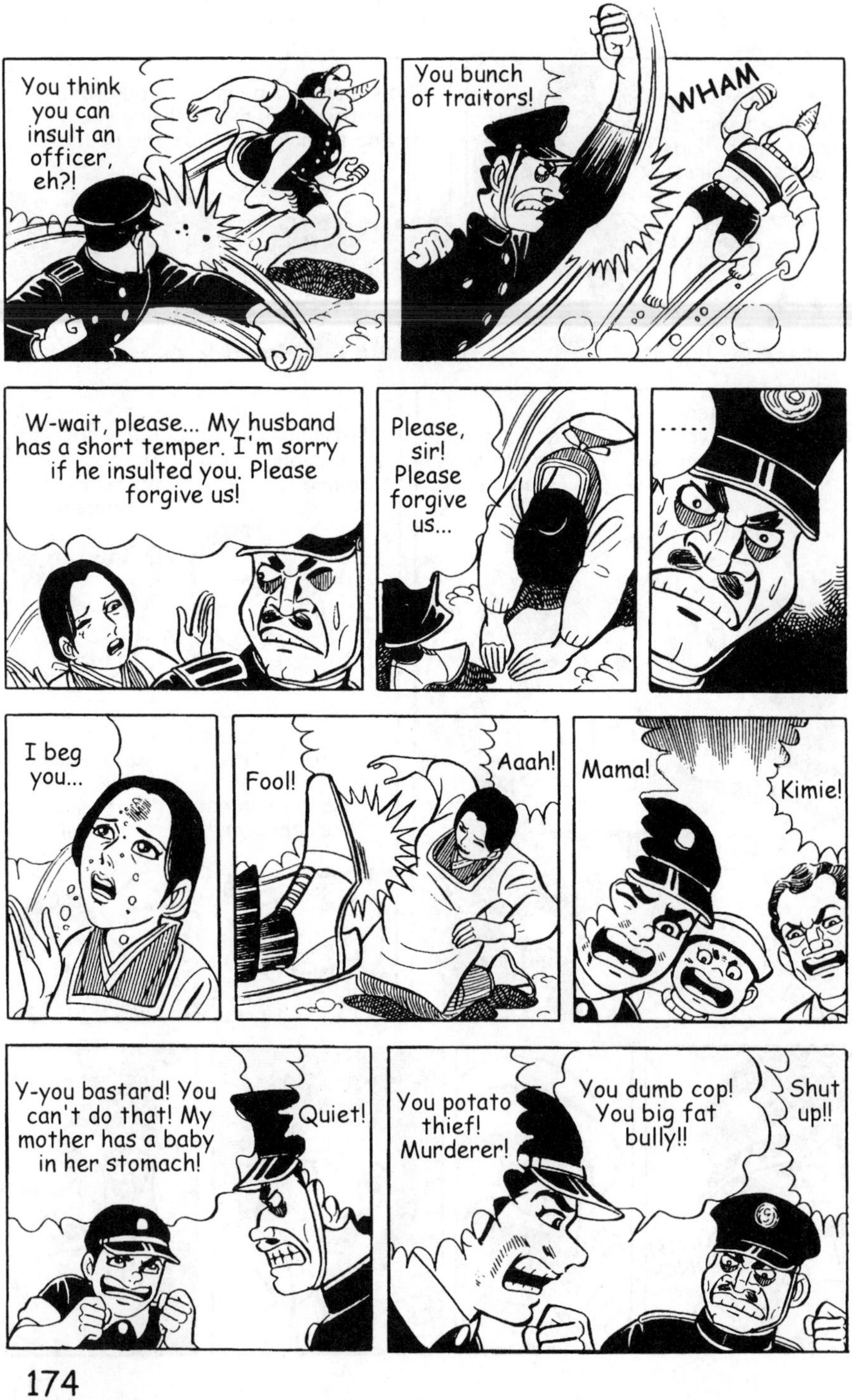
You think you can insult an officer, eh?!
You bunch of traitors!
WHAM
W-wait, please... My husband has a short temper. I'm sorry if he insulted you. Please forgive us!
Please, sir! Please forgive us...
.....
I beg you...
Fool!
Aaah!
Mama!
Kimie!
Y-you bastard! You can't do that! My mother has a baby in her stomach!
Quiet!
You potato thief! Murderer!
You dumb cop! You big fat bully!!
Shut up!!

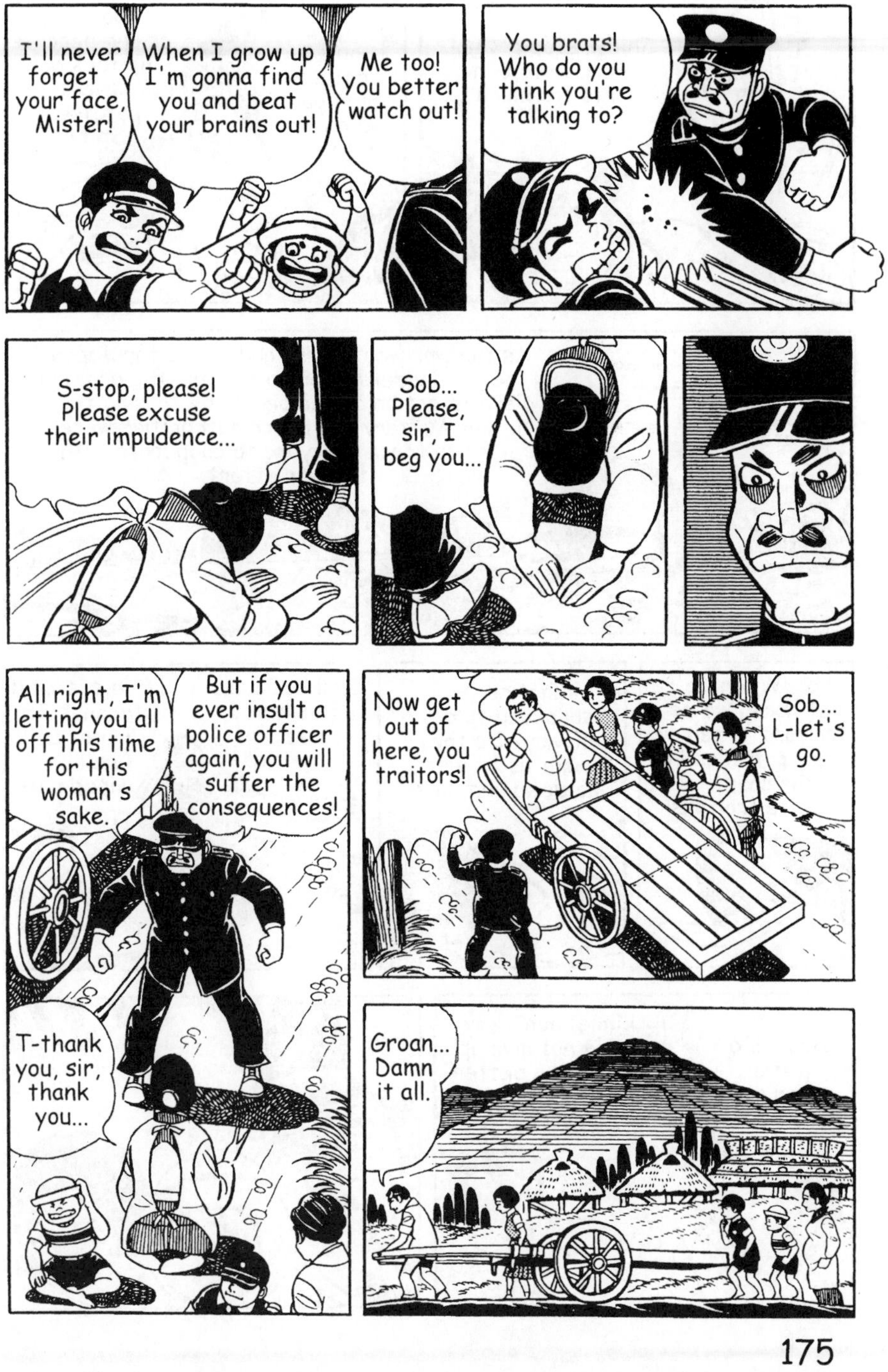

I'll never forget your face, Mister!
When I grow up I'm gonna find you and beat your brains out!
Me too! You better watch out!
You brats! Who do you think you're talking to?
S-stop, please! Please excuse their impudence...
Sob... Please, sir, I beg you...
All right, I'm letting you all off this time for this woman's sake.
But if you ever insult a police officer again, you will suffer the consequences!
T-thank you, sir, thank you...
Now get out of here, you traitors!
Sob... L-let's go.
Groan... Damn it all.

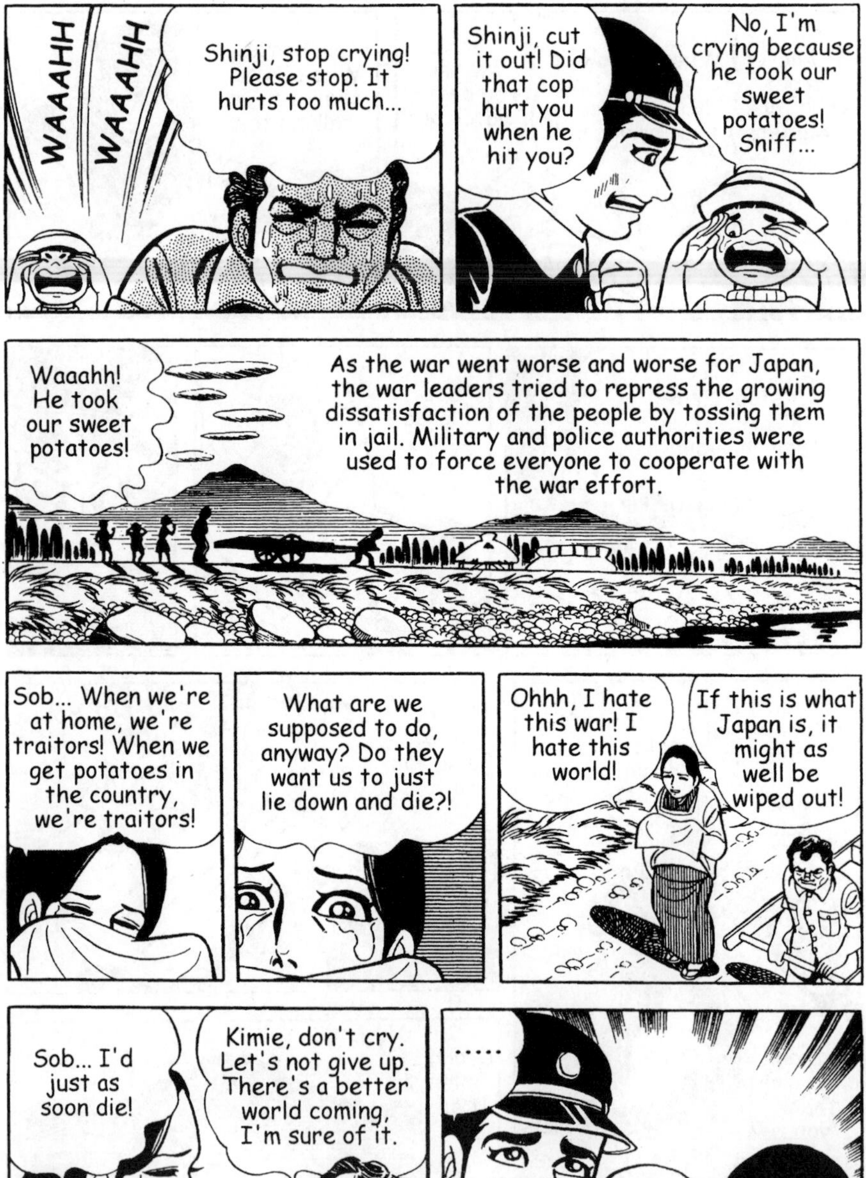
WAAAHH
WAAAHH
Shinji, stop crying! Please stop. It hurts too much...
Shinji, cut it out! Did that cop hurt you when he hit you?
No, I'm crying because he took our sweet potatoes! Sniff...
Waaahh! He took our sweet potatoes!
As the war went worse and worse for Japan, the war leaders tried to repress the growing dissatisfaction of the people by tossing them in jail. Military and police authorities were used to force everyone to cooperate with the war effort.
Sob... When we're at home, we're traitors! When we get potatoes in the country, we're traitors!
What are we supposed to do, anyway? Do they want us to just lie down and die?!
Ohhh, I hate this war! I hate this world!
If this is what Japan is, it might as well be wiped out!
Sob... I'd just as soon die!
Kimie, don't cry. Let's not give up. There's a better world coming, I'm sure of it.
.....

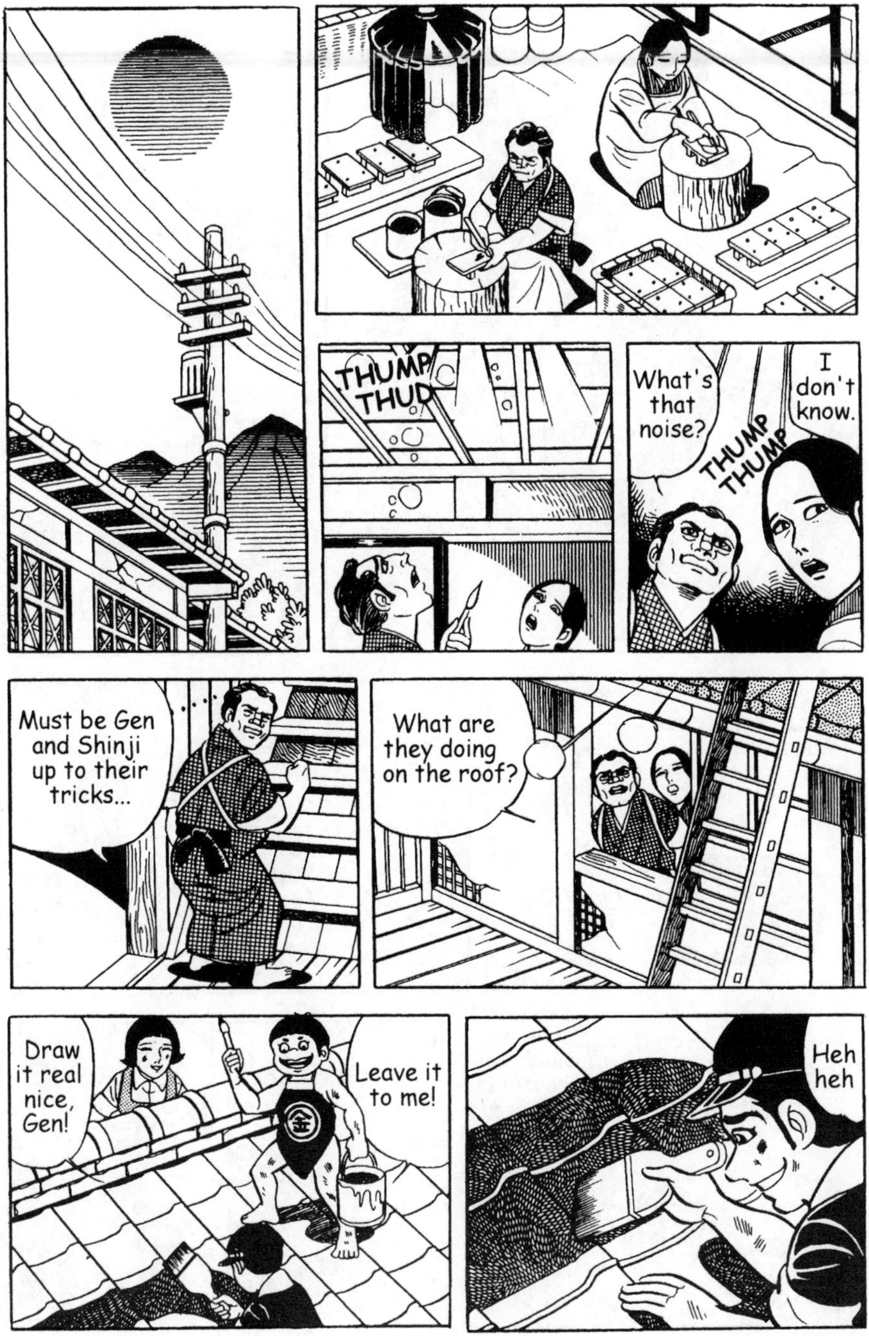
THUMP THUD
What's that noise?
I don't know.
THUMP THUMP
Must be Gen and Shinji up to their tricks...
What are they doing on the roof?
Draw it real nice, Gen!
Leave it to me!
Heh heh

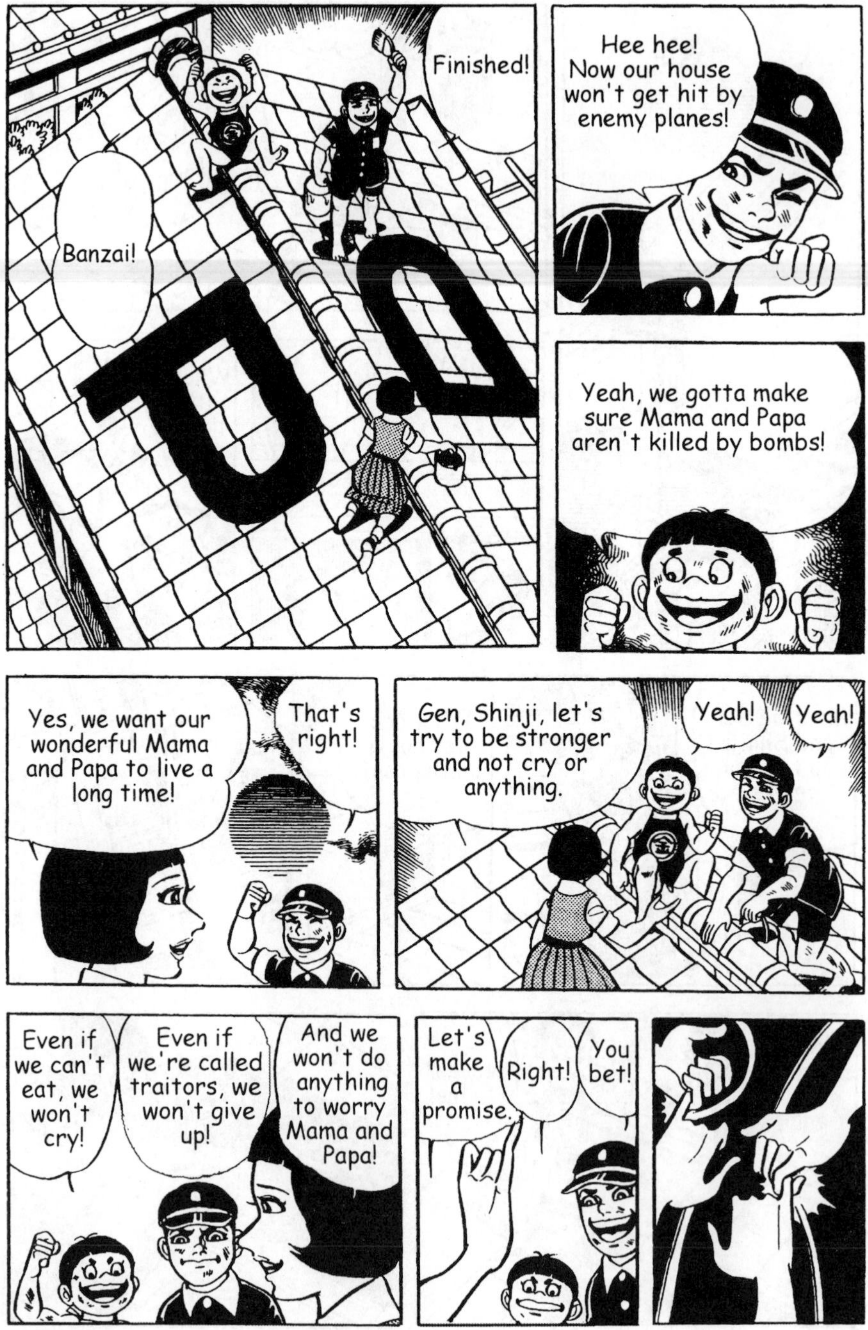
Finished!
Banzai!
Hee hee! Now our house won't get hit by enemy planes!
Yeah, we gotta make sure Mama and Papa aren't killed by bombs!
Yes, we want our wonderful Mama and Papa to live a long time!
That's right!
Gen, Shinji, let's try to be stronger and not cry or anything.
Yeah!
Yeah!
Even if we can't eat, we won't cry!
Even if we're called traitors, we won't give up!
And we won't do anything to worry Mama and Papa!
Let's make a promise.
Right!
You bet!

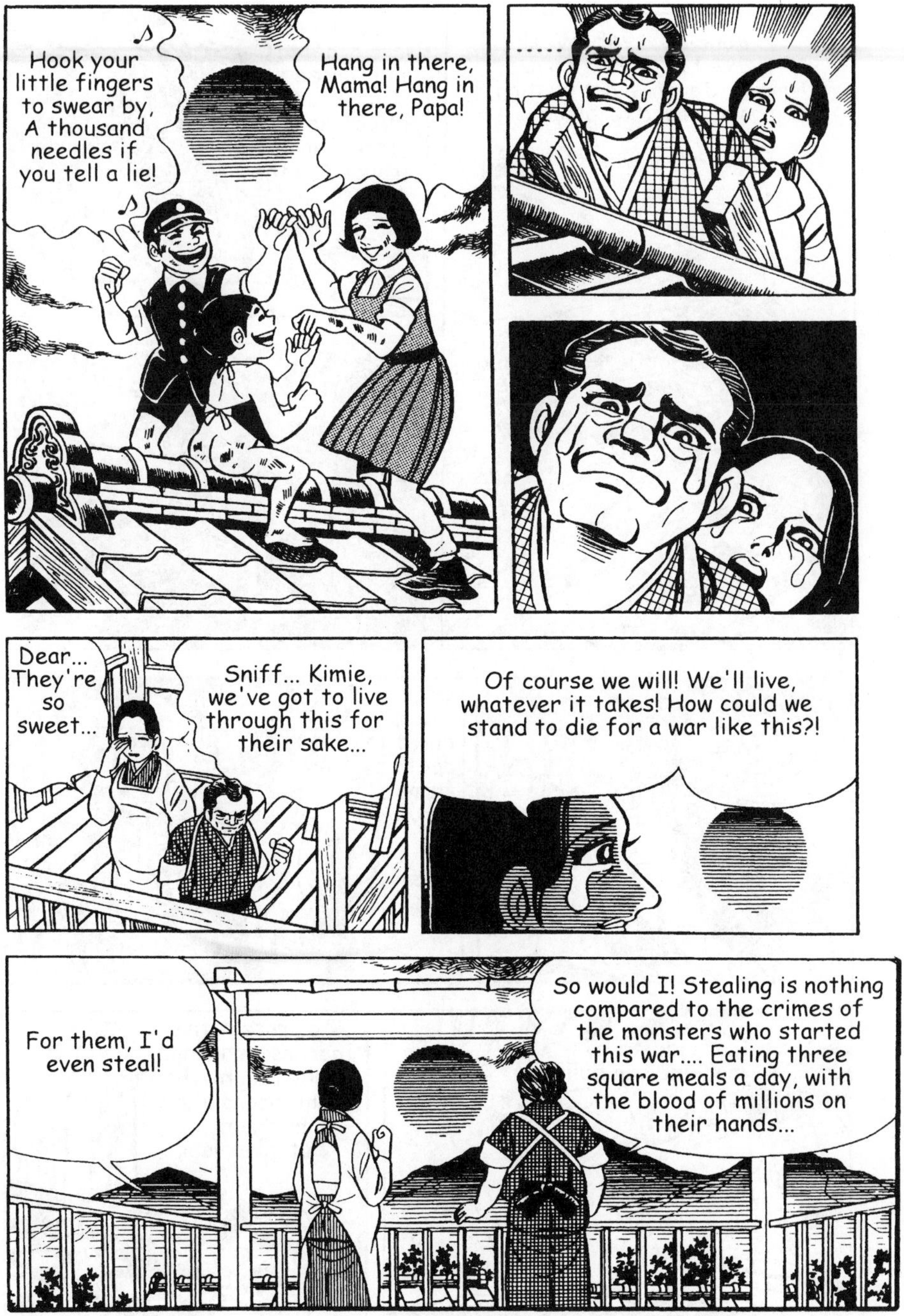
Hook your little fingers to swear by, A thousand needles if you tell a lie!
Hang in there, Mama! Hang in there, Papa!
......
Dear... They're so sweet...
Sniff... Kimie, we've got to live through this for their sake...
Of course we will! We'll live, whatever it takes! How could we stand to die for a war like this?!
For them, I'd even steal!
So would I! Stealing is nothing compared to the crimes of the monsters who started this war.... Eating three square meals a day, with the blood of millions on their hands...

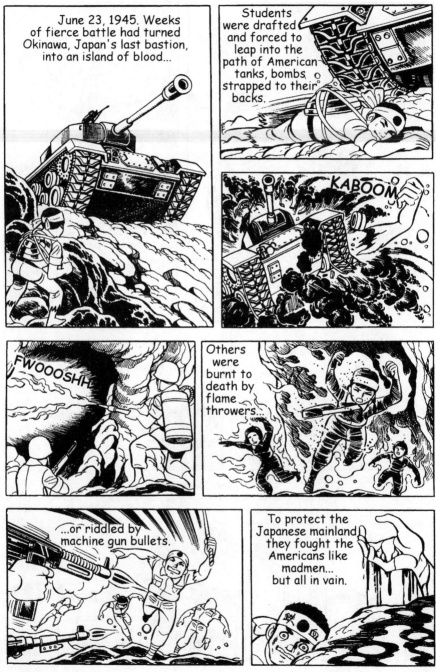

June 23, 1945. Weeks of fierce battle had turned Okinawa, Japan's last bastion, into an island of blood...

Students were drafted and forced to leap into the path of American tanks, bombs strapped to their backs.

KABOOM

FWOOOSHH

Others were burnt to death by flame throwers...

...or riddled by machine gun bullets.

To protect the Japanese mainland they fought the Americans like madmen... but all in vain.

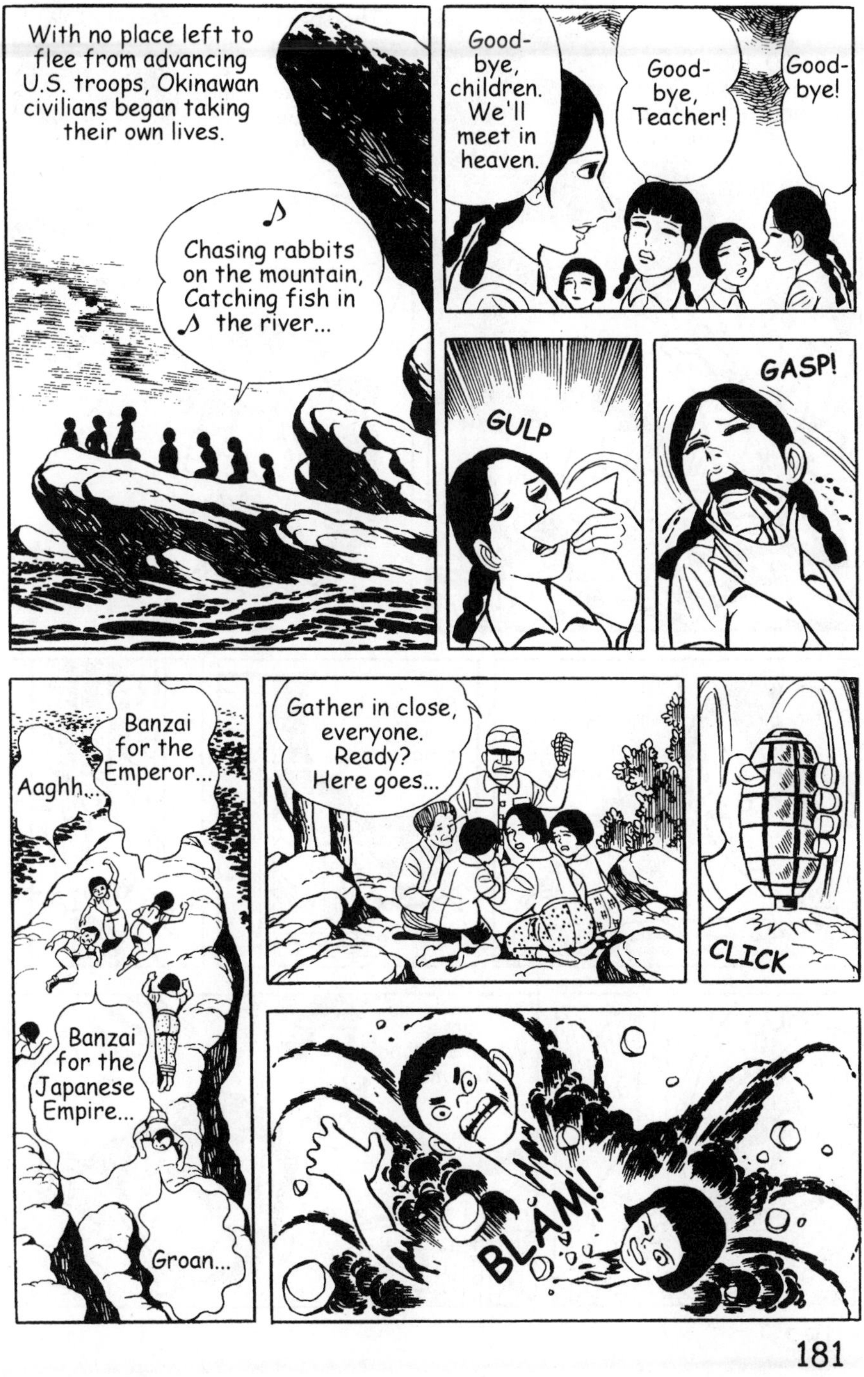
With no place left to flee from advancing U.S. troops, Okinawan civilians began taking their own lives.
♪ Chasing rabbits on the mountain, Catching fish in ♪ the river...
Good-bye, children. We'll meet in heaven.
Good-bye, Teacher!
Good-bye!
GULP
GASP!
Banzai for the Emperor...
Aaghh...
Banzai for the Japanese Empire...
Groan...
Gather in close, everyone. Ready? Here goes...
CLICK
BLAM!

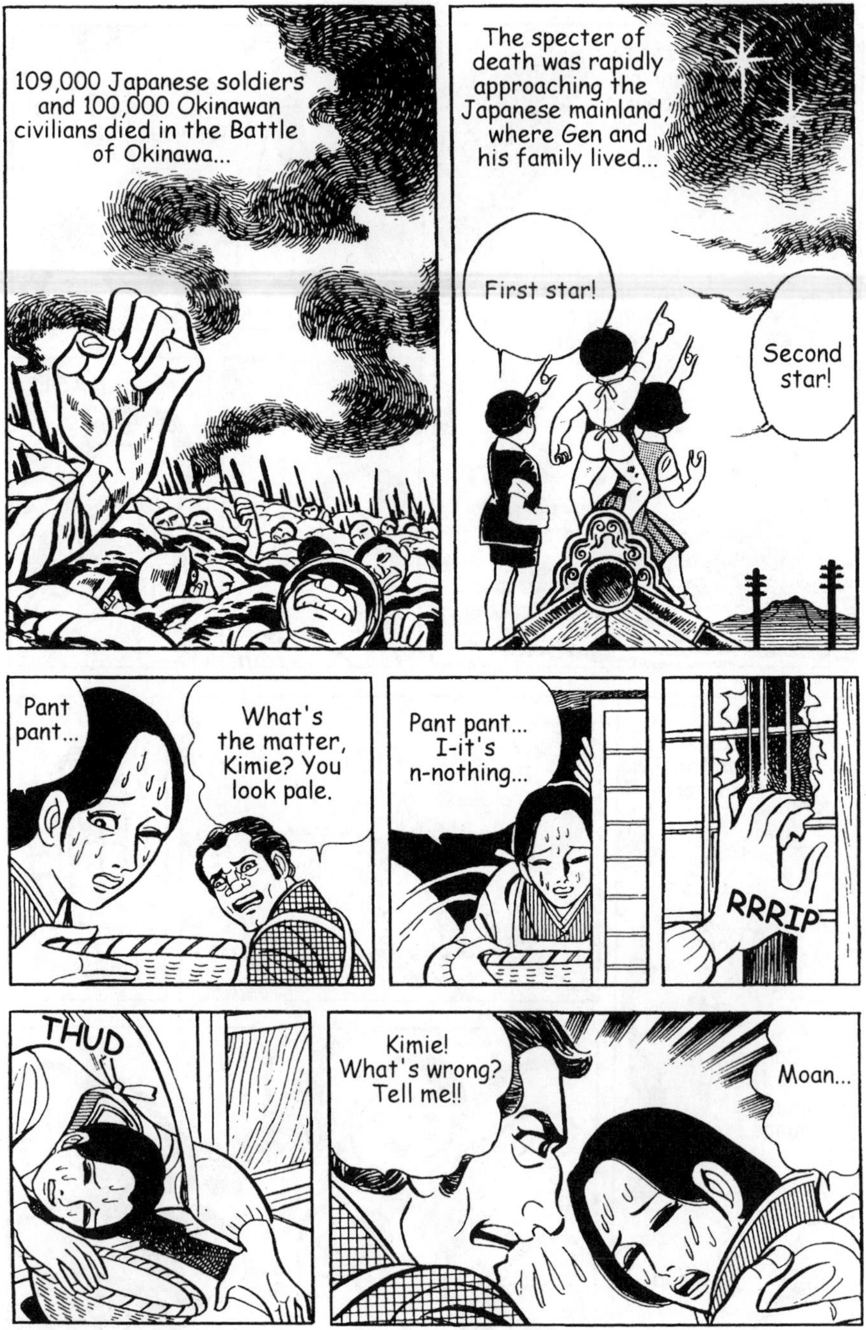
109,000 Japanese soldiers and 100,000 Okinawan civilians died in the Battle of Okinawa...
The specter of death was rapidly approaching the Japanese mainland, where Gen and his family lived...
First star!
Second star!
Pant pant...
What's the matter, Kimie? You look pale.
Pant pant... I-it's n-nothing...
RRRIP
THUD
Kimie! What's wrong? Tell me!!
Moan...

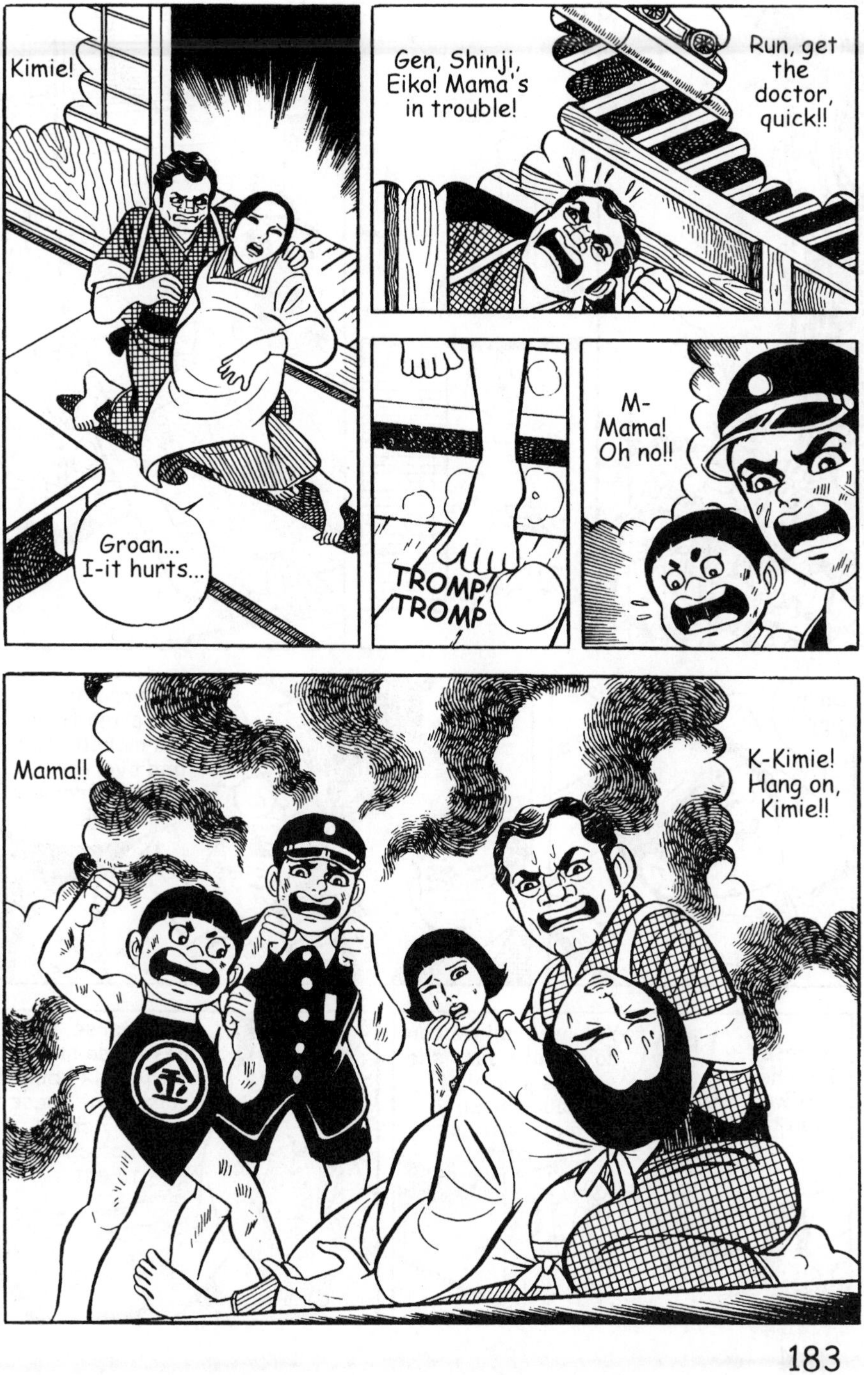
Kimie!
Groan... I-it hurts...
Gen, Shinji, Eiko! Mama's in trouble!
Run, get the doctor, quick!!
TROMP TROMP
M-Mama! Oh no!!
Mama!!
K-Kimie! Hang on, Kimie!!

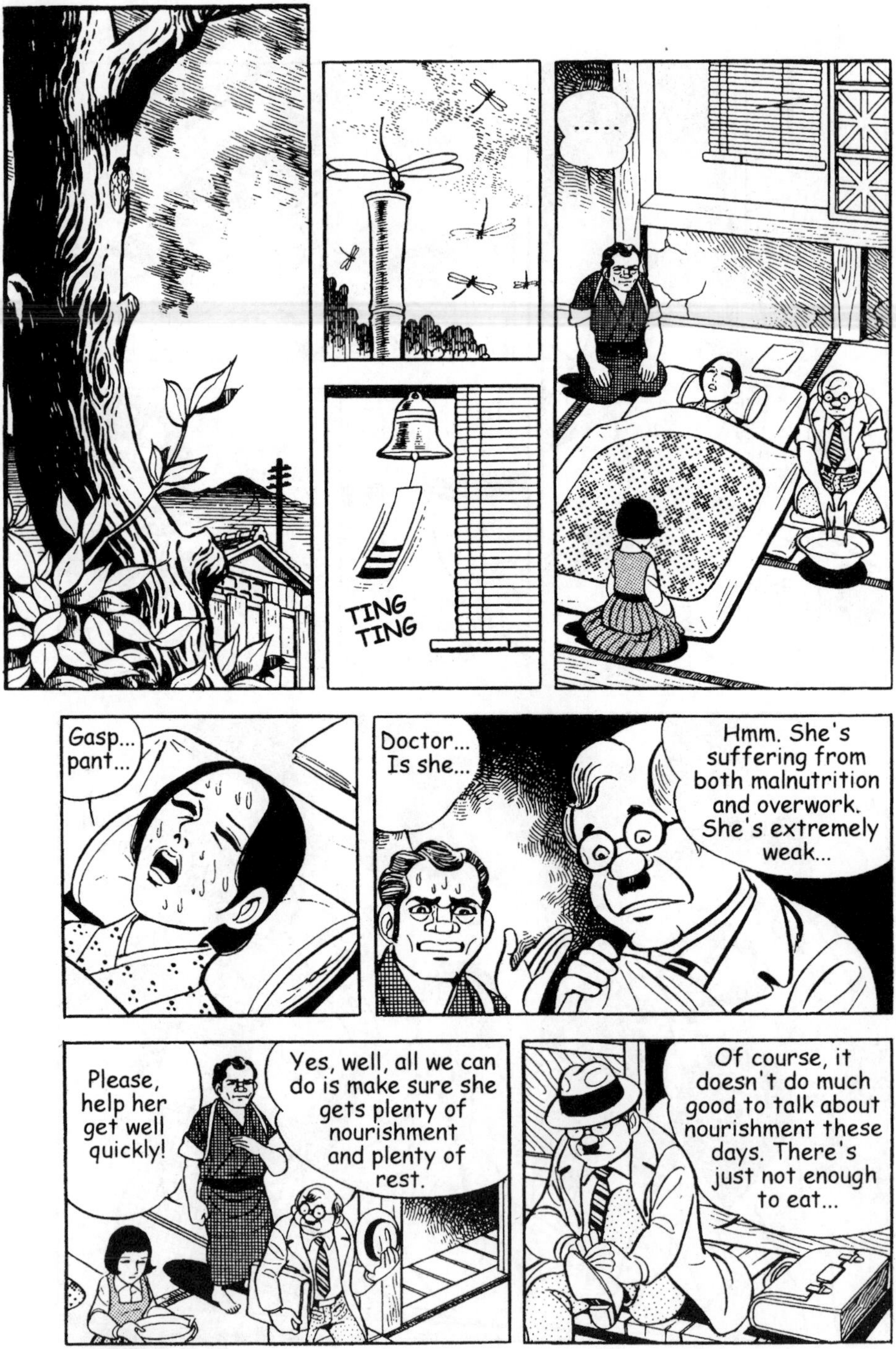
TING TING
.....
Gasp... pant...
Doctor... Is she...
Hmm. She's suffering from both malnutrition and overwork. She's extremely weak...
Please, help her get well quickly!
Yes, well, all we can do is make sure she gets plenty of nourishment and plenty of rest.
Of course, it doesn't do much good to talk about nourishment these days. There's just not enough to eat...

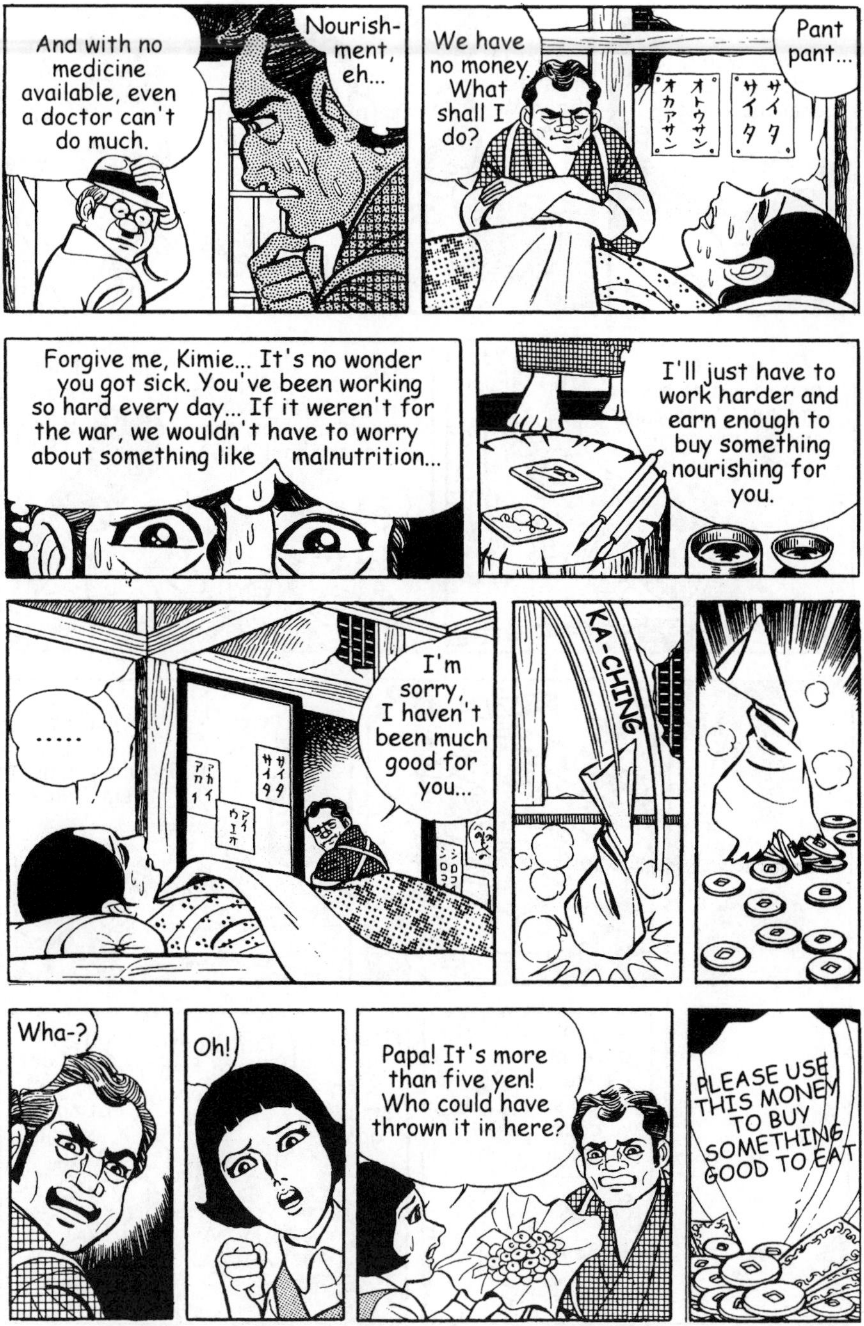
And with no medicine available, even a doctor can't do much.
Nourish-ment, eh...
We have no money. What shall I do?
サイタ サイタ
オトウサン オカアサン
Pant pant...
Forgive me, Kimie... It's no wonder you got sick. You've been working so hard every day... If it weren't for the war, we wouldn't have to worry about something like malnutrition...
I'll just have to work harder and earn enough to buy something nourishing for you.
.....
I'm sorry, I haven't been much good for you...
KA-CHING
Wha-?
Oh!
Papa! It's more than five yen! Who could have thrown it in here?
PLEASE USE THIS MONEY TO BUY SOMETHING GOOD TO EAT

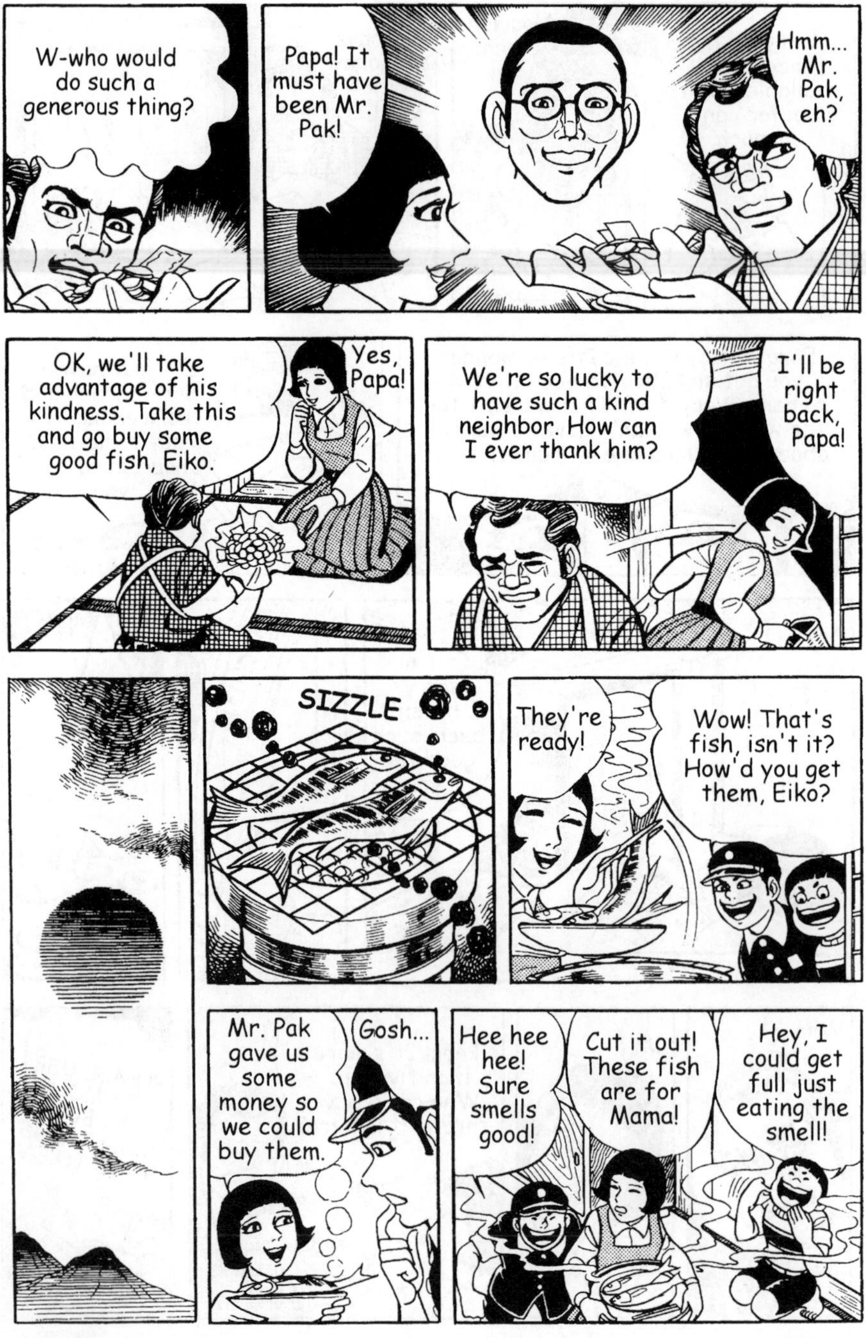
W-who would do such a generous thing?
Papa! It must have been Mr. Pak!
Hmm... Mr. Pak, eh?
OK, we'll take advantage of his kindness. Take this and go buy some good fish, Eiko.
Yes, Papa!
We're so lucky to have such a kind neighbor. How can I ever thank him?
I'll be right back, Papa!
SIZZLE
They're ready!
Wow! That's fish, isn't it? How'd you get them, Eiko?
Mr. Pak gave us some money so we could buy them.
Gosh...
Hee hee hee! Sure smells good!
Cut it out! These fish are for Mama!
Hey, I could get full just eating the smell!

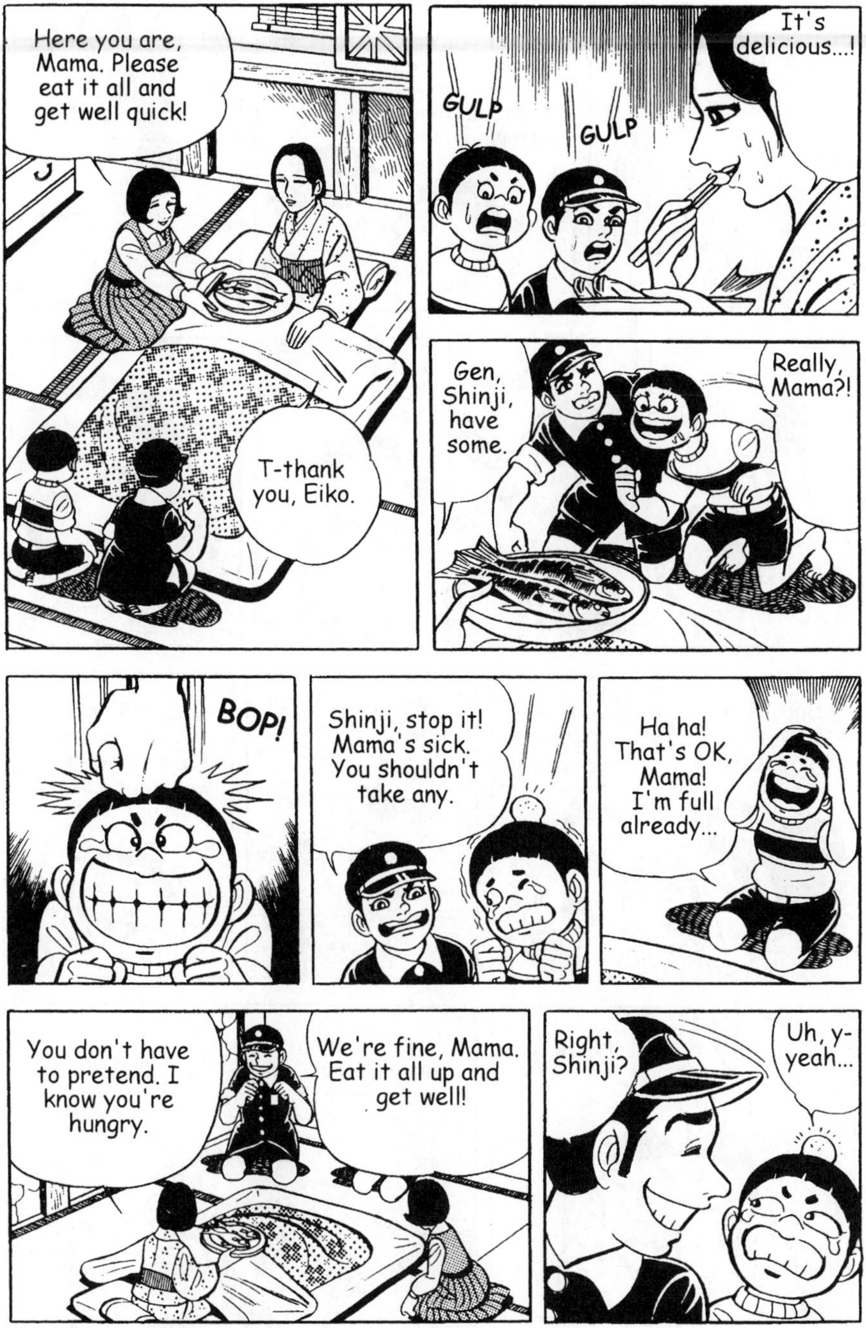

Here you are, Mama. Please eat it all and get well quick!
T-thank you, Eiko.
GULP
GULP
It's delicious...!
Gen, Shinji, have some.
Really, Mama?!
BOP!
Shinji, stop it! Mama's sick. You shouldn't take any.
Ha ha! That's OK, Mama! I'm full already...
You don't have to pretend. I know you're hungry.
We're fine, Mama. Eat it all up and get well!
Right, Shinji?
Uh, y-yeah...

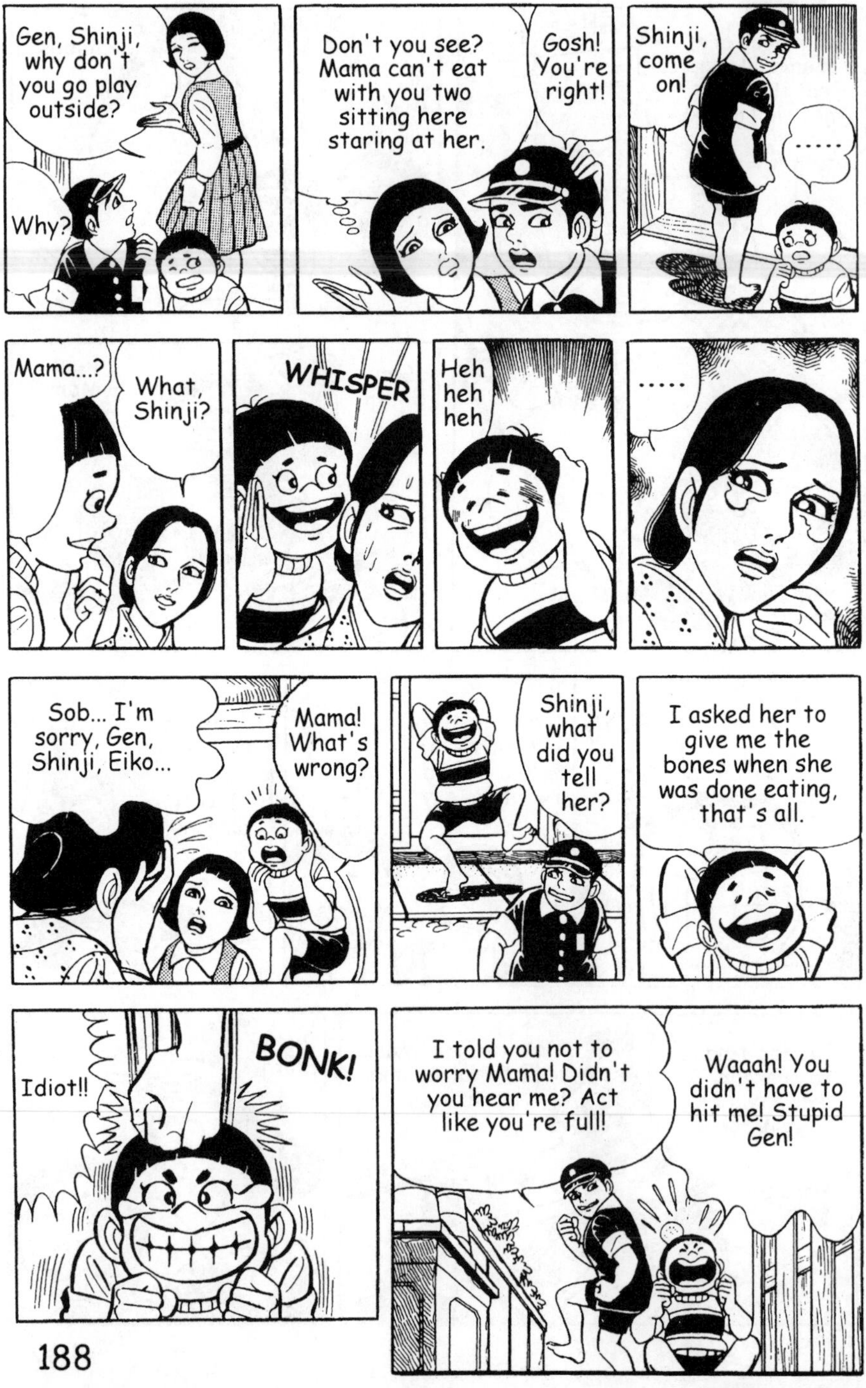
Gen, Shinji, why don't you go play outside?
Why?
Don't you see? Mama can't eat with you two sitting here staring at her.
Gosh! You're right!
Shinji, come on!
.....
Mama...?
What, Shinji?
WHISPER
Heh heh heh
.....
Sob... I'm sorry, Gen, Shinji, Eiko...
Mama! What's wrong?
Shinji, what did you tell her?
I asked her to give me the bones when she was done eating, that's all.
Idiot!!
BONK!
I told you not to worry Mama! Didn't you hear me? Act like you're full!
Waaah! You didn't have to hit me! Stupid Gen!

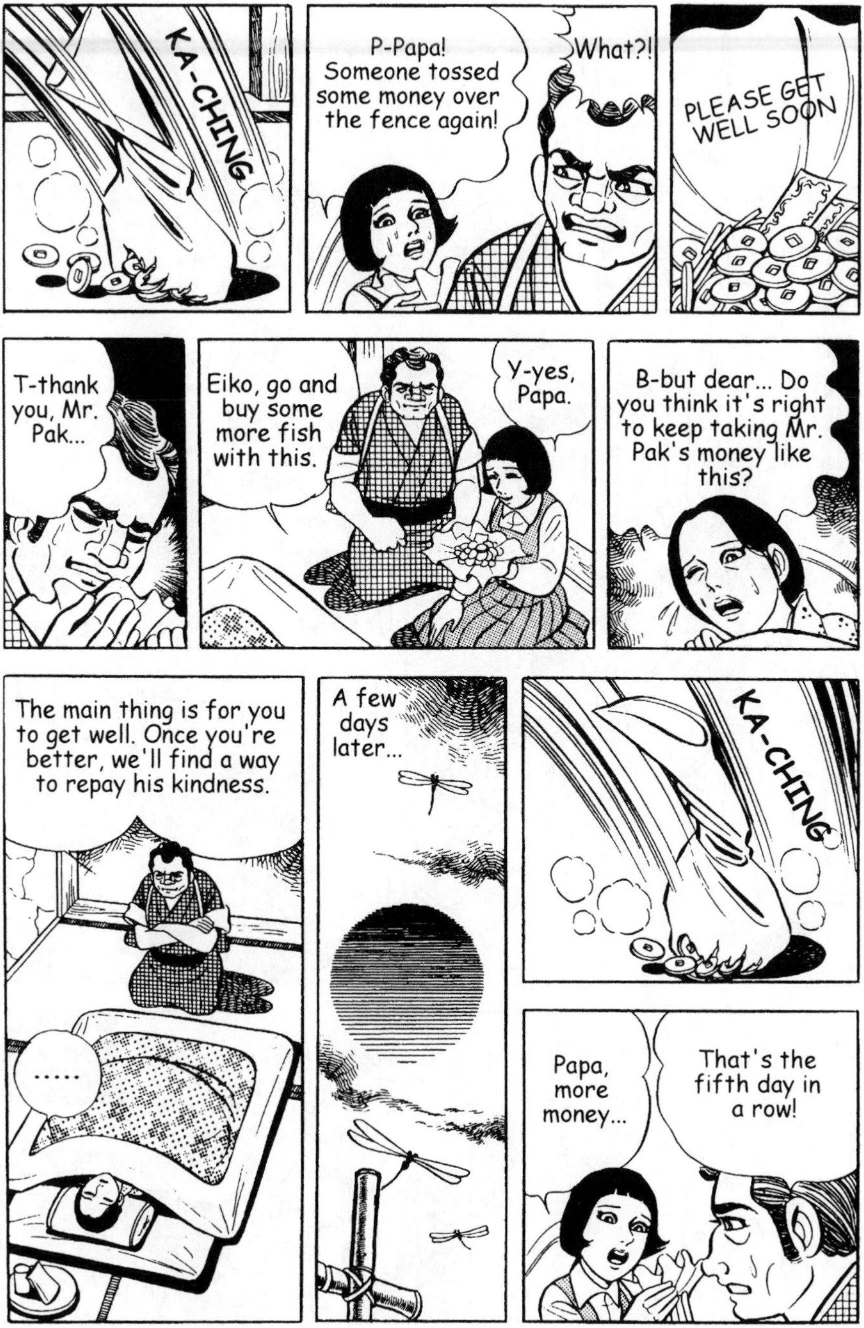
KA-CHING
P-Papa! Someone tossed some money over the fence again!
What?!
PLEASE GET WELL SOON
T-thank you, Mr. Pak...
Eiko, go and buy some more fish with this.
Y-yes, Papa.
B-but dear... Do you think it's right to keep taking Mr. Pak's money like this?
The main thing is for you to get well. Once you're better, we'll find a way to repay his kindness.
......
A few days later...
KA-CHING
Papa, more money...
That's the fifth day in a row!

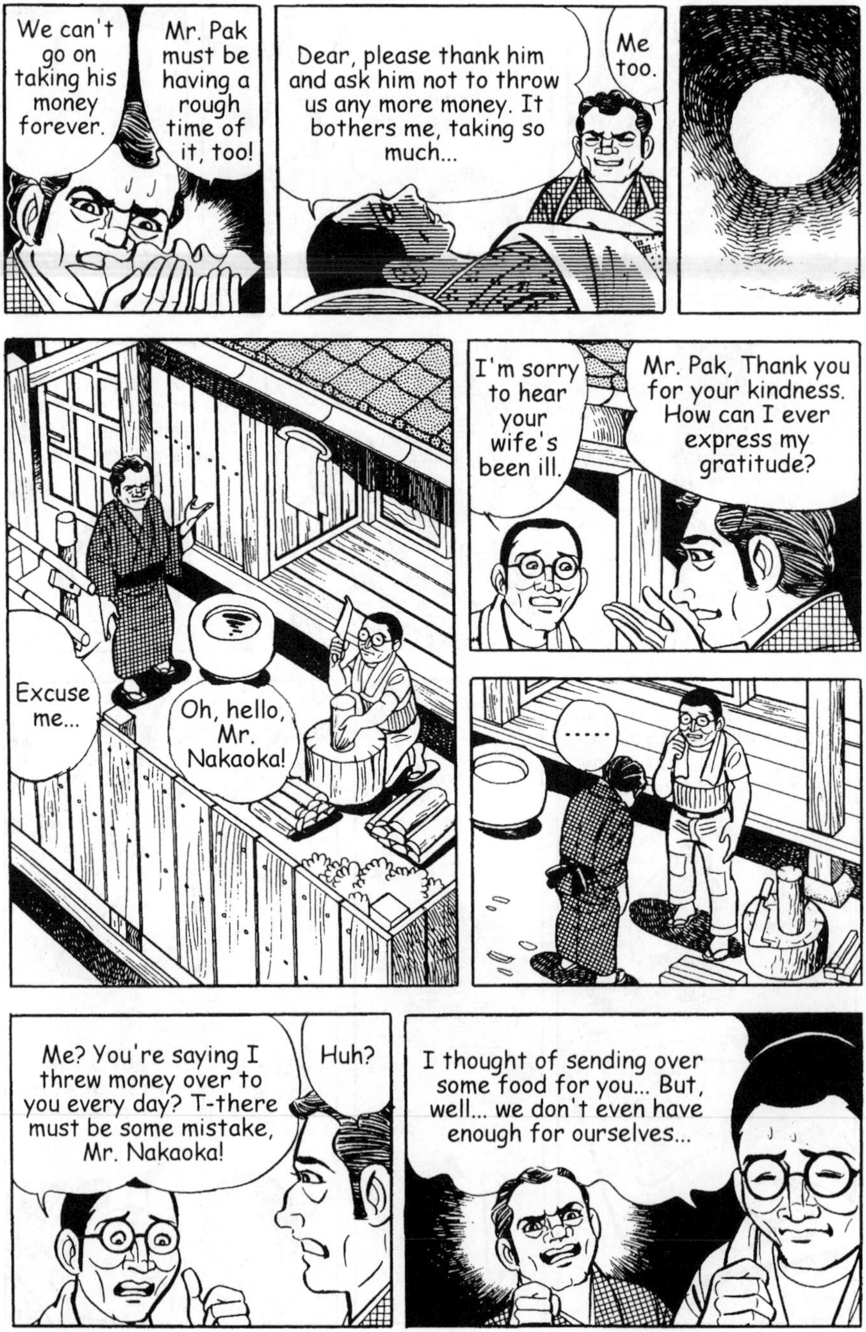
We can't go on taking his money forever.
Mr. Pak must be having a rough time of it, too!
Dear, please thank him and ask him not to throw us any more money. It bothers me, taking so much...
Me too.
Excuse me...
Oh, hello, Mr. Nakaoka!
I'm sorry to hear your wife's been ill.
Mr. Pak, Thank you for your kindness. How can I ever express my gratitude?
.....
Me? You're saying I threw money over to you every day? T-there must be some mistake, Mr. Nakaoka!
Huh?
I thought of sending over some food for you... But, well... we don't even have enough for ourselves...

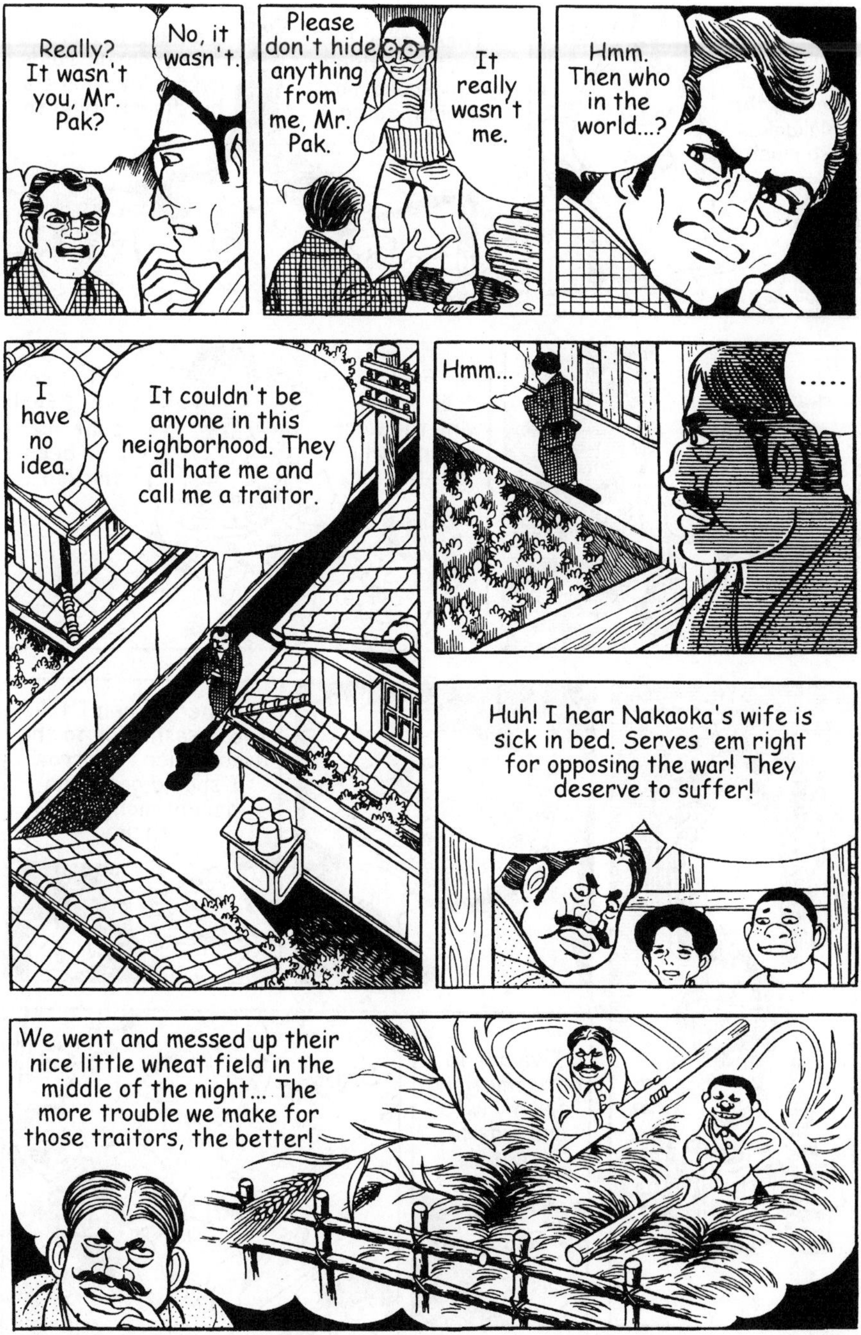
Really? It wasn't you, Mr. Pak?
No, it wasn't.
Please don't hide anything from me, Mr. Pak.
It really wasn't me.
Hmm. Then who in the world...?
I have no idea.
It couldn't be anyone in this neighborhood. They all hate me and call me a traitor.
Hmm...
.....
Huh! I hear Nakaoka's wife is sick in bed. Serves 'em right for opposing the war! They deserve to suffer!
We went and messed up their nice little wheat field in the middle of the night... The more trouble we make for those traitors, the better!

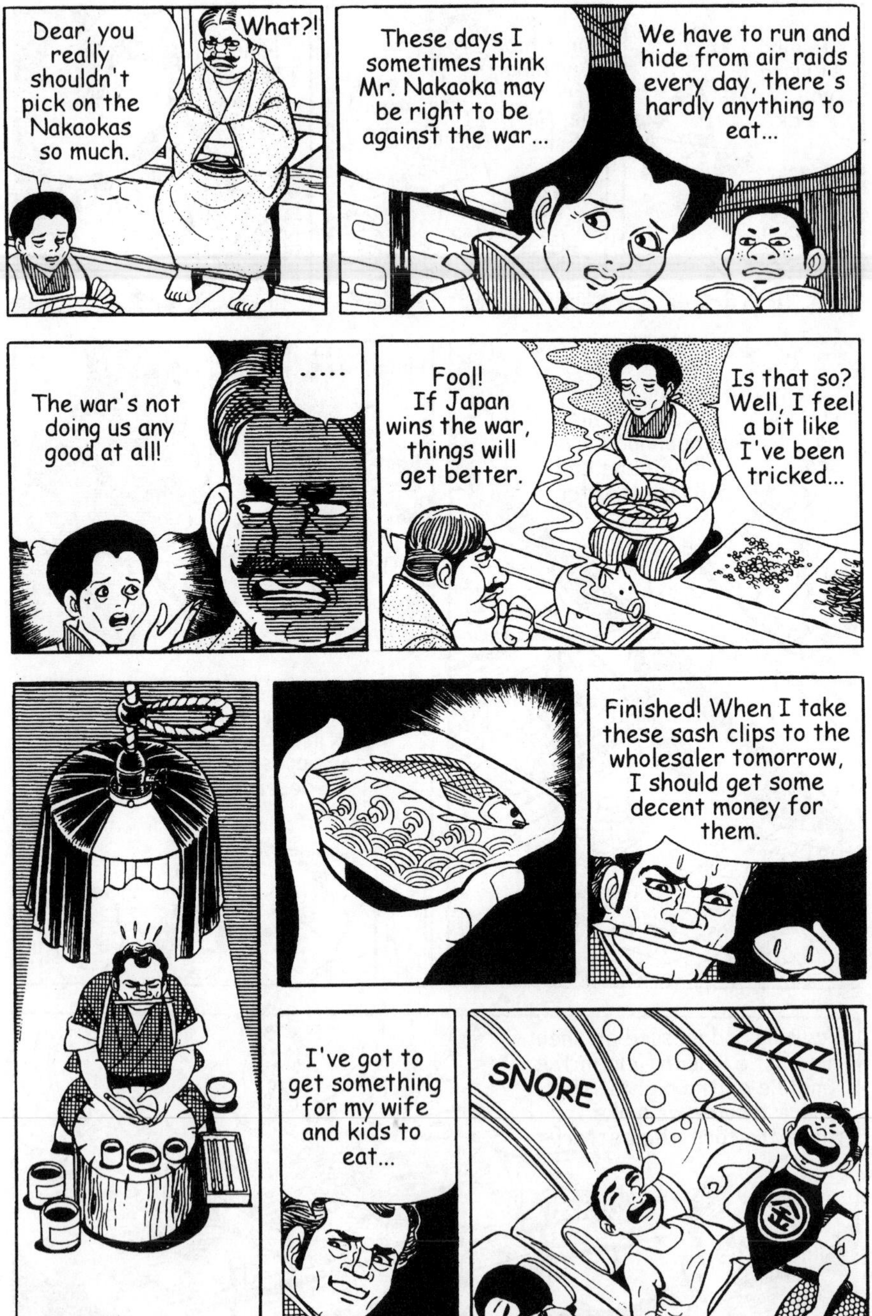
Dear, you really shouldn't pick on the Nakaokas so much.
What?!
These days I sometimes think Mr. Nakaoka may be right to be against the war...
We have to run and hide from air raids every day, there's hardly anything to eat...
The war's not doing us any good at all!
.....
Fool! If Japan wins the war, things will get better.
Is that so? Well, I feel a bit like I've been tricked...
Finished! When I take these sash clips to the wholesaler tomorrow, I should get some decent money for them.
I've got to get something for my wife and kids to eat...
SNORE
ZZZZZ

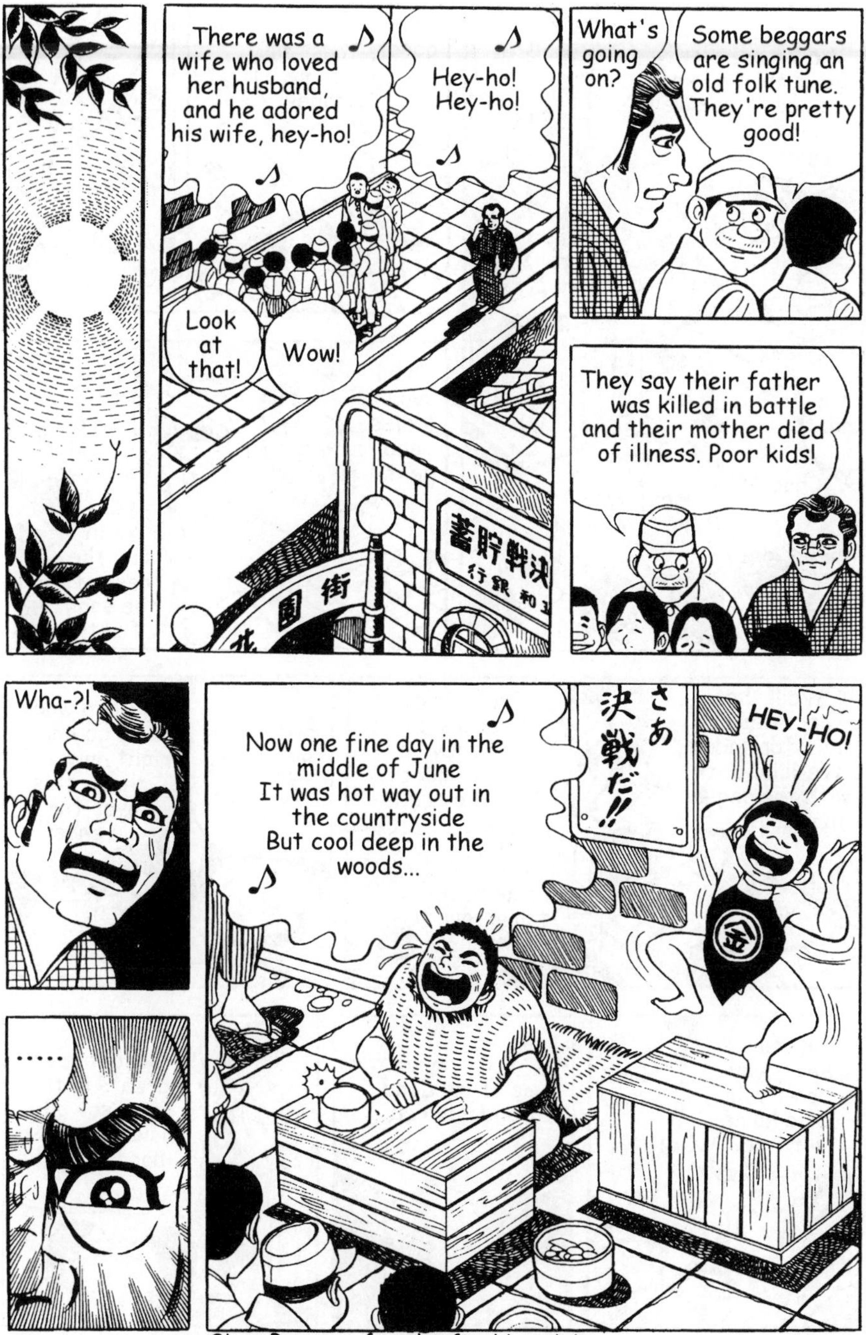
There was a wife who loved her husband, and he adored his wife, hey-ho!
Hey-ho! Hey-ho!
Look at that!
Wow!
What's going on?
Some beggars are singing an old folk tune. They're pretty good!
They say their father was killed in battle and their mother died of illness. Poor kids!
Wha-?!
......
Now one fine day in the middle of June
It was hot way out in the countryside
But cool deep in the woods...
さあ
決戦だ!!
HEY-HO!

Sign: Prepare for the final battle!

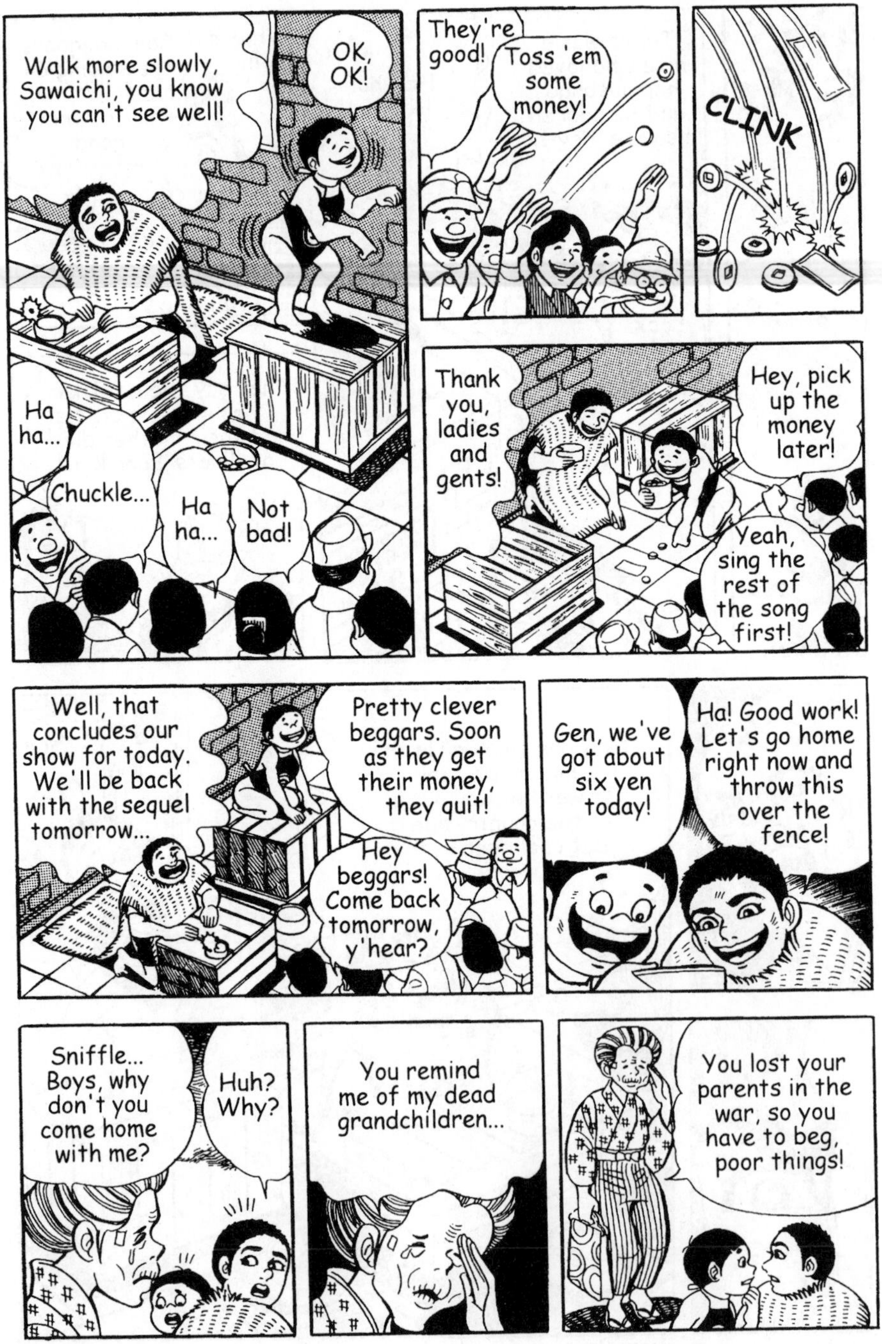

Walk more slowly, Sawaichi, you know you can't see well!
OK, OK!
Ha ha...
Chuckle...
Ha ha...
Not bad!
They're good!
Toss 'em some money!
CLINK
Thank you, ladies and gents!
Hey, pick up the money later!
Yeah, sing the rest of the song first!
Well, that concludes our show for today. We'll be back with the sequel tomorrow...
Pretty clever beggars. Soon as they get their money, they quit!
Hey beggars! Come back tomorrow, y'hear?
Gen, we've got about six yen today!
Ha! Good work! Let's go home right now and throw this over the fence!
Sniffle... Boys, why don't you come home with me?
Huh? Why?
You remind me of my dead grandchildren...
You lost your parents in the war, so you have to beg, poor things!

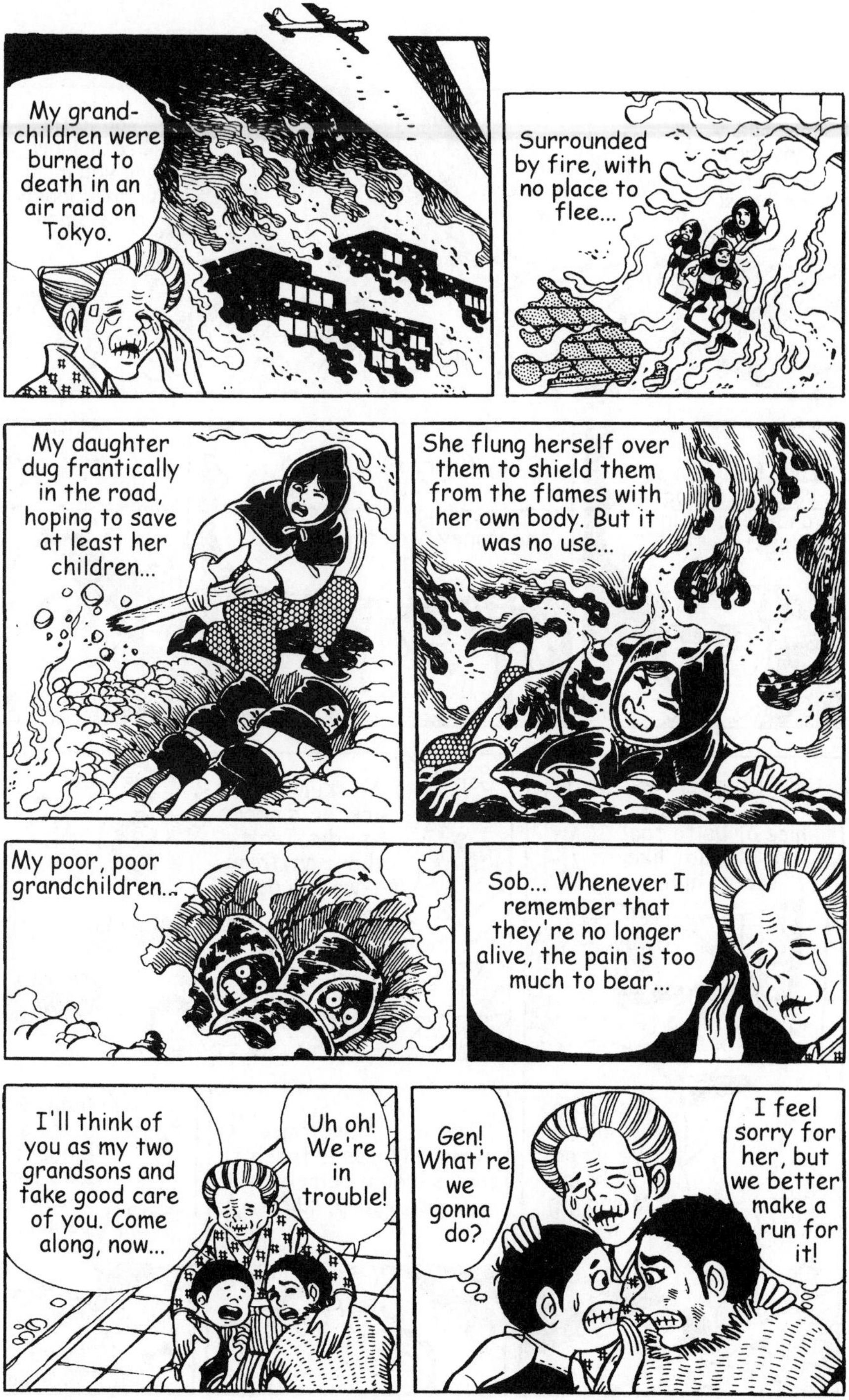
My grand-children were burned to death in an air raid on Tokyo.
Surrounded by fire, with no place to flee...
My daughter dug frantically in the road, hoping to save at least her children...
She flung herself over them to shield them from the flames with her own body. But it was no use...
My poor, poor grandchildren...
Sob... Whenever I remember that they're no longer alive, the pain is too much to bear...
I'll think of you as my two grandsons and take good care of you. Come along, now...
Uh oh! We're in trouble!
Gen! What're we gonna do?
I feel sorry for her, but we better make a run for it!

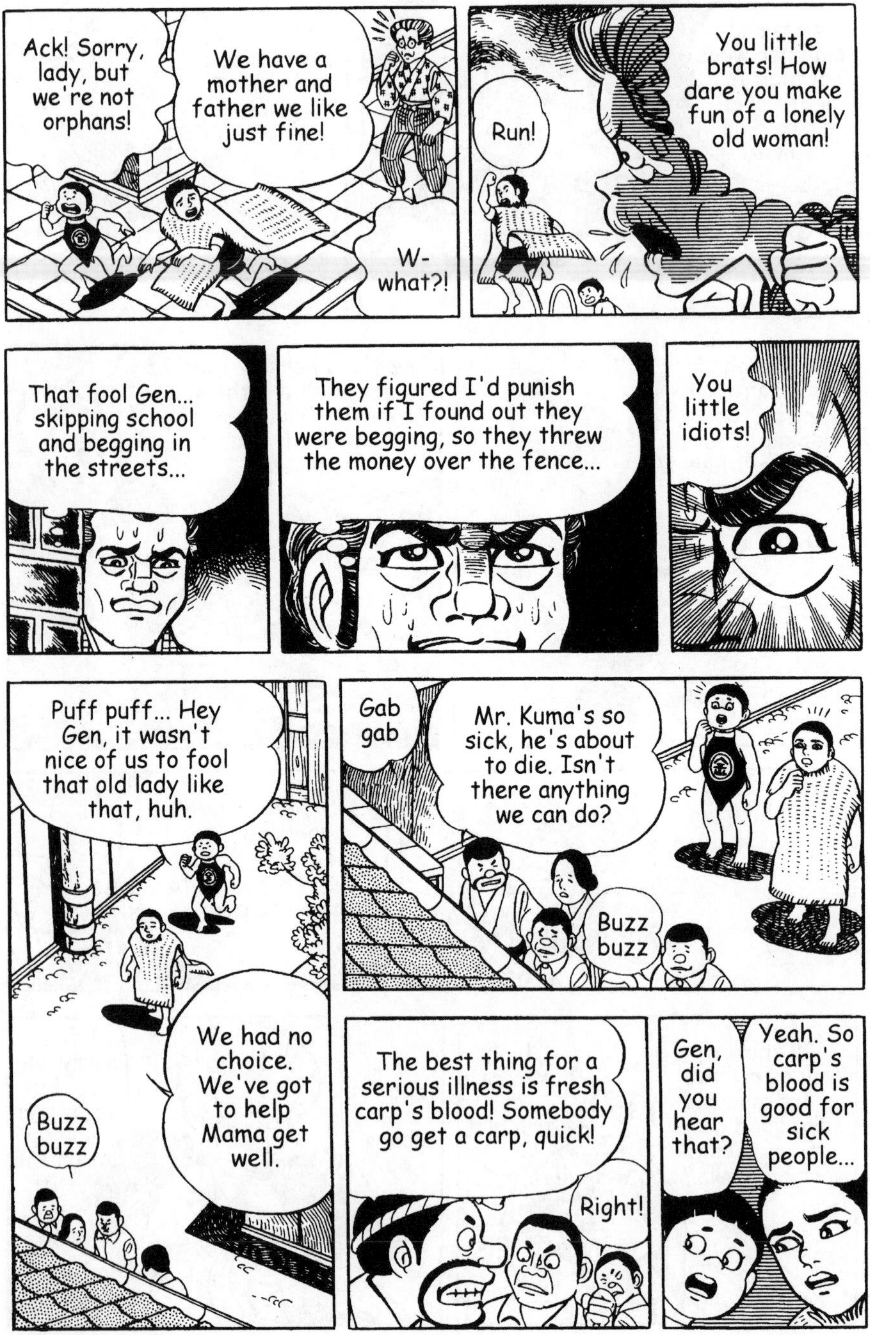
Ack! Sorry, lady, but we're not orphans!
We have a mother and father we like just fine!
W- what?!
Run!
You little brats! How dare you make fun of a lonely old woman!
That fool Gen... skipping school and begging in the streets...
They figured I'd punish them if I found out they were begging, so they threw the money over the fence...
You little idiots!
Puff puff... Hey Gen, it wasn't nice of us to fool that old lady like that, huh.
We had no choice. We've got to help Mama get well.
Buzz buzz
Gab gab
Mr. Kuma's so sick, he's about to die. Isn't there anything we can do?
Buzz buzz
The best thing for a serious illness is fresh carp's blood! Somebody go get a carp, quick!
Right!
Gen, did you hear that?
Yeah. So carp's blood is good for sick people...

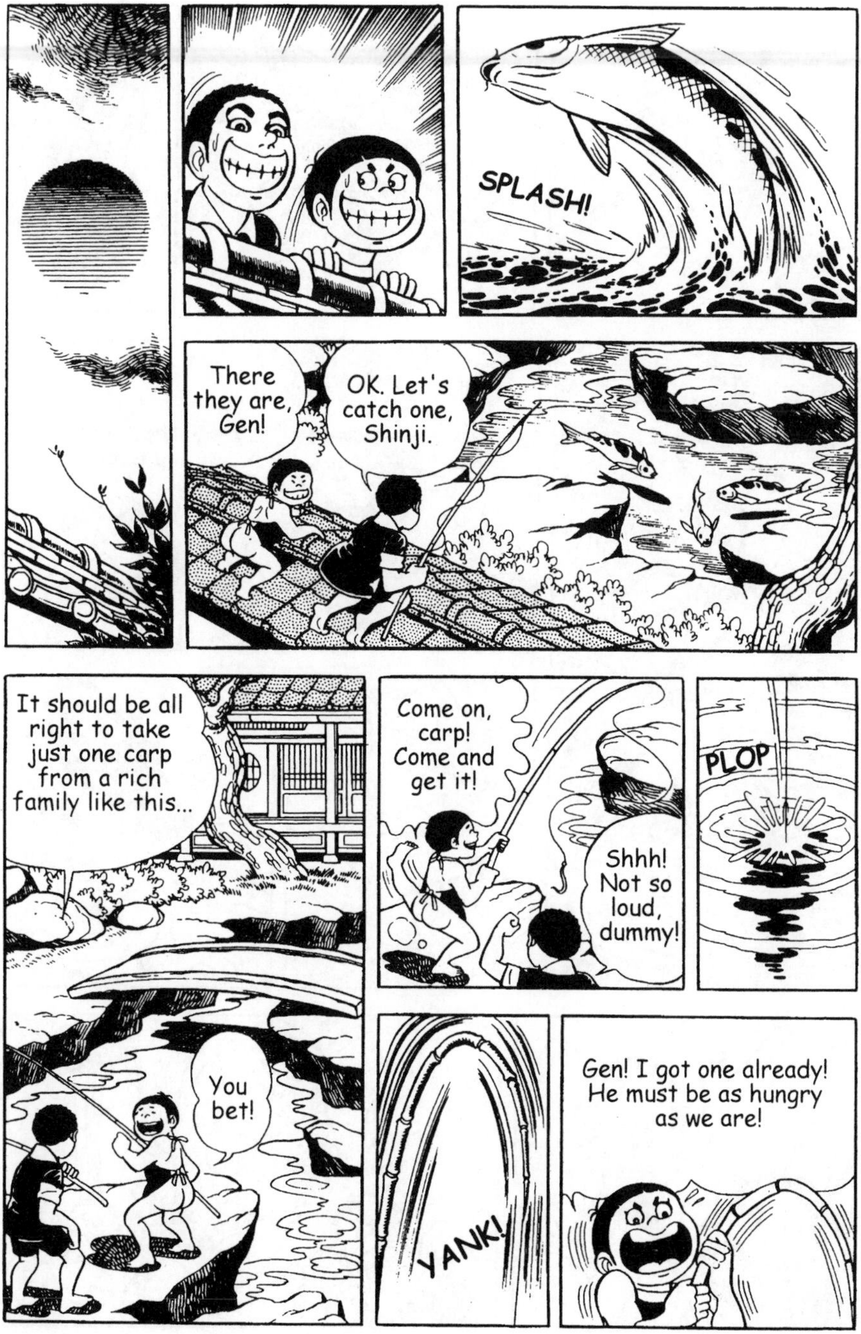
SPLASH!
There they are, Gen!
OK. Let's catch one, Shinji.
It should be all right to take just one carp from a rich family like this...
You bet!
Come on, carp! Come and get it!
Shhh! Not so loud, dummy!
PLOP
YANK!
Gen! I got one already! He must be as hungry as we are!

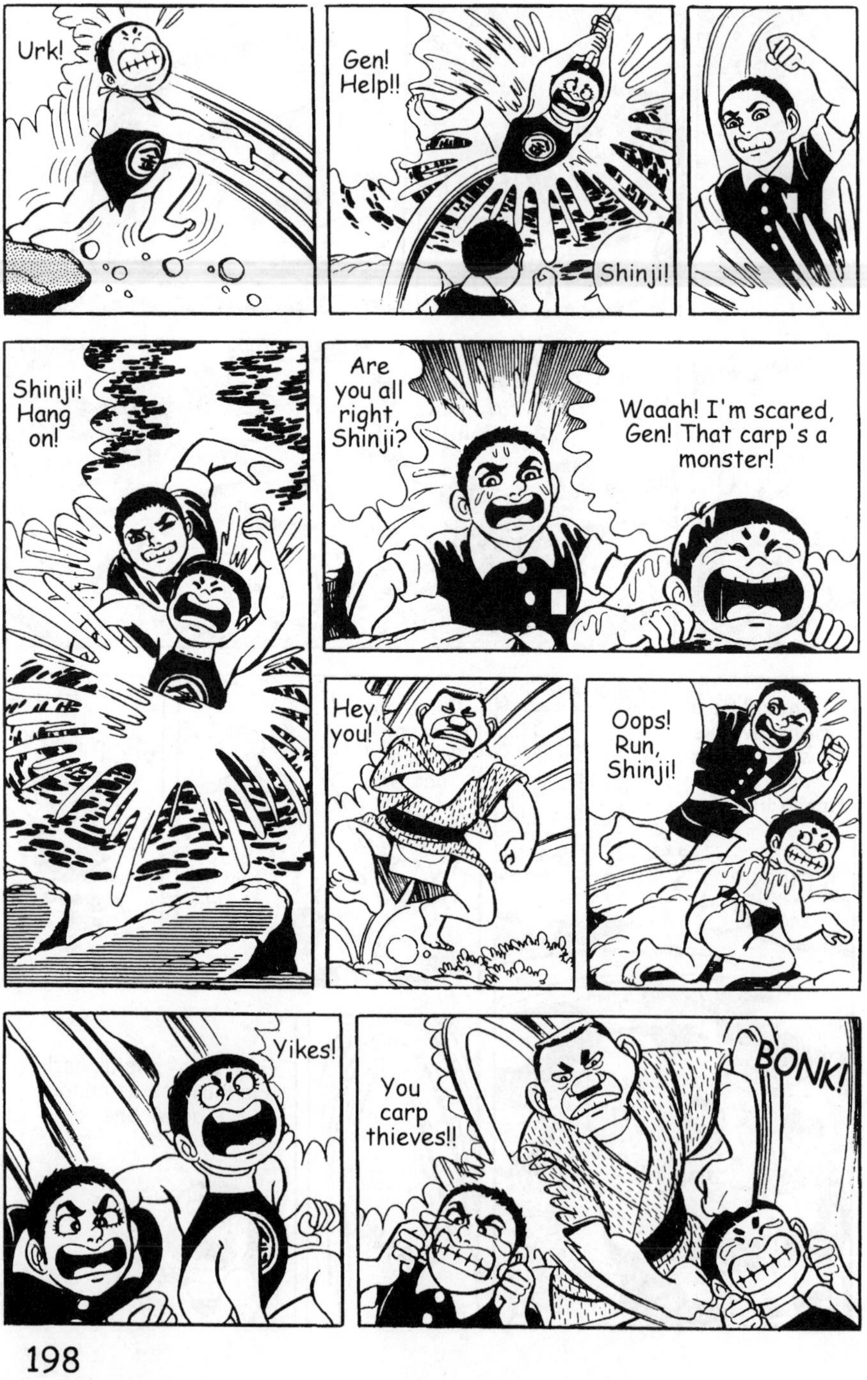
Urk!
Gen! Help!!
Shinji!
Shinji! Hang on!
Are you all right, Shinji?
Waaah! I'm scared, Gen! That carp's a monster!
Hey, you!
Oops! Run, Shinji!
Yikes!
You carp thieves!!
BONK!

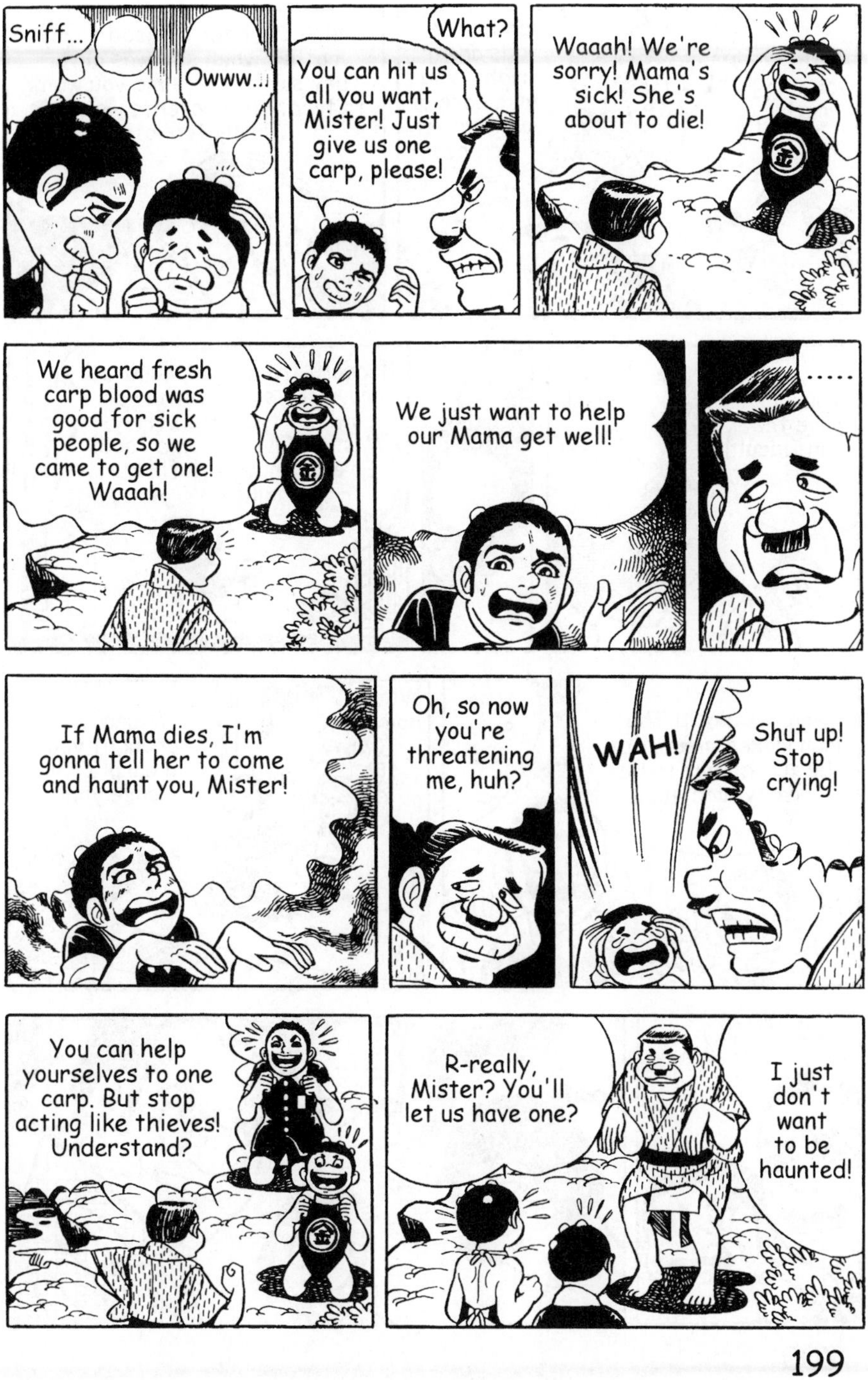
Sniff...
Owww...
What?
You can hit us all you want, Mister! Just give us one carp, please!
Waaah! We're sorry! Mama's sick! She's about to die!
We heard fresh carp blood was good for sick people, so we came to get one! Waaah!
We just want to help our Mama get well!
.....
If Mama dies, I'm gonna tell her to come and haunt you, Mister!
Oh, so now you're threatening me, huh?
WAH!
Shut up! Stop crying!
You can help yourselves to one carp. But stop acting like thieves! Understand?
R-really, Mister? You'll let us have one?
I just don't want to be haunted!

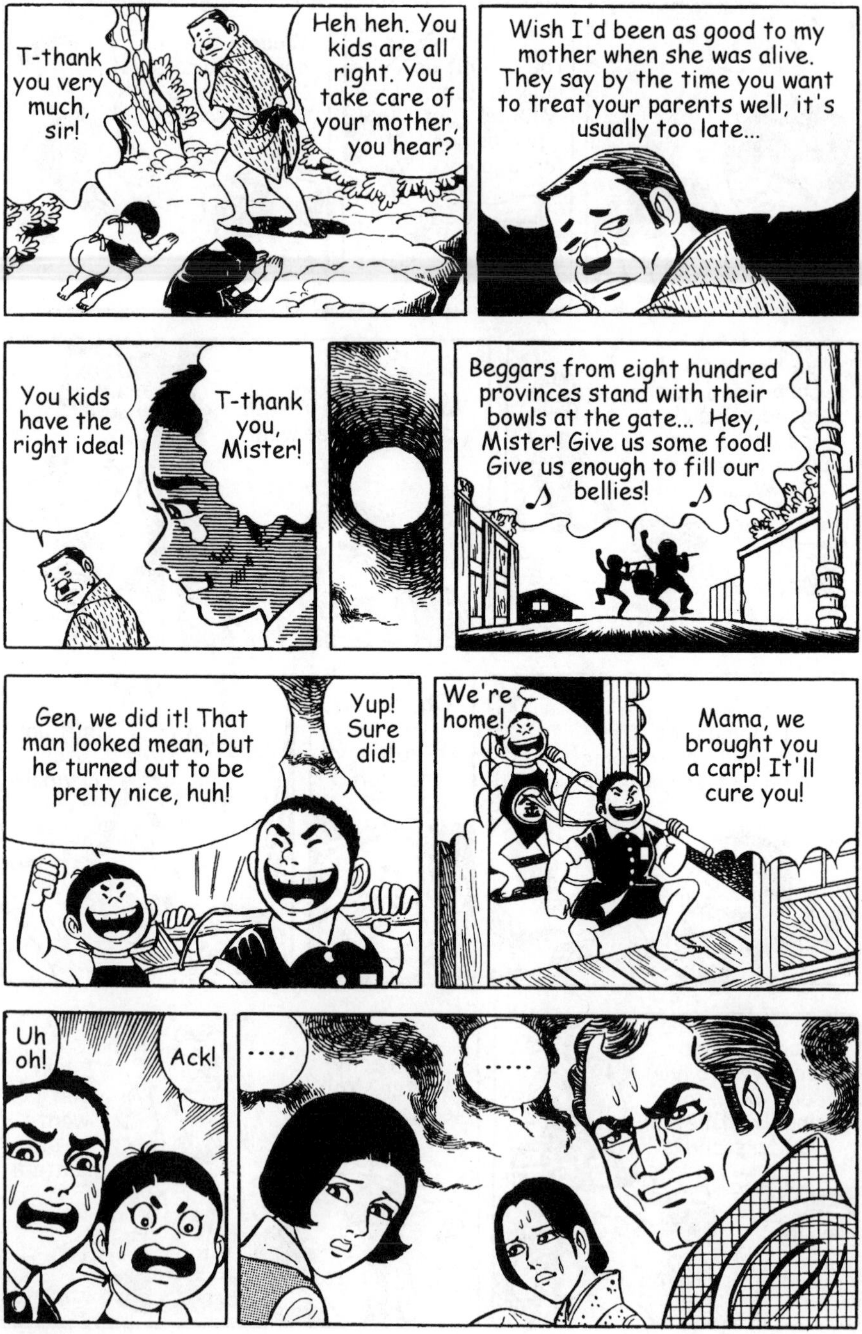
T-thank you very much, sir!
Heh heh. You kids are all right. You take care of your mother, you hear?
Wish I'd been as good to my mother when she was alive. They say by the time you want to treat your parents well, it's usually too late...
You kids have the right idea!
T-thank you, Mister!
Beggars from eight hundred provinces stand with their bowls at the gate... Hey, Mister! Give us some food! Give us enough to fill our bellies! ♪ ♪
Gen, we did it! That man looked mean, but he turned out to be pretty nice, huh!
Yup! Sure did!
We're home!
Mama, we brought you a carp! It'll cure you!
Uh oh!
Ack!
.....
.....

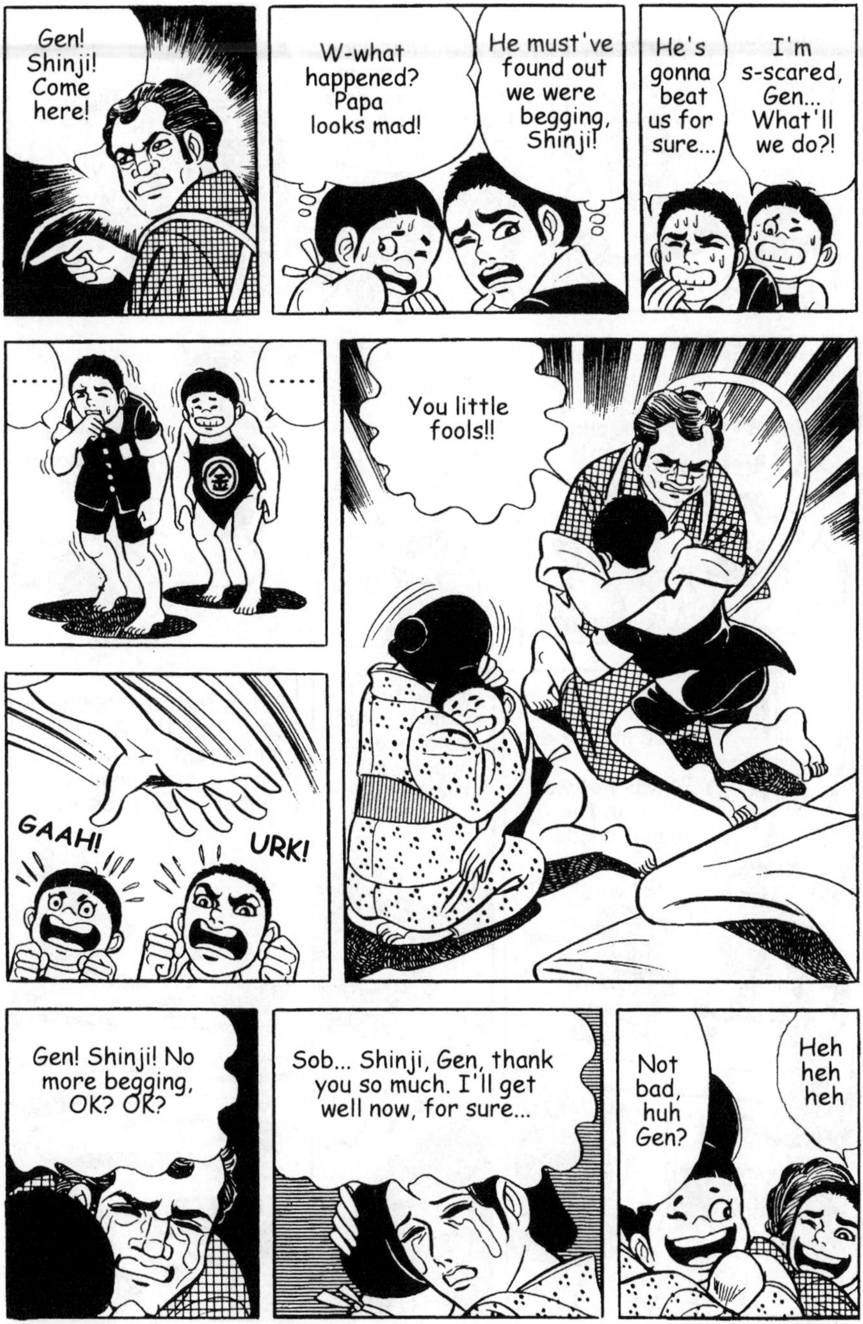
Gen! Shinji! Come here!
W-what happened? Papa looks mad!
He must've found out we were begging, Shinji!
He's gonna beat us for sure...
I'm s-scared, Gen... What'll we do?!
.....
.....
You little fools!!
GAAH!
URK!
Gen! Shinji! No more begging, OK? OK?
Sob... Shinji, Gen, thank you so much. I'll get well now, for sure...
Not bad, huh Gen?
Heh heh heh

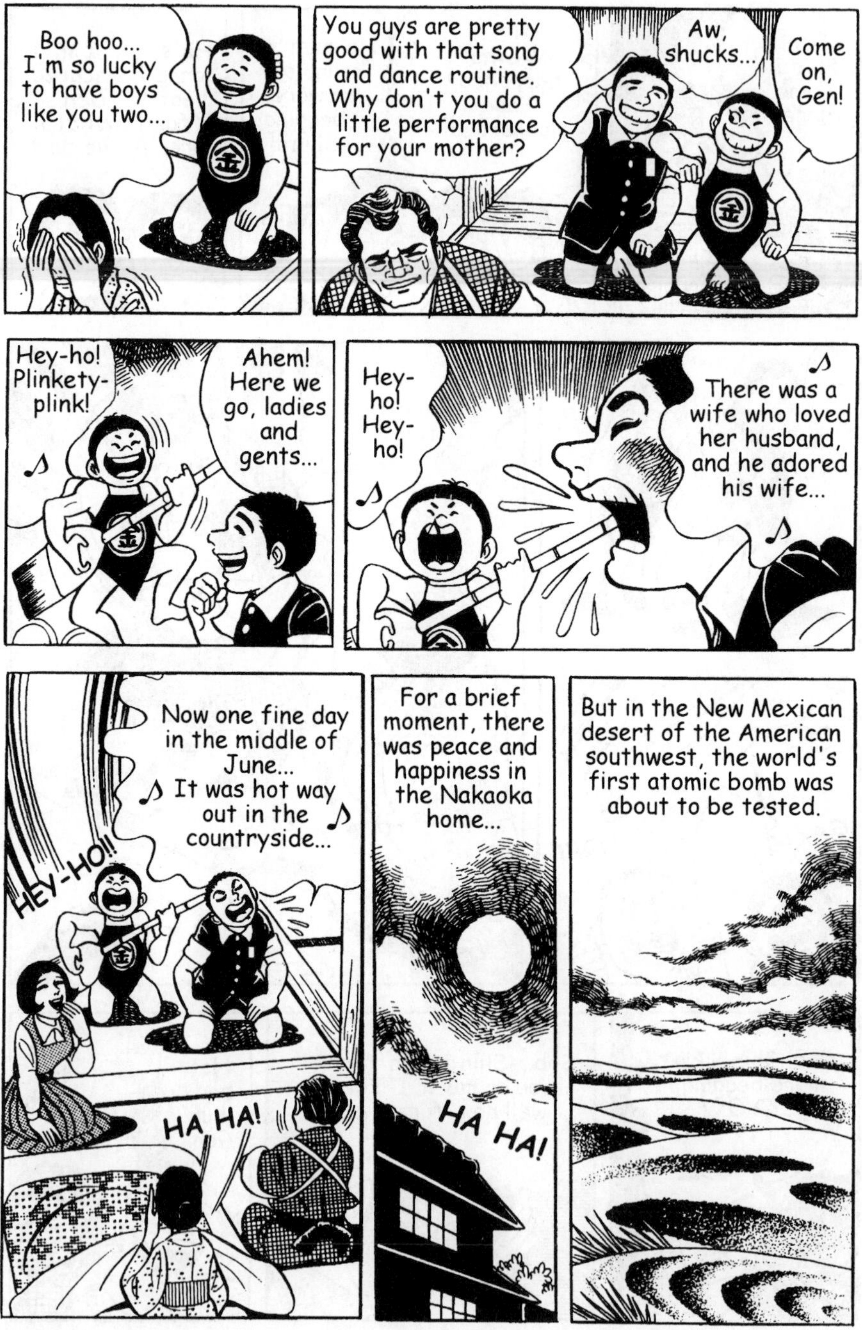
Boo hoo... I'm so lucky to have boys like you two...
You guys are pretty good with that song and dance routine. Why don't you do a little performance for your mother?
Aw, shucks...
Come on, Gen!
Hey-ho! Plinkety-plink!
Ahem! Here we go, ladies and gents...
Hey-ho! Hey-ho!
There was a wife who loved her husband, and he adored his wife...
Now one fine day in the middle of June... It was hot way out in the countryside...
HEY-HO!!
HA HA!
For a brief moment, there was peace and happiness in the Nakaoka home...
HA HA!
But in the New Mexican desert of the American southwest, the world's first atomic bomb was about to be tested.

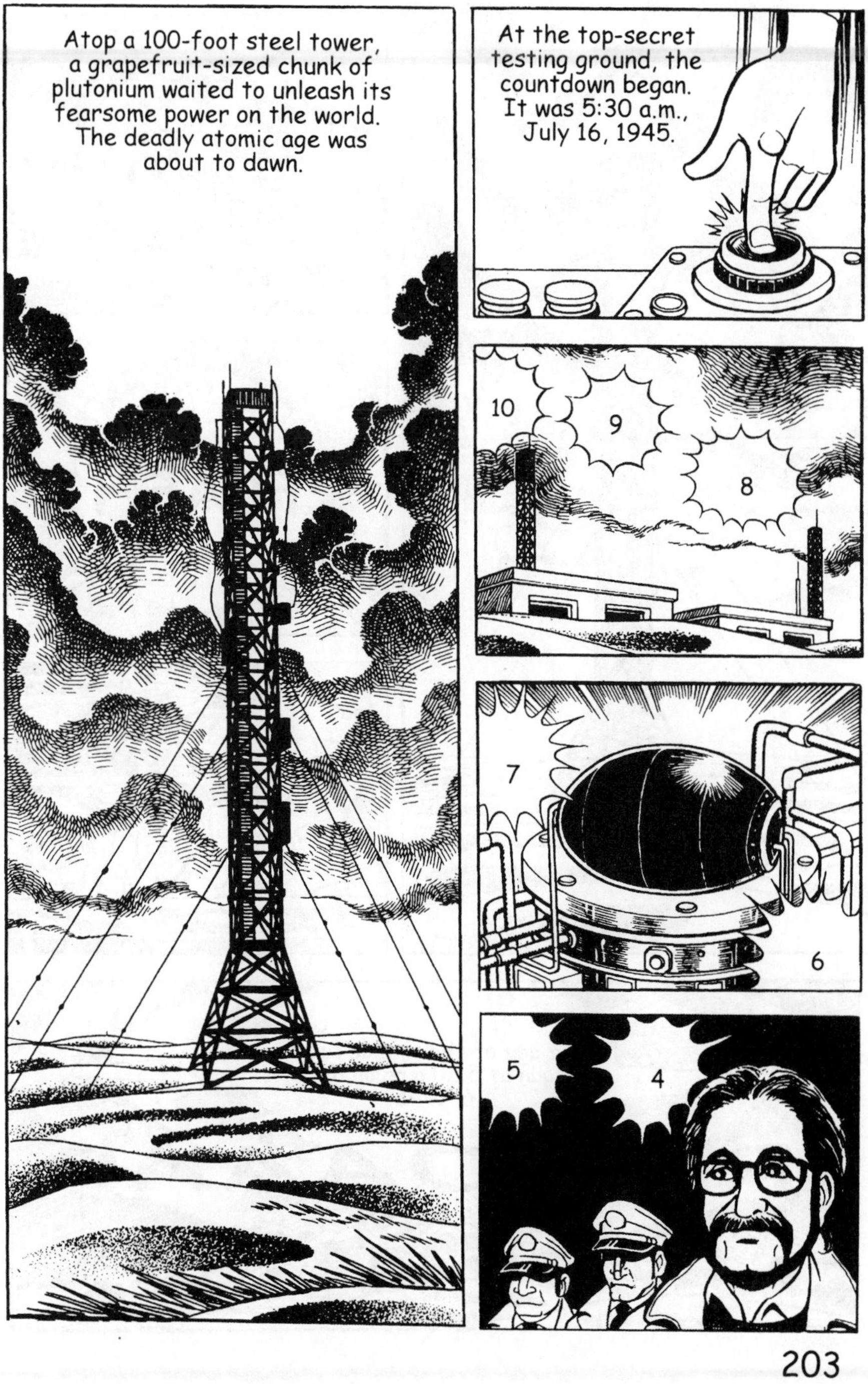
Atop a 100-foot steel tower, a grapefruit-sized chunk of plutonium waited to unleash its fearsome power on the world. The deadly atomic age was about to dawn.
At the top-secret testing ground, the countdown began. It was 5:30 a.m., July 16, 1945.
10
9
8
7
6
5
4

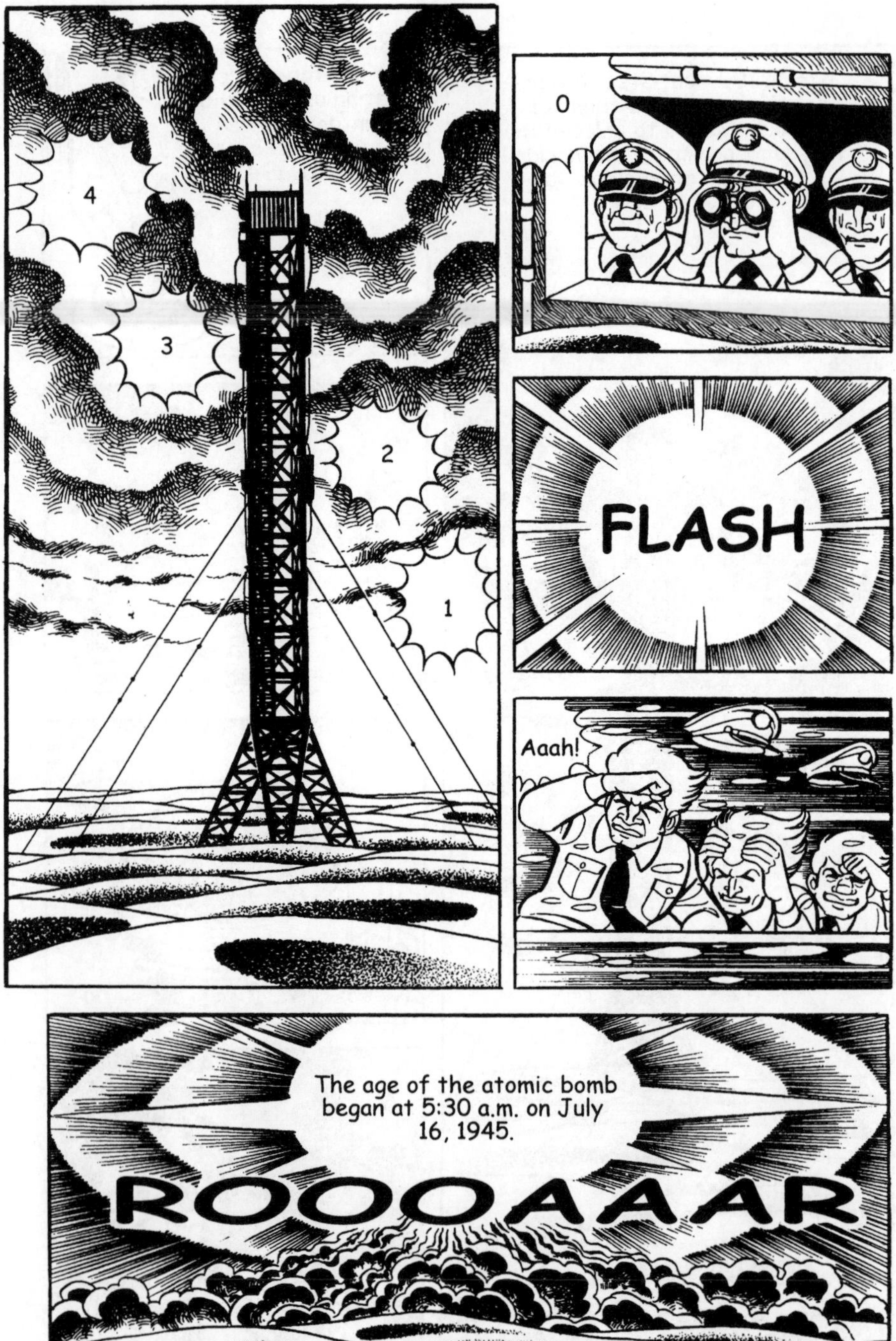

4
3
2
1
0
FLASH
Aaah!
The age of the atomic bomb began at 5:30 a.m. on July 16, 1945.
ROOOAAAR

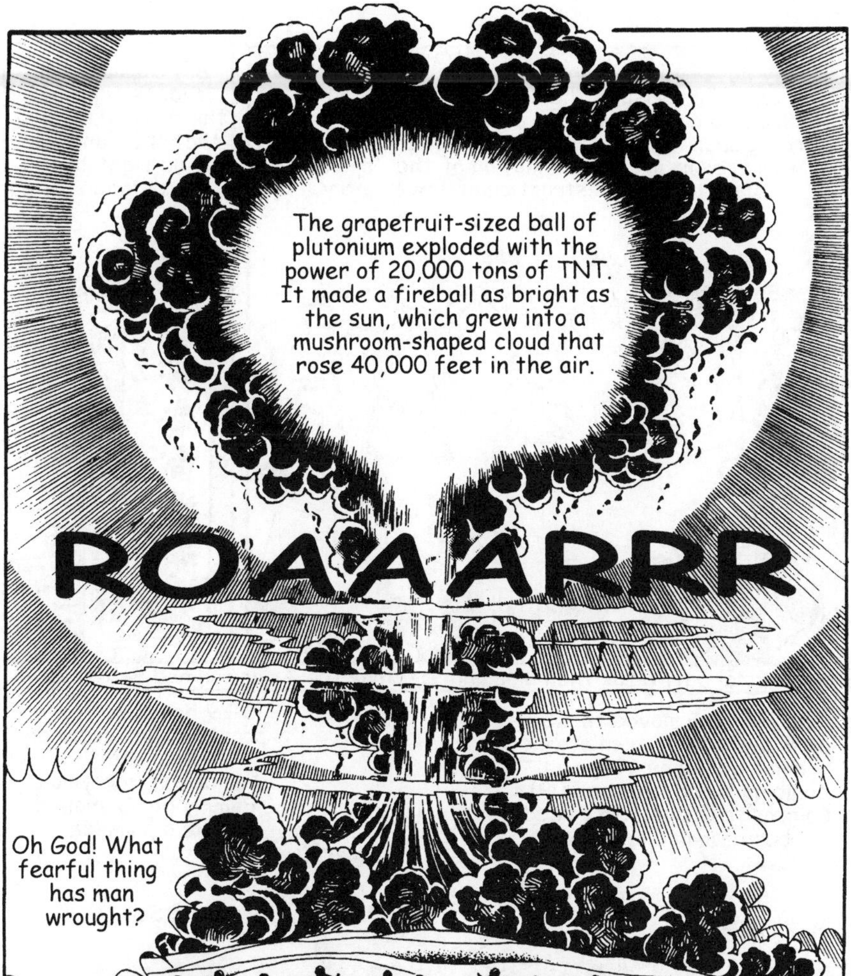
The grapefruit-sized ball of plutonium exploded with the power of 20,000 tons of TNT. It made a fireball as bright as the sun, which grew into a mushroom-shaped cloud that rose 40,000 feet in the air.
ROAAARRR
Oh God! What fearful thing has man wrought?

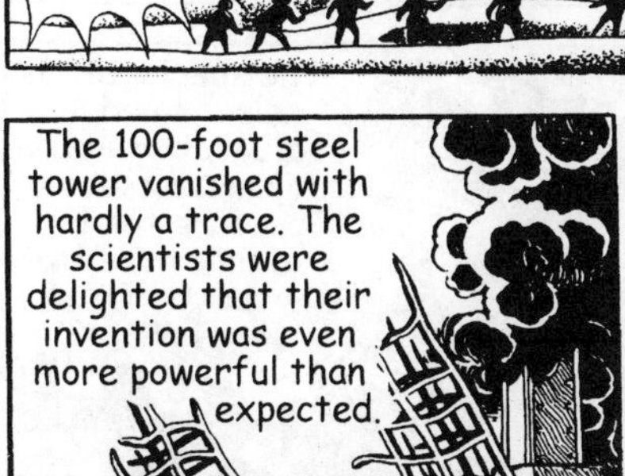
The 100-foot steel tower vanished with hardly a trace. The scientists were delighted that their invention was even more powerful than expected.

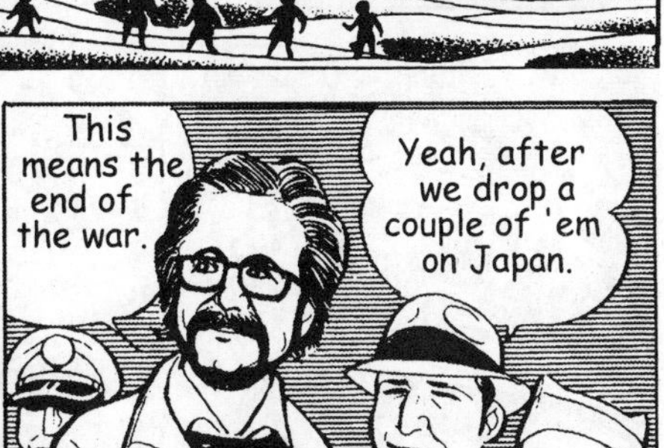
This means the end of the war.
Yeah, after we drop a couple of 'em on Japan.

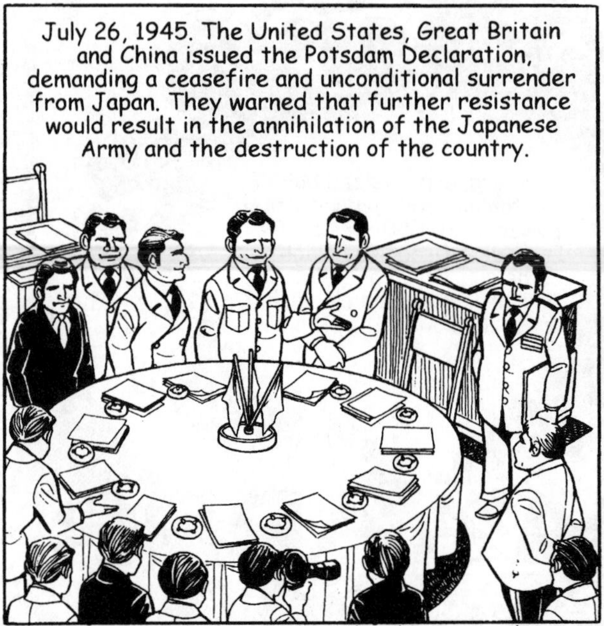
July 26, 1945. The United States, Great Britain and China issued the Potsdam Declaration, demanding a ceasefire and unconditional surrender from Japan. They warned that further resistance would result in the annihilation of the Japanese Army and the destruction of the country.

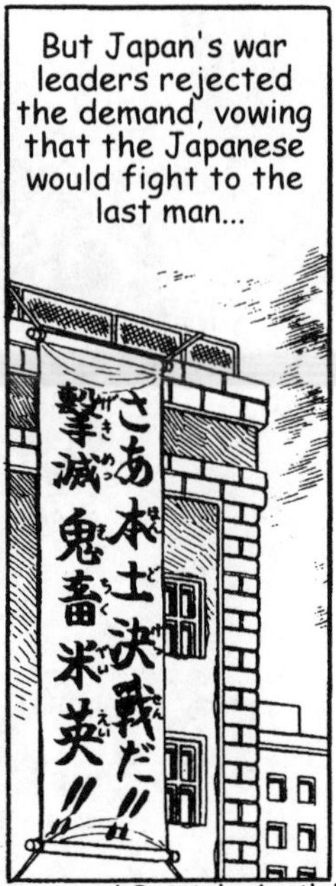
But Japan's war leaders rejected the demand, vowing that the Japanese would fight to the last man...
さあ本土決戦だ!!
撃滅鬼畜米英!!

Banner: Final battle for the homeland! Destroy the American and British devils!

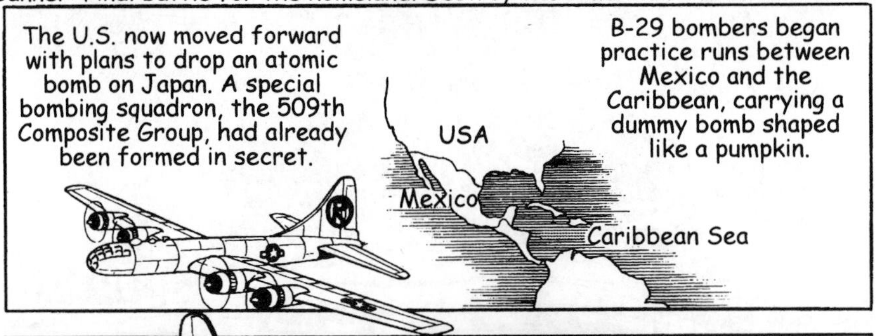
The U.S. now moved forward with plans to drop an atomic bomb on Japan. A special bombing squadron, the 509th Composite Group, had already been formed in secret.
USA
Mexico
Caribbean Sea
B-29 bombers began practice runs between Mexico and the Caribbean, carrying a dummy bomb shaped like a pumpkin.

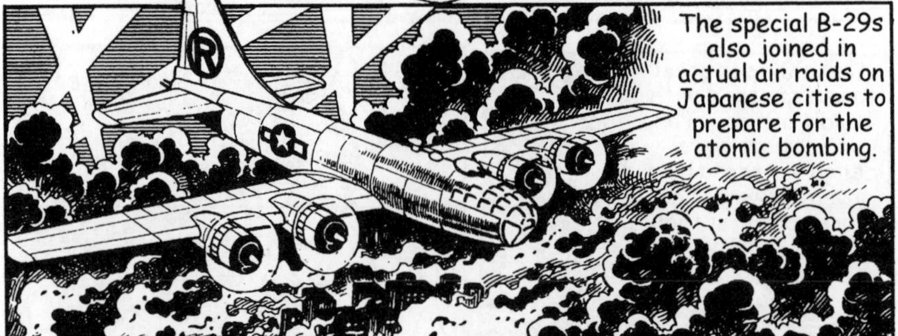
The special B-29s also joined in actual air raids on Japanese cities to prepare for the atomic bombing.

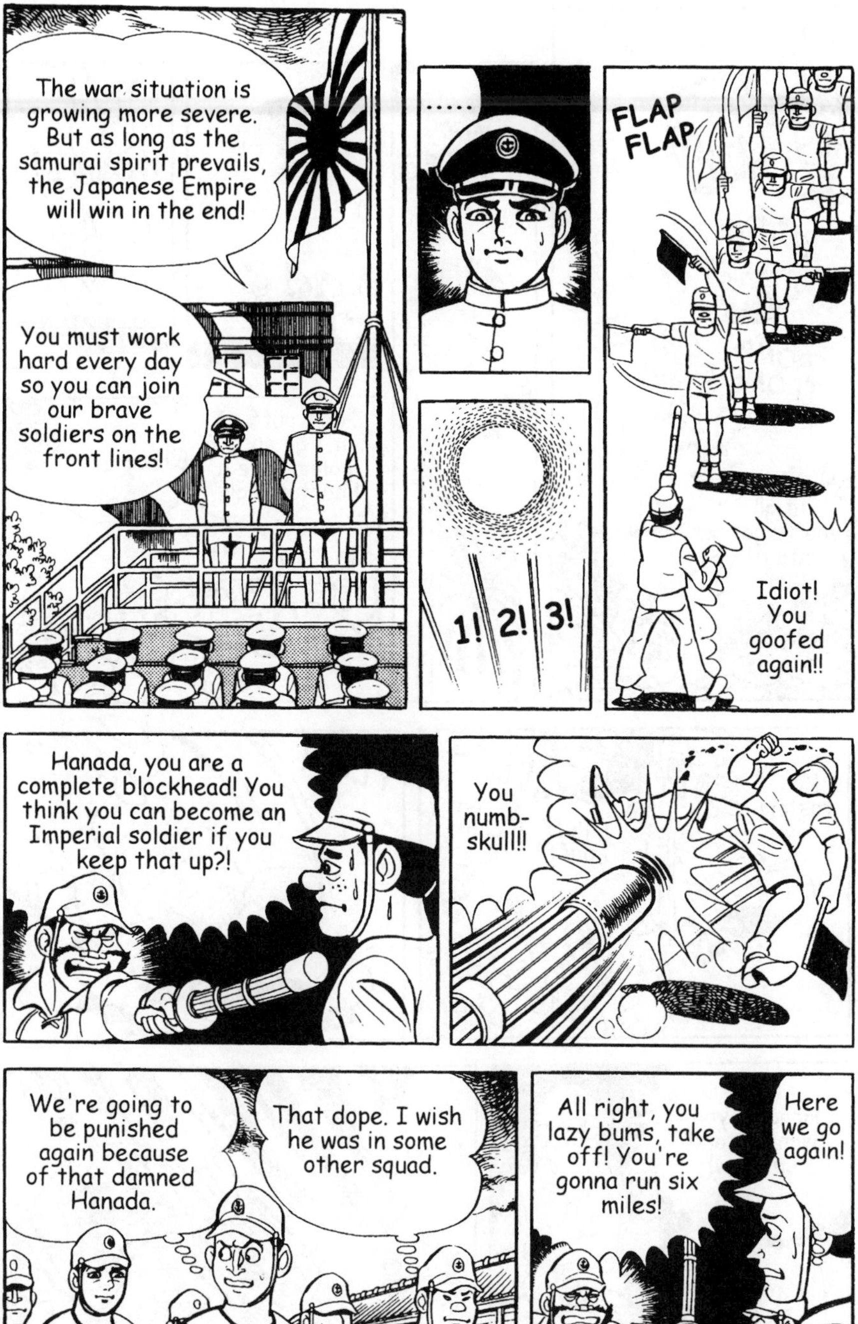
The war situation is growing more severe. But as long as the samurai spirit prevails, the Japanese Empire will win in the end!
You must work hard every day so you can join our brave soldiers on the front lines!
.....
1! 2! 3!
FLAP FLAP
Idiot! You goofed again!!
Hanada, you are a complete blockhead! You think you can become an Imperial soldier if you keep that up?!
You numb-skull!!
We're going to be punished again because of that damned Hanada.
That dope. I wish he was in some other squad.
All right, you lazy bums, take off! You're gonna run six miles!
Here we go again!

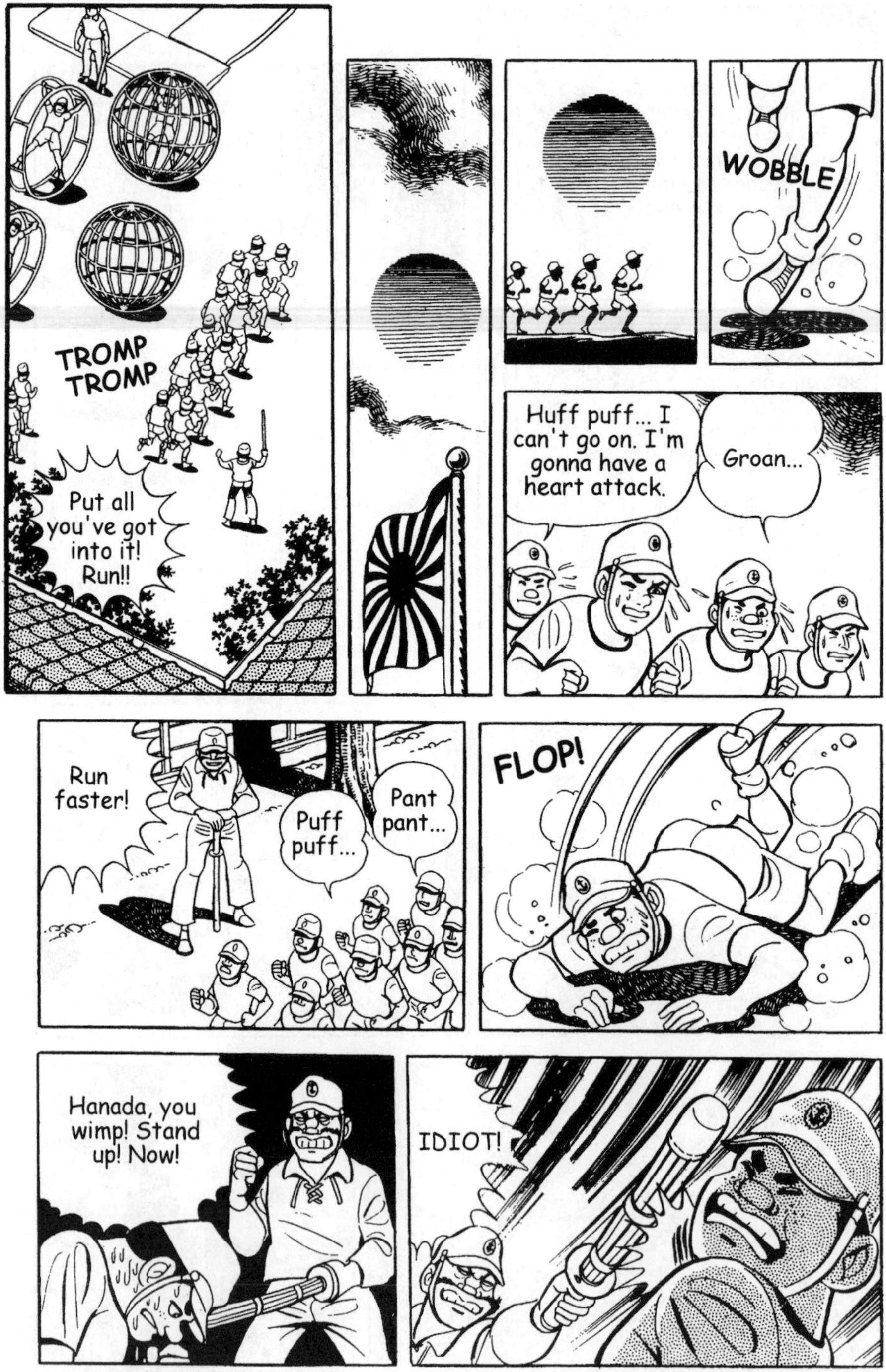
TROMP
TROMP
Put all you've got into it! Run!!
WOBBLE
Huff puff... I can't go on. I'm gonna have a heart attack.
Groan...
Run faster!
Puff puff...
Pant pant...
FLOP!
Hanada, you wimp! Stand up! Now!
IDIOT!

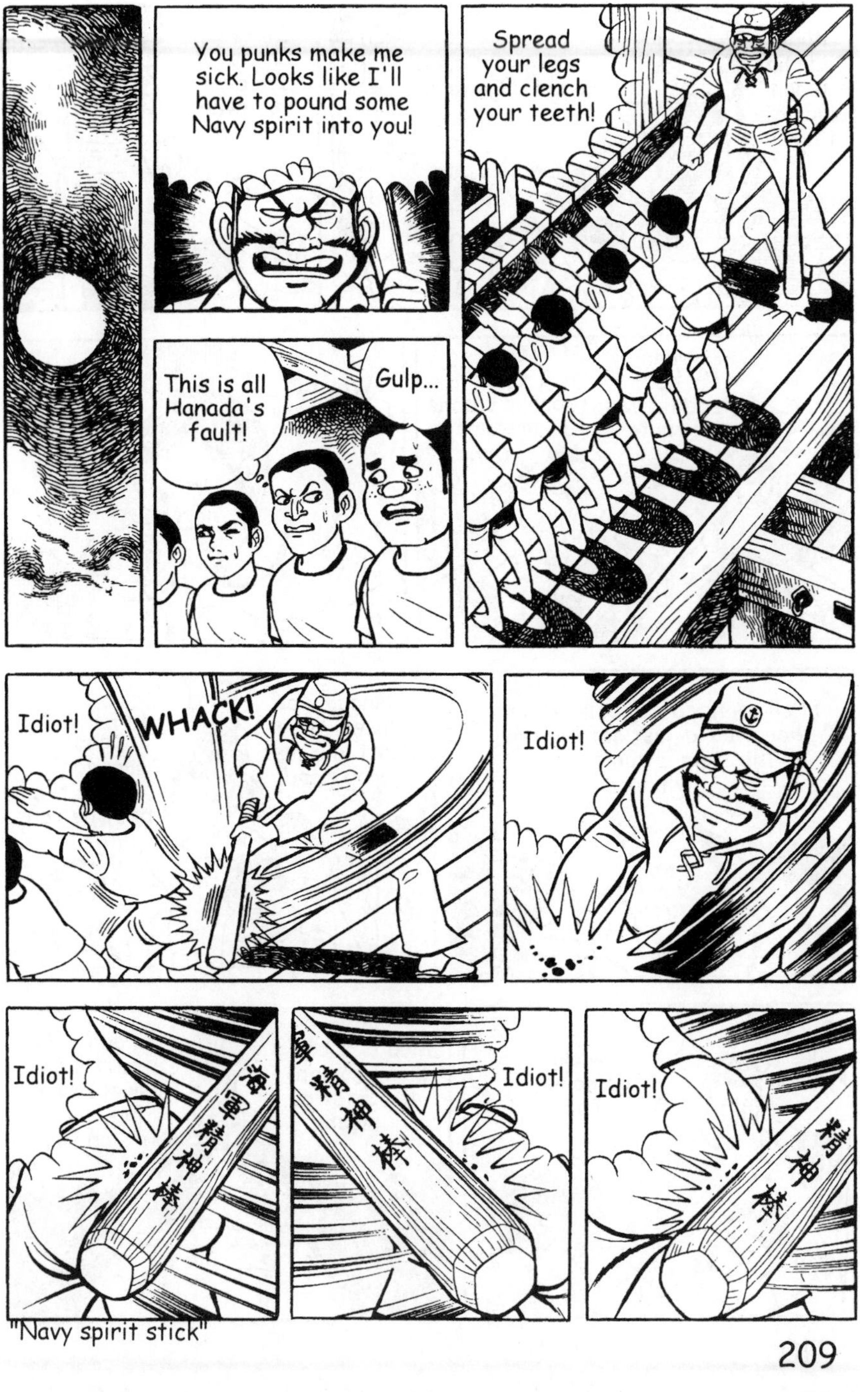
You punks make me sick. Looks like I'll have to pound some Navy spirit into you!
This is all Hanada's fault!
Gulp...
Spread your legs and clench your teeth!
Idiot!
WHACK!
Idiot!
Idiot!
Idiot!
Idiot!
精神棒
"Navy spirit stick"

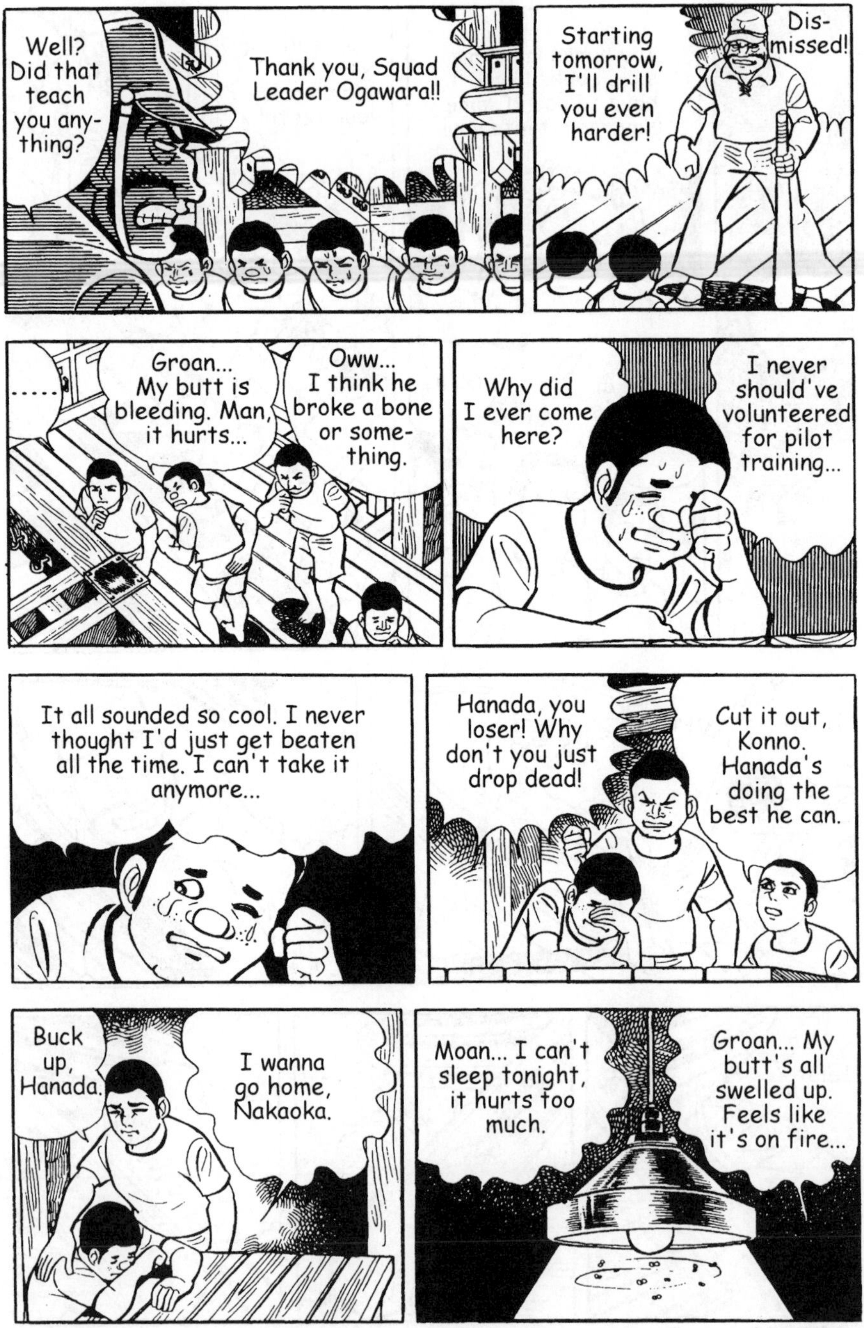
Well? Did that teach you any-thing?
Thank you, Squad Leader Ogawara!!
Starting tomorrow, I'll drill you even harder!
Dis-missed!
.....
Groan... My butt is bleeding. Man, it hurts...
Oww... I think he broke a bone or some-thing.
Why did I ever come here?
I never should've volunteered for pilot training...
It all sounded so cool. I never thought I'd just get beaten all the time. I can't take it anymore...
Hanada, you loser! Why don't you just drop dead!
Cut it out, Konno. Hanada's doing the best he can.
Buck up, Hanada.
I wanna go home, Nakaoka.
Moan... I can't sleep tonight, it hurts too much.
Groan... My butt's all swelled up. Feels like it's on fire...

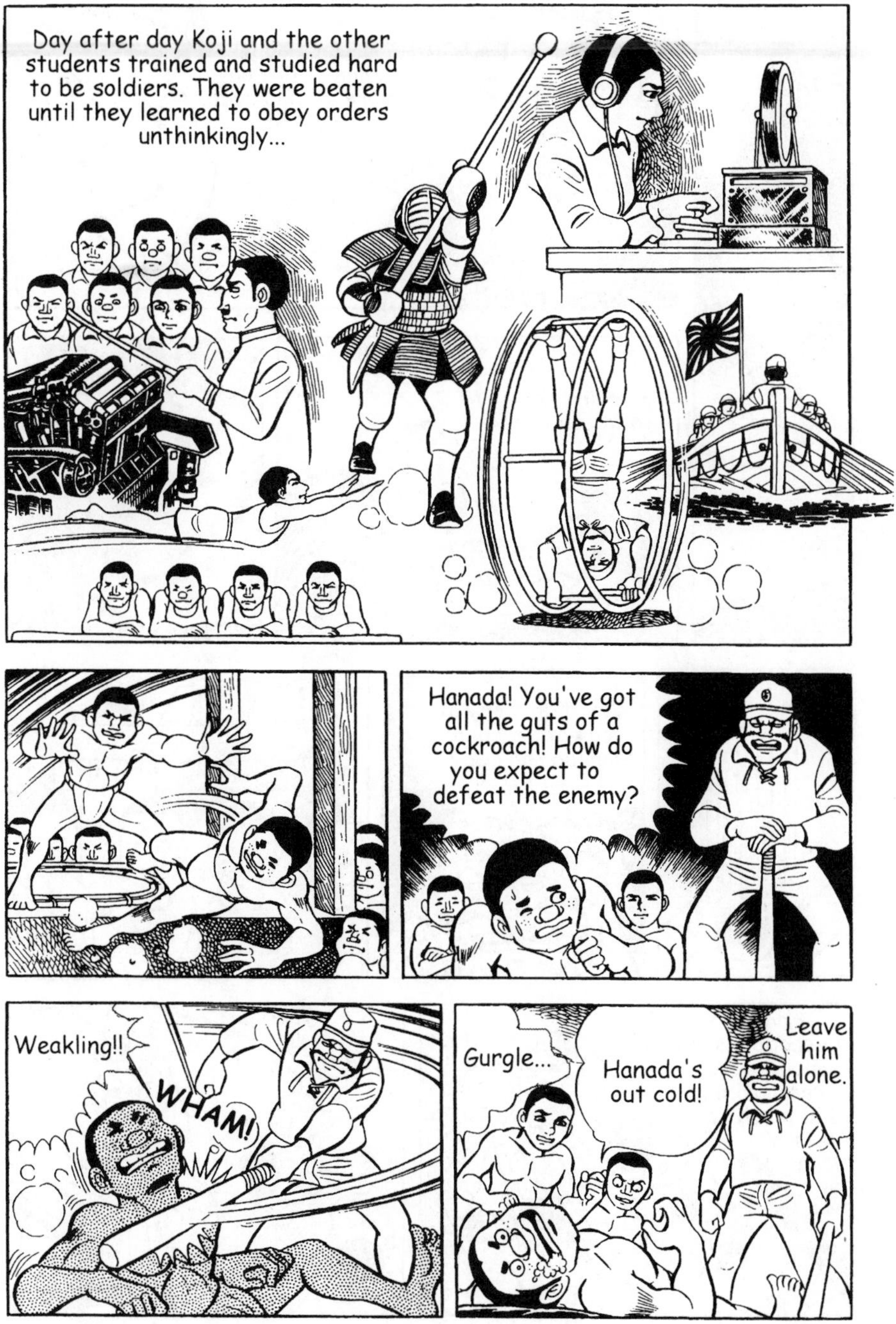
Day after day Koji and the other students trained and studied hard to be soldiers. They were beaten until they learned to obey orders unthinkingly...
Hanada! You've got all the guts of a cockroach! How do you expect to defeat the enemy?
Weakling!!
WHAM!
Gurgle...
Hanada's out cold!
Leave him alone.

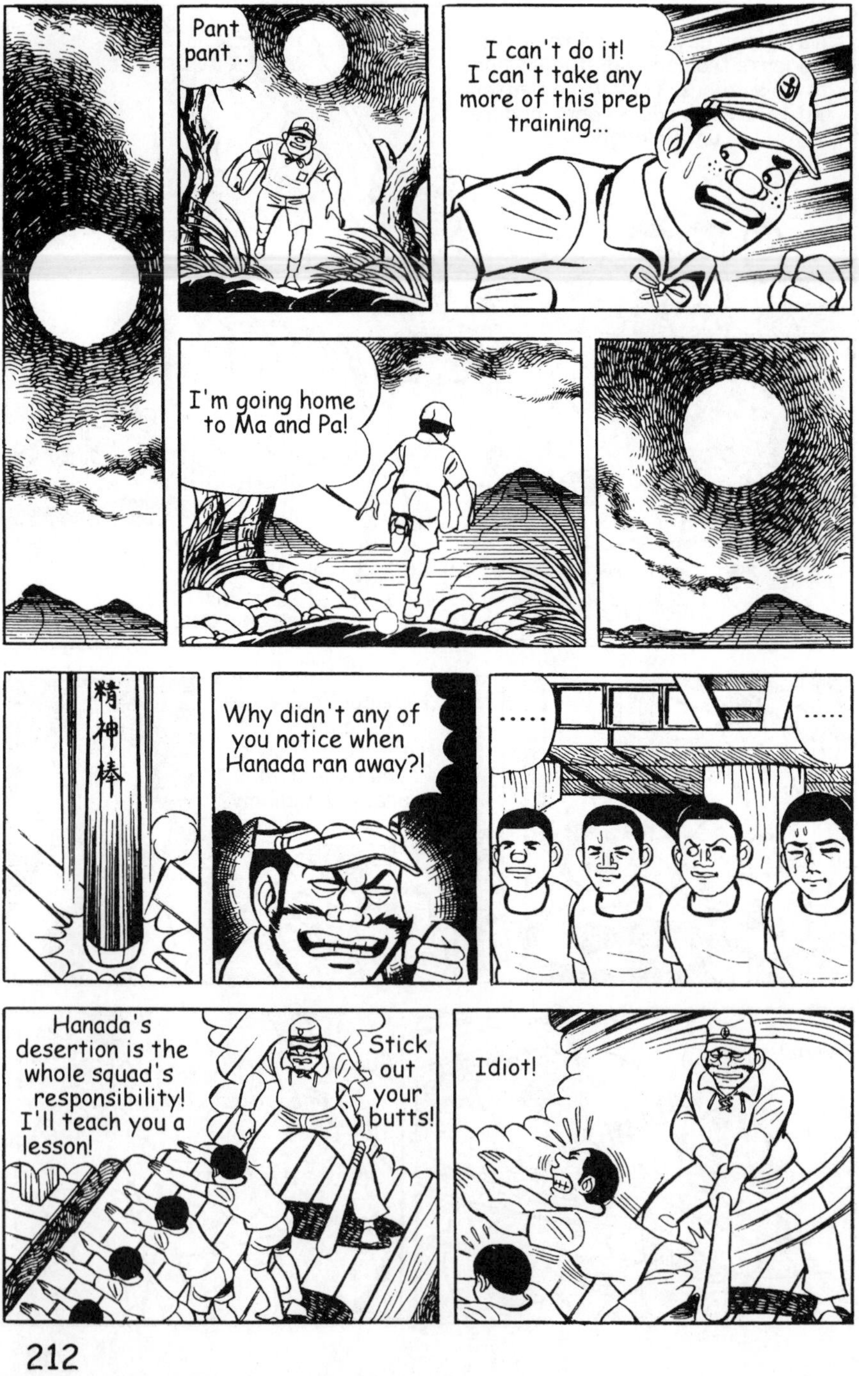
Pant pant...
I can't do it! I can't take any more of this prep training...
I'm going home to Ma and Pa!
精神棒
Why didn't any of you notice when Hanada ran away?!
.....
.....
Hanada's desertion is the whole squad's responsibility! I'll teach you a lesson!
Stick out your butts!
Idiot!

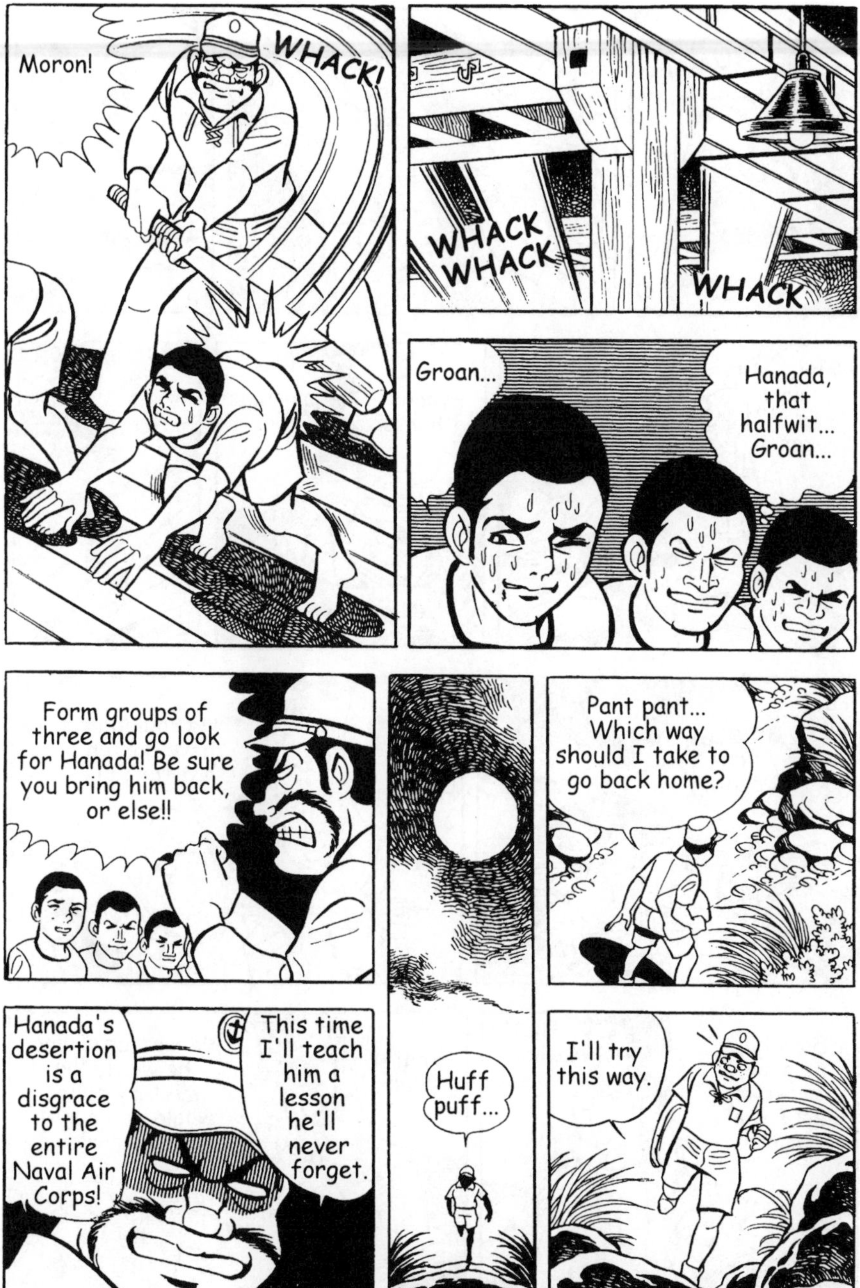

Moron!
WHACK!
WHACK WHACK
WHACK
Groan...
Hanada, that halfwit... Groan...
Form groups of three and go look for Hanada! Be sure you bring him back, or else!!
Pant pant... Which way should I take to go back home?
Hanada's desertion is a disgrace to the entire Naval Air Corps!
This time I'll teach him a lesson he'll never forget.
Huff puff...
I'll try this way.

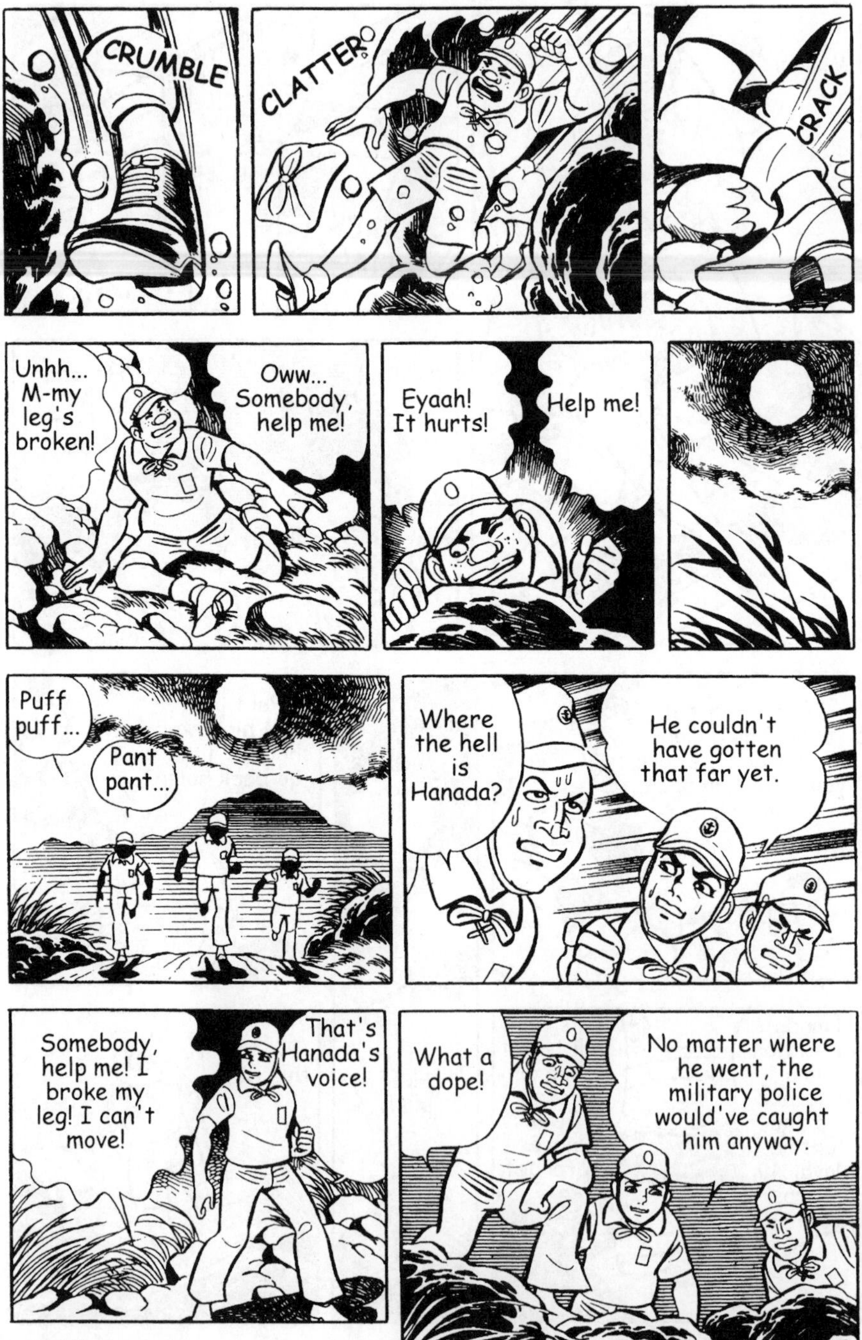
CRUMBLE
CLATTER
CRACK
Unhh... M-my leg's broken!
Oww... Somebody, help me!
Eyaah! It hurts!
Help me!
Puff puff...
Pant pant...
Where the hell is Hanada?
He couldn't have gotten that far yet.
Somebody, help me! I broke my leg! I can't move!
That's Hanada's voice!
What a dope!
No matter where he went, the military police would've caught him anyway.

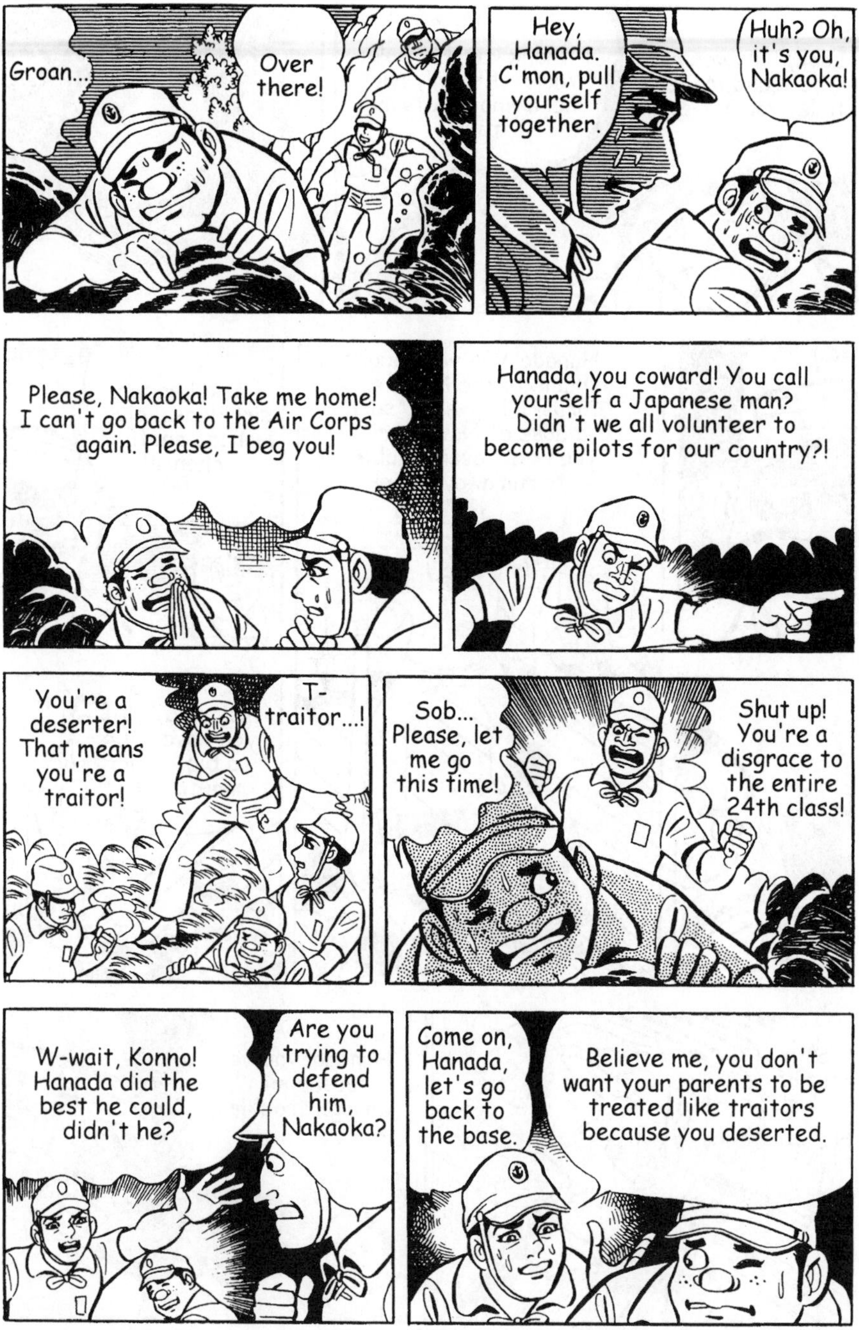
Groan...
Over there!
Hey, Hanada. C'mon, pull yourself together.
Huh? Oh, it's you, Nakaoka!
Please, Nakaoka! Take me home! I can't go back to the Air Corps again. Please, I beg you!
Hanada, you coward! You call yourself a Japanese man? Didn't we all volunteer to become pilots for our country?!
You're a deserter! That means you're a traitor!
T-traitor...!
Sob... Please, let me go this time!
Shut up! You're a disgrace to the entire 24th class!
W-wait, Konno! Hanada did the best he could, didn't he?
Are you trying to defend him, Nakaoka?
Come on, Hanada, let's go back to the base.
Believe me, you don't want your parents to be treated like traitors because you deserted.

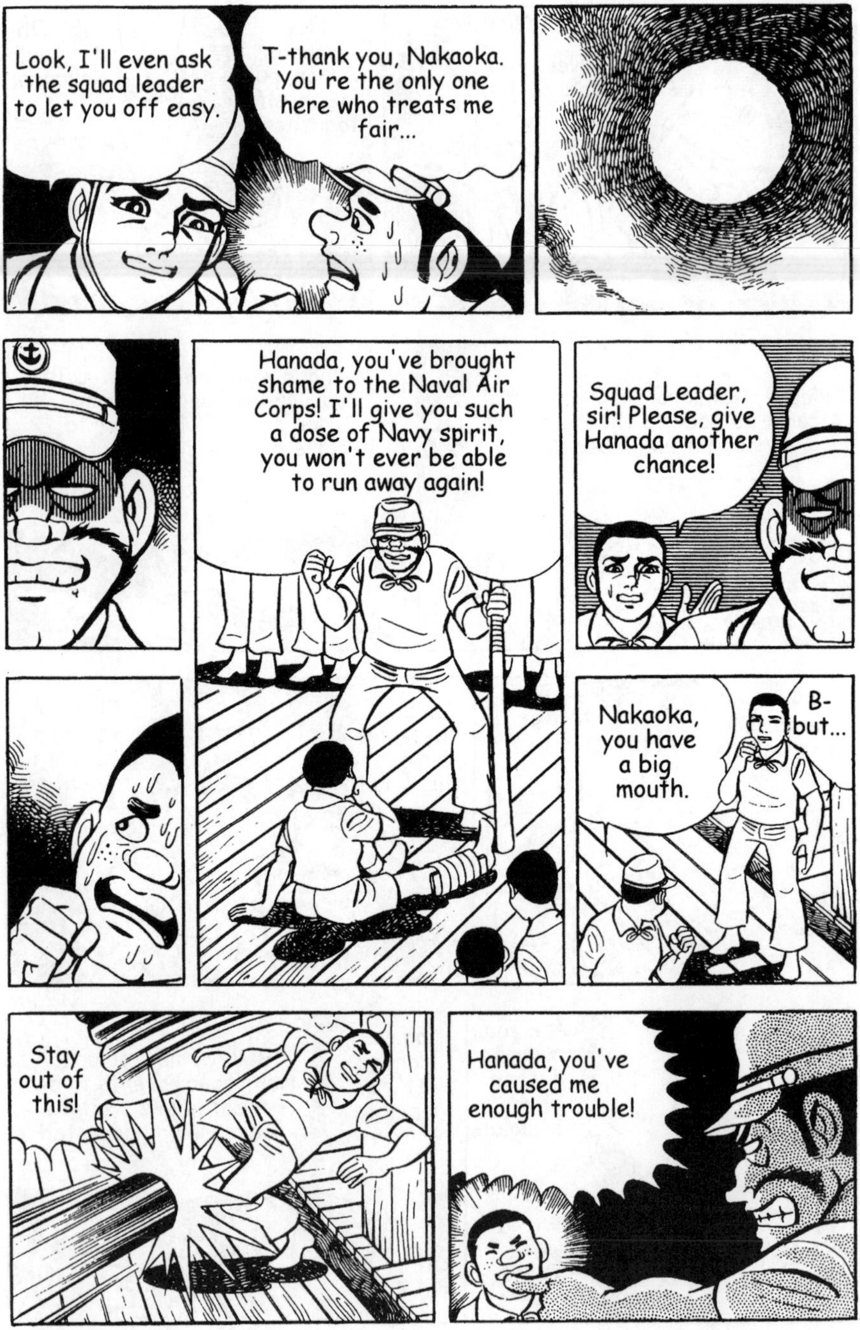
Look, I'll even ask the squad leader to let you off easy.
T-thank you, Nakaoka. You're the only one here who treats me fair...
Hanada, you've brought shame to the Naval Air Corps! I'll give you such a dose of Navy spirit, you won't ever be able to run away again!
Squad Leader, sir! Please, give Hanada another chance!
Nakaoka, you have a big mouth.
B-but...
Stay out of this!
Hanada, you've caused me enough trouble!

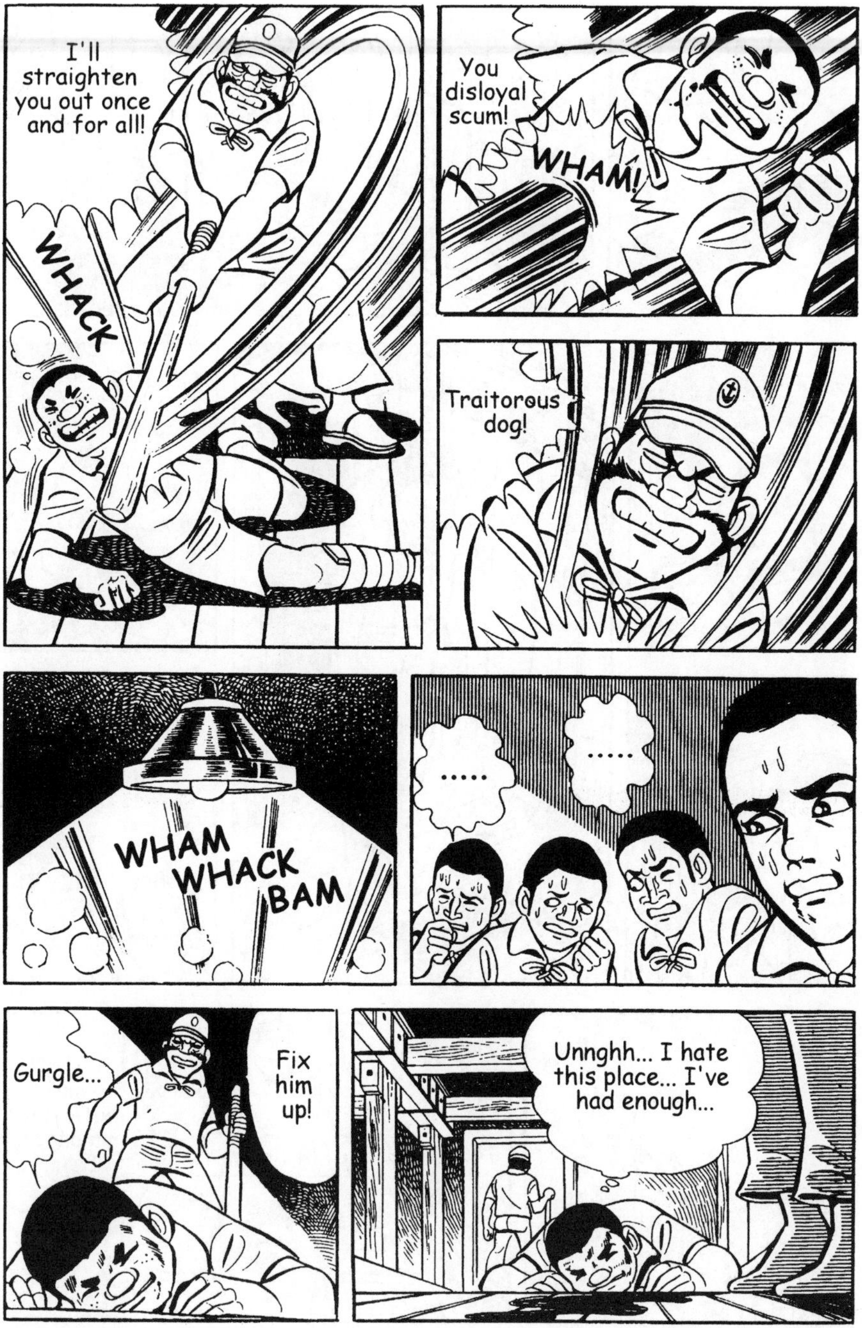
I'll straighten you out once and for all!
WHACK
You disloyal scum!
WHAM!
Traitorous dog!
WHAM
WHACK
BAM
.....
.....
Gurgle...
Fix him up!
Unnghh... I hate this place... I've had enough...

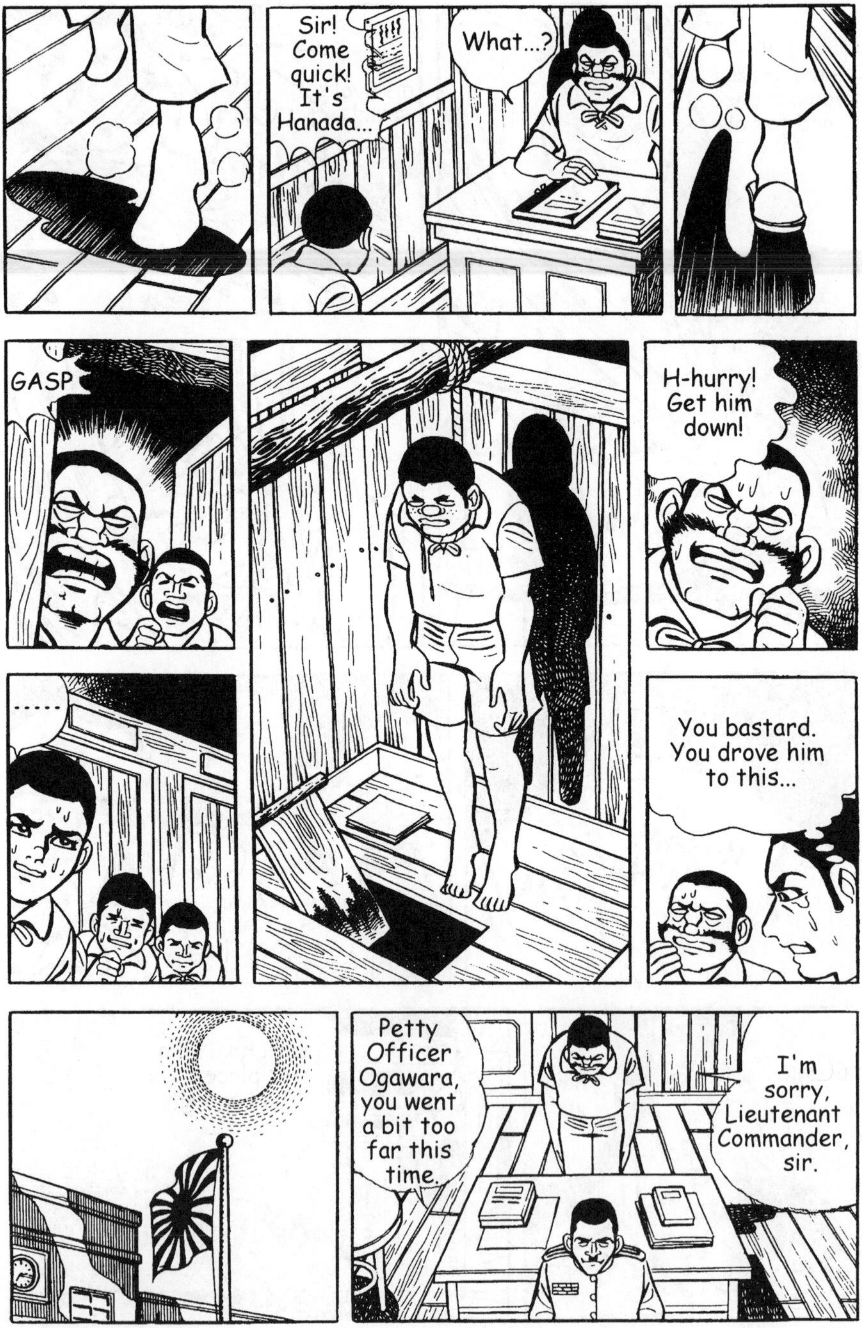
Sir! Come quick! It's Hanada...
What...?
GASP
H-hurry! Get him down!
.....
You bastard. You drove him to this...
Petty Officer Ogawara, you went a bit too far this time.
I'm sorry, Lieutenant Commander, sir.

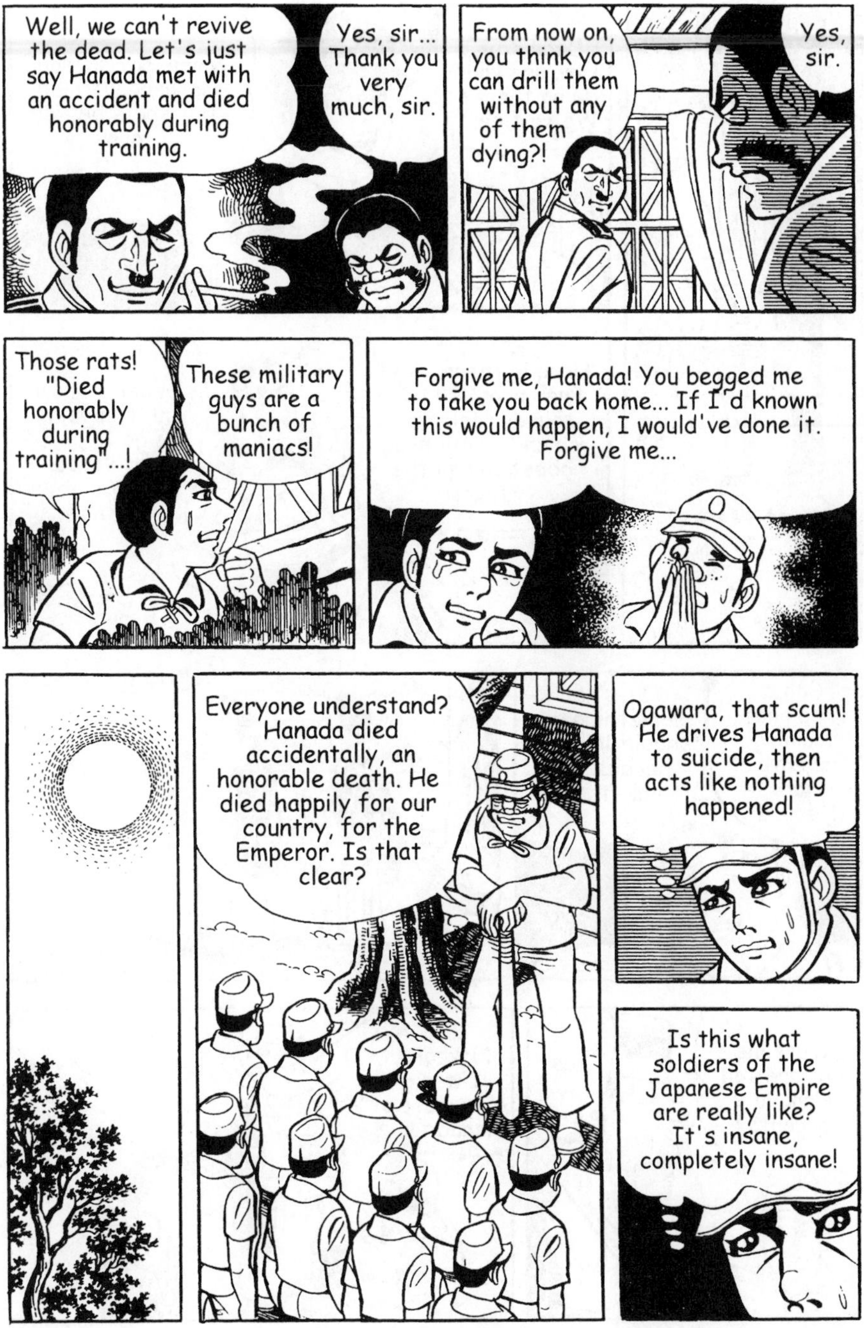
Well, we can't revive the dead. Let's just say Hanada met with an accident and died honorably during training.
Yes, sir... Thank you very much, sir.
From now on, you think you can drill them without any of them dying?!
Yes, sir.
Those rats! "Died honorably during training"...!
These military guys are a bunch of maniacs!
Forgive me, Hanada! You begged me to take you back home... If I'd known this would happen, I would've done it. Forgive me...
Everyone understand? Hanada died accidentally, an honorable death. He died happily for our country, for the Emperor. Is that clear?
Ogawara, that scum! He drives Hanada to suicide, then acts like nothing happened!
Is this what soldiers of the Japanese Empire are really like? It's insane, completely insane!

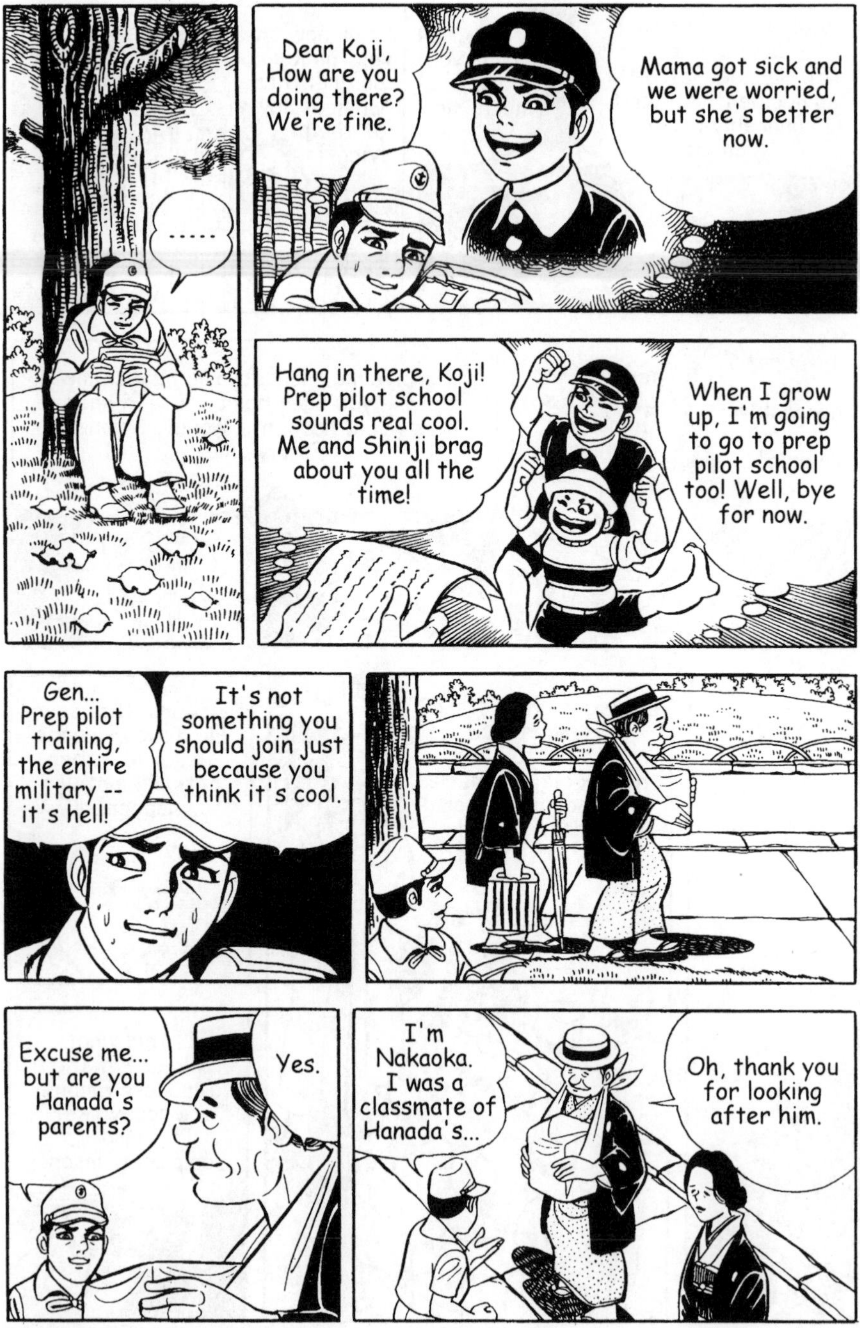

.....
Dear Koji, How are you doing there? We're fine.
Mama got sick and we were worried, but she's better now.
Hang in there, Koji! Prep pilot school sounds real cool. Me and Shinji brag about you all the time!
When I grow up, I'm going to go to prep pilot school too! Well, bye for now.
Gen... Prep pilot training, the entire military -- it's hell!
It's not something you should join just because you think it's cool.
Excuse me... but are you Hanada's parents?
Yes.
I'm Nakaoka. I was a classmate of Hanada's...
Oh, thank you for looking after him.

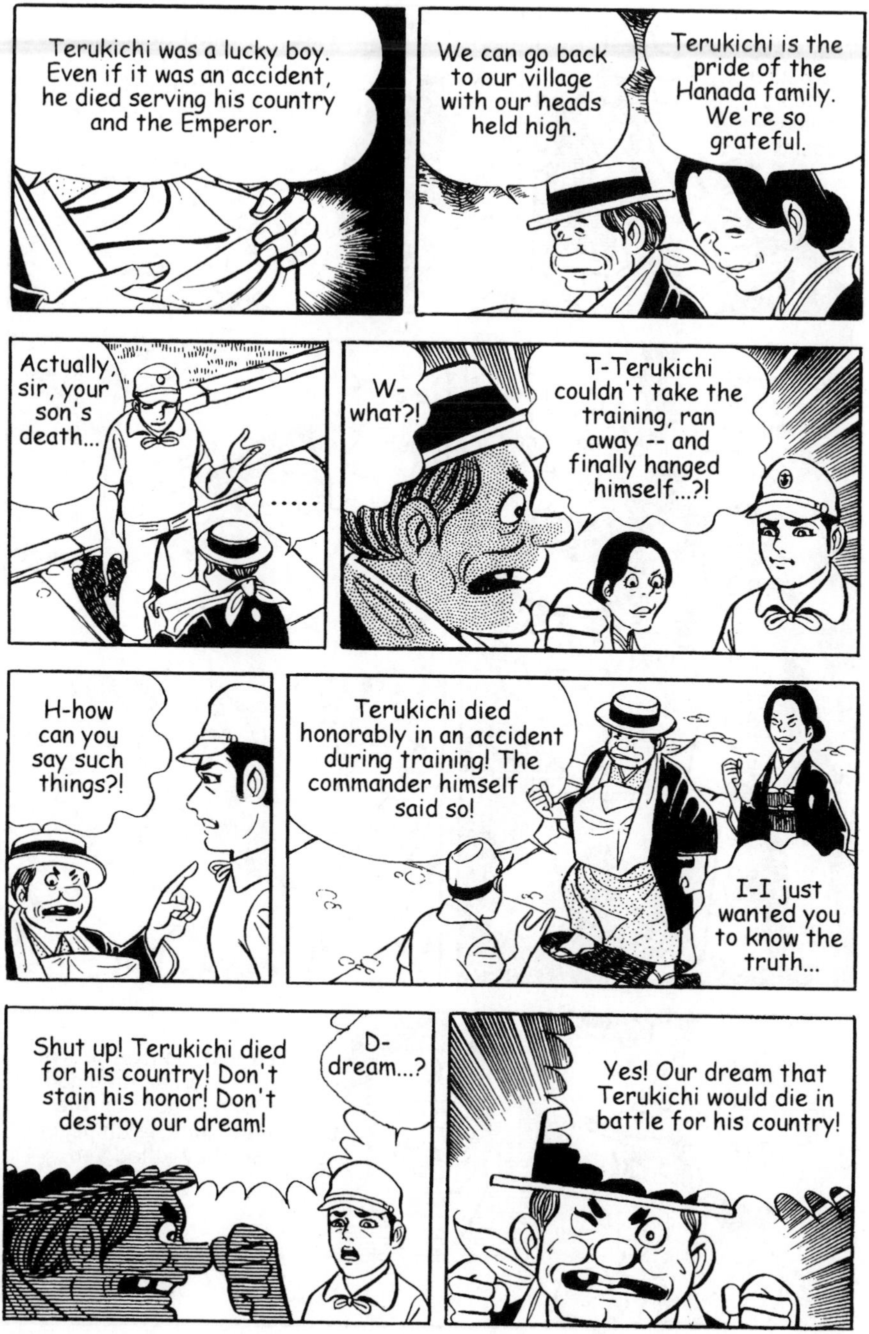
Terukichi was a lucky boy. Even if it was an accident, he died serving his country and the Emperor.
We can go back to our village with our heads held high.
Terukichi is the pride of the Hanada family. We're so grateful.
Actually, sir, your son's death...
......
W- what?!
T-Terukichi couldn't take the training, ran away -- and finally hanged himself...?!
H-how can you say such things?!
Terukichi died honorably in an accident during training! The commander himself said so!
I-I just wanted you to know the truth...
Shut up! Terukichi died for his country! Don't stain his honor! Don't destroy our dream!
D- dream...?
Yes! Our dream that Terukichi would die in battle for his country!

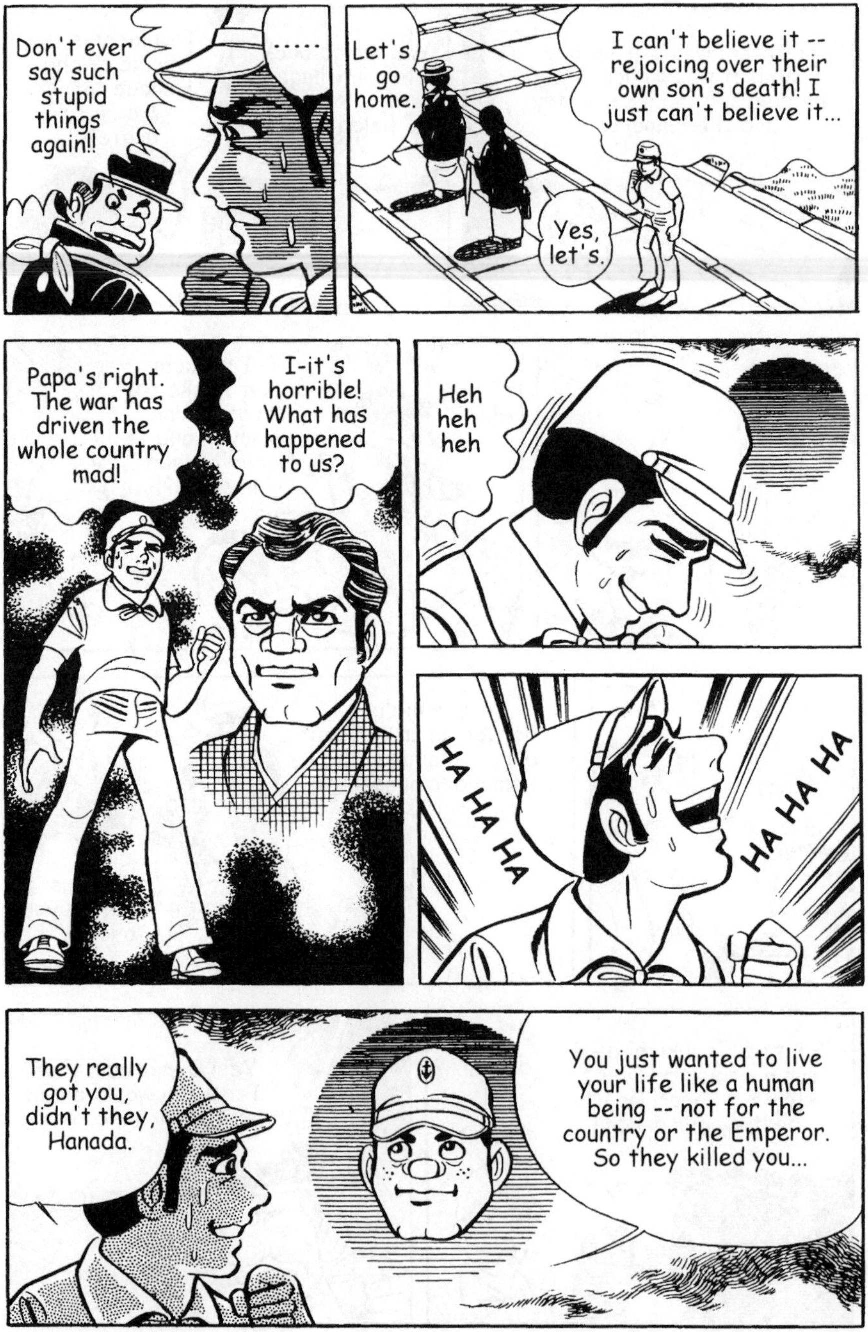
Don't ever say such stupid things again!!
.....
Let's go home.
I can't believe it -- rejoicing over their own son's death! I just can't believe it...
Yes, let's.
Papa's right. The war has driven the whole country mad!
I-it's horrible! What has happened to us?
Heh heh heh
HA HA HA
HA HA HA
They really got you, didn't they, Hanada.
You just wanted to live your life like a human being -- not for the country or the Emperor. So they killed you...

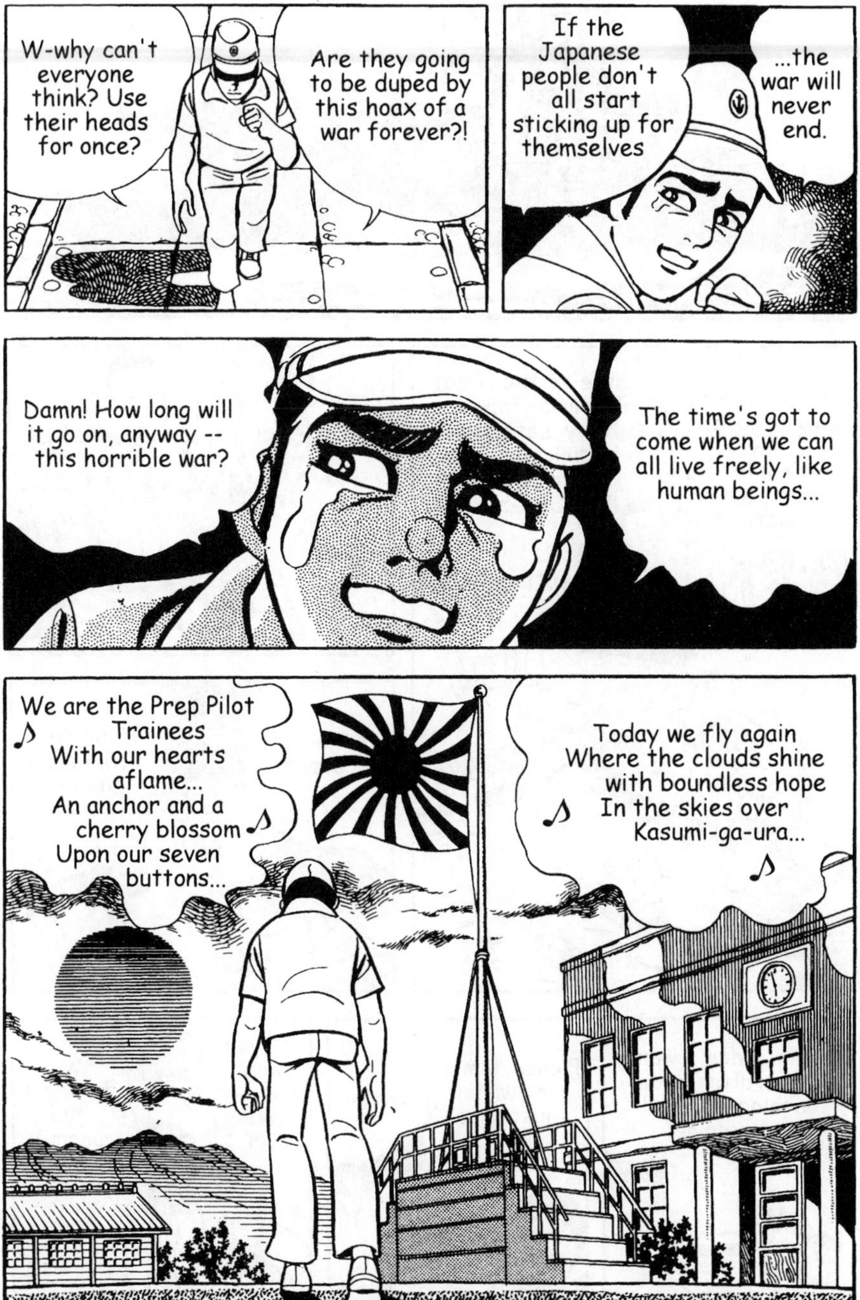

W-why can't everyone think? Use their heads for once?
Are they going to be duped by this hoax of a war forever?!
If the Japanese people don't all start sticking up for themselves
...the war will never end.
Damn! How long will it go on, anyway -- this horrible war?
The time's got to come when we can all live freely, like human beings...
♪ We are the Prep Pilot Trainees With our hearts aflame... An anchor and a cherry blossom ♪ Upon our seven buttons...
♪ Today we fly again Where the clouds shine with boundless hope In the skies over Kasumi-ga-ura... ♪

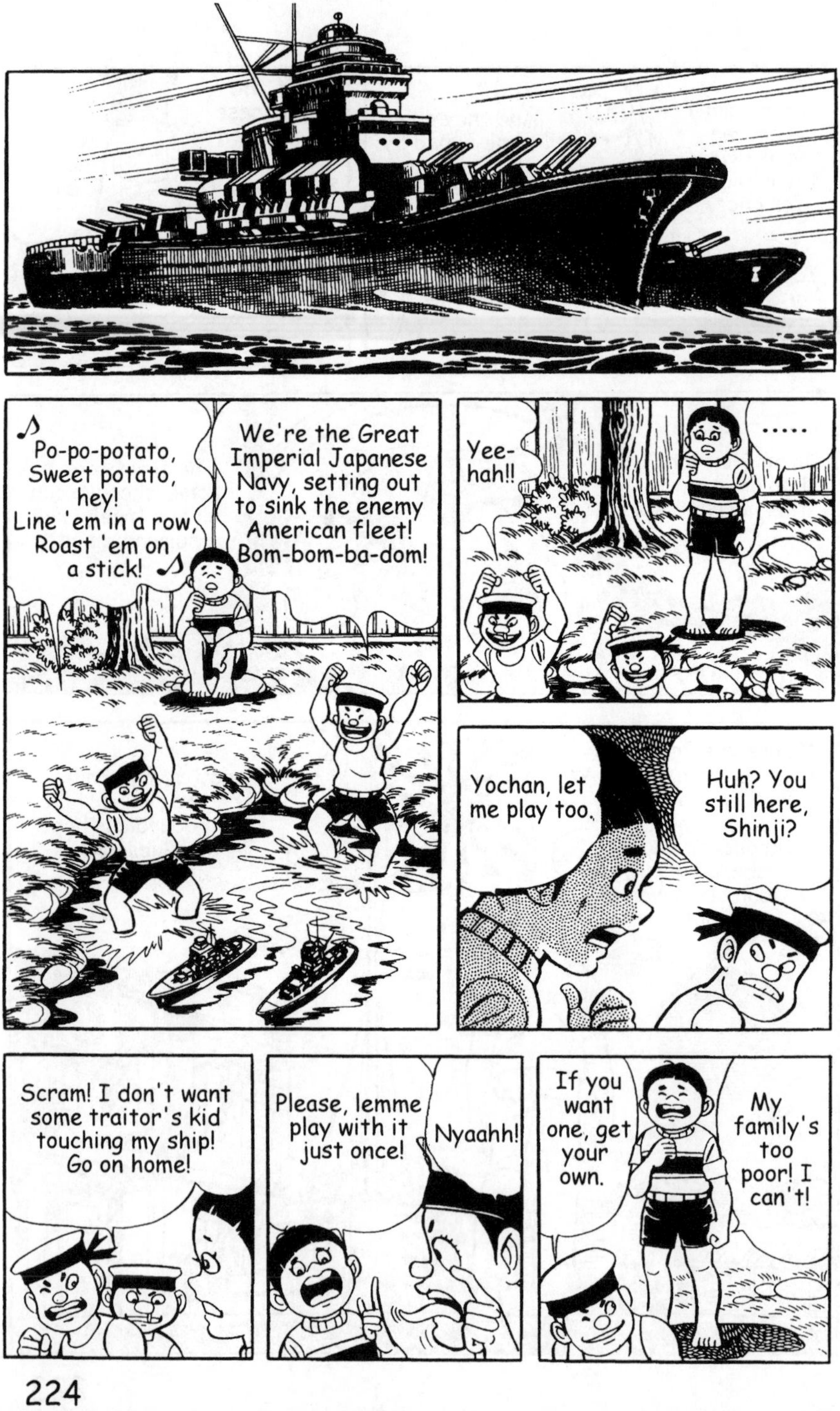

Po-po-potato, Sweet potato, hey! Line 'em in a row, Roast 'em on a stick!
We're the Great Imperial Japanese Navy, setting out to sink the enemy American fleet! Bom-bom-ba-dom!
Yee-hah!!
.....
Yochan, let me play too.
Huh? You still here, Shinji?
Scram! I don't want some traitor's kid touching my ship! Go on home!
Please, lemme play with it just once!
Nyaahh!
If you want one, get your own.
My family's too poor! I can't!

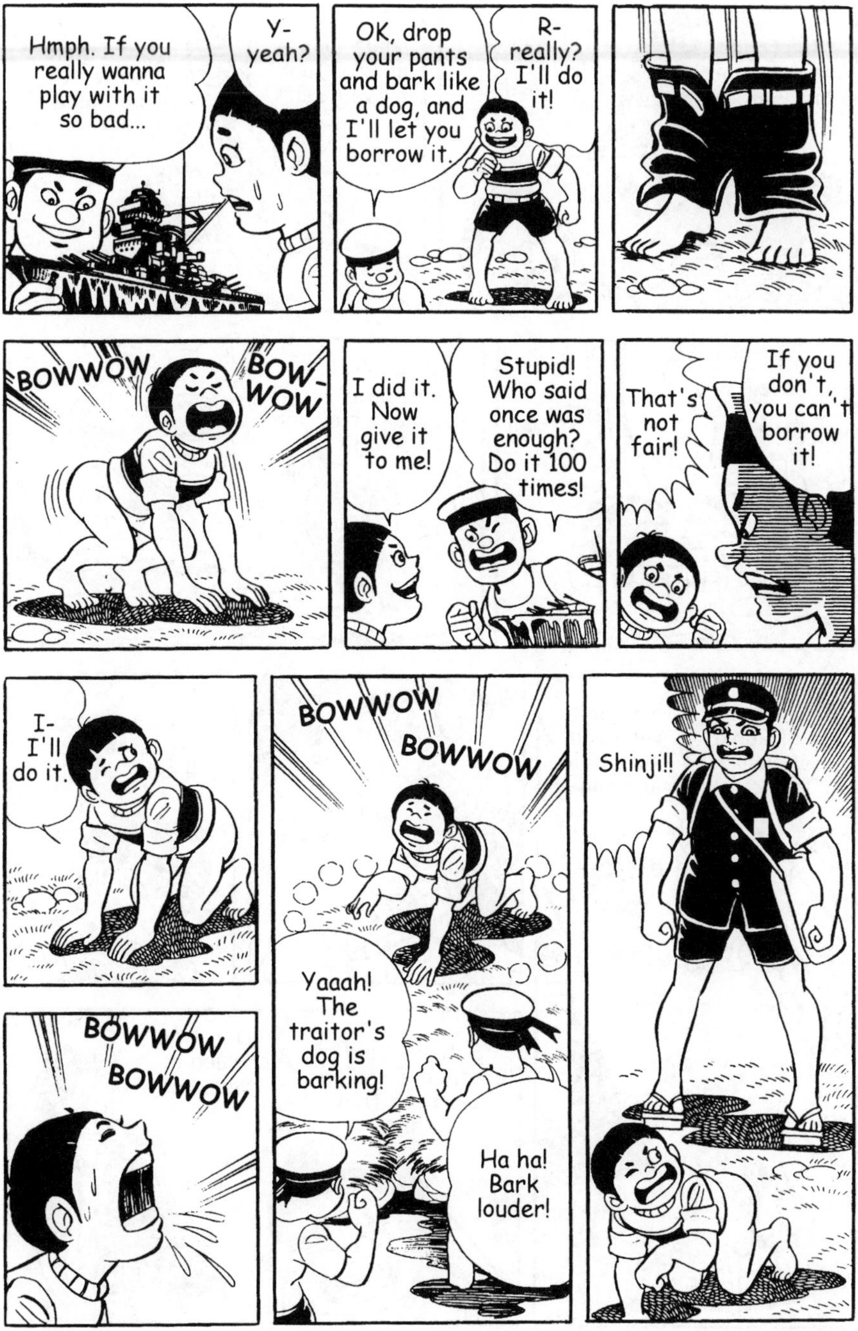
Hmph. If you really wanna play with it so bad...
Y-yeah?
OK, drop your pants and bark like a dog, and I'll let you borrow it.
R-really? I'll do it!
BOWWOW
BOW-WOW
I did it. Now give it to me!
Stupid! Who said once was enough? Do it 100 times!
That's not fair!
If you don't, you can't borrow it!
I-I'll do it.
BOWWOW
BOWWOW
BOWWOW
BOWWOW
Yaaah! The traitor's dog is barking!
Ha ha! Bark louder!
Shinji!!

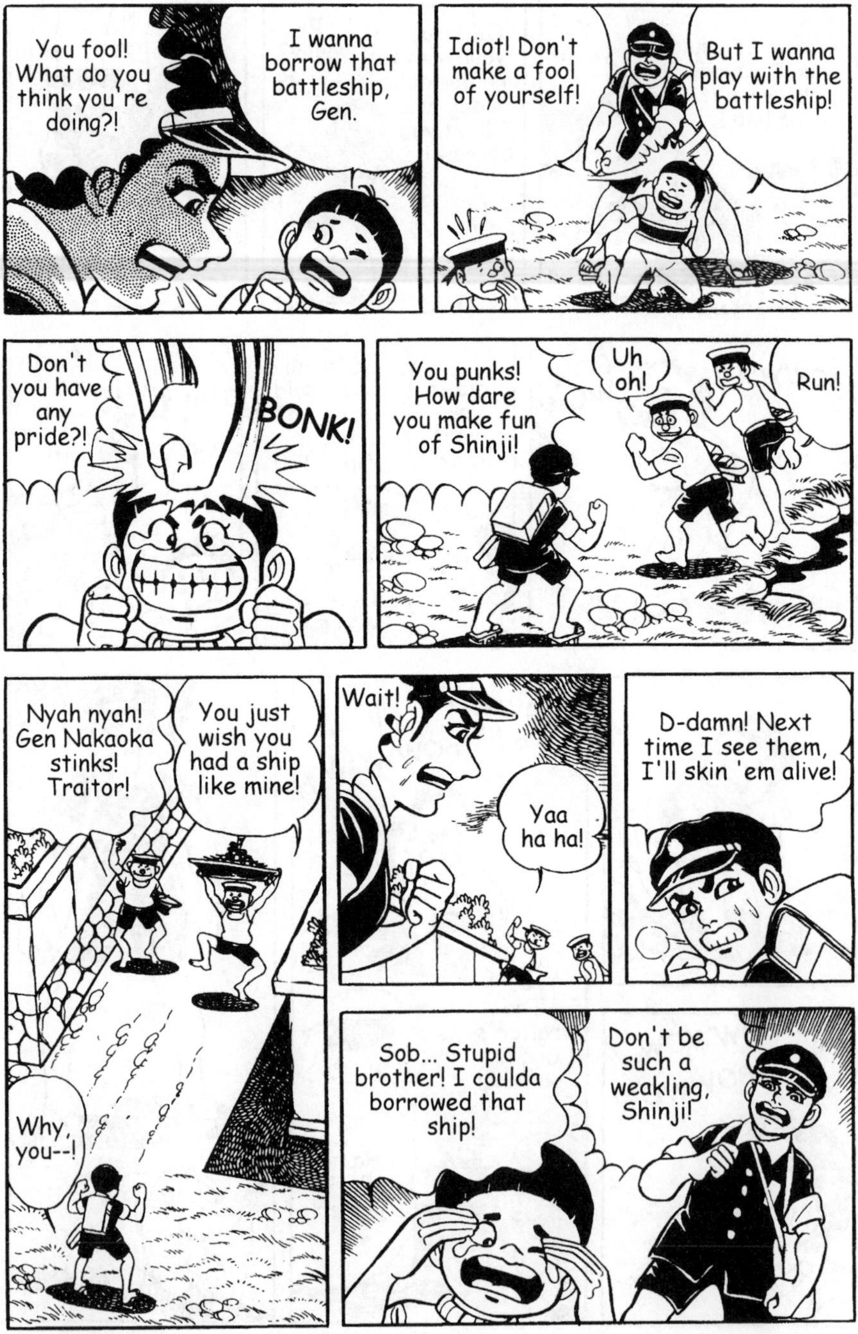
You fool! What do you think you're doing?!
I wanna borrow that battleship, Gen.
Idiot! Don't make a fool of yourself!
But I wanna play with the battleship!
Don't you have any pride?!
BONK!
You punks! How dare you make fun of Shinji!
Uh oh!
Run!
Nyah nyah! Gen Nakaoka stinks! Traitor!
You just wish you had a ship like mine!
Why, you--!
Wait!
Yaa ha ha!
D-damn! Next time I see them, I'll skin 'em alive!
Sob... Stupid brother! I coulda borrowed that ship!
Don't be such a weakling, Shinji!

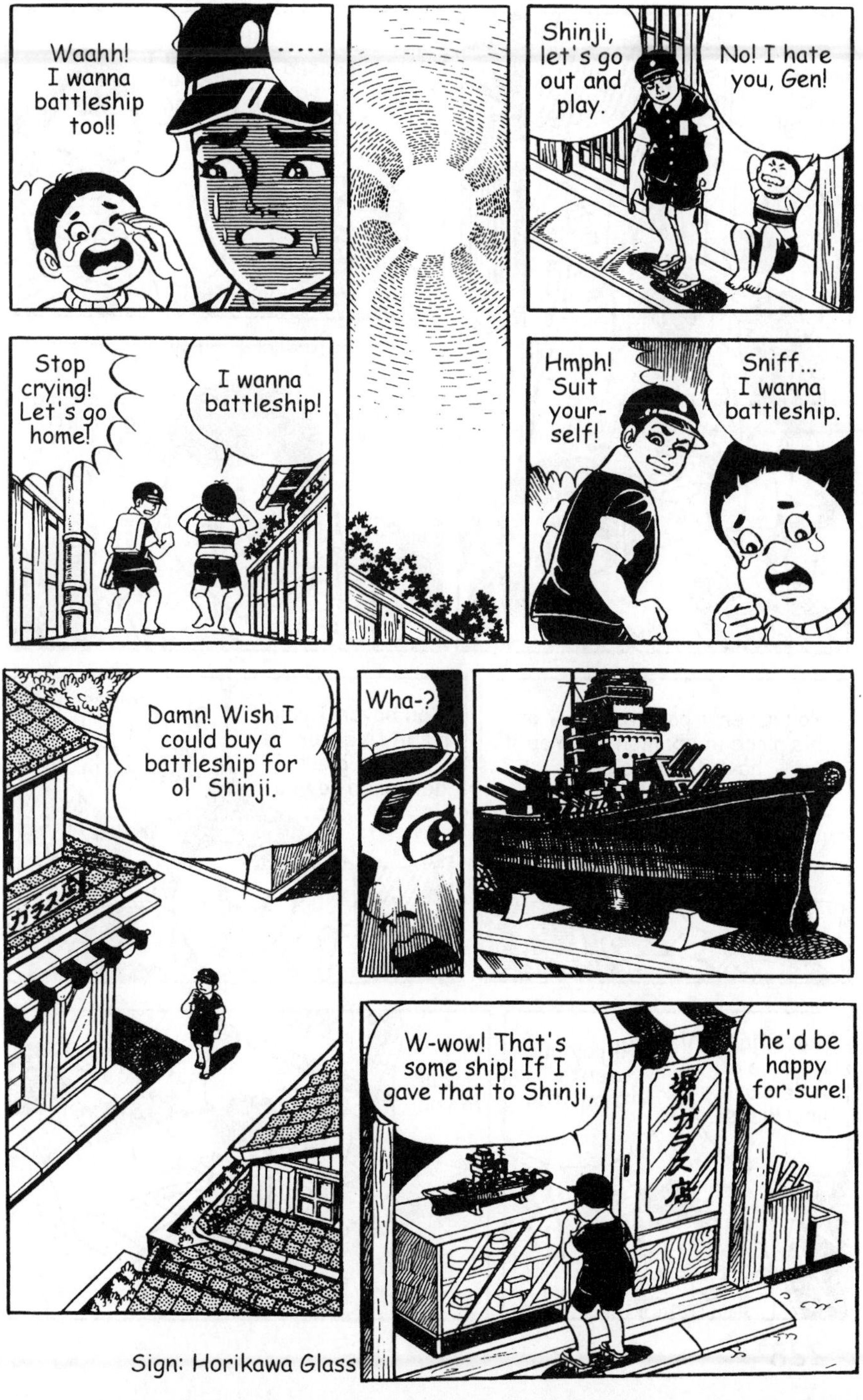
Waahh! I wanna battleship too!!
......
Shinji, let's go out and play.
No! I hate you, Gen!
Stop crying! Let's go home!
I wanna battleship!
Hmph! Suit your-self!
Sniff... I wanna battleship.
Damn! Wish I could buy a battleship for ol' Shinji.
ガラス店
Wha-?
W-wow! That's some ship! If I gave that to Shinji,
he'd be happy for sure!
堀川ガラス店
Sign: Horikawa Glass

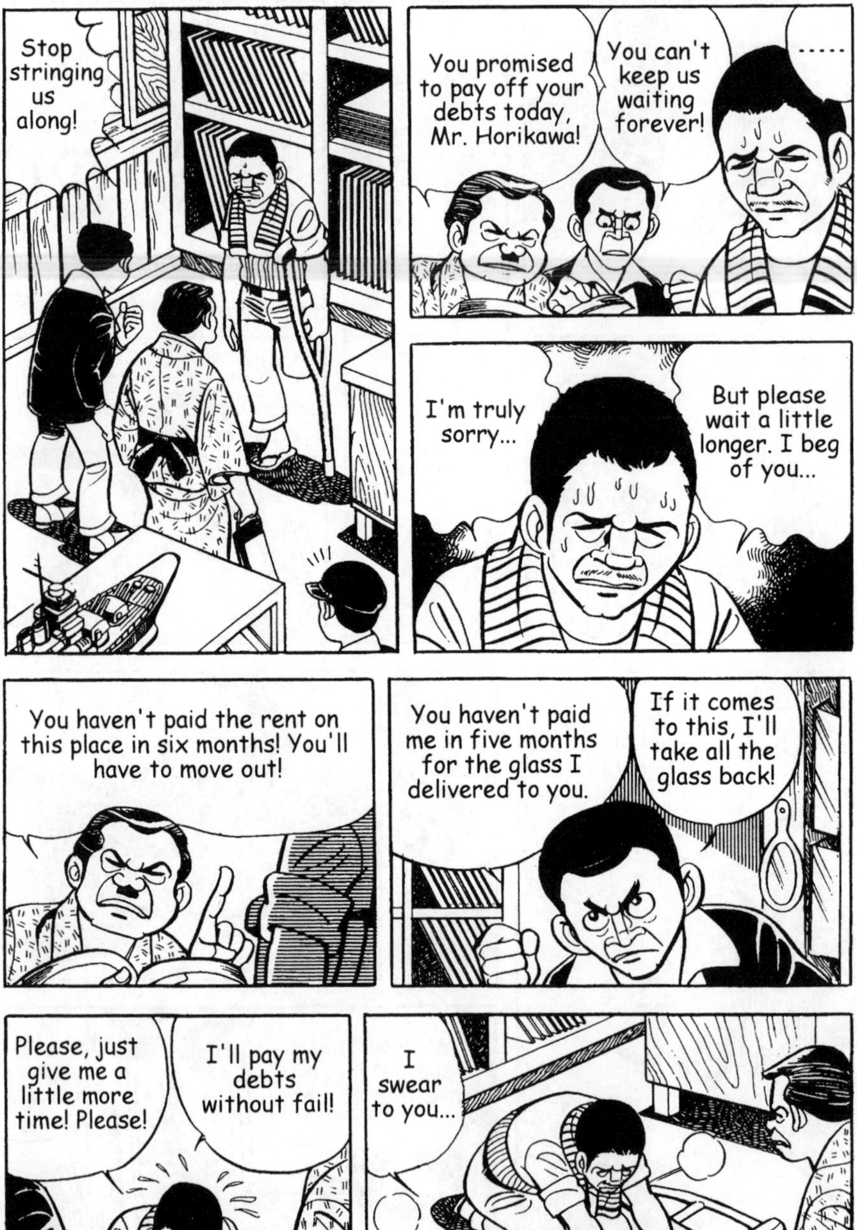
Stop stringing us along!
You promised to pay off your debts today, Mr. Horikawa!
You can't keep us waiting forever!
.....
I'm truly sorry...
But please wait a little longer. I beg of you...
You haven't paid the rent on this place in six months! You'll have to move out!
You haven't paid me in five months for the glass I delivered to you.
If it comes to this, I'll take all the glass back!
Please, just give me a little more time! Please!
I'll pay my debts without fail!
I swear to you...

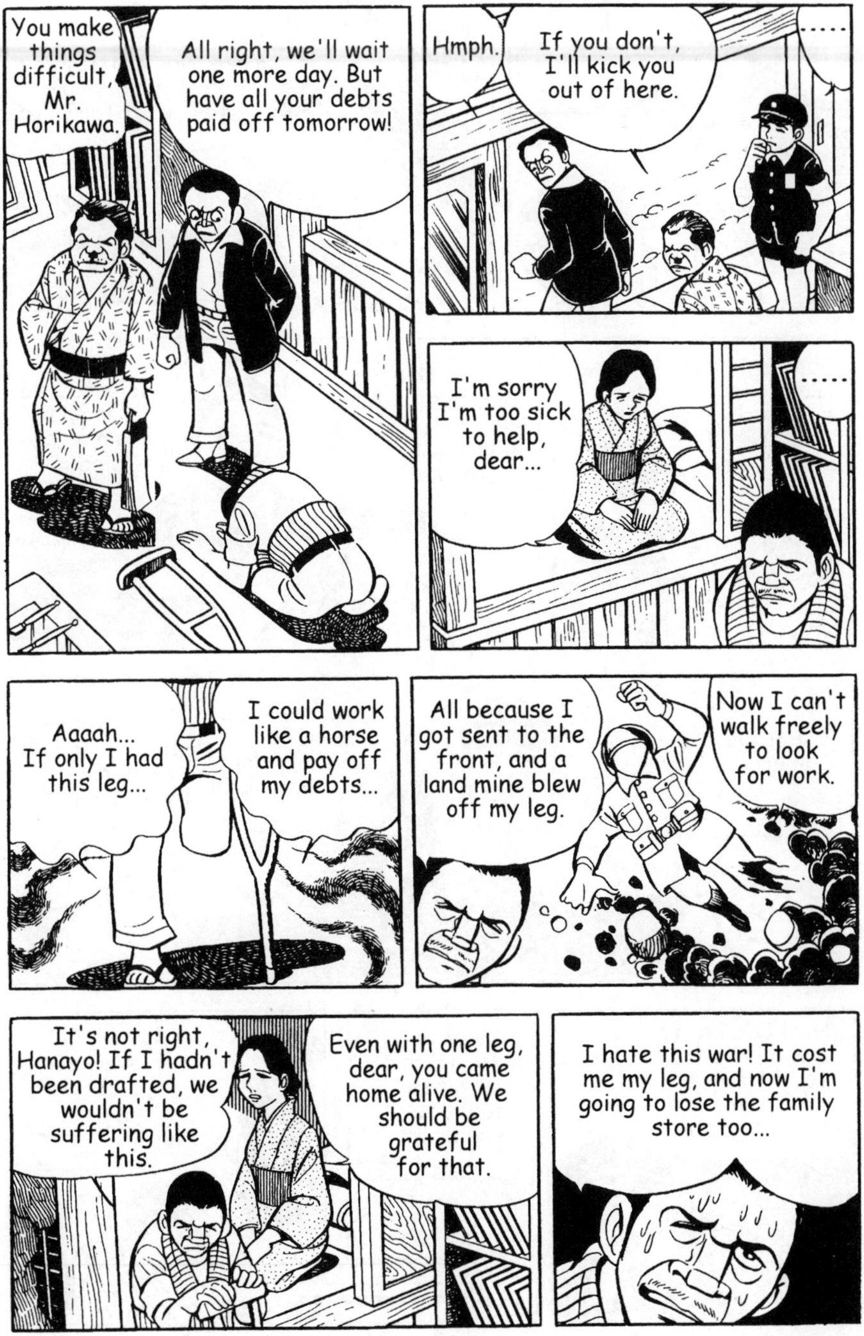
You make things difficult, Mr. Horikawa.
All right, we'll wait one more day. But have all your debts paid off tomorrow!
Hmph.
If you don't, I'll kick you out of here.
.....
I'm sorry I'm too sick to help, dear...
.....
Aaaah... If only I had this leg...
I could work like a horse and pay off my debts...
All because I got sent to the front, and a land mine blew off my leg.
Now I can't walk freely to look for work.
It's not right, Hanayo! If I hadn't been drafted, we wouldn't be suffering like this.
Even with one leg, dear, you came home alive. We should be grateful for that.
I hate this war! It cost me my leg, and now I'm going to lose the family store too...

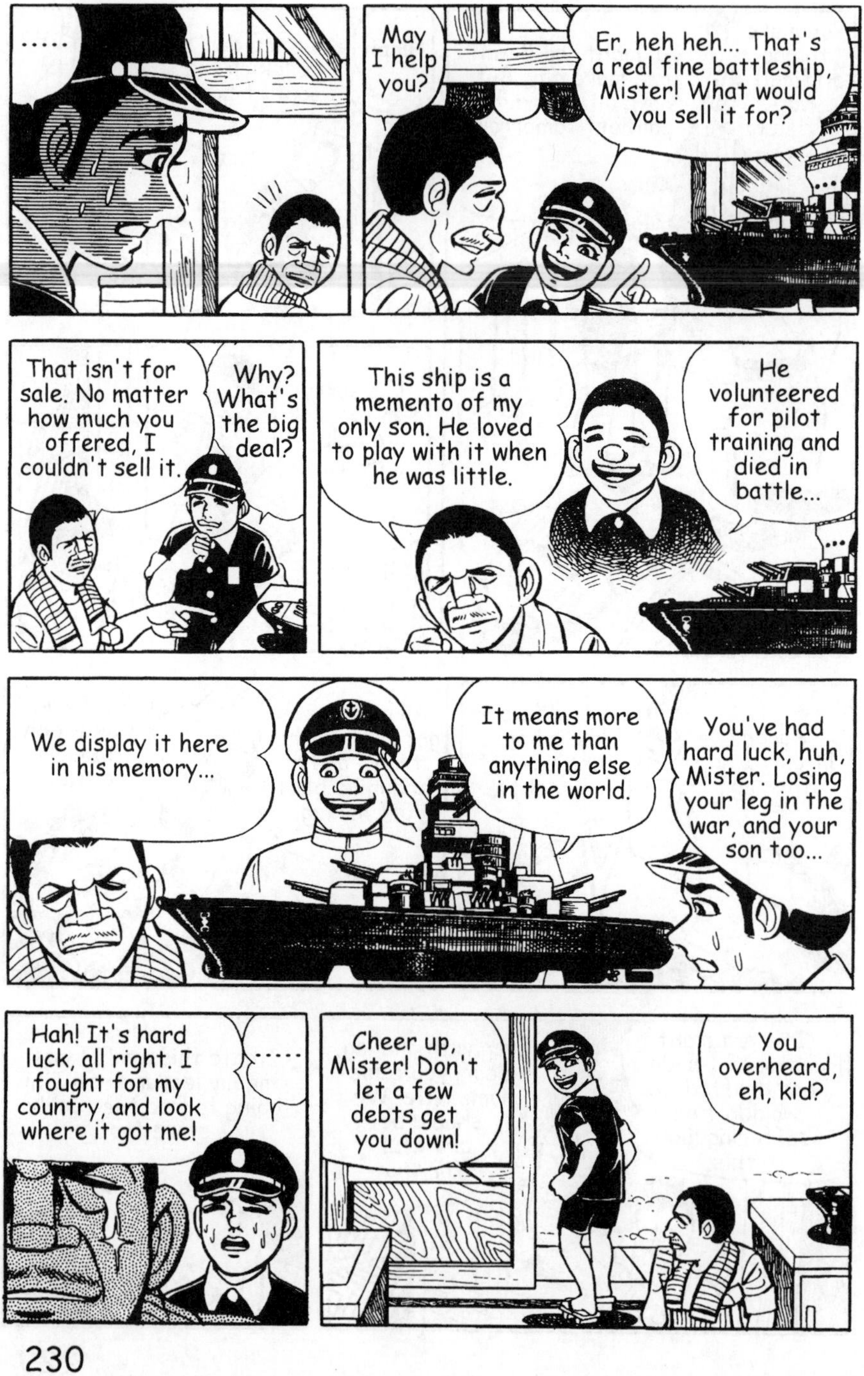
.....
May I help you?
Er, heh heh... That's a real fine battleship, Mister! What would you sell it for?
That isn't for sale. No matter how much you offered, I couldn't sell it.
Why? What's the big deal?
This ship is a memento of my only son. He loved to play with it when he was little.
He volunteered for pilot training and died in battle...
We display it here in his memory...
It means more to me than anything else in the world.
You've had hard luck, huh, Mister. Losing your leg in the war, and your son too...
Hah! It's hard luck, all right. I fought for my country, and look where it got me!
.....
Cheer up, Mister! Don't let a few debts get you down!
You overheard, eh, kid?

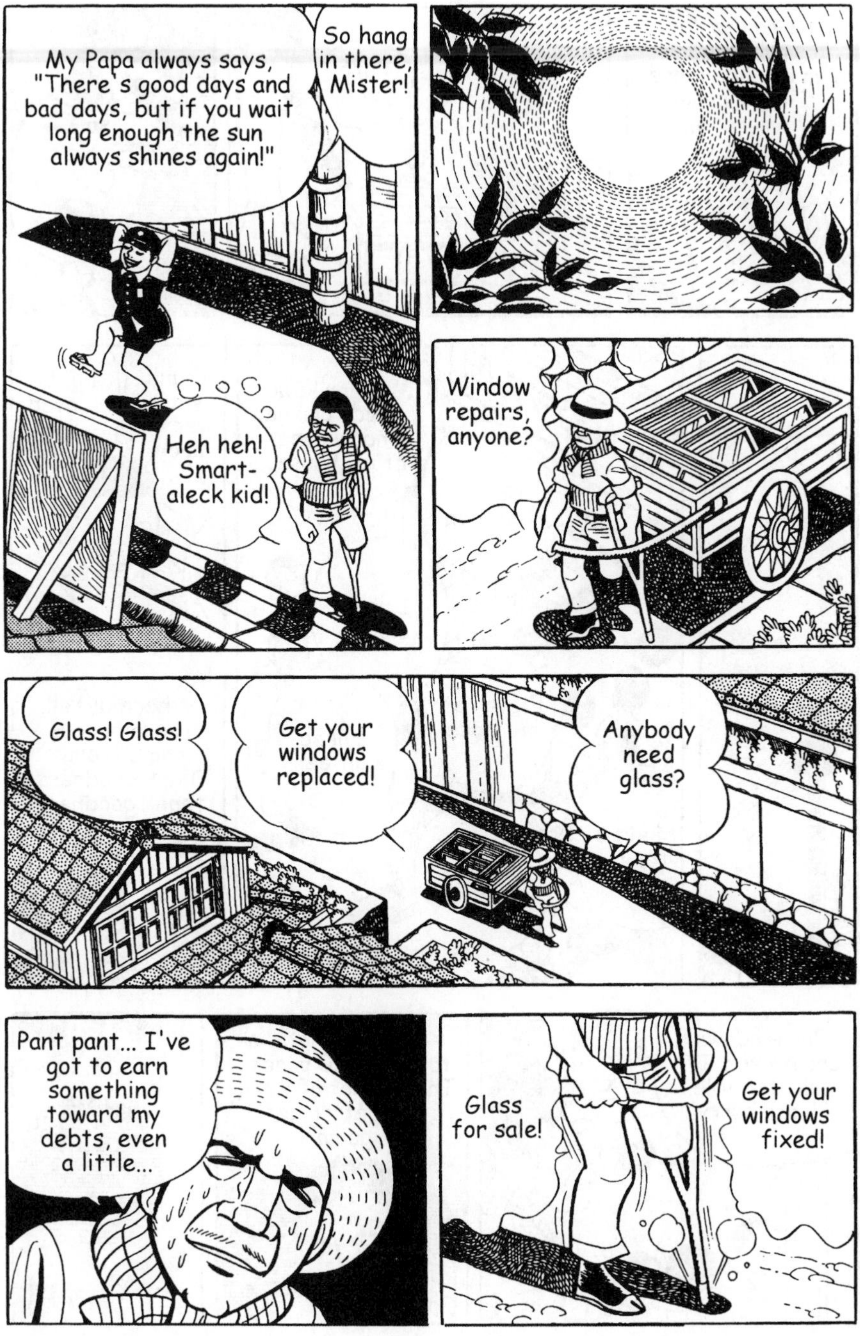
My Papa always says, "There's good days and bad days, but if you wait long enough the sun always shines again!"
So hang in there, Mister!
Heh heh! Smart-aleck kid!
Window repairs, anyone?
Glass! Glass!
Get your windows replaced!
Anybody need glass?
Pant pant... I've got to earn something toward my debts, even a little...
Glass for sale!
Get your windows fixed!

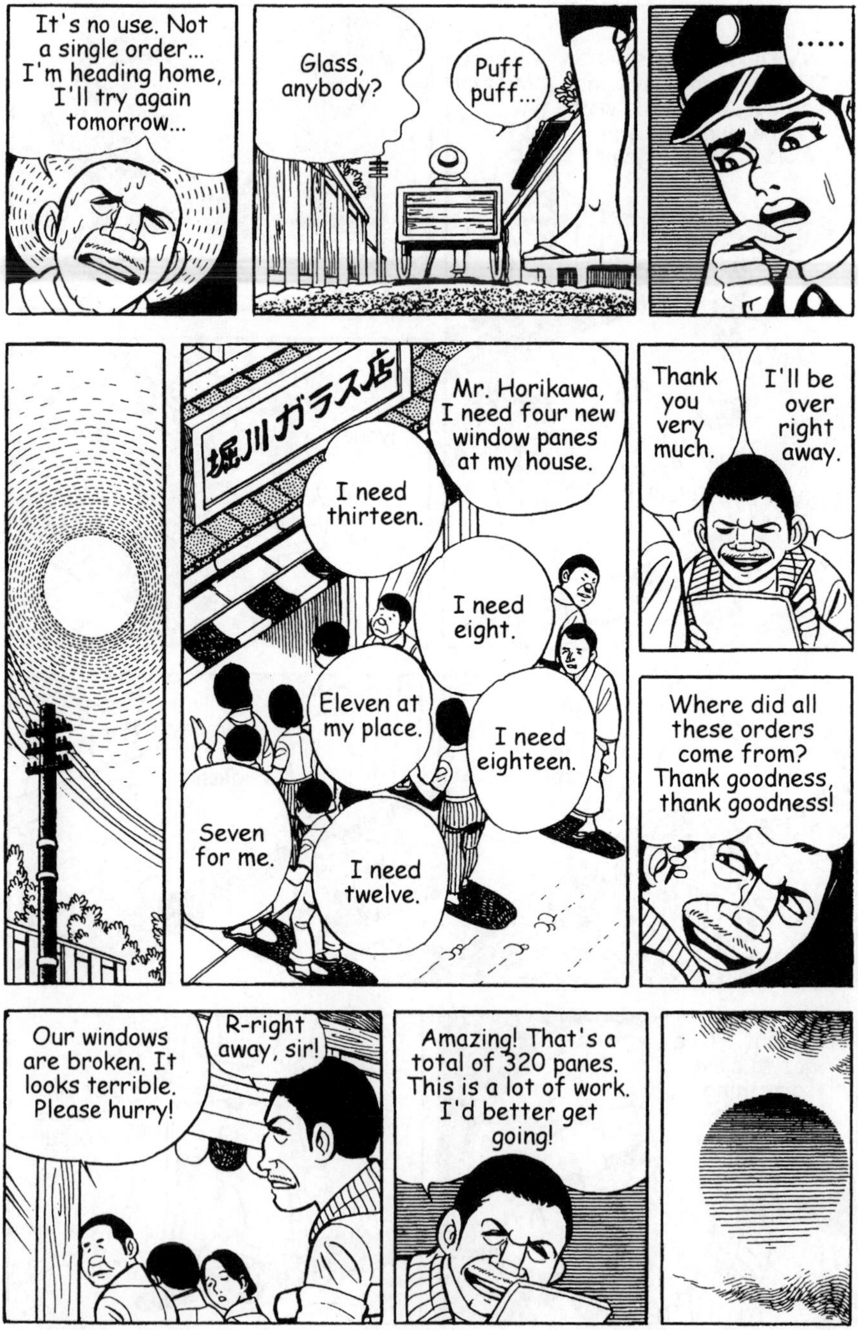
It's no use. Not a single order... I'm heading home, I'll try again tomorrow...
Glass, anybody?
Puff puff...
.....
堀川ガラス店
Mr. Horikawa, I need four new window panes at my house.
I need thirteen.
I need eight.
Eleven at my place.
I need eighteen.
Seven for me.
I need twelve.
Thank you very much.
I'll be over right away.
Where did all these orders come from? Thank goodness, thank goodness!
Our windows are broken. It looks terrible. Please hurry!
R-right away, sir!
Amazing! That's a total of 320 panes. This is a lot of work. I'd better get going!

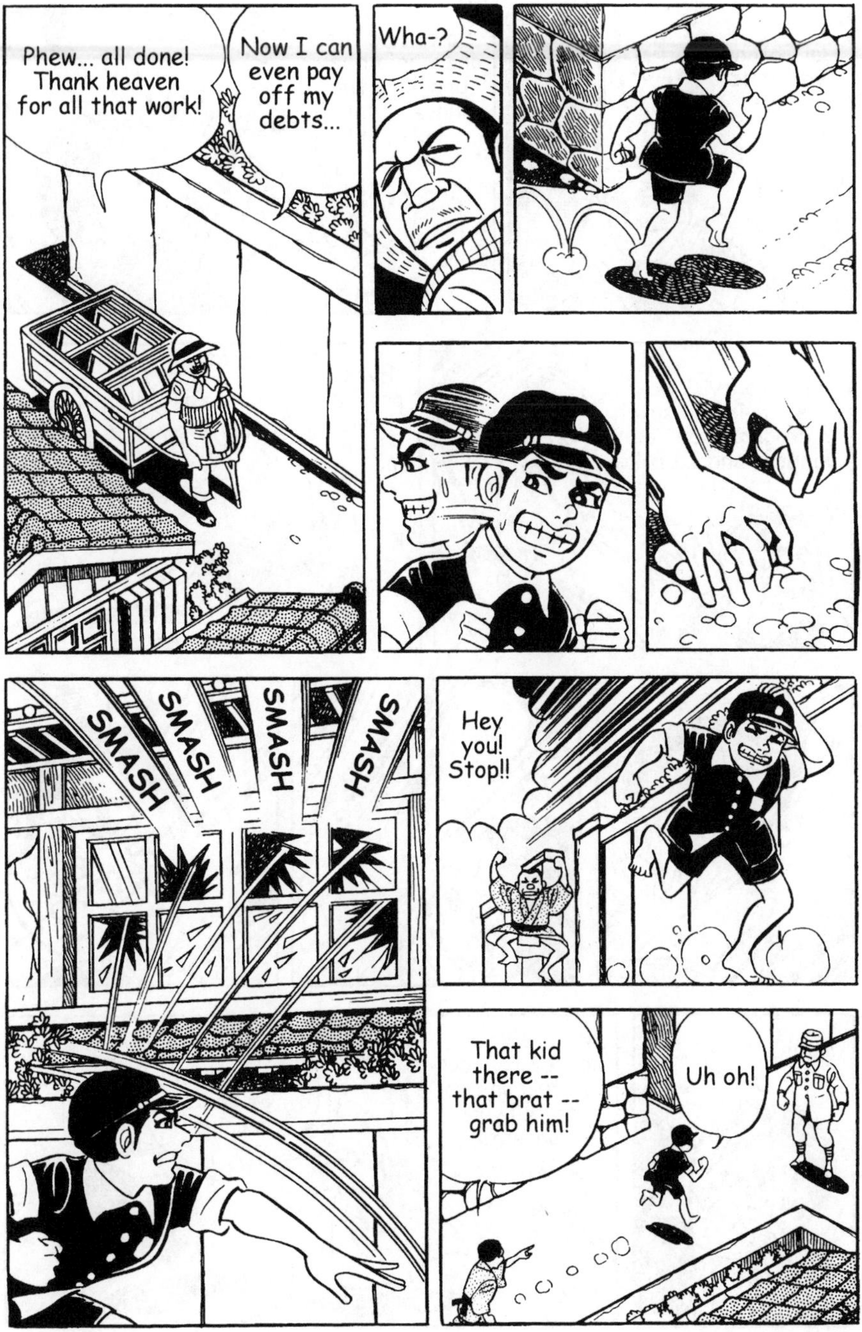

Phew... all done! Thank heaven for all that work!
Now I can even pay off my debts...
Wha-?
SMASH
SMASH
SMASH
SMASH
Hey you! Stop!!
That kid there -- that brat -- grab him!
Uh oh!

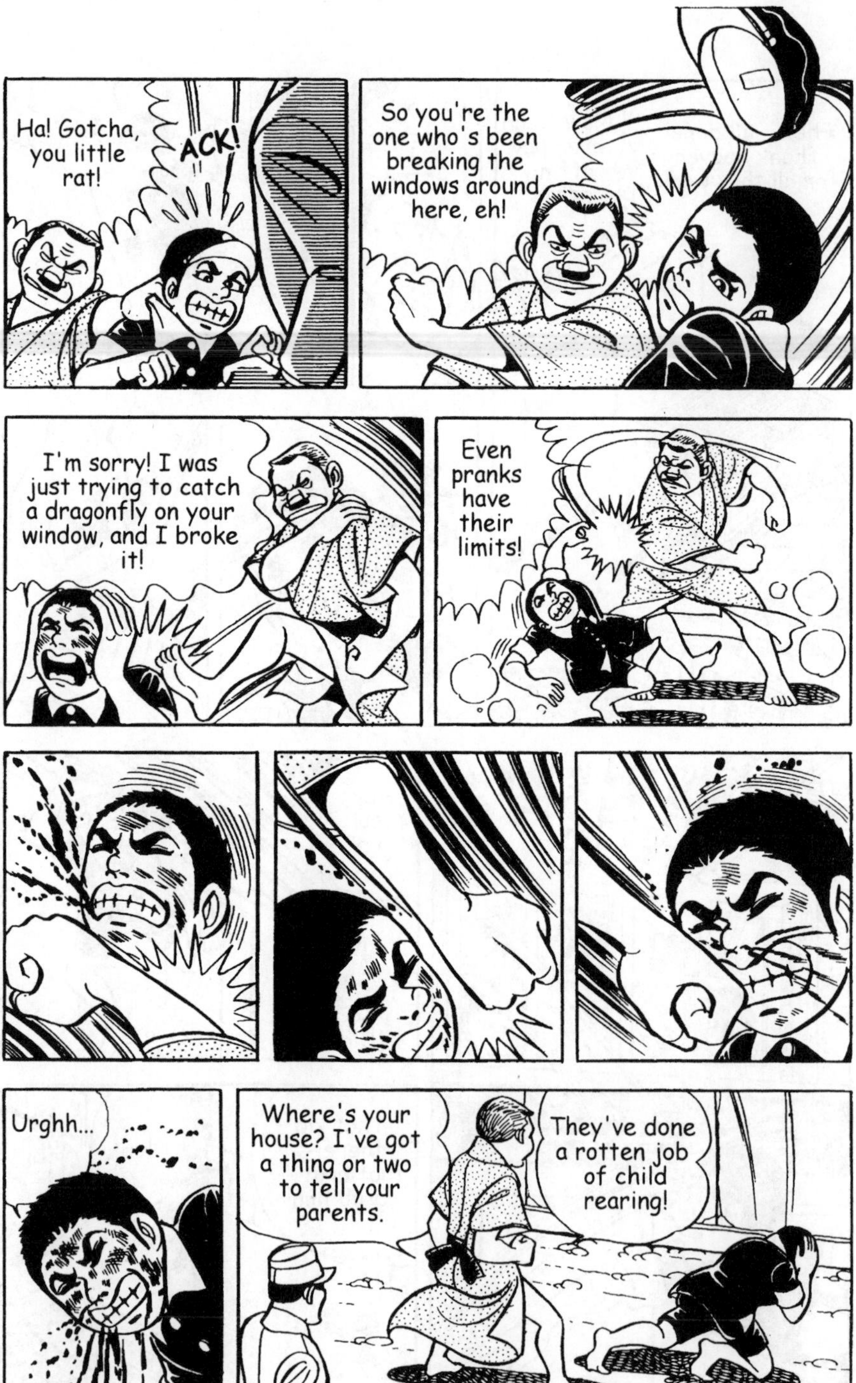
Ha! Gotcha, you little rat!
ACK!
So you're the one who's been breaking the windows around here, eh!
I'm sorry! I was just trying to catch a dragonfly on your window, and I broke it!
Even pranks have their limits!
Urghh...
Where's your house? I've got a thing or two to tell your parents.
They've done a rotten job of child rearing!

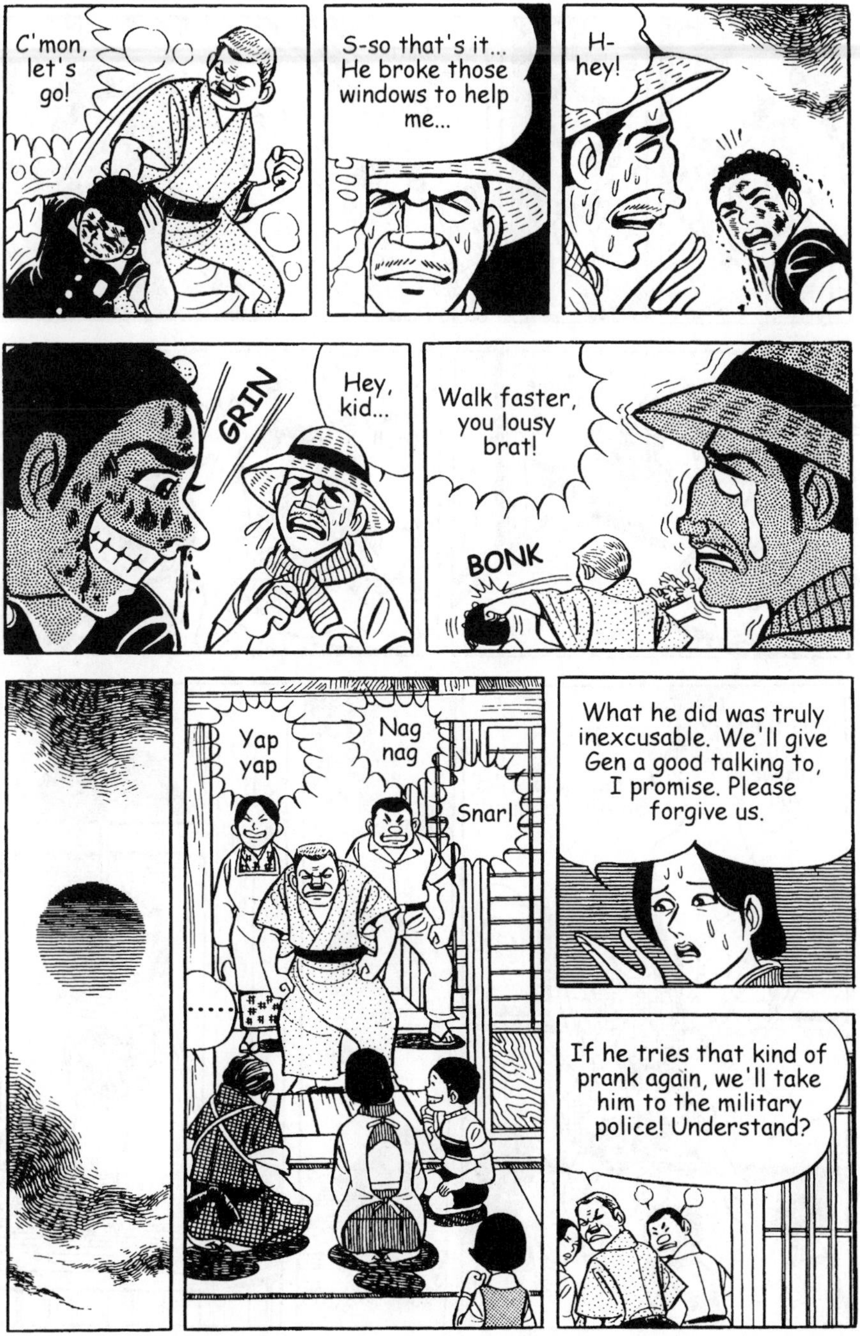
C'mon, let's go!
S-so that's it... He broke those windows to help me...
H-hey!
GRIN
Hey, kid...
Walk faster, you lousy brat!
BONK
Yap yap
Nag nag
Snarl
......
What he did was truly inexcusable. We'll give Gen a good talking to, I promise. Please forgive us.
If he tries that kind of prank again, we'll take him to the military police! Understand?

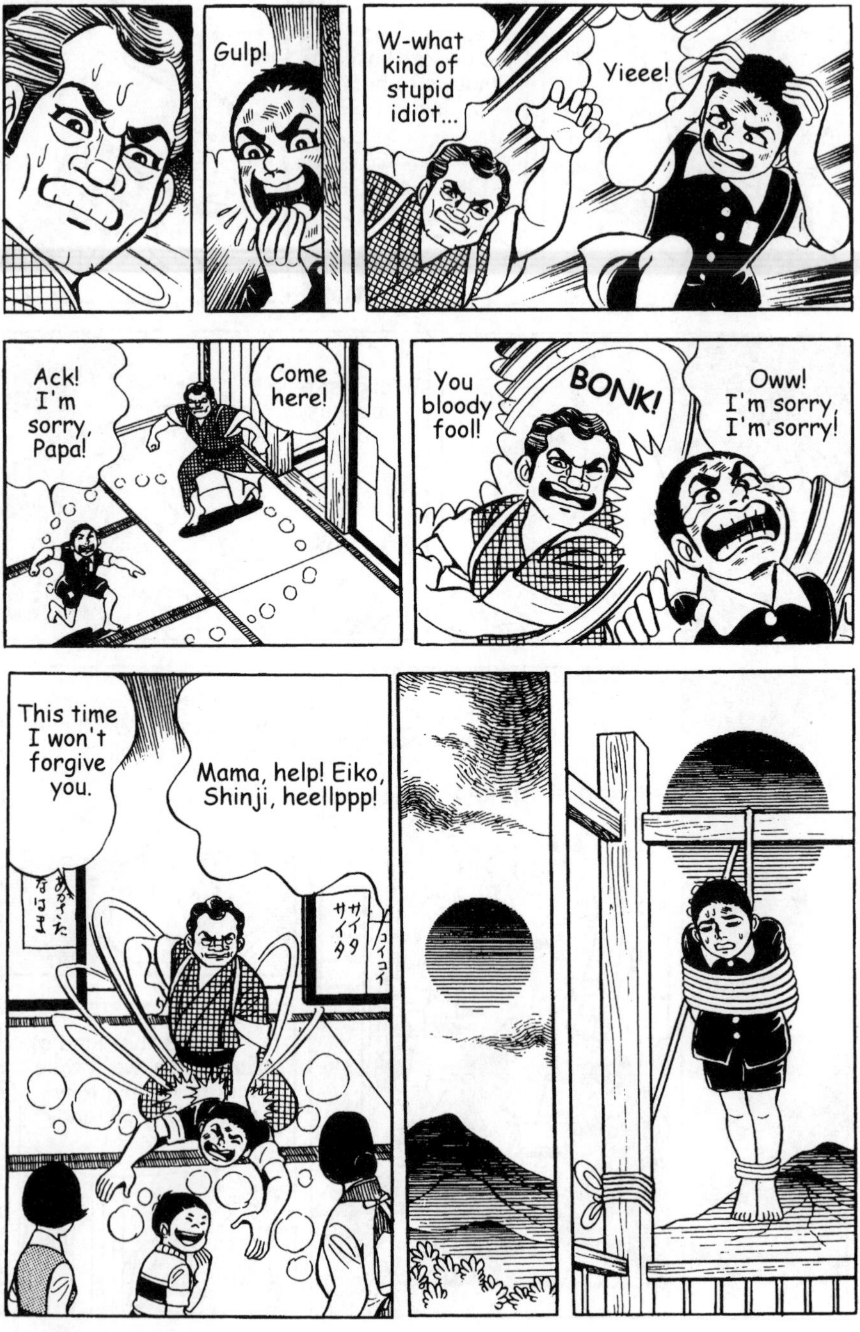
Gulp!
W-what kind of stupid idiot...
Yieee!
Ack! I'm sorry, Papa!
Come here!
You bloody fool!
BONK!
Oww! I'm sorry, I'm sorry!
This time I won't forgive you.
Mama, help! Eiko, Shinji, heellppp!
あかさた
なはま
サイタ
サイタ
コイコイ

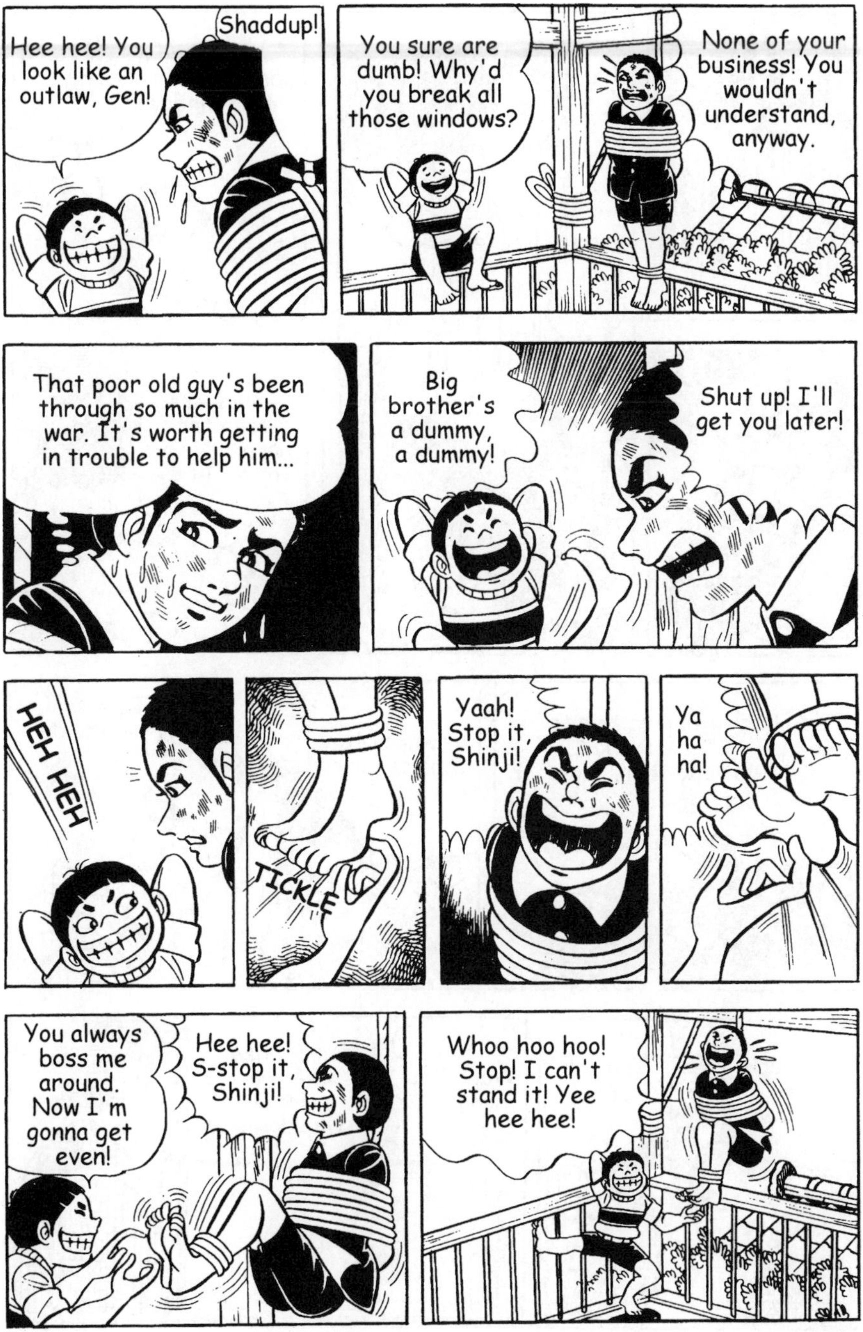
Hee hee! You look like an outlaw, Gen!
Shaddup!
You sure are dumb! Why'd you break all those windows?
None of your business! You wouldn't understand, anyway.
That poor old guy's been through so much in the war. It's worth getting in trouble to help him...
Big brother's a dummy, a dummy!
Shut up! I'll get you later!
HEH HEH
TICKLE
Yaah! Stop it, Shinji!
Ya ha ha!
You always boss me around. Now I'm gonna get even!
Hee hee! S-stop it, Shinji!
Whoo hoo hoo! Stop! I can't stand it! Yee hee hee!

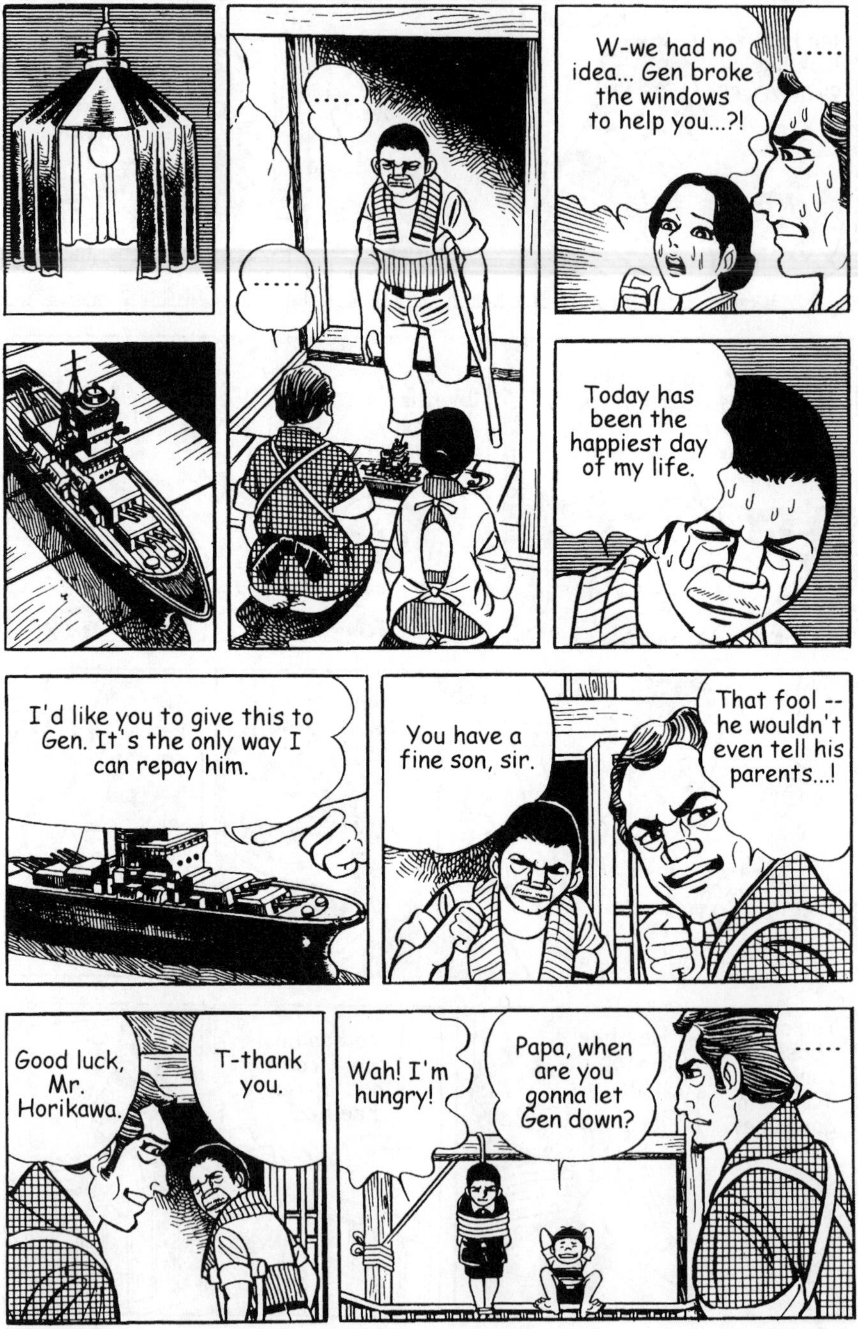
.....
.....
W-we had no idea... Gen broke the windows to help you...?!
.....
Today has been the happiest day of my life.
I'd like you to give this to Gen. It's the only way I can repay him.
You have a fine son, sir.
That fool -- he wouldn't even tell his parents...!
Good luck, Mr. Horikawa.
T-thank you.
Wah! I'm hungry!
Papa, when are you gonna let Gen down?
.....

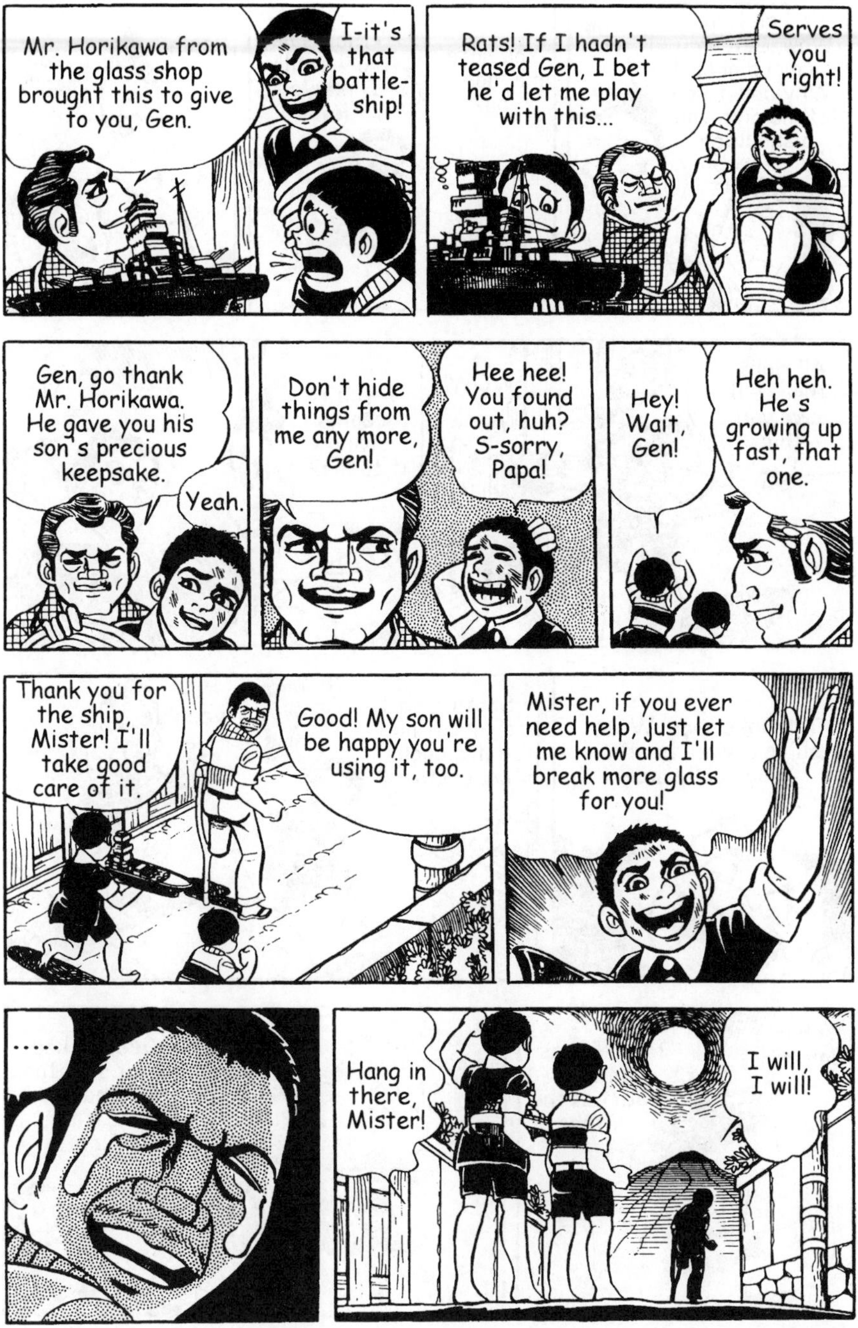
Mr. Horikawa from the glass shop brought this to give to you, Gen.
I-it's that battle-ship!
Rats! If I hadn't teased Gen, I bet he'd let me play with this...
Serves you right!
Gen, go thank Mr. Horikawa. He gave you his son's precious keepsake.
Yeah.
Don't hide things from me any more, Gen!
Hee hee! You found out, huh? S-sorry, Papa!
Hey! Wait, Gen!
Heh heh. He's growing up fast, that one.
Thank you for the ship, Mister! I'll take good care of it.
Good! My son will be happy you're using it, too.
Mister, if you ever need help, just let me know and I'll break more glass for you!
.....
Hang in there, Mister!
I will, I will!

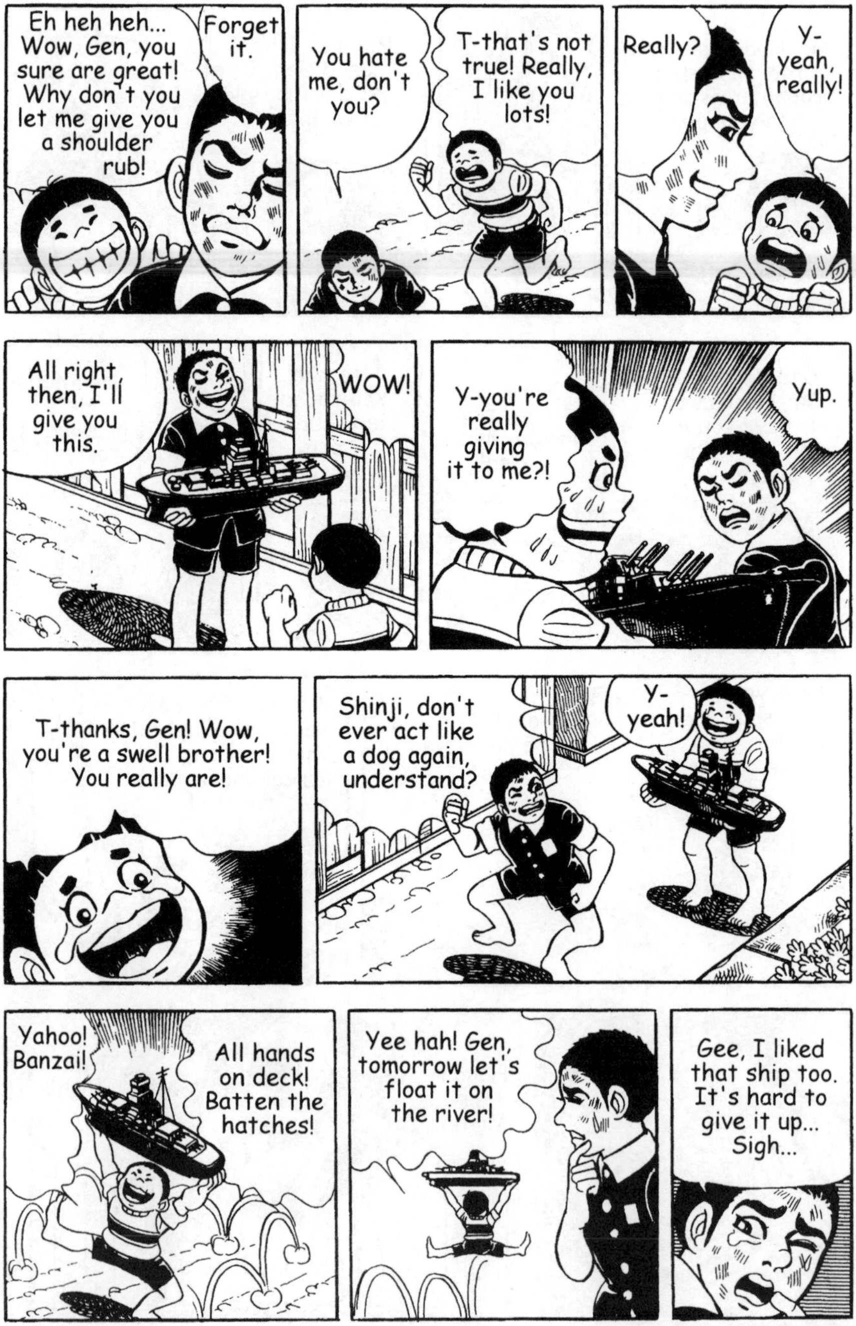
Eh heh heh... Wow, Gen, you sure are great! Why don't you let me give you a shoulder rub!
Forget it.
You hate me, don't you?
T-that's not true! Really, I like you lots!
Really?
Y- yeah, really!
All right, then, I'll give you this.
WOW!
Y-you're really giving it to me?!
Yup.
T-thanks, Gen! Wow, you're a swell brother! You really are!
Shinji, don't ever act like a dog again, understand?
Y- yeah!
Yahoo! Banzai!
All hands on deck! Batten the hatches!
Yee hah! Gen, tomorrow let's float it on the river!
Gee, I liked that ship too. It's hard to give it up... Sigh...

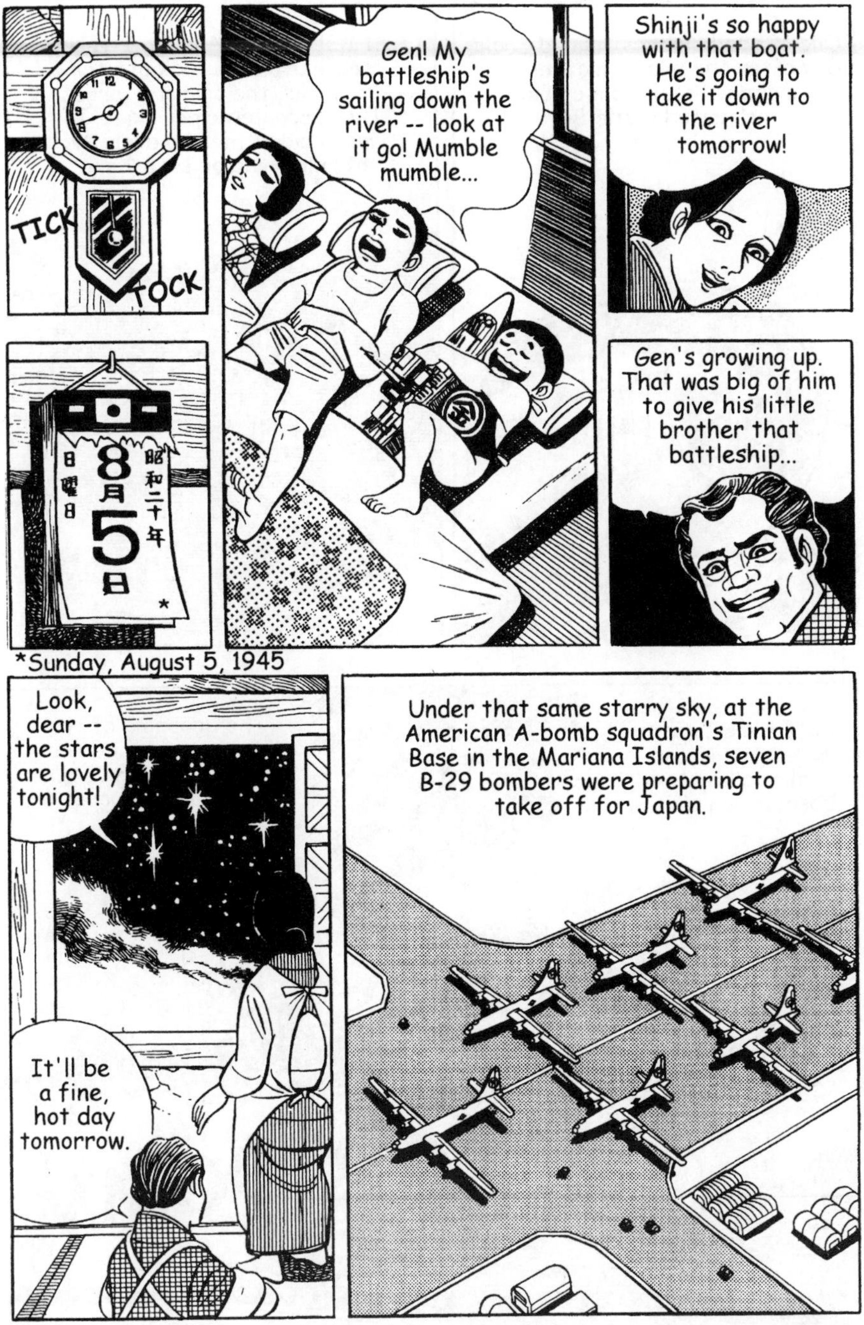
TICK
TOCK
昭和二十年
8月5日
日曜日
*
*Sunday, August 5, 1945
Gen! My battleship's sailing down the river -- look at it go! Mumble mumble...
Shinji's so happy with that boat. He's going to take it down to the river tomorrow!
Gen's growing up. That was big of him to give his little brother that battleship...
Look, dear -- the stars are lovely tonight!
It'll be a fine, hot day tomorrow.
Under that same starry sky, at the American A-bomb squadron's Tinian Base in the Mariana Islands, seven B-29 bombers were preparing to take off for Japan.

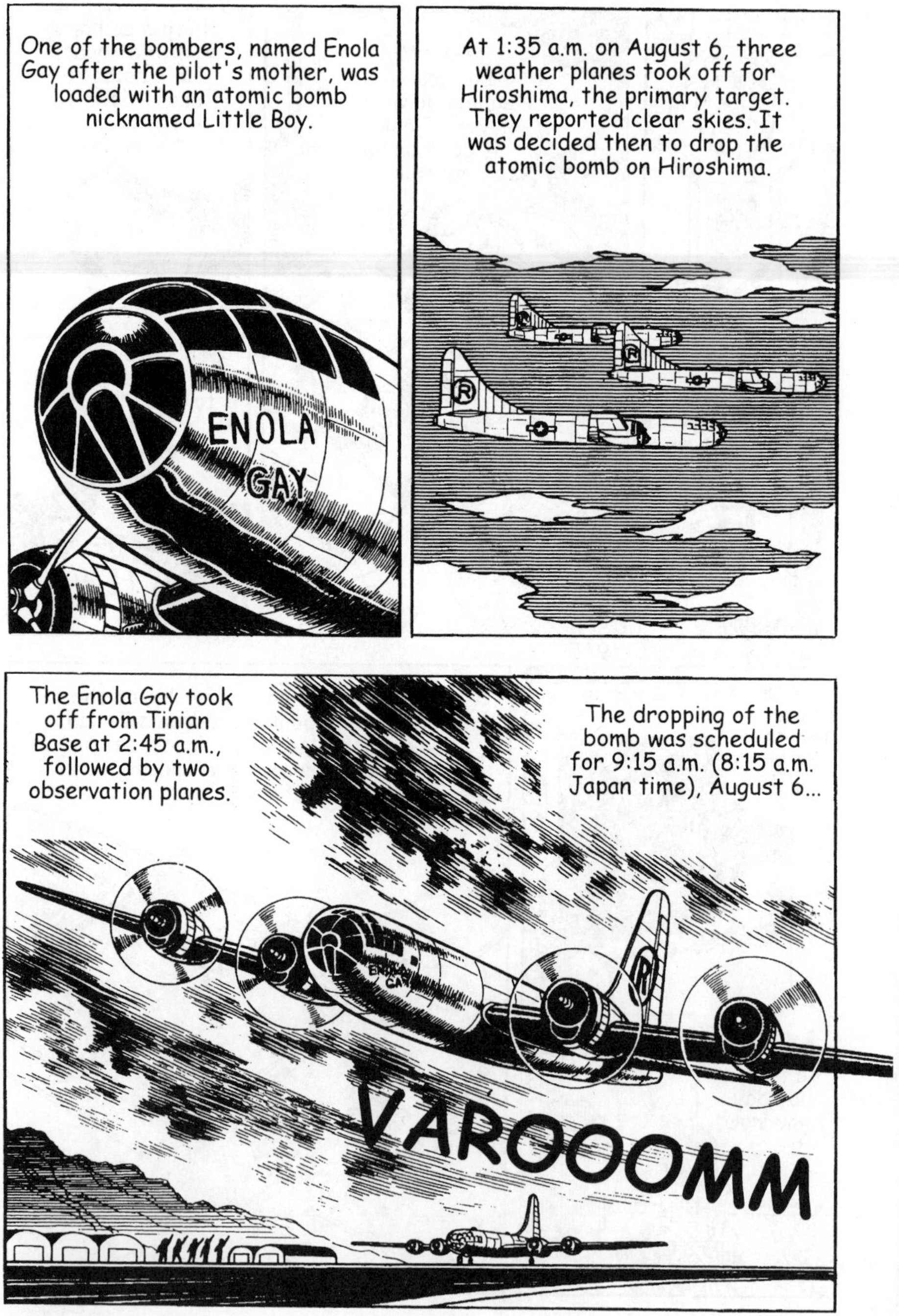
One of the bombers, named Enola Gay after the pilot's mother, was loaded with an atomic bomb nicknamed Little Boy.
ENOLA GAY
At 1:35 a.m. on August 6, three weather planes took off for Hiroshima, the primary target. They reported clear skies. It was decided then to drop the atomic bomb on Hiroshima.
The Enola Gay took off from Tinian Base at 2:45 a.m., followed by two observation planes.
The dropping of the bomb was scheduled for 9:15 a.m. (8:15 a.m. Japan time), August 6...
VAROOOMM

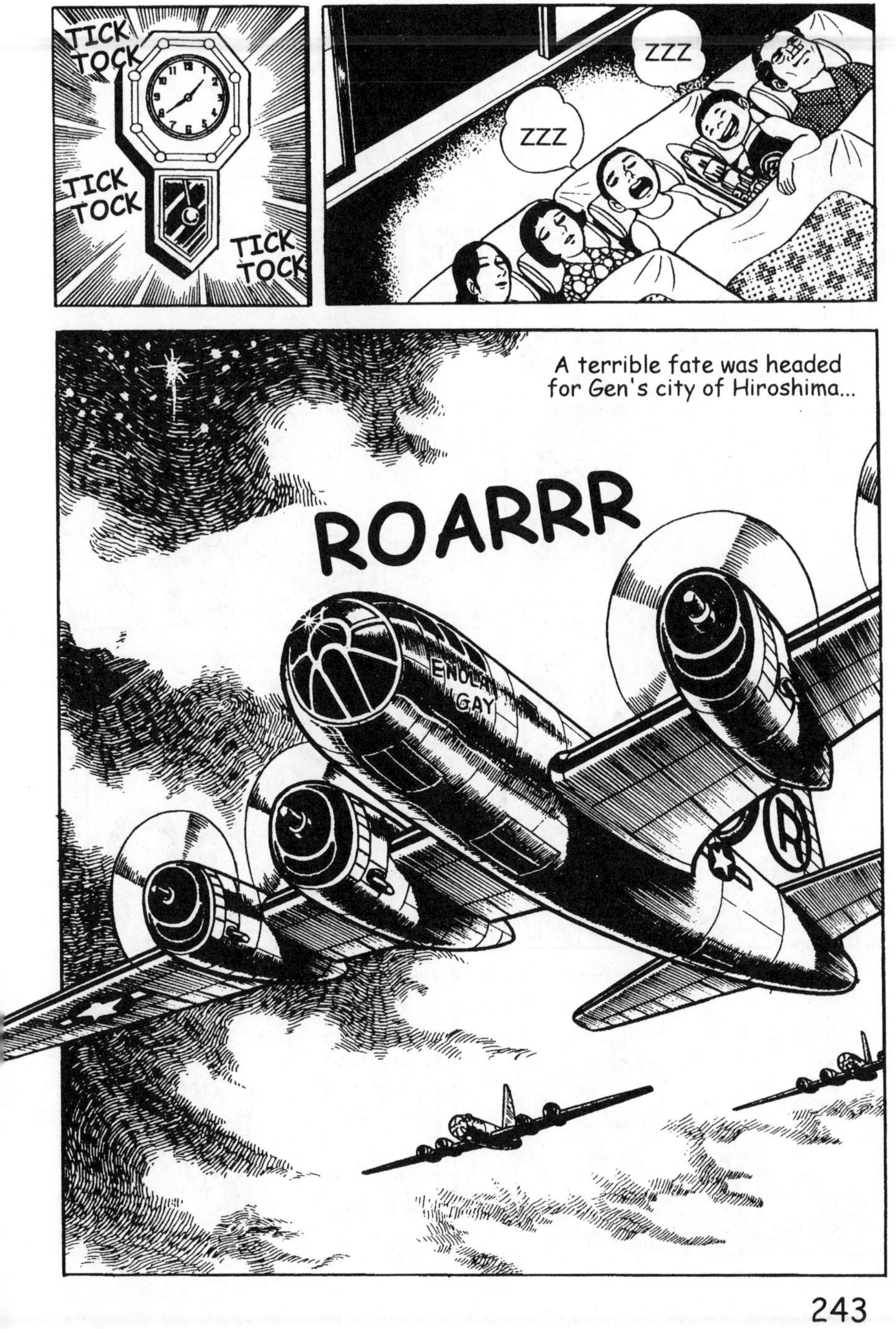
TICK TOCK
TICK TOCK
TICK TOCK
ZZZ
ZZZ
A terrible fate was headed for Gen's city of Hiroshima...
ROARRR
ENOLA GAY

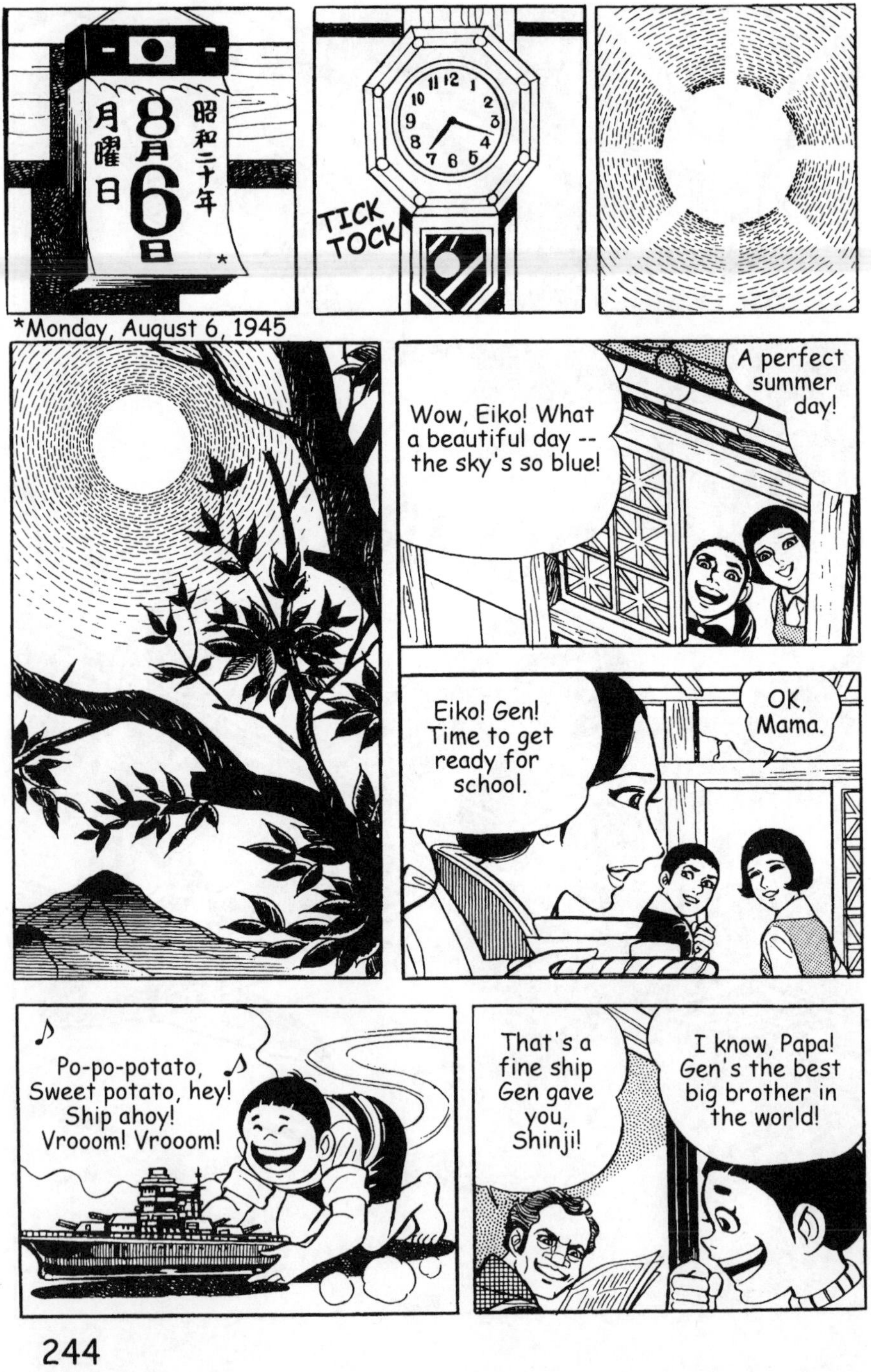
昭和二十年
8月6日
月曜日
*Monday, August 6, 1945
TICK TOCK
Wow, Eiko! What a beautiful day -- the sky's so blue!
A perfect summer day!
Eiko! Gen! Time to get ready for school.
OK, Mama.
Po-po-potato, Sweet potato, hey! Ship ahoy! Vrooom! Vrooom!
That's a fine ship Gen gave you, Shinji!
I know, Papa! Gen's the best big brother in the world!

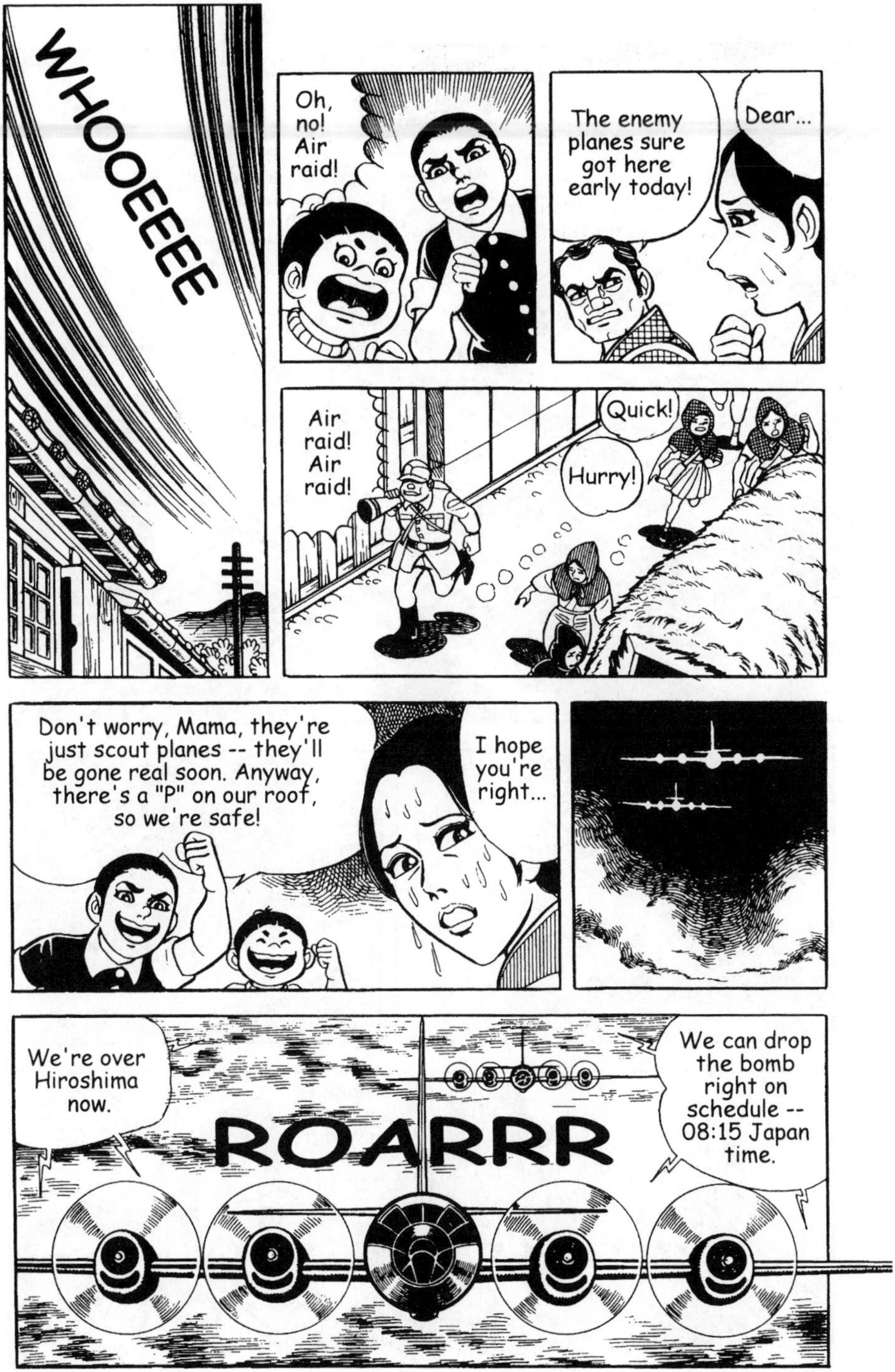
WHOOEEEE
Oh, no! Air raid!
The enemy planes sure got here early today!
Dear...
Air raid! Air raid!
Quick!
Hurry!
Don't worry, Mama, they're just scout planes -- they'll be gone real soon. Anyway, there's a "P" on our roof, so we're safe!
I hope you're right...
We're over Hiroshima now.
ROARRR
We can drop the bomb right on schedule -- 08:15 Japan time.

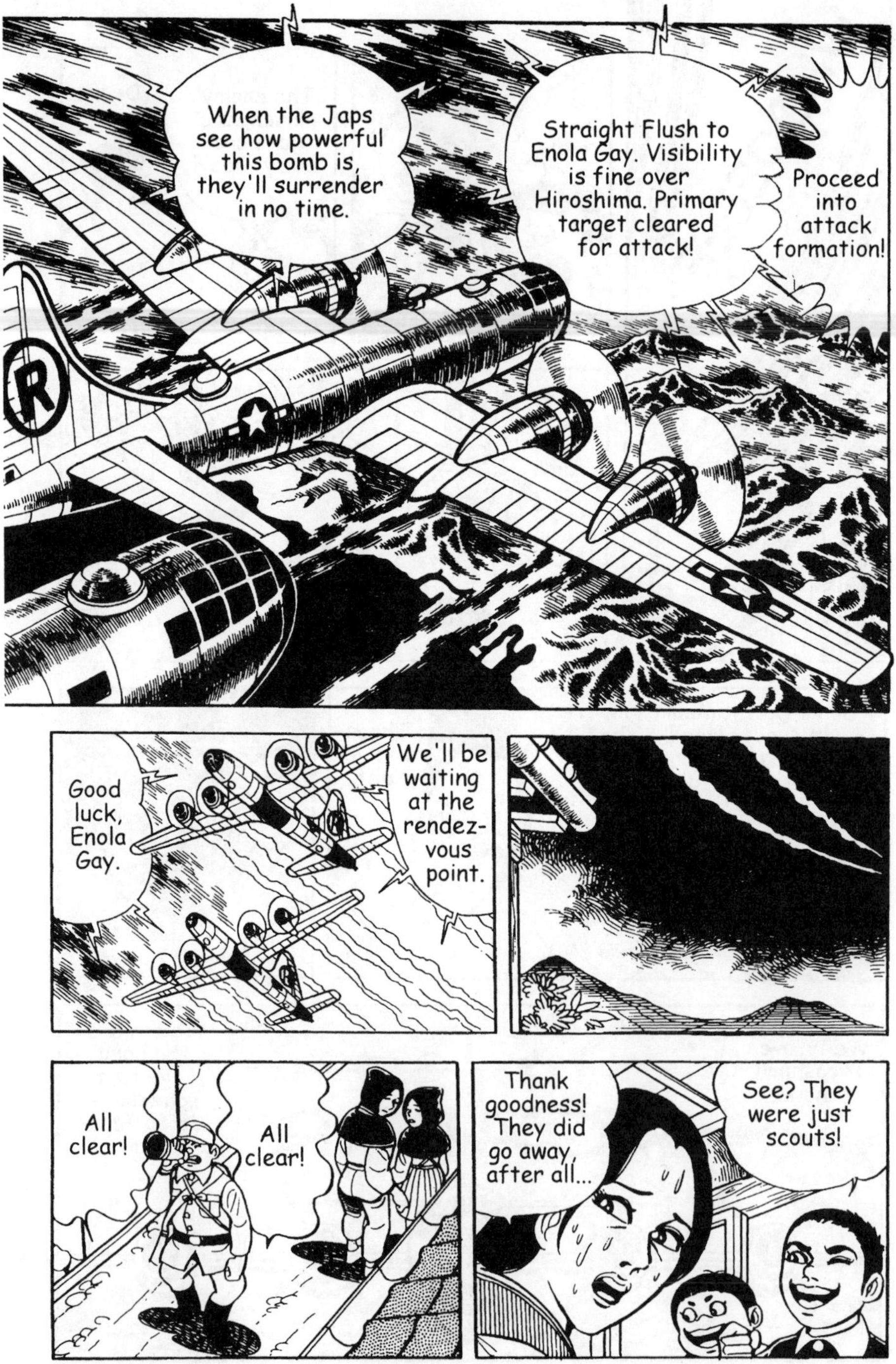
When the Japs see how powerful this bomb is, they'll surrender in no time.
Straight Flush to Enola Gay. Visibility is fine over Hiroshima. Primary target cleared for attack!
Proceed into attack formation!
Good luck, Enola Gay.
We'll be waiting at the rendez-vous point.
All clear!
All clear!
Thank goodness! They did go away after all...
See? They were just scouts!

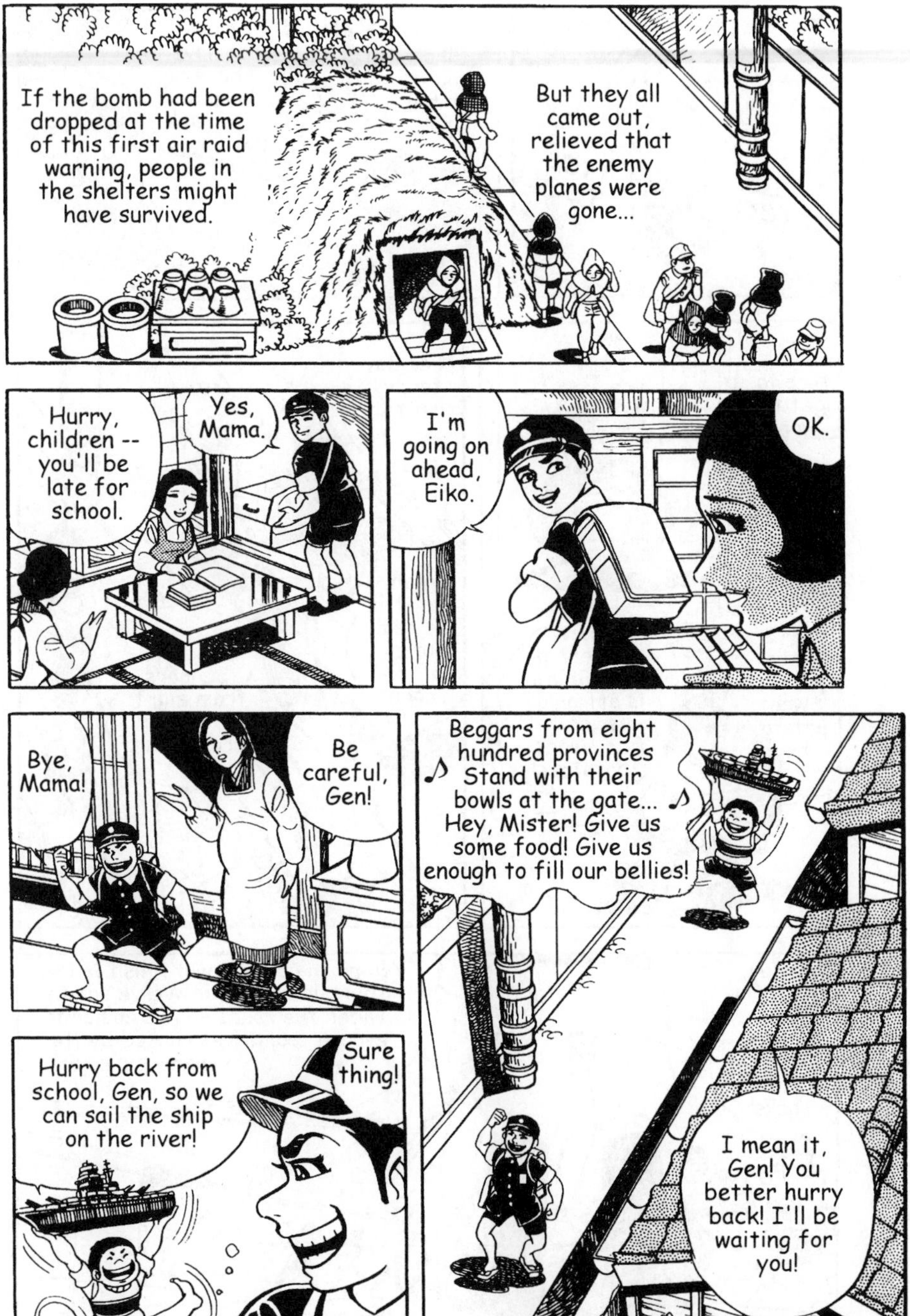
If the bomb had been dropped at the time of this first air raid warning, people in the shelters might have survived.
But they all came out, relieved that the enemy planes were gone...
Hurry, children -- you'll be late for school.
Yes, Mama.
I'm going on ahead, Eiko.
OK.
Bye, Mama!
Be careful, Gen!
Hurry back from school, Gen, so we can sail the ship on the river!
Sure thing!
Beggars from eight hundred provinces Stand with their bowls at the gate... Hey, Mister! Give us some food! Give us enough to fill our bellies!
I mean it, Gen! You better hurry back! I'll be waiting for you!

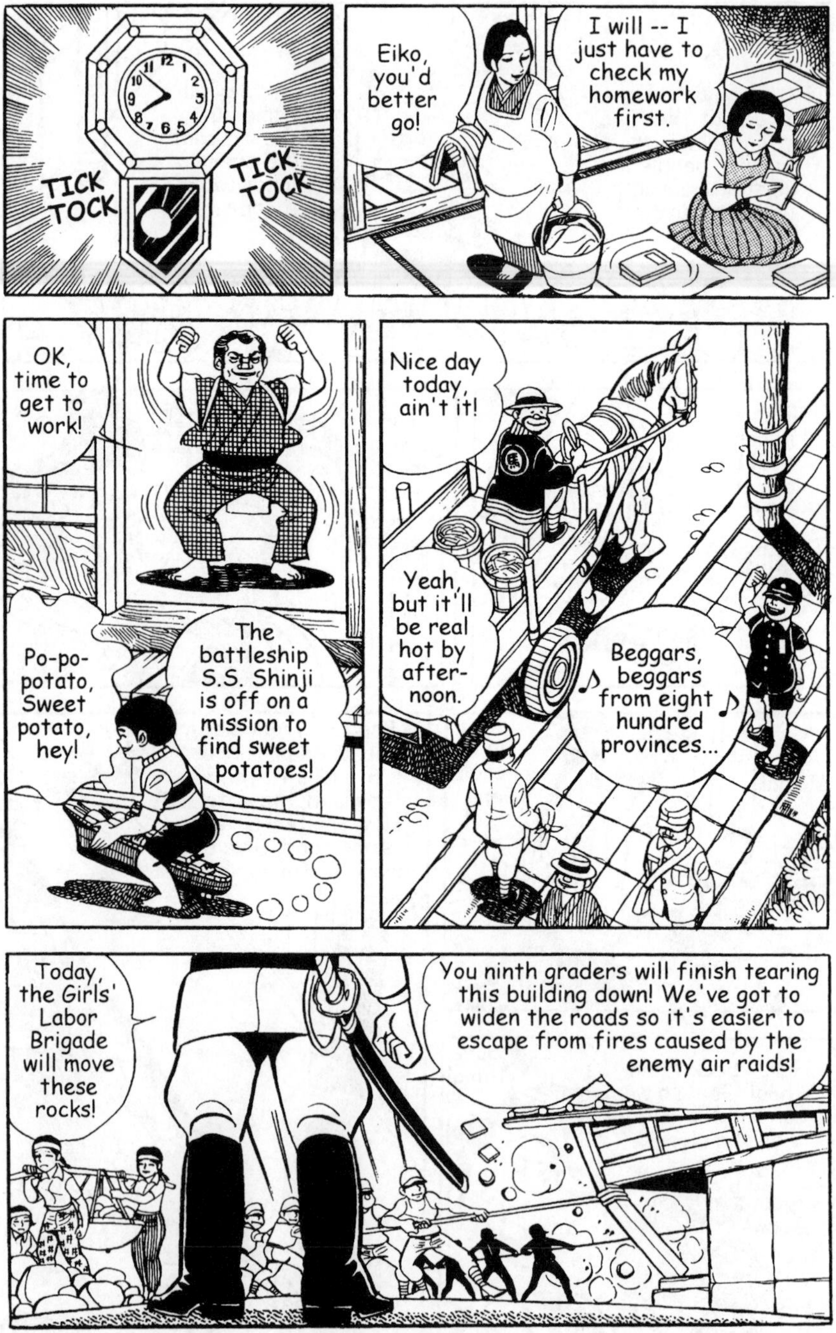
TICK TOCK
TICK TOCK
Eiko, you'd better go!
I will -- I just have to check my homework first.
OK, time to get to work!
Po-po-potato, Sweet potato, hey!
The battleship S.S. Shinji is off on a mission to find sweet potatoes!
Nice day today, ain't it!
Yeah, but it'll be real hot by afternoon.
Beggars, beggars from eight hundred provinces...
Today, the Girls' Labor Brigade will move these rocks!
You ninth graders will finish tearing this building down! We've got to widen the roads so it's easier to escape from fires caused by the enemy air raids!

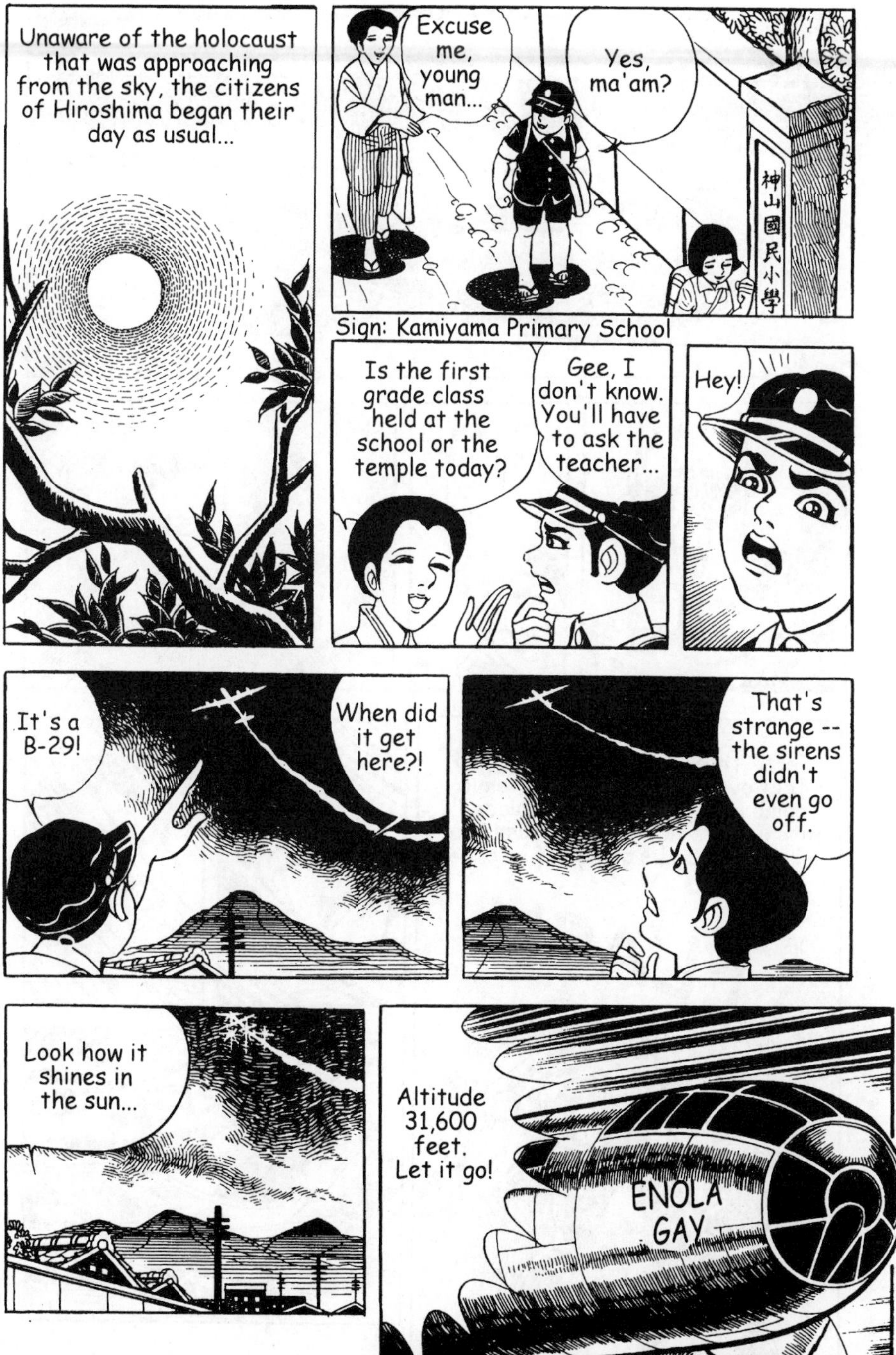
Unaware of the holocaust that was approaching from the sky, the citizens of Hiroshima began their day as usual...
Excuse me, young man...
Yes, ma'am?
神山國民小學
Sign: Kamiyama Primary School
Is the first grade class held at the school or the temple today?
Gee, I don't know. You'll have to ask the teacher...
Hey!
It's a B-29!
When did it get here?!
That's strange -- the sirens didn't even go off.
Look how it shines in the sun...
Altitude 31,600 feet. Let it go!
ENOLA GAY

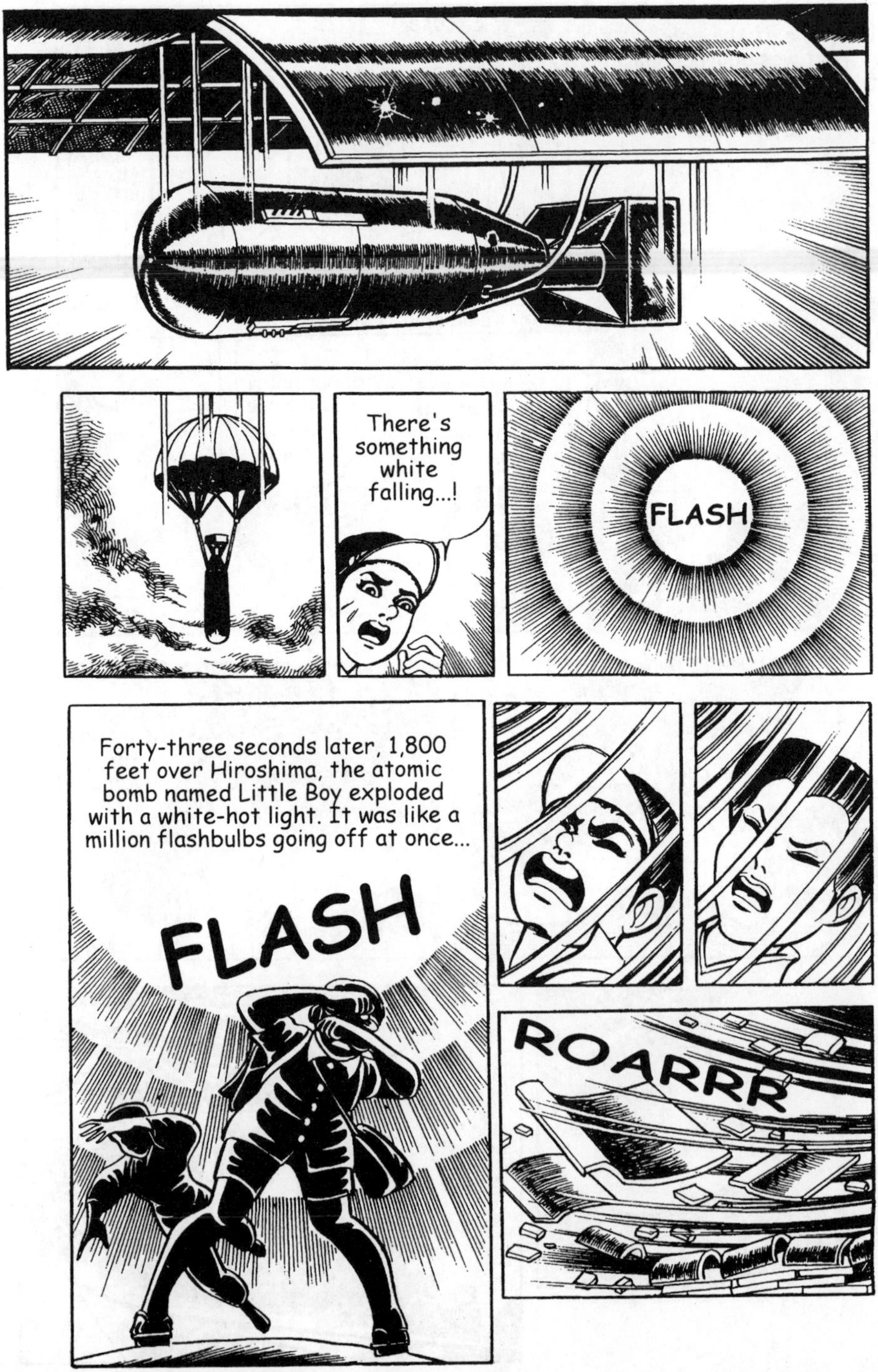
There's something white falling...!
FLASH
Forty-three seconds later, 1,800 feet over Hiroshima, the atomic bomb named Little Boy exploded with a white-hot light. It was like a million flashbulbs going off at once...
FLASH
ROARRR

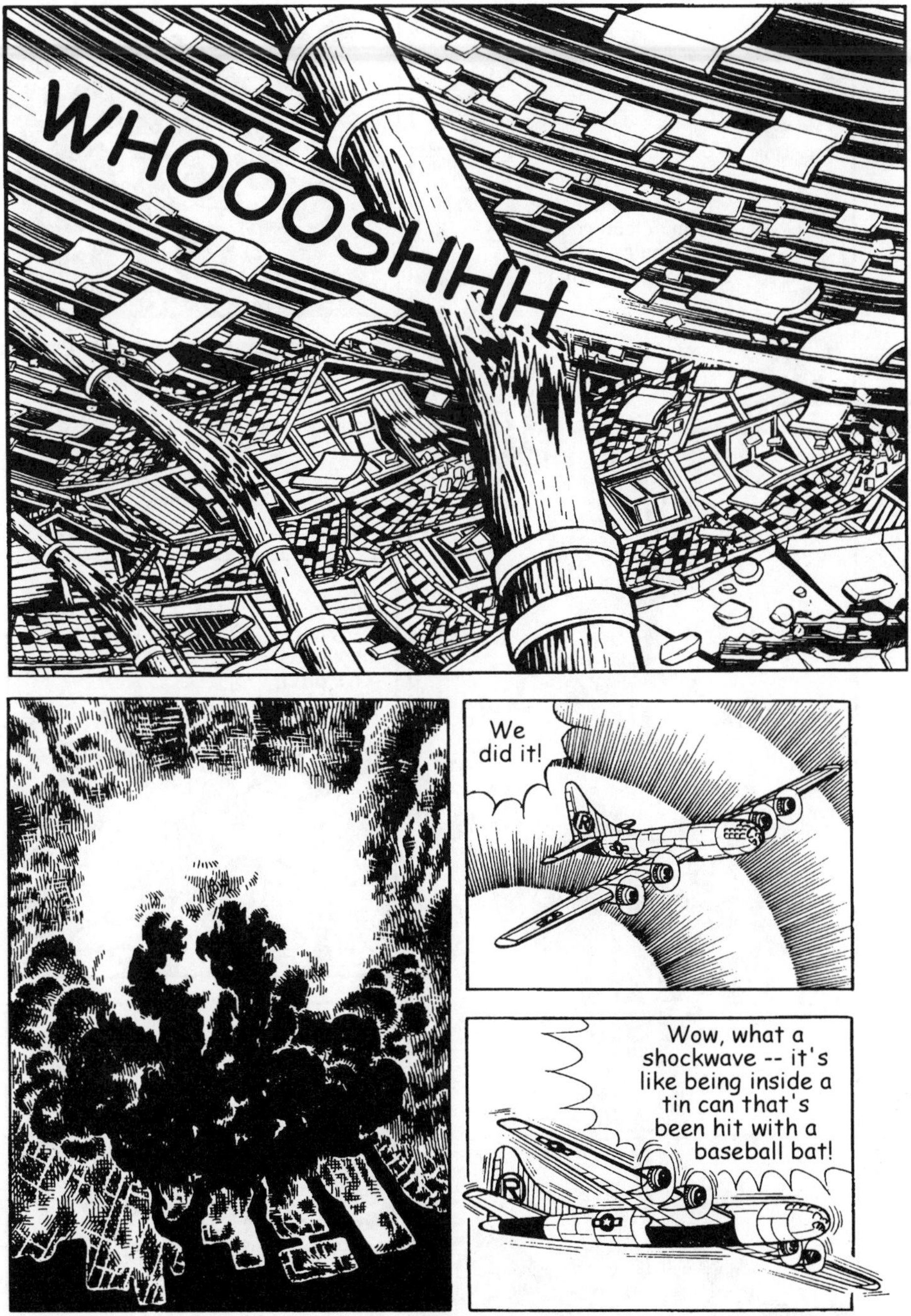
WHOOOSHHH
We did it!
Wow, what a shockwave -- it's like being inside a tin can that's been hit with a baseball bat!

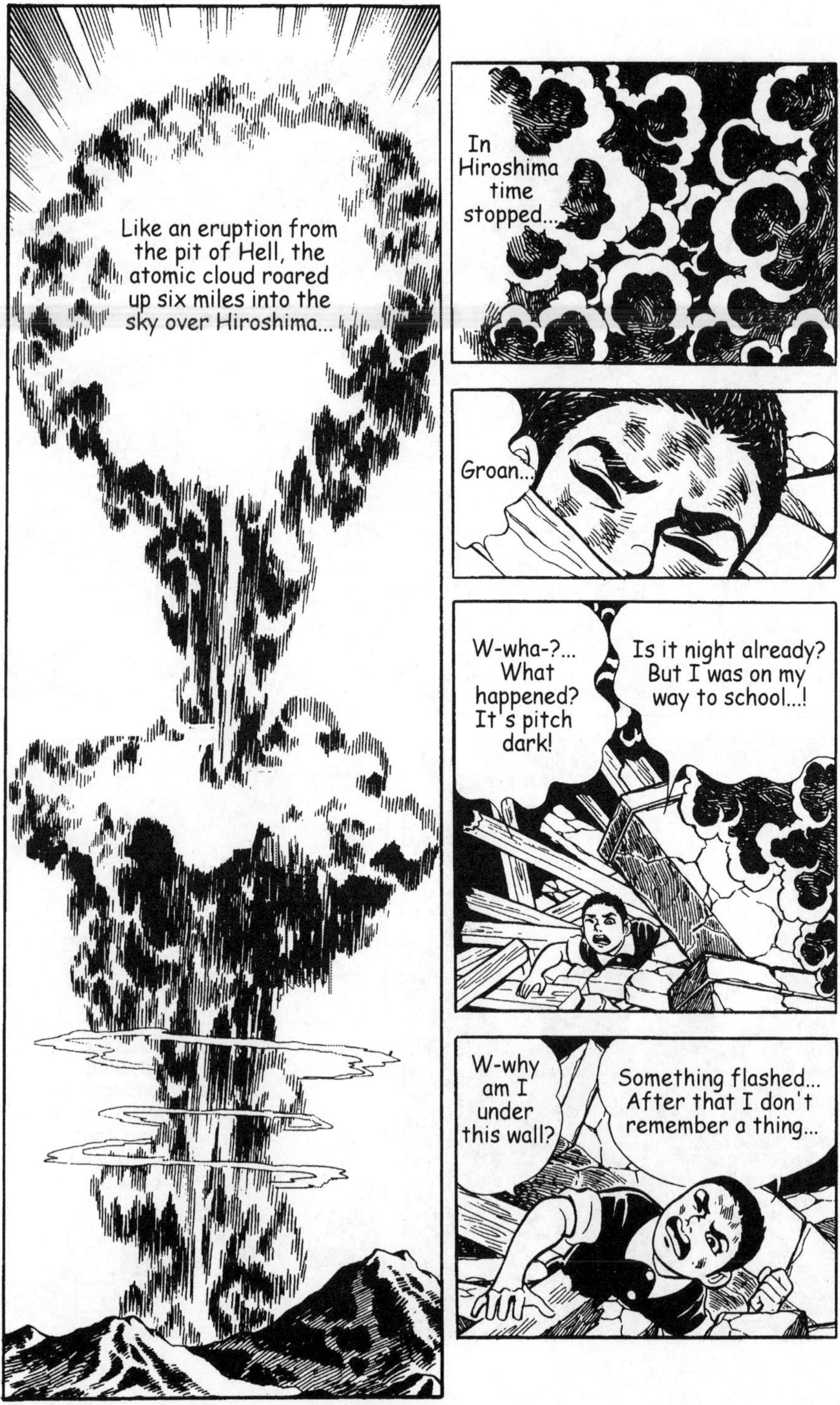
Like an eruption from the pit of Hell, the atomic cloud roared up six miles into the sky over Hiroshima...
In Hiroshima time stopped...
Groan...
W-wha-?... What happened? It's pitch dark!
Is it night already? But I was on my way to school...!
W-why am I under this wall?
Something flashed... After that I don't remember a thing...

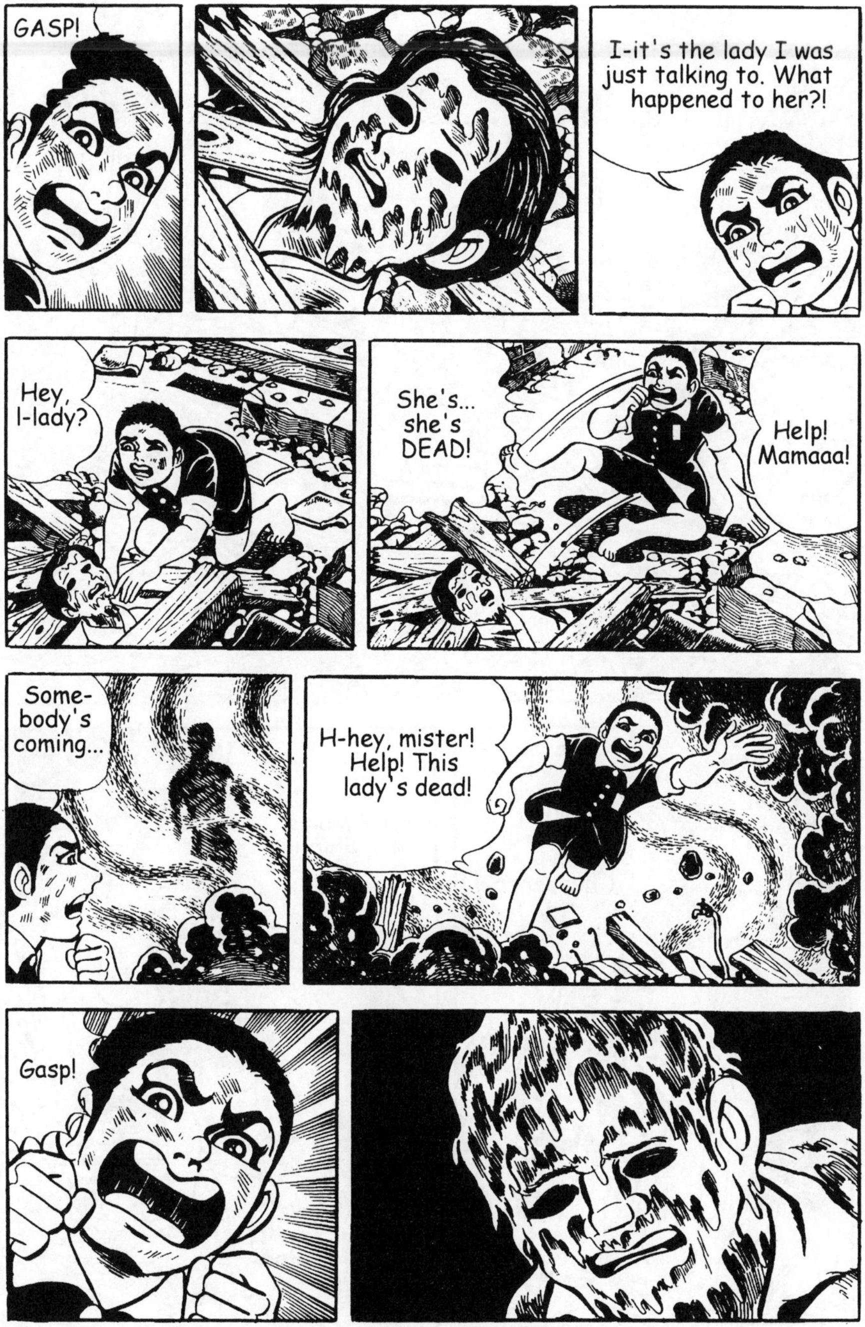
GASP!
I-it's the lady I was just talking to. What happened to her?!
Hey, I-lady?
She's... she's DEAD!
Help! Mamaaa!
Some-body's coming...
H-hey, mister! Help! This lady's dead!
Gasp!

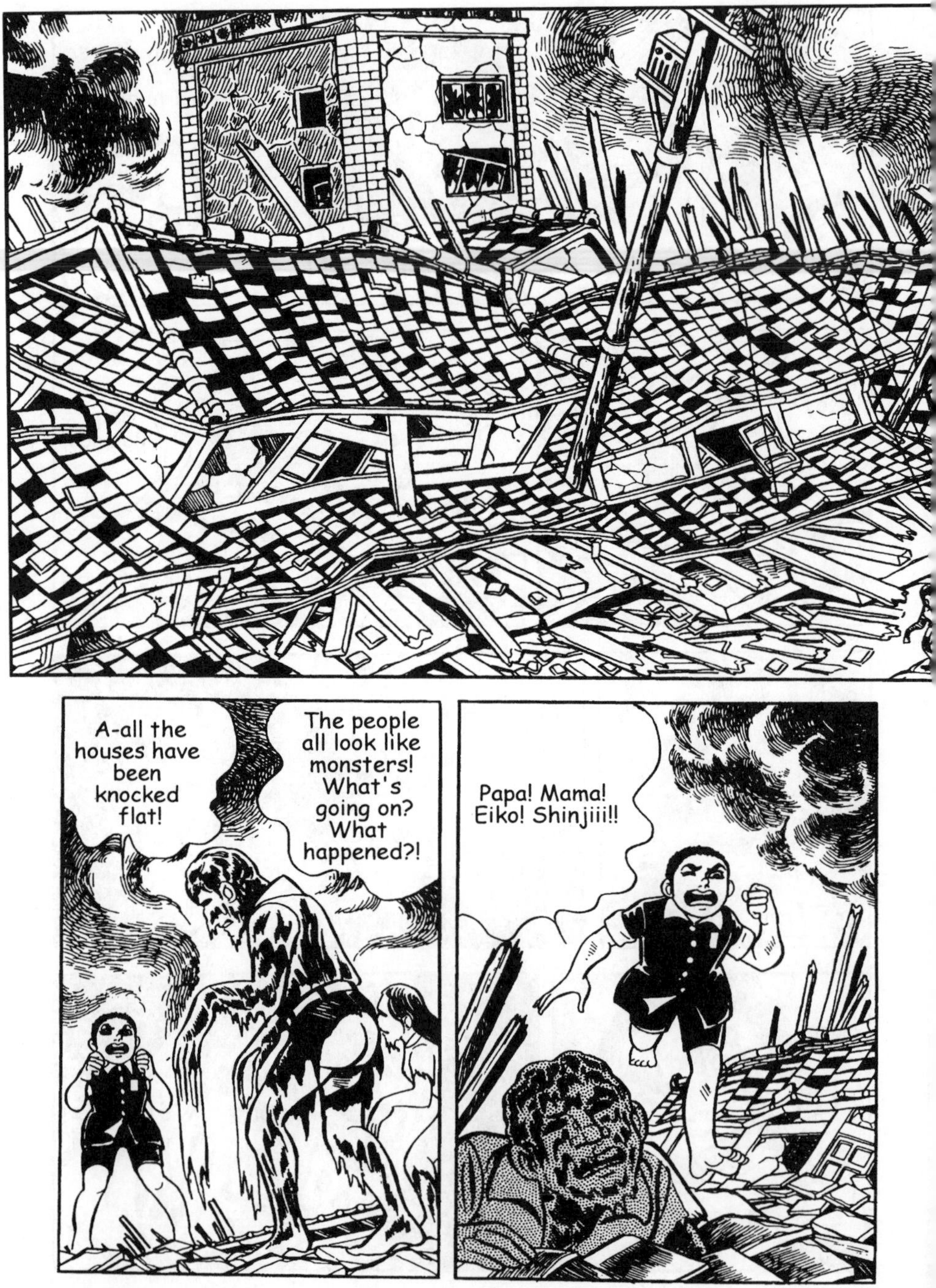
A-all the houses have been knocked flat!
The people all look like monsters! What's going on? What happened?!
Papa! Mama! Eiko! Shinjiii!!

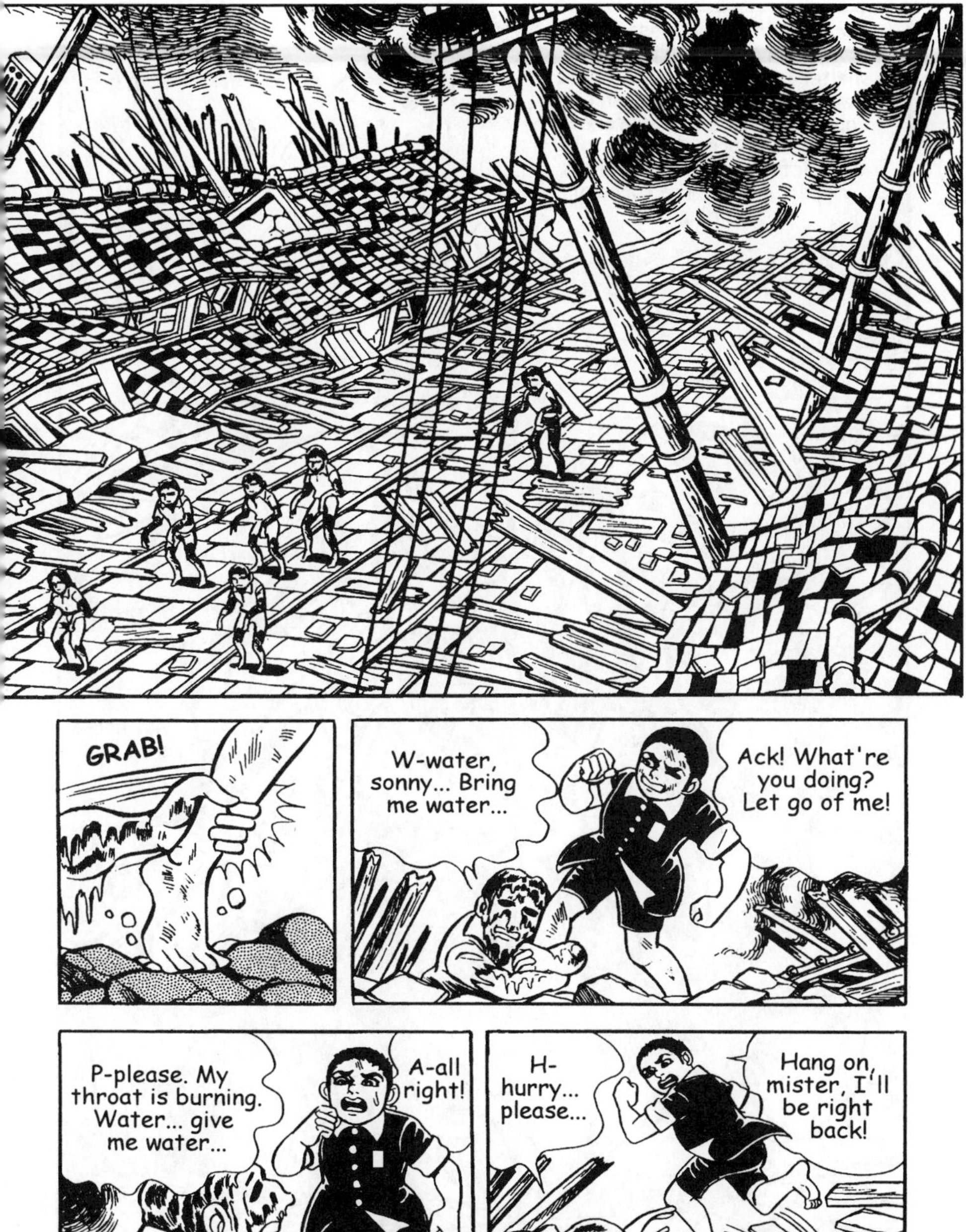
GRAB!
W-water, sonny... Bring me water...
Ack! What're you doing? Let go of me!
P-please. My throat is burning. Water... give me water...
A-all right!
H- hurry... please...
Hang on, mister, I'll be right back!

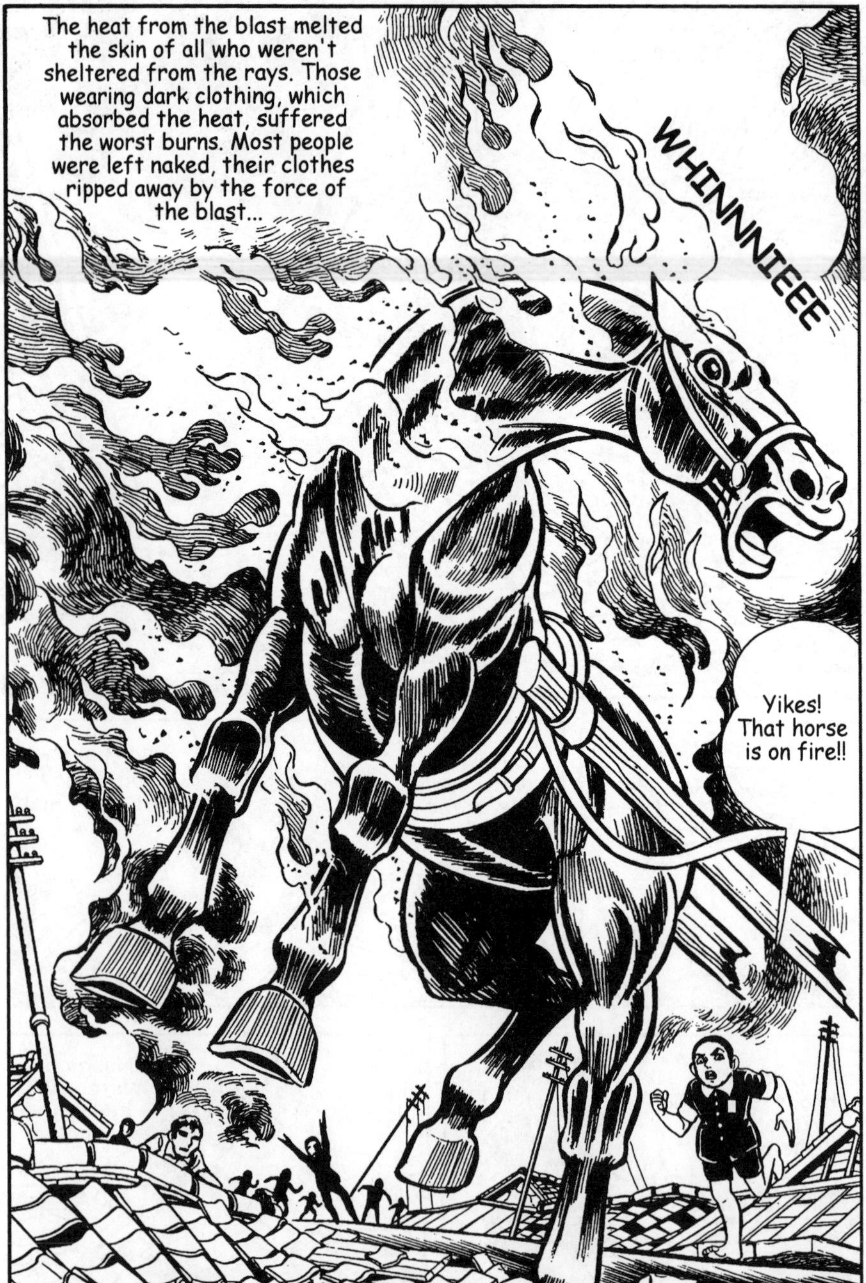
The heat from the blast melted the skin of all who weren't sheltered from the rays. Those wearing dark clothing, which absorbed the heat, suffered the worst burns. Most people were left naked, their clothes ripped away by the force of the blast...
WHINNNIEEE
Yikes! That horse is on fire!!

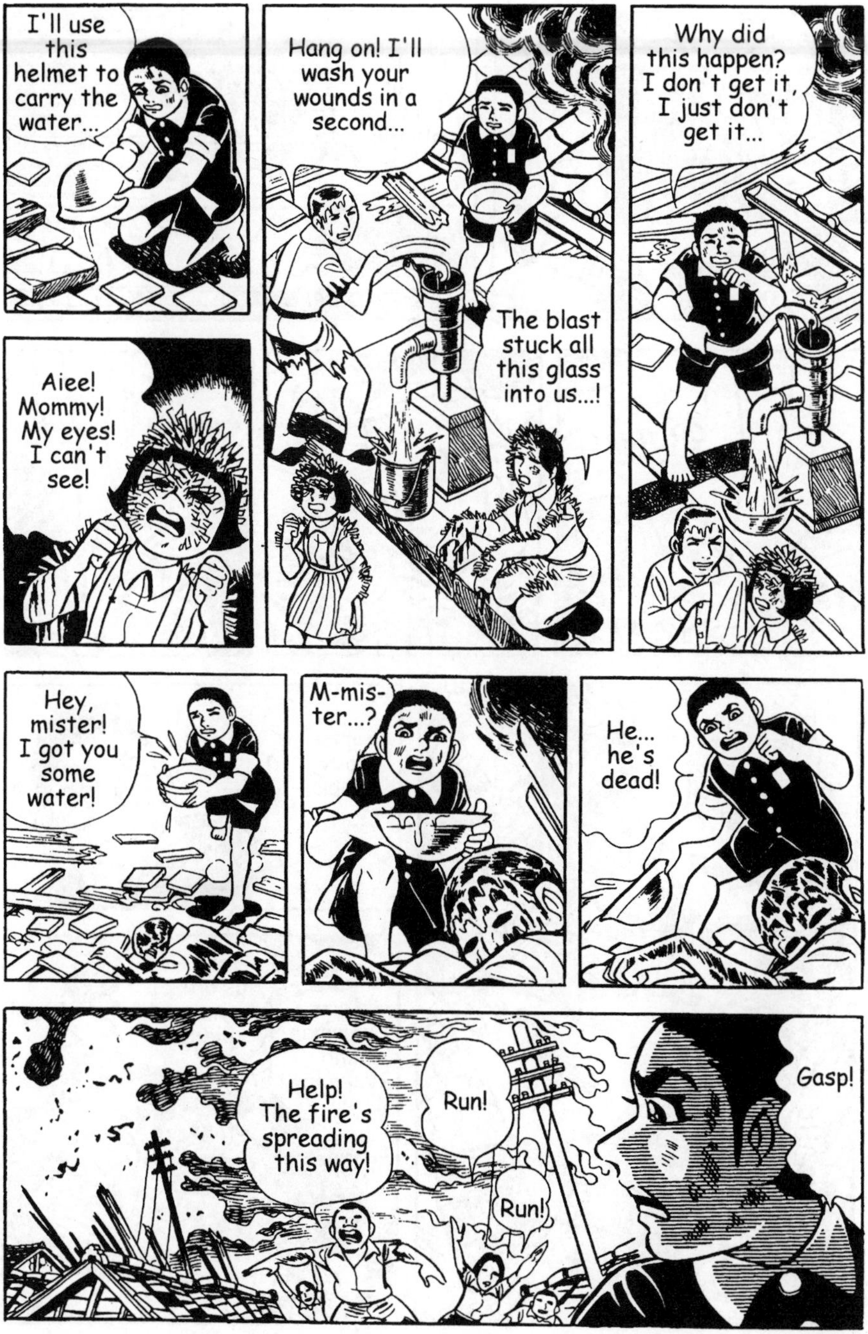
I'll use this helmet to carry the water...
Hang on! I'll wash your wounds in a second...
The blast stuck all this glass into us...!
Why did this happen? I don't get it, I just don't get it...
Aiee! Mommy! My eyes! I can't see!
Hey, mister! I got you some water!
M-mister...?
He... he's dead!
Help! The fire's spreading this way!
Run!
Run!
Gasp!

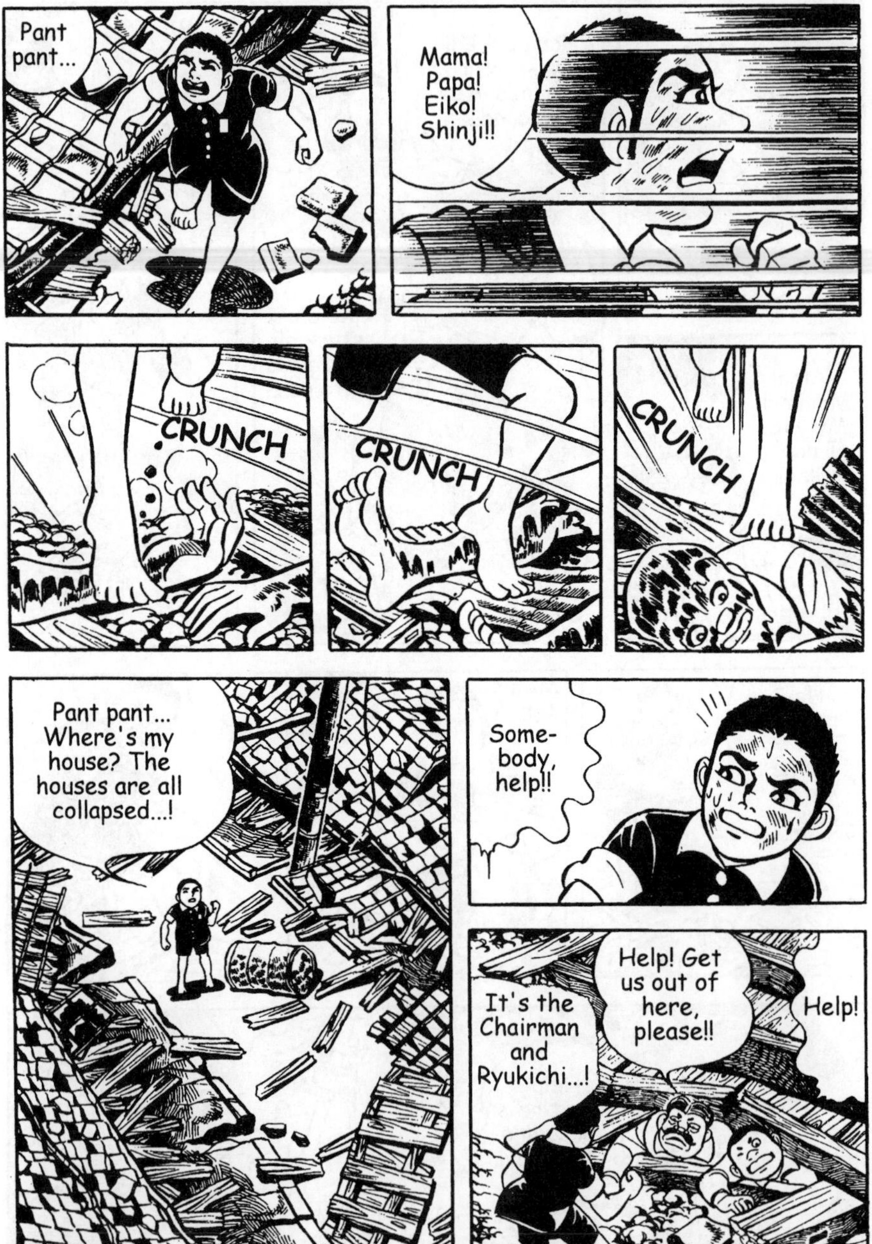
Pant pant...
Mama! Papa! Eiko! Shinji!!
CRUNCH
CRUNCH
CRUNCH
Pant pant... Where's my house? The houses are all collapsed...!
Some-body, help!!
It's the Chairman and Ryukichi...!
Help! Get us out of here, please!!
Help!

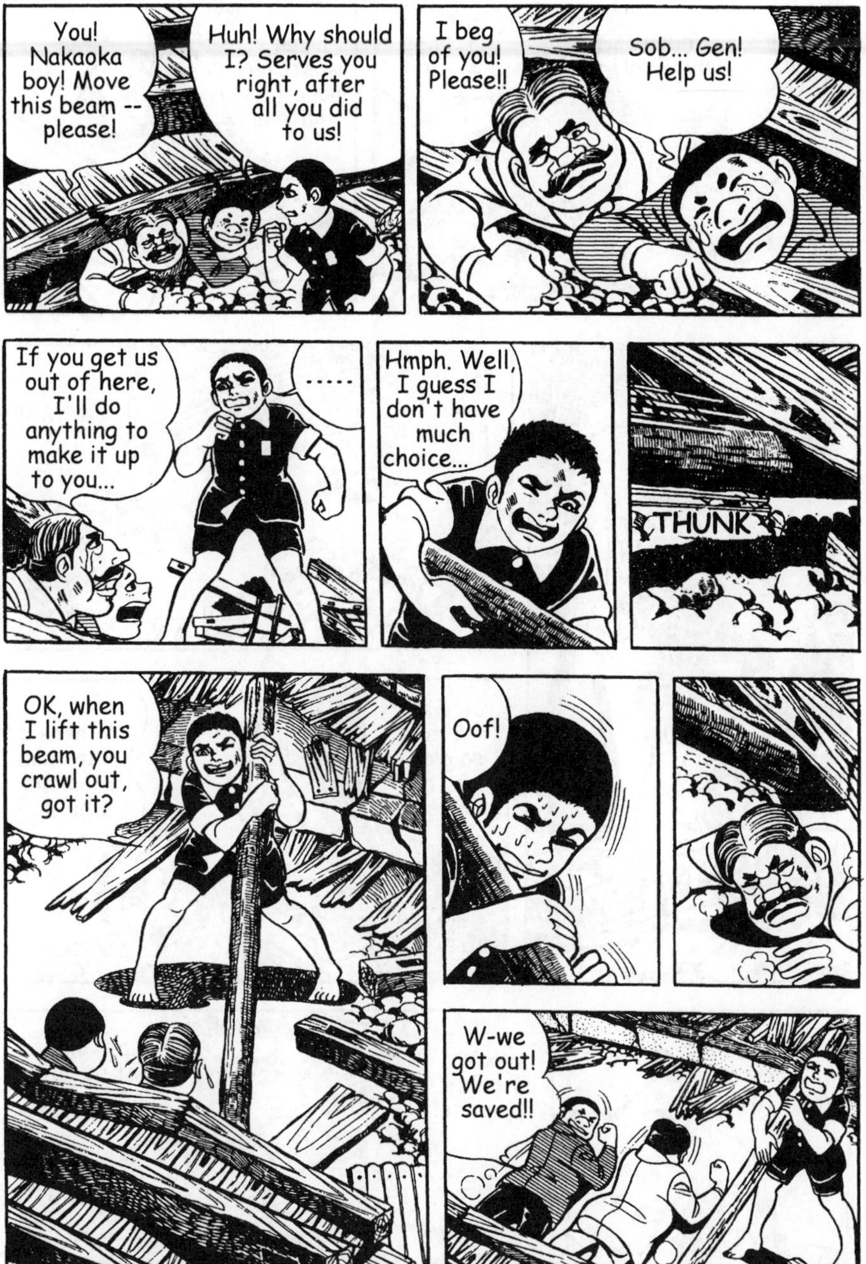
You! Nakaoka boy! Move this beam -- please!
Huh! Why should I? Serves you right, after all you did to us!
I beg of you! Please!!
Sob... Gen! Help us!
If you get us out of here, I'll do anything to make it up to you...

Hmph. Well, I guess I don't have much choice...
THUNK
OK, when I lift this beam, you crawl out, got it?
Oof!
W-we got out! We're saved!!

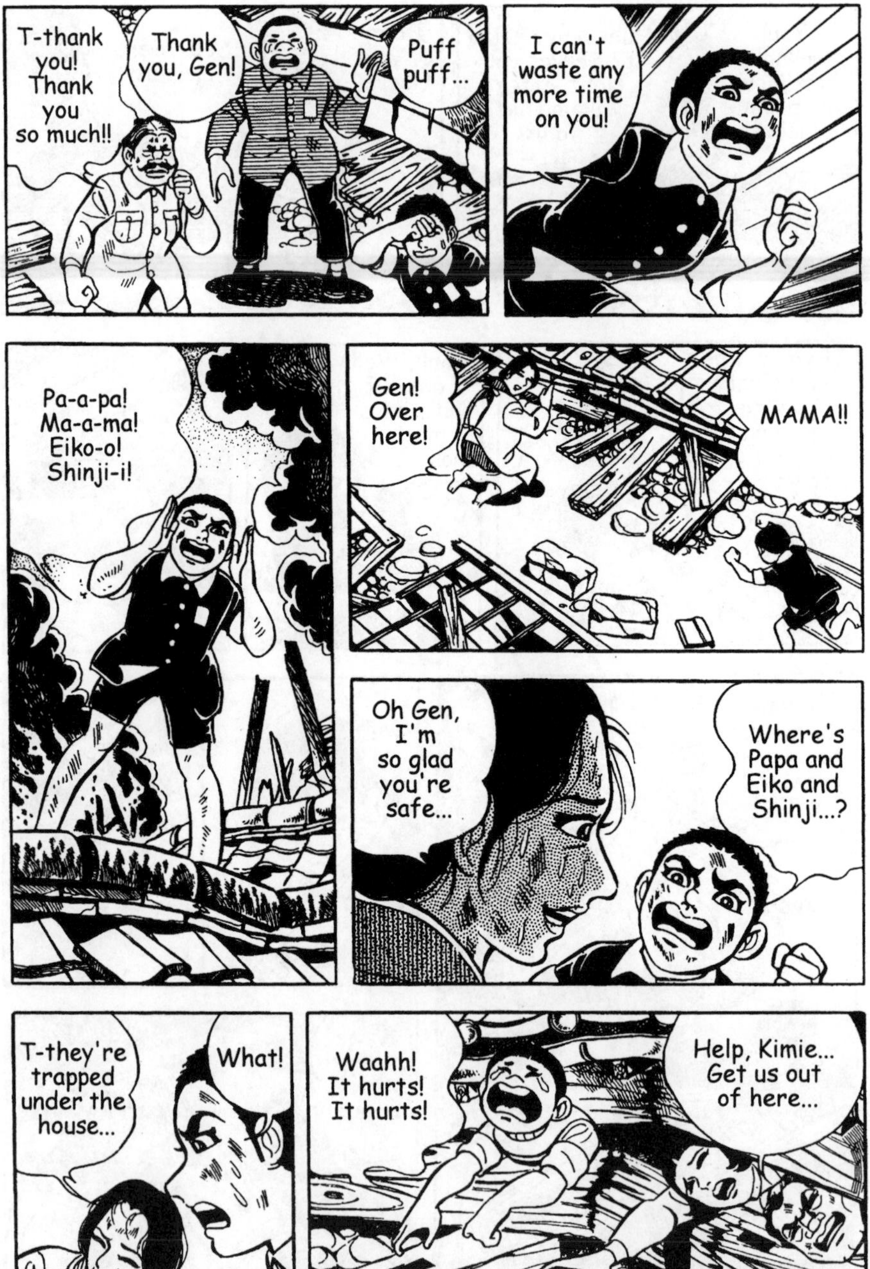
T-thank you! Thank you so much!!
Thank you, Gen!
Puff puff...
I can't waste any more time on you!
Pa-a-pa! Ma-a-ma! Eiko-o! Shinji-i!
Gen! Over here!
MAMA!!
Oh Gen, I'm so glad you're safe...
Where's Papa and Eiko and Shinji...?
T-they're trapped under the house...
What!
Waahh! It hurts! It hurts!
Help, Kimie... Get us out of here...

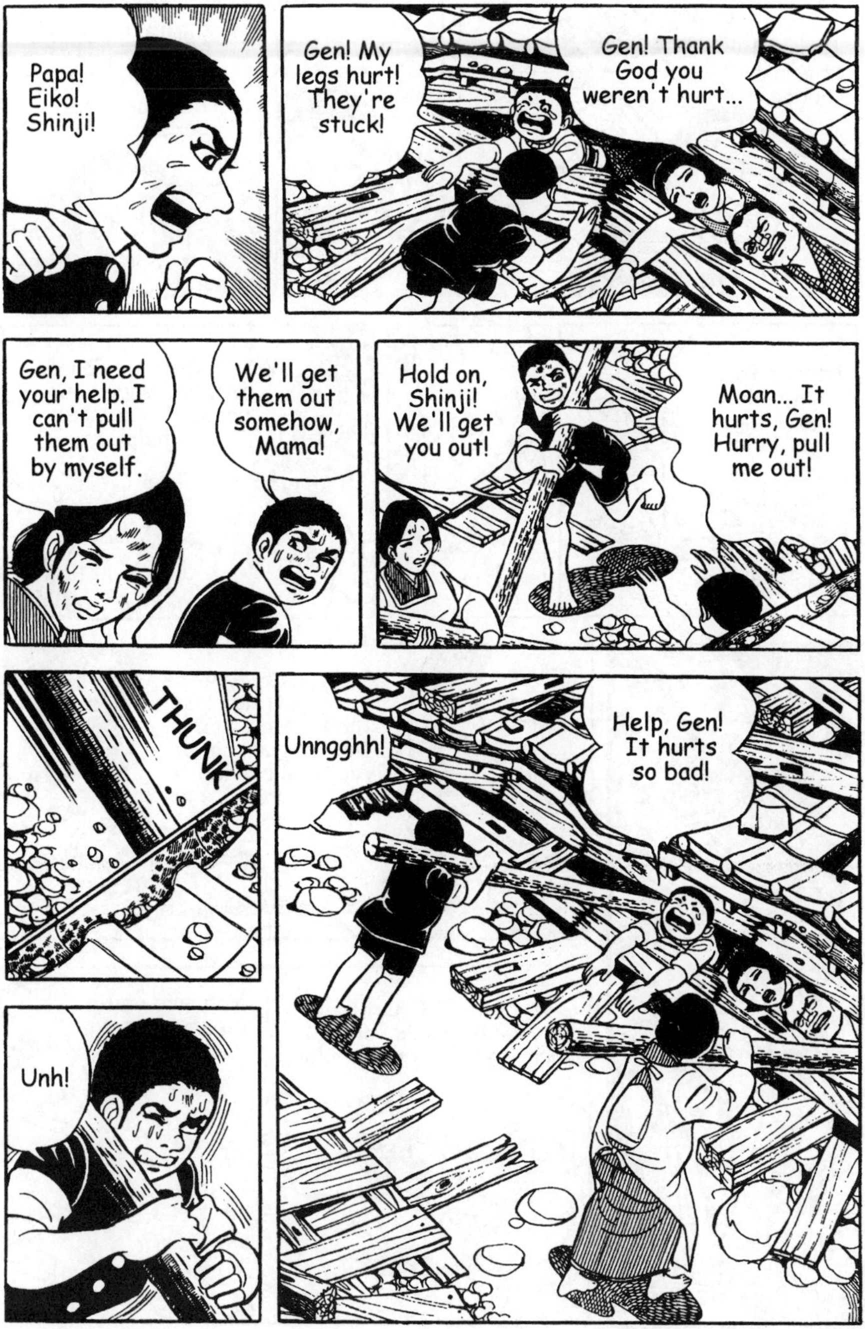
Papa! Eiko! Shinji!
Gen! My legs hurt! They're stuck!
Gen! Thank God you weren't hurt...
Gen, I need your help. I can't pull them out by myself.
We'll get them out somehow, Mama!
Hold on, Shinji! We'll get you out!
Moan... It hurts, Gen! Hurry, pull me out!
THUNK
Unngghh!
Help, Gen! It hurts so bad!
Unh!

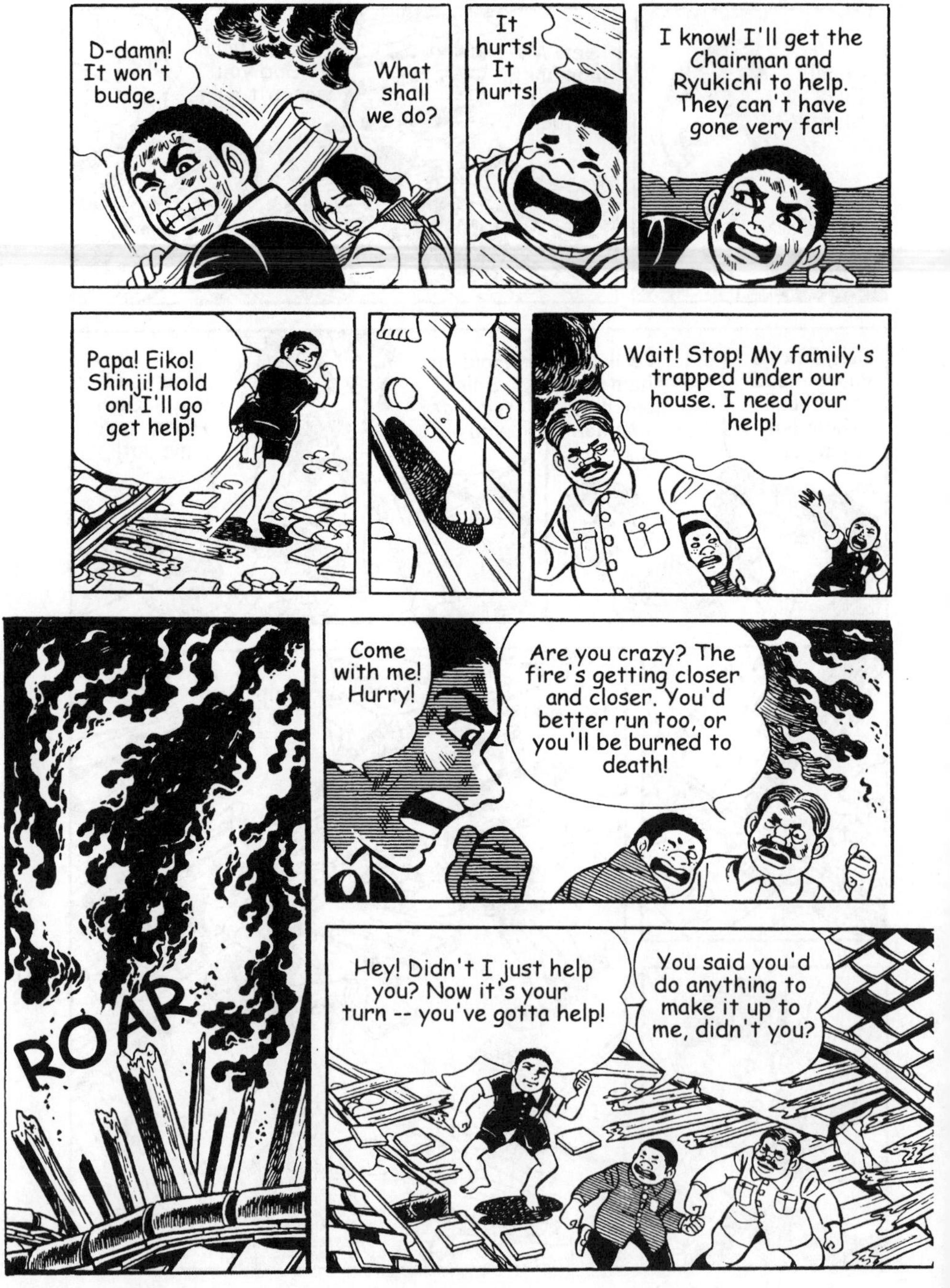
D-damn! It won't budge.
What shall we do?
It hurts! It hurts!
I know! I'll get the Chairman and Ryukichi to help. They can't have gone very far!
Papa! Eiko! Shinji! Hold on! I'll go get help!
Wait! Stop! My family's trapped under our house. I need your help!
ROAR
Come with me! Hurry!
Are you crazy? The fire's getting closer and closer. You'd better run too, or you'll be burned to death!
Hey! Didn't I just help you? Now it's your turn -- you've gotta help!
You said you'd do anything to make it up to me, didn't you?

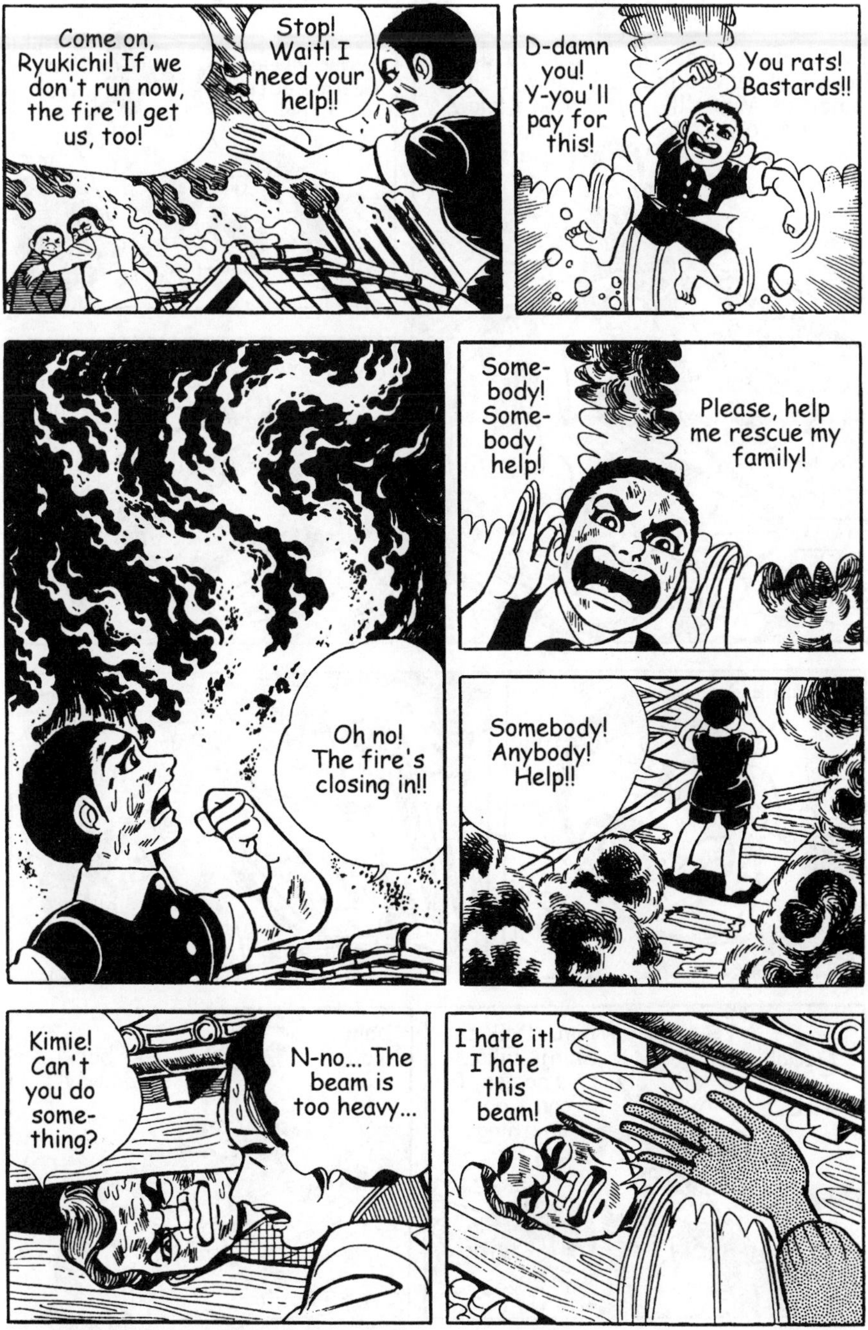
Come on, Ryukichi! If we don't run now, the fire'll get us, too!
Stop! Wait! I need your help!!
D-damn you! Y-you'll pay for this!
You rats! Bastards!!
Oh no! The fire's closing in!!
Some-body! Some-body help!
Please, help me rescue my family!
Somebody! Anybody! Help!!
Kimie! Can't you do some-thing?
N-no... The beam is too heavy...
I hate it! I hate this beam!

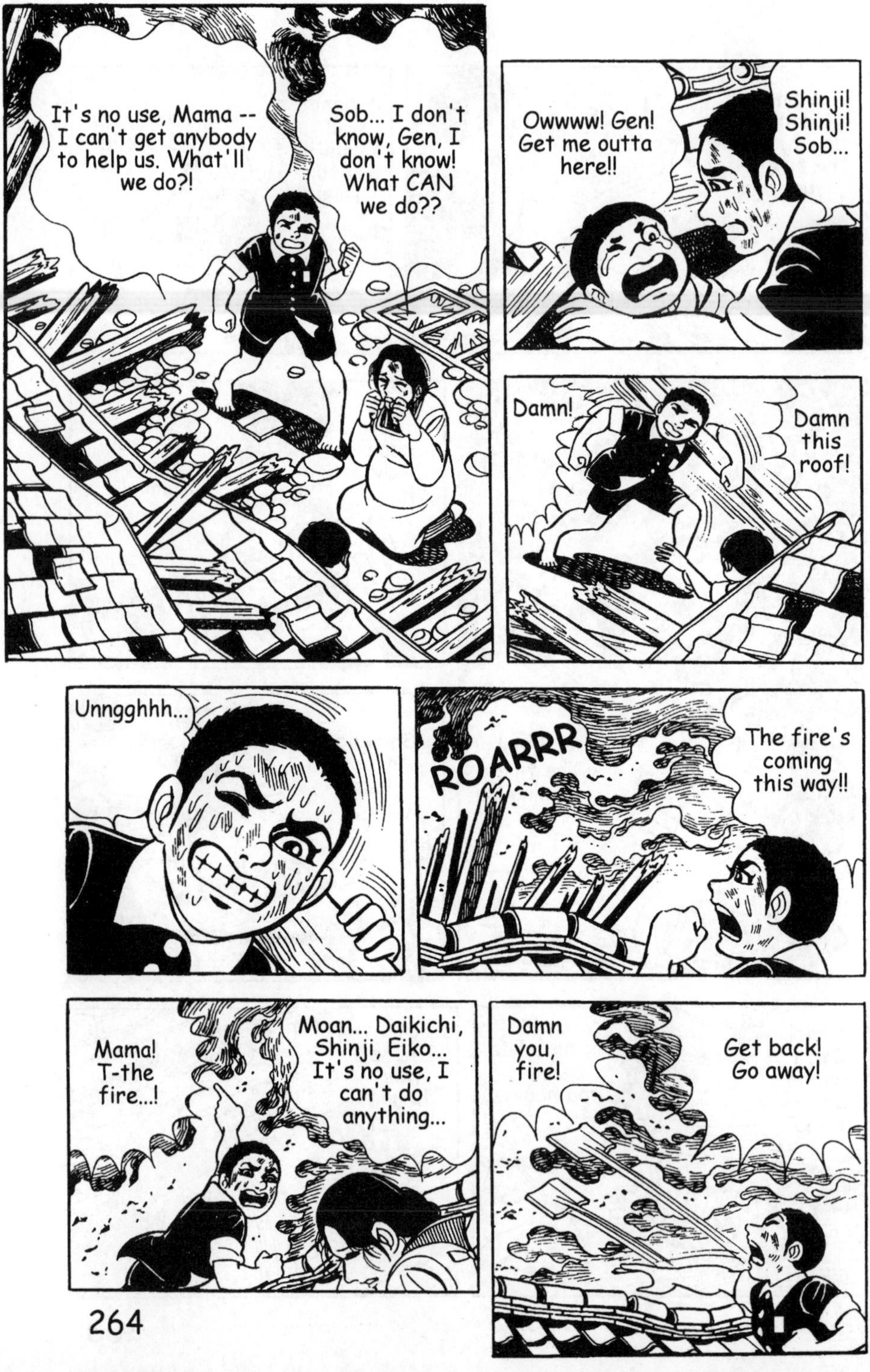
It's no use, Mama -- I can't get anybody to help us. What'll we do?!
Sob... I don't know, Gen, I don't know! What CAN we do??
Owwww! Gen! Get me outta here!!
Shinji! Shinji! Sob...
Damn!
Damn this roof!
Unngghhh...
ROARRR
The fire's coming this way!!
Mama! T-the fire...!
Moan... Daikichi, Shinji, Eiko... It's no use, I can't do anything...
Damn you, fire!
Get back! Go away!

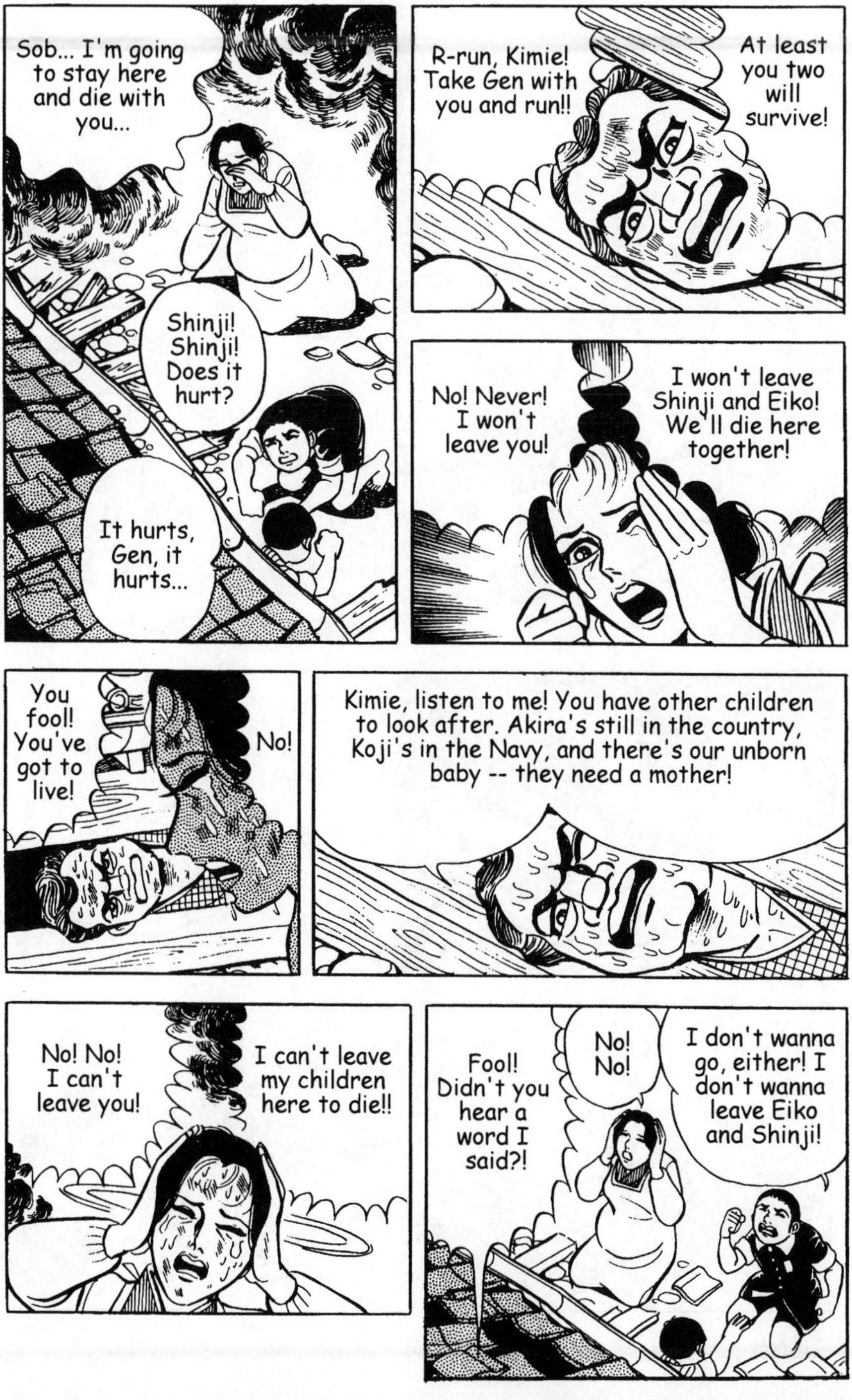
Sob... I'm going to stay here and die with you...
Shinji! Shinji! Does it hurt?
It hurts, Gen, it hurts...
R-run, Kimie! Take Gen with you and run!!
At least you two will survive!
No! Never! I won't leave you!
I won't leave Shinji and Eiko! We'll die here together!
You fool! You've got to live!
No!
Kimie, listen to me! You have other children to look after. Akira's still in the country, Koji's in the Navy, and there's our unborn baby -- they need a mother!
No! No! I can't leave you!
I can't leave my children here to die!!
Fool! Didn't you hear a word I said?!
No! No!
I don't wanna go, either! I don't wanna leave Eiko and Shinji!

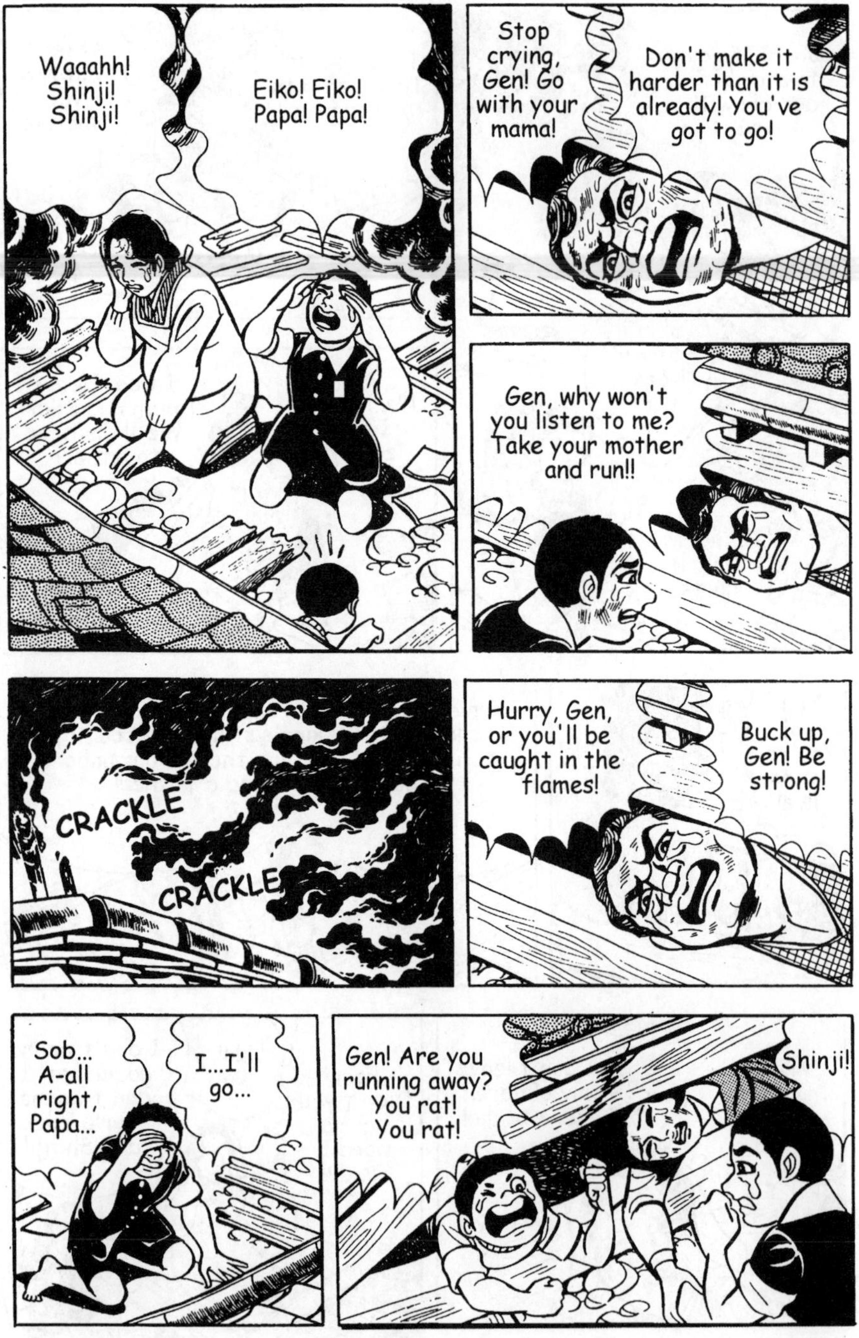
Waaahh! Shinji! Shinji!
Eiko! Eiko! Papa! Papa!
Stop crying, Gen! Go with your mama!
Don't make it harder than it is already! You've got to go!
Gen, why won't you listen to me? Take your mother and run!!
CRACKLE
CRACKLE
Hurry, Gen, or you'll be caught in the flames!
Buck up, Gen! Be strong!
Sob... A-all right, Papa...
I...I'll go...
Gen! Are you running away? You rat! You rat!
Shinji!

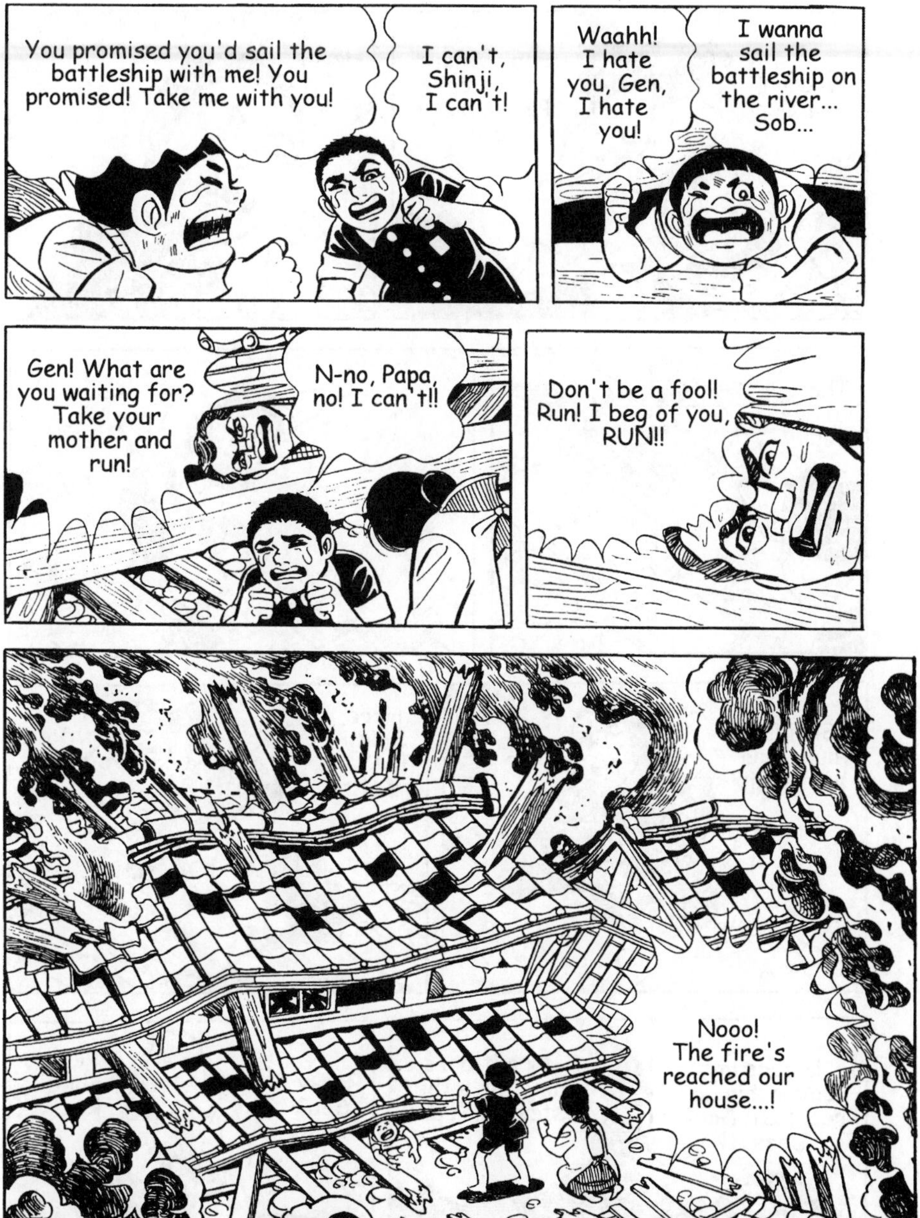
You promised you'd sail the battleship with me! You promised! Take me with you!
I can't, Shinji, I can't!
Waahh! I hate you, Gen, I hate you!
I wanna sail the battleship on the river... Sob...
Gen! What are you waiting for? Take your mother and run!
N-no, Papa, no! I can't!!
Don't be a fool! Run! I beg of you, RUN!!
Nooo! The fire's reached our house...!

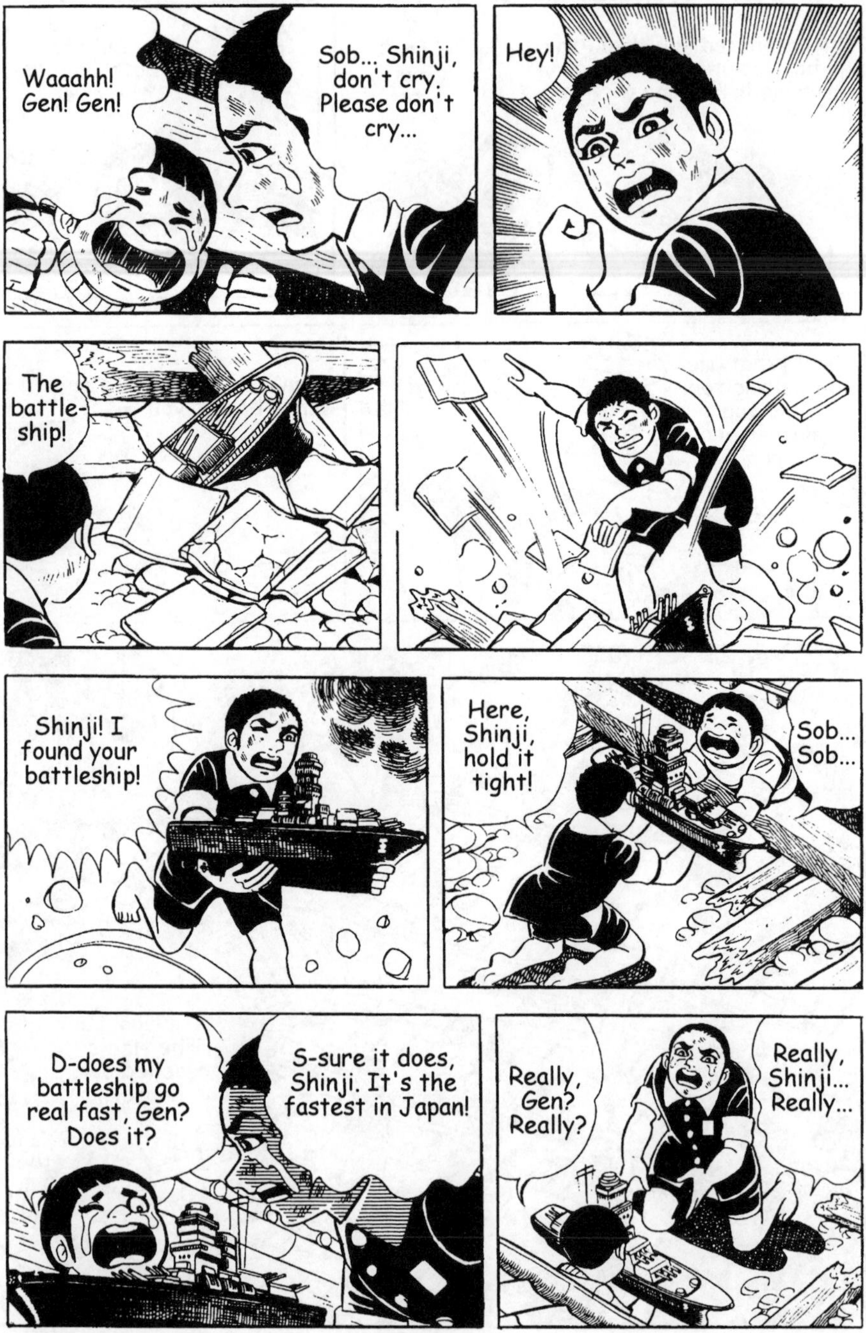
Waaahh! Gen! Gen!
Sob... Shinji, don't cry. Please don't cry...
Hey!
The battle-ship!
Shinji! I found your battleship!
Here, Shinji, hold it tight!
Sob... Sob...
D-does my battleship go real fast, Gen? Does it?
S-sure it does, Shinji. It's the fastest in Japan!
Really, Gen? Really?
Really, Shinji... Really...

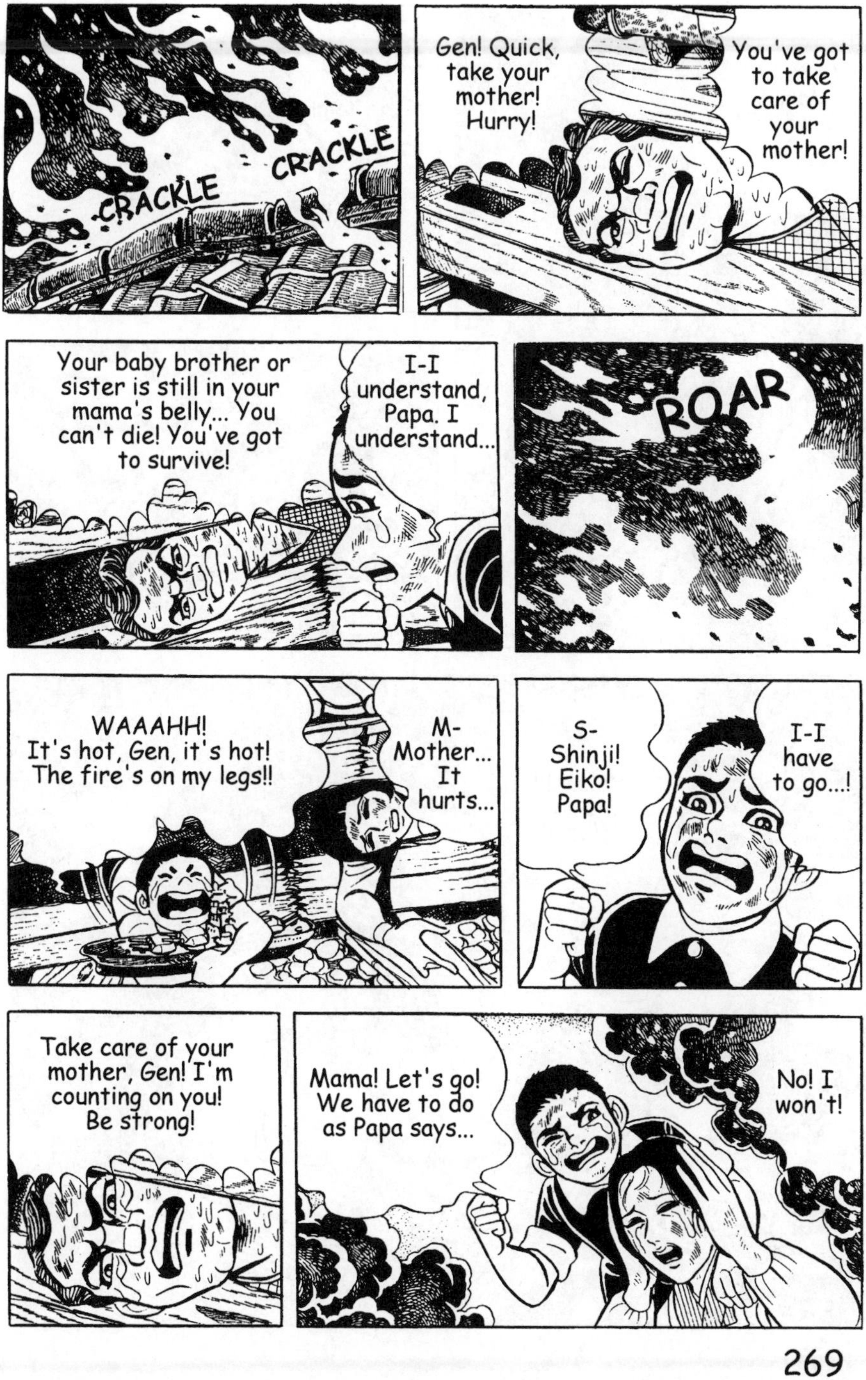
CRACKLE
CRACKLE
Gen! Quick, take your mother! Hurry!
You've got to take care of your mother!
Your baby brother or sister is still in your mama's belly... You can't die! You've got to survive!
I-I understand, Papa. I understand...
ROAR
WAAAHH! It's hot, Gen, it's hot! The fire's on my legs!!
M-Mother... It hurts...
S-Shinji! Eiko! Papa!
I-I have to go...!
Take care of your mother, Gen! I'm counting on you! Be strong!
Mama! Let's go! We have to do as Papa says...
No! I won't!

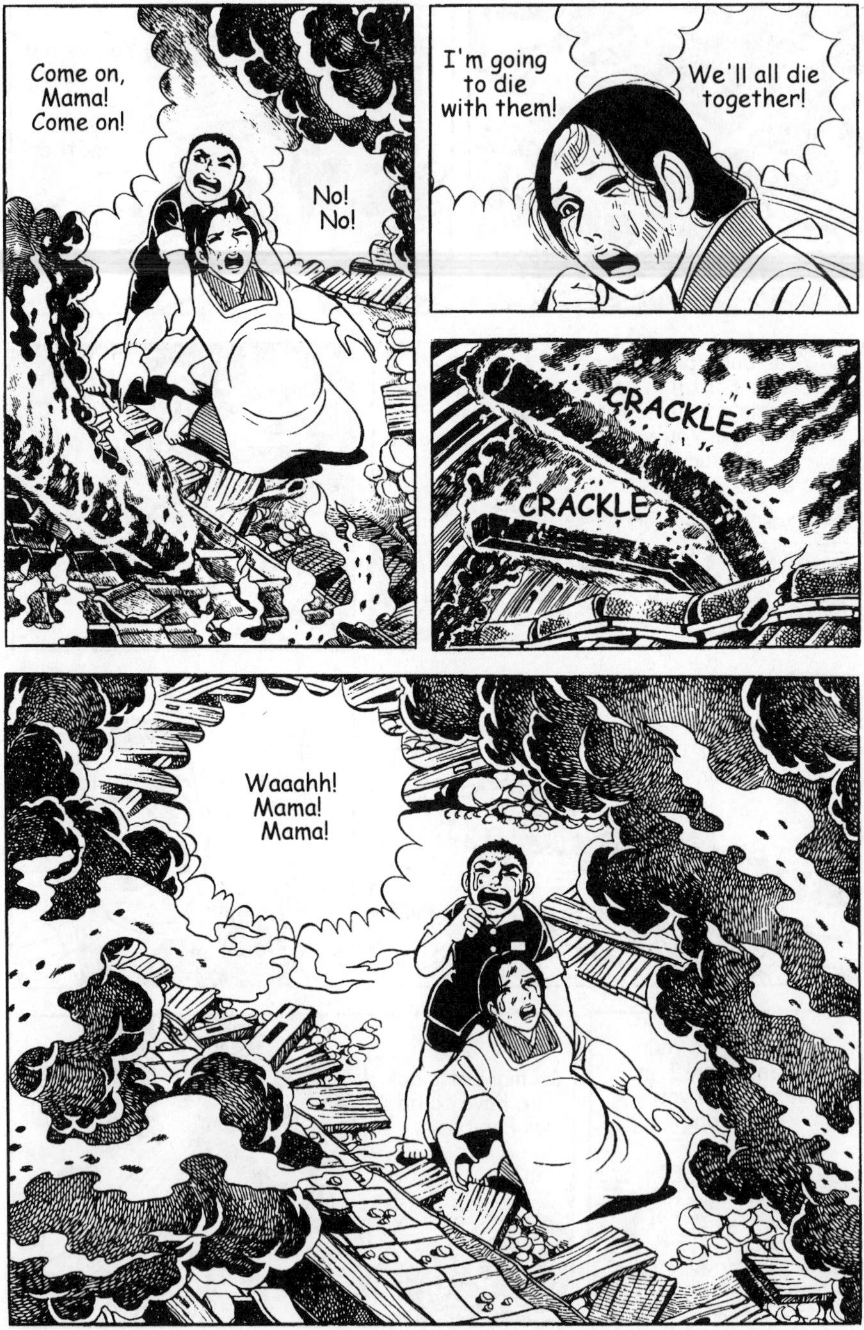
Come on, Mama! Come on!
No! No!
I'm going to die with them!
We'll all die together!
CRACKLE
CRACKLE
Waaahh! Mama! Mama!

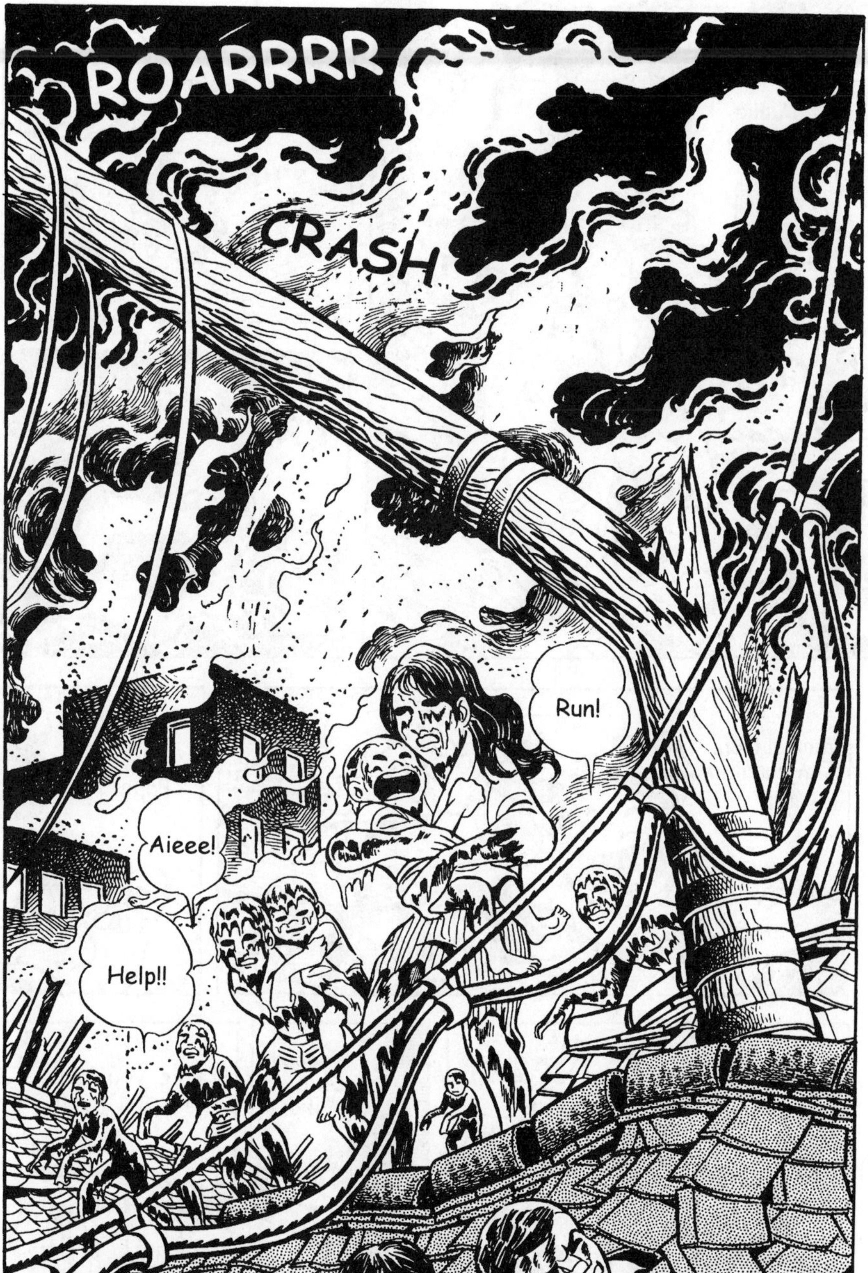
ROARRRR
CRASH
Run!
Aieee!
Help!!

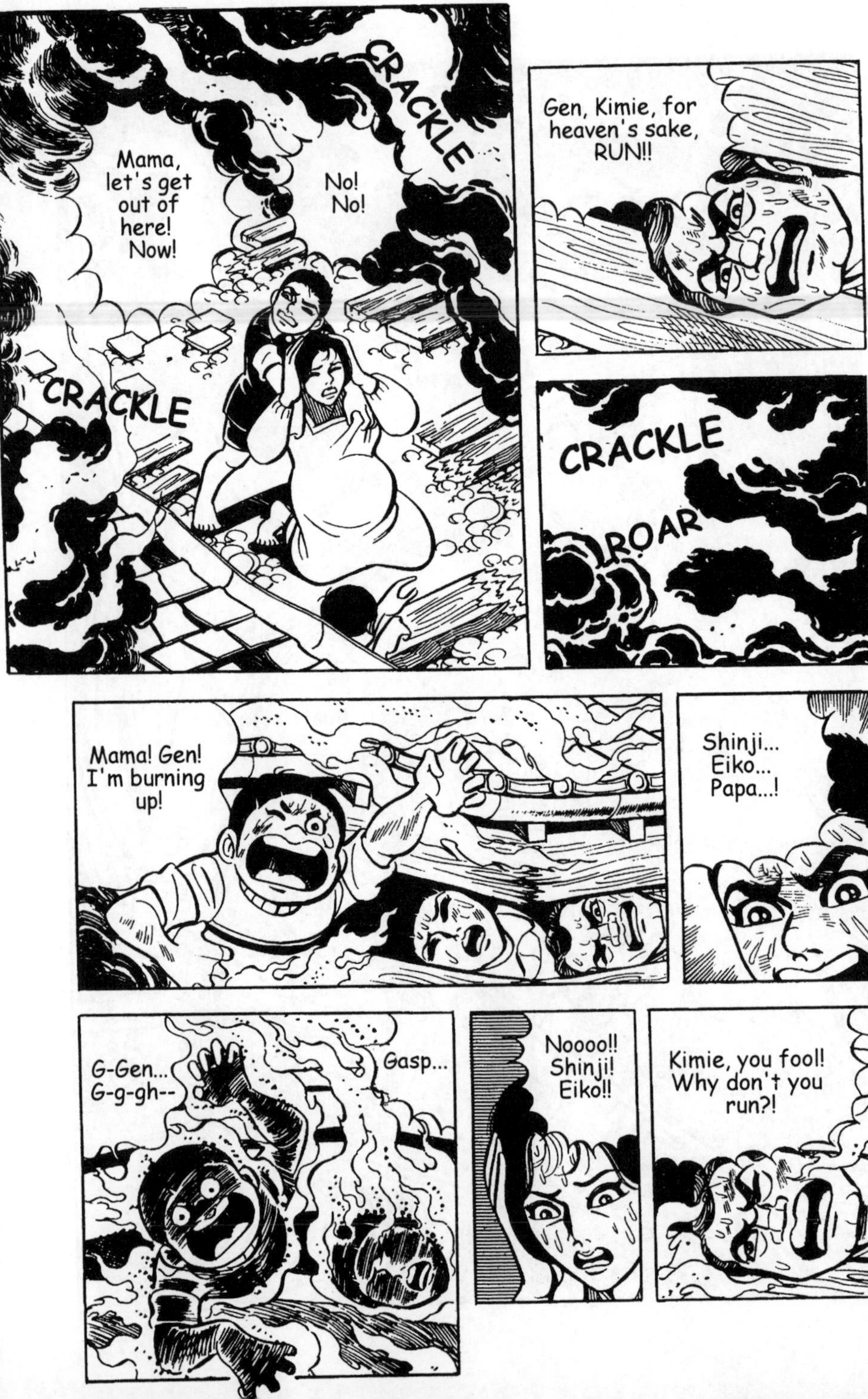
CRACKLE
Mama, let's get out of here! Now!
No! No!
CRACKLE
Gen, Kimie, for heaven's sake, RUN!!
CRACKLE
ROAR
Mama! Gen! I'm burning up!
Shinji... Eiko... Papa...!
G-Gen... G-g-gh--
Gasp...
Noooo!! Shinji! Eiko!!
Kimie, you fool! Why don't you run?!

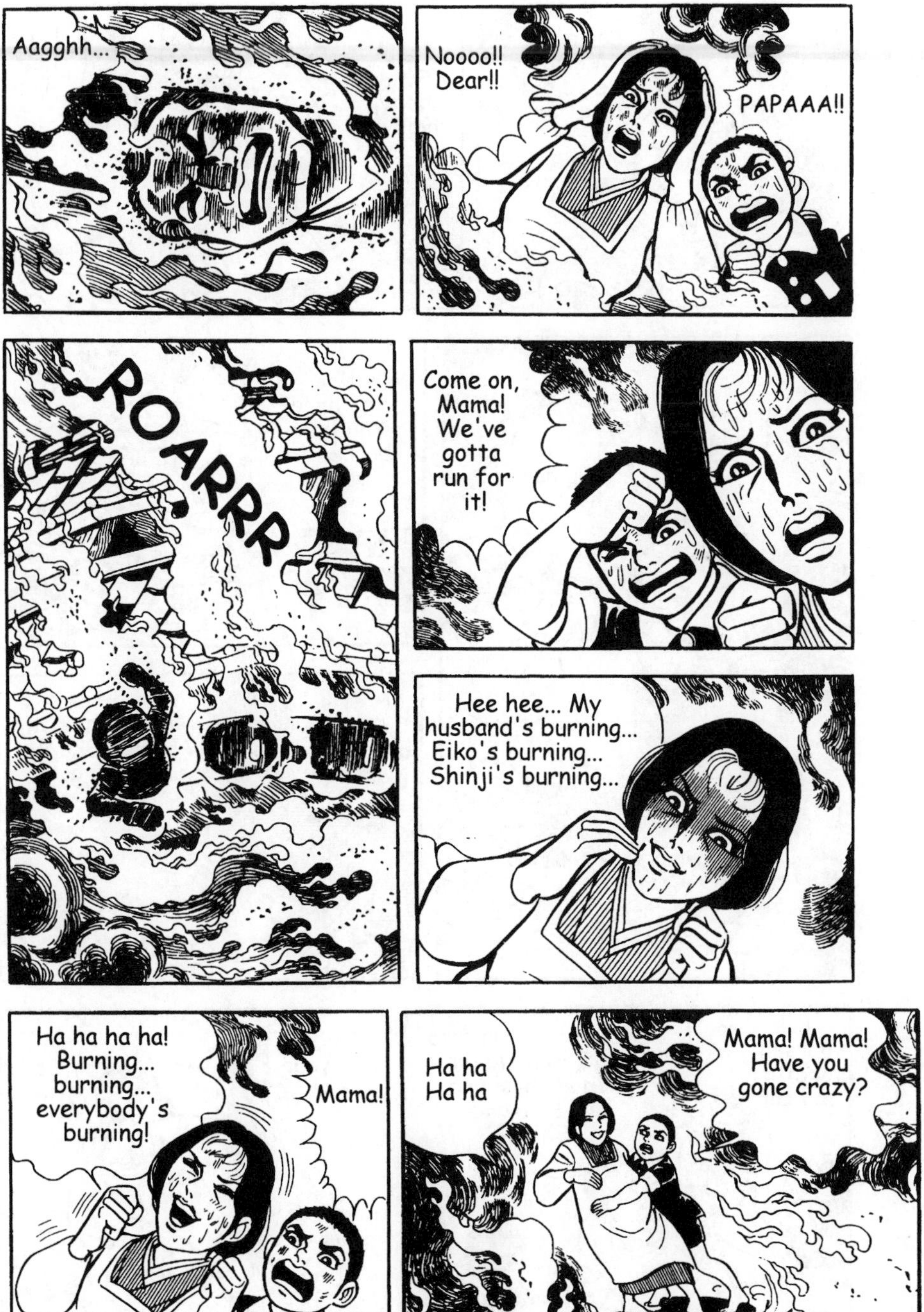

Aagghh...
Noooo!! Dear!!
PAPAAA!!
ROARRR
Come on, Mama! We've gotta run for it!
Hee hee... My husband's burning... Eiko's burning... Shinji's burning...
Ha ha ha ha! Burning... burning... everybody's burning!
Mama!
Ha ha Ha ha
Mama! Mama! Have you gone crazy?

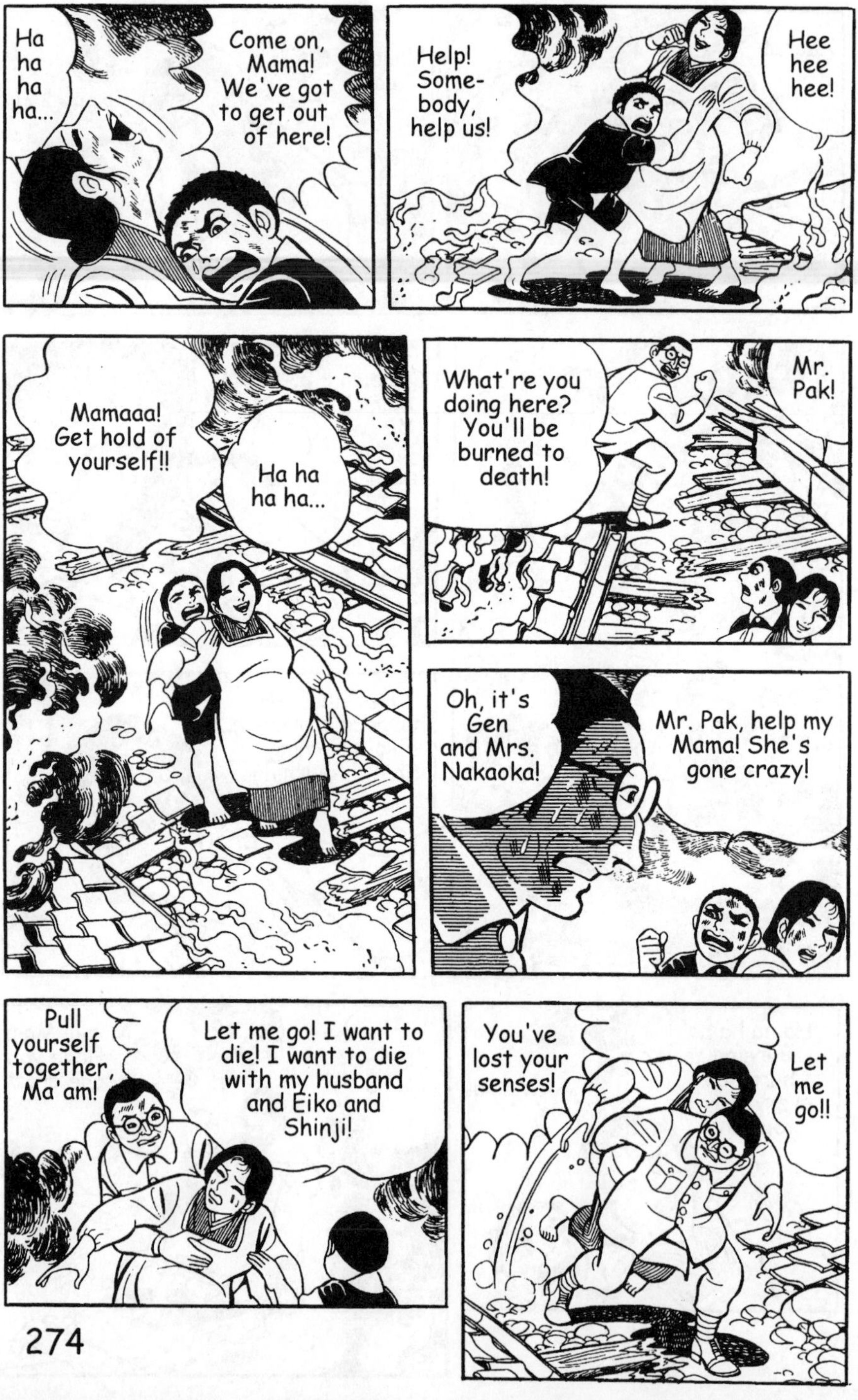
Ha ha ha ha...
Come on, Mama! We've got to get out of here!
Help! Somebody, help us!
Hee hee hee!
Mamaaa! Get hold of yourself!!
Ha ha ha ha...
What're you doing here? You'll be burned to death!
Mr. Pak!
Oh, it's Gen and Mrs. Nakaoka!
Mr. Pak, help my Mama! She's gone crazy!
Pull yourself together, Ma'am!
Let me go! I want to die! I want to die with my husband and Eiko and Shinji!
You've lost your senses!
Let me go!!

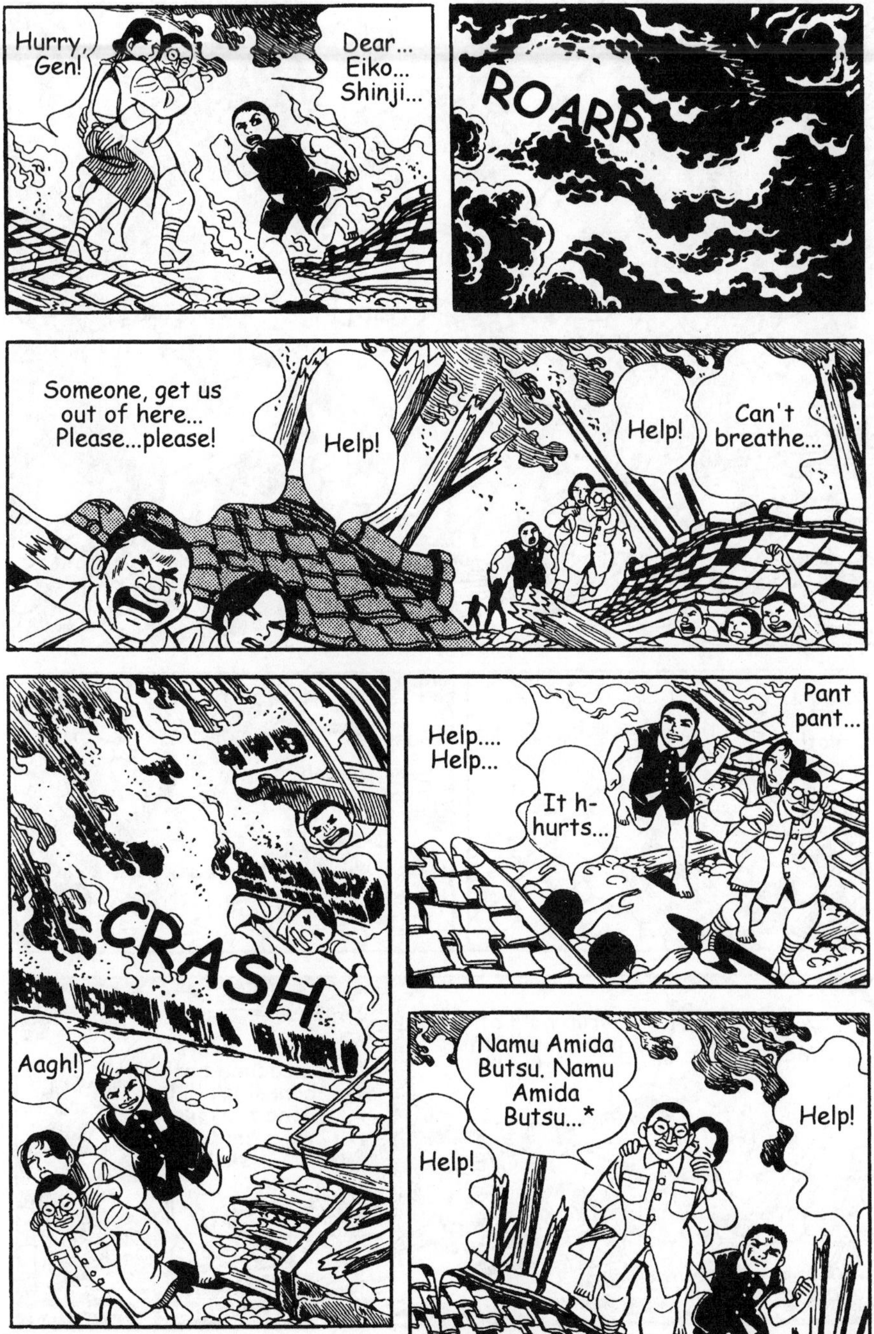
Hurry, Gen!
Dear... Eiko... Shinji...
ROARR
Someone, get us out of here... Please...please!
Help!
Help!
Can't breathe...
CRASH
Aagh!
Help.... Help...
It h-hurts...
Pant pant...
Help!
Namu Amida Butsu. Namu Amida Butsu...*
Help!

*Buddhist prayer

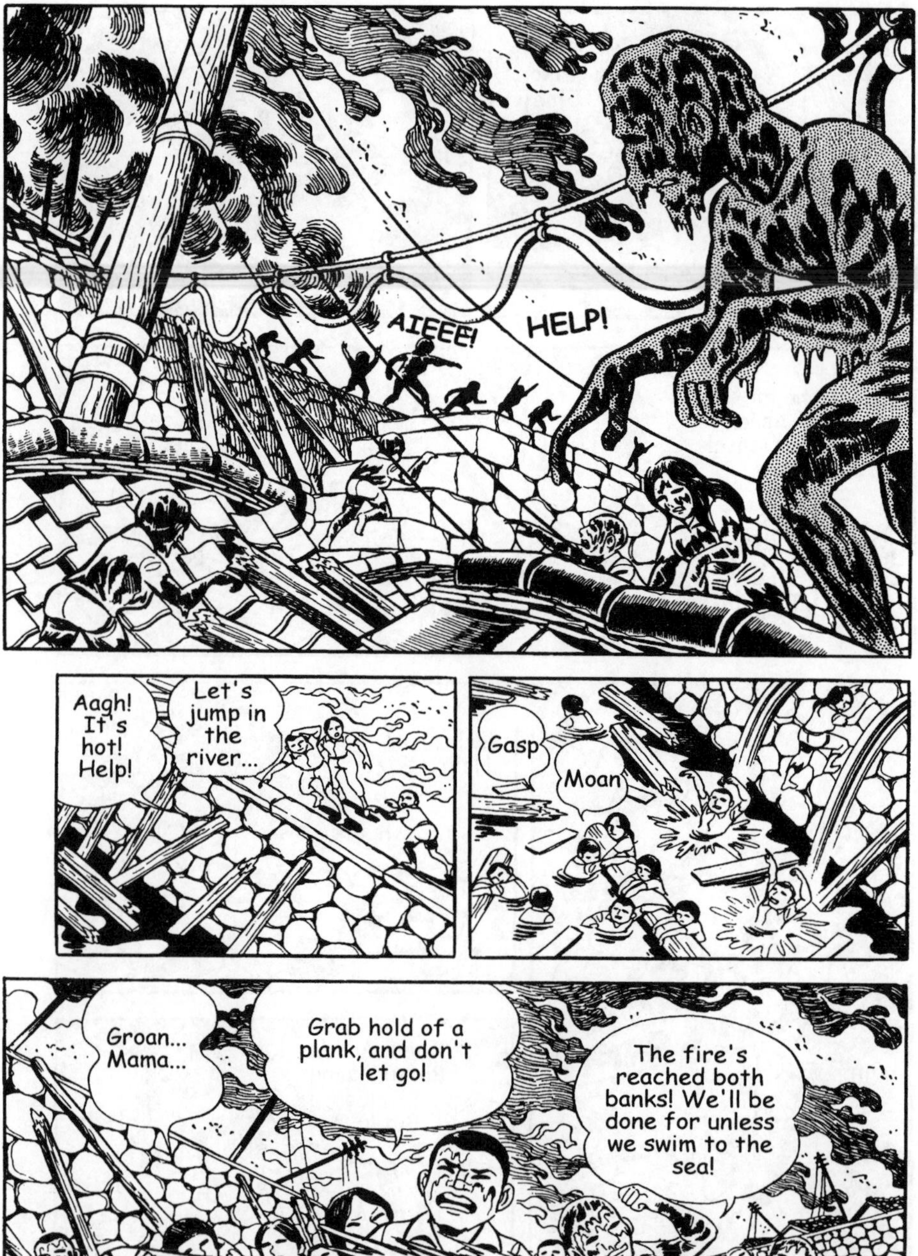
AIEEE!
HELP!
Aagh! It's hot! Help!
Let's jump in the river...
Gasp
Moan
Groan... Mama...
Grab hold of a plank, and don't let go!
The fire's reached both banks! We'll be done for unless we swim to the sea!

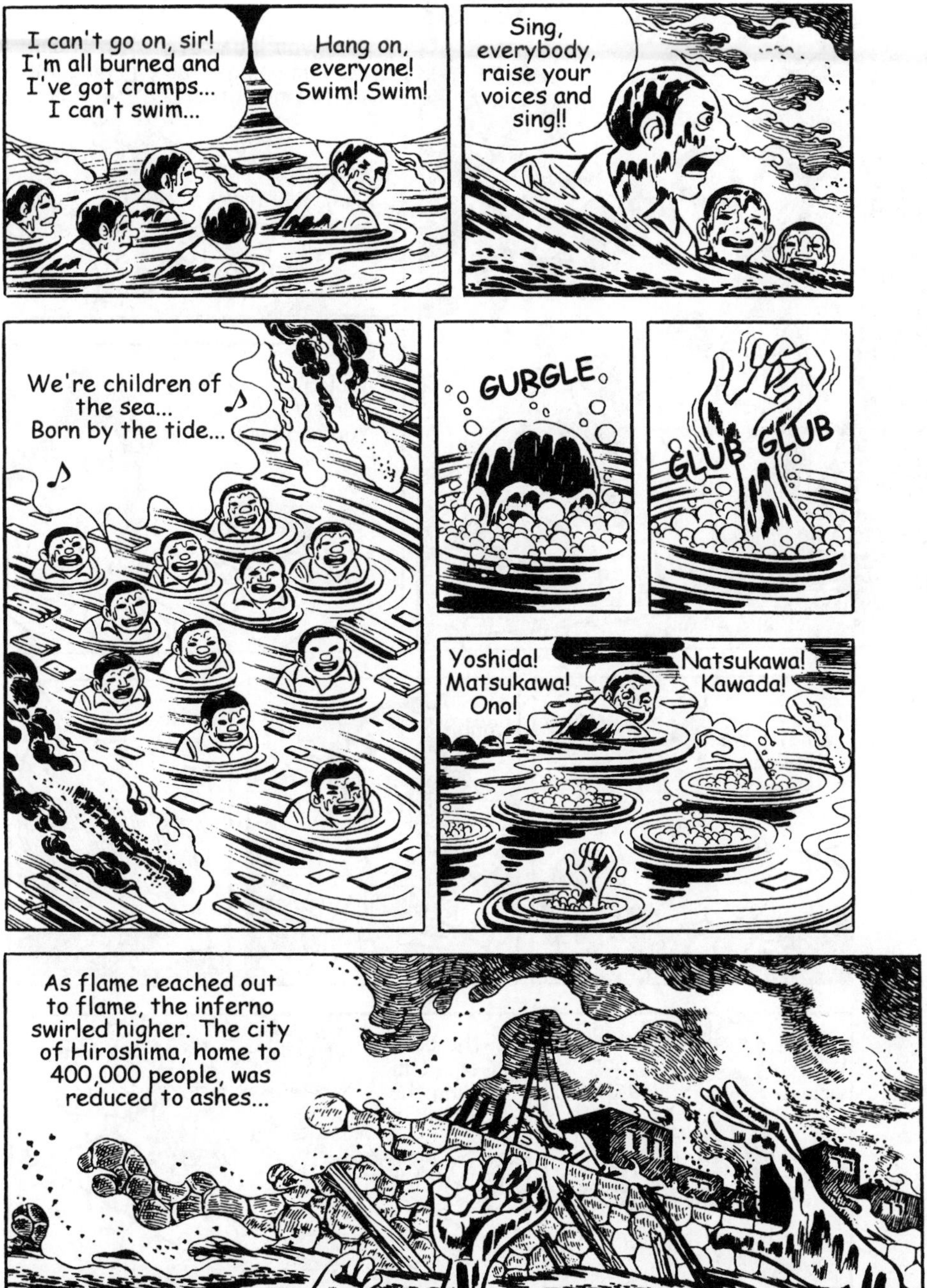
I can't go on, sir! I'm all burned and I've got cramps... I can't swim...
Hang on, everyone! Swim! Swim!
Sing, everybody, raise your voices and sing!!
We're children of the sea... Born by the tide... ♪
♪
GURGLE
GLUB GLUB
Yoshida! Matsukawa! Ono!
Natsukawa! Kawada!
As flame reached out to flame, the inferno swirled higher. The city of Hiroshima, home to 400,000 people, was reduced to ashes...

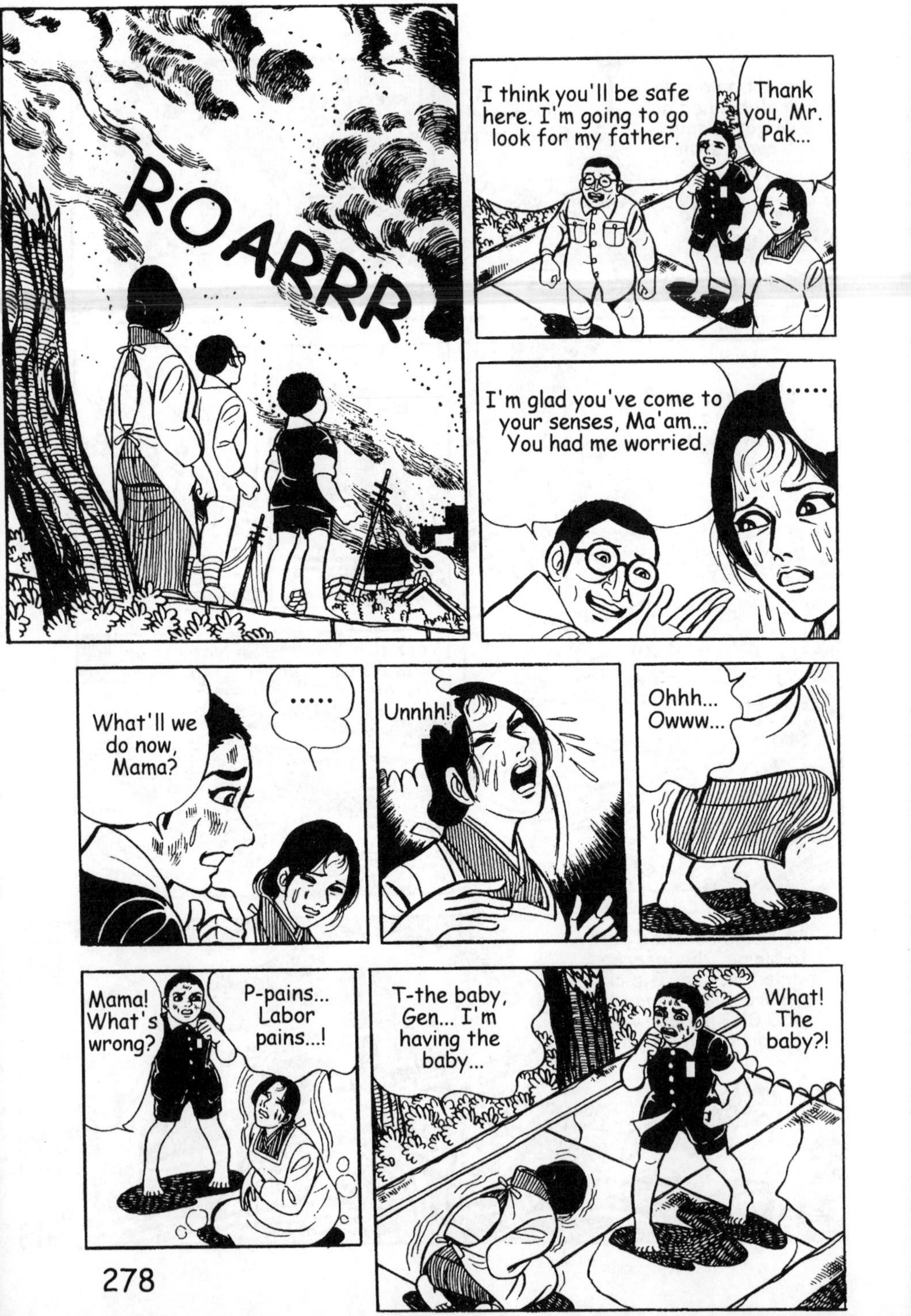
ROARRR
I think you'll be safe here. I'm going to go look for my father.
Thank you, Mr. Pak...
I'm glad you've come to your senses, Ma'am... You had me worried.
.....
What'll we do now, Mama?
.....
Unnhh!
Ohhh... Owww...
Mama! What's wrong?
P-pains... Labor pains...!
T-the baby, Gen... I'm having the baby...
What! The baby?!

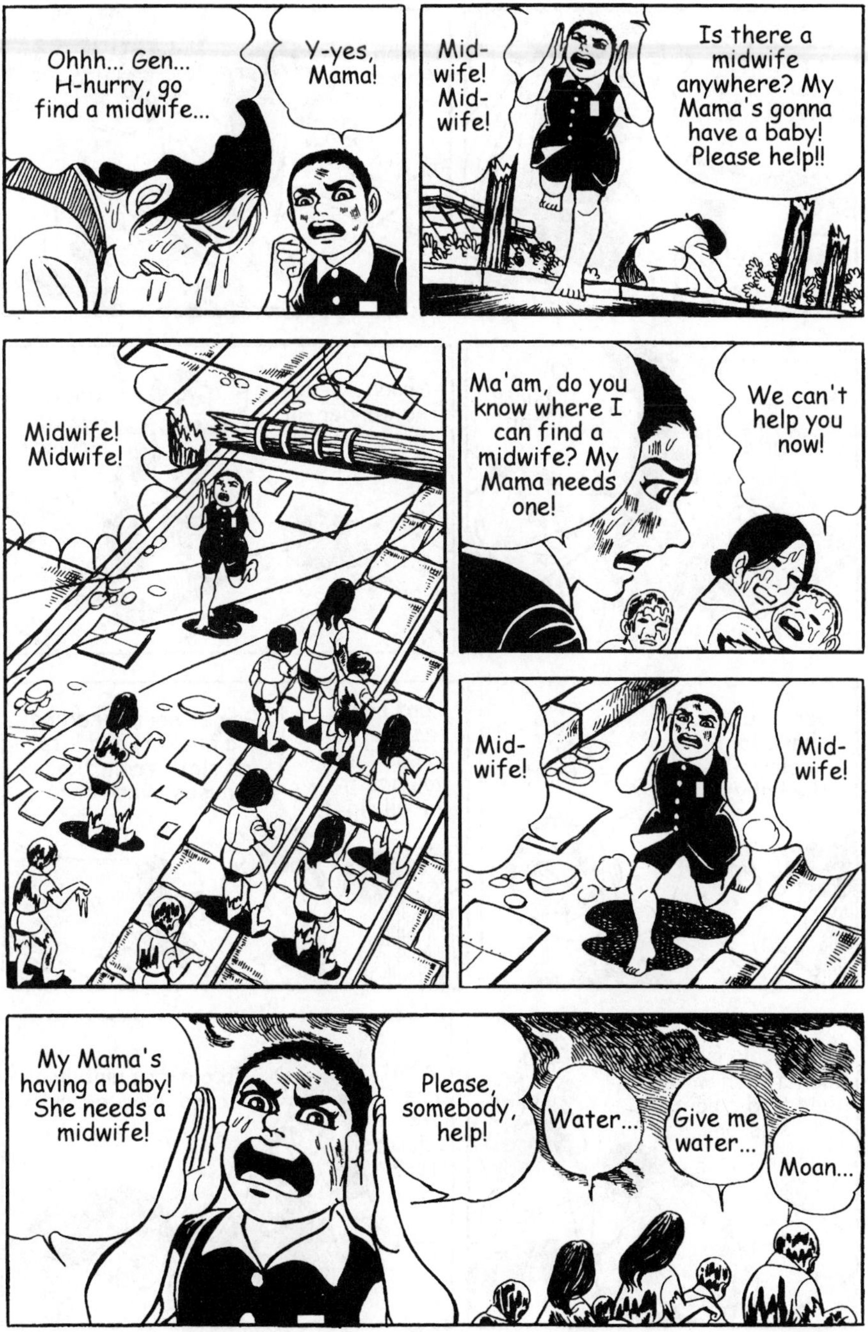
Ohhh... Gen... H-hurry, go find a midwife...
Y-yes, Mama!
Mid-wife! Mid-wife!
Is there a midwife anywhere? My Mama's gonna have a baby! Please help!!
Midwife! Midwife!
Ma'am, do you know where I can find a midwife? My Mama needs one!
We can't help you now!
Mid-wife!
Mid-wife!
My Mama's having a baby! She needs a midwife!
Please, somebody, help!
Water...
Give me water...
Moan...

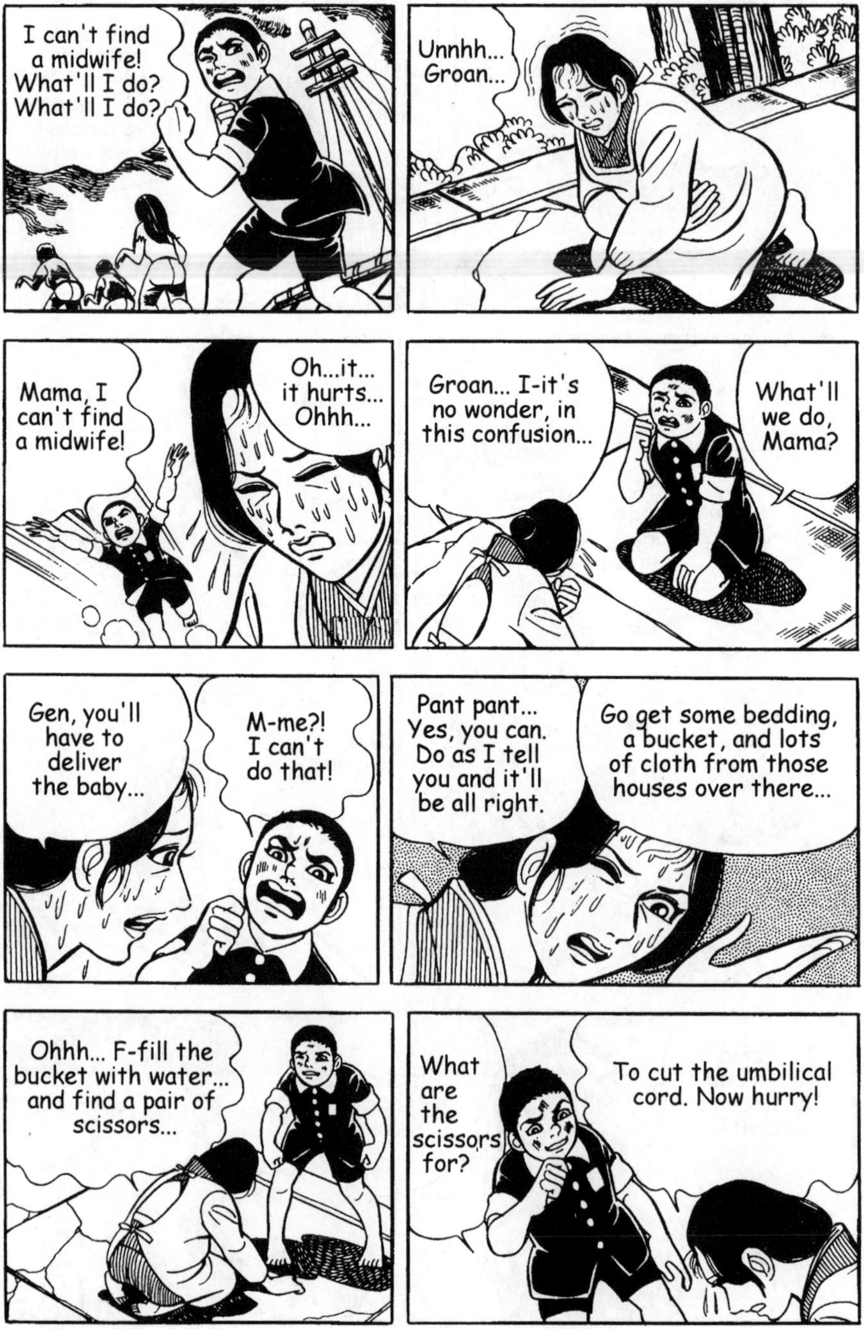
I can't find a midwife! What'll I do? What'll I do?
Unnhh... Groan...
Mama, I can't find a midwife!
Oh...it... it hurts... Ohhh...
Groan... I-it's no wonder, in this confusion...
What'll we do, Mama?
Gen, you'll have to deliver the baby...
M-me?! I can't do that!
Pant pant... Yes, you can. Do as I tell you and it'll be all right.
Go get some bedding, a bucket, and lots of cloth from those houses over there...
Ohhh... F-fill the bucket with water... and find a pair of scissors...
What are the scissors for?
To cut the umbilical cord. Now hurry!

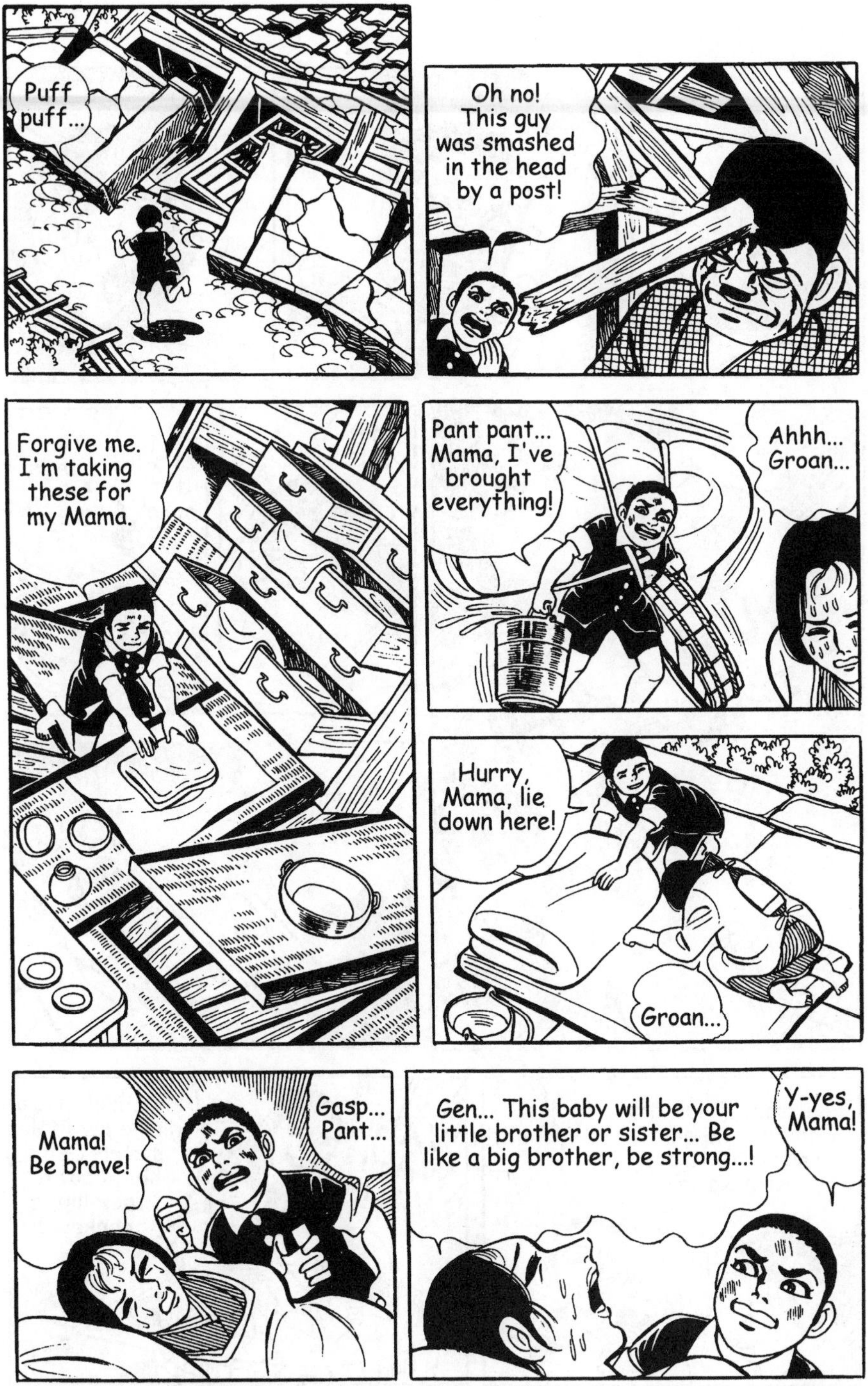
Puff puff...
Oh no! This guy was smashed in the head by a post!
Forgive me. I'm taking these for my Mama.
Pant pant... Mama, I've brought everything!
Ahhh... Groan...
Hurry, Mama, lie down here!
Groan...
Mama! Be brave!
Gasp... Pant...
Gen... This baby will be your little brother or sister... Be like a big brother, be strong...!
Y-yes, Mama!

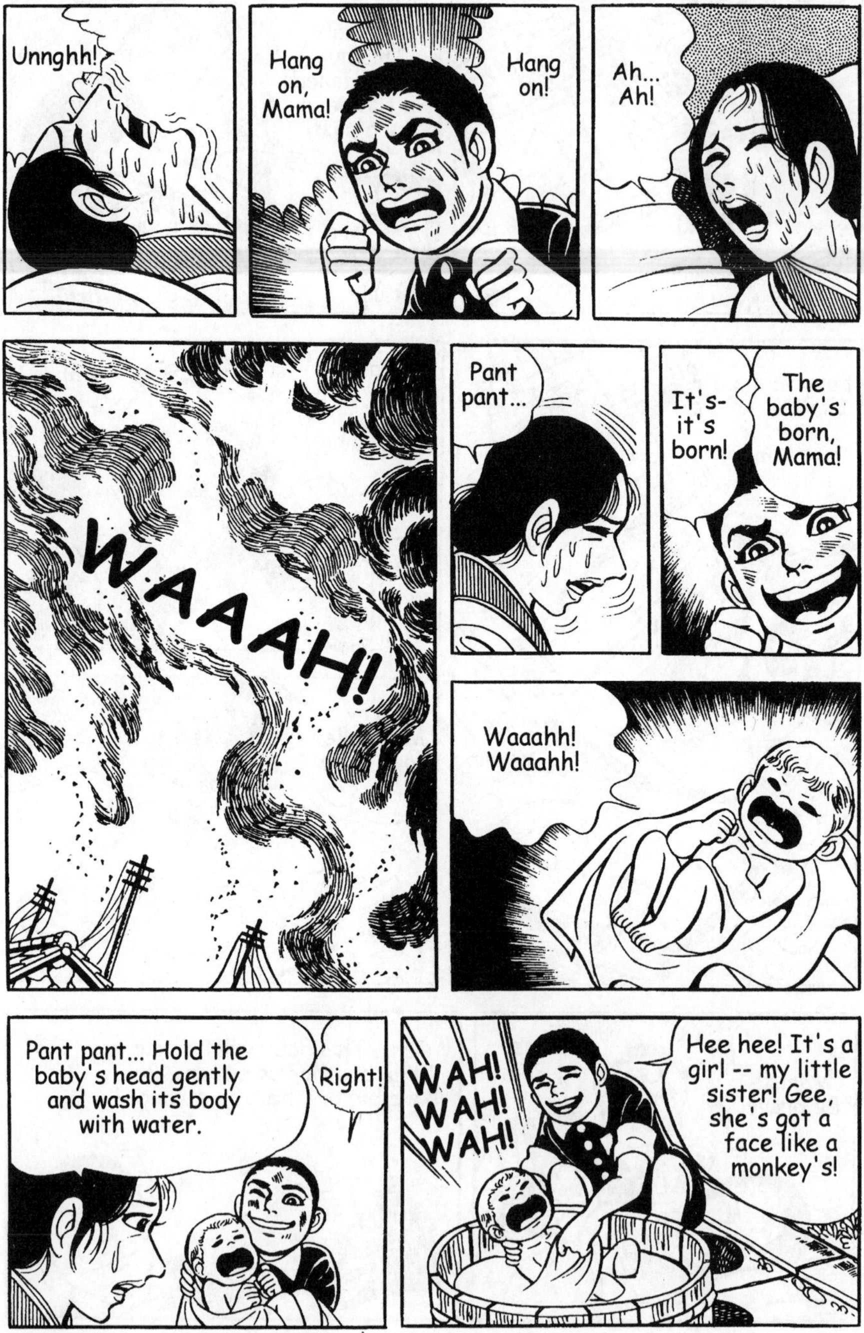
Unnghh!
Hang on, Mama!
Hang on!
Ah... Ah!
WAAAAH!
Pant pant...
It's- it's born!
The baby's born, Mama!
Waaahh! Waaahh!
Pant pant... Hold the baby's head gently and wash its body with water.
Right!
WAH! WAH! WAH!
Hee hee! It's a girl -- my little sister! Gee, she's got a face like a monkey's!

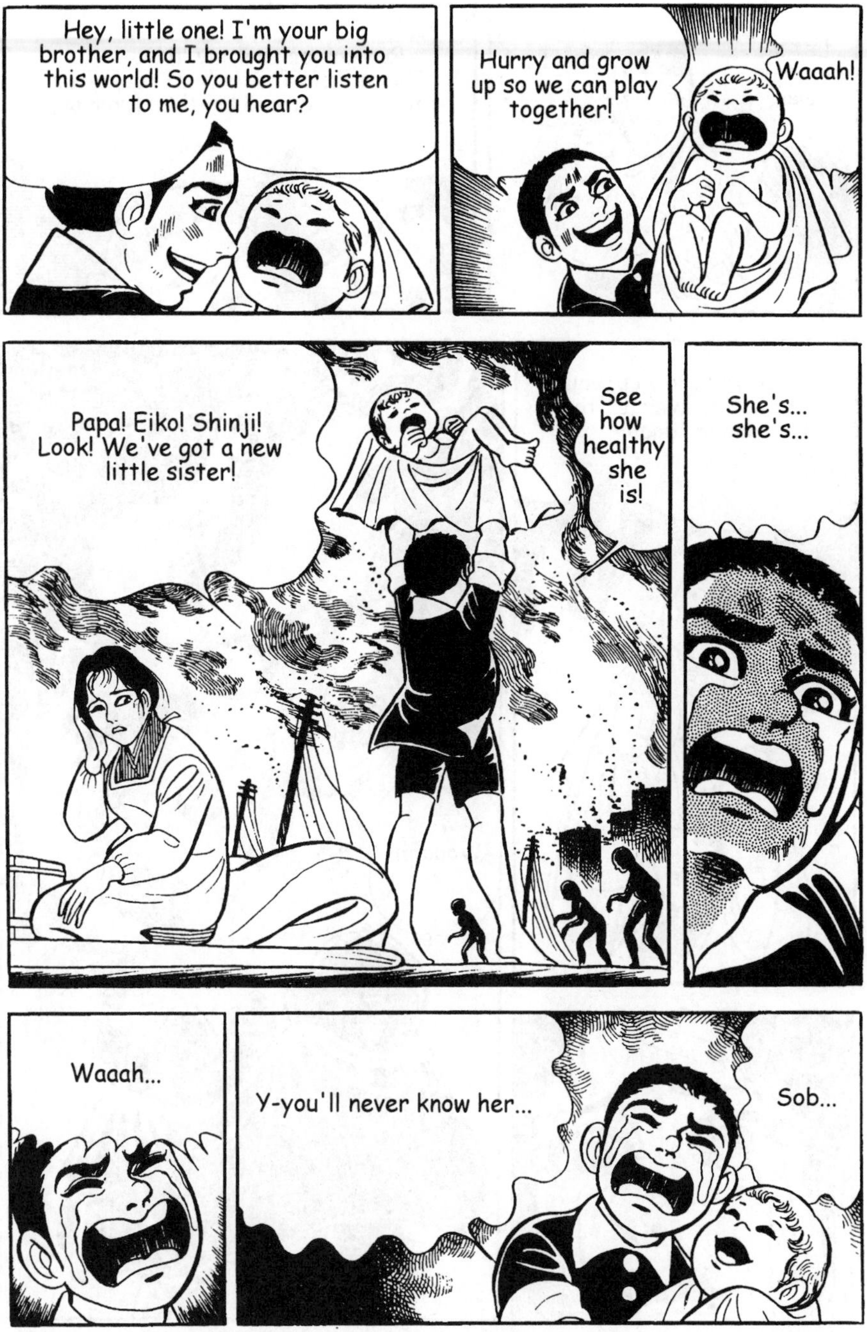
Hey, little one! I'm your big brother, and I brought you into this world! So you better listen to me, you hear?
Hurry and grow up so we can play together!
Waaah!
Papa! Eiko! Shinji! Look! We've got a new little sister!
See how healthy she is!
She's... she's...
Waaah...
Y-you'll never know her...
Sob...

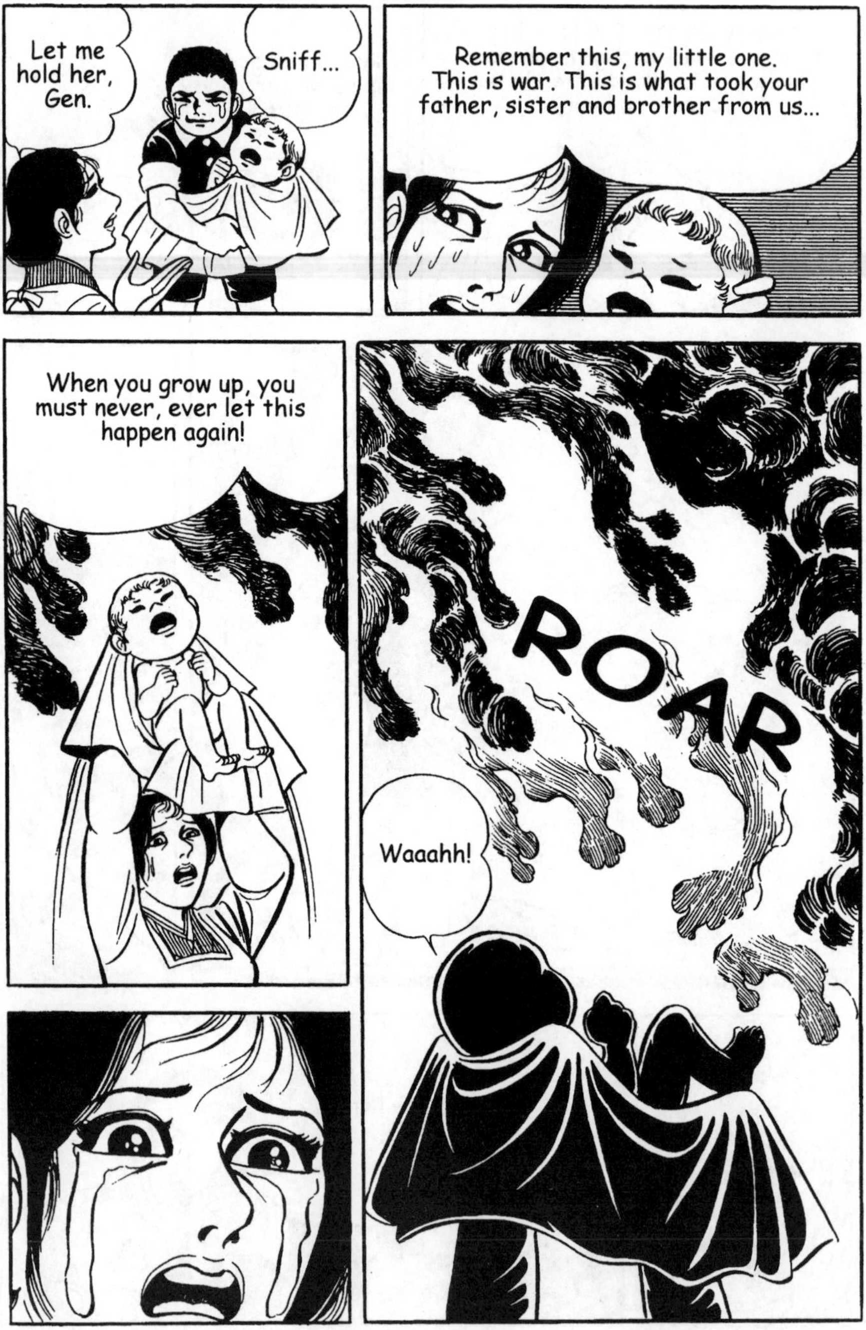
Let me hold her, Gen.
Sniff...
Remember this, my little one. This is war. This is what took your father, sister and brother from us...
When you grow up, you must never, ever let this happen again!
ROAR
Waaahh!

About Project Gen

Namie Asazuma
Former Representative, Project Gen

In the pages of *Barefoot Gen*, Keiji Nakazawa brings to life a tragedy unlike any that has ever befallen the human race before. He does not simply depict the destructive horror of nuclear weapons, but tells of the cruel fate they visited upon victims and survivors in the years to come. Yet Gen, the young hero of this story, somehow manages to overcome one hardship after another, always with courage and humor. *Barefoot Gen*'s tale of hope and human triumph in the face of nuclear holocaust has inspired volunteer translators around the world, as well as people working in a variety of other media. Over the years *Gen* has been made into a three-part live-action film, a feature-length animation film, an opera, and a musical.

The first effort to translate *Barefoot Gen* from the original Japanese into other languages began in 1976, when Japanese peace activists Masahiro Oshima and Yukio Aki walked across the United States as part of that year's Transcontinental Walk for Peace and Social Justice. Their fellow walkers frequently asked them about the atomic bombing of Hiroshima, and one of them happened to have a copy of *Hadashi no Gen* in his backpack. The Americans on the walk, astonished that an atomic bomb survivor had written about it in cartoon form, urged their Japanese friends to translate it into English. Upon returning to Japan, Oshima and Aki founded Project Gen, a non-profit, all-volunteer group of young Japanese and Americans living in Tokyo, to do just that. Project Gen went on to translate the first four volumes of *Barefoot Gen* into English. One or more of these volumes have also been published in French, German, Italian, Portuguese, Swedish, Norwegian, Indonesian, Tagalog, and Esperanto.

By the 1990s Project Gen was no longer active. In the meantime, author Keiji Nakazawa had gone on to complete ten volumes of *Gen*, and expressed his wish to see the entire story made available to non-Japanese readers. Parts of the first four volumes had also been abridged in translation. A new generation of volunteers responded by reviving Project Gen and producing a new, complete and unabridged translation of the entire Gen series.

The second incarnation of Project Gen got its start in Moscow in 1994, when a Japanese student, Minako Tanabe, launched "Project Gen in Russia" to translate *Gen* into Russian. After publishing the first three volumes in Moscow, the project relocated to Kanazawa, Japan, where volunteers Yulia Tachino and Namie Asazuma had become acquainted with *Gen* while translating a story about Hiroshima into Russian. The Kanazawa volunteers, together with Takako Kanekura in Russia, completed Russian volumes 4 through 10 between 1999 and 2001.

In the spring of 2000, the Kanazawa group formally established a new Project Gen in Japan. Nine volunteers spent the next three years translating all ten volumes of *Gen* into English. The translators are Kazuko Futakuchi, Michael Gordon, Kyoko Honda, Yukari Kimura, Nobutoshi Kohara, Kiyoko Nishita, George Stenson, Michiko Tanaka, and Kazuko Yamada.

In 2002, author Keiji Nakazawa put the Kanazawa team in contact with Alan Gleason, a member of the first Project Gen, who introduced them to Last Gasp of San Francisco, publisher of the original English translation of *Gen*. Last Gasp agreed to publish the new, unabridged translation of all ten volumes, of which this book is one.

In the hope that humanity will never repeat the terrible tragedy of the atomic bombing, the volunteers of Project Gen want children and adults all over the world to hear Gen's story. Through translations like this one, we want to help Gen speak to people in different countries in their own languages. Our prayer is that *Barefoot Gen* will contribute in some small way to the abolition of nuclear weapons before this new century is over.

Write to Project Gen at 14-13 Shiragiku-cho, Kanazawa 921-8024, Japan, or projectgenkanazawa@gmail.com

"I named my main character Gen in the hope that he would
become a root or source of strength for a new generation
of mankind—one that can tread the charred soil of
Hiroshima barefoot, feel the earth beneath its feet, and
have the strength to say 'no' to nuclear weapons... I myself
would like to live with Gen's strength—that is my ideal, and
I will continue pursuing it through my work."

— Keiji Nakazawa (1939-2012)

*Keiji Nakazawa retired from cartooning in 2009. He continued
to lecture throughout Japan about the experience of atomic
bomb victims, until his death in Hiroshima in 2012, at age 73.
He is survived by his wife, daughter, and grandchildren.*